ANCIENT
QUOTES
&
ANECDOTES

PUBLISHED VOLUMES

Robert W. Funk, ed., *New Gospel Parallels. Vol. 1: The Synoptic Gospels*
Robert W. Funk, ed., *New Gospel Parallels. Vol. 2: John and the Other Gospels*
John Dominic Crossan, ed., *Sayings Parallels: A Workbook for the Jesus Tradition*
John S. Kloppenborg, *Q Parallels: Synopsis, Critical Notes, and Concordance*
Vernon K. Robbins, *Ancient Quotes & Anecdotes: From Crib to Crypt*

ANCIENT
QUOTES
&
ANECDOTES

FROM CRIB

TO CRYPT

COMPILED & EDITED BY

VERNON K. ROBBINS

SONOMA, CALIFORNIA

Library of Congress Cataloging-in-Publication Data
Ancient quotes & anecdotes : from crib to crypt / [compiled] by Vernon
 K. Robbins.
  p.   cm. — (Foundations & facets. Reference series)
  Bibliography: p.
  Includes index.
  ISBN 0-944344-02-X : $29.95.—ISBN 0-944344-03-8 (pbk.) : $21.95
  1. Conduct of life—Quotations, maxims, etc.—Early works to
1800. 2. Aphorisms and apothegms—Early works to 1800.
I. Robbins, Vernon K. (Vernon Kay), 1939-   . II. Series.
BJ1550.A53   1989
081—dc19   88–12583
                                                            CIP

Printed in the United States of America

In memory of

Howard C. Moritz

and in honor of

Lucille E. Moritz

Contents

Contributors

Preface

The publication of this work has been made possible by a number of individuals and institutions almost too numerous to mention. The history of the project reaches back nearly two decades. The results indicate what scholars can achieve when banded together in collegial endeavor over an extended period of time. Such a collaborative effort is the greatest achievement of all. Nevertheless, it is appropriate to make brief mention of all those who contributed directly and indirectly to its ultimate success. I hope my memory and my records will prevent me from omitting any one who made a significant contribution along the way.

Robert W. Funk conceived the project originally with the organization of the Consultation on Form and Genre in the Religious Literature of Late Mediterranean Antiquity. Robert C. Tannehill was its first director and guided the first phase of the work from its inception to 1981, when I became Director.

Members of the group who contributed indexes or copies of pronouncement stories from various documents and corpora are listed in a separate table of contributors. These are the scholars who put their shoulders to the wheel of the project and caused it to move.

Special mention should be made of active members of the working group during its second phase: James R. Butts, Gary Chamberlain, Mary Dean-Otting, Rod Parrott, Charles J. Reedy, R. Marston Speight, William D. Stroker, and Robert C. Tannehill.

Consultants and reviewers of various aspects of the work included: Burton L. Mack, David E. Aune, Ronald H. Hock, and Thomas M. Conley, along with John Dominic Crossan and Bernard Brandon Scott. Øivind Andersen, Bruce D. Chilton, and John Kampen participated in at least one session of the second phase of the work.

The University of Illinois at Urbana-Champaign has been especially supportive of my role in the project. I am mindful of the encouragement received from colleagues in Religious Studies and Classics during my tenure there.

Under the leadership of David Minter, Dean of the College, Emory University has been no less supportive since the project was moved to Atlanta in 1984.

The National Endowment for the Humanities provided financial assistance for the work. The University of Illinois supplied research assistants and gave me a fellowship in a second discipline in order to read ancient and modern rhetorical theory. I held an SBL—Claremont Fellowship during the spring, 1982. That furnished the opportunity to discuss the work in detail with members of the Institute for Antiquity and Christianity, under the directorship of James M. Robinson.

I enjoyed a Fulbright year at the University of Trondheim, Norway, during 1983–84, a time when Peder Borgen and the computer center at the University accorded me every courtesy.

To fail to mention the clerical and student assistance I have received over the years would be unpardonable. I must mention Elizabeth Woolverton Reis and Mary Crawford at the University of Illinois. Student assistants include: Ann Burger, Richard E. DeMaris, Sarah Glenn DeMaris, and Randall Owen Stewart. Emory University provided the clerical assistance of Karen Hauer, Monica Clay,

Adrienne Freeman, Molly Black, and Lyn Schechtel. More recently, Tasaha DeLaney, William H. Shepherd, Jr., Judith A. Jones, Yun Lak Chung, Martin Wisse, Russell Sisson, David Moenning, and Daniel Ashburn joined the team of students who helped me bring the work to completion.

Among my Emory colleagues, Hendrikus Boers deserves special mention for assistance with computers.

The staff of Polebridge Press has contributed to the organization, legibility, and aesthetic qualities of the work: James R. Butts, Stephanie A. Funk, Helen Melnis, and Charlene Matejovsky.

Finally, I must recognize the continuing assistance of my wife, Deanna, who participated both in the particulars of the project and in its larger dimensions. She, together with Rick and Chimene, our children, have been special conversation partners during the long and sometimes difficult course of this work.

Vernon K. Robbins

Introduction

This book contains stories that reach their high point in a striking saying or action. In New Testament scholarship, this kind of story regularly has been called a pronouncement story, since the sayings or actions in them tend to be "pronouncements" about something in or about the world.[1] The editor of this collection, however, in consultation with the staff of Polebridge Press, decided to use the more widely recognized term "anecdote" in the title for this volume. Since the members of the research group worked under the rubric "pronouncement story," it seems fitting to continue its use throughout this introduction.

A Definition of Pronouncement Story

The following definition of a pronouncement story guided members of the Pronouncement Story Group (cited in detail in the preface) as they collected the anecdotes for this volume.

> A pronouncement story is a brief narrative in which the climactic (and often final) element is a pronouncement either in speech or action or a combination of speech and action. There are two main parts of a pronouncement story: the pronouncement and its setting, i.e., the response and the situation provoking the response. The pronouncement is closely associated with the main character who is the author or recipient of the speech or action. Both the setting and the pronouncement contribute to the rhetorical goal of the story.[2]

Recent research on the literary-rhetorical form ancient rhetoricians called the *chreia* has influenced this version of the definition.[3] Three aspects in the definition are new to research and interpretation.

First is the emphasis on "action or a combination of speech and action" as the means by which the pronouncement occurs. Previous research, unduly influenced by comparison with the apophthegm, focused on sayings alone and paid little attention to actions in pronouncement stories.[4] Such an approach overlooks the

1. Vincent Taylor, *The Formation of the Gospel Tradition* (London: Macmillan, 1933) 30, 63–87 introduced the term to New Testament scholarship.
2. The initial definition can be found in Robert C. Tannehill, "Introduction: The Pronouncement Story and Its Types," *Semeia* 20 (1981): 1. A revised version appeared in Vernon K. Robbins, "A Rhetorical Typology for Classifying and Analyzing Pronouncement Stories," *SBLSP* 23 (1984): 94. Additional revisions, present in the version printed in this volume, were made subsequently by Vernon Robbins.
3. The rhetorician Aelius Theon of Alexandria defined a *chreia* as "a brief statement or action with aptness attributed to some specific person or something analogous to a person." See Ronald F. Hock and Edward N. O'Neil, *The Chreia in Ancient Rhetoric. Volume I: The Progymnasmata* (Atlanta: Scholars, 1986) 83–84; James R. Butts, *The "Progymnasmata" of Theon: A New Text with Translation and Commentary* (Ph.D. diss.; Claremont Graduate School, 1987) 186–187.
4. Rudolf Bultmann was highly responsible for de-emphasizing both actions and situations in pronouncement stories when he called them apophthegms and discussed them under "The Tradition of the Sayings of Jesus" (see *The History of the Synoptic Tradition* [New York: Harper & Row, 1963] 11–69). When Martin Dibelius included a section on the *chreia* in his

fundamental role of situations and actions in communication. Speech occurs at a second level and varies in meaning according to context and attendant actions.[5] Careful analysis of the situations and actions basic to the characterization of different people in Mediterranean antiquity could bring new information to our investigations.

Second, a pronouncement story presents a rhetorical situation, and the responses in the stories have argumentative qualities. This means that expansion or abridgment in the description of a situation and expansion or elaboration in the response have rhetorical significance. All too often, interpreters have considered expansion or elaboration to be unfortunate in a pronouncement story or inconsistent with its true nature. In fact, these rhetorical dimensions are fundamental to the stories. If a story has no witty, figurative, or argumentative qualities, it may be an exemplum or a narrative of an event,[6] but it is not a pronouncement story. When it is a pronouncement story, flexibility in length and detail is characteristic of it, since an essential aspect of rhetorical discourse is adaptation to different circumstances and situations through abridgment, expansion, and elaboration.[7]

Third, the main character in a pronouncement story may be either "the author or recipient of the speech or action" in the story.[8] Previous research often excluded stories in which the main character was the recipient of the speech or action rather than its author. Recent research, however, suggests that stories where an unnamed or general type of speaker performs the saying or action (for example, the baptism of Jesus when a voice from heaven says, "Thou art my beloved Son; with thee I am well pleased") may be pronouncement stories.

Personalities of the Mediterranean World

A basic presupposition of this collection is that people will be interested in other people's stories as well as their own. People who study the thought and action of any person in Mediterranean antiquity, be it Jesus or Hillel, Socrates or Muḥammad, Alexander or Caesar, should have a natural interest in the stories in this book. The collection probably will contain a significant number of stories about the individual the person is studying, and it certainly will contain stories about other individuals in the culture.

---

second edition (1933), he was so influenced by Bultmann's discussion of the apophthegm that he misconstrued the *chreia* as "the reproduction of a short pointed saying of general significance, originating in a definite person and arising out of a definite situation" (see *From Tradition to Gospel* [New York: Charles Scribner's Sons] 152). For further discussion of this, see the first chapter in Burton L. Mack and Vernon K. Robbins, *Patterns of Persuasion in the Gospels* (Sonoma, CA: Polebridge, 1989).

5. See the discussion and references in Carole R. Fontaine, *Traditional Sayings in the Old Testament: A Contextual Study* (Sheffield: Almond, 1982); Vernon K. Robbins, "Picking Up the Fragments: From Crossan's Analysis to Rhetorical Analysis," *Forum* 1,2 (1985): 31–64; Robert de Beaugrande and Wolfgang Dressler, *Introduction to Text Linguistics* (London and New York: Longman, 1981) 131, 163–181.

6. For a definition and discussion of narrative in antiquity, see Butts, The *"Progymnasmata" of Theon*, 291–401.

7. These are terms that come from rhetorical textbooks entitled *Progymnasmata*, written by Aelius Theon of Alexandria (50–100 C.E.) and Hermogenes (2d cent. C.E.). See Hock and O'Neil, *The Chreia* , pp. 100–103, 106–107, 176–177.

8. This observation again comes from the *Progymnasmata*, which present both "active" and "passive" forms of stories. See Hock and O'Neil, *The Chreia*, 88–89; Mack and Robbins, *Patterns of Persuasion in the Gospels*, chap. 6.

A good way to enter other people's stories is through basic social situations in life. All of us interact at some time in our lives with family or relatives, friends or associates, leaders or representatives of groups, specific groups who present a united front, young people, and old people. Likewise, if we live long enough, we will move through stages of life characterized by birth, youth, adulthood, old age, and death. Since these are universal human situations, they represent a good way to enter stories in our own tradition and other people's traditions. Therefore, we have grouped the stories under categories that reflect these situations.

Perhaps an interpreter has not thought about this way of entering other people's stories but looks for topics, stories about specific people, or stories in a particular kind of literature. Indexes in the back of the volume provide ready access to the stories from these angles of interest. There the reader will find:

1. a reference index to specific passages (grouped in sections entitled Hebrew Bible and Apocrypha; Hellenistic, Rabbinic, and Other Jewish Literature; New Testament; Early Christian Literature; Islamic Hadith and Qur'an; Greek and Latin Authors);

2. an index to names and places in the stories (both specific names such as "Socrates" and types such as "Athenian," etc.);

3. a subject index ("divorce," "swimming," "footrace," etc.). It is hoped, therefore, that the book will be useful to people who have an interest in various kinds of stories and that the arrangement may encourage new ways of comparing stories with one another.

The Arrangement of the Stories

After the stories had been collected and printed, Vernon K. Robbins, in consultation with the members of the Group during its second phase (see the preface) and with the assistance of Russell Sisson, established thirteen categories to group the stories from the beginning of a person's life until his or her death. The overall arrangement is based on the life cycle of a human being, because every pronouncement story is about some person. Within the life cycle, the time of one's adult career presents the most occasions for encounter with other people. Very few stories feature only young people interacting with one another. There are seven sub-sections under "adult career" which present an adult interacting with various kinds of individuals or groups. On the basis of five stages in the life cycle of an individual and eight basic kinds of individuals or groups people encounter during their adult career, the overall arrangement of the book is as follows:

1. Birth
2. Youth
3. Adult
   3.1 Friend or Associate
   3.2 Clusters of Friends or Associates
   3.3 Family
   3.4 Women
   3.5 General
   3.6 Leaders
   3.7 Groups
   3.8 Youth
4. Old Age
5. Death

Within each section, the stories are arranged in alphabetical order according to author or, in some instances, type of document. For example, stories in the writings of Babrius occur before stories in the writings of Cicero. Individual documents by these authors appear alphabetically under each author, for example, stories from Plutarch's *Crassus* occur before stories from Plutarch's *Demetrius*. When stories were similar, however, they were grouped together with numbers ending in a, b, c, etc. Within this grouping, alphabetical ordering may not be maintained, and some stories may occur outside their appropriate section in the life cycle. For the convenience of the reader, all stories found in Acts, Gospels, Hadith literature, Mekhilta, Mishnah, Sifre, and Tosefta can be found under these headings. Also for convenience, a list of all the documents in their alphabetical order is presented here:

Acts, Peter
Acts, John
Apocryphal Daniel, Bel and the
   Dragon
Aphrahat, Demonstrations
Augustine, Against Opposition to the
   Law and the Prophets
Babrius, Aesopic Fables
Cassian, John, Conferences
Cicero, Academica
Cicero, De Amicitia
Cicero, De Finibus
Cicero, De Officiis
Cicero, De Senectute
Cicero, Pro Archia
Cicero, Tusculan Disputations
2 Clement
Clement of Alexandria, Stromateis
Diogenes Laertius
Epistle, Pseudo Titus
Eunapius, Lives of the Philosophers
Frontinus, Stratagems
Gellius, Aulus, Attic Nights
Gospel, Egyptians
Gospel, John
Gospel, Luke
Gospel, Mark
Gospel, Matthew
Gospel, Nazoreans
Gospel, Philip
Gospel, Thomas (Coptic)
Hadith, Abū Dawud
Hadith, Albānī
Hadith, Bukhārī
Hadith, Ibn Ḥanbal
Hadith, Mālik
Hadith, Muslim

Hadith, Ṭayālisī
Hadith, Tirmidhī
Hippolytus, On Daniel
Josephus, Against Apion
Josephus, Jewish War
Lives of the Prophets, Daniel
Lucian, Demonax
Macrobius, Saturnalia
Mani, Book of Mysteries
Martyrdom, Peter
Mekhilta, Ish. Pisha
Mekhilta, Ish. Vayassa
Mishnah, Abot
Mishnah, Berakhot
Nepos, Cornelius, Lives of Generals
Papias, from Irenaeus Against
   Heresies
Papyrus Egerton
Papyrus Oxyrhynchus
Phaedrus, Aesopic Fables
Philo, Every Good Man is Free
Philo, On Abraham
Philo, On Providence
Philostratus, Life of Apollonius
Philostratus, Lives of the Sophists
Plutarch, Aemilius Paulus
Plutarch, Agesilaus
Plutarch, Agis
Plutarch, Alcibiades
Plutarch, Alexander
Plutarch, Antony
Plutarch, Aratus
Plutarch, Aristides
Plutarch, Artaxerxes
Plutarch, Brutus
Plutarch, Caesar
Plutarch, Caius Gracchus

Plutarch, Caius Marcius Coriolanus
Plutarch, Caius Marius
Plutarch, Camillus
Plutarch, Cato the Younger
Plutarch, Cicero
Plutarch, Cimon
Plutarch, Cleomenes
Plutarch, Crassus
Plutarch, Demetrius
Plutarch, Demosthenes
Plutarch, Demosthenes and Cicero
Plutarch, Dion
Plutarch, Eumenes
Plutarch, Fabius Maximus
Plutarch, Lucullus
Plutarch, Lycurgus
Plutarch, Lysander
Plutarch, Marcus Cato
Plutarch, Moralia (by LCL volume
  number and paragraph)
Plutarch, Nicias
Plutarch, Nicias and Crassus
Plutarch, Numa
Plutarch, Pelopidas
Plutarch, Pericles

Plutarch, Philopoemen
Plutarch, Phocion
Plutarch, Pompey
Plutarch, Pyrrhus
Plutarch, Sertorius
Plutarch, Solon
Plutarch, Sulla
Plutarch, Themistocles
Plutarch, Theseus
Plutarch, Tiberius Gracchus
Plutarch, Timoleon
Plutarch, Titus Flaminius
Sifra
Sifre, Deuteronomy
Sifre, Numbers
Suetonius, Lives of the Caesars
Testament, Job
Tosefta, Berakhot
Tosefta, Hagigah
Tosefta, Kelim Baba Batra
Tosefta, Nedarim
Tosefta, Pisha
Tosefta, Shebuot
Xenophon, Agesilaus
Xenophon, Memorabilia

Some Statistics About the Collection

The largest number of stories in this volume (ca. 600) feature an adult person interacting with a leader or representative of a group or type of person different from which he himself (or she herself) belongs. This suggests that some of the most important stories from the past show an adult interacting with a person who is in some way "an outsider" to his or her group or type, and he or she in turn is "an outsider" to the other person. The next largest group of stories, however (ca. 450), present an adult interacting with associates or friends. In these, interaction occurs with members of some kind of "inside group." It can be informative in future research to investigate the number and kind of "insider" and "outsider" stories transmitted about various individuals from the past.

The next largest number of stories (more than 200) show an adult interacting with a specified group (i.e., given a specific name like "Athenians" or "slaves"), and these groups often speak as a united front with plural voice. If there is any surprise in this collection, probably this is it. Interpreters of the New Testament have been aware of stories in which disciples, scribes, Pharisees, or Sadducees address Jesus with a united, plural voice. But it may be new information to some interpreters that characterization of a group through a plural voice (like a chorus) is widespread throughout the literature of late Mediterranean antiquity. It would be informative to see studies of the characterization of groups in stories where they speak in plural voice in contrast to other characterizations we possess.

Approximately 175 of the 1750 feature present or refer to a feminine person. It is likely that more than ten percent of the population in late Mediterranean antiquity was feminine, yet they only appear in this disproportionate ratio.

Ten percent of the stories also contain some aspect of interaction or relationship among family members. This percentage, though not exceptionally high, is likely to be similar to the number of stories about family members in our society, since for us, too, stories about interaction among leaders and representatives of various groups are likely to be in the majority.

Approximately seventy-five of the stories contain comments by or about people in the setting of their death. This is more than five times the number of pronouncement stories about people's birth, perhaps because birth stories are limited completely to speech and action by people other than the one who is being born.

The Scope of the Collection

Some may wish to know why stories from these documents and not other documents were chosen for this volume. The project began with a focus on stories between 250 B.C.E. and 250 C.E. in Mediterranean literature. We found a large number of stories in Greek and Latin literature and fewer than we expected in Jewish literature. We have decided to go to print with a less than "complete" collection, since, in the judgment of many, the volume is already large enough. The earliest documents included here are Xenophon's *Agesilaus* and *Memorabilia*. We have not plumbed Plato's *Dialogues* , simply because no one accepted the task. Theon cites a *chreia* in Plato's *Republic* 1.329C (see 598): The writings of Plato and Xenophon (ca. 400–350 B.C.E.) appear to exhibit some of the earliest pronouncement stories in Greek literature.

We have included some stories from Islamic Hadith literature (7–10th century C.E.) because R. Marston Speight became involved in our project, because the stories contain aspects similar to rabbinic tradition, and because it is very important that we become informed about Islamic traditions.

We were amazed at the small number of pronouncement stories in Jewish literature. We are still awaiting a probing analysis of units in the Hebrew Bible that in some way approximate a pronouncement story. The best examples we have seen are in the latest books and the apocrypha.

We have tried to cover known literature in the period from 250 B.C.E. to 250 C.E. to see if pronouncement stories appear with any frequency. There were surprises. We found no pronouncement stories in Herodotus or Polybius. Some interpreters have argued that stories analogous in length and rhetorical quality to stories in the Synoptic Gospels do not appear with any frequency in Greek and Roman literature. The assertion is false. Many stories containing moderate to extensive expansion of units in the Synoptic Gospels do in fact occur.

We have tried to present a complete collection of pronouncement stories from some of the documents we selected. This book contains a virtually complete collection of pronouncement stories from the following literature:

> Christian Apocryphal Literature
> The documents of Cicero listed
> The Gospels listed
> The Rabbinic Literature listed
> Josephus
> Lucian, *Demonax*

Philo
Plutarch, *Parallel Lives* (not the *Moralia*)
The documents of Xenophon listed
Suetonius, *Lives of the Caesars*

For the remaining literature, the selections are representative but may not be complete.

The reasons for a less than complete collection are at least threefold. First, over the twelve year period from 1975 to 1987 the definition of a pronouncement story has been a moving target. It seemed wise to test the stability of the definition among a broader public before attempting a complete collection. Second, a complete collection would expand the publication to more than one volume, and it was decided that we should go to press with a one-volume collection. Third, I prefer, more and more, to print as large a literary context as possible for the story, and this could add many pages to many volumes. It seemed wise, therefore, to proceed with this collection of stories.

Because of the nature of pronouncement stories themselves and of this collection, we recommend that every serious user of this volume investigate the broader literary setting in which the stories exist. The purpose of the volume is to display a wide range of stories. There is, to our knowledge, no parallel collection of such stories available. It is our hope that some truly comprehensive volumes will appear in the future.

Birth

The ancients liked to tell anecdotes about the marvelous conception or birth of famous persons. Conception or birth was often accompanied by omens and portents. Such signs were taken to signal future greatness, or, in rare cases, future misfortune. Only a few of the many birth stories from antiquity incorporate famous sayings, which means that the selection for this volume is severely limited.

Birth

1   *The Birth of Jesus*
Gospel, Matthew 1:18–25

Now the birth of Jesus Christ took place in this way. When his mother Mary had been betrothed to Joseph, before they came together she was found to be with child of the Holy Spirit; and her husband Joseph, being a just man and unwilling to put her to shame, resolved to divorce her quietly. But as he considered this, behold, an angel of the Lord appeared to him in a dream, saying, "Joseph, son of David, do not fear to take Mary your wife, for that which is conceived in her is of the Holy Spirit; she will bear a son, and you shall call his name Jesus, for he will save his people from their sins." All this took place to fulfill what the Lord had spoken by the prophet: "Behold, a virgin shall conceive and bear a son, and his name shall be called Emmanuel" (which means, God with us). When Joseph woke from sleep, he did as the angel of the Lord commanded him; he took his wife, but knew her not until she had borne a son; and he called his name Jesus.

2   *The Wise Men Inquire Where the King of the Jews Has Been Born*
Gospel, Matthew 2:1–6

Now when Jesus was born in Bethlehem of Judea in the days of Herod the king, behold, wise men from the East came to Jerusalem, saying, "Where is he who has been born king of the Jews? For we have seen his star in the East, and have come to worship him."[1] When Herod the king heard this, he was troubled, and all Jerusalem with him; and assembling all the chief priests and scribes of the people, he inquired of them where the Christ was to be born. They told him, "In Bethlehem of Judea; for so it is written by the prophet: 'And you, O Bethlehem, in the land of Judah, are by no means least among the rulers of Judah; for from you shall come a ruler who will govern my people Israel.'"[2]

1. Jeremiah 23:5; Numbers 24:17.
2. Micah 5:2.

3   *Philip's Dream about Olympias' Pregnancy*
Plutarch, Alexander 2.4–5 (2–3)

At a later time, too, after the marriage, Philip dreamed that he was putting a seal upon his wife's womb; and the device of the seal, as he thought, was the figure of a lion. The other seers, now, were led by the vision to suspect that Philip needed to put a closer watch upon his marriage relations; but Aristander of Telmessus said that the woman was pregnant, since no seal was put upon what was empty, and pregnant of a son whose nature would be bold and lion-like.

4   *Delphic Oracle: Loss of Philip's Eye*
Plutarch, Alexander 3.1–2 (1)

However, after his vision, as we are told, Philip sent Chaeron of Megalopolis to Delphi, by whom an oracle was brought him from Apollo, who bade him sacrifice to Ammon and hold that god in greatest reverence, but told him he was to lose that one of his eyes which he had applied to the chink in the door when he espied the god, in the form of a serpent, sharing the couch of his wife.

5   *Burning of the Temple of Artemis at Alexander's Birth*
Plutarch, Alexander 3.5–7 (3–4)

Be that as it may, Alexander was born early in the month Hecatombaeon,[1] the Macedonian name for which is Loüs, on the sixth day of the month, and on this day the temple of Ephesian Artemis was burnt. It was apropos of this that Hegesias the Magnesian made an utterance frigid enough to have extinguished that great conflagration. He said, namely, it was no wonder that the temple of Artemis was burned down, since the goddess was busy bringing Alexander into the world. But all the Magi who were then at Ephesus, looking upon the temple's disaster as a sign of further disaster, ran about beating their faces and crying aloud that woe and great calamity for Asia had that day been born.

> 1. 356 B.C.E. The day of birth has probably been moved back two or three months for the sake of the coincidence mentioned below (vs.5). Hecatombaeon corresponds nearly to July.

6a   *Three Victories on the Day of Alexander's Birth*
Plutarch, Alexander 3.8–9 (4–5)

To Philip, however, who had just taken Potidaea, there came three messages at the same time: the first that Parmenio had conquered the Illyrians in a great battle, the second that his race-horse had won a victory at the Olympic games, while a third announced the birth of Alexander. These things delighted him, of course, and the seers raised his spirits still higher by declaring that the son whose birth coincided with three victories would be always victorious.

6b   *Three Victories on the Day of Alexander's Birth*
Plutarch, Moralia, A Letter to Apollonius II:105A–B

Philip, the king of the Macedonians, happened to have three pieces of good news reported to him all at once: the first, that he was victor at the Olympic games in the race of the four-horse chariots; the second, that Parmenio, his general, had vanquished the Dardanians in battle, and the third, that Olympias had borne him a male child; whereupon, stretching out his hands toward the heavens, he said: "O God, offset all this by some moderate misfortune!" For he well knew that in cases of great prosperity fortune is wont to be jealous.

6c   *Happy Events on a Single Day*
Plutarch, Moralia, Sayings of Kings and Commanders III:177C

When several happy events were reported to him [Philip] within a single day, he said, "O Fortune, do me some little ill to offset so many good things like these!"

7   *Lycurgus Rejoices in the Birth of Charilaüs*
Plutarch, Lycurgus 3.3–4

And it came to pass that as he [Lycurgus] was at supper with the chief magistrates, a male child was born, and his servants brought the little boy to him. He took it in his arms, as we are told, and said to those who were at table with him, "A king is born unto you, O men of Sparta"; then he laid it down in the royal seat and named it Charilaüs, or People's Joy, because all present were filled with joy, admiring as they did his lofty spirit and his righteousness.

8   *Predictions at Nero's Birth*

Suetonius, Lives of the Caesars, Nero 6.6.1

Many people at once made many direful predictions from his [Nero's] horo-scope, and a remark of his father Domitius was also regarded as an omen; for while receiving the congratulations of his friends, he said that "nothing that was not abominable and a public bane could be born of Agrippina and himself."

The stories listed below refer to the birth of a child, but other features in the stories have determined their location in another section.

Diogenes Laertius: 1192
Plutarch: 31

Youth

In ancient lore, the time of youth forecasts what the person will be like as an adult. The precocious and powerful young Jesus becomes the adult Jesus who knows other people's thoughts and tames cosmic powers. The disciplined and skilled Alexander becomes the general who programmatically conquers the world with a demeanor of generosity, fairness, and honor. One or more dramatic events close the period of youth and inaugurate adult life. We have included such transitional events in this section.

Youth

9a *Flutes not for Athenians*
Gellius, Attic Nights 15.17.1–3

Alcibiades the Athenian in his boyhood was being trained in the liberal arts and sciences at the home of his uncle, Pericles; and Pericles had ordered Antigenidas, a player on the pipes, to be sent for, to teach the boy to play on that instrument, which was then considered a great accomplishment. But when the pipes were handed to him and he had put them to his lips and blown, disgusted at the ugly distortion of his face, he threw them away and broke them in two. When this matter was noised abroad, by the universal consent of the Athenians of that time the art of playing the pipes was given up.

9b *Flutes not for Athenians*
Plutarch, Alcibiades 2.4–5

At school, he [Alcibiades] usually paid due heed to his teachers, but he refused to play the flute, holding it to be an ignoble and illiberal thing. The use of the plectrum and the lyre, he argued, wrought no havoc with the bearing and appearance which were becoming to a gentleman; but let a man go to blowing on a flute, and even his own kinsmen could scarcely recognize his features. Moreover, the lyre blended its tones with the voice or song of its master; whereas the flute closed and barricaded the mouth, robbing its master both of voice and of speech. "Flutes, then," said he, "for the sons of Thebes; they know not how to converse. But we Athenians, as our fathers say, have Athene for foundress and Apollo for patron, one of whom cast the flute away in disgust, and the other flayed the presumptious flute-player."[1]

> 1. Athene threw away the flute because she saw her puffed and swollen cheeks reflected in the water of a spring. Marsyas the satyr was vanquished by Apollo in a musical contest, and was flayed alive.

10 *Jesus Raises Zenon*
Gospel, Infancy Thomas 9.1–3

A few days later, Jesus was playing in the upper story of a house. One of the children playing with him fell off the house and was killed. And when the other children saw it they fled; Jesus remained behind. And the parents of the dead child came and accused him of having pushed him off. And Jesus replied: "I did not push him off." But they continued to scold him. Then Jesus jumped down from the roof and stood by the body of the child, and shouted with a loud voice: "Zenon"—for that was his name—"arise and tell me, did I push you off?" And he arose at once and said: "No, Lord, you did not push me off, but raised me up." And when they saw it they were amazed. And the parents of the child glorified God for the miracle that had occurred and worshipped Jesus.

11a *The Coming One*
Gospel, John 1:19–23

And this is the testimony of John, when the Jews sent priests and Levites from Jerusalem to ask him, "Who are you?" He confessed, he did not deny, but confessed, "I am not the Christ." And they asked him, "What then? Are you Elijah?" He said, "I am not." "Are you the prophet?" And he answered, "No." They said to him then, "Who are you? Let us have an answer for those who sent us. What do you say about yourself?" He said, "I am the voice of one crying in the wilderness, 'Make straight the way of the Lord,'¹ as the prophet Isaiah said."

1. Isaiah 40:3.

11b *He Must Increase*
Gospel, John 3:25–30

Now a discussion arose between John's disciples and a Jew over purifying. And they came to John, and said to him, "Rabbi, he who was with you beyond the Jordan, to whom you bore witness, here he is, baptizing, and all are going to him." John answered, "No one can receive anything except what is given him from heaven. You yourselves bear me witness, that I said, I am not the Christ, but I have been sent before him. He who has the bride is the bridegroom; the friend of the bridegroom, who stands and hears him, rejoices greatly at the bridegroom's voice; therefore this joy of mine is now full. He must increase, but I must decrease."

11c *John the Baptist's Call for Repentance*
Gospel, Matthew 3:1–3

In those days came John the Baptist, preaching in the wilderness of Judea, "Repent, for the kingdom of heaven is at hand." For this is he who was spoken of by the prophet Isaiah when he said, "The voice of one crying in the wilderness: Prepare the way of the Lord, make his paths straight."¹

1. Isaiah 40:3.

12a *He of Whom I Spoke*
Gospel, John 1:29–34

The next day he saw Jesus coming toward him, and said, "Behold, the Lamb of God, who takes away the sin of the world! This is he of whom I said, 'After me comes a man who ranks before me, for he was before me.' I myself did not know him; but for this I came baptizing with water, that he might be revealed to Israel." And John bore witness, "I saw the Spirit descend as a dove from heaven, and it remained on him. I myself did not know him; but he who sent me to baptize with water said to me, 'He on whom you see the Spirit descend and remain, this is he who baptizes with the Holy Spirit.' And I have seen and have borne witness that this is the Son of God."

12b *The Coming One*
Gospel, John 1:15

John bore witness to him [Jesus], and cried, "This was he of whom I said, 'He who comes after me ranks before me, for he was before me.'"

12c *The Coming One*
Gospel, Luke 3:15–17

As the people were in expectation, and all men questioned in their hearts concerning John, whether perhaps he were the Christ, John answered them all, "I baptize you with water; but he who is mightier than I is coming, the thong of whose sandals I am not worthy to untie; he will baptize you with the Holy Spirit and with fire. His winnowing fork is in his hand, to clear his threshing floor, and to gather the wheat into his granary, but the chaff he will burn with unquenchable fire."

12d *Baptism of Jesus*
Gospel, Luke 3:21–22

Now when all the people were baptized, and when Jesus also had been baptized and was praying, the heaven was opened, and the Holy Spirit descended upon him in bodily form, as a dove, and a voice came from heaven, "Thou art my beloved Son; with thee I am well pleased."

12e *The Coming One*
Gospel, Mark 1:4–8

John the baptizer appeared in the wilderness, preaching a baptism of repentance for the forgiveness of sins. And there went out to him all the country of Judea, and all the people of Jerusalem; and they were baptized by him in the river Jordan, confessing their sins. Now John was clothed with camel's hair, and had a leather girdle around his waist, and ate locusts and wild honey. And he preached, saying, "After me comes he who is mightier than I, the thong of whose sandals I am not worthy to stoop down and untie. I have baptized you with water; but he will baptize you with the Holy Spirit."

12f *Baptism of Jesus*
Gospel, Mark 1:9–11

In those days Jesus came from Nazareth of Galilee and was baptized by John in the Jordan. And when he came up out of the water, immediately he saw the heavens opened and the Spirit descending upon him like a dove; and a voice came from heaven, "Thou art my beloved Son; with thee I am well pleased."

12g *Baptism of Jesus*
Gospel, Matthew 3:13–15

Then Jesus came from Galilee to the Jordan to John, to be baptized by him. John would have prevented him, saying, "I need to be baptized by you, and do you come to me?" But Jesus answered him, "Let it be so now; for thus it is fitting for us to fulfil all righteousness." Then he consented.

12h *Baptism of Jesus*
Gospel, Matthew 3:16–17

And when Jesus was baptized, he went up immediately from the water, and behold, the heavens were opened and he saw the Spirit of God descending like a dove, and alighting on him; and lo, a voice from heaven saying, "This is my beloved Son, with whom I am well pleased."

12i *Transfiguration of Jesus*
Gospel, Mark 9:2–8

And after six days Jesus took with him Peter and James and John, and led them up a high mountain apart by themselves; and he was transfigured before them, and his garments became glistening, intensely white, as no fuller on earth could bleach them. And there appeared to them Elijah with Moses; and they were talking to Jesus. And Peter said to Jesus, "Master, it is well that we are here; let us make three booths, one for you and one for Moses and one for Elijah." For he did not know what to say, for they were exceedingly afraid. And a cloud overshadowed them, and a voice came out of a cloud, "This is my beloved Son; listen to him." And suddenly looking around they no longer saw any one with them but Jesus only.

12j   On Baptism
Gospel, Nazoreans 2, from Jerome, *Dialogue Against the Pelagians* 3.2
(Migne, PL 23:570–571)

Behold, the mother and brothers of the Lord said to him, "John the Baptist baptizes for the remission of sins. Let us go and be baptized by him." But he replied, "Have I committed a sin that I should go and be baptized by him? Unless what I have just said is a sin of ignorance."

13   The Boy Jesus in the Temple
Gospel, Luke 2:41–51

Now his Jesus' parents went to Jerusalem every year at the feast of the Passover. And when he was twelve years old, they went up according to custom; and when the feast was ended, as they were returning, the boy Jesus stayed behind in Jerusalem. His parents did not know it, but supposing him to be in the company they went a day's journey, and they sought him among their kinsfolk and acquaintances; and when they did not find him, they returned to Jerusalem, seeking him. After three days they found him in the temple, sitting among the teachers, listening to them and asking them questions; and all who heard him were amazed at his understanding and his answers. And when they saw him they were astonished; and his mother said to him, "Son, why have you treated us so? Behold, your father and I have been looking for you anxiously." And he said to them, "How is it that you sought me? Did you not know that I must be in my Father's house?" And they did not understand the saying which he spoke to them. And he went down with them and came to Nazareth, and was obedient to them; and his mother kept all these things in her heart.

14a   Temptation of Jesus
Gospel, Luke 4:1–4

And Jesus, full of the Holy Spirit, returned from the Jordan, and was led by the Spirit for forty days in the wilderness, tempted by the devil. And he ate nothing in those days; and when they were ended, he was hungry. The devil said to him, "If you are the Son of God, command this stone to become bread." And Jesus answered him, "It is written, 'Man shall not live by bread alone.'"[1]

1. Deuteronomy 8:3.

14b   Temptation of Jesus
Gospel, Mark 1:12–13

The Spirit immediately drove him [Jesus] out into the wilderness. And he was in the wilderness forty days, tempted by Satan; and he was with the wild beasts; and the angels ministered to him.

14c *Temptation of Jesus*
Gospel, Matthew 4:1-4

Then Jesus was led up by the Spirit into the wilderness to be tempted by the devil. And he fasted forty days and forty nights, and afterward he was hungry. And the tempter came and said to him, "If you are the Son of God, command these stones to become loaves of bread." But he answered, "It is written, 'Man shall not live by bread alone, but by every word that proceeds from the mouth of God.'"[1]

1. Deuteronomy 8:3.

15a *Temptation of Jesus*
Gospel, Luke 4:5-8

And the devil took him up, and showed him all the kingdoms of the world in a moment of time, and said to him, "To you I will give all this authority and their glory; for it has been delivered to me, and I give it to whom I will. If you, then, will worship me, it shall all be yours." And Jesus answered him, "It is written, 'You shall worship the Lord your God, and him only shall you serve.'"[1]

1. Deuteronomy 6:13.

15b *Temptation of Jesus*
Gospel, Matthew 4:8-11

Again, the devil took him [Jesus] to a very high mountain, and showed him all the kingdoms of the world and the glory of them; and he said to him, "All these I will give you, if you will fall down and worship me." Then Jesus said to him, "Begone, Satan! for it is written, 'You shall worship the Lord your God and him only shall you serve.'"[1] Then the devil left him, and behold, angels came and ministered to him.

1. Deuteronomy 6:13.

16a *Temptation of Jesus*
Gospel, Luke 4:9-13

And he [the devil] took him to Jerusalem, and set him on the pinnacle of the temple, and said to him, "If you are the Son of God, throw yourself down from here; for it is written, 'He will give his angels charge of you, to guard you,' and 'On their hands they will bear you up, lest you strike your foot against a stone.'"[1] And Jesus answered him, "It is said, 'You shall not tempt the Lord your God.'"[2] And when the devil had ended every temptation, he departed from him until an opportune time.

1. Psalm 91:11-12.
2. Deuteronomy 6:16.

16b *Temptation of Jesus*
Gospel, Matthew 4:5-7

Then the devil took him [Jesus] to the holy city, and set him on the pinnacle of the temple, and said to him, "If you are the Son of God, throw yourself down; for it is written, 'He will give his angels charge of you,'[1] and 'On their hands they will bear you up, lest you strike your foot against a stone.'" Jesus said to him, "Again it is written, 'You shall not tempt the Lord your God.'"[2]

1. Psalm 91:11-12.
2. Deuteronomy 6:16.

17a *Beginning of Jesus' Public Ministry*
Gospel, Mark 1:14–15

Now after John was arrested, Jesus came into Galilee, preaching the gospel of God, and saying, "The time is fulfilled, and the kingdom of God is at hand; repent, and believe in the gospel."

17b *Beginning of Jesus' Public Ministry*
Gospel, Matthew 4:17

From that time Jesus began to preach, saying, "Repent, for the kingdom of heaven is at hand."

17c *Commission of Twelve to Lost Sheep of the House of Israel*
Gospel, Matthew 10:5–7

These twelve Jesus sent out, charging them, "Go nowhere among the Gentiles, and enter no town of the Samaritans, but go rather to the lost sheep of the house of Israel. And preach as you go, saying, 'The kingdom of heaven is at hand.'

17d *John the Baptist's Call for Repentance*
Gospel, Matthew 3:1–3

In those days came John the Baptist, preaching in the wilderness of Judea, "Repent, for the kingdom of heaven is at hand." For this is he who was spoken of by the prophet Isaiah when he said, "The voice of one crying in the wilderness: Prepare the way of the Lord, make his paths straight."[1]

> 1. Isaiah 40:3.

18 *Flight to Egypt*
Gospel, Matthew 2:13–15

Now when they [the wise men] had departed, behold, an angel of the Lord appeared to Joseph in a dream and said, "Rise, take the child and his mother, and flee to Egypt, and remain there till I tell you; for Herod is about to search for the child, to destroy him." And he rose and took the child and his mother by night, and departed to Egypt, and remained there until the death of Herod. This was to fulfil what the Lord had spoken by the prophet, "Out of Egypt have I called my son."[1]

> 1. Hosea 11:1; cf. Exodus 4:22.

19 *Herod Kills Male Children*
Gospel, Matthew 2:16–18

Then Herod, when he saw that he had been tricked by the wise men, was in a furious rage, and he sent and killed all the male children in Bethlehem and in all that region who were two years old or under, according to the time which he had ascertained from the wise men. Then was fulfilled what was spoken by the prophet Jeremiah:

> "A voice was heard in Ramah,
> wailing and loud lamentation,
> Rachel weeping for her children;
> she refused to be consoled,
> because they were no more."[1]

> 1. Jeremiah 31:15.

20   *Return to Nazareth*
Gospel, Matthew 2:19–23

But when Herod died, behold, an angel of the Lord appeared in a dream to Joseph in Egypt, saying, "Rise, take the child and his mother, and go to the land of Israel, for those who sought the child's life are dead." And he rose and took the child and his mother, and went to the land of Israel. But when he heard that Archelaus reigned over Judea in place of his father Herod, he was afraid to go there, and being warned in a dream he withdrew to the district of Galilee. And he went and dwelt in a city called Nazareth, that what was spoken by the prophets might be fulfilled, "He shall be called a Nazarene."[1]

1. Cf. Isaiah 11:1; there is a similarity in sound and possibly in meaning between the Aramaic word for Nazareth and the Hebrew word translated branch in this verse.

21   *The Boast of Vatinius*
Macrobius, Saturnalia 2.4.16

As a young man he [Augustus] neatly made fun of one Vatinius who had become crippled by gout but nevertheless wished it to be thought that he had gotten rid of the complaint. The man was boasting that he could walk a mile; "I can well believe it," said Augustus, "the days are getting somewhat longer."

22   *Warming the Water*
Macrobius, Saturnalia 2.7.6

This Publilius was by birth a Syrian, and as a boy he had been brought to his master's patron, whose favor he won as much by his wit and intelligence as by his good looks. For the patron one day happened to see a slave of his who suffered from dropsy lying on the ground and angrily asked what the fellow was doing in the sun: "Warming the water," replied Publilius.

23   *Gout in the Feet*
Macrobius, Saturnalia 2.7.6

On another occasion, when various answers were being given to a question asked in jest at dinner—what was meant by the expression "troublesome idleness,"[1] Publilius said: "Gout in the feet."

1. *Molestum otium*: perhaps Catullus 51.13 (*otium, Catulle, tibi molestum est*) was being discussed. This is not a wordplay, but is a witty explanation for not getting up and doing things.

24   *Harlot and Young Man*
Phaedrus, Aesopic Fables, Appendix 29

When a treacherous harlot was wheedling a young man and he, though wronged by her many times and in many ways, nevertheless allowed himself to be her easy victim, the insidious creature made this remark: "Though many rivals compete with gifts, still I think most of you." The young man, recalling how many times he had been fooled, said: "I take pleasure in hearing those words, my love, not because they are sincere but because they make me happy."

25   *Varus and Polemo*
Philostratus, Lives of the Sophists 1.25 (540–541)

There was an Ionian youth who was indulging in a life of dissipation at Smyrna to a degree not customary with the Ionians, and was being ruined by his great wealth, which is a vicious teacher of ill-regulated natures. Now the youth's name was Varus, and he had been so spoiled by parasites that he had convinced himself that he was the fairest of the fair, the tallest of the tall, and the noblest and most expert of the youths at the wrestling-ground, and that not even the Muses could strike up a prelude more sweetly than he, whenever he had a mind to sing. He had the same notions about the sophists; that is to say, that he could outstrip even their tongues whenever he declaimed—and he actually used to declaim—and those who borrowed money from him used to reckon their attendance at his declamations as part of the interest. Even Polemo, when he was still a young man and not yet an invalid, was induced to pay this tribute, for he had borrowed money from him, and when he did not pay court to him or attend his lectures, the youth resented it and threatened him with a summons to recover the debt. This summons is a writ issued by the law court proclaiming judgement by default against the debtor who fails to pay. Thereupon his friends reproached Polemo with being morose and discourteous, seeing that when he could avoid being sued and could profit by the young man's money by merely giving him an amiable nod of approval, he would not do this, but provoked and irritated him. Hearing this sort of thing said, he did indeed come to the lecture, but when, late in the evening, the youth's declamation was still going on, and no place of anchorage for his speech was in sight, and everything he said was full of solecisms, barbarisms, and inconsistencies, Polemo jumped up, and stretching out his hands, cried: "Varus, bring your summons."

26   *The Eloquence of Hermogenes*
Philostratus, Lives of the Sophists 2.7 (577–578)

The following will show the kind of eloquence that he [Hermogenes] affected. In a speech that he was delivering before Marcus, he said, "You see before you, Emperor, an orator who still needs an attendant to take him to school, an orator who still looks to come of age." He said much more of this sort and in the same facetious vein. He died at a ripe old age, but accounted as one of the rank and file, for he became despised when his skill in his art deserted him.

27   *The Inimitable Herodes*
Philostratus, Lives of the Sophists 2.10 (586)

Adrian the Phoenician was born at Tyre, but he was trained in rhetoric at Athens. For, as I used to hear from my own teachers, he came to Athens in the time of Herodes and there displayed a great natural talent for sophistic, and it was generally held that he would rise to greatness in his profession. For he began to attend the school of Herodes when he was perhaps eighteen years old, was very soon admitted to the same privileges as Sceptus and Amphicles, and was enrolled among the pupils belonging to the Clepsydrion. Now the Clepsydrion was conducted in the following manner. After the general lecture which was open to all, ten of the pupils of Herodes, that is to say those who were proved worthy of a reward for excellence, used to dine for a period limited by a water-clock timed to last through a hundred verses; and these verses Herodes used to expound with copious comments, nor would he allow any applause from his hearers, but was wholly intent on what he was saying. And since he had enjoined on his pupils not to be idle even when it was the hour for drinking, but at that time also to pursue some sort of study over their wine, Adrian used to drink with the pupils of the clepsydra as their partner in a great and mysterious rite. Now a discussion was once going on about the style of all the sophists, when Adrian came forward in their midst, and said, "I will now give a sketch of their types of style, not by quoting from memory brief phrases of theirs or smart sayings, or clauses or rhythmical effects. But I will undertake to imitate them, and will reproduce extempore the style of every one of them, with an easy flow of words and giving the rein to my tongue." But in doing this he left out Herodes, and Amphicles asked him to explain why he had omitted their own teacher, seeing that he himself was enamoured of his style of eloquence, and saw that they were likewise enamoured. "Because," said he, "these fellows are the sort that lend themselves to imitation, even when one is drunk. But as for Herodes, the prince of eloquence, I should be thankful if I could mimic him when I have had no wine and am sober."

28   Alcibiades Bites as Lion Does
Plutarch, Alcibiades 2.2

He [Alcibiades] was once hard pressed in wrestling, and to save himself from getting a fall, set his teeth in his opponent's arms, where they clutched him, and was like to have bitten through them. His adversary, letting go his hold, cried: "You bite, Alcibiades, as women do!" "Not I," said Alcibiades, "but as lions do."

29   Alcibiades Leaves Home
Plutarch, Alcibiades 3.1

Among the calumnies which Antiphon[1] heaps upon him it is recorded that, when he [Alcibiades] was a boy, he ran away from home to Democrates, one of his lovers, and that Ariphron was all for having him proclaimed by town crier as a castaway. But Pericles would not suffer it. "If he is dead," said he, "we shall know it only a day the sooner for the proclamation; whereas, if he is alive, he will, in consequence of it, be as good as dead for the rest of his life."

> 1. An abusive oration of Antiphon the Rhamnusian against Alcibiades, cited in Athenaeus 12.525B, was probably a fabrication and falsely attributed to him. It is not extant.

30a   Alcibiades Accosts Teachers
Plutarch, Alcibiades 7.1

Once, as he [Alcibiades] was getting on past boyhood, he accosted a school-teacher, and asked him for a book of Homer. The teacher replied that he had nothing of Homer's, whereupon Alcibiades fetched him a blow with his fist, and went his way. Another teacher said he had a Homer which he had corrected himself. "What!" said Alcibiades, "are you teaching boys to read when you are competent to edit Homer? You should be training young men."

30b   Alcibiades Accosts Teachers
Plutarch, Moralia, Sayings of Kings and Commanders III:186E (3)

Coming upon a schoolroom, he asked for a book of the *Iliad*, and when the teacher said that he had nothing of Homer's, Alcibiades[1] hit him a blow with his fist and passed on.[2]

> 1. Rich and erratic ward of Pericles.
> 2. Cf. Aelian, *Varia Historia* 13.38.

31a *Alexander Not Son of Zeus*
Plutarch, Alexander 3.3–4 (2)

Moreover, Olympias, as Eratosthenes says, when she sent Alexander forth upon his great expedition, told him, and him alone, the secret of his begetting, and bade him have purposes worthy of his birth. Others, on the contrary, say that she repudiated the idea, and said: "Alexander must cease slandering me to Hera."[1]

    1. The lawful spouse of Zeus Ammon.

31b *Alexander Not Son of Jupiter*
Gellius, Attic Nights 13.4.1–3

In many of the records of Alexander's deeds, and not long ago in the book of Marcus Varro entitled *Orestes or On Madness*, I have read that Olympias, the wife of Philip, wrote a very witty reply to her son Alexander. For he had addressed his mother as follows: "King Alexander, son of Jupiter Hammon, greets his mother Olympias." Olympias replied to this effect: "Pray, my son," said she, "be silent, and do not slander me or accuse me before Juno; undoubtedly she will take cruel vengeance on me, if you admit in your letters that I am her husband's paramour." This courteous reply of a wise and prudent woman to her arrogant son seemed to warn him in a mild and polite fashion to give up the foolish idea which he had formed from his great victories, from the flattery of his courtiers, and from his incredible success—that he was the son of Jupiter.

32a *Young Alexander Refuses Olympic Footrace*
Plutarch, Alexander 4.8–10 (4–5)

But while he [Alexander] was still a boy his self-restraint showed itself in the fact that, although he was impetuous and violent in other matters, the pleasures of the body had little hold upon him, and he indulged in them with great moderation, while his ambition kept his spirit serious and lofty in advance of his years. For it was neither every kind of fame nor fame from every source that he courted, as Philip did, who plumed himself like a sophist on the power of his oratory, and took care to have the victories of his chariots at Olympia engraved upon his coins; nay, when those about him inquired whether he would be willing to contend in the foot-race at the Olympic games, since he was swift of foot, "Yes," said he, "if I could have kings as my contestants."

32b *Young Alexander Refuses Olympic Footrace*
Plutarch, Moralia, Sayings of Kings and Commanders III:179D (2)

Being nimble and swift of foot, he was urged by his father to run in the foot-race at the Olympic games. "Yes, I would run," said he, "if I were to have kings as competitors."

32c *Young Alexander Refuses Olympic Footrace*
Plutarch, Moralia, Fortune of Alexander IV:331B (9a)

Since he was the swiftest of foot of all the young men of his age, his comrades urged him to enter the Olympic games. He asked if the competitors were kings, and when his friends replied that they were not, he said that the contest was unfair, for it was one in which a victory would be over commoners, but a defeat would be the defeat of a king.

33   *Young Alexander Amazes Persian Envoys*
Plutarch, Alexander 5.1–3 (1)

He [Alexander] once entertained the envoys from the Persian king who came during Philip's absence, and associated with them freely. He won upon them by his friendliness, and by asking no childish or trivial questions, but by inquiring about the length of the roads and the character of the journey into the interior, about the king himself, what sort of a warrior he was, and what the prowess and might of the Persians. The envoys were therefore astonished and regarded the much-talked-of ability of Philip as nothing compared with his son's eager disposition to do great things.

34a   *Alexander's Complaint about Philip's Achievements*
Plutarch, Alexander 5.4 (2)

At all events, as often as tidings were brought that Philip had either taken a famous city or been victorious in some celebrated battle, Alexander was not very glad to hear them, but would say to his comrades: "Boys, my father will anticipate everything; and for me he will leave no great or brilliant achievement to be displayed to the world with your aid."

34b   *Alexander's Complaint about Philip's Achievements*
Plutarch, Moralia, Sayings of Kings and Commanders III:179D (1)

While Alexander was still a boy and Philip was winning many successes, he was not glad, but said to his playmates, "My father will leave nothing for me to do." "But," said the boys, "he is acquiring all this for you." "But what good is it," said Alexander, "if I possess much and accomplish nothing?"

35   *Young Alexander Tames Bucephalus*
Plutarch, Alexander 6.1–8 (1–5)

Once upon a time Philoneicus the Thessalian brought Bucephalus, offering to sell him to Philip for thirteen talents, and they went down into the plain to try the horse, who appeared to be savage and altogether intractable, neither allowing any one to mount him, nor heeding the voice of any of Philip's attendants, but rearing up against all of them. Then Philip was vexed and ordered the horse to be led away, believing him to be altogether wild and unbroken; but Alexander, who was near by, said: "What a horse they are losing, because, for lack of skill and courage, they cannot manage him!" At first, then, Philip held his peace; but as Alexander many times let fall such words and showed great distress, he said: "Dost thou find fault with thine elders in the belief that thou knowest more than they do or art better able to manage a horse?" "This horse, at any rate," said Alexander, "I could manage better than others have." "And if thou shouldst not, what penalty wilt thou undergo for thy rashness?" "Indeed," said Alexander, "I will forfeit the price of the horse." There was laughter at this, and then an agreement between father and son as to the forfeiture, and at once Alexander ran to the horse, took hold of his bridle-rein, and turned him towards the sun; for he had noticed, as it would seem, that the horse was greatly disturbed by the sight of his own shadow falling in front of him and dancing about. And after he had calmed the horse a little in this way, and had stroked him with his hand, when he saw that he was full of spirit and courage, he quietly cast aside his mantle and with a light spring safely bestrode him. Then, with a little pressure of the reins on the bit, and without striking or tearing his mouth, he held him in hand; but when he saw that the horse was rid of the fear that had beset him, and was impatient for the course, he gave him his head, and at last urged him on with sterner tone and thrust of foot. Philip and his company were speechless with anxiety at first; but when Alexander made the turn in proper fashion and came back towards them proud and exultant, all the rest broke into loud cries, but his father, as we are told, actually shed tears of joy, saying: "My son, seek thee out a kingdom equal to thyself; Macedonia has not room for thee."

36   *Alexander Writes to Aristotle*
Plutarch, Alexander 7.4–9 (3–5)

Well, then, as a place where master and pupil could labor and study, he [Philip] assigned them [Alexander and Aristotle] the precinct of the nymphs near Mieza, where to this day the visitor is shown the stone seats and shady walks of Aristotle. It would appear, moreover, that Alexander not only received from his master his ethical and political doctrines, but also participated in those secret and more profound teachings which philosophers designate by the special terms "acroamatic" and "epoptic,"[1] and do not impart to many. For after he had already crossed into Asia, and when he learned that certain treatises on these recondite matters had been published in books by Aristotle, he wrote him a letter on behalf of philosophy, and put it in plain language. And this is a copy of the letter. "Alexander, to Aristotle, greeting. Thou hast not done well to publish thy acroamatic doctrines; for in what shall I surpass other men if those doctrines wherein I have been trained are to be all men's common property? But I had rather excel in my acquaintance with the best things than in my power. Farewell." Accordingly, in defending himself, Aristotle encourages the ambition of Alexander by saying that the doctrines of which he spoke were both published and not published; for in truth his treatise on metaphysics is of no use for those who would either teach or learn the science, but is written as a memorandum for those already trained therein.

     1. I.e., fit for oral teaching only, and for the initiated; "esoteric," as opposed to "exoteric" doctrines.

37a   *Alexander Loved Aristotle More Than Philip*
Plutarch, Alexander 8.4 (3)

Aristotle he [Alexander] admired at the first, and loved him, as he himself used to say, more than he did his father, for that the one had given him life, but the other had taught him a noble life.

37b   *Teachers Deserve More Honor than Parents*
Diogenes Laertius, Lives of the Eminent Philosophers 5.19

Teachers who educated children deserved, he [Aristotle] said, more honor than parents who merely gave them birth; for bare life is furnished by the one, the other ensures a good life.

38   *Philip Rejoices in Macedonians' Praise of Alexander*
Plutarch, Alexander 9.4 (3)

In consequence of these exploits, then, as was natural, Philip was excessively fond of his son, so that he even rejoiced to hear the Macedonians call Alexander their king, but Philip their general.

39   *Philip Draws Sword against Alexander*
Plutarch, Alexander 9.6–10 (4–5)

The most open quarrel was brought on by Attalus at the marriage of Cleopatra, a maiden whom Philip was taking to wife, having fallen in love with the girl when he was past the age for it. Attalus, now, was the girl's uncle, and being in his cups, he called upon the Macedonians to ask of the gods that from Philip and Cleopatra there might be born a legitimate successor to the kingdom. At this Alexander was exasperated, and with the words, "But what of me, base wretch? Dost thou take me for a bastard?" threw a cup at him. Then Philip rose up against him with drawn sword, but, fortunately for both, his anger and his wine made him trip and fall. Then Alexander, mocking over him, said: "Look now, men! here is one who was preparing to cross from Europe into Asia; and he is upset in trying to cross from couch to couch."

40a   *Demaratus Rebukes Philip*
Plutarch, Alexander 9.12–14 (6)

Meanwhile Demaratus the Corinthian, who was a guest-friend of the house and a man of frank speech, came to see Philip. After the first greetings and welcomes were over, Philip asked him how the Greeks were agreeing with one another, and Demaratus replied: "It is surely very fitting, Philip, that thou shouldst be concerned about Greece, when thou hast filled thine own house with such great dissension and calamities." Thus brought to his senses, Philip sent and fetched Alexander home, having persuaded him to come through the agency of Demaratus.

40b   *Demaratus Rebukes Philip*
Plutarch, Moralia, Sayings of Kings and Commanders III:179C (30)

At a time when he was at odds with Olympias, his wife, and with his son, Demaratus of Corinth arrived, and Philip inquired of him how the Greeks were feeling towards one another. And Demaratus said, "Much right have you to talk about the harmony of the Greeks when the dearest of your own household feel so towards you!" Philip, taking the thought to heart, ceased from his anger, and became reconciled with them.

40c   *Demaratus Rebukes Philip*
Plutarch, Moralia, How to Tell a Flatterer I:70C (30)

Demaratus is said to have come to Macedonia during the time when Philip was at odds with his wife and son. Philip, after greeting him, inquired how well the Greeks were at harmony together; and Demaratus, who knew him well and wished him well said, "A glorious thing for you, Philip, to be inquiring about the concord of Athenians and Peloponnesians, while you let your own household be full of all this quarrelling and dissension!"

41   *Pixodarus and Philip Plan Alliance by Marriage*
Plutarch, Alexander 10.1

But when Pixodarus, the satrap of Caria, trying by means of a tie of relationship to steal into a military alliance with Philip, wished to give his eldest daughter in marriage to Arrhidaeus the son of Philip, and sent Aristocritus to Macedonia on this errand, once more slanderous stories kept coming to Alexander from his friends and his mother, who said that Philip, by means of a brilliant marriage and a great connection, was trying to settle the kingdom upon Arrhidaeus.

42 *Alexander Plots with Pixodarus*
Plutarch, Alexander 10.2

Greatly disturbed by these stories, Alexander sent Thessalus, the tragic actor, to Caria, to argue with Pixodarus that he ought to ignore the bastard brother, who was also a fool, and make Alexander his connection by marriage.

43 *Philip Upbraids Alexander for His Plot*
Plutarch, Alexander 10.2–3

And this plan was vastly more pleasing to Pixodarus than the former. But Philip, becoming aware of this, went to Alexander's chamber, taking with him one of Alexander's friends and companions, Philotas the son of Parmenio, and upbraided his son severely, and bitterly reviled him as ignoble and unworthy of his high estate, in that he desired to become the son-in-law of a man who was a Carian and a slave to a barbarian king.

44 *Cassius and Faustus*
Plutarch, Brutus 9.2–4

For when Faustus blustered among the boys and bragged about his father's absolute power, Cassius sprang and gave him a thrashing. The guardians and relatives of Faustus wished to carry the matter into court, but Pompey forbade it, and after bringing the two boys together, questioned them both about the matter. Then as the story goes, Cassius said: "Come now, Faustus, have the courage to utter in this man's presence that speech which angered me, and I will smash your face again."

45a *More than one Marius*
Plutarch, Caesar 1.2–3

Moreover, Caesar was not satisfied to be overlooked at first by Sulla, who was busy with a multitude of proscriptions, but he came before the people as candidate for a priesthood, although he was not yet much more than a stripling. To this candidacy Sulla secretly opposed himself, and took measures to make Caesar fail in it, and when he was deliberating about putting him to death and some said there was no reason for killing a mere boy like him, he declared that they had no sense if they did not see in this boy many Mariuses.

45b *More than one Marius*
Suetonius, Lives of the Caesars, Julius 1.1.3

Everyone knows that when Sulla had long held out against the most devoted and eminent men of his party who interceded for Caesar, and they obstinately persisted, he at last gave way and cried, either by divine inspiration or by a shrewd forecast: "Have your way and take him; only bear in mind that the man you are so eager to save will one day deal the death blow to the cause of the aristocracy, which you have joined with me in upholding; for in this Caesar there is more than one Marius."

46   *The Dream of Cicero*
Plutarch, Cicero 44.3–4 (2–4)

For it would appear that while Pompey and Caesar were still living Cicero dreamed that someone invited the sons of the senators to the Capitol, on the ground that Jupiter was going to appoint one of their number ruler of Rome; and that the citizens eagerly ran and stationed themselves about the temple, while the youths, in their purple-bordered togas, seated themselves there in silence. Suddenly the door of the temple opened, and one by one the youths rose and walked around past the god, who reviewed them all and sent them away sorrowing. But when this young Caesar advanced into his presence the god stretched out his hand and said: "O Romans, ye shall have an end of civil wars when this youth has become your ruler."

47a   *Antigonus on Hearing the Trumpet*
Plutarch, Demetrius 28.5

At all events, we are told that Demetrius, when he was still a stripling, asked his father when they were going to break camp; and that Antigonus replied in anger: "Art thou in distress lest thou alone shouldst not hear the trumpet?"

47b   *Crassus on Hearing the Trumpet*
Frontinus, Stratagems 1.1.13

When Marcus Licinius Crassus was asked at what time he was going to break camp, he replied: "Are you afraid you'll not hear the trumpet?"

48   *Dercyllidas Scorned for Having No Son*
Plutarch, Lycurgus 15.2

Therefore there was no one to find fault with what was said to Dercyllidas, reputable general though he was. As he entered a company, namely, one of the younger men would not offer him his seat, but said: "Indeed, thou hast begotten no son who will one day give his seat to me."

49a   *Boy Steals Fox*
Plutarch, Lycurgus 18.1

The [Spartan] boys make such a serious matter of their stealing, that one of them, as the story goes, who was carrying concealed under his cloak a young fox which he had stolen, suffered the animal to tear out his bowels with its teeth and claws, and died rather than have his theft detected. And even this story gains credence from what their youths now endure, many of whom I have seen expiring under the lash at the altar of Artemis Orthia.

49b   *Boy Steals Fox*
Plutarch, Moralia, Sayings of Spartans III:234A–B (35)

In the case of another boy, when the time had arrived during which it was the custom for the free boys to steal whatever they could, and it was a disgrace not to escape being found out, when the boys with him had stolen a young fox alive, and given it to him to keep, and those who had lost the fox came in search for it, the boy happened to have slipped the fox under his garment. The beast, however, became savage and ate through his side to the vitals; but the boy did not move or cry out, so as to avoid being exposed, and later, when they had departed, the boys saw what had happened, and blamed him, saying that it would have been better to let the fox be seen than to hide it even unto death; but the boy said, "Not so, but better to die without yielding to the pain than through being detected because of weakness of spirit to gain a life to be lived in disgrace."

50a *Pytheas Opposes Deification of Alexander*
Plutarch, Moralia, Sayings of Kings and Commanders III:187E

Pytheas,[1] while still young, came forward in the Assembly to oppose the resolutions proposed in honor of Alexander. When someone said, "Have you the audacity, young as you are, to speak about such important matters?" he replied, "As a matter of fact, Alexander, whom your resolutions declare to be a god, is younger than I am."[2]

1. Unprincipled Athenian orator, opponent of Demosthenes.
2. Similar derisive remarks about the deification of Alexander are attributed to other sharp-tongued Greeks. Cf. Diogenes Laertius 6.8; Aelian, *Varia Historia* 2.19 and 5.12; Valerius Maximus 7.2; externa 13.

50b *Pytheas Opposes Deification of Alexander*
Plutarch, Moralia, Precepts of Statecraft X:804B (8)

So also when Pytheas the orator was speaking in opposition to the granting of honors to Alexander and someone said to him, "Do you, at your age, dare to speak on such important matters?" he replied: "And yet Alexander is younger than I, and you are voting to make him a god."

50c *Diogenes and the Deification of Alexander*
Diogenes Laertius, Lives of the Eminent Philosophers 6.63

When the Athenians gave Alexander the title of Dionysus, he [Diogenes] said, "Me too you might make Sarapis."[1]

1. "Sarapis" was represented, like Pluto, as seated with an animal by his side having the head of a dog, lion, or wolf combined in a three-headed Cerberus.

51a *The Last a Place of Honor*
Plutarch, Moralia, Sayings of Spartans III:208D–E (6)

When he [Agesilaus] was still a boy, at a celebration of the festival of the naked boys the director of the dance assigned him to an inconspicuous place; and he obeyed, although he was already destined to be king,[1] saying, "Good! I shall show that it is not the places that make men to be held in honor, but the men the places."

1. Plutarch, in his *Agesilaus* 1.1–4.1, says that Agesilaus was brought up as a private citizen, and did not become king until after the death of Agis.

51b *The Last a Place of Honor*
Plutarch, Moralia, Dinner of the Seven Wise Men II:149A (3)

"So then," said Thales, "as the Egyptians say of the stars, when they gain or lose altitude in their courses, that they are growing better or worse than they were before, do you fear that the obscuration and degradation affecting you because of your place at table will be brought about in a similar way? And you will be contemptible when compared with the Spartan who in a chorus was put by the director in the very last place, whereupon he exclaimed, 'Good! You have found out how this may be made a place of honor.'"

51c   *The Last a Place of Honor*
Plutarch, Moralia, Sayings of Spartans III:219E

Damonidas, being assigned to the last place in the chorus by the director, exclaimed, "Good! You have discovered, sir, how this place which is without honor may be made a place of honor."

51d   *The Last a Place of Honor*
Plutarch, Moralia, Sayings of Kings and Commanders III:191F

When Damonidas was assigned to the last place in the chorus by the director, he said, "Good! You have discovered a way by which even this place may come to be held in honor."

51e   *The Last a Place of Honor*
Diogenes Laertius, Lives of the Eminent Philosophers 2.73

Being once compelled by Dionysius to enunciate some doctrine of philosophy, "It would be ludicrous," he [Aristippus] said, "that you should learn from me what to say, and yet instruct me when to say it." At this, they say, Dionysius was offended and made him recline at the end of the table. And Aristippus said, "You must have wished to confer distinction on the last place."

52   *Bravery of Acrotatus*
Plutarch, Pyrrhus 28.1–3

Pyrrhus himself, then, with his men at arms, tried to force his way directly against the many shields of the Spartans which confronted him and over a trench which was impassable and afforded his soldiers no firm footing owing to the freshly turned earth. But his son Ptolemy, with two thousand Gauls and picked Chaonians, went round the trench and tried to force a passage where the wagons were. These, however, being so deeply planted in the earth and so close together, made not only his onset, but also the counter-efforts of the Lacedaemonians, a difficult matter. The Gauls pulled the wheels up and were dragging the wagons down into the river; but the young Acrotatus saw the danger, and running through the city with three hundred men got round behind Ptolemy without being seen by him, owing to some depressions in the ground, and at last fell upon his rear ranks and forced them to turn about and fight with him. And now the Barbarians crowded one another into the trench and fell among the wagons, and finally, after great slaughter, were successfully driven back. The elderly men and the host of women watched the brilliant exploit of Acrotatus. And when he went back again through the city to his allotted post, covered with blood and triumphant, elated with his victory, the Spartan women thought that he had become taller and more beautiful than ever, and envied Chilonis her lover. Moreover, some of the elderly men accompanied him on his way, crying: "Go, Acrotatus, and take to thyself Chilonis; only, see that thou begettest brave sons for Sparta."

53a   *Sword Will Achieve the Demand*
Suetonius, Lives of the Caesars, Augustus 2.26.1

He [Augustus] received offices and honors before the usual age, and some of a new kind and for life. He usurped the consulship in the twentieth year of his age, leading his legions against the city as if it were that of an enemy, and sending messengers to demand the office for him in the name of his army; and when the Senate hesitated, his centurion, Cornelius, leader of the deputation, throwing back his cloak and showing the hilt of his sword, did not hesitate to say in the House, "This will make him consul, if you do not."

53b   *Sword Will Achieve the Demand*
Plutarch, Caesar 29.7 (5)

Nay, we are told that one of the centurions sent to Rome by Caesar, as he stood in front of the senate-house and learned that the senate would not give Caesar an extension of his term of command, slapped the handle of his sword and said: "But this will give it."

53c   *Sword Will Achieve the Demand*
Plutarch, Pompey 58.2

It was said, indeed, that one of Caesar's centurions who had come back to Rome and was standing near the senate-house, when he heard that the senate would not give Caesar a prolongation of his term of office, struck his hand upon his sword and said: "But this will give it."

53d   *On Boundaries*
Plutarch, Lysander 22.1

For instance, when the Argives were disputing about boundaries, and thought they made a juster plea than the Lacedaemonians, he [Lysander] pointed to his sword, and said to them: "He who is master of this discourses best about boundaries."

53e   *On Boundaries*
Plutarch, Moralia, Sayings of Kings and Commanders III:190E (3)

When the Argives seemed to make out a better case than the Spartans about the territory in dispute, he [Lysander] drew his sword, and said to them, "He who is master of this talks best about boundaries of land."

53f   *Spear as Boundary*
Plutarch, Moralia, Sayings of Spartans III:210E (28)

Being asked once how far the bounds of Sparta extended, he [Agesilaus] said, with a flourish of his spear, "As far as this can reach."

53g   *Spear as Boundary*
Plutarch, Moralia, Sayings of Spartans III:217E (7)

He [Antalcidas] used to say that the young men were the walls of Sparta, and the points of their spears it boundaries.

53h   *Spear as Boundary*
Plutarch, Moralia, Sayings of Spartans III:218F (2)

Being asked how much land the Spartans controlled, he [Archidamus, son of Agesilaus] said, "As much as they can reach with the spear."

53i   *Spear as Boundary*
Plutarch, Moralia, Sayings of Spartans III:229C (6)

In answer to the Argives, who were disputing with the Spartans in regard to the boundaries of their land and said that they had the better of the case, he [Lysander] drew his sword and said, "He who is master of this talks best about boundaries of land."

53j   *Spear as Boundary*
Plutarch, Moralia, Roman Questions IV:267C (15)

Is it that Romulus placed no boundary-stones for his country, so that Romans might go forth, seize land, and regard all as theirs, as the Spartan said, which their spears could reach?

53k   *Spear as Boundary*
Cicero, De Re Publica 3.9.15

Indeed, men's principles of life are so different that the Cretans and Aetolians[1] consider piracy and brigandage honorable, and the Spartans used to claim as their own all the territory they could touch with their spears.

> 1. In regard to the Aetolians compare Thucydides 1.5. The Cretans allied themselves with the Cilician pirates against the Romans.

54   *Galba to Nibble*
Suetonius, Lives of the Caesars, Galba 7.4.1

It is well known that when he [Galba] was still a boy and called to pay his respects to Augustus with others of his age, the emperor pinched his cheek and said in Greek: "Thou too, child, wilt have a nibble at this power of mine."

55   *Galba Does Not Concern Tiberius*
Suetonius, Lives of the Caesars, Galba 7.4.1

Tiberius, too, when he heard that Galba was destined to be emperor, but in his old age, said: "Well, let him live then, since that does not concern me."

56   *When a Mule Has a Foal*
Suetonius, Lives of the Caesars, Galba 7.4.2

Again, when Galba's grandfather was busy with a sacrifice for a stroke of lightning, and an eagle snatched the intestines from his hand and carried them to an oak full of acorns, the prediction was made that the highest dignity would come to the family, but late; whereupon he said with a laugh: "Very likely, when a mule has a foal."[1]

> 1. Proverbial for "never," like the Greek Kalends (Suetonius, *Lives of the Caesars, Augustus* 2.87.1).

57   *Nero Lies to Preceptor*
Suetonius, Lives of the Caesars, Nero 6.22.1

Once when he [Nero] was lamenting with his fellow pupils the fate of a charioteer of the "Greens," who was dragged by his horses, and his preceptor scolded him, he told a lie and pretended that he was talking of Hector.

The stories listed below contain an action or refer to the character of a youth or young adult, but other features in the stories have determined their location in another section.

Eunapius: 363
Josephus: 1232
Phaedrus: 372
Philostratus: 884, 1410
Plutarch: 165, 308, 397, 908a, 1007, 1100b, 1293, 1319a, 1419
Suetonius: 420

Adult

Illustrious persons in antiquity were known, in part, for their wit and repartee in the company of friends and associates. Many anecdotes record scenes of this type. The eminent and powerful also enjoyed confronting important people outside their immediate circles, either to shame them or to strike a bargain. Family members, too, are caught in acts of conflict and tension, of love and reconciliation in their exchanges. Youth and women rarely received special attention in common yarns, but occasionally we catch glimpses of them in these tales.

Adult: Friend or Associate

The anecdotes in our collection reveal that persons of importance surrounded themselves with friends and associates. The stories exhibit situations in which the famous chide and rebuke, poke fun at and rib, and applaud and commend those closest to them. Now and then a friend occasions the downfall of the powerful friend. Loyalty and trust form a two-edged sword, it seems.

58 *Theophrastus and Callisthenes*
Cicero, Tusculan Disputations 3.10.21

The same person therefore is susceptible of pity and envy. For the man who is pained by another's misfortunes is also pained by another's prosperity. For instance, Theophrastus in lamenting the death of his friend Callisthenes[1] is vexed at the prosperity of Alexander; and so he says that Callisthenes fell in with a man of supreme power and unparalleled good fortune, but one who did not know how to turn prosperity to good account. And yet, as compassion is distress due to a neighbor's misfortunes, so envy is distress due to a neighbor's prosperity. Therefore the man who comes to feel compassion comes also to feel envy. The wise man, however, does not come to feel envy; therefore he does not come to feel compassion either. But if the wise man were accustomed to feel distress he would also be accustomed to feel compassion. Therefore distress keeps away from the wise man.

> 1. Callisthenes was fellow-pupil with Alexander the Great of Aristotle. He was put to death by Alexander in Asia on a charge of conspiracy. Theophrastus of Lesbos, cf. Cicero, *Tusculan Disputations* 5.24, a pupil of Plato and Aristotle, wrote a book in memory of his friend.

59 *Lesson from Anaxagoras*
Cicero, Tusculan Disputations 3.14.30

[Euripides] had been a pupil of Anaxagoras, who, according to the story, said when he heard of his son's death, "I knew that I had begotten a mortal." This saying shows that such events are cruel for those who have not reflected that everything which is thought evil is more grievous if it comes unexpectedly. And so, though this is not the one cause of the greatest distress, yet as foresight and anticipation have considerable effect in lessening pain, a human being should ponder all the vicissitudes that fall to man's lot. And do not doubt that here is found the ideal of that wisdom which excels and is divine, namely in the thorough study and comprehension of human vicissitudes, in being astonished at nothing when it happens, and in thinking, before the event is come, that there is nothing which may not come to pass.

60 *Socrates on the Greatest Gift*
Diogenes Laertius, Lives of the Eminent Philosophers 2.34

Aeschines said to him [Socrates], "I am a poor man and have nothing else to give, but I offer you myself," and Socrates answered, "Nay, do you not see that you are offering me the greatest gift of all?"

61a *Xenophon Follows Socrates*
Diogenes Laertius, Lives of the Eminent Philosophers 2.48

The story goes that Socrates met him [Xenophon] in a narrow alley, and that he stretched out his staff to bar the way, while he inquired where each kind of food was sold. Upon receiving a reply, he put another question, "And where do men become good and honorable?" But when Xenophon was puzzled, Socrates said, "Then follow me and learn." From that time on he was a disciple of Socrates.

61b *Diogenes Becomes Antisthenes' Disciple*
Diogenes Laertius, Lives of the Eminent Philosophers 6.21

On reaching Athens he [Diogenes] fell in with Antisthenes. Being repulsed by him, because he never welcomed pupils, by sheer persistence Diogenes wore him out. Once when he stretched out his staff against him, the pupil offered his head with the words, "Strike, for you will find no wood hard enough to keep me away from you, so long as I think you have something to say." From that time on he was his disciple.

61c *Diogenes' Friendship Broken by Fish*
Diogenes Laertius, Lives of the Eminent Philosophers 6.36

Someone wanted to study philosophy under him. Diogenes gave him a fish to carry and told him to follow him. But the man threw it away out of shame and departed. Some time later Diogenes met him and laughed and said, "Our friendship was broken by a fish."

61d *Zeno Follows Socrates*
Diogenes Laertius, Lives of the Eminent Philosophers 7.2–3

Zeno went up to Athens and sat down in a bookseller's shop, being then a man of thirty. As he was reading the second book of Xenophon's *Memorabilia*, he was so pleased that he inquired where men like Socrates were to be found. Just then Crates passed by and the bookseller pointed to him and said, "Follow that man." From that day on he became Crates' disciple.

61e *Crates Shows His Possessions*
Diogenes Laertius, Lives of the Eminent Philosophers 6.96

Hipparchia fell in love with the discourses and the life of Crates, and would not pay attention to any of her suitors, their wealth, their high birth, or their beauty. But to her Crates was everything. She even used to threaten her parents that she would do away with herself unless she were given in marriage to him. Crates therefore was implored by her parents to dissuade the girl, and did all he could, and at last, failing to persuade her, got up, took off his clothes before her face and said, "This is the bridegroom, here are his possessions; make your choice accordingly; for you will be no helpmate of mine unless you share my pursuits."

61f   *John's Disciples Go Over to Jesus*
Gospel, John 1:35–42

The next day again John was standing with two of his disciples; and he looked at Jesus as he walked, and said, "Behold, the Lamb of God!" The two disciples heard him say this, and they followed Jesus. Jesus turned, and saw them following, and said to them, "What do you seek?" And they said to him, "Rabbi" (which means Teacher), "where are you staying?" He said to them, "Come and see." They came and saw where he was staying; and they stayed with him that day, for it was about the tenth hour. One of the two who heard John speak, and followed him, was Andrew, Simon Peter's brother. He first found his brother Simon, and said to him, "We have found the Messiah" (which means Christ). He brought him to Jesus. Jesus looked at him, and said, "So you are Simon the son of John? You shall be called Cephas" (which means Peter).

61g   *Calling of Simon, James and John*
Gospel, Luke 5:1–11

While the people pressed upon him to hear the word of God, he [Jesus] was standing by the lake of Gennesaret. And he saw two boats by the lake; but the fishermen had gone out of them and were washing their nets. Getting into one of the boats, which was Simon's, he asked him to put out a little from the land. And he sat down and taught the people from the boat. And when he had ceased speaking, he said to Simon, "Put out into the deep and let down your nets for a catch." And Simon answered, "Master, we toiled all night and took nothing! But at your word I will let down the nets." And when they had done this, they enclosed a great shoal of fish; and as their nets were breaking, they beckoned to their partners in the other boat to come and help them. And they came and filled both the boats, so that they began to sink. But when Simon Peter saw it, he fell down at Jesus' knees, saying, "Depart from me, for I am a sinful man, O Lord." For he was astonished, and all that were with him, at the catch of fish which they had taken; and so also were James and John, sons of Zebedee, who were partners with Simon. And Jesus said to Simon, "Do not be afraid; henceforth you will be catching men." And when they had brought their boats to land, they left everything and followed him.

61h   *Calling of Simon and Andrew*
Gospel, Mark 1:16–18

And passing along by the Sea of Galilee, he [Jesus] saw Simon and Andrew the brother of Simon casting a net in the sea; for they were fishermen. And Jesus said to them, "Follow me and I will make you become fishers of men." And immediately they left their nets and followed him.

61i   *Calling of Simon and Andrew*
Gospel, Matthew 4:18–20

As he [Jesus] walked by the Sea of Galilee, he saw two brothers, Simon who is called Peter and Andrew his brother, casting a net into the sea; for they were fishermen. And he said to them, "Follow me, and I will make you fishers of men." Immediately they left their nets and followed him.

61j *Calling of James and John*
Gospel, Mark 1:19–20

And going on a little farther, he saw James the son of Zebedee and John his brother, who were in their boat mending the nets. And immediately he called them; and they left their father Zebedee in the boat with the hired servants, and followed him.

61k *Calling of James and John*
Gospel, Matthew 4:21–22

And going on from there he [Jesus] saw two other brothers, James the son of Zebedee and John his brother, in the boat with Zebedee their father, mending their nets, and he called them. Immediately they left the boat and their father, and followed him.

61l *Calling of Levi*
Gospel, Luke 5:27–28

After this he [Jesus] went out, and saw a tax collector, named Levi, sitting at the tax office; and he said to him, "Follow me." And he left everything, and rose and followed him.

61m *Calling of Levi*
Gospel, Mark 2:13–14

He [Jesus] went out again beside the sea; and all the crowd gathered about him, and he taught them. And as he passed on, he saw Levi the son of Alphaeus sitting at the tax office, and he said to him, "Follow me." And he rose and followed him.

61n *Calling of Matthew*
Gospel, Matthew 9:9

As Jesus passed on from there, he saw a man called Matthew sitting at the tax office; and he said to him, "Follow me." And he rose and followed him.

61o *Jesus and Nathaniel*
Gospel, John 1:43–51

The next day Jesus decided to go to Galilee. And he found Philip and said to him, "Follow me." Now Philip was from Bethsaida, the city of Andrew and Peter. Philip found Nathanael, and said to him, "We have found him of whom Moses in the law and also the prophets wrote, Jesus of Nazareth, the son of Joseph." Nathanael said to him, "Can anything good come out of Nazareth?" Philip said to him, "Come and see." Jesus saw Nathanael coming to him, and said of him, "Behold, an Israelite indeed, in whom is no guile!" Nathanael said to him, "How do you know me?" Jesus answered him, "Before Philip called you, when you were under the fig tree, I saw you." Nathanael answered him, "Rabbi, you are the Son of God! You are the King of Israel!" Jesus answered him, "Because I said to you, I saw you under the fig tree, do you believe? You shall see greater things than these." And he said to him, "Truly, truly, I say to you, you will see heaven opened, and the angels of God ascending and descending upon the Son of man."

62   *Lost Notes*

Diogenes Laertius, Lives of the Eminent Philosophers 6.5

When a friend complained to him [Antisthenes] that he had lost his notes, "You should have inscribed them," said he, "on your mind instead of on paper."

63   *Lambs and Wolves*

Epistle, 2 Clement 5.2–4 (Funk-Bihlmeyer: 73)

For the Lord said, "You will be as lambs in the midst of wolves."[1] And Peter answered and said to him, "If then the wolves tear the lambs?" Jesus said to Peter, "Let the lambs have no fear of the wolves after their death. And you, have no fear of those that slay you and can do nothing more to you. Fear, rather, him who after your death has power over body and soul, to cast them into the fiery hell."

     1. Cf. Matthew 10:16a; Luke 10:3.

64   *Metellus Pius on Secrecy*

Frontinus, Stratagems 1.1.12

When Metellus Pius was in Spain and was asked what he was going to do the next day, he replied: "If my tunic could tell, I would burn it."[1]

     1. 79–72 B.C.E. Cf. Valerius Maximus 7.4.5.

65   *Sneeze Signals Retreat*

Frontinus, Stratagems 1.12.11

When Timotheus, the Athenian, was about to contend against the Corcyreans in a naval battle, his pilot, hearing one of the rowers sneeze, started to give the signal for retreat, just as the fleet was setting out; whereupon Timotheus exclaimed: "Do you think it strange if one out of so many thousands has had a chill?"[1]

     1. 375 B.C.E. Cf. Polyaenus 3.10.2.

66   *Pyrrhus Makes Big Men Brave*

Frontinus, Stratagems 4.1.3

Pyrrhus is said to have remarked to his recruiting officer: "You pick out the big men! I'll make them brave."

67a   *Trusted Shield*

Frontinus, Stratagems 4.1.5

Scipio Africanus, noticing the shield of a certain soldier rather elaborately decorated, said he didn't wonder the man had adorned it with such care, seeing that he put more trust in it than in his sword.[1]

     1. 134 B.C.E. Cf. Livy, *Periochae* 57; Polyaenus 8.16.3, 4.

67b   *Trusted Shield*

Plutarch, Moralia, Sayings of Romans III:201D (18)

When another man showed him [Scipio the Younger] a shield beautifully ornamented, he said, "A fine shield, young sir; but it is more fitting that a Roman rest his hopes in his right hand rather than in his left."

68   *No Pillaging*
Frontinus, Stratagems 4.1.9

Lysander, the Spartan, once flogged a soldier who had left the ranks while on the march. When the man said that he had not left the line for the purpose of pillage, Lysander retorted: "I won't have you look as if you were going to pillage."

69   *Lagging Soldier Made Example*
Frontinus, Stratagems 4.1.33

On one occasion when Marcus Cato, who had lingered for several days on a hostile shore, had at length set sail, after three times giving the signal for departure, and a certain soldier, who had been left behind, with cries and gestures from the land, begged to be picked up, Cato turned his whole fleet back to the shore, arrested the man, and commanded him to be put to death, thus preferring to make an example of the fellow than to have him ignominiously put to death by the enemy.[1]

1. 471 B.C.E. Cf. Livy 2.59; Dionysius 9.50; Zonaras 7.17.

70a   *Spartans Fight Better in Shade*
Frontinus, Stratagems 4.5.13

Leonidas, the Spartan, in reply to the statement that the Persians would create clouds by the multitude of their arrows, is reported to have said: "We shall fight all the better in the shade."[1]

1. Cf. Valerius Maximus 3.7, externa 8.

70b   *Spartans Fight Better in Shade*
Cicero, Tusculan Disputations 1.42.101

Of like spirit were the Lacedaemonians who fell at Thermopylae, on whose tomb Simonides wrote:

Stranger, the Spartans tell that here in the grave you beheld us

Keeping the laws of our land by an obedience due. One of them, when a Persian foeman in conversation had said in boast, "You will not see the sun for the number of our javelins and arrows," "Then," said he, "we shall fight in the shade."[1]

1. Herodotus 7.266 states that the conversation was held not with a Persian but with a Greek.

71   *Sitting in the King's Seat*
Frontinus, Stratagems 4.6.3

When Alexander was marching at the head of his troops one winter's day, he sat down by a fire and began to review the troops as they passed by. Noticing a certain soldier who was almost dead with the cold, he bade him sit in his place, adding: "If you had been born among the Persians, it would be a capital crime for you to sit on the king's seat; but since you were born in Macedonia, that privilege is yours."[1]

1. Cf. Valerius Maximus 5.1, externa 1; Curtius Rufus 8.4.15–17.

72   *Vespasian Settles with Youth*
Frontinus, Stratagems 4.6.4

When the Deified Vespasianus Augustus learned that a certain youth, of good birth, but ill adapted to military service, had received a high appointment because

of his straitened circumstances, Vespasian settled a sum of money on him, and
gave him an honorable discharge.

73a *Philip Helps Pythias*
Frontinus, Stratagems 4.7.37

Philip,[1] having heard that a certain Pythias, an excellent warrior, had become
estranged from him because he was too poor to support his three daughters, and
was not assisted by the king, and having been warned by certain persons to be on
his guard against the man, replied: "What! If part of my body were diseased, should
I cut it off, rather than give it treatment?" Then, quietly drawing Pythias aside for a
confidential talk, and learning the seriousness of his domestic embarassments, he
supplied him with funds, and found in him a better and more devoted adherent
than before the estrangement.

> 1. The father of Alexander.

73b *Philip and Nicanor*
Plutarch, Moralia, Sayings of Kings and Commanders III:177D–E (6)

When Smicythus remarked maliciously of Nicanor that he was always speaking
ill of Philip,[1] and Philip's companions thought that he ought to send for Nicanor
and punish him, Philip said, "But really Nicanor is not the worst of the Macedonians. We must investigate therefore whether something is not happening for
which we are responsible." When he learned therefore that Nicanor was hard
pressed by poverty, and had been neglected by him, he directed that a present be
given to the man. So when again Smicythus said that Nicanor was continually
sounding the praises of Philip to everybody in a surprising way, Philip said, "You
all see that we ourselves are responsible for the good and the ill that is said of us."[2]

> 1. King of Macedonia, 359–336 B.C.E.
> 2. Cf. Themistius, *Oration* 7.95 B.

74 *Xanthippe, the Impudent Wife of Socrates*
Gellius, Attic Nights 1.17.1–3

Xanthippe, the wife of the philosopher Socrates, is said to have been ill-tem-
pered and quarrelsome to a degree, with a constant flood of feminine tantrums and
annoyances day and night. Alcibiades, amazed at this outrageous conduct of hers
toward her husband, asked Socrates what earthly reason he had for not showing so
shrewish a woman the door. "Because," replied Socrates, "it is by enduring such a
person at home that I accustom and train myself to bear more easily away from
home the impudence and injustice of other persons."

75 *Mind as Mellow Fruit*
Gellius, Attic Nights 13.2.1–6

Those who have had leisure and inclination to inquire into the life and times of
learned men and hand them down to memory have related the following anecdote
of the tragic poets Marcus Pacuvius and Lucius Accius: "Pacuvius," they say,
"when already enfeebled by advanced age and constant bodily illness, had withdrawn from Rome to Tarentum. Then Accius, who was a much younger man,
coming to Tarentum on his way to Asia, visited Pacuvius, and being hospitably
received and detained by him for several days, at his request read him his tragedy
entitled *Atreus*." Then they say that Pacuvius remarked that what he had written

seemed sonorous and full of dignity, but that nevertheless it appeared to him somewhat harsh and rugged. "What you say is true," replied Accius, "and I do not greatly regret it; for it gives me hope that what I write hereafter will be better. For they say it is with the mind as it is with fruits; those which are at first harsh and bitter, later become mild and sweet; but those which at once grow mellow and soft, and are juicy in the beginning, presently become, not ripe, but decayed. Accordingly, it has seemed to me that something should be left in the products of the intellect for time and age to mellow."

76a   *Peter's Declaration about Jesus*
Gospel, John 6:66–71

After this many of his disciples drew back and no longer went about with him. Jesus said to the twelve, "Do you also wish to go away?" Simon Peter answered him, "Lord, to whom shall we go? You have the words of eternal life; and we have believed, and have come to know, that you are the Holy One of God." Jesus answered them, "Did I not choose you, the twelve, and one of you is a devil?" He spoke of Judas the son of Simon Iscariot, for he, one of the twelve, was to betray him.

76b   *Peter's Declaration about Jesus*
Gospel, Luke 9:18–22

Now it happened that as he [Jesus] was praying alone the disciples were with him; and he asked them, "Who do the people say that I am?" And they answered, "John the Baptist; but others say, Elijah; and others, that one of the old prophets has risen." And he said to them, "But who do you say that I am?" And Peter answered, "The Christ of God." But he charged and commanded them to tell this to no one, saying, "The Son of man must suffer many things, and be rejected by the elders and chief priests and scribes, and be killed, and on the third day be raised."

76c   *Peter's Declaration about Jesus*
Gospel, Mark 8:27–30

And Jesus went on with his disciples, to the villages of Caesarea Philippi; and on the way he asked his disciples, "Who do men say that I am?" And they told him, "John the Baptist; and others say, Elijah; and others one of the prophets." And he asked them, "But who do you say that I am?" Peter answered him, "You are the Christ." And he charged them to tell no one about him.

76d   *Peter's Declaration about Jesus*
Gospel, Thomas 13

Jesus said to his disciples, "Compare me with someone, and tell me whom I am like." Simon Peter said to him, "You are like a just angel." Matthew said to him, "You are like a wise philospher." Thomas said to him, "Teacher, my mouth is utterly unable to say whom you are like." Jesus said, "I am not your teacher. Because you have drunk, you have become intoxicated from the bubbling spring that I have tended." And he took him, and withdrew, and spoke three sayings to him. When Thomas came back to his friends, they asked him, "What did Jesus say to you?" Thomas said to them, "If I tell you one of the sayings he spoke to me, you will pick up rocks and stone me, and fire will come from the rocks and devour you."

77a *The World's Light*
Gospel, John 11:5-16

Now Jesus loved Martha and her sister and Lazarus. So when he heard that he was ill, he stayed two days longer in the place where he was. Then after this he said to the disciples, "Let us go into Judea again." The disciples said to him, "Rabbi, the Jews were but now seeking to stone you, and are you going there again?" Jesus answered, "Are there not twelve hours in the day? If any one walks in the day, he does not stumble, because he sees the light of this world. But if any one walks in the night, he stumbles, because the light is not in him." Thus he spoke, and then he said to them, "Our friend Lazarus has fallen asleep, but I go to awake him out of sleep." The disciples said to him, "Lord, if he has fallen asleep, he will recover." Now Jesus had spoken of his death, but they thought that he meant taking rest in sleep. Then Jesus told them plainly, "Lazarus is dead; and for your sake I am glad that I was not there, so that you may believe. But let us go to him." Thomas, called the Twin, said to his fellow disciples, "Let us also go, that we may die with him."

77b *The World's Light*
Gospel, Thomas 24

His disciples said, "Show us the place where you are, for we must seek it." He said to them, "Whoever has ears ought to listen. There is light within a person of light, and it (or: he) shines on the whole world. If it (or: he) does not shine, it is dark."

77c *The World's Light*
Gospel, John 8:12-20

Again Jesus spoke to them, saying, "I am the light of the world; he who follows me will not walk in darkness, but will have the light of life." The Pharisees then said to him, "You are bearing witness to yourself; your testimony is not true." Jesus answered, "Even if I do bear witness to myself, my testimony is true, for I know whence I have come and whither I am going, but you do not know whence I come or whither I am going. You judge according to the flesh, I judge no one. Yet even if I do judge, my judgment is true, for it is not I alone that judge, but I and he who sent me. In your law it is written that the testimony of two men is true; I bear witness to myself, and the Father who sent me bears witness to me." They said to him therefore, "Where is your Father?" Jesus answered, "You know neither me nor my Father; if you knew me, you would know my Father also." These words he spoke in the treasury; but no one arrested him, because his hour had not yet come.

77d *The World's Light*
Gospel, John 12:37-50

Though he [Jesus] had done so many signs before them, they did not believe in him; it was that the word spoken by the prophet Isaiah might be fulfilled:
"Lord, who has believed our report,
and to whom has the arm of the Lord been revealed?"
Therefore they could not believe. For Isaiah again said,
"He has blinded their eyes and hardened their heart,
lest they should see with their eyes and perceive with their heart,
and turn for me to heal them."

Isaiah said this because he saw his glory and spoke of him. Nevertheless many even of the authorities believed in him, but for fear of the Pharisees they did not confess it, lest they should be put out of the synagogue: for they loved the praise of men more than the praise of God. And Jesus cried out and said, "He who believes in me, believes not in me but in him who sent me. And he who sees me sees him who sent me. I have come as light into the world, that whoever believes in me may not remain in darkness. If any one hears my sayings and does not keep them, I do not judge him; for I did not come to judge the world but to save the world. He who rejects me and does not receive my sayings has a judge; the word that I have spoken will be his judge on the last day. For I have not spoken on my own authority; the Father who sent me has himself given me commandment what to say and what to speak. And I know that his commandment is eternal life. What I say, therefore, I say as the Father has bidden me."

77e   *The World's Light*
Gospel, Thomas 77

Jesus said, "I am the light that is over all things. I am all: all came forth from me, and all attained to me. Split a piece of wood; I am there. Pick up a stone, and you will find me there."

78a   *Woman with Ointment*
Gospel, John 12:1–8

Six days before the Passover, Jesus came to Bethany, where Lazarus was, whom Jesus had raised from the dead. There they made him a supper; Martha served, and Lazarus was one of those at table with him. Mary took a pound of costly ointment of pure nard and anointed the feet of Jesus and wiped his feet with her hair; and the house was filled with the fragrance of the ointment. But Judas Iscariot, one of his disciples (he who was to betray him), said, "Why was this ointment not sold for three hundred denarii and given to the poor?" This he said, not that he cared for the poor but because he was a thief, and as he had the money box he used to take what was put into it. Jesus said, "Let her alone, let her keep it for the day of my burial. The poor you always have with you, but you do not always have me."

78b   *Woman with Ointment*
Gospel, Luke 7:36–50

One of the Pharisees asked him [Jesus] to eat with him, and he went into the Pharisee's house, and sat at table. And behold, a woman of the city, who was a sinner, when she learned that he was sitting at table in the Pharisee's house, brought an alabaster flask of ointment, and standing behind him at his feet, weeping, she began to wet his feet with her tears, and wiped them with the hair of her head, and kissed his feet, and anointed them with the ointment. Now when the Pharisee who had invited him saw it, he said to himself, "If this man were a prophet, he would have known who and what sort of woman this is who is touching him, for she is a sinner." And Jesus answering said to him, "Simon, I have something to say to you." And he answered, "What is it, Teacher?" "A certain creditor had two debtors; one owed five hundred denarii, and the other fifty. When they could not pay, he forgave them both. Now which of them will love him more?" Simon answered, "The one, I suppose, to whom he forgave more." And he said to him, "You have judged rightly." Then turning toward the woman he said to

Simon, "Do you see this woman? I entered your house, you gave me no water for my feet, but she has wet my feet with her tears and wiped them with her hair. You gave me no kiss, but from the time I came in she has not ceased to kiss my feet. You did not anoint my head with oil, but she has anointed my feet with ointment. Therefore I tell you, her sins, which are many, are forgiven, for she loved much; but he who is forgiven little, loves little." And he said to her, "Your sins are forgiven." Then those who were at table with him began to say among themselves, "Who is this, who even forgives sins?" And he said to the woman, "Your faith has saved you; go in peace."

78c *Woman with Ointment*
Gospel, Mark 14:3–9

And while he [Jesus] was at Bethany in the house of Simon the leper, as he sat at table, a woman came with an alabaster flask of ointment of pure nard, very costly, and she broke the flask and poured it over his head. But there were some who said to themselves indignantly, "Why was the ointment wasted? For this ointment might have been sold for more than three hundred denarii, and given to the poor." And they reproached her. But Jesus said, "Let her alone; why do you trouble her? She has done a beautiful thing to me. For you always have the poor with you, and whenever you will, you can do good to them; but you will not always have me. She has done what she could; she has anointed my body beforehand for burying. And truly, I say to you, wherever the gospel is preached in the whole world, what she has done will be told in memory of her.

78d *Woman With Ointment*
Gospel, Matthew 26:6–13

Now when Jesus was at Bethany in the house of Simon the leper, a woman came up to him with an alabaster flask of very expensive ointment, and she poured it on his head, as he sat at table. But when the disciples saw it, they were indignant, saying, "Why this waste? For this ointment might have been sold for a large sum, and given to the poor." But Jesus, aware of this, said to them, "Why do you trouble the woman? For she has done a beautiful thing to me. For you always have the poor with you, but you will not always have me. In pouring this ointment on my body she has done it to prepare me for burial. Truly, I say to you, wherever this gospel is preached in the whole world, what she has done will be told in memory of her."

79a *Leader as Servant*
Gospel, John 13:1–20

Now before the feast of the Passover, when Jesus knew that his hour had come to depart out of this world to the Father, having loved his own who were in the world, he loved them to the end. And during supper, when the devil had already put it into the heart of Judas Iscariot, Simon's son, to betray him, Jesus, knowing that the Father had given all things into his hands, and that he had come from God and was going to God, rose from supper, laid aside his garments, and girded himself with a towel. Then he poured water into a basin, and began to wash the disciples' feet and to wipe them with the towel with which he was girded. He came to Simon Peter; and Peter said to him, "Lord, do you wash my feet?" Jesus answered him, "What I am doing you do not know now, but afterward you will understand." Peter said to him, "You shall never wash my feet." Jesus answered him, "If I do not wash you, you have no part in me." Simon Peter said to him, "Lord, not my feet only but also my hands and my head!" Jesus said to him, "He who has bathed does not need to wash, except for his feet, but he is clean all over; and you are clean, but not every one of you." For he knew who was to betray him; that was why he said, "You are not all clean."

When he had washed their feet, and taken his garments, and resumed his place, he said to them, "Do you know what I have done to you? You call me Teacher and Lord; and you are right, for so I am. If I then, your Lord and Teacher, have washed your feet, you also ought to wash one another's feet. For I have given you an example, that you also should do as I have done to you. Truly, truly, I say to you, a servant is not greater than his master; nor is he who is sent greater than he who sent him. If you know these things, blessed are you if you do them. I am not speaking of you all; I know whom I have chosen; it is that the scripture may be fulfilled, 'He who ate my bread has lifted his heel against me.' I tell you this now, before it takes place, that when it does take place you may believe that I am he. Truly, truly, I say to you, he who receives any one whom I send receives me; and he who receives me receives him who sent me."

79b *Leader as Servant*
Gospel, Luke 22:24–27

A dispute also arose among them [the disciples], which of them was to be regarded as the greatest. And he [Jesus] said to them, "The kings of the Gentiles exercise lordship over them; and those in authority over them are called bene-factors. But not so with you; rather let the greatest among you become as the youngest, and the leader as one who serves. For which is the greater, one who sits at table, or one who serves? Is it not the one who sits at table? But I am among you as one who serves."

79c *Jesus Denounces Scribes and Pharisees*
Gospel, Matthew 23:1–12

Then said Jesus to the crowds and to his disciples, "The scribes and the Pharisees sit on Moses' seat; so practice and observe whatever they tell you, but not what they do; for they preach, but do not practice. They bind heavy burdens, hard to bear, and lay them on men's shoulders; but they themselves will not move them with their finger. They do all their deeds to be seen by men; for they make their phylacteries broad and their fringes long, and they love the place of honor at feasts and the best seats in the synagogues, and salutations in the market places, and being called rabbi by men. But you are not to be called rabbi, for you have one teacher, and you are all brethren. And call no man your father on earth, for you have one Father, who is in heaven. Neither be called masters, for you have one master, the Christ. He who is greatest among you shall be your servant; whoever exalts himself will be humbled, and whoever humbles himself will be exalted.

79d *Exalting the Humble*
Gospel, Luke 14:7–11

Now he [Jesus] told a parable to those who were invited, when he marked how they chose the places of honor, saying to them, "When you are invited by anyone to a marriage feast, do not sit down in a place of honor, lest a more eminent man than you be invited by him; and he who invited you both will come and say to you, 'Give place to this man,' and then you will begin with shame to take the lowest place. But when you are invited, go and sit in the lowest place, so that when your host comes he may say to you, 'Friend, go up higher'; then you will be honored in the presence of all who sit at table with you. For every one who exalts himself will be humbled, and he who humbles himself will be exalted."

79e   *Exalting the Humble*
Gospel, Luke 18:9–14

He [Jesus] also told this parable to some who trusted in themselves that they were righteous and despised others: "Two men went up into the temple to pray, one a Pharisee and the other a tax collector. The Pharisee stood and prayed thus with himself, 'God, I thank thee that I am not like other men, extortioners, unjust, adulterers, or even like this tax collector. I fast twice a week, I give tithes of all that I get.' But the tax collector, standing far off, would not even lift up his eyes to heaven, but beat his breast, saying, 'God, be merciful to me a sinner!' I tell you, this man went down to his house justified rather than the other; for every one who exalts himself will be humbled, but he who humbles himself will be exalted."

79f   *Exalting the Humble*
Suetonius, Lives of the Caesars, Julius 1.72.1

His friends he [Julius] treated with invariable kindness and consideration. When Gaius Oppius was his companion on a journey through a wild, woody country and was suddenly taken ill, Caesar gave up to him the only shelter there was, while he himself slept on the ground out-of-doors. Moreover, when he came to power, he advanced some of his friends to the highest positions, even though they were of the humblest origin, and when taken to task for it, flatly declared that if he had been helped in defending his honor by brigands and cut-throats, he would have requited even such men in the same way.

79g   *Exalting the Humble*
Diogenes Laertius, Lives of the Eminent Philosophers 1.69

The tale is also told that he [Chilon] inquired of Aesop what Zeus was doing and received the answer: "He is humbling the proud and exalting the humble."

80   *Peter's Betrayal Foretold*
Gospel, John 13:36–38

Simon Peter said to him, "Lord, where are you going?" Jesus answered, "Where I am going you cannot follow me now; but you shall follow afterward." Peter said to him, "Lord, why cannot I follow you now? I will lay down my life for you." Jesus answered, "Will you lay down your life for me? Truly, truly, I say to you, the cock will not crow, till you have denied me three times."

81   *Jesus Arrested*
Gospel, John 18:1–12

When Jesus had spoken these words, he went forth with his disciples across the Kidron valley, where there was a garden, which he and his disciples entered. Now Judas, who betrayed him, also knew the place; for Jesus often met there with his disciples. So Judas, procuring a band of soldiers and some officers from the chief priests and the Pharisees, went there with lanterns and torches and weapons. Then Jesus, knowing all that was to befall him, came forward and said to them, "Whom do you seek?" They answered him, "Jesus of Nazareth." Jesus said to them, "I am he." Judas, who betrayed him, was standing with them. When he said to them, "I am he," they drew back and fell to the ground. Again he asked them, "Whom do you seek?" They answered him, "Jesus of Nazareth." Jesus answered, "I told you that I am he; so, if you seek me, let these men go." This was to fulfil the word which he had spoken, "Of those whom thou gavest me I lost not one." Then Simon Peter, having a sword drew it and struck the high priest's slave and cut off his right ear. The slave's name was Malchus. Jesus said to Peter, "Put your sword into its sheath; shall I not drink the cup which the Father has given me?"

So the band of soldiers and their captain and the officers of the Jews seized Jesus and bound him.

82 *Faith against Sight*
Gospel, John 20:24–29

Now Thomas, one of the twelve, called the Twin, was not with them when Jesus came. So the other disciples told him, "We have seen the Lord." But he said to them, "Unless I see in his hands the print of the nails, and place my finger in the mark of the nails, and place my hand in his side, I will not believe." Eight days later, his disciples were again in the house, and Thomas was with them. The doors were shut, but Jesus came and stood among them, and said, "Peace be with you." Then he said to Thomas, "Put your finger here, and see my hands; and put out your hand, and place it in my side; do not be faithless, but believing." Thomas answered him, "My Lord and my God!" Jesus said to him, "Have you believed because you have seen me? Blessed are those who have not seen and yet believe."

83 *He Will Remain until I Come*
Gospel, John 21:20–23

Peter turned and saw following them the disciple whom Jesus loved, who had lain close to his breast at the supper and had said, "Lord, who is it that is going to betray you?" When Peter saw him, he said to Jesus, "Lord, what about this man?" Jesus said to him, "If it is my will that he remain until I come, what is that to you? Follow me!" The saying spread abroad among the brethren that this disciple was not to die; yet Jesus did not say to him that he was not to die, but, "If it is my will that he remain until I come, what is that to you?"

84a *He Who Is Not against You Is for You*
Gospel, Luke 9:49–50

John answered, "Master, we saw a man casting out demons in your name, and we forbade him, because he does not follow with us." But Jesus said to him, "Do not forbid him; for he that is not against you is for you."

84b *He Who Is Not against Us Is for Us*
Gospel, Mark 9:38–41

John said to him, "Teacher, we saw a man casting out demons in your name, and we forbade him, because he was not following us." But Jesus said, "Do not forbid him; for no one who does a mighty work in my name will be able soon after to speak evil of me. For he that is not against us is for us. For truly, I say to you, whoever gives you a cup of water to drink because you bear the name of Christ, will by no means lose his reward."

85 *Teaching about Prayer*
Gospel, Luke 11:1–13

He [Jesus] was praying in a certain place, and when he ceased, one of his disciples said to him, "Lord, teach us to pray, as John taught his disciples." And he said to them, "When you pray, say: Father, hallowed be thy name. Thy kingdom come. Give us each day our daily bread; and forgive us our sins, for we ourselves forgive every one who is indebted to us; and lead us not into temptation." And he said to them, "Which of you who has a friend will go to him at midnight and say to him, 'Friend, lend me three loaves; for a friend of mine has arrived on a journey, and I have nothing to set before him'; and he will answer from within, 'Do not bother me; the door is now shut, and my children are with me in bed; I cannot get up and give you anything'? I tell you, though he will not get up and give him anything because he is his friend, yet because of his importunity he will rise and give him whatever he needs. And I tell you, Ask, and it will be given you; seek, and you will find; knock, and it will be opened to you. For every one who asks receives, and he who seeks finds, and to him who knocks it will be opened. What father among you, if his son asks for a fish, will instead of a fish give him a serpent; or if he asks for an egg, will give him a scorpion? If you then, who are evil, know how to give good gifts to your children, how much more will the heavenly Father give the Holy Spirit to those who ask him?"

86a *Jesus Foretells His Death and Resurrection*
Gospel, Mark 8:31–33

And he [Jesus] began to teach them that the Son of man must suffer many things, and be rejected by the elders and the chief priests and the scribes, and be killed, and after three days rise again. And he said this plainly. And Peter took him, and began to rebuke him. But turning and seeing his disciples, he rebuked Peter, and said, "Get behind me, Satan! For you are not on the side of God, but of men."

86b *Jesus Foretells His Death and Resurrection*
Gospel, Mark 9:30–32

They went on from there and passed through Galilee. And he [Jesus] would not have any one know it; for he was teaching his disciples, saying to them, "The Son of man will be delivered into the hands of men, and they will kill him; and when he is killed, after three days he will rise." But they did not understand the saying, and they were afraid to ask him.

86c *Jesus Foretells His Death and Resurrection*
Gospel, Mark 10:32–34

And they were on the road, going up to Jerusalem, and Jesus was walking ahead of them; and they were amazed, and those who followed were afraid. And taking the twelve again, he began to tell them what was to happen to him, saying, "Behold, we are going up to Jerusalem; and the Son of man will be delivered to the chief priests and the scribes, and they will condemn him to death, and deliver him to the Gentiles; and they will mock him, and spit upon him, and scourge him, and kill him; and after three days he will rise."

86d *Jesus Fortells His Death and Resurrection*
Gospel, Matthew 17:22–23
As they were gathering in Galilee, Jesus said to them, "The Son of man is to be delivered into the hands of men, and they will kill him, and he will be raised on the third day." And they were greatly distressed.

86e *Jesus Fortells His Death and Resurrection*
Gospel, Matthew 20:17–19
And as Jesus was going up to Jerusalem, he took the twelve disciples aside, and on the way he said to them, "Behold, we are going up to Jerusalem; and the Son of man will be delivered to the chief priests and scribes, and they will condemn him to death, and deliver him to the Gentiles to be mocked and scourged and crucified, and he will be raised on the third day."

86f *Jesus Foretells His Death*
Gospel, Matthew 26:1–2
When Jesus had finished all these sayings he said to his disciples, "You know that after two days the Passover is coming, and the Son of man will be delivered up to be crucified."

87a *Foxes Have Holes*
Gospel, Matthew 8:18–20
Now when Jesus saw great crowds around him, he gave orders to go over to the other side. And a scribe came up and said to him, "Teacher, I will follow you wherever you go." And Jesus said to him, "Foxes have holes, and birds of the air have nests; but the Son of man has nowhere to lay his head."

87b *Leave the Dead*
Gospel, Matthew 8:21–22
Another of the disciples said to him, "Lord, let me first go and bury my father." But Jesus said to him, "Follow me, and leave the dead to bury their own dead."

87c *Foxes Have Holes; Leave the Dead*
Gospel, Luke 9:57–62
As they were going along the road, a man said to him, "I will follow you wherever you go." And Jesus said to him, "Foxes have holes, and birds of the air have nests: but the Son of man has nowhere to lay his head."
To another he said, "Follow me." But he said, "Lord, let me first go and bury my father. But he said to him, "Leave the dead to bury their own dead: but as for you, go and proclaim the kingdom of God."
Another said, "I will follow you, Lord; but let me first say farewell to those at my home." Jesus said to him, "No one who puts his hand to the plow and looks back is fit for the kingdom of God."

87d *Foxes Have Holes*
Gospel, Thomas 86
Jesus said, "[Foxes have] their dens and birds have their nests, but the son of man has no place to lay his head and rest."

88a The Half-Shekel Tax
Gospel, Matthew 17:24–27

When they came to Capernaum, the collectors of the half-shekel tax went up to Peter and said, "Does not your teacher pay the tax?" He said, "Yes." And when he came home, Jesus spoke to him first saying, "What do you think, Simon? From whom do kings of the earth take toll or tribute? From theirs or from others?" And when he said, "From others," Jesus said unto him, "Then the sons are free. However, not to give offense to them, go to the sea and cast a hook, and take the first fish that comes up, and when you open its mouth you will find a shekel; take that and give it to them for me and for yourself."

88b The Half-Shekel Tax
Gospel, Matthew 17:24–27 <Codex 713; see also Latin mss. b, ff>
(Aland: 245)

And when they came to Capernaum, those who collect the half-shekel tax approached Peter and said, "Does your teacher not pay the half-shekel?" He said, "Yes." And when he came into the house, Jesus spoke to him first, saying, "Simon, what do you think? From whom do the kings of the earth collect tribute? From their own sons or from foreigners?" He said, "From foreigners." Jesus said to him, "Are the sons then free?" Simon said, "Yes." Jesus said, "Therefore give as though you were a foreigner to them. And lest we offend them, go to the sea and cast a hook, and take the first fish that comes up, and when you open its mouth, you will find a shekel. Take that and give it to them for me and for you."

89a On Forgiveness
Gospel, Matthew 18:21–22

Then Peter came up and said to him, "Lord, how often shall my brother sin against me, and I forgive him? As many as seven times?" Jesus said to him, "I do not say to you seven times, but seventy times seven."

89b On Forgiveness
Gospel, Nazoreans 15, from Jerome, *Dialogue Against the Pelagians* 3.2
(Migne, PL 23:571)

Jesus said, "If your brother has committed a verbal sin and has sought your pardon, acknowledge him seven times a day." Simon his disciple said to him, "Seven times a day?" The Lord answered him, "I tell you, as many as seventy times seven times. For after the prophets were anointed with the Holy Spirit, a verbal sin was also found in their discourse."

90 Something of the World
Gospel, Philip 34 (CG II, 59:18b–27)

The saints are served by evil powers, for they are blinded by the Holy Spirit into thinking they are serving a man whenever they do something for the saints. Because of this a disciple asked the Lord one day for something of the world. He said to him, "Ask your mother, and she will give you that which belongs to another."

91a *Women Not Worthy*
Gospel, Thomas 114

Simon Peter said to them, "Let Mary leave us, because females are not worthy of life." Jesus said, "Behold, I shall guide her so as to make her male, that she too may become a living spirit like you males. For every female who makes herself male will enter the kingdom of heaven."

91b *Neither Male Nor Female*
Gospel, Egyptians 5, from Clement, *Stromateis* 3.13.92
(Staehlin-Fruechtel 2.3:238)

Therefore Cassianus says, When Salome asked when the things would be known that she had inquired about, the Lord said, "When you (pl.) have trampled on the garment of shame and when the two become one and the male with the female is neither male nor female."

92 *Prophet without Irritation*
Hadith, Bukhārī, adab, 38

Mūsā b. Ismā'īl related to us that he heard Sallām b. Miskīn say: I heard Thābit say: Anas (may God be pleased with him) told us saying, I worked for the Prophet for ten years and he never said to me, "Uff,"[1] nor did he ever blame me saying, "Why did you do thus and so?" or "Why did you not do thus and so?"

   1. A harsh word expressing irritation.

93 *Moses Showed Forbearance*
Hadith, Bukhārī, adab, 53

Muḥammad b. Yūsuf and Sufyān related to us from Al-A'mash, Abū Wā'il and Ibn Mas'ūd, who said: One time the Messenger of God divided the booty of battle. One of the men of the Helpers said, "By God, Muḥammad did not please God by that division of booty!" I came to the Messenger of God and told him about it. His face showed anger, and he said, "May God be merciful to Moses, for he was hurt more than this, and he showed forbearance."

94 *On Vows*
Hadith, Bukhārī, nudhūr, 26

Yaḥyā b. Ṣāliḥ and Fulayḥ b. Sulaymān informed us that Sa'īd b. al-Ḥārith heard Ibn 'Umar say: "Is it not forbidden to make vows?" The Prophet said, "A vow neither hastens nor delays anything, but by means of a vow a miser can be separated from his wealth."

95 *Both Escape*
Hadith, Bukhārī, ṣayd, 7

'Umar b. Ḥafṣ b. Ghiyāth and his father reported to us that Al-A'mash said: Ibrāhīm told me on the authority of Al-Aswad that 'Abd Allāh (may God be pleased with him) said: While we were with the Prophet in a cave at Mina, the Sura, "Wa-l-Mursalāt" was revealed to him. He recited it, and I heard it directly from his mouth, while the inspiration was still fresh. Then a snake sprang at us. The Prophet said, "Kill it!" We hurried to do so, but it ran away. The Prophet said, "It has escaped your evil, even as you have escaped its evil."

96 Word More Precious
Hadith, Bukhārī, tawḥīd, 49

Abū al-Nuʿmān and Jarīr b. Ḥāzim related to us on the authority of Al-Ḥasan, who had it from ʿAmr b. Taghlib who said: Some property was given to the Prophet, and he gave some of it to certain people and not to others. He learned that the latter were blaming him. He said, "I give to one person and I withhold from another. The one from whom I withhold is dearer to me than the one to whom I give. I give to some people because of the anxiety and restlessness which are in their hearts and I do not give to others because of the contentment and goodness which God has put in their hearts. One of these is ʿAmr b. Taghlib." ʿAmr said, "The word of the Messenger of God is more precious to me than the possession of red camels."

97 On Kindness
Hadith, Tirmidhī, birr, 12

Ibn abī ʿUmar and Saʿīd b. ʿAbd al-Raḥmān said they heard from Sufyān and Al-Zuhrī, who reported from Abū Salama from Abū Hurayra, who said: Al-Aqraʿ b. Ḥābis saw the Prophet kissing al-Ḥasan (Ibn abī ʿUmar said, al-Ḥasan or al-Ḥusayn). Then al-Aqraʿ said, "I have ten children, and I have never kissed one of them." The Messenger of God replied, "Verily, he who shows no kindness will have no kindness shown him."

98 Do Not Sell that which You Do Not Have
Hadith, Tirmidhī, buyūʿ, 19

Qutayba and Hushaym reported from Abū Bishr and Yūsuf b. Māhak from Ḥakīm b. Ḥizām who said, I asked the Messenger of God, "If a man should come to me and ask me to sell him something which I do not have, may I purchase it later and then deliver it to him?" He replied, "Do not sell that which you do not have."

99 The Worthy Will See
Hippolytus, On Daniel 4.60 (Bonwetsch and Achelis: 338)

When the Lord was describing the coming kingdom of the saints to the disciples, that it would be glorious and wonderful, Judas, being astounded at the things spoken, said, "And who will see these things?" The Lord said, "Those who become worthy will see these things."

100 The Hearing Powers of Asclepius
Lucian, Demonax 27

When one of his friends said, "Demonax, let's go to the Asclepeion and pray for my son," he replied, "You must think Asclepius very deaf, that he can't hear our prayers from where we are!"

101 Good-For-Nothing Not Great
Lucian, Demonax 30

Cethegus the ex-consul, going by way of Greece to Asia to be his father's lieutenant, did and said many ridiculous things. One of the friends of Demonax, looking on, said that he was a great good-for-nothing. "No, he isn't either," responded Demonax, "not a great one!"

102 *Demonax Does Not Fear Fish*
Lucian, Demonax 35

When he [Demonax] was intending to make a voyage in winter, one of his friends remarked, "Aren't you afraid the boat will capsize and the fishes will eat you?" "I should be an ingrate," he replied, "if I were afraid of the fishes eating me, when I have eaten so many of them!"

103 *Drinking and Running*
Macrobius, Saturnalia 2.2.7

After the rout at Mutina . . . people were asking what Antonius was doing, and the story went that an acquaintance of his replied: "What dogs do in Egypt—drinking and running away"; since it is well known that in those parts dogs drink as they run, for fear of being caught by a crocodile.[1]

> 1. Cf. Pliny, *Natural History* 8.61.148. Antony was a notorious drunkard.

104a *Young for Age*
Macrobius, Saturnalia 2.3.2

When he [Cicero] was dining at the house of Damasippus, his host produced a very ordinary wine, saying, "Try this Falernian; it is forty years old." "Young for its age," replied Cicero.

104b *Small for Age*
Athenaeus, Deipnosophists 13.584B–C

When some one poured into her [Gnathaena's] cup, which was small,[1] some small wine, with the remark that it was sixteen years old, she said, "It's small indeed, considering how many years old it is."

> 1. Here the cup is a small specimen of the class known as "cooler." The wine itself was thin and cheap (*mikros*).

105 *Cicero Jeers Caesar's Appointment*
Macrobius, Saturnalia 2.3.11

There was another occasion on which Cicero openly jeered at the readiness with which Caesar admitted new members to the Senate; for, asked by his host Publius Mallius to procure the office of decurion[1] for his stepson, he said in the presence of a large company: "Senatorial rank? Well, at Rome he shall certainly have it, if you so wish; but at Pompeii it isn't easy."

> 1. A member of the legislative council (corresponding to the Roman Senate) of a provincial township the inhabitants of which enjoyed a large measure of local self-government.

106 *Don't Believe It*
Macrobius, Saturnalia 2.4.4

When Pacuvius Taurus was asking him [Augustus] for a gift of money and added that it was common gossip that he had already received a considerable sum from him, Augustus replied: "Don't you believe it."

107 *A Prefect Claims Pension*
Macrobius, Saturnalia 2.4.5

To another prefect of cavalry who had been relieved of his command but nevertheless claimed a pension, saying that he made the request not for the sake of the money but that it might be thought that he had resigned his commission and had been adjudged worthy of the gift by the emperor, Augustus retorted: "Tell everybody that you have had it. I shall deny that I gave it."

108   Charmer of Unfaithful Wives
Macrobius, Saturnalia 2.4.12

Again, knowing that his friend Maecenas wrote in a loose, effeminate, and languishing style, he [Augustus] would often affect a similar style in the letters which he wrote to him; and, in contrast to the restrained language of his other writings, an intimate letter to Maecenas contained, by way of a joke, a flood of such expressions as these: "Good-by, my ebony of Medullia, ivory from Etruria, silphium of Aretium, diamond of the Adriatic, pearl from the Tiber, Cilnian emerald, jasper of the Iguvians, Porsenna's beryl, Italy's carbuncle—in short, you charmer of unfaithful wives."[1]

> 1. The reference to pearl, emerald, jasper, and beryl suggest that Augustus is here making fun of some lines, addressed by Maecenas to Horace, in which these jewels are named. The lines are preserved in Isidore of Seville 19.32.6.

109   The Poor Meal
Macrobius, Saturnalia 2.4.13

He [Augustus] hardly ever refused to accept hospitality; and having been entertained to a very frugal and, so to speak, everyday dinner, he just whispered in his host's ear, as he was saying good-by after the poor and ill-appointed meal: "I didn't think that I was so close a friend of yours."

110   Playing with One Hand?
Macrobius, Saturnalia 2.6.5

To others who used to play at ball with him Gaius Caesar had made a gift of a hundred thousand sesterces, but Lucius Caecilius got only fifty thousand. "What is the meaning of this?" said Caecilius, "Do I play with only one hand?"

111   Warm Hands
Macrobius, Saturnalia 7.3.15

The praetor Lucius Quinctius,[1] soon after his return from a province which he had governed with the highest integrity—a matter for surprise in the days of Domitian—being in poor health, remarked to a friend sitting next to him at dinner that his hands were cold. Whereupon the other replied with a smile: "And yet they were warm enough when you came home from your province a short time ago." Quinctius was delighted by the quip and laughed, for he was the very last man on whom suspicion of speculation could fall. But, if those words had been addressed to a man with a guilty conscience and a memory of dishonest practices, they would have moved the hearer to anger.

> 1. Macrobius has Quintus, but a "gentile" name is needed.

112   Grown from the Same Seed
Macrobius, Saturnalia 7.3.20

A gibe too becomes agreeable if the party who makes it and the party at whom it is directed are of the same condition in life, as, for example, if a man of slender means were to chaff another with his poverty, or if a man of obscure birth were to make fun of another's humble origin. Thus Amphias of Tarsus, who from a market gardener became a person of importance, after some reference to a friend's low estate, went on to say: "But there, we are both grown from the same seed," a remark which gave pleasure to all alike.

113 *Those Who Come Will See*
Papias, from Irenaeus, *Against Heresies* 5.33.4 (Harvey 2:418):

And he [Papias] added a saying: "These things are indeed believable to those who have faith." And when Judas the betrayer did not believe and asked how such things would be accomplished by the Lord (God), the Lord (Jesus) said, "Those who come to these things will see."

114 *Musonius Digs*
Philostratus, Life of Apollonius 5.19

Demetrius said that he had fallen in with Musonius at the Isthmus, where he was fettered and under orders to dig; and that he addressed to him such consolations as he could, but Musonius took his spade and stoutly dug it into the earth, and then looking up, said: "You are distressed, Demetrius, to see me digging through the Isthmus for Greece; but if you saw me playing the harp like Nero, what would you feel then?"

115 *Wisdom Greater Than Colossus*
Philostratus, Life of Apollonius 5.21

As he [Apollonius] approached the image of the Colossus, Damis asked him if he thought anything could be greater than that and he replied: "Yes, a man who loves wisdom in a sound and innocent spirit."

116 *The Silent Arguments of Marcus*
Philostratus, Lives of the Sophists 1.24 (528–529)

The expression of his brows and the gravity of his countenance proclaimed Marcus a sophist, and indeed his mind was constantly brooding over some theme, and he was always training himself in the methods that prepare one for extempore speaking. This was evident from the steady gaze of his eyes which were usually intent on secret thoughts, and, moreover, it was admitted by the man himself. For when one of his friends asked him how he declaimed the day before, he replied, "To myself, well enough, but to my pupils not so well." And when the other expressed surprise at the answer, Marcus said, "I work even when I am silent, and I keep myself in practice with two or three arguments beside the one that I maintain in public."

117 *Polemo Takes Fee*
Philostratus, Lives of the Sophists 1.25 (538)

Herodes says that in payment for this [Polemo's declamation] he sent him [Polemo] 150,000 drachmae, and called this the fee for his lectures. But since he did not accept it, Herodes thought that he had been treated with contempt, but Munatius the critic, when drinking with him (this man came from Tralles), remarked, "Herodes, I think that Polemo dreamed of 250,000 drachmae, and so thinks that he is being stinted because you did not send so large a sum." Herodes says that he added the 100,000 drachmae, and that Polemo took the money without the least hesitation, as though he were receiving only what was his due.

118 *The Disease of Polemo*
Philostratus, Lives of the Sophists 1.25 (543)

And in writing to Herodes about this disease[1] he [Polemo] sent this bulletin: "I must eat, but I have no hands; I must walk, but I have no feet; I must endure pain, and then I find I have both feet and hands."

1. Polemo suffered from a hardening of the joints.

119 *Herodes Stops Mourning*
Philostratus, Lives of the Sophists 2.1 (557)

And this incident must not be omitted from my narrative, since it is held worthy of mention by learned writers. For this Lucius ranked among men renowned for learning, and since he had been trained in philosophy by Musonius of Tyre, his repartees were apt to hit the mark, and he practised a wit well suited to the occasion. Now, as he was very intimate with Herodes, he was with him when he was most deeply afflicted by his grief, and used to give him good advice to the following effect: "Herodes, in every matter that which is enough is limited by the golden mean, and I have often heard Musonius argue on this theme, and have often discoursed on it myself; and, moreover, I used to hear you also, at Olympia, commending the golden mean to the Greeks, and at that time you would even exhort rivers to keep their course in mid channel between their banks. But what has now become of all this advice? For you have lost your self-control, and are acting in a way that we must needs deplore, since you risk your great reputation." He said more to the same effect. But since he could not convince him, he went away in anger. And he saw some slaves at a well that was in the house, washing radishes, and asked them for whose dinner they were intended. They replied that they were preparing them for Herodes. At this Lucius remarked, "Herodes insults Regilla by eating white radishes in a black house." This speech was reported indoors to Herodes, and when he heard it he removed the signs of mourning from his house, for fear he should become the laughing-stock of wise men.

120 *Herodes Rebukes Sceptus*
Philostratus, Lives of the Sophists 2.5 (573)

When the declamation [of Alexander] was over, Herodes called together the more advanced of his own pupils and asked them what was their opinion of the sophists; and when Sceptus of Corinth said that he had found the clay but had still to find the Plato,[1] Herodes cut him short, and said, "Do not talk like that to anyone else, for," said he, "you will incriminate yourself as an illiterate critic. Nay rather follow me in thinking him a more sober Scopelian."

1. Alexander was generally nicknamed "Clay-Plato."

121 *The Temper of Philagrus*
Philostratus, Lives of the Sophists 2.8 (580–581)

In height Philagrus was below the average, his brow was stern, his eye alert and easily roused to anger, and he was himself conscious of his morose temper. Hence when one of his friends asked him why he did not enjoy bringing up a family, he replied, "Because I do not even enjoy myself."

122 *Adrian Jests with Student*
Philostratus, Lives of the Sophists 2.10 (590)

They slander him [Adrian] too in saying that he had shameless manners because, when one of his pupils sent him a present of fish lying on a silver plate embossed with gold, he was enchanted with the plate and so did not return it, and in acknowledging the present to the sender, he said, "It was indeed kind of you to send the fish as well." But it is said that he made this jest as a sarcasm against one of his pupils who had been reported to him as using his wealth in a miserly fashion, and that he gave back the piece of silver after he had castigated the student in this witty manner.

123 *Unhappy Marriage of Hermocrates*
Philostratus, Lives of the Sophists 2.25 (610)

After Antipater had been promoted to be Imperial Secretary he desired to arrange a marriage between Hermocrates and his daughter who was very unattractive in appearance. But Hermocrates did not jump at the chance to share Antipater's prosperity, but when the woman who was arranging the affair called his attention to the great resources of which Antipater was then possessed, he replied that he could never become the slave of a large dowry and a father-in-law's swollen pride. And though his relatives tried to push him into this marriage, and regarded Antipater as "Corinthus, son of Zeus,"[1] he did not give way until the Emperor Severus summoned him to the East and gave him the girl in marriage. Then, when one of his friends asked him when he was going to celebrate the unveiling of the bride, Hermocrates replied with ready wit, "Say rather the veiling, when I am taking a wife like that." And it was not long before he dissolved the marriage, on finding that she had neither a pleasing appearance nor an agreeable disposition.

> 1. This popular proverb was used in two ways: of empty boasting, because the Corinthians boasted that their eponymous hero was Corinthus, son of Zeus; and to express aimless iteration as in Pindar, *Nemean* 7.105; but here it merely implies exaggerated respect for Antipater.

124 *Misfortunes of Heracleides*
Philostratus, Lives of the Sophists 2.26 (614)

It is said that for cutting down sacred cedars he [Heracleides] was punished by the confiscation of a great part of his estate. On that occasion, as he was leaving the law-court, his pupils were in attendance to comfort and sustain him, and one of them said, "But your ability to declaim no one will ever take from you, Heracleides, nor the fame you have won thereby." And he went on to recite over him the verse, "One methinks is still detained in a wide"—"privy purse,"[1] interrupted Heracleides, thus wittily jesting at his own misfortunes.

> 1. This quotation was popular because it was easily parodied; here the pupil means that Heracleides and his fame survive, but the sophist by his allusion to the confiscation of his property to the Emperor, alters the sense of the verb to mean "is checked by," and changes the last word from "sea" to "privy purse."

125a *Hard to Be Merciful and Sensible*
Plutarch, Agesilaus 13.4

Of this he [Agesilaus] gave an instance when, as he was decamping in some haste and confusion, he left his favorite behind him sick. The sick one besought him loudly as he was departing, but he merely turned and said that it was hard to be compassionate and at the same time prudent.

125b *Hard to Be Merciful and Sensible*
Plutarch, Moralia, Sayings of Spartans III:209F (17)

Such, then, was Agesilaus in his friends' behalf in most matters; but there are instances when, in meeting a critical situation, he showed more regard for the general welfare. At any rate, on a time when camp was being broken in some disorder, and Agesilaus was leaving behind his loved one who was ill, and the loved one implored him and called him back with tears, Agesilaus, turning round, exclaimed, "How hard it is to be merciful and sensible at the same time!"

125c *Hard to Be Merciful and Sensible*
Plutarch, Moralia, Sayings of Kings and Commanders III:191A (4)

When he [Agesilaus] was about to break camp in haste by night to leave the enemy's country, and saw his favorite youth, owing to illness, being left behind all in tears, he said, "It is hard to be merciful and sensible at the same time."

126 *Agesilaus Plays with Children*
Plutarch, Agesilaus 25.5

A story is told of his [Agesilaus'] joining in their childish play. Once, when they were very small, he bestrode a stick, and was playing horse with them in the house, and when he was spied doing this by one of his friends, he entreated him not to tell any one, until he himself should be a father of children.

127a *Phocion Not Both Friend and Flatterer*
Plutarch, Agis 2.2

[This is] what Phocion said to Antipater, who demanded from him some dishonorable service, "Thou canst not have Phocion as thy friend and at the same time thy flatterer."

127b *Phocion Not Both Friend and Flatterer*
Plutarch, Phocion 30.2

Again, when Antipater desired him [Phocion] to do something that was not seemly, he gave him a sharper answer, saying: "Antipater cannot have from me the services of friend and flatterer at once." And Antipater himself once said, as we are told, that he had two friends at Athens, Phocion and Demades; one he could never persuade to take anything, the other he could never satisfy with his gifts.

128 *Alexander's Allotment to His Soldiers*
Plutarch, Alexander 15.1–7 (1–3)

As to the number of his [Alexander's] forces, those who put it at the smallest figure mention thirty thousand foot and four thousand horse; those who put it at the highest, forty-three thousand foot and five thousand horse.[1] To provision these forces, Aristobulus says he had not more than seventy talents; Duris speaks of maintenance for only thirty days; and Onesicritus says he owed two hundred talents besides. But although he set out with such meager and narrow resources, he would not set foot upon his ship until he had enquired into the circumstances of his companions and allotted to one a farm, to another a village, and to another the revenue from some hamlet or harbor. And when at last nearly all of the crown property had been expended or allotted, Perdiccas said to him: "But for thyself, O king, what art thou leaving?" And when the king answered, "My hopes." "In these, then," said Perdiccas, "we also will share who make the expedition with thee." Then he declined the possessions which had been allotted to him, and some of the other friends of Alexander did likewise. But upon those who wanted and would accept his favors Alexander bestowed them readily, and most of what he possessed in Macedonia was used up in these distributions. Such was the ardor and such the equipment with which he crossed the Hellespont.

> 1. "Not much more than thirty thousand foot, including light-armed troops and archers, and over five thousand horse (Arrian, *Anabasis*. 1.2.3)".

129 *Alexander's Crossing of the Granicus*
Plutarch, Alexander 16.1–3 (1–2)

Meanwhile the generals of Darius had assembled a large force and set it in array at the crossing of the river Granicus, so that it was practically necessary to fight, as it were at the gates of Asia, for entrance and dominion there. But most of the Macedonian officers were afraid of the depth of the river, and of the roughness and unevenness of the farther banks, up which they would have to climb while fighting. Some, too, thought they ought to observe carefully the customary practice in regard to the month (for in the month of Daesius the kings of Macedonia were not wont to take the field with an army). This objection Alexander removed by bidding them call the month a second Artemisius; and when Parmenio, on the ground that it was too late in the day, objected to their risking the passage, he declared that the Hellespont would blush for shame, if, after having crossed that strait, he should be afraid of the Granicus, and plunged into the stream with thirteen troops of horsemen.

130 *Alexander Conquers But Does Not Capture Darius*
Plutarch, Alexander 20.10–12 (5–7)

Although he [Alexander] won a brilliant victory and destroyed more than a hundred and ten thousand of his enemies, he did not capture Darius, who got a start of four or five furlongs in his flight; but he did take the king's chariot, and his bow, before he came back from the pursuit. He found his Macedonians carrying off the wealth from the camp of the Barbarians, and the wealth was of surpassing abundance, although its owners had come to the battle in light marching order and had left most of their baggage in Damascus; he found, too, that his men had picked out for him the tent of Darius, which was full to overflowing with gorgeous servitors and furniture, and many treasures. Straightway, then, Alexander put off his armor and went to the bath, saying: "Let us go and wash off the sweat of the battle in the bath of Darius." "No, indeed," said one of his companions, "but rather in that of Alexander; for the property of the conquered must belong to the conqueror, and be called his."

131 *Alexander Rebukes Hagnon*
Plutarch, Alexander 22.3 (2)

He [Alexander] severely rebuked Hagnon also for writing to him that he wanted to buy Crobylus, whose beauty was famous in Corinth, as a present for him.[1]

> 1. Cf. 632a, e–f.

132 Alexander Respects Wife of Darius
Plutarch, Alexander 22.4–5 (2–3)

Furthermore, on learning that Damon and Timotheus, two Macedonian soldiers under Parmenio's command, had ruined the wives of certain mercenaries, he [Alexander] wrote to Parmenio ordering him, in case the men were convicted, to punish them and put them to death as wild beasts born for the destruction of mankind. In this letter he also wrote expressly concerning himself: "As for me, indeed, it will be found not only that I have not seen the wife of Darius or desired to see her, but that I have not even allowed people to speak to me of her beauty."

133 Alexander Sleeps before Battle with Darius
Plutarch, Alexander 32.1–4 (1–2)

After the men were gone, Alexander lay down in his tent, and is said to have passed the rest of the night in a deeper sleep than usual, so that when his officers came to him in the early morning they were amazed, and on their own authority issued orders that the soldiers should first take breakfast. Then, since the occasion was urgent, Parmenio entered the tent, and standing by his couch called Alexander twice or thrice by name; and when he had thus roused him, he asked him how he could possibly sleep as if he were victorious, instead of being about to fight the greatest of all his battles. Then Alexander said with a smile: "What, pray? Dost thou not think that we are already victorious, now that we are relieved from wandering about in a vast and desolated country in pursuit of a Darius who avoids a battle?" And not only before the battle, but also in the very thick of the struggle did he show himself great, and firm in his confident calculations.

134 Alexander's Concern over Refusal of Gifts
Plutarch, Alexander 39.4 (3)

Furthermore, he [Alexander] was generally more displeased with those who would not take his gifts than with those who asked for them. And so he wrote to Phocion in a letter that he would not treat him as a friend in the future if he rejected his favors.

135 Alexander Forgives Proteas with a Gift
Plutarch, Alexander 39.6 (4)

With Proteas, however, a clever wag and boon companion, he [Alexander] appeared to be angry; but when the man's friends begged his forgiveness, as did Proteas himself with tears, the king said that he was his friend again, whereat Proteas said: "In that case, O King, give me something to prove it first." Accordingly, the king ordered that five talents should be given him.

136 Alexander Charges Hephaestion with Secrecy
about Olympias' Letters
Plutarch, Alexander 39.8 (5)

Olympias often wrote him in like vein, but Alexander kept her writings secret, except once when Hephaestion, as was his wont, read with him a letter which had been opened; the king did not prevent him, but took the ring from his own finger and applied its seal to the lips of Hephaestion.

137   *Alexander Defends Olympias against Antipater*
Plutarch, Alexander 39.13 (7)

Once, however, after reading a long letter which Antipater had written in denunciation of her [Olympias], he [Alexander] said Antipater knew not that one tear of a mother effaced ten thousand letters.

138   *Alexander Rebukes Peucestas concerning Hunting Accident*
Plutarch, Alexander 41.4 (2)

He [Alexander] found fault with Peucestas by letter because, after being bitten by a bear, he wrote about it to the rest of his friends but did not tell him. "Now, however," said he, "write me how you are, and tell me whether any of your fellow-huntsmen left you in the lurch, that I may punish them."

139   *Alexander Helps Eurylochus Woo Telesippa*
Plutarch, Alexander 41.9–10 (5)

When he [Alexander] was sending home his aged and infirm soldiers, Eury-lochus of Aegae got himself enrolled among the sick, and then, when it was discovered that he had nothing the matter with him, confessed that he was in love with Telesippa, and was bent on following along with her on her journey to the seaboard. Alexander asked of what parentage the girl was, and on hearing that she was a free-born courtesan, said: "I will help you, O Eurylochus, in your amour; but see to it that we try to persuade Telesippa either by arguments or by gifts, since she is free-born."

140a   *Craterus and Hephaestion*
Plutarch, Alexander 47.9–10 (5)

Moreover, when he [Alexander] saw that among his chiefest friends Hephaes-tion approved his course and joined him in changing his mode of life, while Craterus clung fast to his native ways, he employed the former in his business with the Barbarians, the latter in that with the Greeks and Macedonians. And in general he showed most affection for Hephaestion, but most esteem for Craterus, thinking and constantly saying, that Hephaestion was a friend of Alexander, but Craterus a friend of the king.

140b   *Craterus and Hephaestion*
Plutarch, Moralia, Sayings of Kings and Commanders III:181D (29)

Of his foremost and most influential friends he [Alexander] seems to have honored Craterus most and to have loved Hephaestion best. "For," said he, "Craterus is fond of the king, but Hephaestion is fond of Alexander."[1]

1. Cf. Diodorus 17.114.

141   *Generosity of Philotas*
Plutarch, Alexander 48.1–2

Now, Philotas, the son of Parmenio, had a high position among the Mace-donians; for he was held to be valiant and able to endure hardship, and, after Alexander himself, no one was so fond of giving and so fond of his comrades. At any rate, we are told that when one of his intimates asked him for some money, he ordered his steward to give it him, and when the steward said he had none to give, "What meanest thou?" cried Philotas, "hast thou not even plate or clothing?"

142   *Alexander Refuses to Let Callisthenes Kiss Him*
Plutarch, Alexander 54.4–6 (3–4)

Chares of Mitylene says that once at a banquet Alexander, after drinking, handed the cup to one of his friends, and he, on receiving it, rose up so as to face the household shrine, and when he had drunk, first made obeisance to Alexander, then kissed him, and then resumed his place upon the couch. As all the guests were doing this in turn, Callisthenes took the cup, the king not paying attention, but conversing with Hephaestion, and after he had drunk went towards the king to kiss him; but Demetrius, surnamed Pheido, cried: "O King, do not accept his kiss, for he alone has not done thee obeisance." So Alexander declined the kiss, at which Callisthenes exclaimed in a loud voice: "Well, then, I'll go away the poorer by a kiss."[1]

1. Cf. Arrian, *Anabasis* 4.12.

143   *Alexander Purified after Seeing Deformed Lamb*
Plutarch, Alexander 57.4 (3)

When a sheep gave birth to a lamb which had upon its head what looked like a tiara in form and color, with testicles on either side of it, Alexander was filled with loathing at the portent, and had himself purified by the Babylonians, whom he was accustomed to take along with him for such purposes; and in conversation with his friends he said that he was not disturbed for his own sake, but for theirs, fearing lest after his death Heaven might devolve his power upon an ignoble and impotent man.

144   *Alexander Takes Sisimithres' Citadel*
Plutarch, Alexander 58.3–4 (2–3)

It is said that when he [Alexander] was besieging the citadel of Sisimithres, which was steep and inaccessible, so that his soldiers were disheartened, he asked Oxyartes what sort of a man Sisimithres himself was in point of spirit. And when Oxyartes replied that he was most cowardly of men, "Thy words mean," said Alexander, "that we can take the citadel, since he who commands it is a weak thing." And indeed he did take the citadel by frightening Sisimithres.

145   *Alexander Grieves over Death of Namesake*
Plutarch, Alexander 58.5 (3)

Again, after attacking another citadel equally precipitous, he [Alexander] was urging on the younger Macedonians, and addressing one who bore the name of Alexander, said: "It behooves thee, at least, to be a brave man, even for thy name's sake." And when the young man, fighting gloriously, fell, the king was pained beyond measure.

146   *Many Suppers Arranged*
Plutarch, Antony 28.2–3

At any rate, Philotas, the physician of Amphissa, used to tell my grandfather Lamprias that he was in Alexandria at this time, studying his profession, and that having got well acquainted with one of the royal cooks, he was easily persuaded by him (young man that he was) to take a view of the extravagant preparations for a royal supper. Accordingly, he was introduced into the kitchen, and when he saw all the other provisions in great abundance and eight wild boars a-roasting, he expressed his amazement at what must be the number of guests. But the cook burst out laughing and said: "The guests are not many, only about twelve; but every thing that is set before them must be at perfection, and this an instant of time reduces. For it might happen that Antony would ask for supper immediately and after a little while perhaps, would postpone it and call for a cup of wine, or engage in conversation with someone. Wherefore," he said, "not one, but many suppers are arranged; for the precise time is hard to hit."

147   *Give Us Land*
Plutarch, Antony 64.1–2

It was on this occasion [the decision to engage in a sea battle], we are told, that an infantry centurion, a man who had fought many a battle for Antony and was covered with scars, burst into laments as Antony was passing by, and said: "Imperator, why dost thou distrust these wounds and this sword and put thy hopes in miserable logs of wood? Let Egyptians and Phoenicians do their fighting at sea, but give us land, on which we are accustomed to stand and either conquer enemies or die." To this Antony made no reply, but merely encouraged the man by a gesture and a look to be of good heart, and passed on.

148   *Timon's Symposium*
Plutarch, Antony 70.2

Apemantus alone of all men Timon would sometimes admit into his company, since Apemantus was like him and tried sometimes to imitate his mode of life; and once, at the festival of The Pitchers, the two were feasting by themselves, and Apemantus said: "Timon, what a fine symposium ours is!" "It would be," said Timon, "if thou were not here."

149   *A Caesar Too Many*
Plutarch, Antony 81.1–2

As for the children of Antony, Antyllus, his son by Fulvia, was betrayed by Theodorus his tutor and put to death; and after the soldiers had cut off his head, his tutor took away the exceeding precious stone which the boy wore about his neck and sewed it into his own girdle; and though he denied the deed, he was convicted of it and crucified. Cleopatra's children, together with their attendants, were kept under guard and had generous treatment. But Caesarion, who was said to be Cleopatra's son by Julius Caesar, was sent by his mother, with much treasure, into India, by way of Ethiopia. There Rhodon, another tutor like Theodorus, persuaded him to go back, on the ground that Caesar invited him to take the kingdom. But while Caesar was deliberating on the matter, we are told that Areius said: "Not a good thing were a Caesar too many."[1]

1. [A pun on the Greek of] Homer, *Iliad* 2.204.

150   *Cyrus Not Unworthy of Kingdom*
Plutarch, Artaxerxes 8.2

And we are told that Cyrus, before the battle, when Clearchus besought him to remain behind the combatants and not risk his life, replied: "What sayest thou,

Clearchus? Dost thou bid me, who am reaching out for a kingdom, to be unworthy of a kingdom?"

151   *King or Gods to Reward Giver*
Plutarch, Artaxerxes 12.3–4

Meanwhile, since the king [Artaxerxes] was almost dead with thirst, Satibarznes the eunuch ran about in quest of a drink for him; for the place had no water, and the camp was far away. At last, then, he came upon one of those low Caunians who had vile and polluted water in a wretched skin, about two quarts in all; this he took, brought it to the king, and gave it to him. After the king had drunk it all off, the eunuch asked him if he was not altogether disgusted with the drink. But the king swore by the gods that he had never drunk wine, or the lightest or purest water, with so much pleasure. "Therefore," said the king, "if I should be unable to find and reward the man who gave thee this drink, I pray the gods to make him rich and happy."

152   *Ligarius Recovers for Brutus*
Plutarch, Brutus 11.1–3

There was a certain Caius Ligarius among the friends of Pompey, who had been denounced as such, but pardoned by Caesar. This man, cherishing no gratitude for his pardon, but rather offended by the power which had put his life in jeopardy, was an enemy of Caesar, and one of the most familiar friends of Brutus. Once, when this man was sick, Brutus came to see him, and said: "O Ligarius, what a time this is to be sick!" Ligarius at once raised himself on his elbow, clasped Brutus by the hand and said: "Nay, Brutus, if thou hast a purpose worthy of thyself, I am well."

153   *Porcia Valiant*
Plutarch, Brutus 23.5–6

And when Acilius, one of the friends of Brutus, recited the verses containing Andromache's words to Hector,
>"But, Hector, thou to me art father and honored mother
>And brother; my tender husband, too, art thou,"

Brutus smiled and said: "But I, certainly, have no mind to address Porcia in the words of Hector,
>'Ply loom and distaff and give orders to thy maids,'[1]

for though her body is not strong enough to perform such heroic tasks as men do, still, in spirit she is valiant in defense of her country, just as we are."

1. Homer, *Iliad* 6.429f., 491.

154   *Cassius Trusts Fortune*
Plutarch, Brutus 40.1–3

But Cassius, as Messala tells us, supped in private with a few of his intimates, and was seen to be silent and pensive, contrary to his usual nature. When supper was over, he grasped Messala's hand warmly, and speaking in Greek, as was his custom when he would show affection, said: "I call thee to witness, Messala, that I am in the same plight as Pompey the Great, in that I am forced to hazard the fate of my country on the issue of a single battle. With good courage, however, let us fix our waiting eyes on Fortune, of whom, even though our counsels be infirm, it is not right that we should be distrustful."

155 *Brutus and Cassius Go into Battle*
Plutarch, Brutus 40.5–9

As soon as it was day, a scarlet tunic, the signal for battle, was displayed before the camps of Brutus and Cassius, and they themselves came together into the space between their armies. Here Cassius said: "May we be victorious, Brutus, and ever afterwards share a mutual prosperity; but since the most important of human affairs are most uncertain, and since, if the battle goes contrary to our wishes, we shall not easily see one another again, what is thy feeling about flight and death?" And Brutus made answer: "When I was a young man, Cassius, and without experience of the world, I was led, I know not how, to speak too rashly for a philosopher. I blamed Cato for making away with himself, on the ground that it was impious and unmanly to yield to one's evil genius, not accepting fearlessly whatever befalls, but running away. In my present fortunes, however, I am become of a different mind; and if God does not decide the present issue in our favor, I do not ask once more to put fresh hopes and preparations to the test, but I will go hence with words of praise for Fortune; on the Ides of March I gave my own life to my country, and since then, for her sake, I have lived another life of liberty and glory." At these words Cassius smiled, and after embracing Brutus, said: "Thus minded, let us go against the enemy; for either we shall be victorious, or we shall not fear the victors."

156a *Came, Saw, Conquered*
Plutarch, Caesar 50:1–3 (1–2)

On leaving that country and traversing Asia, he [Caesar] learned that Domitius had been defeated by Pharnaces the son of Mithridates and had fled from Pontus with a few followers; also that Pharnaces, using his victory without waiting, and occupying Bithynia and Cappadocia, was aiming to secure the country called Lesser Armenia, and was rousing to revolt all the princes and tetrarchs there. At once, therefore, Caesar marched against him with three legions, fought a great battle with him near the city of Zela, drove him in flight out of Pontus, and annihilated his army. In announcing the swiftness and fierceness of this battle to one of his friends at Rome, Amantius, Caesar wrote three words: "Came, saw, conquered."[1]

1. *Veni, vidi, vici.*

156b *Came, Saw, Conquered*
Plutarch, Moralia, Sayings of Romans III:206E (12)

After he [Caesar] had conquered Pharnaces of Pontus by a swift drive against him, he wrote to his friends, "I came, saw, conquered."[1]

1. In 47 B.C.E. Cf. Appian, *The Civil Wars* 2.91; Dio Cassius 42.48.

156c *Came, Saw, Conquered*
Suetonius, Julius Caesar 1.37

In his Pontic triumph he displayed among the show-pieces of the procession an inscription of but three words, "I came, I saw, I conquered," not indicating the events of the war, as the others did, but the speed with which it was finished.

157 *Yonder Is the Enemy*
Plutarch, Caesar 52.9 (6)

On one occasion, too, in another battle, the enemy got the advantage in the encounter, and here it is said that Caesar seized by the neck the fugitive standard-bearer, faced him about, and said: "Yonder is the enemy."

158 *Caesar Strives for Life*
Plutarch, Caesar 56.2–4 (2–3)

The great battle was joined near the city of Munda, and here Caesar, seeing his own men hard pressed and making a feeble resistance, asked in a loud voice as he ran through the armed ranks whether they felt no shame to take him and put him in the hands of those boys. With difficulty and after much strenuous effort he repulsed the enemy and slew over thirty thousand of them, but he lost one thousand of his own men, and those the very best. As he was going away after battle he said to his friends that he had often striven for victory, but now first for his life.

159 *Cato's Silence*
Plutarch, Cato the Younger 4.2

Indeed, to one of his companions who said, "Men find fault with thee, Cato, for thy silence," he replied: "Only let them not blame my life. I will begin to speak when I am not going to say what were better left unsaid."

160 *Cato to Be Tamed*
Plutarch, Cato the Younger 14.4

For Curio, annoyed at the severity of Cato, who was his intimate friend, had asked him whether he was desirous of seeing Asia after his term of service in the army. "Certainly I am," said Cato. "That's right," said Curio, "for you will come back from there more agreeable and more tame."

161a *No Secrets, Please*
Plutarch, Demetrius 12.5

On one occasion Lysimachus wished to do him a kindness, and said: "Philippides, what have I that I can share with thee?" "O King," said Philippides, "anything but one of thy state secrets."

161b *No Secrets, Please*
Plutarch, Moralia, Sayings of Kings and Commanders III:183E (2)

To Philippides the comic poet who was his friend and intimate he [Lysimachus[1]] said, "What of mine shall I share with you?" And the other replied, "What you will, except your secrets."

1. One of Alexander's generals; later king of Thrace.

161c *No Secrets, Please*
Plutarch, Moralia, Concerning Talkativeness VI:508C (12)

Philippides, the comic poet, therefore, made the right answer when King Lysimachus courteously asked him, "What is there of mine that I may share with you?" and he replied, "Anything you like, Sire, except your secrets."

161d *No Secrets, Please*
Plutarch, Moralia, On Being a Busybody VI:517B (4)

Philippides, the comic poet, made an excellent reply when King Lysimachus once said to him, "Which one of my possessions may I share with you?" "Anything, Sire," said Philippides, "except your secrets."

162 *No Account of Perdition*
Plutarch, Eumenes 8.4

Because he was superior in cavalry, Eumenes wished to give battle in the plains of Lydia about Sardis, and at the time he was ambitious to make a display of his forces before Cleopatra; but at the request of that princess, who was afraid to give Antipater any cause for complaint, he marched away into upper Phrygia and wintered at Celaenae. Here Alcetas, Polemon, and Docimus strove emulously with him for the chief command, whereupon he said: "This bears out the saying 'Of perdition no account is made.'"

163 *No Gisco*
Plutarch, Fabius Maximus 15.2

When one of his companions, named Gisco, a man of his own rank, remarked that the number of the enemy amazed him, Hannibal put on a serious look and said: "Gisco, another thing has escaped your notice which is more amazing still." And when Gisco asked what it was, "It is the fact," said he, "that in all this multitude there is no one who is called Gisco."

164 *No Use for Victory*
Plutarch, Fabius Maximus 17.1

In view of such a complete success, Hannibal's friends urged him to follow up his good fortune and dash into their city on the heels of the flying enemy, assuring him in that case that on the fifth day after his victory he would sup on the Capitol. It is not easy to say what consideration turned him from this course, nay, it would rather seem that his evil genius, or some divinity, interposed to inspire him with the hesitation and timidity which he now showed. Wherefore, as they say, Barca, the Carthaginian, said to him angrily: "Thou canst win a victory, but thy victory thou canst not use."[1]

1. Livy 22.51.

165 *Archelaus Notes Charilaüs' Lack of Severity*
Plutarch, Lycurgus 5.5

Archelaus, his royal colleague, is said to have remarked to those who were extolling the young king, "How can Charilaüs be a good man, when he has no severity even for the bad?

166 *Useless and Superfluous Things Bring Happiness*
Plutarch, Marcus Cato 18.3–4

This, we are told, is what most astonished Ariston the philosopher, namely, that those possessed of the superfluities of life should be counted happy, rather than those well provided with life's necessary and useful things. Scopas the Thessalian, when one of his friends asked for something of his which was of no great service to him, with the remark that he asked for nothing that was necessary and useful, replied: "And yet my wealth and happiness are based on just such useless and superfluous things."

167   *Paid to Fight*
Plutarch, Moralia, Sayings of Kings and Commanders III:174C

Memnon, who was waging war against Alexander on the side of King Darius,[1] when one of his mercenary soldiers said many libelous and indecent things of Alexander, struck the man with his spear, saying, "I pay you to fight Alexander, not to malign him."

1. Circa 333 B.C.E.

168   *Better to Die Than to Watch Friends*
Plutarch, Moralia, Sayings of Kings and Commanders III:176F–177A

When Dion, who expelled Dionysius from his kingdom, heard that a plot against him was being set on foot by Callippus, in whom he placed the greatest trust above all other friends, both those at home and those from abroad, he could not bring himself to investigate, but said, "It is better to die than to live in a state of continual watchfulness not only against one's enemies but also against one's friends."[1]

1. Cf. Plutarch, *Dion* 56.1–6 (982 D). The story of the plot and the death of Dion is in chapters 54–57. Cf. also Valerius Maximus 3.8, externa 5.

169   *Rights to Ask and Receive*
Plutarch, Moralia, Sayings of Kings and Commanders III:177A (1)

When Archelaus,[1] at a convivial gathering, was asked for a golden cup by one of his acquaintances of a type not commendable for character, he bade the servant give it to Euripides; and in answer to the man's look of astonishment, he said, "It is true that you have a right to ask for it, but Euripides has a right to receive it even though he did not ask for it."

1. King of Macedonia, 413–399 B.C.E.

170   *Enough to Give*
Plutarch, Moralia, Sayings of Kings and Commanders III:179F (6)

When Perillus, one of his friends, asked him for dowry for his girls, Alexander bade him accept ten thousand pounds. He said that two thousand would be enough; but Alexander said, "Enough for you to accept, but not enough for me to give."

171   *City Keeps Holiday*
Plutarch, Moralia, Sayings of Kings and Commanders III:192E (6)

While the city was keeping holiday, and all were busy with drinking and social enjoyment, Epameinondas,[1] as he was walking along unwashed and absorbed in thought, met one of his intimate friends, who inquired in surprise why it was that he alone was going about in that state. "So that all of you," said he, "may get drunk and have a holiday."[2]

1. Famous Theban general and statesman, 420–362 B.C.E. These sayings were doubtless incorporated in Plutarch's *Epameinondas*, now lost. A collection of stories about Epameinondas will be found in Polyaenus, *Strategemata* 2.3.
2. Cf. Themistius, *Oration* 7.88 C.

172a *Wound a Tuition Fee*
Plutarch, Pelopidas 15.1–2

The Thebans, too, by always engaging singly in Boeotia with the Lacedaemonians, and by fighting battles which, though not important in themselves, nevertheless afforded them much practice and training, had their spirits roused and their bodies thoroughly inured to hardships, and gained experience and courage from their constant struggles. For this reason Antalcidas the Spartan, we are told, when Agesilaus came back from Boeotia with a wound, said to him: "Indeed, this is a fine tuition-fee which thou art getting from the Thebans, for teaching them how to war and fight when they did not wish to do it."

172b *Wound a Tuition Fee*
Plutarch, Agesilaus 26.2

One day when he [Agesilaus] was wounded, Antalcidas said to him: "Indeed, this is a fine tuition fee which thou art getting from the Thebans, for teaching them how to fight when they did not wish to do it, and did not even know how."

172c *Wound a Tuition Fee*
Plutarch, Lycurgus 13.6

And this was the special grievance which they [Lycurgus's followers] had against King Agesilaus in later times, namely, that by his continual and frequent incursions and expeditions into Boeotia he rendered the Thebans a match for the Lacedaemonians. And therefore, when Antalcidas saw the king wounded, he said: "This is a fine tuition-fee which thou art getting from the Thebans, for teaching them how to fight, when they did not wish to do it, and did not know how."

173 *More to Conquer*
Plutarch, Pelopidas 32.1

Accordingly, when he [Pelopidas] was come to Pharsulus, he assembled his forces and marched at once against Alexander. Alexander, also, seeing that there were only a few Thebans with Pelopidas, while his own men at arms were more than twice as many as the Thessalians, advanced as far as the temple of Thetis to meet him. When Pelopidas was told that the tyrant was coming up against him with a large force, "All the better," he said, "for there will be more for us to conquer."

174 *Eclipse No Portent*
Plutarch, Pericles 35.1–2

Desiring to heal these evils, and at the same time to inflict some annoyance upon the enemy, he [Pericles] manned a hundred and fifty ships of war, and, after embarking many brave hoplites and horsemen, was on the point of putting out to sea, affording great hope to the citizens, and no less fear to the enemy in consequence of so great a force. But when the ships were already manned, and Pericles had gone aboard his own trireme, it chanced that the sun was eclipsed and darkness came on, and all were thoroughly frightened, looking upon it as great portent. Accordingly, seeing that his steersman was timorous and utterly perplexed, Pericles held up his cloak before the man's eyes, and, thus covering them, asked him if he thought it anything dreadful, or portentous of anything dreadful. "No," said the steersman. "How then," said Pericles, "is yonder event different from this, except that it is something rather larger than my cloak which has caused the obscurity?"

175 *Pericles Falls Ill*
Plutarch, Pericles 38.1–2

At this time, it would seem, the plague laid hold of Pericles, not with a violent attack, as in the case of others, nor acute, but one which, with a kind of sluggish distemper that prolonged itself through varying changes, used up his body slowly and undermined the loftiness of his spirit. Certain it is that Theophrastus, in his "Ethics," querying whether one's character follows the bent of one's fortunes and is forced by bodily sufferings to abandon its high excellence, records this fact, that Pericles, as he lay sick, showed one of his friends who was coming to see him an amulet that the women had hung around his neck, as much as to say that he was very badly off to put up with such folly as that.

176 *Philopoemen Pays Penalty for Ill Looks*
Plutarch, Philopoemen 2.1–2

In looks he [Philopoemen] was not, as some suppose, ill favored; for a statue of him is still to be seen at Delphi; and the mistake of his Megarian hostess was due, as we are told, to a certain indifference and simplicity on his part. This woman, learning that the general of the Achaeans was coming to her house, in great confusion set about preparing supper; besides, her husband chanced to be away from home. Just then Philopoemen came in, wearing a simple soldier's cloak, and the woman, thinking him to be one of his servants who had been sent on in advance, invited him to help her in her housework. So Philopoemen at once threw off his cloak and fell to splitting wood. Then his host came in, and seeing him thus employed, said: "What does this mean, Philopoemen?" "What else," said Philopoemen in broad Doric, "than that I am paying a penalty for my ill looks?"

177 *Philopoemen Lacks Belly*
Plutarch, Philopoemen 2.3

And once Titus Flamininus, making fun of certain parts of his figure, said: "Philopoemen, what fine arms and legs thou hast; but belly thou hast not"; for Philopoemen was quite slender at the waist. This piece of fun, however, was aimed the rather at his resources. For though he had excellent men-at-arms and horsemen, he was often at a loss for money.

178 *Chabrias' Friendship a Burden*
Plutarch, Phocion 7.2

Once, however, we are told, when the young man [Ctesippus] was troublesome to him [Phocion] on an expedition, and plied him with unseasonable questions and advice, like one making corrections and sharing in the command, he cried: "O Chabrias, Chabrias, surely I make thee a large return for thy friendship in enduring thy son."

179 *Soldier Abandons Two Posts*
Plutarch, Phocion 25.2

Again, after he [Phocion] had drawn up his men at arms, one of them went out far in advance of the rest, and then was stricken with fear when an enemy advanced to meet him, and went back again to his post. "Shame on thee, young man," said Phocion, "for having abandoned two posts, the one which was given thee by thy general, and the one which thou didst give thyself."

180a *Praise Whether Alive or Dead*
Plutarch, Pompey 71.1–3

So then, when the Pharsalian plain was filled with men and horses and arms and the signals for battle had been lifted on both sides, the first to rush out from Caesar's lines was Caius Crassianus,[1] a centurion in command of one hundred and twenty men, who was thus redeeming a great promise made to Caesar. For he had been the first man whom Caesar saw as he issued from the camp, and addressing him, he had asked him what he thought about the battle. The centurion stretched forth his right hand and cried with a loud voice: "Thou wilt win a splendid victory, O Caesar; and I shall have thy praise today, whether I live or die." Mindful now of these words of his, he rushed forward, carrying many along with him, and threw himself into the midst of the enemy. The combatants at once took to their swords and many were slain, and as the centurion was forcing his way along and cutting down the men in the front ranks, one of them confronted him and drove his sword in at his mouth with such force that its point went through to the nape of his neck.[2]

1. The name is Crastinus in Caesar's own story of the battle (*Civil Wars* 3.91).
2. Cf. Caesar, *Civil Wars* 3.99, where Caesar gives Crastinus that high praise for which he was willing to die.

180b *Bravery of Caius Crassinius*
Plutarch, Caesar 44.9–12 (5–6)

As Caesar himself was about to move his lines of legionaries, and was already going forward into action, he saw first one of his centurions, a man experienced in war and faithful to him, encouraging his men and challenging them to vie with him in prowess. Him Caesar addressed by name and said: "Caius Crassinius, what are our hopes, and how does our confidence stand?" Then Crassinius, stretching forth his right hand, said with a loud voice: "We shall win a glorious victory, O Caesar, and thou shalt praise me today, whether I am alive or dead." So saying, he plunged foremost into the enemy at full speed, carrying along with him the one hundred and twenty soldiers under his command. But after cutting his way through the first rank, and while he was forging onwards with great slaughter, he was beaten back by the thrust of a sword through his mouth, and the point of the sword actually came out at the back of his neck.

181 *On Golden Bracelets and Collars*
Plutarch, Themistocles 18.2

Surveying once the dead bodies of the Barbarians which had been cast up along the sea, he [Themistocles] saw that they were decked with golden bracelets and collars, and yet passed on by them himself, while to a friend who followed he pointed them out and said: "Help thyself, thou art not Themistocles."

182 *Student Sinks*
Sifra 58b–c

A certain student said before R. Aqiba: "I must say what I have learned: [*When a woman at childbirth bears a male] she shall be unclean seven days. . . . And on the eighth day [the flesh of his foreskin] shall be circumcised* (Lev. 12:2–3). One might think [that he should be circumcised] fifteen days [after his birth; that is, the] eighth [day after her] seven days [of uncleanness; however] Scripture says, *on that day* [which proves that circumcision is on the eighth day after birth]." R. Aqiba said to him: "You sink in mighty waters and you bring clay up in your hands. For is it not already said: *And a son eight days old you shall circumcise, all the males forever* (Gen. 17:12)?"

183   *The Understanding Man*
Sifre, Deuteronomy 13

[*Choose] wise, understanding, [and experienced] men* (Deut. 1:13). This is the question which Arios asked R. Yose; [Arios] said to him: "Which is a wise man?" [Yose] said to him: "He who practices that which he teaches. Or perhaps [such a person] is [referred to] rather [as] an understanding man?" [Arios] said to him: "*Understanding men* is already said [in the above verse]. What is the difference between a wise man and an understanding man?" [Yose said to him:] "A wise man is similar to a rich [gold] smith. When [others] bring him [gold] to examine (lit.: see), he examines [it]. When [others] do not bring him [gold] to examine, he takes out his own [gold] and examines [it]. An understanding man is similar to a poor [gold] smith. When [others] bring him [gold] to examine, he examines [it]. When [others] do not bring him [gold] to examine, he must sit and be idle."

184   *Gamaliel Serves*
Sifre, Deuteronomy 38

One time R. Eliezer and R. Zadok were reclining at a feast for the son of Rabban Gamaliel. Rabban Gamaliel mixed a glass [of wine] for R. Eliezer, but he did not wish to accept it. R. Joshua accepted it. R. Eliezer said to him: "What is this, Joshua? Is it right that we should recline and Gamaliel beRabbi should stand and serve us?" R. Joshua said to him: "Leave him alone that he might serve [us]. Abraham, the great one of the world, served the ministering angels, even though he thought that they were Arab idolaters, for it is said, *And he lifted his eyes and looked, and behold, three men stood in front of him* (Gen. 18:2). And is it not an *a fortiori* [argument]? Now if Abraham, the great one of the world, served the ministering angels, and he thought that they were Arab idolaters, should not Gamaliel beRabbi serve us?"

185   *Aqiba Laughs*
Sifre, Deuteronomy 43

And one time Rabban Gamaliel, R. Joshua, R. Eleazar b. Azzariah and R. Aqiba entered Rome. They heard a din from Petilon, 120 miles away. They began crying, but R. Aqiba laughed. They said to him: "Aqiba, why are we crying, but you are laughing?" [Aqiba] said to them: "And you, why are you crying?" They said to him: "Should we not cry, for the gentile idolaters, who offer sacrifices to [false] gods and prostrate themselves before idols, sit in peace and ease. But the House which was the footstool of our God is burned with fire and has become a dwelling place for beasts of the field." [Aqiba] said to them: "It is even for that reason that I laugh. If [God] acted thus towards those who anger Him, how much the more [will He act in this way] towards those who do His will, [so that Israel eventually will also dwell in peace and ease]."

186 *Israel Equal to Torah*
Sifre, Deuteronomy 80

One time R. Judah b. Bathyra, R. Mattyah b. Harash, R. Hananyah b. Ahai, R. Joshua and R. Yonatan were leaving the Land of [Israel]. When they reached Palton, they recalled the Land of Israel and they stood erect while their eyes shed tears. They rent their garments and recited this verse: "[*You shall indeed cross the Jordan to enter and to make the land your own that the Lord your God is giving you.*] *You shall possess it and shall live in it and you must keep and observe all the laws . . .*" (Deut. 11:31). They said: "Living in the Land of Israel is equal to observing all of the [other] commandments [stated] in the Torah."

187 *Tarfon Praises Aqiba*
Sifre, Numbers 75

[*And the sons of Aaron*], *the priests*, [*shall blow the trumpets*] (Num. 10:3). "Whether blemished or unblemished"—the words of R. Tarfon. R. Aqiba says: "*Priests* is said here, and *priests* is said elsewhere (Lev. 1:11). Just as *priests* which is said elsewhere [refers to] unblemished [priests] and not to blemished [priests], also here [*priests* refers to] unblemished [priests] and not to blemished [priests]." R. Tarfon said to him: "How long will you rake [words] together and bring them against us, Aqiba?" He was unable to bear up. "I swear by the life of my children that I saw Simon, my mother's brother, who girded his feet [for he was blemished] standing and blowing the trumpets." [Aqiba] said to him: "Yes, [but] perhaps [he did this only] on Rosh HaShanah, Yom Kippur or the Jubilee year?" [Tarfon] said to him: "You are not refuted. Happy are you, Abraham, our father, for Aqiba has come out of your loins. Tarfon saw and forgot, [but] Aqiba explained [it] on his own and made [it] agree with the law. Behold, anyone who separates himself from you [Aqiba], it is as if he separated himself from his own life."

188 *Caesar Builds Alone*
Suetonius, Lives of the Caesars, Julius 1.10.1

When aedile, Caesar decorated not only the Comitium and the Forum with its adjacent basilicas, but the Capitol as well, building temporary colonnades for the display of a part of his material. He exhibited combats with wild beasts and stageplays too, both with his colleague and independently. The result was that Caesar alone took all the credit even for what they spent in common, and his colleague Marcus Bibulus openly said that his was the fate of Pollux: "For," said he, "just as the temple erected in the Forum to the twin brethren, bears only the name of Castor, so the joint liberality of Caesar and myself is credited to Caesar alone."

189 *Moderate Caesar*
Suetonius, Lives of the Caesars, Julius 1.53.1

That he [Julius] drank very little wine not even his enemies denied. There is a saying of Marcus Cato that Caesar was the only man who undertook to overthrow the state when sober. Even in the matter of food Gaius Oppius tells us that he was so indifferent, that once when his host served stale oil instead of fresh, and the other guests would have none of it, Caesar partook even more plentifully than usual, not to seem to charge his host with carelessness or lack of manners.

190 *Eliezar Expounds and Lives Well*
Tosefta, Hagigah 2:1

One time R. Yohanan b. Zakkai was riding on his donkey, and R. Eleazar b. Arak was close behind him. [Eleazar] said to him: "Rabbi, teach me one section of the Ma'aseh Merkavah." [Yohanan] said to him: "No! Thus I have said to you previously, that they do not teach about the Merkavah to an individual unless he is a sage who understands his own knowledge." [Eleazar] said to him: "Now I wish to discuss with you." [Yohanan] said to him: "Speak." R. Eleazar b. Arak opened [his discourse] and expounded the Ma'aseh Merkavah. R. Yohanan b. Zakkai got down from his donkey and wrapped himself in his prayer shawl, and both of them sat on a stone under an olive tree, and he discussed before him. [Yohanan] stood and kissed him on his head and said: "Blessed is the Lord, the God of Israel, who gave a son to Abraham, our father, who knows [how] to understand and to explain the glory of our Father in heaven. There are those who expound well but do not live well. There are those who live well but do not expound well. But Eleazar b. Arak expounds well and lives well. Happy are you, Abraham our father, for Eleazar b. Arak, who knows how to understand and to explain the glory of our Father in heaven, came out of your loins."

191 *Hananyah the Nazarite*
Tosefta, Nedarim 5:15

It happened to Hananyah b. Hananyah that his father dedicated him to be a Nazarite. He brought him before Rabban Gamaliel, [and] Rabban Gamaliel examined him to see if he were of age. [Hananyah] said to him: "Why are you worried? [Are you worried that] I am [not] under my father's authority? [If] I am under my father's authority, behold, I am a Nazarite. But if I am under my own authority, behold, I am a Nazarite from this moment [forward]." [Gamaliel] stood and kissed him on the head. He said: "I am certain that you will be an authoritative teacher in Israel before you die." And he did become an authoritative teacher in Israel before his death.

192a *The Battle of the Kiss*
Xenophon, Agesilaus 5.4–5

His [Agesilaus'] habitual control of his affections surely deserves a tribute of admiration, if worthy of mention on no other ground. That he should keep at arms' length those whose intimacy he did not desire may be thought only human. But he loved Megabates, the handsome son of Spithridates, with all the intensity of an ardent nature. Now it is the custom[1] among the Persians to bestow a kiss on those whom they honor. Yet when Megabates attempted to kiss him, Agesilaus resisted his advances with all his might—an act of punctilious moderation surely! Megabates, feeling himself slighted, tried no more to kiss him, and Agesilaus approached one of his companions with a request that he would persuade Megabates to show him honor once again. "Will you kiss him," asked his companion, "if Megabates yields?" After a deep silence, Agesilaus gave his reply: "By the twin gods, no, not if I were straightway to be the fairest and strongest and fleetest man on earth! By all the gods I swear that I would rather fight that same battle over again than that everything I see should turn into gold."[1]

> 1. Xenophon, *Cyropaedia* 1.4.27.

192b *The Battle of the Kiss*
Plutarch, Agesilaus 11.5-7

Indeed, when Megabates once came up and offered to embrace and kiss him [Agesilaus], he declined his caresses. The boy was mortified at this, and desisted, and afterwards kept his distance when addressing him, whereupon Agesilaus, distressed now and repentant for having avoided his kiss, pretended to wonder what ailed Megabates that he did not greet him with a kiss. "It is thy fault," the king's companions said; "thou didst not accept, but didst decline the fair one's kiss in fear and trembling; yet even now he might be persuaded to come within range of thy lips; but see that thou dost not again play the coward." Then, after some time spent in silent reflection, Agesilaus said: "There is no harm in your persuading him; for I think I would more gladly fight that battle of the kiss over again than possess all the gold I have ever seen."

193 *Generalship: Expanded Statement (It Persuaded the Man)*
Xenophon, Memorabilia 3.1.1-3

I will now explain how he [Socrates] helped those who were eager to win distinction by making them qualify themselves for the honors they coveted. He once heard that Dionysodorus had arrived at Athens, and gave out that he was going to teach generalship. Being aware that one of his companions wished to obtain the office of general from the state, he addressed him thus: "Young man, surely it would be disgraceful for one who wishes to be a general in the state to neglect the opportunity of learning the duties, and he would deserve to be punished by the state much more than one who carved statues without having learned to be a sculptor. For in the dangerous times of war the whole state is in the general's hands, and great good may come from his success and great evil from his failure. Therefore anyone who exerts himself to gain the votes, but neglects to learn the business, deserves punishment."

An individual associate or friend is present or referred to in the stories listed below, but some other feature has determined their location in another section.

Cicero: 196, 680, 1462
Diogenes Laertius: 61e
Eunapius: 198a
Gellius: 559, 1467
Gospel: 12e, 91b, 430a, 430b, 430c, 430d, 434, 435, 438, 742b, 742d, 1208
Hadith: 257, 265
Macrobius: 817, 826, 827
Nepos: 1474
Philostratus: 27, 867, 870, 1274, 1409
Plutarch: 40a, 41, 280, 293, 912b, 934, 937, 938, 990, 1058, 1072, 1073, 1095, 1289, 1411, 1416
Sifra: 1366

Adult: Clusters of Friends or Associates

In ancient anecdotes, friends and associates often speak as a chorus with a single voice to the famous and powerful. A renowned person may give advice to companions or disciples, issue orders to soldiers and allies, or punish any group for recklessness or inattention. Seriousness sometimes gives way to frivolity: the master teases and jests even while handing out special privileges.

194a *If You Have Faith*
Aphrahat, Demonstrations 1.17 (Parisot: 42)

And when the apostles asked of the Lord, they requested nothing from him, except that they said to him, "Increase our faith." He said to them, "If there were faith in you, even a mountain would move away from before you." And he said, "Do not doubt, lest you sink in the world, even as Simon, when he doubted, began to sink in the sea."[1]

> 1. Matthew 14:28–33.

194b *If You Have Faith*
Gospel, Luke 17:5–6

The apostles said to the Lord, "Increase our faith!" And the Lord said, "If you had faith as a grain of mustard seed, you could say to this sycamine tree, 'Be rooted up, and be planted in the sea,' and it would obey you."

194c *If You Have Faith*
Gospel, Matthew 21:18–22

In the morning, as he [Jesus] was returning to the city, he was hungry. And seeing a fig tree by the wayside he went to it, and found nothing on it but leaves only. And he said to it, "May no fruit ever come from you again!" And the fig tree withered at once. When the disciples saw it they marveled, saying, "How did the fig tree wither at once?" And Jesus answered them, "Truly, I say to you, if you have faith and never doubt, you will not only do what has been done to this fig tree, but even if you say to this mountain, 'Be taken up and cast into the sea;' it will be done. And whatever you ask in prayer, you will receive, if you have faith."

195a *Living One Forsaken*
Augustine, Against Opposition to the Law and the Prophets 2.4.14 (Migne, PL 42.647)

But, he [Jesus] said, when the apostles asked how the Jewish prophets were to be regarded, who were thought to have proclaimed his coming beforehand, our Lord, disturbed that they still held this conception, answered, "You have forsaken the living one who is before you and speak about the dead."

195b *Living One Forsaken*
Gospel, Thomas 52

His [Jesus'] disciples said to him, "Twenty-four prophets have spoken in Israel, and they all spoke of (lit.: in) you." He said to them, "You have disregarded the living one who is in your presence, and have spoken of the dead."

196 *Alexander at Achilles' Tomb*
Cicero, Pro Archia 24

We read that Alexander the Great carried in his train numbers of epic poets and historians. And yet, standing before the tomb of Achilles at Sigeum, he exclaimed, "Fortunate youth, to have found in Homer an herald of thy valor!" Well might he so exclaim, for had the *Iliad* never existed, the same mound which covered Achilles' bones would also have overwhelmed his memory. Again, did not he to whom our own age has accorded the title of Great, whose successes have been commensurate with his high qualities, present with the citizenship before a mass meeting of his troops Theophanes of Mytilene, the historian of his campaigns? Were not our brave fellows, soldiers and peasants though they were, so smitten with the glamor of renown that they loudly applauded the act, feeling that they too had a share in the glory that had been shed upon their leader?

197 *Lions Are Not Slaves*
Diogenes Laertius, Lives of the Eminent Philosophers 6.75

Cleomenes in his work entitled *Concerning Pedagogues* says that the friends of Diogenes wanted to ransom him, whereupon he called them simpletons; for, said he, lions are not the slaves of those who feed them, but rather those who feed them are at the mercy of the lions: for fear is the mark of the slave, whereas wild beasts make men afraid of them.

198a *Iamblichus Senses Impurity*
Eunapius, Lives of the Philosophers 458–459

The sun was traveling towards the limits of the Lion at the time when it rises along with the constellation called the Dog. It was the hour for sacrifice, and this had been made ready in one of the suburban villas belonging to Iamblichus. Presently when the rites had been duly performed and they were returning to the city, walking slowly and at their leisure,—for indeed their conversation was about the gods as was in keeping with the sacrifice—suddenly Iamblichus even while conversing was lost in thought, as though his voice were cut off, and for some moments he fixed his eyes steadily on the ground[1] and then looked up at his friends and called to them in a loud voice: "Let us go by another road, for a dead body has lately been carried along this way." After saying this he turned into another road which seemed to be less impure,[2] and some of them turned aside with him, who thought it was a shame to desert their teacher. But the greater number and the more obstinate of his disciples, among whom was Aedesius, stayed where they were, ascribing the occurrence to a portent and scenting like hounds for the proof.[3] And very soon those who had buried the dead man came back. But even so the disciples did not desist but inquired whether they had passed along this road. "We had to," they replied, for there was no other road.

1. This seems to imitate Plutarch, *Moralia*, Sign of Socrates VII:580.
2. It was a Pythagorean doctrine that a funeral contaminates the bystander.
3. A favorite Platonic simile, frequently echoed by the sophists.

198b *Socrates Senses Swine*
Plutarch, Moralia, Sign of Socrates VII:580

I [Theocritus] was myself present (I had come to visit Euthyphron the sooth-sayer) when Socrates—you recall the incident, Simmias—happened to be making the ascent toward the Symbolon and the house of Andocides putting some question to Euthyphron the while and sounding him out playfully. Suddenly he stopped short and fell silent, lost for a good time in thought; at last he turned back, taking the way through the street of the cabinetmakers, and called out to the friends who had already gone onward to return, saying that the sign had come to him. Most turned back with him, I with the rest, clinging close to Euthyphron; but certain young fellows went straight ahead, imagining that they would discredit Socrates' sign, and drew along Charillus the flute-player who had also come to Athens with me to visit Cebes. As they were walking along the street of the statuaries past the law-courts, they were met by a drove of swine, covered with mud and so numerous that they pressed against one another; and as there was nowhere to step aside, the swine ran into some and knocked them down, and befouled the rest. Charillus came home like the others, his legs and clothes covered with mud; so that we always mentioned Socrates' sign with laughter, at the same time marveling that Heaven never deserted or neglected him."

199 *The Ghost of a Gladiator*
Eunapius, Lives of the Philosophers 473

Likewise the famous Iamblichus, as I have handed down in my account of his life, when a certain Egyptian invoked Apollo, and to the great amazement of those who saw the vision, Apollo came: "My friends," said he, "cease to wonder; this is only the ghost of a gladiator."

200a *Alexander Refuses Water before Troops*
Frontinus, Stratagems 1.7.7

This place, I think, is not inappropriate for recounting that famous deed of Alexander of Macedon. Marching along the desert roads of Africa, and suffering in common with his men from most distressing thirst, when some water was brought him in a helmet by a soldier, he poured it out upon the ground in the sight of all, in this way serving his soldiers better by his example of restraint than if he had been able to share the water with the rest.[1]

> 1. 332–331 B.C.E. Polyaenus 4.3.25 and Curtius Rufus 7.5.9–12 have a slightly different version.

200b *Alexander Refuses Water before Troops*
Plutarch, Alexander 42.6–10 (3–6)

In consequence of the pursuit of Darius, which was long and arduous (for in eleven days he [Alexander] rode thirty-three hundred furlongs), most of his horsemen gave out, and chiefly for lack of water. At this point some Macedonians met him who were carrying water from the river in skins upon their mules. And when they beheld Alexander, it being now midday, in a wretched plight from thirst, they quickly filled a helmet and brought it to him. To his inquiry for whom they were carrying the water, they replied: "For our own sons; but if thou livest, we can get other sons, even if we lose these." On hearing this he took the helmet into his hands, but when he looked around and saw the horsemen about him all stretching out their heads and gazing at the water, he handed it back without drinking any, but with praises for the men who had brought it; "For," said he, "if I should drink of it alone, these horsemen of mine will be out of heart." But when they beheld his self-control and loftiness of spirit, they shouted out to him to lead them forward boldly, and began to goad their horses on, declaring that they would not regard themselves as weary, or thirsty, or as mortals at all, so long as they had such a king.

201a *Sertorius and Parable of Horse's Tail*
Frontinus, Stratagems 1.10.1

After Quintus Sertorius had learned by experience that he was by no means a match for the whole Roman army, in order to prove this to the Barbarians also, who were rashly demanding battle, he brought into their presence two horses, one very strong, the other very feeble. Then he brought up two youths of corresponding physique, one robust, the other slight. The stronger youth was commanded to pull out the entire tail of the feeble horse, while the slight youth was commanded to pull out the hairs of the strong horse one by one. Then, when the slight youth had succeeded in his task, while the strong one was still vainly struggling with the tail of the weak horse, Sertorius observed: "By this illustration I have exhibited to you, my men, the nature of the Roman cohorts. They are invincible to him who attacks them in a body; yet he who assails them by groups will tear and rend them."[1]

> 1. 80–72 B.C.E. Cf. Valerius Maximus 7.3.6; Horace, *Epistles* 2.1.45ff; Pliny, *Epistles* 3.9.11.

201b *Sertorius and Parable of Horse's Tail*
Plutarch, Sertorius 16.3–5

So after a few days he [Sertorius] called a general assembly and introduced before it two horses, one utterly weak and already quite old, the other large-sized and strong, with a tail that was astonishing for the thickness and beauty of its hair. By the side of the feeble horse stood a man who was tall and robust, and by the side of the powerful horse another man, small and of a contemptible appearance. At a signal given them, the strong man seized the tail of his horse with both hands and tried to pull it towards him with all his might, as though he would tear it off; but the weak man began to pluck out the hairs in the tail of the strong horse one by one. The strongest man gave himself no end of trouble to no purpose, made the spectators laugh a good deal, and then gave up his attempt; but the weak man, in a trice and with no trouble, stripped his horse's tail of its hair. Then Sertorius rose up and said: "Ye see, men of my allies, that perseverance is more efficacious than violence, and that many things which cannot be mastered when they stand together yield when one masters them little by little. For irresistible is the force of continuity, by virtue of which advancing Time subdues and captures every power; and Time is a kindly ally for all who act as diligent attendants upon opportunity, but a most bitter enemy for all who urge matters on unseasonably."

202a *Tenth Legion Alone*
Frontinus, Stratagems 1.11.3

Gaius Caesar, when about to fight the Germans and their king, Ariovistus, at a time when his own men had been thrown into panic, called his soldiers together and declared to the assembly that on that day he proposed to employ the services of the tenth legion alone. In this way he caused the soldiers of this legion to be stirred by his tribute to their unique heroism, while the rest were overwhelmed with mortification to think that reputation for courage should rest with others.[1]

1. 58 B.C.E. Cf. Caesar, *Gallic War* 1.39.7, 40.1, 14ff.

202b *Tenth Legion Alone*
Plutarch, Caesar 19.3–4 (2–3)

Seeing that his officers were inclined to be afraid, and particularly all the young men of high rank who had come out intending to make the campaign with Caesar an opportunity for high-living and money-making, he called them together and bade them be off, since they were so unmanly and effeminate, and not to force themselves to face danger; as for himself, he said he would take the tenth legion alone and march against the Barbarians; the enemy would be no better fighters than the Cimbri, and he himself was no worse a general than Marius.

203a *Agesilaus Strips Prisoners*
Frontinus, Stratagems 1.11.7

Agesilaus, the Spartan, on one occasion captured certain Persians. The appearance of these people, when dressed in uniform, inspired great terror. But Agesilaus stripped his prisoners and exhibited them to his soldiers, in order that their delicate white bodies might excite contempt.[1]

1. 395 B.C.E. Cf. Polyaenus 2.1.6; Xenophon, *Hellenica* 3.4.19.

203b *Agesilaus Strips Prisoners*
Plutarch, Agesilaus 9.5

And once when, by his orders, his [Agesilaus'] prisoners of war were stripped of their clothing and offered for sale by the vendors of booty, their clothing found many purchasers, but their naked bodies, which were utterly white and delicate, owing to their effeminate habits, were ridiculed as useless and worthless. Then Agesilaus, noticing, said: "These are the men with whom you fight, and these the things for which you fight."

203c *Gelo Strips Prisoners*
Frontinus, Stratagems 1.11.18

Gelo, tyrant of Syracuse, having undertaken war against the Carthaginians, after taking many prisoners, stripped all the feeblest, especially from among the auxiliaries, who were very swarthy, and exhibited them nude before the eyes of his troops, in order to convince his men that their foes were contemptible.[1]

1. 480 B.C.E.

204 *No Reliance on Ships*
Frontinus, Stratagems 1.11.21

Fabius Maximus, fearing that his troops would fight less resolutely in consequence of their reliance on their ships to which it was possible to retreat, ordered the ships to be set on fire before the battle began.[1]

1. 315 B.C.E. Cf. Livy 9.23.

205a *Caesar Interprets Omens Favorably*
Frontinus, Stratagems 1.12.2

Gaius Caesar, having slipped as he was about to embark on ship, exclaimed: "I hold thee fast, Mother Earth." By this interpretation of the incident he made it seem that he was destined to come back to the lands from which he was setting out.

205b *Caesar Interprets Omens Favorably*
Suetonius, Lives of the Caesars, Julius 1.59.1

No regard for religion ever turned him [Julius] from any undertaking, or even delayed him. Though the victim escaped as he was offering sacrifice, he did not put off his expedition against Scipio and Juba. Even when he had a fall as he disembarked, he gave the omen a favorable turn by crying: "I hold thee fast, Africa."

206 *Bloody Shields and Horses*
Frontinus, Stratagems 1.12.4

Sertorius, when by a sudden prodigy the outsides of the shields of his cavalrymen and the breasts of their horse showed marks of blood, interpreted this as a mark of victory, since those were the parts which were wont to be spattered with the blood of the enemy.

207 *Tombs Decorated*
Frontinus, Stratagems 1.12.5

Epaminondas, the Theban, when his soldiers were depressed because the decoration hanging from his spear like a fillet had been torn away by the wind and carried to the tomb of a certain Spartan, said: "Do not be concerned, comrades! Destruction is foretold for the Spartans. Tombs are not decorated except for funerals."[1]

> 1. 371 B.C.E. Cf. Diodorus 15.52.5ff.

208 *Light from Powers Above*
Frontinus, Stratagems 1.12.6

The same Epaminondas, when a meteor fell from the sky by night and struck terror to the hearts of those who noticed it, exclaimed: "It is a light sent us from the powers above."

209 *Forbidden to Sit*
Frontinus, Stratagems 1.12.7

When the same Epaminondas was about to open battle against the Spartans, the chair on which he had sat down gave way beneath him, whereat all the soldiers, greatly troubled, interpreted this as an unlucky omen. But Epaminondas exclaimed: "Not at all; we are simply forbidden to sit."[1]

> 1. I.e., "we must be up and doing."

210 *Jupiter Reveals Power*
Frontinus, Stratagems 1.12.12

As Chabrias, the Athenian, was about to fight a naval battle, a thunderbolt fell directly across the path of his ship. When the soldiers were filled with dismay at such a portent, he said: "Now is the very time to begin battle, when Jupiter, mightiest of the gods, reveals that his power is present with our fleet."[1]

1. 391–357 B.C.E.

211a *Water Towards the Enemy*
Frontinus, Stratagems 2.7.12

When Marius was fighting against the Cimbrians and Teutons, his engineers on one occasion had heedlessly chosen such a site for the camp that the barbarians controlled the water supply. In response to the soldiers' demand for water, Marius pointed with his finger toward the enemy and said: "There is where you must get it." Thus inspired, the Romans straightway drove the Barbarians from the place.[1]

1. 102 B.C.E. Cf. Florus 3.3.7–10.

211b *Water Towards the Enemy*
Plutarch, Caius Marius 18.3–4

Thus the two armies went on until they came to the place called Aquae Sextiae, from which they had to march only a short distance and they would be in the Alps. For this reason, indeed, Marius made preparations to give battle here, and he occupied for his camp a position that was strong, but poorly supplied with water, wishing, as they say, by this circumstance also to incite his soldiers to fight. At any rate, when many of them were dissatisfied and said they would be thirsty there, he pointed to a river that ran near the barbarian fortifications, and told them they could get water there, but the price of it was blood. "Why, then," they said, "dost thou not lead us at once against the enemy, while our blood is still moist?" To which Marius calmly replied: "We must first make our camp strong."

212a *Fighting in Boeotia*
Frontinus, Stratagems 2.8.12

When Sulla's legions broke before the hosts of Mithridates led by Archelaus, Sulla advanced with drawn sword into the first line and, addressing his troops, told them, in case anybody asked where they had left their general, to answer: "Fighting in Boeotia." Shamed by these words, they followed him to a man.[1]

1. 85 B.C.E. Cf. Polyaenus 8.9.2; Appian, *Mithridates* 49.

212b *Betrayed at Orchomenus*
Plutarch, Sulla 21.1–2

When the two armies had encamped near each other, Archelaus lay still, but Sulla proceeded to dig trenches on either side, in order that, if possible, he might cut the enemy off from the solid ground which was favorable for cavalry, and force them into the marshes. The enemy, however, would not suffer this, but when their generals sent them forth, charged impetuously and at full speed, so that not only Sulla's laborers were dispersed, but also the greater part of the corps drawn up to protect them was thrown into confusion and fled. Then Sulla threw himself from his horse, seized an ensign, and pushed his way through the fugitives against the enemy, crying: "For me, O Romans, an honorable death here; but you, when men ask you where you betrayed your commander, remember to tell them, at Orchomenus."

213   *Four Days' March in Two*
Frontinus, Stratagems 3.1.2

Marcus Cato, when in Spain, saw that he could gain possession of a certain town, if only he could assault the enemy by surprise. Accordingly, having in two days accomplished a four days' march through rough and barren districts, he crushed his foes, who were fearing no such event. Then, when his men asked the reason of so easy a success, he told them that they had won a victory as soon as they had accomplished the four days' march in two.[1]

> 1. 195 B.C.E.

214   *Prices of Young Men Up*
Frontinus, Stratagems 3.5.3

When Aulus Torquatus was besieging a Greek city and was told that the young men of the city were engaged in earnest practice with the javelin and bow, he replied: "Then the price at which I shall presently sell them shall be higher."

215   *Sleeping Guard Stabbed*
Frontinus, Stratagems 3.12.2

When Iphicrates, the Athenian general, was holding Corinth with a garrison and on one occasion personally made the rounds of the sentries as the enemy were approaching, he found one of the guards asleep at his post and stabbed him with his spear. When certain ones rebuked this procedure as cruel, he answered: "I left him as I found him."[1]

> 1. 393–391 B.C.E. Cf. Nepos 11, *Iphicrates* 2.1–2.

216   *Theagenes Assigns Places*
Frontinus, Stratagems 4.1.8

When Theagenes, the Athenian, was leading his troops towards Megara, and his men inquired as to their place in the ranks, he told them he would assign them their places when they arrived at their destination. Then he secretly sent the cavalry ahead and commanded them, in the guise of enemies, to turn back and attack their comrades. When this plan was carried out and the men whom he had with him made preparations for an encounter with the foe, he permitted the battle-line to be drawn up in such a way that each man took his place where he wished, the most cowardly retiring to the rear, the bravest rushing to the front. He thereupon assigned to each man, for the campaign, the same position in which he had found him.[1]

> 1. Polyaenus 5.28.1 attributes this to Theognis; in 3.9.10, he attributes it to Iphicrates.

217   *Survivors Carry Tidings*
Frontinus, Stratagems 4.7.15

When Marcus Livius had routed Hasdrubal, and certain persons urged him to pursue the enemy to annihilation, he answered: "Let some survive to carry to the enemy the tidings of our victory!"[1]

> 1. 207 B.C.E. Cf. Livy 27.49.

218   *Herodes and the Vagabond Philosopher*
Gellius, Attic Nights 9.2.1–7

To Herodes Atticus, the ex-consul, renowned for his personal charm and his Grecian eloquence, there once came, when I was present, a man in a cloak, with long hair and a beard that reached almost to his waist, and asked that money be given him for bread. Then Herodes asked him who on earth he was, and the man, with anger in his voice and expression, replied that he was a philosopher, adding that he wondered why Herodes thought it necessary to ask what was obvious. "I see," said Herodes, "a beard and a cloak; the philosopher I do not yet see. Now, I pray you, be so good as to tell me by what evidence you think we may recognize you as a philosopher." Meanwhile some of Herodes' companions told him that the fellow was a vagabond of worthless character, who frequented foul dives and was in the habit of being shamefully abusive if he did not get what he demanded. Thereupon, Herodes said: "Let us give him some money, whatever his character may be, not because he is a man, but because we are men," and he ordered enough money to be given him to buy bread for thirty days.

219   *Musonius and the Fakir*
Gellius, Attic Nights 9.2.8–9

Then, turning to those of us who were with him, he [Herodes Atticus] said: "Musonius ordered a thousand sesterces to be given to a fakir of this sort who posed as a philosopher, and when several told him that the fellow was a rascal and knave and deserving of nothing good, Musonius, they say, replied with a smile: 'Then he deserves the money.' But," said Herodes, "it is rather this that causes me resentment and vexation, that foul and evil beasts of this sort usurp a most sacred name and call themselves philosophers."

220   *Romulus Drinks All He Wants*
Gellius, Attic Nights 11.14.1–2

Lucius Piso Frugi has shown an elegant simplicity of diction and thought in the first book of his *Annals*, when writing of the life and habits of King Romulus. His words are as follows: "They say also of Romulus, that being invited to dinner, he drank but little there, giving the reason that he had business for the following day. They answer: 'If all men were like you, Romulus, wine would be cheaper.' 'Nay, expensive,' answered Romulus, 'if each man drank as much as he wished; for I drank as much as I wished.'"

221   *Marcus Cicero Refutes the Charge of a Direct Falsehood*
Gellius, Attic Nights 12.12.1–4

This also is a part of rhetorical training, cunningly and cleverly to admit charges not attended with danger, so that if something base is thrown up to you which cannot be denied, you may turn it off by a jocular reply, making the thing seem deserving of laughter rather than censure. This we read that Cicero did, when by a witty and clever remark he put aside what could not be denied. For when he wished to buy a house on the Palatine, and did not have the ready money, he received a loan of 2,000,000 sesterces privately from Publius Sulla, who was at the time under accusation.[1] But before he bought the house, the transaction became known and reached the ears of the people, and he was charged with having received money from an accused man for the purpose of buying a house. Then

Cicero, disturbed by the unexpected reproach, said that he had not received the money and also declared he had no intention of buying a house, adding: "Therefore, if I buy a house, let it be considered that I did receive the money." But when later he had bought the house and was twitted in the senate with this falsehood by friends, he laughed heartily, saying as he did so: "You are men devoid of common sense, if you do not know that it is the part of a prudent and careful head of a family to get rid of rival purchasers by declaring that he does not intend to buy something that he wishes to purchase."

1. He was charged with participation in the conspiracy of Catiline.

222a   *Harvest Is Great*
Gospel, John 4:31–38

Meanwhile the disciples besought him [Jesus], saying, "Rabbi, eat." But he said to them, "I have food to eat of which you do not know." So the disciples said to one another, "Has any one brought him food?" Jesus said to them, "My food is to do the will of him who sent me, and to accomplish his work. Do you not say, 'There are yet four months, then comes the harvest'? I tell you, lift up your eyes, and see how the fields are already white for harvest. He who reaps receives wages, and gathers fruit for eternal life, so that sower and reaper may rejoice together. For here the saying holds true, 'One sows and another reaps.' I sent you to reap that for which you did not labor; others have labored, and you have entered into their labor."

222b   *Harvest Is Great*
Gospel, Matthew 9:35–38

And Jesus went about all the cities and villages, teaching in their synagogues and preaching the gospel of the kingdom, and healing every disease and every infirmity. When he saw the crowds, he had compassion for them, because they were harassed and helpless, like sheep without a shepherd. Then he said to his disciples, "The harvest is plentiful, but the laborers are few; pray therefore the Lord of the harvest to send out laborers into his harvest."

223   *Binding and Loosing*
Gospel, John 20:19–23

On the evening of that day, the first day of the week, the doors being shut where the disciples were, for fear of the Jews, Jesus came and stood among them and said to them, "Peace be with you." When he had said this, he showed them his hands and his side. Then the disciples were glad when they saw the Lord. Jesus said to them again, "Peace be with you. As the Father has sent me, even so I send you." And when he had said this, he breathed on them, and said to them, "Receive the Holy Spirit. If you forgive the sins of any, they are forgiven; if you retain the sins of any, they are retained."[1]

1. Cf. Matthew 16:19; 18:18.

224a   *Who Is the Greatest?*
Gospel, Luke 9:46–48

And an argument arose among them [the disciples] as to which of them was the greatest. But when Jesus perceived the thought of their hearts, he took a child and put him by his side, and said to them, "Whoever receives this child in my name receives me, and whoever receives me receives him who sent me; for he who is least among you all is the one who is great."

224b *Jesus Blesses Children*
Gospel, Luke 18:15–17

Now they were bringing even infants to him that he might touch them; and when the disciples saw it, they rebuked them. But Jesus called them to him, saying, "Let the children come to me, and do not hinder them; for to such belongs the kingdom of God. Truly, I say to you, whoever does not receive the kingdom of God like a child shall not enter it."

224c *Who Is the Greatest?*
Gospel, Mark 9:33–37

And they came to Capernaum; and when he [Jesus] was in the house he asked them, "What were you discussing on the way?" But they were silent; for on the way they had discussed with one another who was the greatest. And he sat down and called the twelve; and he said to them, "If any one would be first, he must be last of all and servant of all." And he took a child, and put him in the midst of them; and taking him in his arms, he said to them, "Whoever receives one such child in my name receives me; and whoever receives me, receives not me but him who sent me."

224d *Jesus Blesses Children*
Gospel, Mark 10:13–16

And they were bringing children to him, that he [Jesus] might touch them; and the disciples rebuked them. But when Jesus saw it he was indignant, and said to them, "Let the children come to me, do not hinder them; for to such belongs the kingdom of God. Truly, I say to you, whoever does not receive the kingdom of God like a child shall not enter it." And he took them in his arms and blessed them, laying his hands upon them.

224e *Who Is the Greatest?*
Gospel, Matthew 18:1–4

At that time the disciples came to Jesus, saying, "Who is the greatest in the kingdom of heaven?" And calling to him a child, he put him in the midst of them, and said, "Truly, I say to you, unless you turn and become like children, you will never enter the kingdom of heaven. Whoever humbles himself like this child, he is the greatest in the kingdom of heaven.

224f *Jesus Blesses Children*
Gospel, Matthew 19:13–15

Then children were brought to him that he might lay his hands on them and pray. The disciples rebuked the people; but Jesus said, "Let the children come to me, and do not hinder them; for to such belongs the kingdom of heaven." And he laid his hands on them and went away.

224g Shall We Enter the Kingdom?
Gospel, Thomas 22

Jesus saw some babies nursing. He said to his disciples, "These nursing babies are like those who enter the kingdom." They said to him, "Then shall we enter the kingdom as babies?" Jesus said to them, "When you make the two into one, and when you make the inner like the outer and the outer like the inner, and the upper like the lower, and when you make male and female into a single one, so that the male will not be male nor the female be female, when you make eyes in place of an eye, a hand in place of a hand, a foot in place of a foot, an image in place of an image, then you will enter [the kingdom]."

225 A Samaritan Village Refuses to Receive Jesus
Gospel, Luke 9:51–56

When the days drew near for him to be received up, he [Jesus] set his face to go to Jerusalem. And he sent messengers ahead of him, who went and entered a village of the Samaritans, to make ready for him; but the people would not receive him, because his face was set toward Jerusalem. And when his disciples James and John saw it, they said, "Lord, do you want us to bid fire come down from heaven and consume them?" But he turned and rebuked them.[1] And they went on to another village.

>   1. Cf. 2 Kings 1:9–12.

226 The Return of the Seventy-Two
Gospel, Luke 10:17–20

The seventy returned with joy, saying, "Lord, even the demons are subject to us in your name!" And he said to them, "I saw Satan fall like lightning from heaven. Behold, I have given you authority to tread upon serpents and scorpions,[1] and over all the power of the enemy; and nothing shall hurt you. Nevertheless do not rejoice in this, that the spirits are subject to you; but rejoice that your names are written in heaven."

>   1. Cf. Psalm 9:13.

227a Beware of the Scribes
Gospel, Luke 20:45–47

And in the hearing of all the people he [Jesus] said to his disciples, "Beware of the scribes, who like to go about in long robes, and love salutations in the market places and the best seats in the synagogues and the places of honor at feasts, who devour widow's houses and for a pretense make long prayers. They will receive the greater condemnation."

227b Jesus Denounces Scribes and Pharisees
Gospel, Matthew 23:1–12

Then said Jesus to the crowds and to his disciples, "The scribes and the Pharisees sit on Moses' seat; so practice and observe whatever they tell you, but not what they do; for they preach, but do not practice. They bind heavy burdens, hard to bear, and lay them on men's shoulders; but they themselves will not move them with their finger. They do all their deeds to be seen by men; for they make their phylacteries broad and their fringes long, and they love the place of honor at feasts and the best seats in the synagogues, and salutations in the market places, and being called rabbi by men. But you are not to be called rabbi, for you have one teacher, and you are all brethren. And call no man your father on earth, for you have one Father, who is in heaven. Neither be called masters, for you have one master, the Christ. He who is greatest among you shall be your servant; whoever exalts himself will be humbled, and whoever humbles himself will be exalted.

228a *Teaching about Divorce*
Gospel, Mark 10:10-12

And in the house the disciples asked him [Jesus] again about this matter [divorce]. And he said to them, "Whoever divorces his wife and marries another, commits adultery against her; and if she divorces her husband and marries another, she commits adultery."

228b *Teaching about Divorce*
Gospel, Matthew 19:7-9

They [Pharisees] said to him, "Why then did Moses command one to give a certificate of divorce, and to put her away?"[1] He [Jesus] said to them, "For your hardness of heart Moses allowed you to divorce your wives, but from the beginning it was not so. And I say to you: whoever divorces his wife, except for unchastity, and marries another, commits adultery."

1. Deuteronomy 24:1-4.

228c *Teaching about Divorce*
Gospel, Matthew 5:31-32

"It was also said, "Whoever divorces his wife, let him give her a certificate of divorce." But I say to you that every one who divorces his wife, except on the ground of unchastity, makes her an adulteress; and whoever marries a divorced woman commits adultery.

228d *Teaching about Divorce*
Gospel, Luke 16:18

"Every one who divorces his wife and marries another commits adultery, and he who marries a woman divorced from her husband commits adultery."

228e *Teaching about Divorce*
1 Corinthians 7:10-11

To the married I give charge, not I but the Lord, that the wife should not separate from her husband (but if she does, let her remain single or else be reconciled to her husband) and that the husband should not divorce his wife.

229a *Triumphal Entry into Jerusalem*
Gospel, Mark 11:1-10

And when they drew near to Jerusalem, to Bethphage and Bethany, at the Mount of Olives, he [Jesus] sent two of his disciples, and said to them, "Go into the village opposite you, and immediately as you enter it you will find a colt tied, on which no one has ever sat; untie it and bring it. If any one says to you, 'Why are you

doing this?' say, 'The Lord has need of it and will send it back here immediately.'"
And they went away, and found a colt tied at the door out in the open street; and
they untied it. And those who stood there said to them, "What are you doing,
untying the colt?" And they told them what Jesus had said; and they let them go.
And they brought the colt to Jesus, and threw their garments on it; and he sat upon
it. And many spread their garments on the road, and others spread leafy branches
which they had cut from the fields. And those who went before and those who
followed cried out, "Hosanna! Blessed is he who comes in the name of the Lord!
Blessed is the kingdom of our father David that is coming! Hosanna in the
highest!"[1]

1. Psalm 118:26; Zechariah 9:9.

229b *Triumphal Entry into Jerusalem*
Gospel, Luke 19:37–40

As he [Jesus] was now drawing near, at the descent of the Mount of Olives, the
whole multitude of the disciples began to rejoice and praise God with a loud voice
for all the mighty works that they had seen, saying, "Blessed be the King who
comes in the name of the Lord! Peace in heaven and glory in the highest!" And
some of the Pharisees in the multitude said to him, "Teacher, rebuke your disciples." He answered, "I tell you, if these were silent, the very stones would cry
out."

230a *Widow's Offering*
Gospel, Mark 12:41–44

And he [Jesus] sat down opposite the treasury, and watched the multitude
putting money into the treasury. Many rich people put in large sums. And a poor
widow came, and put in two copper coins, which make a penny. And he called his
disciples to him, and said to them, "Truly, I say to you, this poor widow has put in
more than all those who are contributing to the treasury. For they all contributed
out of their abundance; but she out of her poverty has put in everything she had,
her whole living."

230b *Widow's Offering*
Gospel, Luke 21:1–4

He [Jesus] looked up and saw the rich putting their gifts into the treasury; and he
saw a poor widow put in two copper coins. And he said, "Truly I tell you, this poor
widow has put in more than all of them; for they all contributed out of their
abundance, but she out of her poverty put in all the living that she had."

231 *Passover with the Disciples*
Gospel, Mark 14:17–21

And when it was evening he came with the twelve. And as they were at table
eating, Jesus said, "Truly, I say to you, one of you will betray me, one who is eating
with me."[1] They began to be sorrowful, and to say to him one after another, "Is it
I?" He said to them, "It is one of the twelve, one who is dipping bread into the dish
with me. For the Son of man goes as it is written of him, but woe to that man by
whom the Son of man is betrayed! It would have been better for that man if he had
not been born."

1. Psalm 41:9.

232 *Institution of the Lord's Supper*
Gospel, Mark 14:22–25

And as they were eating, he [Jesus] took bread, and blessed, and broke it, and gave it to them, and said, "Take; this is my body." And he took a cup, and when he had given thanks he gave it to them, and they all drank of it. And he said to them, "This is my blood of the covenant, which is poured out for many. Truly, I say to you, I shall not drink again of the fruit of the vine until that day when I drink it new in the kingdom of God."

233a *Mother and Brothers of Jesus*
Gospel, Matthew 12:46–50

While he [Jesus] was still speaking to the people, behold, his mother and his brothers stood outside, asking to speak to him. But he replied to the man who told him, "Who is my mother, and who are my brothers?" And stretching out his hand toward his disciples, he said, "Here are my mother and my brothers! For whoever does the will of my Father in heaven is my brother, and sister, and mother."

233b *Mother and Brothers of Jesus*
Gospel, Thomas 99

The disciples said to him, "Your brothers and your mother are standing outside." He said to them, "Those here who do the will of my Father are my brothers and my mother. They are the ones who will enter the kingdom of my Father."

233c *Mother and Brothers of Jesus*
Gospel, Luke 8:19–21

Then his mother and his brothers came to him but they could not reach him for the crowd. And he [Jesus] was told, "Your mother and your brothers are standing outside, desiring to see you." But he said to them, "My mother and my brothers are those who hear the word of God and do it."

233d *Mother and Brothers of Jesus*
Gospel, Mark 3:31–35

And his mother and his brothers came; and standing outside they sent to him and called him. And a crowd was sitting about him; and they said to him, "Your mother and your brothers are outside, asking for you." And he replied, "Who are my mother and my brothers?" And looking around on those who sat about him, he said, "Here are my mother and my brothers! Whoever does the will of God is my brother, and sister, and mother."

233e *Blessed Is the Womb*
Gospel, Luke 11:27–28

As he [Jesus] said this, a woman in the crowd raised her voice and said to him, "Blessed is the womb that bore you, and the breasts that you sucked!" But he said, "Blessed rather are those who hear the word of God and keep it!"

233f *Blessed Is the Womb*
Gospel, Thomas 79

A woman in the crowd said to him, "Blessed are the womb that bore you and the breasts that fed you." He said to [her], "Blessed are those who have heard the word of the Father and have truly kept it. For the days will come when you will say, 'Blessed are the womb that has not conceived and the breasts that have not produced milk.'"

234a *Destruction of Temple Foretold*
Gospel, Matthew 24:1-2

Jesus left the temple and was going away, when his disciples came to point out to him the buildings of the temple. But he answered them, "You see all these, do you not? Truly, I say to you, there will not be left here one stone upon another, that will not be thrown down."

234b *Destruction of Temple Foretold*
Gospel, Luke 21:5-6

And as some spoke of the temple, how it was adorned with noble stones and offerings, he [Jesus] said, "As for these things which you see, the days will come when there shall not be left here one stone upon another that will not be thrown down."

235 *Commission to Disciples*
Gospel, Matthew 28:16-20

Now the eleven disciples went to Galilee, to the mountain to which Jesus had directed them. And when they saw him they worshiped him; but some doubted. And Jesus came and said to them, "All authority in heaven and on earth has been given to me. Go therefore and make disciples of all nations, baptizing them in the name of the Father and of the Son and of the Holy Spirit, teaching them to observe all that I have commanded you; and lo, I am with you always, to the close of the age."

236 *Christ and Mary Magdalene*
Gospel, Philip 55 (CG II, 63:32-64.5)

And the companion of Christ is Mary Magdalene. [The Lord loved Mary] more than [all] the disciples, [and] kissed her on her [mouth many] times. The other [disciples saw] him [loving Mary]. They said to him, "Why do you love her more than all of us?" The Savior answered and said to them, "Why do I not love you as I do her?"

237 *Nothing Hidden that Shall Not Be Revealed*
Gospel, Thomas 6

His disciples asked him and said to him, "Do you want us to fast? How shall we pray? Shall we give alms? What diet shall we observe?" Jesus said, "Do not lie, and do not do what you hate, because all things are disclosed before heaven. For there is nothing hidden that will not be revealed, and there is nothing covered that will remain without being disclosed."[1]

1. Cf. Matthew 10:26; Mark 4:21-22; Luke 8:17; 12:2.

238 *James the Just Chosen Leader*
Gospel, Thomas 12

The disciples said to Jesus, "We know that you will leave us. Who is going to be our leader?" Jesus said to them, "No matter where you are, you are to go to James the Just, for whose sake heaven and earth came into being."

239 *Fasting, Alms and Defilement*
Gospel, Thomas 14

Jesus said to them, "If you fast, you will bring sin upon yourselves. If you pray, you will be condemned. If you give alms, you will harm your spirits. When you go into any country and walk from place to place, when the people receive you, eat what they serve you and heal the sick among them. For what goes into your mouth will not defile you; rather, it is what comes out of your mouth that will defile you."

240 *The Beginning and the End*
Gospel, Thomas 18

The disciples said to Jesus, "Tell us how our end will be." Jesus said, "Have you already discovered the beginning, that you are seeking after the end? For where the beginning is, the end will be. Blessed is one who stands at the beginning: that one will know the end, and will not taste death."[1]

1. Cf. Matthew 16:28; Mark 9:1; Luke 9:27.

241 *Mustard Seed*
Gospel, Thomas 20

The disciples said to Jesus, "Tell us what the kingdom of heaven is like." He said to them, "It is like a mustard seed, the tiniest of all seeds. But when it falls on prepared soil, it produces a large plant and becomes a shelter for birds of heaven."[1]

1. Cf. Matthew 13:31–32; Mark 4:30–32; Luke 13:18–19.

242a *Children Take Clothes Off*
Gospel, Thomas 37

His disciples said, "When will you appear to us, and when shall we see you?" Jesus said, "When you strip and are not ashamed, and you take your clothes and put them under your feet like little children and trample them, then [you] will see the son of the living one and you will not be afraid."

242b *Children Take Clothes Off*
Gospel, Thomas 21

Mary said to Jesus, "Whom are your disciples like?" He said, "They are like little children living in a field that is not theirs. When the owners of the field come, they will say, 'Give our field back to us.' They (the children) take off their clothes in their presence in order to give the field back and return it to them. For this reason I say, if the owner of a house knows that a thief is coming, the owner will be on guard before the thief arrives, and will not let the thief break into his house of his domain and steal his possessions. As for you, then, be on guard against the world. Gird yourselves with great strength, lest the robbers find a way to get to you, for the trouble you expect will come. Let there be among you a person who understands. When the crop ripened, one came quickly with sickle in hand and harvested it. Whoever has ears to hear ought to listen."

243 *Who Are You?*
Gospel, Thomas 43

His disciples said to him, "Who are you to say these things to us?" <Jesus said to them,> "You do not know who I am from what I say to you. Rather, you have become like the Jews, for they love the tree but hate its fruit, or they love the fruit but hate the tree."[1]

    1. Cf. Matthew 7:15–20; 12:33; Luke 6:43–45.

244a *Coming of Kingdom*
Gospel, Thomas 51

His disciples said to him, "When will the rest for the dead take place, and when will the new world come?" He said to them, "What you look for has come, but you do not know it."

244b *Coming of Kingdom*
Gospel, Thomas 113

His disciples said to him, "When will the kingdom come?" <Jesus said,> "It will not come by looking for it, nor will it be said, 'Behold, over here!' or 'Behold, over there!' Rather, the kingdom of the Father is spread out on the earth, but people do not see it."

244c *Coming of Kingdom*
Gospel, Luke 17:20–21

Being asked by the Pharisees when the kingdom of God was coming, he [Jesus] answered them, "The kingdom of God is not coming with signs to be observed; nor will they say, 'Lo, here it is!' or 'There!' for behold, the kingdom of God is in the midst of you."[1]

    1. Cf. Gospel, Thomas 3.

245 *On Circumcision*
Gospel, Thomas 53

His disciples said to him, "Is circumcision useful or not?" He said to them, "If it were useful, the father would produce them (children) already circumcised from their mother. Rather, the circumcision in spirit has become profitable in every respect."[1]

    1. Romans 2:25–29; 1 Corinthians 7:17–19; Galatians 6:15; Philippians 3:3; Colossians 2:11–14.

246a *Devouring the Dead*
Gospel, Thomas 60

<They saw> a Samaritan carrying a lamb and going to Judea. He said to his disciples, "(Why is) that person (carrying) the lamb around?" They said to him, "So that he may kill it and eat it." He said to them, "He will not eat it while it is alive, but only after he has killed it and it has become a carcass." They said, "Otherwise he cannot do it." He said to them, "So also with you, seek a place of rest for yourselves, lest you become a carcass and be eaten."

246b *Devouring the Dead*
Gospel, Thomas 11

Jesus said, "This heaven will pass away, and the one above it will pass away. The dead are not alive, and the living will not die. During the days when you ate what is dead, you made it alive. When you are in the light, what will you do? On the day when you were one, you became two. But when you become two, what will you do?"

247a *I Am No Divider*
Gospel, Thomas 72

A [person said] to him, "Tell my brothers to divide my father's property with me." He said to the person, "Sir, who made me a divider?" He turned to his disciples and said to them, "I am not a divider, am I?"

247b *Parable of the Rich Fool*
Gospel, Luke 12:13–21

One of the multitude said to him [Jesus], "Teacher, bid my brother divide the inheritance with me." But he said to him, "Man, who made me a judge or divider over you?" And he said to them, "Take heed, and beware of all covetousness; for a man's life does not consist in the abundance of his possessions." And he told them a parable, saying, "The land of a rich man brought forth plentifully; and he thought to himself, 'What shall I do, for I have nowhere to store my crops?' And he said, 'I will do this: I will pull down my barns, and build larger ones; and there I will store all my grain and my goods. And I will say to my soul, Soul, you have ample goods laid up for many years; take your ease, eat, drink, be merry.'[1] But God said to him, 'Fool! This night your soul is required of you; and the things you have prepared, whose will they be?' So is he who lays up treasure for himself, and is not rich toward God."

1. Cf. 1 Corinthians 15:32.

247c *Parable of the Rich Fool*
Gospel, Thomas 63

Jesus said, "There was a rich person who had a great deal of money. He said 'I shall invest my money so that I may sow, reap, plant, and fill my storehouses with produce, that I may lack nothing.' These were his plans, but that very night he died. Whoever has ears ought to listen."

248a *Tell Us Who You Are*
Gospel, Thomas 91

They said to him, "Tell us who you are so that we may believe in you." He said to them, "You examine the face of heaven and earth, but you have not come to know the one who is in your presence, and you do not know how to examine this moment."

248b *Demand for a Sign*
Gospel, Mark 8:11–13

The Pharisees came and began to argue with him [Jesus], seeking from him a sign from heaven, to test him. And he sighed deeply in his spirit, and said, "Why does this generation seek a sign? Truly, I say to you, no sign shall be given to this generation." And he left them, and getting into the boat again he departed to the other side.

248c *Demand for a Sign*

Gospel, Matthew 12:38-42

Then some of the scribes and Pharisees said to him, "Teacher, we wish to see a sign from you." But he [Jesus] answered them, "An evil and adulterous generation seeks for a sign; but no sign shall be given to it except the sign of the prophet Jonah. For as Jonah was three days and three nights in the belly of the whale, so will the Son of man be three days and three nights in the heart of the earth.[1] The men of Nineveh will arise at the judgment with this generation and condemn it; for they repented at the preaching of Jonah, and behold, something greater than Jonah is here. The queen of the South will arise at the judgment with this generation and condemn it; for she came from the ends of the earth to hear the wisdom of Solomon, and behold, something greater than Solomon is here."

1. Cf. Gospel, Nazoreans 11.

248d *Demand for a Sign*

Gospel, Matthew 16:1-4

And the Pharisees and Sadducees came, and to test him they asked him to show them a sign from heaven. He [Jesus] answered them, "When it is evening, you say, 'It will be fair weather; for the sky is red.' And in the morning, 'It will be stormy today, for the sky is red and threatening.' You know how to interpret the appearance of the sky, but you cannot interpret the signs of the times.[1] An evil and adulterous generation seeks for a sign, but no sign shall be given to it except the sign of Jonah." So he left them and departed.

1. Cf. Gospel, Nazoreans 13.

249a *On Taxes*

Gospel, Thomas 100

They showed Jesus a gold coin and said to him, "Caesar's people demand taxes from us." He said to them, "Give Caesar the things that are Caesar's, give God the things that are God's, and give me what is mine."

249b *On Taxes*

Papyrus Egerton 2, 2 recto 43-59 (Bell and Skeat: 11-13)

They came to him to test him with questions, [saying], "Teacher Jesus, we know that you are come [from God], for what you do [testifies] above all the prophets. [Tell] us, [therefore], is it lawful to [give] to kings what pertains to their rule? Shall we [pay] them or not?" And Jesus, knowing their thoughts, was moved with indignation and said [to them], "Why do you call me teacher with your mouth and do not hear what I say? Well did [Isaiah] prophesy [of] you when he said, '[This people honors] me with their lips, [but] their [heart is far] from [me]. In vain [they worship me], (teaching as doctrines) the precepts (of men). . . .'"

249c *On Taxes*

Gospel, Luke 20:19-26

The scribes and the chief priests tried to lay hands on him [Jesus] at that very hour, but they feared the people; for they perceived that he had told this parable against them. So they watched him, and sent spies, who pretended to be sincere, that they might take hold of what he said, so as to deliver him up to the authority and jurisdiction of the governor. They asked him, "Teacher, we know that you speak and teach rightly, and show no partiality, but truly teach the way of God. Is it lawful for us to give tribute to Caesar, or not?" But he perceived their craftiness, and said to them, "Show me a coin. Whose likeness and inscription has it?" They said, "Caesar's." He said to them, "Then render to Caesar the things that are Caesar's, and to God the things that are God's." And they were not able in the presence of the people to catch him by what he said; but marveling at his answer they were silent.

249d   On Taxes
Gospel, Mark 12:13–17

And they sent to him [Jesus] some of the Pharisees and some of the Herodians, to entrap him in his talk. And they came and said to him, "Teacher, we know that you are true, and care for no man; for you do not regard the position of men, but truly teach the way of God. Is it lawful to pay taxes to Caesar, or not? Should we pay them, or should we not?" But knowing their hypocrisy, he said to them, "Why put me to the test? Bring me a coin, and let me look at it." And they brought one. And he said to them, "Whose likeness and inscription is this?" They said to him, "Caesar's." Jesus said to them, "Render to Caesar the things that are Caesar's, and to God the things that are God's." And they were amazed at him.

249e   On Taxes
Gospel, Matthew 22:15–22

Then the Pharisees went and took counsel how to entangle him in his talk. And they sent their disciples to him, along with the Herodians saying, "Teacher, we know that you are true, and teach the way of God truthfully, and care for no man; for you do not regard the position of men. Tell us, then, what you think. Is it lawful to pay taxes to Caesar or not?" But Jesus, aware of their malice, said, "Why put me to the test, you hypocrites? Show me the money for the tax." And they brought him a coin. And Jesus said to them, "Whose likeness and inscription is this?" They said, "Caesar's." Then he said to them, "Render therefore to Caesar the things that are Caesar's, and to God the things that are God's." When they heard it, they marveled and they left him and went away.

250a   On Fasting
Gospel, Thomas 104

They said [to Jesus], "Come, let us pray today, and let us fast." Jesus said, "What sin have I committed, or how have I been undone? Rather, when the bridegroom leaves the wedding chamber, then let people fast and pray."

250b   On Fasting
Gospel, Luke 5:33–39

And they said to him [Jesus], "The disciples of John fast often and offer prayers, and so do the disciples of the Pharisees, but yours eat and drink." And Jesus said to them, "Can you make wedding guests fast while the bridegroom is with them? The days will come, when the bridegroom is taken away from them, and then they will fast in those days."[1] He told them a parable also: "No one tears a piece from a new garment and puts it upon an old garment; if he does, he will tear the new, and the piece from the new will not match the old. And no one puts new wine into old wineskins; if he does the new wine will burst the skins and it will be spilled, and the skins will be destroyed. But new wine must be put into fresh wineskins. And no one after drinking old wine desires new; for he says, 'The old is good.'"[2]

1. Cf. Gospel, Thomas 27.
2. Cf. Gospel, Thomas 47.

250c   *On Fasting*
Gospel, Mark 2:18–22

Now John's disciples and the Pharisees were fasting; and people came and said to him, "Why do John's disciples and the disciples of the Pharisees fast, but your disciples do not fast?" And Jesus said to them, "Can the wedding guests fast while the bridegroom is with them? As long as they have the bridegroom with them, they cannot fast. The days will come, when the bridegroom is taken away from them, and then they will fast in that day. No one sews a piece of unshrunk cloth on an old garment; if he does, the patch tears away from it, the new from the old, and a worse tear is made. And no one puts new wine into old wineskins; if he does, the wine will burst the skins, and the wine is lost, and so are the skins; but new wine is for fresh skins."

250d   *On Fasting*
Gospel, Matthew 9:14–17

Then the disciples of John came to him saying, "Why do we and the Pharisees fast, but your disciples do not fast?" And Jesus said to them, "Can the wedding guests mourn as long as the bridegroom is with them? The days will come, when the bridegroom is taken away from them, and then they will fast. And no one puts a piece of unshrunk cloth on an old garment, for the patch tears away from the garment, and a worse tear is made. Neither is new wine put into old wineskins; if it is, the skins burst, and the wine is spilled, and the skins are destroyed; but new wine is put into fresh wineskins, and so both are preserved."

251   *Regard for Dumb Animals*
Hadith, Abū Dawud, jihād, 23

'Abd Allāh b. Muḥammad al-Nufaylī related to us that Maskīn (that is, Ibn Bukayr) reported that Muḥammad b. Muhājir said, reporting from Rabī'a b. Yazīd, who himself had it from Abū Kabsha al-Salūlī, reporting from Sahl b. al-Ḥan-ẓalīya, who said, The Messenger of God passed by a camel so thin that its back met its abdomen. He said, "For God's sake, show regard for these dumb animals. Ride them properly and feed them properly."

252   *On Alms*
Hadith, Bukhārī, adab, 33

Adam, Shu'ba, and Sa'īd b. abī Burda b. abī Mūsā al-Ash'arī reported to us from the latter's father and grandfather, who said: The Prophet said, "Every Muslim must give alms." The people said, "And if one has nothing?" He replied, "Then he should work with his hands to benefit himself and give to charity." They said, "And if he cannot or does not work?" He replied, "Then he should help a needy or unhappy person." They: "If he does not do it?" He: "Then he should enjoin what is good (or: What is fitting)"[1] They: "If he does not do that?" He: "Then let him refrain from doing evil, and that will be considered as a contribution to charity."

1. Variant reading.

253 *People Turn from Prayer*
Hadith, Bukhārī, buyū', 7

Talaq b. Ghannām and Zā'ida related to us from Ḥusayn and Sālim, who reported that Jābir said: While we were praying with the Prophet a caravan from Syria drew near, carrying food. So many people turned toward the caravan that there were only twelve persons left with the Prophet. Then was revealed the verse: "But when they see a business transaction or some amusement they disperse for one or the other."[1]

1. Qur'ān 62:11.

254 *Information Withheld*
Hadith, Bukhārī, tarāwīḥ, 5

Muḥammad b. al-Muthannā, Khālid b. al-Ḥārith, Ḥumayd and Anas are our authorities, who reported on the authority of 'Ubāda b. al-Ṣāmit, who said: The Prophet went out to inform us about the Night of Destiny, but two Muslims were insulting each other. He said, "I came out to tell you about the Night of Destiny, but so-and-so and so-and-so were insulting each other. So the information about it has been taken away. Perhaps that is better for you. Look for it on the twenty-ninth, the twenty-seventh and the twenty-fifth of Ramadan."

255 *On Pagan Meat*
Hadith, Bukhārī, tawḥīd, 13

Yūsuf b. Mūsā related to us from Abū Khālid al-Aḥmar, who said: I heard Hishām b. 'Urwa telling on his father's authority, who had it from 'Ā'isha, who said: People said: "O Messenger of God, here are some people who only recently came out of paganism. They brought us some meat and we do not know whether they pronounced the name of God while slaughtering the animals or not." He said, "Pronounce the name of God yourselves and eat."

256 *A Place Assigned*
Hadith, Bukhārī, tawḥīd, 54

Muḥammad b. Bashshār, Ghundar and Shu'ba reported from Manṣūr and Al-A'mash, who heard Sa'd b. 'Ubayda report from Abū 'Abd al-Raḥmān from 'Alī, who reported that: While the Prophet was in a funeral procession he took a stick and began to scratch on the ground with it. He said, "Every one of you has a place assigned in Hell or in Paradise." The people said, "Shall we simply depend on that?" He said, "Keep on doing your works, for all have the way made easy which will lead to the destined place for which they have been created." Then the Prophet recited the verse, "Yet he who gives to others and fears God . . ."[1]

1. Qur'ān, 92.5.

257 *The Man with the Sword*
Hadith, Muslim, faḍā'il, 4

'Abdu b. Ḥumayd, 'Abd al-Razzāq, Ma'mar b. al-Zuhrī related to us from Abū Salama who had it from Jābir b. 'Abd Allāh who said: We went on an expedition with the Messenger of God in the direction of Najd. He came up to us in a valley full of thorny trees. There the Messenger of God rested under a tree, hanging his sword on one of its branches. The people scattered out in the valley to rest under the trees. Later the Messenger of God said, "A man came up to me while I was asleep. He took my sword, and as I woke up he was standing at my head. As I came to full consciousness I realized that the sword was drawn. The man said, 'Who can protect you from me?' I said, 'God.' He said again, 'Who can protect you from us?' I said, 'God.' He put the sword back in its sheath, and that man is sitting here." Then the Messenger of God called no more attention to him.

258   *I Am the Brick*
Hadith, Muslim, faḍā'il, 7

'Amr b. Muḥammad al-Nāqid and Sufyān b. 'Uyayna informed us from Abū al-Zanād, who had it from Al-A'raj upon the authority of Abū Hurayra, that the Prophet said, The relationship between the previous Prophets and me is comparable to a person who built a building, finishing and embellishing it well. People went around it saying, "We have never seen a building as fine as this one, except for one brick." I am that brick.

259   *The Most Noble People*
Hadith, Muslim, faḍā'il, 44

Zuhayr b. Ḥarb, Muḥammad b. al-Muthannā and 'Ubayd Allāh b. Sa'īd reported to us on the authority of Yaḥyā b. Sa'īd, 'Ubayd Allāh, Sa'īd b. abī Sa'īd, his father and Abū Hurayra, who said: Some people asked, "O Messenger of God, who is the most noble of people?" He replied, "The most God-fearing among you." They: "That is not what we are asking about." He: "Well, it is Joseph, the Prophet of God and the son of God's Prophet, who was the son of the Friend of God." They: "That is not what we are asking about." He: "Are you asking about the Arab tribes? The best of them in the Age of Ignorance will be the best in Islam, when they understand."

260   *He Is Delivered, We Are Delivered*
Hadith, Muslim, janā'iz, 21

Qutayba b. Sa'īd related to us from Mālik b. Anas, as has been transmitted concerning him, from Muḥammad b. 'Amr b. Ḥalḥala, Ma'bad b. Ka'b b. Mālik and Abū Qatāda b. Rib'ī, that he [Anas] used to tell: A funeral procession passed by the Messenger of God and he said, "He is delivered; we are delivered." He was asked, "O Messenger of God, what do you mean by 'He is delivered; we are delivered?'" He answered, "In the case of a believing man, he is delivered from the evils of this world, but in the case of a wicked man, his fellows, the country and all of nature are delivered from him."

261   *On Obedience*
Hadith, Ṭayālisī, 109

Shu'ba b. 'Ubayda informed us from Abū 'Abd al-Raḥmān al-Salamī from 'Alī that: The Prophet sent out a raiding party and put someone in charge of it, commanding the men to obey him. A fire broke out in the party and their leader ordered them to defy danger to put it out. Some did so, but others said, "We fled from the fire and refused to obey." Later they came to the Messenger of God and told him what had happened. The Messenger of God said, "Even if they had had to enter the fire, their obligation to obey orders would have held and it will hold until the day of resurrection. There shall be no obedience to man if it involves disobedience to God (may He be praised and exalted), but obedience is necessary in that which is good."

262 God Is Peace
Hadith, Ṭayālisī, 249

Hishām reported from Ḥammād who had it from Abū Wā'il from 'Abd Allāh (Ibn Mas'ūd), who said: When we were praying behind the Messenger of God we said, "Peace be upon God, peace be upon Gabriel, peace be upon Michael." Then the Messenger of God turned to us and said, "Do not say, peace be upon God, for God is peace; but say, greetings, prayers and good things to God; peace be upon you, O Prophet, with God's mercy and blessings; peace be upon us and upon the righteous servants of God; I witness that there is no deity but God, and that Muhammad is His servant and His messenger."

263 On Punishment
Hadith, Ṭayālisī, 260

Shu'ba informed us from Al-A'mash, who said, We heard Abū Wā'il recount from 'Abd al-Rahmān, saying: We said, "O Messenger of God, will what we did in the Time of Ignorance be held against us?" The Messenger of God replied, "Whoever does good in Islam will not be punished for what he did either in the Time of Ignorance or in Islam; but whoever does evil in Islam will be punished both for what he did in the Time of Ignorance and in Islam."

264 The Greatest Sins
Hadith, Tirmidhī, birr, 4

Ḥumayd b. Mas'ada informed us from Bishr b. al-Mufaḍḍal from Al-Jarīrī from 'Abd al-Rahmān b. Abī Bakra from his father who said: The Messenger of God said: "Shall I not tell you about the most serious of the great sins?" His listeners replied, "Yes, indeed, O Messenger of God." He said, "Making someone an associate with God in His sovereignty, then disobedience to parents,"—here he sat up from his reclining position—"then false testimony or untrue words." And the Messenger of God kept on talking about the great sins until we wished he would stop.

265 On the Punishment for Theft
Hadith, Tirmidhī, ḥudūd, 5

Qutayba and Al-Layth reported from Ibn Shihāb, 'Urwa and 'Ā'isha that: The Quraysh were concerned about the case of the Makhzumīya woman who had stolen. They said, "Who will speak to the Messenger of God on her behalf?" Others said, "Who would be bold enough to do it but Usāma b. Zayd, the dear friend of the Messenger of God." So Usāma spoke to him. The Messenger of God said, "Are you interceding regarding the legal punishment for infraction of a divine statute?" He got up and addressed the people, saying, "Verily what caused those who lived before to perish was that when one of their nobles stole, they let him go. But when one of their lowly ones stole they carried out the sentence against him. I swear by

God, that even if the thief is Fāṭima the daughter of Muḥammad, I shall cut off her hand.

266 *On Old Age and Medicines*
Hadith, Tirmidhī, ṭibb, 2

Bishr b. Muʿādh al-ʿAqadī al-Baṣrī and Abū ʿAwāna reported to us from Ziyād b. ʿIlāqa from Usāma b. Sharīk who said: The Bedouins asked the Messenger of God, "Shall we not use medicines?" He said, "Yes, O people of God, use medicines. God provides either healing or a remedy for each disease, that is, except one." They said, "O Messenger of God, what is that one?" He said, "Old age."

267 *Vespasian Counsels Romans to Think of Safety*
Josephus, Jewish War 3.207–210 (7.18)

The Romans suffered from these sallies, for they were ashamed to fly before Jews, and when they put the latter to flight the weight of their arms impeded them in the pursuit, while the Jews always did some mischief before the enemy could retaliate, and then took refuge in the town. In view of this, Vespasian ordered his legionaries to shun these attacks and not to be drawn into an engagement with men who were bent on death. "Nothing," he said, "is more redoubtable than despair, and their impetuosity, deprived of an objective, will be extinguished, like fire for lack of fuel. Besides, it becomes even Romans to think of safety as well as victory, since they make war not from necessity, but to increase their empire."

268 *Titus Amazed at Towers*
Josephus, Jewish War 6.409–411 (7.2–3)

Titus, on entering the town [Jerusalem], was amazed at its strength, but chiefly at the towers, which the tyrants, in their infatuation, had abandoned. Indeed, when he beheld their solid lofty mass, the magnitude of each block and the accuracy of the joinings, and marked how great was their breadth, how vast their height, "God indeed," he exclaimed, "has been with us in the war. God it was who brought down the Jews from these strongholds; for what power have human hands or engines against these towers?"

269 *Theocritus' Unhappy Witticism*
Macrobius, Saturnalia 7.3.12

But, on the other hand, to taunt a man with the loss of an eye is bound to stir up strong feeling. Thus it was that King Antigonus, although he had sworn to spare the life of Theocritus of Chios, put him to death on account of just such a gibe made at his expense by that man. For when Theocritus was being held before Antigonus, as though for punishment, and his friends were encouraging him with the assurance that he would certainly meet with mercy as soon as the king had set eyes upon him, he replied: "You are telling me, then, that it is all up with me." The jest was ill-timed, for Antigonus had lost an eye, and the unhappy witticism cost Theocritus his life.

270 *Life of Inanimate Nature*
Mani, Book of Mysteries (trans. from Sachau, 1:48)

The apostles asked Jesus about the life of inanimate nature, whereupon he said, "If that which is inanimate is separated from the living element which is commingled with it, and appears alone by itself, it is again inanimate and is not capable of living, whilst the living element which has left it, retaining its vital energy unimpaired, never dies."

271 *Weak Souls Perish*
Mani, Book of Mysteries (trans. from Sachau: 1:54–55)

He [Mani] says in the *Book of Mysteries*: Since the apostles knew that the souls are immortal, and that in their migrations they array themselves in every form, that they are shaped in every animal, and are cast in the mold of every figure, they asked Messiah what would be the end of those souls which did not receive the truth nor learn the origin of their existence. Whereupon he said, "Any weak soul which has not received all that belongs to her of truth perishes without any rest or bliss."

272 *Joshua Praises Eleazar*
Mekhilta, Ish. Pisha 16

One time the students spent the Sabbath in Yavneh, but R. Joshua did not spend the Sabbath there. When his students came to him, he said to them: "What new thing did you [learn] in Yavneh?" They said to him: "After you, Rabbi." He said to them: "Who spent the Sabbath there?" They said to him: "R. Eleazar b. Azzariah." He said to them: "Is it possible that R. Eleazar b. Azzariah spent the Sabbath there and you did not [learn] anything new!" They said to him: "[He stated] this general statement [when] he explained [Deuteronomy 29:9–10]: '*You are standing today all of you . . . your little ones and your wives.* Now did a little one actually know [enough] to understand [the difference] between good and evil? Rather, [they were mentioned in the verse] to give a reward for those who brought them [and] to increase the reward for those who do His will to establish what is said, *The Lord was pleased for his righteousness' sake*'" (Isaiah 42:21). He said to them: "This is a new teaching and more than that, [for] behold, I was like a person seventy years old, but I was not worthy [to understand] this thing until today. Happy are you, Abraham, our father, for Eleazar b. Azzariah came out of your loins. The generation is not an orphan generation, for Eleazar b. Azzariah dwells in it."

273 *Student Lengthens Prayers*
Mekhilta, Ish. Vayassa 1

Again it once happened that a student went [before the ark to lead the service] in the presence of R. Eliezer, and [the student] lengthened his prayers. [Eliezer]'s students said to him: "Our Rabbi, you saw that so-and-so lengthened his prayers. ". . . [Eliezer] said to them: "He did not lengthen [them] more than Moses, for it is said: *So I fell down before the Lord forty days . . .*" (Deuteronomy 9:25). For R. Eliezer used to say: "There is a time to shorten [one's prayers] and a time to lengthen [them]."

274 *Gamaliel Recites Shema on Wedding Night*
Mishnah, Berakhot 2:5

There was an incident concerning Rabban Gamaliel, who recited the *Shema* on the night of his wedding. His students said to him: "Did you not teach us, our Rabbi, that the groom is exempt from reciting the *Shema* on the night of his marriage?" He said to them: "I will not listen to you so that I would remove the Kingdom of Heaven from me for even one hour!"

275 *Gamaliel of Feeble Health*
Mishnah, Berakhot 2:6

[Gamaliel] washed on the first night after his wife had died. His students said to him: "Did you not teach us, our Rabbi, that a mourner is forbidden to wash?" He said to them: "I am not like other men, for I am of feeble health."

276 *Slave Ritually Fit*
Mishnah, Berakhot 2:7

And when Tabi his slave died, [Gamaliel] received consolation because of him. His students said to him: "Did you not teach us, our Rabbi, that one does not receive consolation on account of slaves?" He said to them: "Tabi was not like other slaves; he was ritually fit."

277 *Apollonius and Weak Followers*
Philostratus, Life of Apollonius 1.18

And he [Apollonius] announced his intention to his followers, who were seven in number; but when they tried to persuade him to adopt another plan, in hopes of drawing him off from his resolution, he said: "I have taken the gods into counsel and have told you their decision; and I have made trial of you to see if you are strong enough to undertake the same things as myself. Since therefore you are so soft and effeminate, I wish you very good health and that you may go on with your philosophy; but I must depart whither wisdom and the gods lead me."

278 *The Loftiest Spot*
Philostratus, Life of Apollonius 4.23

And as he [Apollonius] was coming to the mound where the Lacedaemonians are said to have been overwhelmed by the bolts which the enemy rained upon them, he heard his companions dicussing with one another which was the loftiest hill in Hellas, this topic being suggested it seems by the sight of the mountain of Oeta which rose before their eyes; so ascending the mound, he said: "I consider this the loftiest spot of all, for those who fell here in defense of freedom raised it to a level with Oeta and carried it to a height surpassing many mountains like Olympus. It is these men that I admire, and beyond any of them Megistias the Acarnanian; for he knew the death that they were about to die, and deliberately made up his mind to share in it with these heroes, fearing not so much death, as the prospect that he should miss death in such company."

279 *Agesilaus Returns Home*
Plutarch, Agesilaus 15.4

Agesilaus, however, never performed a nobler or a greater deed than in returning home as he now did, nor was there ever a fairer example of righteous obedience to authority. For Hannibal, though he was already in an evil plight and on the point of being driven out of Italy, could with the greatest difficulty bring himself to obey his summons to the war at home; and Alexander actually went so far as to jest when he heard of Antipater's battle with Agis,[1] saying: "It would seem, my men, that while we were conquering Darius here, there has been a battle of mice there in Arcadia."

1. At Megalopolis, in Arcadia, 331 B.C.E., Agis fell fighting, and the Spartan rebellion at once collapsed. Alexander had not the slightest thought of returning home to help Antipater.

280   Alcibiades Leaves Half
Plutarch, Alcibiades 4.5

This man [Anytus] was a lover of his, who, entertaining some friends, asked Alcibiades also to the dinner. Alcibiades declined the invitation, but after having drunk deep at home with some friends, went in revel rout to the house of Anytus, took his stand at the door of the men's chamber, and observing the tables full of gold and silver beakers, ordered his slaves to take half of them and carry them home for him. He did not deign to go in, but played this prank and was off. The guests were naturally indignant, and declared that Alcibiades had treated Anytus with gross and overweening insolence. "Not so," said Anytus, "but with moderation and kindness; he might have taken all there were: he has left us half."

281   Nothing Worse Said
Plutarch, Alcibiades 9.1

Possessing a dog of wonderful size and beauty, which had cost him seventy minas, he [Alcibiades] had its tail cut off, and a beautiful tail it was, too. His comrades chided him for this, and declared that everybody was furious about the dog and abusive of its owner. But Alcibiades burst out laughing and said: "That's just what I want; I want Athens to talk about this, that it may say nothing worse about me."

282   Alexander's Admiration of Darius' Captured Camp
Plutarch, Alexander 20.13 (8)

And when he [Alexander] saw the basins and pitchers and tubs and caskets, all of gold, and curiously wrought, while the apartment was marvelously fragrant with spices and unguents, and when he passed from this into a tent which was worthy of admiration for its size and height, and for the adornment of the couch and tables and banquet prepared for him, he turned his eyes upon his companions and said: "This, as it would seem, is to be a king."

283a   Alexander Has Blood, Not Ichor
Plutarch, Alexander 28.3 (2)

At a later time, however, when he [Alexander] had been hit by an arrow and was suffering great pain, he said: "This, my friends, that flows here, is blood, and not 'Ichor, such as flows from the veins of the blessed gods.'"[1]

1. Homer, Iliad 5.340; the "spirit fluid" in the gods' veins was called "ichor," not blood.

283b   Alexander Has Blood, Not Ichor
Plutarch, Moralia, Sayings of Kings and Commanders III:180E (16)

When he [Alexander] was hit in the leg by an arrow, and many of those who were oftentimes wont to hail him as a god hurried up to him, he, relaxing his countenance, said, "This is blood, as you see, and not 'Ichor, like that which flows from the wounds of the blessed immortals.'"[1]

1. The story is often repeated: cf. for example, Dio Chrysostom, Oration 44 (498); Seneca, Epistulae Morales 6.7.12.

283c *Alexander Has Blood, Not Ichor*
Plutarch, Moralia, Fortune of Alexander IV:341B (9)

Among the Assacenians his [Alexander's] ankle was wounded by an Indian arrow; that was the time when he smilingly said to his flatters, "this that you see is blood, not 'Ichor, that which flows from the wounds of the blessed immortals.'"

283d *Alexander Has Blood, Not Ichor*
Diogenes Laertius, Lives of the Eminent Philosophers 9.60

He [Anaxarchus] had, too, the capacity of bringing anyone to reason in the easiest possible way. At all events he succeeded in diverting Alexander when he had begun to think himself a god; for, seeing blood running from a wound he had sustained, he pointed to him with his finger and said, "See, there is blood and not 'Ichor which courses in the veins of the blessed gods.'" Plutarch reports this as spoken by Alexander to his friends.

283e *Alexander Has Blood, Not Ichor*
Athenaeus, Deipnosophists 6.251A

And Aristobulus of Cassandreia says[1] that the Athenian pancratiast Dioxippus, when Alexander was woulded and his blood was flowing, quoted the line, "Ichor, such as floweth in the blessed gods."

> 1. Frag. 28B Müller.

284 *Alexander Refuses to Steal Victory over Darius by Night*
Plutarch, Alexander 31.10–13 (5–7)

Meanwhile the older of his [Alexander's] companions, and particularly Parmenio, when they saw the plain between the Niphates and the Gordyaean mountains all lighted up with the barbarian fires, while an indistinguishably mingled and tumultuous sound of voices arose from their camp as if from a vast ocean, were astonished at their multitude and argued with one another that it was a great and grievous task to repel such a tide of war by engaging in broad daylight. They therefore waited upon the king when he had finished his sacrifices, and tried to persuade him to attack the enemy by night, and so to cover up with darkness the most fearful aspect of the coming struggle. But he gave them the celebrated answer, "I will not steal my victory"; whereupon some thought that he had made a vainglorious reply, and was jesting in the presence of so great a peril. Others, however, thought that he had confidence in the present situation and estimated the future correctly, not offering Darius in case of defeat an excuse to pluck up courage again for another attempt, by laying the blame this time upon darkness and night, as he had before upon mountains, defiles, and sea.[1]

> 1. Cf. Arrian, *Anabasis* 3.10, where it is Parmenio who advises a night attack.

285 *Alexander Rebukes His Favorites for Their Extravagant Life Styles*
Plutarch, Alexander 40.1–3

He [Alexander] saw that his favorites had grown altogether luxurious, and were vulgar in the extravagance of their ways of living. For instance, Hagnon the Teian used to wear silver nails in his boots; Leonnatus had dust for his gymnastic exercises brought to him on many camels from Egypt; Philotas had hunting-nets a hundred furlongs long; when they took their exercise and their baths, more of them actually used myrrh than olive oil, and they had in their train masseurs and chamberlains. Alexander therefore chided them in gentle and reasonable fashion. He was amazed, he said, that after they had undergone so many and so great contests they did not remember that those who conquer by toil sleep more sweetly than those who are conquered by their toil, and did not see, from a comparison of their own lives with those of the Persians, that it is a very servile thing to be luxurious, but a very royal thing to toil. "And yet," said he, "how can a man take care of his own horse or furbish up his spear and helmet, if he is unaccustomed to using his hands on his own dear person? Know ye not," said he, "that the end and object of conquest is to avoid doing the same thing as the conquered?"

286a *Good Deeds of King Maligned*
Plutarch, Alexander 41.1–2 (1)

Alexander, then, in exercising himself and at the same time inciting others to deeds of valor, was wont to court danger; but his friends, whose wealth and magnificence now gave them a desire to live in luxury and idleness, were impatient of his long wanderings and military expeditions, and gradually went so far as to abuse him and speak ill of him. He, however, was very mildly disposed at first toward this treatment of himself, and used to say that it was the lot of a king to confer favors and be ill-spoken of therefor.

286b *Good Deeds of King Maligned*
Plutarch, Moralia, Sayings of Kings and Commanders III:181F (32)

Learning that he [Alexander] was being maligned by a certain man, he said, "It is kingly to be ill spoken of for doing good."[1]

> 1. An oft-repeated aphorism; cf. for example, Plutarch, *Pro Nobilitate* 19 (Bernardakis ed. 7.268); Epictetus, *Discourses* 4.6; Marcus Aurelius Antoninus 7.36.

286c *Good Deeds of King Maligned*
Diogenes Laertius, Lives of the Eminent Philosophers 6.3

Being told that Plato was abusing him, he [Antisthenes] remarked, "It is a royal privilege to do good and be ill spoken of."

286d *Good Deeds of King Maligned*
Dio Chrysostom 47.25

However that may be, some one[1] has said that being roundly abused, though doing kindly deeds, is also a mark of royalty.

> 1. Alexander the Great, according to Plutarch; Antisthenes, according to Marcus Aurelius.

287 *Pep Talk from Alexander to Macedonian Soldiers*
Plutarch, Alexander 47.1–3 (1–2)

Fearing that his Macedonians might tire of the rest of his expedition, he [Alexander] left the greater part of them in quarters, and while he had the best of them with him in Hyrcania, twenty thousand foot and three thousand horse, he addressed them, saying that at present they were seen by the Barbarians as in a dream, but that if they should merely throw Asia into confusion and then leave it they would be attacked by them as if they were women. However, he said, he allowed those who wished it to go away, calling them to witness that while he was winning the inhabited world for the Macedonians he had been left behind with his friends and those who were willing to continue the expedition. This is almost word for word what he wrote in his letter to Antipater, and he adds that after he had thus spoken all his hearers cried out to him to lead them to whatever part of the world he wished.

288   *Death of Philotas And Parmenio Worries Alexander's Friends*
Plutarch, Alexander 49.14–15 (7)

After Philotas had been put to death, Alexander sent at once into Media and dispatched Parmenio also, a man whose achievements with Philip had been many, and who was the only one of Alexander's older friends, or the principal one, to urge his crossing into Asia, and who, of the three sons that were his, had seen two killed on the expedition before this, and was now put to death along with the third. These actions made Alexander an object of fear to many of his friends, and particularly to Antipater, who sent secretly to the Aetolians and entered into an alliance with them. For the Aetolians also were in fear of Alexander, because they had destroyed the city of the Oeniadae, and because Alexander, on learning of it, had said that it would not be the sons of the Oeniadae, but he himself who would punish the Aetolians.

289   *Alexander Bemoans His Inability to Swim*
Plutarch, Alexander 58.6 (4)

And at another time, when his Macedonians hesitated to advance upon the citadel called Nysa because there was a deep river in front of it, Alexander, halting on the bank, cried: "Most miserable man that I am, why, pray, have I not learned to swim?" and at once, carrying his shield, he would have tried to cross.

290a   *Artaxerxes Buys Victory*
Plutarch, Artaxerxes 20.3–4

Artaxerxes considered how he must carry on the war with Agesilaus, and sent Timocreon the Rhodian into Greece with a great sum of money, bidding him use it for the corruption of the most influential men in the cities there, and for stirring up the Greeks to make war upon Sparta. Timocrates did as he was bidden, the most important cities conspired together against Sparta, Peloponnesus was in a turmoil, and the Spartan magistrates summoned Agesilaus home from Asia. It was at this time, as we are told, and as he was going home, that Agesilaus said to his friends; "The king has driven me out of Asia with thirty thousand archers"; for the Persian coin has the figure of an archer stamped upon it.

290b   *Artaxerxes Buys Victory*
Plutarch Agesilaus 15.6

Persian coins were stamped with the figure of an archer, and Agesilaus said, as he was breaking camp, that the King was driving him out of Asia with ten thousand "archers"; for so much money had been sent to Athens and Thebes and distributed among the popular leaders there, and as a consequence those peoples made war upon the Spartans.[1]

1. Agesilaus followed "the very route taken by the Great King when he invaded Hellas" (Xenophon, *Hellenica* 4.2.8).

291 *Brutus Wants Much*
Plutarch, Brutus 6.7

And it is said that Caesar, when he first heard Brutus speak in public, said to his friends: "I know not what this young man wants, but all that he wants he wants very much."

292 *Brutus Wins Praetorship*
Plutarch, Brutus 7.4

But others say that this rivalry [between Brutus and Cassius for the praetorship of the city] was the work of Caesar, who secretly favored the hopes of each until, thus induced and incited, they entered into competition with one another. Brutus, however, made the contest supported only by his fair fame and his virtue, as against many brilliant and spirited exploits of Cassius in the Parthian War. But Caesar, after hearing the claims of each, said, in council with his friends: "Cassius makes the juster plea, but Brutus must have the first praetorship."

293 *The Capture of Lucilius*
Plutarch, Brutus 50.1–8

Now there was a certain Lucilius, a brave man, among the comrades of Brutus. This man, seeing some barbarian horsemen ignoring all others in their pursuit and riding impetuously after Brutus, determined at the risk of his life to stop them. So falling behind a little, he told them that he was Brutus. The Barbarians believed him because he asked them to conduct him to Antony, pretending to be afraid of Octavius but to have no fear of Antony. They were delighted with their unexpected prize, and thinking themselves amazingly fortunate, led Lucilius along in the darkness which had now fallen, after sending ahead some messages to Antony. Antony himself was pleased, of course, and set out to meet the escort, and all the rest also who learned that Brutus was being brought in alive flocked together, some thinking him to be pitied for his misfortune, others that he was unworthy of his fame in thus allowing his love of life to make him a prey of Barbarians. When they were near, however, Antony paused, at a loss to know how he ought to receive Brutus; but Lucilius, as he was brought forward, said with great boldness: "Marcus Brutus, O Antony, no foe has taken or can take; may fortune not so far prevail over virtue! Nay, he will be found living or possibly even lying dead as becomes him. It is by cheating these soldiers of thine that I am come, and I am ready to suffer for it any fatal penalty." When Lucilius had thus spoken and all were in amazement, Antony turned to his conductors and said: "I suppose, my fellow soldiers, you are vexed at your mistake and think that you have been flouted; but be assured that you have taken a better prey than that you sought. For you sought an enemy, but you come bringing me a friend. Since, by the gods, I know not how I could have treated Brutus, had he come into my hands alive; but such men as this I would have my friends rather than my enemies."

294 *First Rather Than Second*
Plutarch, Caesar 11.3–4 (2)

We are told that, as he [Caesar] was crossing the Alps and passing by a barbarian village which had very few inhabitants and was a sorry sight, his companions asked with mirth and laughter, "Can it be that here too there are ambitious strifes for office, struggles for primacy, and mutual jealousies of powerful men?" Whereupon Caesar said to them in all seriousness, "I would rather be first here than second in Rome."

295a *No Brilliant Success*
Plutarch, Caesar 11.5–6 (3)

In like manner we are told again that, in Spain, when he [Caesar] was at leisure and was reading from the history of Alexander, he was lost in thought for a long time, and then burst into tears. His friends were astonished, and asked the reason for his tears. "Do you not think," said he, "it is a matter for sorrow that while Alexander, at my age, was already king of so many peoples, I have as yet achieved no brilliant success?"[1]

> 1. Suetonius, *Lives of the Caesars*, Julius 1.7.1–2 and Dio Cassius 37.52.2 connect this anecdote more properly with Caesar's quaestorship in Spain (67 B.C.E.), when he was thirty-three years of age, the age at which Alexander died.

295b *Julius Destined to Rule*
Suetonius, Lives of the Caesars, Julius 1.7.1–2

As quaestor it fell to his [Julius'] lot to serve in Farther Spain. When he was there, while making the circuit of the assize-towns, to hold court under commission from the praetor, he came to Gades, and noticing a statue of Alexander the Great in the temple of Hercules, he heaved a sigh, and as if out of patience with his own incapacity in having as yet done nothing noteworthy at a time of life when Alexander had already brought the world to his feet, he straightway asked for his discharge, to grasp the first opportunity for greater enterprises at Rome. Furthermore, when he was dismayed by a dream the following night (for he thought that he had offered violence to his mother) the soothsayers inspired him with high hopes by their interpretation, which was: that he was destined to rule the world, since the mother whom he had seen in his power was none other than the earth, which is regarded as the common parent of all mankind.

296 *On Ill-Breeding*
Plutarch, Caesar 17.9–10 (5–6)

When the host who was entertaining him in Mediolanum, Valerius Leo, served up asparagus dressed with myrrh instead of olive oil, Caesar ate of it without ado, and rebuked his friends when they showed displeasure. "Surely," said he, "it were enough not to eat what you don't like; but he who finds fault with ill-breeding like this is ill-bred himself."

297 *Necessities to Weakest*
Plutarch, Caesar 17.11 (6)

Once, too, upon a journey, he [Caesar] and his followers were driven by a storm into a poor man's hut, and when he found that it consisted of one room only, and that one barely able to accommodate a single person, he said to his friends that honors must be yielded to the strongest, but necessities to the weakest, and bade Oppius lie down there, while he himself with the rest of his company slept in the porch.

298 Charge on Foot

Plutarch, Caesar 18.2–3 (2)

The Tigurini were crushed at the river Arar, not by Caesar himself, but by Labienus, his deputy; the Helvetii, however, unexpectedly attacked Caesar himself on the march, as he was leading his forces towards a friendly city, but he succeeded in reaching a strong place of refuge. Here, after he had collected and arrayed his forces, a horse was brought to him. "This horse," said he, "I will use for the pursuit after my victory; but now let us go against the enemy," and accordingly led the charge on foot.

299a Caesar Crosses Rubicon

Plutarch, Caesar 32.5–6 (4–6)

He [Caesar] himself mounted one of the hired carts and drove at first along another road, then turned towards Ariminum. When he came to the river which separates Cisalpine Gaul from the rest of Italy (it is called the Rubicon), and began to reflect, now that he drew nearer to the fearful step and was agitated by the magnitude of his ventures, he checked his speed. Then, halting in his course, he communed with himself a long time in silence as his resolution wavered back and forth, and his purpose then suffered change after change. For a long time, too, he discussed his perplexities with his friends who were present, among whom was Asinius Pollio, estimating the great evils for all mankind which would follow their passage of the river, and the wide fame of it which they would leave to posterity. But finally, with a sort of passion, as if abandoning calculation and casting himself upon the future, and uttering the phrase with which men usually prelude their plunge into desperate and daring fortunes, "Let the die be cast," he hastened to cross the river; and going at full speed now for the rest of the time, before daybreak he dashed into Ariminum and took possession of it.

299b Caesar Crosses Rubicon

Plutarch, Moralia, Sayings of Romans III:206C (7)

And he [Caesar] crossed the river Rubicon from his province in Gaul against Pompey, saying before all, "Let the die be cast."[1]

> 1. Cf. Suetonius, *Lives of the Caesars*, *Julius* 1.32.1 "*iacta alea est*" or "*esto.*" The expression seems to have been proverbial; cf. Leutsch and Schneidewin, *Paroemiographi Graeci*, 1.383 and the references; Aristophanes, *Fragment* 673 T. Kock, *Comicorum Atticorum Fragmenta* 1.557 and Menander, *Fragment* 65, ibid. 3.22.

299c Caesar Crosses Rubicon

Plutarch, Pompey 60.2

When he [Caesar] was come to the river Rubicon, which was the boundary of the province allotted to him, he stood in silence and delayed to cross, reasoning with himself, of course, upon the magnitude of his adventure. Then, like one who casts himself from a precipice into a yawning abyss, he closed the eyes of reason, and put a veil between them and his peril, and calling out in Greek to the bystanders these words only, "Let the die be cast," he set his army across.

299d Caesar Crosses Rubicon

Suetonius, Lives of the Caesars, Julius 1.32.1

As he [Julius] stood in doubt, this sign was given him. On a sudden there appeared hard by a being of wondrous stature and beauty, who sat and played upon a reed; and when not only the shepherds flocked to hear him, but many of the soldiers left their posts, and among them some of the trumpeters, the apparition snatched a trumpet from one of them, rushed to the river, and sounding the war-note with mighty blast, strode to the opposite bank. Then Caesar cried: "Take we the course which the signs of the gods and the false dealing of our foes point out. The die is cast," said he.

300 *Caesar at Appollonia*
Plutarch, Caesar 38.1–7 (1–4)

At Apollonia, since the force which he had with him was not a match for the enemy and the delay of his troops on the other side caused him perplexity and distress, Caesar conceived the dangerous plan of embarking in a twelve-oared boat, without anyone's knowledge, and going over to Brundisium, though the sea was encompassed by such large armaments of the enemy. At night, accordingly, after disguising himself in the dress of a slave, he went on board, threw himself down as one of no account, and kept quiet. While the river Aoüs was carrying the boat down towards the sea, the early morning breeze, which at that time usually made the mouth of the river calm by driving back the waves, was quelled by a strong wind which blew from the sea during the night; the river therefore chafed against the inflow of the sea and the opposition of its billows, and was rough, being beaten back with a great din and violent eddies, so that it was impossible for the master of the boat to force his way along. He therefore ordered the sailors to come about in order to retrace his course. But Caesar, perceiving this, disclosed himself, took the master of the boat by the hand, who was terrified at the sight of him, and said: "Come, good man, be bold and fear naught; thou carryest Caesar and Caesar's fortune in thy boat." The sailors forgot the storm, and laying to their oars, tried with all alacrity to force their way down the river. But since it was impossible, after taking much water and running great hazard at the mouth of the river, Caesar very reluctantly suffered the captain to put about. When he came back, his soldiers met him in throngs, finding much fault and sore displeased with him because he did not believe that even with them alone he was able to conquer, but was troubled, and risked his life for the sake of the absent as though distrusting those who were present.

301a *No Victor in Command*
Plutarch, Caesar 39.4–8 (3–5)

There were constant skirmishings about the fortifications of Pompey, and in all of them Caesar got the better except one, where there was a great rout of his men and he was in danger of losing his camp. For when Pompey attacked, not one of Caesar's men stood his ground, but the moats were filled with the slain, and others were falling at their own ramparts and walls, whither they had been driven in headlong flight. And though Caesar met the fugitives and tried to turn them back, he availed nothing, nay, when he tried to lay hold of the standards the bearers threw them away, so that the enemy captured thirty-two of them. Caesar himself, too, narrowly escaped being killed. For as a tall and sturdy man was running away past him, he laid his hand upon him and bade him stay and face about upon the enemy; and the fellow, full of panic at the threatening danger, raised his sword to smite Caesar, but before he could do so Caesar's shield-bearer lopped off his arm at the shoulder. So completely had Caesar given up his cause for lost that, when

Pompey, either from excessive caution or by some chance, did not follow up his great success, but withdrew after he had shut up the fugitives within their entrenchments, Caesar said to his friends as he left them: "Today victory had been with the enemy, if they had had a victor in command."

301b *No Victor in Command*
Plutarch, Pompey 65.5

Once he [Caesar] narrowly escaped being utterly crushed and losing his army, for Pompey made a brilliant fight and at last routed Caesar's whole force and killed two thousand of them. He did not, however, force his way into their camp with the fugitives, either because he could not, or because he feared to do so, and this led Caesar to say to his friends: "Today victory would have been with the enemy if they had had a victor in command."

302 *Pompey Flees*
Plutarch, Caesar 45.7–8 (4–5)

When Pompey, on the other wing, saw his horsemen scattered in flight, he was no longer the same man, nor remembered that he was Pompey the Great, but more like one whom Heaven has robbed of his wits than anything else, he went off without a word to his tent, sat down there, and awaited what was to come, until his forces were all routed and the enemy were assailing his ramparts and fighting with their defenders. Then he came to his senses, as it were, and with this one ejaculation, as they say, "What, even to my quarters?" took off his fighting and general's dress, put on one suitable for a fugitive, and stole away.

303a *Condemned if Dismissed Army*
Plutarch, Caesar 46.1

But Caesar, when he reached Pompey's ramparts and saw those of the enemy who were already lying dead there and those who were still falling, said·with a groan: "They would have it so; they brought me to such a pass that if I, Caius Caesar, after waging successfully the greatest wars, had dismissed my forces, I should have been condemned in their courts."

303b *Condemned if Dismissed Army*
Suetonius, Lives of the Caesars, Julius 1.30.4

[This is] the assertion of Asinius Pollio, that when Caesar at the battle of Pharsalus saw his enemies slain or in flight, he said, word for word: "They would have it so. Even I, Gaius Caesar, after so many great deeds, should have been found guilty, if I had not turned to my army for help."

304a *Caesar Sets Up Statues*
Plutarch, Caesar 57.6–7 (4)

The statues of Pompey, too, which had been thrown down, he [Caesar] would not suffer to remain so, but set them up again, at which Cicero said that in setting up Pompey's statues Caesar firmly fixed his own. When his friends thought it best that he should have a bodyguard, and many of them volunteered for this service, he would not consent, saying that it was better to die once for all than to be always expecting death.

304b   *Caesar Sets Up Statues*
Plutarch, Cicero 40.4–5 (4)

Of this sort is what he said about the statues of Pompey. These Caesar ordered to be set up again after they had been thrown down and taken away; and they were set up again. What Cicero said was that by this act of generosity Caesar did indeed set up the statues of Pompey, but firmly planted his own also.

305a   *Pale Ones*
Plutarch, Caesar 62.9 (5)

Moreover, Caesar actually suspected him [Cassius], so that he once said to his friends: "What, think ye, doth Cassius want? I like him not over much, for he is much too pale."

305b   *Pale Ones*
Plutarch, Caesar 62.10 (5)

And again, we are told that when Antony and Dolabella were accused to him of plotting revolution, Caesar said: "I am not much in fear of these fat, long-haired fellows, but rather of those pale, thin ones," meaning Brutus and Cassius.

306   *The Best Death*
Plutarch, Caesar 63.7 (4)

Moreover, on the day before, when Marcus Lepidus was entertaining him at supper, Caesar chanced to be signing letters, as his custom was, while reclining at table, and the discourse turned suddenly upon the question what sort of death was the best; before any one else could answer Caesar cried out: "That which is unexpected."

307   *Two Cowardly Armies*
Plutarch, Caius Marius 33.3

And at another time, when the enemy had given him [Marius] an opportunity to attack them, but the Romans had played the coward, and both sides had withdrawn, he called an assembly of his soldiers and said to them: "I do not know whether to call the enemy or you the greater cowards; for they were not able to see your backs, nor you their napes."

308   *Cato Tested*
Plutarch, Cato the Younger 2.1–4

While Cato was still a boy, the Italian allies of the Romans were making efforts to obtain Roman citizenship. One of their number, Pompaedius Silo, a man of experience in war and of the highest position, was a friend of Drusus, and lodged at his house for several days. During this time he became familiar with the children, and said to them once: "Come beg your uncle to help us in our struggle for citizenship." Caepio, accordingly, consented with a smile, but Cato made no reply and gazed fixedly and fiercely upon the strangers. Then Pompaedius said: "But thou, young man, what sayest thou to us? Canst thou not take the part of the strangers with thy uncle, like thy brother?" And when Cato said not a word but by his silence and the look on his face seemed to refuse the request, Pompaedius lifted him up through a window, as if he would cast him out, and ordered him to consent, or he would throw him down, at the same time making the tone of his voice harsher, and frequently shaking the boy as he held his body out at the window. But when Cato had endured his treatment for a long time without showing fright or fear, Pompaedius put him down, saying quietly to his friends: "What a piece of good fortune it is for Italy that he is a boy; for if he were a man, I do not think we could get a single vote among the people."[1]

1. The story is told also in Valerius Maximus 3.1.2.

309 Love Of Command Lives amid Destruction
Plutarch, Cato the Younger 65.1–2

After this discourse to the three hundred, he [Cato] withdrew; and on learning that Caesar with all his army was already on the march, "Aha!" he said, "he thinks we are men!" Then turning to the senators he bade them not delay, but save themselves while the horsemen were still there. He also closed the other gates of the city, and stationing himself at the one leading to the sea, he assigned transports to those under his command, and tried to keep things in order, stopping deeds of wrong, quelling tumults, and supplying stores to those who were destitute. And when Marcus Octavius with two legions encamped near by and sent to Cato demanding that he come to terms with him about the command in the province, Cato would make no reply to him, but said to his friends: "Can we wonder that our cause is lost, when we see that the love of command abides with us though we are standing on the brink of destruction."

310 Cicero, Vatinius, and Crassus
Plutarch, Cicero 26.1–3 (1–2)

When Crassus was about to set out for Syria, wishing that Cicero should be a friend rather than an enemy, he said to him in a friendly manner that he wished to dine with him; and Cicero readily received him into his house. But a few days afterwards, when some friends interceded with him for Vatinius, saying that the man sought reconciliation and friendship (for he was an enemy), "It surely cannot be," said Cicero, "that Vatinius also wishes to dine with me." Such, then, was his treatment of Crassus.

311 Lucius Cotta the Censor
Plutarch, Cicero 27.3–4 (2)

Again, Lucius Cotta, who held the office of censor, was very fond of wine, and Cicero, when canvassing for the consulship, was thirsty, and as his friends stood about him while he drank, said: "You have good reason to fear that the censor will deal harshly with me—for drinking water."

312 Cicero a Philosopher
Plutarch, Cicero 32.6 (4–5)

And yet he [Cicero] often asked his friends not to call him an orator, but a philosopher, because he had chosen philosophy as an occupation, but used oratory merely as an instrument for attaining the needful ends of a political career.

313 *Cleomenes Exhorts Army*
Plutarch, Cleomenes 4.5

He [Cleomenes] would often remind them [the army] of one of their ancient kings who said, and not idly either, "The Lacedaemonians are wont to ask, not how many, but where, their enemies are."

314 *Veterans Desire More Land*
Plutarch, Crassus 2.8

Far different was the opinion of Marius, who said, after distributing to each of his veterans fourteen acres of land and discovering that they desired more, "May no Roman ever think that land too small which suffices to maintain him."

315a *Phocion Chops Speeches*
Plutarch, Demosthenes 10.4–5 (2–3)

Indeed, we are told that even Demosthenes himself, whenever Phocion mounted the bema to reply to him, would say to his intimates: "Here comes the chopper of my speeches." Now it is not clear whether Demosthenes had this feeling towards Phocion because of his oratory, or because of his life and reputation, believing that a single word or nod from a man who is trusted has more power than very many long periods.

315b *Phocion Chops Speeches*
Plutarch, Phocion 5.3–4

Indeed, it is said that once upon a time, when the theater was filling up with people, Phocion himself was walking about behind the scenes lost in thought, and that when one of his friends remarked: "You seem to be considering, Phocion," he replied: "Yes, indeed, I am considering whether I can shorten the speech which I am to deliver to the Athenians." And Demosthenes, who held the other orators in great contempt, when Phocion rose to speak, was wont to say quietly to his friends: "Here comes the pruning knife of my speeches." But perhaps this must be referred to Phocion's character; since a word or a nod merely from a good man is of more convincing weight than any number of elaborate periods.

315c *Demosthenes, Demades and Phocion*
Plutarch, Demosthenes 10.2–3 (1–2)

And Ariston the Chian records an opinion which Theophrastus also passed upon the two orators. When he was asked, namely, what sort of an orator he thought Demosthenes was, he replied: "Worthy of the city"; and what Demades, "Too good for the city." And the same philosopher tells us that Polyeuctus the Sphettian, one of the political leaders of that time at Athens, declared that Demosthenes was the greatest orator, but Phocion the most influential speaker; since he expressed most sense in the fewest words.

316 *Visit to Ptoeodorus*
Plutarch, Dion 17.9–10

And it is related that Dion once went to pay a visit to Ptoeodorus the Megarian, upon his invitation. Now Ptoeodorus, it would seem, was one of the wealthy and influential men of the city; and when, therefore, Dion saw a crowd of people at his door, and a press of business, which made him difficult of access and hard to come at, he turned to his friends, who were vexed and indignant at it, and said: "Why should we blame this man? For we ourselves used to do just so in Syracuse."

317   *Plato and Dionysius*
Plutarch, Dion 19.4–8

After the first acts of kindness, however, Plato introduced the subject of Dion, and then there were postponements at first on the part of Dionysius, and afterwards faultfindings and disagreements. These were unnoticed by outsiders, since Dionysius tried to conceal them, and sought by the rest of his kind attentions and honorable treatment to draw Plato away from his goodwill towards Dion. And even Plato himself did not at first reveal the tyrant's perfidy and falsehood, but bore with it and dissembled his resentment. But while matters stood thus between them, and no one knew of it, as they supposed, Helicon of Cyzicus, one of Plato's intimates, predicted an eclipse of the sun. This took place as he had predicted, in consequence of which he was admired by the tyrant and presented with a talent of silver. Thereupon Aristippus, jesting with the rest of the philosophers, said that he himself also could predict something strange. And when they besought him to tell what it was, "Well, then," said he, "I predict that before long Plato and Dionysius will become enemies." At last Dionysius sold the estate of Dion and appropriated the money, and removing Plato from his lodging in the palace guard, put him in charge of his mercenaries, who had long hated the philosopher and sought to kill him, on the ground that he was trying to persuade Dionysius to renounce the tyranny and live without a bodyguard.

318   *No Fetters for Eumenes*
Plutarch, Eumenes 9.6

And it is said that when Menander bore witness of these things to Antigonus, and the Macedonians began to praise Eumenes and felt more kindly towards him, because, when it was in his power to enslave their children and outrage their wives, he had spared them and let them go. Antigonus said: "Nay, my good men, that fellow did not let them go out of regard for you, but because he was afraid to put such fetters on himself in his flight."

319   *A Litter Arrayed against Antigonus*
Plutarch, Eumenes 15.1–2

Now Antigonus, hearing from his prisoners that Eumenes was sick and in such wretched plight as to be borne along in a litter, thought it no great task to crush the other commanders if Eumenes was sick. He therefore hastened to lead his army to battle. But when, as the enemy were forming in battle order, he had ridden past their lines and observed their shape and disposition, he was amazed, and paused for some time; then the litter was seen as it was carried from one wing to the other. At this, Antigonus gave a loud laugh, as was his wont, and after saying to his friends, "This litter, it would seem, is what is arrayed against us," immediately retired with his forces and pitched his camp.

320   *Cloud Bursts*
Plutarch, Fabius Maximus 12.4

It is said that as Hannibal withdrew, he addressed to his friends some such pleasantry as this about Fabius: "Verily, did I not often prophesy to you that the cloud which we saw hovering above the heights would one day burst upon us in a drenching and furious storm?"

321   *Horsemen Dismount*
Plutarch, Fabius Maximus 16.4

It is said, further, that a strange calamity befell the Roman cavalry also. The horse of Paulus, as it appears, was wounded and threw his rider off, and one after another of his attendants dismounted and sought to defend the consul on foot. When the horsemen saw this, supposing that a general order had been given, they all dismounted and engaged the enemy on foot. On seeing this, Hannibal said: "This is more to my wish than if they had been handed over to me in fetters."[1]

1. Livy 22.49.

322   *Hannibal Loses Tarentum*
Plutarch, Fabius Maximus 23.1

It is said that Hannibal had got within five miles of Tarentum when it fell, and that openly he merely remarked: "It appears, then, that the Romans have another Hannibal, for we have lost Tarentum even as we took it"; but that in private he was then for the first time led to confess to his friends that he had long seen the difficulty, and now saw the impossibility of their mastering Italy with their present forces.

323   *Nearer Things Reserved for Victors*
Plutarch, Lucullus 24.6–8

Accordingly, he [Lucullus] took advantage of his opportunity and put his troops across, and a favorable sign accompanied his crossing. Heifers pasture there which are sacred to Persia Artemis, a goddess whom the Barbarians on the further side of the Euphrates hold in the highest honor. These heifers are used only for sacrifice, and at other times are left to roam about the country at large, with brands upon them in the shape of the torch of the goddess. Nor is it a slight or easy matter to catch any of them when they are wanted. One of these heifers, after the army had crossed the Euphrates, came to a certain rock which is deemed sacred to the goddess, and stood upon it, and lowering its head without any compulsion from the usual rope, offered itself to Lucullus for sacrifice. He also sacrificed a bull to the Euphrates, in acknowledgment of his safe passage. Then, after encamping there during that day, on the next and the succeeding days he advanced through Sophene. He wrought no harm to the inhabitants, who came to meet him and received his army gladly. Nay, when his soldiers wanted to take a certain fortress which was thought to contain much wealth, "Yonder lies the fortress which we must rather bring low," said he, pointing to the Taurus in the distance; "these nearer things are reserved for the victors."

324   *Lucullus to Make Day Lucky*
Plutarch, Lucullus 27.7

As Lucullus was about to cross the river, some of his officers advised him to beware of the day, which was one of the unlucky days—the Romans call them "black days." For on that day Caepio and his army perished in the battle with the Cimbri.[1] But Lucullus answered with the memorable words: "Verily, I will make this day, too, a lucky one for the Romans."

> 1. The sixth of October, B.C.E. 105. Cf. Plutarch, *Camillus* 19.7.

325   *Hares Sleep on Walls*
Plutarch, Lysander 22.2

And once when the Corinthians had revolted, and, on coming to their walls, he [Lysander] saw that the Lacedaemonians hesitated to make an assault, a hare was seen leaping across the moat; whereupon he said: "Are ye not ashamed to fear enemies who are so lazy that hares sleep on their walls?"

326a   *Two Pups*
Plutarch, Moralia, The Education of Children I:3A–B

Lycurgus, lawgiver of the Spartans, took two puppies of the same litter, and reared them in quite different ways, so that from the one he produced a mischievous and greedy cur, and from the other a dog able to follow a scent and to hunt. And then at a time when the Spartans were gathered together, he said, "Men of Sparta, of a truth habit and training and teaching and guidance in living are a great influence toward engendering excellence, and I will make this evident to you at once." Thereupon producing the two dogs, he let them loose, putting down directly in front of them a dish of food and a hare. The one dog rushed after the hare, and the other made for the dish. While the Spartans were as yet unable to make out what import he gave to this, and with what intent he was exhibiting the dogs, he said, "These dogs are both of the same litter, but they have received a different bringing-up, with the result that the one has turned out a glutton and the other a hunter."

326b   *Two Pups*
Plutarch, Moralia, Sayings of Spartans III:225F, 226A–B

Lycurgus, the lawgiver, wishing to recall the citizens from the mode of living then existent, and to lead them to a more sober and temperate order of life, and to render then good and honorable men (for they were living a soft life), reared two puppies of the same litter; and one he accustomed to dainty food, and allowed it to stay in the house; the other he took afield and trained in hunting. Later he brought them into the public assembly and put down some bones and dainty food and let loose a hare. Each of the dogs made for that to which it was accustomed, and, when the one of them had overpowered the hare, he said, "You see, fellow-citizens, that these dogs belong to the same stock, but by virtue of the discipline to which they have been subjected they have turned out utterly different from each other, and you also see that training is more effective than Nature for good."

327   *Pyrrho on Indifference*
Plutarch, Moralia, Progress in Virtue I:82F

And the story about Pyrrho is that when he was on a voyage, and in peril during a storm, he pointed to a little pig contentedly feeding upon some barley which had been spilled near by, and said to his companions that a similar indifference must be acquired from reason and philosophy by the man who does not wish to be disturbed by anything that may befall him.

328a   *Leave Room for Cake*
Plutarch, Moralia, Advice about Keeping Well II:123E–F

It was in this wise: A man had invited Philip to dinner in the country, assuming that he had but a few with him, but when later the host saw Philip bringing a great company, no great preparations having been made, he was much perturbed. Philip, becoming aware of the situation, sent word privately to each of his friends to "leave room for cake." They, following the advice, and looking for more to come, ate sparingly of what was before them, and so the dinner was ample for all. In this manner, then, we ought to prepare ourselves in anticipation of our imperative round of social engagements by keeping room in the body for elaborate dishes and pastry, and, I dare to say it, for indulgence in strong drink also, by bringing to these things an appetite fresh and willing.

328b   *Leave Room for Cake*
Plutarch, Moralia, Sayings of Kings and Commanders III:178D–E (20)

Once when he [Philip] was on the march, and was invited to dinner by a man of the land, he took a good many persons with him; and when he saw that his host was much perturbed, since the preparations that had been made were inadequate, he sent word in advance to each of his friends, and told them to "leave room for cake." They took his advice and, expecting more to follow, did not eat much, and thus there was enough for all.

328c   *Leave Room for Cake*
Plutarch, Moralia, Table-Talk 7 IX:707B (1)

He [Philip] came with a large number, but dinner had not been prepared for so many; so, seeing that his host was embarrassed, he passed the word quietly to his friends to "save room for cake." Looking forward to this, they ate sparingly of what lay before them, and in this way there was enough for everyone.

329   *Water Thrown*
Plutarch, Moralia, Sayings of Kings and Commanders III:177B (5)

When somebody had thrown water upon him [Archelaus], and he was incited by his friends against the man, he said, "But it was not upon me that he threw it, but upon the man he thought me to be."

330a   *Living to Suit Asses*
Plutarch, Moralia, Sayings of Kings and Commanders III:178A (13)

When he [Philip] was about to pitch his camp in an excellent place, he learned that there was no grass for the pack-animals. "What a life is ours," he said, "if we must live to suit the convenience of the asses!"[1]

1. Cf. Eunapius, Fragment 56 in Dindorf, *Historici Graeci Minores* 1.249.

330b   *Living to Suit Asses*
Plutarch, Moralia, Old Men in Public Affairs X:790B (11)

And Philip, we are told, when he heard, as he was on the point of encamping in a suitable place, that there was no fodder for the beasts of draught, exclaimed: "O Hercules, what a life is mine, if I must needs live to suit the convenience even of my asses!"

331a   *Antipater Awake*
Plutarch, Moralia, Sayings of Kings and Commanders III:179B (27)

Once on a campaign he [Philip] slept for an unusually long time, and later, when he arose, he said, "I slept safely, for Antipater was awake."

331b   *Antipater Sober*
Athenaeus, Deipnosophists 10.435D

When Philip made up his mind to get drunk, he used to say, "Now we must drink; for it is enough that Antipater is sober."

332   *More Kingly to Enrich*
Plutarch, Moralia, Sayings of Kings and Commanders III:181F (34)

Ptolemy,[1] son of Lagus, used, as a rule, to dine and sleep at his friends' houses; and if ever he gave a dinner, he would send for their dishes and linen and tables, and use them for the occasion. He himself owned no more than were required for everyday use; and he used to say that it was more kingly to enrich than to be rich.[2]

> 1. Ptolemy Soter, king of Egypt, 323–285 (or 283) B.C.E.
> 2. Cf. Aelian, *Varia Historia* 13.13.

333   *Antigonus Replaces Drinkers with Ballplayers*
Plutarch, Moralia, Sayings of Kings and Commanders III:182A (2)

Seeing some of his soldiers playing ball in their breastplates and helmets, he [Antigonus[1]] was much pleased and sent for their officers, wishing to commend them. But when he heard that they were engaged in drinking, he gave their positions to their soldiers.

> 1. The "One-Eyed"; one of Alexander's generals; ruler in Asia Minor, 323–301 B.C.E.

334a   *Mouse Saves Life*
Plutarch, Moralia, Sayings of Kings and Commanders III:190B

Brasidas[1] caught a mouse among some dry figs, and, getting bitten, let it go. Then, turning to those who were present, he said, "There is nothing so small that it cannot save its life, if it has the courage to defend itself against those who would lay hand on it."

> 1. Spartan general in Peloponnesian War.

334b   *Mouse Saves Life*
Plutarch, Moralia, Sayings of Spartans III:208F (9)

At another time he saw a mouse being dragged from a hole by a boy who had hold of him, and the mouse turned and bit the hand that held him and escaped; whereupon Agesilaus called the attention of the bystanders to this, and said, "When the smallest animal thus defends itself against those who do it wrong, consider what it becomes men to do."

334c *Mouse Saves Life*
Plutarch, Moralia, Progress in Virtue I:79E (8)

Brasidas caught a mouse among some dried figs, got bitten, and let it go; thereupon he said to himself, "Heavens, there is nothing so small or weak that it will not save its life if it has courage to defend itself."

334d *Mouse Saves Life*
Plutarch, Moralia, Sayings of Spartans III:219C (1)

Brasidas caught a mouse among some figs, and when he got bitten, let it go. Then, turning to those who were present, he said, "There is nothing so small that it does not save its life if it has the courage to defend itself against those who would lay hand on it."

335a *Agis Outnumbered*
Plutarch, Moralia, Sayings of Kings and Commanders III:190C (2)

At Mantineia, when efforts were made to dissuade him [Agis[1]] from risking a battle with the enemy who outnumbered his own men, he said, "He who would rule over many must fight with many."

> 1. Son of Archidamus. There were two kings of Sparta of this name: Agis II, 427–401 B.C.E., and Agis III, 338–331 B.C.E., and there is some confusion as to which said which!

335b *Agesilaus Outnumbered*
Plutarch, Moralia, Sayings of Spartans III:215D (4)

When, at Mantineia, he [Agesilaus] was not permitted to risk a decisive battle with the enemy, who outnumbered his men, he said, "He who would rule over many must fight with many."

336 *Indulgence Chastised*
Plutarch, Moralia, Sayings of Kings and Commanders III:193A–B (11)

It was his [Epameinondas'] habit to appear at all times with a well-groomed body and a cheerful countenance, but on the day after that battle [in which he defeated the Spartans at Leuctra] he went forth unwashed and with a look of dejection. When his friends asked if anything distressing had befallen him, he said, "Nothing; but yesterday I found myself feeling a pride greater than is well. Therefore today I am chastising my immoderate indulgence in rejoicing."

337 *Blind Wealth*
Plutarch, Moralia, Sayings of Spartans III:226E–F (5)

Having made wealth unenviable, since nobody could make any use or show of it, he [Lycurgus] said to his intimate friends, "What a good thing it is, my friends, to show in actual practice the true characteristic of wealth, that it is blind!"[1]

> 1. Plutarch amplifies this account in his *Lycurgus* 10.2–3 (45 C).

338 *Eumenes Pretends Craterus Is Neoptolemus*
Plutarch, Moralia, Concerning Talkativeness VI:506D–E

And Eumenes,[1] when he heard that Craterus was advancing, told none of his friends, but pretended that it was Neoptolemus. For his soldiers despised Neoptolemus, but both respected the reputation of Craterus and admired his valor. No one else knew the truth, and they joined battle, won the victory, killed Craterus without knowing it, and only recognized him when he was dead. So successfully did silence maneuver the contest and keep hidden so formidable an opponent that his friends admired Eumenes for not forewarning them rather than blamed him. And even if some do blame you, it is better that men should criticize you when they are already saved through mistrust than that they should accuse you when they are being destroyed because you did trust them.

1. Cf. Plutarch, *Eumenes* 6.4–7.8 (586 Bff.).

339   *Young Enemy Commands Macedonians*
Plutarch, Philopoemen 6.6–7

After his victory, therefore, Antigonus put his Macedonians to the question, and asked them why, without his orders, they had brought the cavalry into action. They defended themselves by saying that they had been forced against their will to attack the enemy, because a young man of Megapolis had first led a charge against them. At this Antigonus gave a laugh and said: "Well, then, that young man behaved like a great commander."

340   *Approval a Bad Sign?*
Plutarch, Phocion 8.3

And when, as he [Phocion] was once delivering an opinion to the people, he met with their approval, and saw that all alike had accepted his argument, he turned to his friends and said: "Can it possibly be that I am making a bad argument without knowing it?"

341   *Phocion Aids Adversaries*
Plutarch, Phocion 10.4

Phocion, then, wrought no injury to any one of his fellow citizens out of enmity, nor did he regard any one of them as his enemy; but he was harsh, obstinate and inexorable only so far as was necessary to struggle successfully against those who opposed his efforts in behalf of the country, and in other relations of life showed himself well-disposed to all, accessible, and humane, so that he gave aid to his adversaries when they were in trouble or danger of being brought to account. When his friends chided him for pleading the cause of some worthless man, he said that good men needed no aid.

342   *Aristogeiton in Prison*
Plutarch, Phocion 10.5

Again when Aristogeiton the public informer, who was under condemnation, sent and asked him [Phocion] to come to him, he obeyed the summons and set out for the prison; and when his friends sought to prevent him, he said: "Let me go, my good men; for where could one take greater pleasure in meeting Aristogeiton?"

343   *Justice Reversed*
Plutarch, Phocion 24.2

Again, when the Athenians were bent on making an expedition against the Boeotians, at first he [Phocion] opposed it; and when his friends told him that he would be put to death by the Athenians if he offended them, "That will be unjust," said he, "if I act for their advantage; but if I play them false, it will be just."

344   *Many Generals, Few Soldiers*
Plutarch, Phocion 25.1

However, when their seacoast was being devastated by Micion, who landed at Rhamnus with a horde of Macedonians and mercenaries and overran the adjacent territory, Phocion led the Athenians out against him. And as they marched, men would run up to their general from all sides and show him what to do. He was advised to seize a hill here, to send his horsemen around thither, or to make his attack upon the enemy there. "O, Heracles," said Phocion, "how many generals I see, and how few soldiers."

345   *Roman Discipline Surprising*
Plutarch, Pyrrhus 16.4–5

When he [Pyrrhus] learned that the Romans were near and lay encamped on the further side of the river Siris, he rode up to the river to get a view of them; and when he had observed their discipline, the appointment of their watches, their order, and the general arrangement of their camp, he was amazed, and said to the friend who was nearest him: "The discipline of these Barbarians is not barbarous; but the result will show us what it amounts to."

346   *Sicily a Wrestling Ground*
Plutarch, Pyrrhus 23.6

And it is said that at the time of his departure he [Pyrrhus] looked back at the island [Sicily] and said to those about him: "My friends, what a wrestling ground for Carthaginians and Romans we are leaving behind us!"

347   *The Old Woman and the Boy*
Plutarch, Sertorius 19.2–6

Now, the battle on the Sucro[1] is said to have been precipitated by Pompey, in order that Metellus might not share in the victory. Sertorius, too, wished to fight the issue out with Pompey before Metellus came up, and therefore drew out his forces when evening was already at hand, and began the engagement, thinking that, since his enemies were strangers and unacquainted with the region, darkness would be a hindrance to them either in flight or in pursuit. When the fighting was at close quarters, it happened that Sertorius was not himself engaged with Pompey at first, but with Afranius, who commanded Pompey's left, while Sertorius himself was stationed on the right. Hearing, however, that those of his men who were engaged with Pompey were yielding before his onset and being worsted, he put his right wing in command of other generals, and hastened himself to the help of the wing that was suffering defeat. Those of his men who were already in retreat he rallied, those who were still keeping their ranks he encouraged, then charged anew upon Pompey, who was pursuing, and put his men to a great rout, in which Pompey also came near being killed, was actually wounded, and had a marvelous escape. For the Libyans with Sertorius, after getting Pompey's horse, which had golden decorations and was covered with costly trappings, were so busy distributing the booty and quarrelling with one another over it, that they neglected the pursuit. Afranius, however, as soon as Sertorius had gone off to the other wing with aid and succor, routed his opponents and drove them headlong into their camp; and dashing in with the fugitives, it being now dark, he began to plunder, knowing nothing of Pompey's flight and having no power to keep his soldiers from their pillaging. But meanwhile Sertorius came back from his victory on the other wing, and falling upon the straggling and confused soldiers of Afranius, slew great numbers of them. In the morning, moreover, he armed his troops and came out for battle; then learning that Metellus was near, he broke up his array and decamped, saying: "But as for this boy, if that old woman had not come up, I should have given him a sound beating and sent him back to Rome."

1. Cf. Plutarch, *Pompey* 19.

348   *No Way Down from Tyranny*
Plutarch, Solon 14.5

To his friends he [Solon] said, as we are told, that a tyranny was a lovely place, but there was no way down from it.

349a   *Ajax Falls on Sponge*
Suetonius, Lives of the Caesars, Augustus 2.85.2

Though he [Augustus] began a tragedy with much enthusiasm, he destroyed it because his style did not satisfy him, and when some of his friends asked him what in the world had become of Ajax, he answered that "his Ajax had fallen on his sponge."

349b   *Ajax Falls On Sponge*
Macrobius, Saturnalia 2.4.2

He [Augustus] had written a tragedy entitled *Ajax* but, dissatisfied with it, had rubbed it out. And, when the tragedian Lucius Varius asked him afterward how his Ajax was getting on, he replied: "He has fallen on his sponge."

350   *Caligula Claims Victory*
Suetonius, Lives of the Caesars, Caligula 4.46.1

Finally, as if he [Caligula] intended to bring the war to an end, he drew up a line of battle on the shore of the Ocean, arranging his ballistas[1] and other artillery; and when no one knew or could imagine what he was going to do, he suddenly bade them gather shells and fill their helmets and the folds of their gowns, calling them "spoils from the Ocean, due to the Capitol and Palatine." As a monument of his victory he erected a lofty tower, from which lights were to shine at night to guide the course of ships, as from the Pharos.[2] Then, promising the soldiers a gratuity of a hundred denarii each, as if he had shown unprecedented liberality, he said, "Go your way happy; go your way rich."

1. The ballista cast stones.
2. The lighthouse at Alexandria.

351   *Caesar Reaches the Rubicon*
Suetonius, Lives of the Caesars, Julius 1.31.2

It was not until after sunset that he [Julius] set out very secretly with a small company, taking the mules from a bakeshop nearby and harnessing them to a carriage; and when his lights went out and he lost his way, he was astray for some time, but at last found a guide at dawn and got back to the road on foot by narrow bypaths. Then, overtaking his cohorts at the river Rubicon, which was the boundary of his province, he paused for a while, and realising what a step he was taking, he turned to those about him and said: "Even yet we may draw back; but once cross yon little bridge, and the whole issue is with the sword."

352   *Caesar Attacks Pompey in Spain*
Suetonius, Lives of the Caesars, Julius 1.34.2

After vainly trying by every kind of hindrance to prevent their sailing, he [Julius] marched off to Rome, and after calling the senate together to discuss public business, went to attack Pompey's strongest forces, which were in Spain under command of three of his lieutenants—Marcus Petreius, Lucius Afranius, and Marcus Varro—saying to his friends before he left, "I go to meet an army without a leader, and I shall return to meet a leader without an army."

353   *Caesar Exaggerates Danger*
Suetonius, Lives of the Caesars, Julius 1.66.1

When they were in a panic through reports about the enemy's numbers, he [Julius] used to rouse their courage not by denying or discounting the rumors, but by falsely exaggerating the true danger. For instance, when the anticipation of Juba's coming filled them with terror, he called the soldiers together and said: "Let me tell you that within the next few days the king will be here with ten legions, thirty thousand horsemen, a hundred thousand light-armed troops, and three hundred elephants. Therefore some of you may as well cease to ask further questions or make surmises and may rather believe me, since I know all about it. Otherwise, I shall surely have them shipped on some worn-out craft and carried off to whatever lands the wind may blow them."

354   *Nero Tires of Octavia*
Suetonius, Lives of the Caesars, Nero 6.35.1

He [Nero] soon grew tired of living with Octavia, and when his friends took him to task, replied that "she ought to be content with the insignia of wifehood."

355   *Titus Loses Day*
Suetonius, Lives of the Caesars, Titus 8.8.1

On another occasion, remembering at dinner that he [Titus] had done nothing for anybody all that day, he gave utterance to that memorable and praiseworthy remark: "Friends, I have lost a day."

356   *Light Given*
Suetonius, Lives of the Caesars, Vitellius 7.8.2

He [Vitellius] did not return to headquarters until the dining-room caught fire from the stove and was ablaze; and then, when all were shocked and troubled at what seemed a bad omen, he said: "Be of good cheer; to us light is given."

357   *Sweet Odor of Corpses*
Suetonius, Lives of the Caesars, Vitellius 7.10.3

When he [Vitellius] came to the plains where the battle was fought and some shuddered with horror at the moldering corpses, he had the audacity to encourage them by the abominable saying, that the odor of a dead enemy was sweet and that of a fellow-citizen sweeter still.

358 *Lizard Bites Ben Dosa*
Tosefta, Berakhot 3:20

They said about R. Haninah b. Dosa that he was praying when a lizard bit him; however, he did not stop praying. His students went and found it dead. They said: "Woe to the man whom a lizard bites; woe to the lizard that bites Ben Dosa."

359 *Critias Has Feelings of a Pig for Euthydemus*
Xenophon, Memorabilia 1.2.29–30

Nevertheless, although he [Socrates] was himself free from vice, if he saw and approved of base conduct in them, he would be open to censure. Well, when he found that Critias loved Euthydemus[1] and wanted to lead him astray, he tried to restrain him by saying that it was mean and unbecoming in a gentleman to sue like a beggar to the object of his affection, whose good opinion he coveted, stooping to ask a favor that it was wrong to grant. As Critias paid no heed whatever to this protest, Socrates, it is said, exclaimed in the presence of Euthydemus and many others, "Critias seems to have the feelings of a pig: he can no more keep away from Euthydemus than pigs can help rubbing themselves against stones."

    1. Xenophon, *Memorabilia* 4.2.1.

360 *Self-Control at Dinners*
Xenophon, Memorabilia 1.3.6–7

Whenever he [Socrates] accepted an invitation to dinner, he resisted without difficulty the common temptation to exceed the limit of satiety; and he advised those who could not do likewise to avoid appetizers that encouraged them to eat and drink what they did not want: for such trash was the ruin of stomach and brain and soul. "I believe," he said in jest, "it was by providing a feast of such things that Circe made swine; and it was partly by the prompting of Hermes,[1] partly through his own self-restraint and avoidance of excessive indulgence in such things, that Odysseus was not turned into a pig."

    1. Homer, *Odyssey* 10.281f.

361 *On Sensual Passion*
Xenophon, Memorabilia 1.3.8

Of sensual passion he [Socrates] would say: "Avoid it resolutely: it is not easy to control yourself once you meddle with that sort of thing."

362 *Best Road to Glory*
Xenophon, Memorabilia 1.7.1

For he [Socrates] always said that the best road to glory is the way that makes a man as good as he wishes to be thought.

A group of associates or friends is present or referred to in the stories listed below, but some other feature has determined their location in another section.

Frontinus: 69, 71, 1195
Gellius: 1201, 1467
Gospel: 76a, 76b, 76c, 77a, 78d, 79a, 229b, 250c, 1203a, 1213b, 1224
Hadith: 96
Papyrus Oxyrhynchus: 838
Phaedrus: 1247

Philostratus: 25, 27, 120, 867
Plutarch: 41, 128, 164, 905, 912a, 947, 966, 1119, 1290
Sifra: 1366
Suetonius: 647

Adult: Family

In the ancient world, as in the modern world, members of a family were often rivals. Although conflict in these stories is common, these tales also reveal touching moments of love, admiration, and forgiveness between and among siblings and parents. Both the agony of sorrow and the joy of celebration leap off the page and cross the centuries.

363 Aedesius Reveres His Father
Eunapius, Lives of the Philosophers 461

Aedesius the Cappadocian succeeded to the school of Iamblichus and his circle of disciples. He was extremely well born, but his family was not possessed of great wealth, and therefore his father sent him away from Cappadocia to Greece to educate himself with a view to making money, thinking that he would find a treasure in his son. But on his return, when he discovered that he was inclined to philosophy, he drove him out of his house as useless.[1] And as he drove him forth he asked: "Why, what good does philosophy do you?" Whereupon his son turned round and replied: "It is no small thing, Father, to have learned to revere one's father even when he is driving one forth." When his father heard this, he called his son back and expressed his approval of his virtuous character.

> 1. A similar story is told of an unnamed youth by Aelian, Fragment 1038, and it may be imitated here by Eunapius.

364 Advantage Too Expensive
Frontinus, Stratagems 4.6.1

Quintus Fabius,[1] upon being urged by his son to seize an advantageous position at the expense of losing a few men, asked: "Do you want to be one of those few?"

> 1. Quintus Fabius Maximus Cunctator. Cf. Silius Italicus 7.539ff.

365 Fight from Necessity or Opportunity
Gellius, Attic Nights 13.3.6

I have written this with regard to the lack of distinction between these two words [*necessitudo* and *necessitas*] as the result of reading the fourth book of the *History* of Sempronius Asellio, an early writer, in which he wrote as follows about Publius Africanus, the son of Paulus: "For he had heard his father, Lucius Aemilius Paulus, say that a really able general never engaged in a pitched battle, unless the utmost necessity [*necessitudo*] demanded, or the most favorable opportunity offered."

366 Jesus Remains in Galilee
Gospel, John 7:1–9 (NIV)

After this, Jesus went around in Galilee, purposely staying away from Judea because the Jews there were waiting to take his life. But when the Jewish Feast of

Tabernacles was near, Jesus' brothers said to him, "You ought to leave here and go to Judea, so that your disciples may see the miracles you do. No one who wants to become a public figure acts in secret. Since you are doing these things, show yourself to the world." For even his own brothers did not believe in him.

Therefore Jesus told them, "The right time for me has not yet come: for you any time is right. The world cannot hate you, but it hates me because I testify that what it does is evil. You go to the Feast. I am not yet going up to this Feast, because for me the right time has not yet come." Having said this, he stayed in Galilee.

367 The Beelzebul Controversy
Gospel, Mark 3:19b–35 (NIV)

Then Jesus entered a house, and again a crowd gathered, so that he and his disciples were not even able to eat. When his family heard about this, they went to take charge of him, for they said, "He is out of his mind." And the teachers of the law who came down from Jerusalem said, "He is possessed by Beelzebub! By the prince of demons he is driving out demons."

So Jesus called them and spoke to them in parables: "How can Satan drive out Satan? If a kingdom is divided against itself that kingdom cannot stand. If a house is divided against itself, that house cannot stand. And if Satan opposes himself and is divided, he cannot stand; his end has come. In fact, no one can enter a strong man's house and carry off his possesions unless he ties up the strong man. Then he can rob his house. I tell you the truth, all the sins and blasphemies of men will be forgiven them. But whoever blasphemes against the Holy Spirit will never be forgiven; he is guilty of an eternal sin." He said this because they were saying, "He has an evil spirit."

Then Jesus' mother and brothers arrived. Standing outside, they sent someone in to call him. A crowd was sitting around him, and they told him, "Your mother and brothers are outside looking for you." "Who are my mother and my brothers?" he asked. Then he looked at those seated in a circle around him and said, "Here are my mother and my brothers! Whoever does God's will is my brother and sister and mother."

368 Son-In-Law Buckled to Sword
Macrobius, Saturnalia 2.3.3

Seeing his son-in-law Lentulus (who was a very short man) wearing a long sword, he [Cicero] said: "Who has buckled my son-in-law to that sword?"

369 Half Greater Than Whole
Macrobius, Saturnalia 2.3.4

He [Cicero] did not spare even his brother Quintus but was just as sarcastic about him, for on seeing, in the province which Quintus had governed, a half-length portrait of him, painted as usual on a shield and very much larger than life, he remarked (since Quintus was a small man): "With my brother it would seem that the half is greater than the whole."

370 Obligation to Recite Shema
Mishnah, Berakhot 1:1

One time [R. Gamaliel]'s sons returned [after midnight] from a wedding feast. They said to him: "We have not yet recited the Shema." He said to them: "If the morning star has not risen, you [still] are obligated to recite it."

371   *Mnestheus Thinks More of Mother Than of Father*
Nepos 11, Iphicrates 3.4

He [Iphicrates] left a son—Mnestheus, the offspring of a Thracian woman, the daughter of King Cotus.[1] When Mnestheus was once asked whether he thought more of his father or of his mother, he answered: "My mother." When everyone expressed surprise at his reply, he added: "I have good reason for that; for my father did everything in his power to make me a Thracian; my mother, on the contrary, made me an Athenian."

> 1. Cotys (Cotyis) is the proper form of the name.

372   *Brother and Sister*
Phaedrus, Aesopic Fables 3.8

Be warned by this lesson and examine yourself often. A certain man had a very ugly daughter, and also a son remarkable for the beauty of his features. These two, while at their childish play, happened to look into a mirror which had been placed on their mother's boudoir chair. The boy made much of his own good looks; the girl was angry and could not bear the quips of her proud brother, construing everything he said—what else would you expect?—as a reproach against herself. Accordingly, she ran off to her father, bent on getting back at her brother. Full of malice, she pressed her charge against the boy, that he, though a male, had been meddling with something that belongs only to women. The father took both in his arms and, as he kissed them, sharing his warm love between the two, he said: "I want you both to use the mirror every day; you, that you may not spoil your beauty by the vices of profligacy; you, that you may overcome by virtuous qualities the handicap of your looks."

373   *Dardanian Children Spared from Slavery by Drowning*
Philo, Every Good Man Is Free 115

There is also the story of the Dardanian women taken prisoners by the Macedonians, how holding slavery to be the worst disgrace, they threw the children which they were nurturing into the deepest part of the river, exclaiming, "You at least shall not be slaves, but ere you have begun your life of misery shall cut short your destined span and pass still free along the final road which all must tread."

374   *Porus Loses and Wins*
Philostratus, Life of Apollonius 2.21

And after the battle, in which his [Porus'] conduct struck Alexander as divine and superhuman, when one of his relations said to him: "If you had only paid homage to him after he had crossed, O Porus, you would not yourself have been defeated in battle, nor would so many Indians have lost their lives, nor would you yourself have been wounded," he said: "I knew from report that Alexander was so fond of glory that, if I did homage to him, he would regard me as a slave, but if I fought him, as a king. And I much preferred his admiration to his pity, nor was I wrong in my calculation. For by showing myself to be such a man as Alexander found me, I both lost and won everything in one day."

375   *The Pedigree of Braduas*
Philostratus, Lives of the Sophists 2.1 (555)

A charge of murder was also brought against Herodes, and it was made up in this way. His wife Regilla, it was said, was in the eighth month of her pregnancy, and Herodes ordered his freedman Alcimedon to beat her for some slight fault, and the woman died in premature childbirth from a blow in the belly. On these grounds, as though true, Regilla's brother Braduas brought a suit against him for murder. He was a very illustrious man of consular rank, and the outward sign of his high birth, a crescent-shaped ivory buckle, was attached to his sandal. And when Braduas appeared before the Roman tribunal he brought no convincing proof of the charge that he was making, but delivered a long panegyric on himself dealing with his own family. Whereupon Herodes jested at his expense and said, "You have your pedigree on your toe-joints."[1]

1. I.e., there was no need to talk about it.

376 Braduas Cites Benefactions
Philostratus, Lives of the Sophists 2.1 (555–556)
And when his accuser [Braduas] boasted too of his benefactions to one of the cities of Italy, Herodes said with great dignity, "I too could have recited many such actions of my own in whatever part of the earth I were now being tried."

377 Proclus and Son
Philostratus, Lives of the Sophists 2.21 (603)
He [Proclus of Naucratis] had a son who dissipated his fortune in breeding fighting-cocks, quails, dogs, puppies, and horses, but instead of rebuking him he used to join him in these youthful pursuits. And when many people blamed him for this, he said, "He will stop playing with old men sooner than he will with those of his own age."

378 Quirinus Faces Death of Son
Philostratus, Lives of the Sophists 2.29 (621)
When his relatives tried to console him [Quirinus] for the death of his son, he said, "When, if not now, shall I prove myself a man?"

379 Olympias' Concern over Alexander's Generosity
Plutarch, Alexander 39.7 (4–5)
What lofty airs his [Alexander's] friends and bodyguards were wont to display over the wealth bestowed by him, is plain from a letter which Olympias wrote to him. She says: "I beg thee to find other ways of conferring favors on those thou lovest and holdest in honor; as it is, thou makest them all the equals of kings and providest them with an abundance of friends, whilst thyself thou strippest bare."

380 Alexander Bears Patiently Olympias' Advice
Plutarch, Alexander 39.12 (7)
To his mother, also, he [Alexander] sent many presents, but would not suffer her to meddle in affairs nor interfere in his campaigns; and when she chided him for this, he bore her harshness patiently.

381 Parmenio Rebukes Philotas for Showing Off
Plutarch, Alexander 48.3 (2)
However, he [Philotas] displayed a pride of spirit, an abundance of wealth, and a care of the person and mode of life which were too offensive for a private man, and at this time particularly his imitation of majesty and loftiness was not successful at

all, but clumsy, spurious, and devoid of grace, so that he incurred suspicion and envy, and even Parmenio once said to him: "My son, pray be less of a personage."

382   *Olympias and Cleopatra Divide Antipater's Realm*
Plutarch, Alexander 68.3–5 (2–5)

In a word, restlessness and a desire for change spread everywhere. For even against Antipater, Olympias and Cleopatra had raised a faction, and had divided his realm[1] between them, Olympias taking Epirus, and Cleopatra Macedonia. When he heard of this, Alexander said that his mother had made the better choice; for the Macedonians would not submit to be reigned over by a woman.

> 1. During Alexander's campaign in the East Antipater was governor of Macedonia and 'general of Europe.'

383   *The Revenge of Parysatis*
Plutarch, Artaxerxes 17.1–5

And now there was one mark left for the vengeance of Parysatis—the man who had cut off the head and right hand of Cyrus, Masabetes, an eunuch of the king...So, one day, finding Artaxerxes trying to amuse himself in a vacant hour, she challenged him to play at dice for a thousand darics, allowed him to win the game, and paid the money down. Then, pretending to be chagrined at her loss and to seek revenge, she challenged the king to play a second game, with an eunuch for the stake, and the king consented. They agreed that both might reserve five of their most trusty eunuchs, but that from the rest the loser must give whichever one the winner might select, and on these conditions played their game. Parysatis took the matter much to heart and was in great earnest with her playing, and since the dice also fell in her favor, she won the game, and selected Masabates; for he was not among those who had been excepted. And before the king suspected her design, she put the eunuch in the hands of the executioners, who were ordered to flay him alive, to set up his body slantwise on three stakes, and to nail his skin to the fourth. This was done, and when the king was bitterly incensed at her, she said to him, with a mocking laugh: "What a blessed simpleton thou art, to be incensed on account of a wretched old eunuch, when I, who have diced away a thousand darics, accept my loss without a word."

384   *Porcia Superior to Pain*
Plutarch, Brutus 13.3–10

Porcia, as has been said, was a daughter of Cato, and when Brutus, who was her cousin, took her to wife, she was not a virgin; she was however, still very young, and had by her deceased husband a little son whose name was Bibulus. A small book containing memoirs of Brutus was written by him, and is still extant. Porcia, being of an affectionate nature, fond of her husband, and full of sensible pride, did not try to question her husband about his secrets until she had put herself to the following test. She took a little knife, such as barbers use to cut the fingernails, and after banishing all her attendants from her chamber, made a deep gash in her thigh, so that there was a copious flow of blood, and after a little while violent pains and chills and fever followed from the wound. Seeing that Brutus was disturbed and greatly distressed, in the height of her anguish she spoke to him thus: "Brutus, I am Cato's daughter, and I was brought into thy house, not, like a mere concubine, to share thy bed and board merely, but to be a partner in thy joys, and a partner in thy troubles. Thou indeed, art faultless as a husband; but how can I show thee any grateful service if I am to share neither thy secret sufferings nor the anxiety which craves a loyal confidant? I know that woman's nature is thought too weak to endure a secret; but good rearing and excellent companionship go far towards strengthening the character, and it is my happy lot to be both the daughter of Cato and the wife of Brutus. Before this I put less confidence in these advantages, but now I know that I am superior even to pain."

385   Either Pontifex Maximus or Exile
Plutarch, Caesar 7.3

The day for the election came, and as Caesar's mother accompanied him to the door in tears, he kissed her and said: "Mother, today thou shalt see thy son either pontifex maximus or an exile."

386   Tiberius Appears to Caius in Dream
Plutarch, Caius Gracchus 1.6

And Cicero the orator also relates that Caius declined all office and had chosen to live a quiet life, but that his brother appeared to him in a dream and addressed him, saying: "Why, pray, dost thou hesitate, Caius? There is no escape; one life is fated for us both, and one death as champions of the people."

387   Mother Becomes Hostage
Plutarch, Cleomenes 22.3–4

Now, Ptolemy the king of Egypt promised him [Cleomenes] aid and assistance, but demanded his mother and his children as hostages. For a long time, therefore, he was ashamed to tell his mother, and though he often went to her and was at the very point of letting her know, he held his peace, so that she on her part became suspicious and inquired of his friends whether there was not something which he wished to impart to her but hesitated to do so. Finally, when Cleomenes plucked up courage to speak of the matter, his mother burst into a hearty laugh and said: "Was this the thing which thou wast often of a mind to tell me but lost thy courage? Make haste, put me on board a vessel and send this frail body wheresoever thou thinkest it will be of most use to Sparta, before old age destroys it sitting idly here."

388   Kissing Lamia
Plutarch, Demetrius 19.4

And we are told that once, after Lamia was known of all men to be in complete control of Demetrius, he came home from abroad and greeted his father with a kiss, whereupon Antigonus said with a laugh, "One would think, my son, that thou wert kissing Lamia."

389   Demetrius Revels
Plutarch, Demetrius 19.4

Again, on another occasion, when Demetrius had been at his revels for several days, and excused his absence by saying that he was troubled with a flux, "So I learned," said Antigonus, "but was it Thasian or Chian wine that flowed?"

390   Fever Leaves
Plutarch, Demetrius 19.5

And again, learning that the son was sick, Antigonus was going to see him, and met a certain beauty at his door; he went in, however, sat down by his son, and felt his pulse. "The fever has left me now," said Demetrius. "No doubt, my boy," said Antigonus, "I met it just now at the door as it was going away."

391 *Philip in Narrow Quarters*
Plutarch, Demetrius 23.3–4

And yet on one occasion when his [Demetrius'] father understood that his brother Philip was quartered in a house occupied by three young women, he said not a word to Philip himself, but in his presence said to the quartermaster whom he had summoned, "See here, wilt thou not remove my son from his narrow quarters?"

392 *No Rations for Dead*
Plutarch, Demetrius 40.1–2

But Pyrrhus now overran Thessaly and was seen as far south as Thermopylae; Demetrius therefore left Antigonus to conduct the siege of Thebes, and himself set out against this new foe. Pyrrhus, however, made a swift retreat, whereupon Demetrius stationed ten thousand men-at-arms and a thousand horsemen in Thessaly and once more devoted himself to Thebes. Here he brought up against the city his famous City-taker, but this was so laboriously and slowly propelled, owing to its weight and great size, that in the space of two months it hardly had advanced two furlongs. Besides, the Boeotians made a stout resistance and Demetrius many times, out of contumacy rather than from need, forced his soldiers to risk their lives in battle. Antigonus saw that they were falling in great numbers, and in great concern said: "Why, my father, should we suffer these lives to be squandered without any necessity for it?" But Demetrius was incensed, and said: "Why, pray, art thou disturbed at this? Are rations due from thee to the dead?"

393 *Polyxenus Leaves Wife Behind*
Plutarch, Dion 21.7–8

When, therefore, Polyxenus was moved by fear to run away and go into exile from Sicily, the tyrant sent for his sister and upbraided her because she had been privy to her husband's flight and had not told her brother about it. But she, without consternation, and, indeed, without fear, replied: "Dost thou think me, Dionysius, such a mean and cowardly wife that, had I known beforehand of my husband's flight, I would not have sailed off with him and shared his fortunes? Indeed, I did not know about it; since it would have been well for me to be called the wife of Polyxenus the exile, rather than the sister of Dionysius the tyrant."

394 *King Theopompus Rebuts Wife*
Plutarch, Lycurgus 7.2

This king [Theopompus], they say, on being reviled by his wife because the royal power, when he handed it over to his sons, would be less than when he received it, said: "Nay, but greater, in that it will last longer."

395 *Aristippus Charges for Education*
Plutarch, Moralia, The Education of Children I:4F–5A

Many fathers, however, go so far in their devotion to money as well as in animosity toward their chidren, that in order to avoid paying a larger fee, they select as teachers for their children men who are not worth any wage at all—looking for ignorance, which is cheap enough. Wherefore Aristippus not inelegantly, in fact very cleverly, rebuked a father who was devoid both of mind and sense. For when a man asked him what fee he should require for teaching his child, Aristippus replied, "A thousand drachmas"; but when the other exclaimed, "Great Heavens! what an excessive demand! I can buy a slave for a thousand," Aristippus retorted, "Then you will have two slaves, your son and the one you buy."

396a   *Nothing Makes Horse Fat as King's Eye*
Plutarch, Moralia, The Education of Children I:9D

It is right to rebuke some fathers who, after entrusting their sons to attendants and masters, do not themselves take cognizance at all of their instruction by means of their own eyes or their own ears. Herein they most fail in their duty; for they ought themselves every few days to test their children, and not rest their hopes upon the disposition of a hired person; for even those persons will devote more attention to the children if they know they must from time to time render an account. And in this connection there is point as well as wit in the remark of the groom who said that nothing makes the horse so fat as the king's eye.[1]

396b   *Nothing Makes Horse Fat as King's Eye*
Xenophon, Oeconomicus 12.20

[Ischomachus]: "I like the answer that is attributed to the Persian. The king, you know, had happened on a good horse, and wanted to fatten him as speedily as possible. So he asked one who was reputed clever with horses what is the quickest way of fattening a horse. 'The master's eye,' replied the man. I think we may apply the answer generally, Socrates, and say that the master's eye in the main does the good and worthy work."

397   *Son of Despot*
Plutarch, Moralia, Sayings of Kings and Commanders III:175E (3)

Learning that his son, to whom he [Dionysius the Elder] was intending to bequeath his empire, had debauched the wife of a free citizen, he asked the young man, with some heat, what act of his father's he knew of like that! And when the youth answered, "None, for you did not have a despot for a father." "Nor will you have a son," was the reply, "unless you stop doing this sort of thing."

398   *Peisistratus Gives Daughter to Thrasybulus*
Plutarch, Moralia, Sayings of Kings and Commanders III:189C (3)

When Thrasybulus, who was in love with the daughter of Peisistratus,[1] kissed her one day on meeting her, Peisistratus, when incited by his wife against the man, said, "If we hate them that love us, what shall we do to them that hate us?" And thereupon he gave the maiden as wife to Thrasybulus.[2]

> 1. Ruler of Athens, at times between 560 and 528 B.C.E.
> 2. Cf. Valerius Maximus 5.1, externa 2.

399a   *Lesson of the Javelins*
Plutarch, Moralia, Concerning Talkativeness VI:511C–D

And Scilurus, king of the Scythians, left behind him eighty sons; when he was dying, he asked for a bundle of spear-shafts and bade his sons take it and break it in pieces, tied closely together as the shafts were. When they gave up the task, he himself drew all the spears out one by one and easily broke them in two, thus revealing that the harmony and concord of his sons was a strong and invincible thing, but that their disunion would be weak and unstable.

399b *Lesson of the Javelins*
Plutarch, Moralia, Sayings of Kings and Commanders III:174F

Scilurus,[1] who left eighty sons surviving him, when he was at the point of death handed a bundle of javelins to each son in turn and bade him break it. After they had all given up, he took out the javelins one by one and easily broke them all, thereby teaching the young men that, if they stood together, they would continue strong, but that they would be weak if they fell out and quarreled.

> 1. King of the Scythians, second or first century B.C.E.

400 *Celebration to Ruin Victory?*
Plutarch, Phocion 20.1–3

When Phocus his son wished to compete at the Panathenaic festival as a vaulting rider of horses, Phocion permitted it, not because he was ambitious for the victory, but in order that care and training of the body might make his son a better man; for in general the youth was fond of wine and irregular in his habits. The youth was victorious, and many asked him to their houses for the victor's banquet; but Phocion declined the other invitations and granted the coveted honor to one host only. And when he went to the banquet and saw the general magnificence of the preparations, and particularly the foot-basins of spiced wine that were brought to the guests as they entered, he called his son and said: "Phocus, do not let thy companion ruin thy victory."

401 *Justice before Family*
Plutarch, Phocion 22.3

However, when Charicles was brought to trial for his dealings with Harpalus, and begged Phocion to help him and go with him into the court-room, Phocion refused, saying: "I made thee my son-in-law, Charicles, for none but just purposes."

402 *The Marriage of Demeas*
Plutarch, Phocion 30.3

Again, when he [Demades] was bringing home a wife for his son Demeas, he said to him: "When I married thy mother, my son, not even a neighbor noticed it; but to thy nuptials kings and potentates are contributing."

403 *Kingdom for Sharpest Son*
Plutarch, Pyrrhus 9.2

It is said, for instance, that when he [Pyrrhus] was asked by one of them [his sons], who was still a boy, to whom he would leave his kingdom, he replied: "To that one of you who keeps his sword the sharpest."

404a *The Powerful Boy*
Plutarch, Themistocles 18.5

Of his son, who lorded it over his mother, and through her over himself, he [Themistocles] said, jestingly, that the boy was the most powerful of all the Hellenes; for the Hellenes were commanded by the Athenians, the Athenians by himself, himself by the boy's mother, and the mother by her boy.

404b *The Powerful Boy*
Plutarch, Marcus Cato 8.3

This, however, is a translation from the sayings of Themistocles. He [Cato] finding himself much under his son's orders through the lad's mother, said: "Wife, the Athenians rule the Hellenes, I rule the Athenians, thou rulest me, and thy son thee. Therefore let him make sparing use of that authority which makes him, child though he is, the most powerful of the Hellenes."

405 *Undone Before*
Plutarch, Themistocles 29.7

And Themistocles himself, they say, now become great and courted by many, said to his children, when a splendid table was once set for him: "My children, we should now have been undone, had we not been undone before."

406 *Appius Betroths Daughter to Tiberius*
Plutarch, Tiberius Gracchus 4.1–2

For Appius, who had been consul and censor, had been made Dean of the Roman senate by virtue of his dignity, and in loftiness of spirit far surpassed his contemporaries, at a banquest of the augurs addressed Tiberius with words of friendship and asked him to become the husband of his daughter. Tiberius gladly accepted the invitation, and the betrothal was thus arranged, and when Appius returned home, from the doorway where he stood he called his wife and cried in a loud voice: "Antistia, I have betrothed our Claudia." And Antistia, in amazement, said: "Why so eager, or why so fast? If thou hadst only found Tiberius Gracchus for betrothal to her!"

407 *All The World Praises Lycurgus*
Plutarch, Titus Flaminius 12.4

Xenocrates the philosopher, as the story runs, was once being hauled away to prison by the tax-collectors for not having paid the alien's tax, but was rescued out of their hands by Lycurgus the orator, who also visited the officials with punishment for their impudence. Xenocrates afterwards met the sons of Lycurgus, and said: "My boys, I am making a noble return to your father for his kindness towards me; for all the world is praising him for what he did."

408 *Joseph Has Operation*
Sifra 94a

One time an ulcer formed on the leg of Joseph b. Pakas, and he asked the doctor to operate. He said to him: "Let me know when [you] finish the operation and [the leg] remains [hanging] as if by a hair." The doctor [finished the operation and] left [the leg hanging] as if by a hair, and he made this known to him. [Joseph] called to his son, Nahunyah. He said to him: "Hunyah, my son, until now you have been obligated to care for me. From now on, go away, for one does not defile [himself] by the limb of a living person, even his father's." And when the matter came before the sages, they said that it was said [about him]: "*There is a righteous man that perishes in his righteousness* (Qoh. 7:15), [which means] the righteous one is lost, and his righteousness [is lost] with him."

409   *Augustus Exalts Priests and Vestal Virgins*
Suetonius, Lives of the Caesars, Augustus 2.31.3

He [Augustus] increased the number and importance of the priests, and also their allowances and privileges, in particular those of the Vestal virgins. Moreover, when there was occasion to choose another Vestal in place of one who had died, and many used all their influence to avoid submitting their daughters to the hazard of the lot, he solemnly swore that if anyone of his granddaughters were of eligible age, he would have proposed her name.

410   *Augustus Recommends Water*
Suetonius, Lives of the Caesars, Augustus 2.42.1

But to show that he [Augustus] was a prince who desired the public welfare rather than popularity, when the people complained of the scarcity and high price of wine, he sharply rebuked them by saying: "My son-in-law Agrippa has taken good care, by building several aqueducts, that men shall not go thirsty."

411   *Augustus Shamed*
Suetonius, Lives of the Caesars, Augustus 2.65.2

He [Augustus] bore the death of his kin with far more resignation than their misconduct. For he was not greatly broken by the fate of Gaius and Lucius, but he informed the senate of his daughter's fall through a letter read in his absence by a quaestor, and for very shame would meet no one for a long time, and even thought of putting her to death. At all events, when one of her confidantes, a freedwoman called Phoebe, hanged herself at about that same time, he said: "I would rather have been Phoebe's father."

412   *Immobility of Caligula*
Suetonius, Lives of the Caesars, Caligula 4.29.1

He [Caligula] added to the enormity of his crimes by the brutality of his language. He used to say that there was nothing in his own character which he admired and approved more highly than what he called his "immobility,"[1] that is to say, his shameless impudence. When his grandmother Antonia gave him some advice, he was not satisfied merely not to listen but replied: "Remember that I have the right to do anything to anybody."

> 1. "Immobility" was a Stoic virtue. In Gaius this took the form of callous indifference to suffering and to public opinion.

413   *Antidote against Caesar*
Suetonius, Lives of the Caesars, Caligula 4.29.1–2

When he [Caligula] was on the point of killing his brother, and suspected that he had taken drugs as a precaution against poison, he cried: "What! an antidote against Caesar?"

414   *Caligula Threatens Sisters*
Suetonius, Lives of the Caesars, Caligula 4.29.2

After banishing his sisters, he made the threat that he [Caligula] not only had islands, but swords as well.

415a *Caligula's Women*
Suetonius, Lives of the Caesars, Caligula 4.33.1
Whenever he [Caligula] kissed the neck of his wife or sweetheart, he would say:
"Off comes this beautiful head whenever I give the word." He even used to
threaten now and then that he would resort to torture[1] if necessary, to find out from
his dear Caesonia why he loved her so passionately.

> 1. Literally, "the cords," as an instrument of torture.

415b *Tiberius Tortures*
Suetonius, Lives of the Caesars, Tiberius 3.62.3
At Capreae they still point out the scene of his executions, from which he
[Tiberius] used to order that those who had been condemned after long and
exquisite tortures be cast headlong into the sea before his eyes, while a band of
marines waited below for the bodies and broke their bones with boathooks and
oars, to prevent any breath of life from remaining in them. Among various forms of
torture he had devised this one: he would trick men into loading themselves with
copious draughts of wine, and then on a sudden tying up their private parts, would
torment them at the same time by the torture of the cords and of the stoppage of
their water. And had not death prevented him, and Thrasyllus, purposely it is said,
induced him to put off some things through hope of a longer life, it is believed that
still more would have perished, and that he would not even have spared the rest of
his grandsons; for he had his suspicions of Gaius and detested Tiberius as the fruit
of adultery. And this is highly probable, for he used at times to call Priam happy,
because he had outlived all his kindred.

416 *Claudius Meets Britannicus*
Suetonius, Lives of the Caesars, Claudius 5.43
Shortly afterwards meeting Britannicus, he [Claudius] hugged him close and
urged him to grow up and receive from his father an account of all that he had
done, adding in Greek, "He who dealt the wound will heal it."[1]

> 1. A proverbial expression, derived from the story of Telephus, who when wounded
> by Achilles was told by the oracle that he could be cured only by the one who dealt the
> blow. Achilles cured him by applying rust from his spear to the wound.

417 *Not Good Is a Number of Rulers*
Suetonius, Lives of the Caesars, Domitian 8.12.3
He [Domitian] was vexed that his brother's son-in-law had attendants clad in
white, as well as he, and uttered the words
"Not good is a number of rulers."[1]

> 1. Homer, *Iliad* 2.204.

418 *Julius Wins Election*
Suetonius, Lives of the Caesars, Julius 1.13.1
After giving up hope of the special commission, he [Julius] announced his
candidacy for the office of pontifex maximus, resorting to the most lavish bribery.
Thinking on the enormous debt which he had thus contracted, he is said to have
declared to his mother on the morning of the election, as she kissed him when he
was starting for the polls, that he would never return except as pontifex. And in fact
he so decisively defeated two very strong competitors (for they were greatly his

superiors in age and rank), that he polled more votes in their tribes than were cast for both of them in all the tribes.

419   *Nero Marries Boy*
Suetonius, Lives of the Caesars, Nero 6.28.1

He [Nero] castrated the boy Sporus and actually tried to make a woman of him; and he married him with all the usual ceremonies, including a dowry and a bridal veil, took him to his house attended by a great throng, and treated him as his wife. And the witty jest that someone made is still current, that it would have been well for the world if Nero's father Domitius had had that kind of wife.

420   *Nero Murders Aunt*
Suetonius, Lives of the Caesars, Nero 6.34.5

To matricide he [Nero] added the murder of his aunt. When he once visited her as she was confined to her bed from costiveness, and she, as old ladies will, stroking his downy beard (for he was already well grown) happened to say fondly: "As soon as I receive this,[1] I shall gladly die," he turned to those with him and said as if in jest: "I'll take it off at once." Then he bade the doctors give the sick woman an overdose of physic and seized her property before she was cold, suppressing her will, that nothing might escape him.

> 1. That is, "When I see you arrived at man's estate." The first shaving of the beard by a young Roman was a symbolic act, usually performed at the age of twenty-one with due ceremony; see Suetonius, *Lives of the Caesars*, Nero 6.12.3.

421   *Money from Urine*
Suetonius, Lives of the Caesars, Vespasian 8.23.3

When Titus found fault with him for contriving a tax upon public conveniences, he [Vespasian] held a piece of money from the first payment to his son's nose, asking whether its odor was offensive to him. When Titus said "No," he replied, "Yet it comes from urine."

422   *Spouse as Slave*
Testament, Job 21:1-4

And I spent forty-eight years sitting on the dung heap outside the city with the plague so that I saw, my children, with my own eyes my humiliated wife carrying water into the house of some disgraceful person as a maidservant until she could get bread and bring it to me. And I was stunned and said: "O the pretentiousness of the rulers of this city. I do not even consider them worthy to be my roving dogs. For how can they treat my spouse like a female slave?" And after this I adopted a rational composure.

A family member is present or referred to in the stories listed below, but some other feature has determined their location in another section.

Cicero: 502, 1396, 1423, 1075b
Diogenes Laertius: 61e, 1192
Epistle: 712
Frontinus: 690b
Gellius: 74
Gospel: 233a, 233b, 242b, 433, 434, 735, 737a

Adult: Women

Young girls and women were often objects of humor in antiquity. Nevertheless, in these anecdotes women also regularly display wit, wisdom, and courage that expose the frailties and follies of men.

423   Aphrodite and the Slave Girl
Babrius, Aesopic Fables 10

A certain man having fallen in love with an ugly and ill-natured slave girl, one of his own, was wont to give her everything she asked for without delay. And she, bedecked with golden ornaments and trailing a delicate crimson robe about her shanks, would take every occasion to quarrel with the mistress of the house. It was Aphrodite whom she regarded as the author of these blessings, and her she honored at night by the burning of love-lamps, and every day she sacrificed, made vows and supplications, asked for favors or advice, until at length the goddess came as the pair slept and appearing to the slave girl said: "Be not thankful unto me, as though I were making you beautiful; I'm angry with your bedfellow for thinking you beautiful."

424   Why Spartan Women Bore Sons
Cicero, Tusculan Disputations 1.42.102

I am quoting examples of men: of what temper, pray, was the Spartan woman? When she had sent her son to battle and heard the news of his death, "To that end," said she, "had I borne him, to be a man who should not hesitate to meet death for his country."

425   Pettiness of Demosthenes
Cicero, Tusculan Disputations 5.36.103

Will then obscurity, insignificance, unpopularity prevent the wise man from being happy? Beware lest the favor of the crowd and the glory we covet be more of a burden than a pleasure. Surely it was petty of my favorite Demosthenes to say he was delighted with the whispered remark of a poor woman carrying water, as is the custom in Greece, and whispering in her fellow's ear—"Here is the great Demosthenes!" What could be more petty? "Ah, but how consummate an orator!" Yes! but assuredly he had learnt how to speak before others, not to commune much with himself.

426   Pleasure in the Night
Cicero, Tusculan Disputations 5.38.112

For if night does not put a stop to happy life why should a day that resembles night stop it? For the remark of the Cyrenaic Antipater is, it is true, a bit coarse, but its purport is not pointless; when his womenfolk were bemoaning his blindness,

"What is the matter?" he said: "is it that you think there is no pleasure in the night?"

427 *Thales Cannot See What Is before His Feet*
Diogenes Laertius, Lives of the Eminent Philosophers 1.34

It is said that once, when he [Thales] was taken out of doors by an old woman in order that he might observe the stars, he fell into a ditch, and his cry for help drew from the old woman the retort, "How can you expect to know all about the heavens, Thales, when you cannot even see what is just before your feet?"

428 *Sosipatra Appears as Goddess*
Eunapius, Lives of the Philosophers 470

Now there was one Philometor, a kinsman of hers [Sosipatra], who, overcome by her beauty and eloquence, and recognizing the divinity of her nature, fell in love with her; and his passion possessed him and completely overmastered him. Not only was he completely conquered by it but she also felt its onslaught. So she said to Maximus, who was one of the most distinguished pupils of Aedesius and was moreover his kinsman: "Maximus, pray find out what ailment I have, that I may not be troubled by it." When he inquired: "Why, what ails you?" she replied: "When Philometor is with me he is simply Philometor, and in no way different from the crowd. But when I see that he is going away my heart within me is wounded and tortured till it tries to escape from my breast. Do you exert yourself on my behalf," she added, "and so display your piety." When he had heard this, Maximus went away puffed up with pride as though he were now associating with the gods, because so wonderful a woman had put such faith in him. Meanwhile Philometor pursued his purpose, but Maximus having discovered by his sacrificial lore what was the power that Philometor possessed, strove to counteract and nullify the weaker spell by one more potent and efficacious. When Maximus had completed this rite he hastened to Sosipatra, and bade her observe carefully whether she had the same sensations in future. But she replied that she no longer felt them, and described to Maximus his own prayer and the whole ceremony; she also told him the hour at which it took place, as though she had been present, and revealed to him the omens that had appeared. And when he fell to the earth in amazement and proclaimed Sosipatra visibly a goddess, she said: "Rise, my son. The gods love you if you raise your eyes to them and do not lean towards earthly and perishable riches."

429a *Price Too High*
Gellius, Attic Nights 1.8.3-6

In the book, *The Horn of Plenty*, is found the following anecdote about the orator Demosthenes and the courtesan Lais: "Lais of Corinth," he says, "used to gain a great deal of money by the grace and charm of her beauty, and was frequently visited by wealthy men from all over Greece; but no one was received that did not give what she demanded, and her demands were extravagant enough." He says that this was the origin of the proverb common among the Greeks:

Not every man may fare to Corinth town,[1] for in vain would any man go to Corinth to visit Lais who could not pay her price. "The great Demosthenes approached her secretly and asked for her favors. But Lais demanded ten thousand drachmas"—a sum equivalent in our money to ten thousand denarii. "Amazed and shocked at the woman's great impudence and the vast sum of money demanded,

Demosthenes turned away, remarking as he left her: 'I will not buy regret at such a price.'" But the Greek words which he is said to have used are neater; he said: "I will not buy regret for ten thousand drachmas."

1. Cf. Horace, *Epistles* 1.17.36.

429b *Price Too High*
Macrobius, Saturnalia 2.2.11

Demosthenes, . . . attracted by the fame of Lais, whose beauty at that time was the wonder of Greece, went to enjoy her vaunted favors himself. But, when he heard that her company for a single night would cost him half a talent, he went away, saying: "I find that too high a price to pay for what I should regret."

430a *Death as long as Women Bear Children*
Gospel, Egyptians 6, from Clement, *Excerpts from Theodotus* 67
(Staehlin-Fruechtel 3.2:129)

And when the Savior says to Salome that there will be death as long as women bear children, he does not speak reproachfully of procreation, for that is necessary for the salvation of believers.

430b *Death as long as Women Bear Children*
Gospel, Egyptians 1, from Clement, *Stromateis* 3.6.45
(Staehlin-Fruechtel 2.3:217)

When Salome asked, "How long will death have power?" the Lord said, "As long as you women bear children," not as if life were bad and creation evil, but as teaching the sequence of nature. For death always follows birth.

430c *Death as long as Women Bear Children*
Gospel, Egyptians 3, from Clement, *Stromateis* 3.9.64
(Staehlin-Fruechtel 2.3:225)

It is probably because the Word had spoken concerning the consummation that Salome said, "Until when will men die?" Scripture speaks of man in two ways, the visible appearance and the soul, and again, the one who is being saved and the one who is not. And sin is said to be the death of the soul. Therefore the Lord answered very carefully, "As long as women bear children," that is, as long as the desires are active.

430d *Eat Every Plant*
Gospel, Egyptians 4, from Clement, *Stromateis* 3.9.66
(Staehlin-Fruechtel 2.3:226)

For when she [Salome] said, "I have done well then in not having borne children," as if it were improper to engage in procreation, then the Lord answered and said, "Eat every plant, but do not eat the one which contains bitterness."

431a *Living Water*
Gospel, John 4:1–15 (NIV)

The Pharisees heard that Jesus was gaining and baptizing more disciples than John, although in fact it was not Jesus who baptized, but his disciples. When the Lord learned of this, he left Judea and went back once more to Galilee. Now he had to go through Samaria. So he came to a town in Samaria called Sychar, near the plot of ground Jacob had given to his son Joseph. Jacob's well was there, and

Jesus, tired as he was from the journey sat down by the well. It was about the sixth hour. When a Samaritan woman came to draw water Jesus said to her, "Will you give me a drink?" (His disciples had gone into the town to buy food.) The Samaritan woman said to him, "You are a Jew and I am a Samaritan woman. How can you ask me for a drink?" (For Jews do not associate with Samaritans.) Jesus answered her, "If you knew the gift of God and who it is that asks you for a drink, you would have asked him and he would have given you living water." "Sir," the woman said, "you have nothing to draw with and the well is deep. Where can you get this living water? Are you greater than our father Jacob, who gave us the well and drank from it himself, as did also his sons and his flocks and herds?" Jesus answered, "Everyone who drinks this water will be thirsty again, but whoever drinks the water I give him will never thirst. Indeed, the water I give him will become in him a spring of water welling up to eternal life." The woman said to him, "Sir, give me this water so that I won't get thirsty and have to keep coming here to draw water."

431b   Drink From Jesus' Mouth
Gospel, Thomas 108

Jesus said, "Whoever drinks from my mouth will become like me; I myself shall become that person, and the hidden things will be revealed to that one."

432   Adulterous Woman Forgiven
Gospel, John 7:53–8:11 (NIV)

Then each went to his own home. But Jesus went to the Mount of Olives. At dawn he appeared again in the temple courts, where all the people gathered around him, and he sat down to teach them. The teachers of the law and the Pharisees brought in a woman caught in adultery. They made her stand before the group and said to Jesus, "Teacher this woman was caught in the act of adultery. In the Law Moses commanded us to stone such women. Now what do you say?" They were using this question as a trap, in order to have a basis for accusing him. But Jesus bent down and started to write on the ground with his finger. When they kept on questioning him, he straightened up and said to them, "If any one of you is without sin, let him be the first to throw a stone at her." Again he stooped down and wrote on the ground. At this, those who heard began to go away one at a time, the older ones first, until only Jesus was left, with the woman still standing there. Jesus straightened up and asked her, "Woman, where are they? Has no one condemned you?" "No one, sir," she said. "Then neither do I condemn you," Jesus declared. "Go now and leave your life of sin."

433   Lazarus' Illness for Glory of God
Gospel, John 11:1–4 (NIV)

Now a man named Lazarus was sick. He was from Bethany, the village of Mary and her sister Martha. This Mary, whose brother Lazarus now lay sick, was the same one who poured perfume on the Lord and wiped his feet with her hair. So the sisters sent word to Jesus, "Lord, the one you love is sick." When he heard this, Jesus said, "This sickness will not end in death. No, it is for God's glory so that God's Son may be glorified through it." Jesus loved Martha and her sister and Lazarus. Yet when he heard that Lazarus was sick, he stayed where he was two more days.

434   *Behold, Your Mother*
Gospel, John 19:25b-27 (NIV)

Near the cross of Jesus stood his mother, his mother's sister, Mary the wife of Clopas, and Mary Magdalene. When Jesus saw his mother there, and the disciple whom he loved standing nearby, he said to his mother, "Dear woman, here is your son," and to the disciple, "Here is your mother." From that time on, this disciple took her into his home.

435   *Visiting Martha and Mary*
Gospel, Luke 10:38-42 (NIV)

As Jesus and his disciples were on their way, he came to a village where a woman named Martha opened her home to him. She had a sister called Mary, who sat at the Lord's feet listening to what he said. But Martha was distracted by all the preparations that had to be made. She came to him and asked, "Lord, don't you care that my sister has left me to do the work by myself? Tell her to help me!" "Martha, Martha," the Lord answered, "you are worried and upset about many things, but only one thing is needed. Mary has chosen what is better, and it will not be taken away from her."

436   *Healing of a Crippled Woman on the Sabbath*
Gospel, Luke 13:10-17 (NIV)

On a Sabbath Jesus was teaching in one of the synagogues, and a woman was there who had been crippled by a spirit for eighteen years. She was bent over and could not straighten up at all. When Jesus saw her, he called her forward and said to her, "Woman, you are set free from your infirmity." Then he put his hands on her and immediately she straightened up and praised God. Indignant because Jesus had healed on the Sabbath the synagogue ruler said to the people, "There are six days for work. So come and be healed on those days, not on the Sabbath." The Lord answered him, "You hypocrites! Doesn't each of you on the Sabbath untie his ox or donkey from the stall and lead it out to give it water? Then should not this woman, a daughter of Abraham, whom Satan has kept bound for eighteen long years, be set free on the Sabbath day from what bound her?" When he said this, all his opponents were humiliated, but the people were delighted with all the wonderful things he was doing.

437a   *The Road to Golgotha*
Gospel, Luke 23:27-31 (NIV)

A large number of people followed him, including women who mourned and wailed for him. Jesus turned and said to them, "Daughters of Jerusalem, do not weep for me; weep for yourselves and for your children. For the time will come when you will say, 'Blessed are the barren women, the wombs that never bore and the breasts that never nursed!' Then "'they will say to the mountains, "Fall on us!" and to the hills, "Cover us!"' For if men do these things when the tree is green, what will happen when it is dry?"

437b   *Blessed Is the Womb*
Gospel, Thomas 79

A woman in the crowd said to him, "Blessed are the womb that bore you and the breasts that fed you." He said to [her], "Blessed are those who have heard the word of the Father and have truly kept it. For the days will come when you will say, 'Blessed are the womb that has not conceived and the breasts that have not produced milk."

437c *Jesus Weeps over Jerusalem*
Gospel, Luke 19:41–44 (NIV)

As he approached Jerusalem and saw the city, he wept over it and said, "If you, even you, had only known on this day what would bring you peace—but now it is hidden from your eyes. The days will come upon you when your enemies will build an embankment against you and encircle you and hem you in on every side. They will dash you to the ground, you and the children within your walls. They will not leave one stone on another, because you did not recognize the time of God's coming to you."

438 *Salome a Disciple*
Gospel, Thomas 61b

Salome said, "Who are you, sir? You climbed on my couch and ate from my table as if you are somebody (uncertain; lit.: as if from one)." Jesus said to her, "I am from one that is whole. I was granted from the things of my Father." "I am your disciple." "For this reason I say, if one is <whole> (text: desolate), one will be filled with light, but if one is fragmented, one will be filled with darkness."

439 *Two Lies*
Hadith, Bukhārī, Tawḥīd, 4

Muḥammad b. Yūsuf and Sufyān related to us from Ismāʿīl, Al-Shaʿbī, and Masrūq, on the authority of ʿĀʾisha (may God be pleased with her), who said: Whoever says that Muḥammad has seen his Lord is a liar, for God says, "No vision can reach Him."[1] And whoever says that Muḥammad had perceived the unseen is a liar, for God says, "No one perceives the unseen except God."

> 1. Qurʾān 6:103.

440 *Demonax and Danae*
Lucian, Demonax 47

When a woman named Danae had a dispute with her brother, he [Demonax] said: "Go to law! Though your name be Danae, you are not the daughter of Acrisius (Lawless)."

441 *Stain and Fuller*
Macrobius, Saturnalia 2.2.9

Sulla's son Faustus . . . hearing that his sister was having an affair with two lovers at the same time—with Fulvius (a fuller's son) and Pompeius surnamed Macula [a stain]—declared: "I am surprised to find my sister with a stain, seeing that she has the services of a fuller."

442 *Walk Like Your Husband*
Macrobius, Saturnalia 2.3.16

Cicero, seeing his son-in-law Piso walking in a somewhat effeminate manner and his daughter striding more briskly along, said to her: "Walk like your husband."

443   *Two Spoiled Daughters*
Macrobius, Saturnalia 2.5.3–4

Again and again her father [Augustus] had referred to the extravagance of her [Julia's] dress and the notoriety of her companions and had urged her in language at once tender and grave to show more restraint. But at the same time the sight of his many grandchildren and their likeness to their father, Agrippa, forbade him for very shame's sake to entertain any doubt about his daughter's virtue. And so he flattered himself that her high spirits, even if they gave the impression of a wanton, were in fact blameless, and he ventured to regard her as a latter day Claudia.[1] Thus it was once observed, when talking among some friends, that he had two spoiled daughters to put up with—Rome and Julia.

> 1. See Ovid, *Fasti* 4.305–344. Under cover of this story of Claudia Ovid defends the character of Julia, about whom scandal was current when he wrote it.

444   *Julia's Dress*
Macrobius, Saturnalia 2.5.5

She [Julia] came one day into her father's presence wearing a somewhat immodest dress. Augustus was shocked but said nothing. On the next day, to his delight, she wore a different kind of dress and greeted him with studied demureness. Although the day before he had repressed his feelings, he was now unable to contain his pleasure and said: "This dress is much more becoming in the daughter of Augustus." But Julia had an excuse ready and replied: "Yes, for today I am dressed to meet my father's eyes; yesterday it was for my husband's."

445   *Old Friends*
Macrobius, Saturnalia 2.5.6

Here is another well-known saying of hers. At a display of gladiators the contrast between Livia's suite and Julia's had caught the eye, for the former was attended by a number of grown-up men of distinction but the latter was seated surrounded by young people of the fast set. Her father sent Julia a letter of advice, bidding her mark the difference between the behavior of the two chief ladies of Rome, to which she wrote this neat reply: "These friends of mine will be old men too, when I am old."

446   *Gray or Bald?*
Macrobius, Saturnalia 2.5.7

Her [Julia's] hair began to go gray at an early age, and she used secretly to pull the gray hairs out. One day her maids were surprised by the unexpected arrival of her father, who pretended not to see the gray hairs on her women's dresses and talked for some time on other matters. Then, turning the conversation to the subject of age, he asked whether she would prefer eventually to be gray or bald. She replied that for her part she would rather be gray. "Why then," said her father, thus rebuking her deceit, "are those women of yours in such a hurry to make you bald?"

447   *Caesar's Daughter*
Macrobius, Saturnalia 2.5.8

Moreover, to a seriousminded friend who was seeking to persuade her that she [Julia] would be better advised to order her life to conform to her father's simple tastes she replied: "He forgets that he is Caesar, but I remember that I am Caesar's daughter."

448   *Hold Is Full*
Macrobius, Saturnalia 2.5.9

To certain persons who knew of her infidelities and were expressing surpise at her children's likeness to her husband Agrippa, since she was free with her favors, she [Julia] said: "Passengers are never allowed on board until the hold is full."

449   *The Lower Animals*
Macrobius, Saturnalia 2.5.10

[This saying is] ascribed to Populia (daughter of Marcus), who, to someone asking in surprise why it was that among the lower animals the female sought to mate with the male only when she wished to conceive, replied: "Because they *are* the lower animals."

450   *A Woman in Childbirth*
Phaedrus, Aesopic Fables 1.18

No one else likes to revisit the place which has brought him injury. Her months of pregnancy having duly gone by, a woman on the point of giving birth was lying on the ground uttering piteous moans. Her husband urged her to lay her body on the bed, where she might better deposit the burden of nature. "I'm not at all convinced," said she, "that my troubles can end in the very place where they began."

451   *Mercury and the Two Women*
Phaedrus, Aesopic Fables, Appendix 4

Once two women entertained Mercury in a mean and shabby fashion. One of them had a little son in the cradle, the other was pleased to follow the trade of a prostitute. Accordingly, in order to make them a suitable return for their services, Mercury, as he was about to leave and was already crossing the threshold, said: "In me you behold a god, I will give each of you at once whatever she may wish." The mother in her petition asks that she may see her son with a beard as soon as possible, the prostitute that whatever she touches may follow her. Mercury flies away and the women return indoors. Behold the baby now bearded starting to bawl. While the prostitute was enjoying a hearty laugh at this it happened that her nasal passages got clogged with mucus, as will happen. Intending, therefore, to blow her nose, she took hold of it with her hand and pulled it out longer and longer, clear to the floor. Thus, while laughing at another she herself became an object of laughter.

452   *No Smoke Seen*
Plutarch, Agesilaus 31.5

He [Agesilaus] was also distressed at the thought of what his fame would be, because he had taken command of the city when she was greatest and most powerful, and now saw her reputation lowered, and her proud boast made empty, which boast he himself also had often made, saying that no Spartan woman had ever seen the smoke of an enemy's fires.

453 *Alexander Respects the Persian Women Captives*
   Plutarch, Alexander 21.7-11 (4-5)

But Alexander, as it would seem, considering the mastery of himself a more kingly thing than the conquest of his enemies, neither laid hands upon these women, nor did he know any other before marriage, except Barsiné. This woman, Memnon's widow, was taken prisoner at Damascus. And since she had received a Greek education, and was of an agreeable disposition, and since her father, Artabanus, was son of a king's daughter, Alexander determined (at Parmenio's instigation, as Aristobulus says) to attach himself to a woman of such high birth and beauty. But as for the other captive women, seeing that they were surpassingly stately and beautiful, he merely said jestingly that Persian women were torments to the eyes. And displaying in rivalry with their fair looks the beauty of his own sobriety and self-control, he passed them by as though they were lifeless images for display.

454 *Lucius Caesar Saved by Sister*
   Plutarch, Antony 20.3

His [Antony's] uncle, Lucius Caesar, being sought for and pursued, took refuge with his sister. She, when the executioners were at hand and trying to force their way into her chamber, stood in the doorway, spread out her arms and cried repeatedly: "Ye shall not slay Lucius Caesar, unless ye first slay me, the mother of your imperator."

455 *Antony No Fisherman*
   Plutarch, Antony 29.3-4

Now to recount the greater part of his boyish pranks would be great nonsense. One instance will suffice. He [Antony] was fishing once, and had bad luck, and was vexed at it because Cleopatra was there to see. He therefore ordered his fishermen to dive down and secretly fasten to his hook some fish that had been previously caught, and pulled up two or three of them. But the Egyptian saw through the trick, and pretending to admire her lover's skill, told her friends about it, and invited them to be spectators of it on the following day. So great numbers of them got into the fishing boats, and when Antony had let down his line, she ordered one of her own attendants to get the start of him by swimming to his hook and fastening on it a salted Pontic herring. Antony thought he had caught something, and pulled it up, whereupon there was great laughter, as was natural, and Cleopatra said: "Imperator, hand over thy fishing-rod to the fishermen of Pharos and Conopus; thy sport is the hunting of cities, realms and continents."

456 *Geminus Blames Cleopatra*
   Plutarch, Antony 59.2-3

Once, however, at a supper, being bidden to tell the reasons for his coming, he [Geminus] replied that the rest of his communication required a sober head, but one thing he knew, whether he was drunk or sober, and that was that all would be well if Cleopatra was sent off to Egypt. At this, Antony was wroth, and Cleopatra said: "Thou hast done well, Geminus, to confess the truth without being put to the torture."

457 *Caesar At Ladle*
Plutarch, Antony 62.3

But while Antony was lying at anchor off Actium, where now Nicopolis stands, Caesar got the start of him by crossing the Ionian sea and occupying a place in Epeirus called Toruné (that is, ladle); and when Antony and his friends were disturbed by this, since their infantry forces were belated, Cleopatra said jestingly, "What is there dreadful in Caesar's sitting at a ladle?"

458 *No Faith in Laws or Gods after Murder of Tiberius*
Plutarch, Caius Gracchus 15.1–3

When day came, Fulvius was with difficulty roused from his drunken sleep by his partisans, who armed themselves with the spoils of war about his house, which he had taken after a victory over the Gauls during his consulship, and with much threatening and shouting went to seize the Aventine hill. Caius, on the other hand, was unwilling to arm himself, but went forth in his toga, as though on his way to the forum, with only a short dagger on his person. As he was going out of the door, his wife threw herself in his way, and with one arm around her husband and the other round their little son said: "Not to the rostra, O Caius, do I now send thee forth, as formerly, to serve as tribune and law-giver, nor yet to a glorious war, where, shouldst thou die (and all men must die), thou wouldst at all events leave me an honored sorrow; but thou art exposing thyself to the murderer of Tiberius, and thou doest well to go unarmed, that thou mayest suffer rather than inflict wrong; but thy death will do the state no good. The worst has at last prevailed; by violence and the sword men's controversies are now decided. If thy brother had only fallen at Numantia, his dead body would have been given back to us by terms of truce; but as it is, perhaps I too shall have to supplicate some river or sea to reveal to me at last thy body in its keeping. Why, pray, should men longer put faith in laws or gods, after the murder of Tiberius?"

459 *Cleonice and Pausanias*
Plutarch, Cimon 6.4–5

It is said that a maiden of Byzantium, of excellent parentage, Cleonice by name, was summoned by Pausanias for a purpose that would disgrace her. Her parents, influenced by constraint and fear, abandoned their daughter to her fate, and she, after requesting the attendants before his chamber to remove the light, in darkness and silence at length drew near the couch on which Pausanias was asleep, but accidentally stumbled against the lamp-holder and upset it. Pausanias, startled by the noise, drew the dagger which lay at his side, with the idea that some enemy was upon him, and smote and felled the maiden. After her death in consequence of the blow, she gave Pausanias no peace, but kept coming into his sleep by night in phantom form, wrathfully uttering this verse:
"Draw thou nigh to thy doom; 'tis evil for men to be wanton."

460 *A Statesman's Ball*
Plutarch, Demetrius 11.2

He [Stratocles] had taken up with a mistress named Phylacion; and one day when she had bought in the market-place for his supper some brains and neck-bones, "Aha!" he cried, "thou hast bought just such delicacies for me as we statesmen used to play ball with."

461 *Lamia Deprecated*
Plutarch, Demetrius 27.3–4

At all events, some ambassadors from him [Demetrius] once came to Lysimachus, and Lysimachus, in an hour of leisure, showed them on his thighs and shoulders deep scars of wounds made by a lion's claws; he also told them about the battle he had fought against the beast, with which he had been caged by Alexander the king. Then they laughingly told him that their own king also carried, on his neck, the bites of a dreadful wild beast, a Lamia.[1] And it was astonishing that while in the beginning he was displeased at Phila's disparity in years, he was vanquished by Lamia, and loved her so long, although she was already past her prime. At all events, when Lamia was playing on the flute at a supper, and Demetrius asked Demo, surnamed Mania, what she thought of her, "O King," said Mania, "I think her an old woman."

> 1. The name of Demetrius' courtesan; also a fabled monster.

462 *Mania Insults Lamia Again*
Plutarch, Demetrius 27.4

And at another time, when some sweetmeats were served up, and Demetrius said to Mania, "Dost thou see how many presents I get from Lamia?" "My mother," said Mania, "will send thee more, if thou wilt make her also thy mistress."

463a *The Insistent Woman*
Plutarch, Demetrius 42.3–4

An old woman once assailed Demetrius as he was passing by, and demanded many times that he give her a hearing. "I have no time," said Demetrius. "Then don't be king," screamed the old woman. Demetrius was stung to the quick, and after thinking upon the matter went to his house, and postponing everything else, for several days devoted himself entirely to those who wished audience of him, beginning with the old woman who had rebuked him.

463b *The Insistent Woman*
Plutarch, Moralia, Sayings of Kings and Commanders III:179C–D (31)

When a poor old woman insisted that her case should be heard before him, and often caused him annoyance, he said he had no time to spare, whereupon she burst out, "Then give up being king." Philip, amazed at her words, proceeded at once to hear not only her case but those of the others.[1]

> 1. Stobaeus, *Florilegium* 33.28, quotes Serenus, who states that a peasant made this remark to Antipater.

463c *The Insistent Man*
Gospel, Luke 11:5–8 (NIV)

Then he said to them, "Suppose one of you has a friend, and he goes to him at midnight and says, 'Friend, lend me three loaves of bread, because a friend of mine on a journey has come to me, and I have nothing to set before him.' "Then the one inside answers, 'Don't bother me. The door is already locked, and my children are with me in bed. I can't get up and give you anything.' I tell you, though he will not get up and give him the bread because he is his friend, yet because of the man's boldness he will get up and give him as much as he needs."

464 *Priestess Hails Lycurgus*
Plutarch, Lycurgus 5.3

Full of this determination, he [Lycurgus] first made a journey to Delphi, and after sacrificing to the god and consulting the oracle, he returned with that famous response in which the Pythian priestess addressed him as "beloved of the gods, and rather god than man," and said that the god had granted his prayer for good laws, and promised him a constitution which should be the best in the world.

465a *Spartan Women Rule Men*
Plutarch, Lycurgus 14.4

Wherefore they [Spartan women] were led to think and speak as Gorgo, the wife of Leonidas, is said to have done. When some foreign woman, as it would seem, said to her: "You Spartan women are the only ones who rule their men," she answered: "Yes, we are the only ones that give birth to men."

465b *Spartan Women Rule Men*
Plutarch, Moralia, Sayings of Spartans III:227E (13)

Wherefore is recorded also in regard to Gorgo, the wife of Leonidas, a saying to this effect: when some woman, a foreigner presumably, remarked to her, "You Spartan women are the only women that lord it over your men," she replied, "Yes, for we are the only women that are mothers of men!"

465c *Spartan Women Rule Men*
Plutarch, Moralia, Sayings of Spartan Women III:240E (5)

Being asked by a woman from Attica, "Why is it that you Spartan women are the only women that lord it over your men," she [Gorgo] said, "Because we are the only women that are mothers of men."

466 *Wives Rule*
Plutarch, Marcus Cato 8.2

Discoursing on the power of women, he [Cato] said: "All other men rule their wives; we rule all other men, and our wives rule us."

467 *Message to Greedy King*
Plutarch, Moralia, Sayings of Kings and Commanders III:173B

Semiramis caused a great tomb to be prepared for herself,[1] and on it this inscription: "Whatsoever king finds himself in need of money may break into this monument and take as much as he wishes." Darius accordingly broke into it, but found no money; he did, however, come upon another inscription reading as follows: "If you were not a wicked man with an insatiate greed for money, you would not be disturbing the places where the dead are laid."

1. Herodotus, 1.187, says that Nitocris built the tomb above the gates of Babylon. Stobaeus, 10.53, copies Plutarch word for word.

468a *All Men Smell*
> Plutarch, Moralia, Sayings of Kings and Commanders III:175C (3)

On being reviled by someone for his offensive breath, he [Hiero[1]] blamed his wife for never having told him about this; but she said, "I supposed that all men smelled so.[2]"

> 1. Ruler of Gela and Syracuse, 478–467 B.C.E.
> 2. Cf. Lucian, *Hermotimus* 34. Aristotle tells the same story of Gelon according to Stobaeus, *Florilegium* 5.83.

468b *All Men Smell*
> Plutarch, Moralia, How to Profit by One's Enemies II:90B (7)

Hiero was reviled by one of his enemies for his offensive breath; so when he went home he said to his wife, "What do you mean? Even you never told me of this." But she being virtuous and innocent said, "I supposed that all men smelt so." Thus it is that things which are perceptible, material, and evident to all the world, may sooner be learned from our enemies than from our friends and close associates.

469a *Parting Words*
> Plutarch, Moralia, Sayings of Spartan Women III:240E (6)

As she [Gorgo] was encouraging her husband Leonidas, when he was about to set out for Thermopylae, to show himself worthy of Sparta, she asked what she should do; and he said, "Marry a good man, and bear good children."

469b *Parting Words*
> Plutarch, Moralia, Sayings of Spartans III:225A (2)

His [Leonidas'] wife Gorgo inquired, at the time when he was setting forth to Thermopylae to fight the Persian, if he had any instructions to give her, and he said, "To marry good men and bear good children."

470a *Death of Sons Accepted*
> Plutarch, Moralia, Sayings of Spartan Women III:241C (7)

One woman sent forth her sons, five in number, to war, and, standing in the outskirts of the city, she awaited anxiously the outcome of the battle. And when someone arrived and, in answer to her inquiry, reported that all her sons had met death, she said, "I did not inquire about that, you vile varlet, but how fares our country?" And when he declared that it was victorious, "Then," she said, "I accept gladly also the death of my sons."

470b *Death of Sons Accepted*
> Plutarch, Agesilaus 29.5

And a still greater difference was to be seen (or heard about) in the women; she who expected her son back from the battle alive was dejected and silent, but the mothers of those reported to have fallen immediately frequented the temples, and visited one another with an air of gladness and pride.

471a Remember Valor

Plutarch, Moralia, Sayings of Spartan Women III:241E (13)

Another, as she accompanied a lame son on his way to the field of battle, said, "At every step, my child, remember your valor."[1]

1. Cf. Stobaeus, *Florilegium* 7.29; Cicero, *De Oratore* 2.61 (249).

471b Remember Valor

Plutarch, Moralia, Sayings of Spartan Women III:241F (14)

Another, when her son came back to her from the field of battle wounded in the foot, and in great pain, said, "If you remember your valor, my child, you will feel no pain, and be quite cheerful."

471c Remember Valor

Plutarch, Moralia, Fortune of Alexander IV:331B (9b)

When the thigh of his father Philip had been pierced by a spear in battle with the Triballians, and Philip, although he escaped with his life, was vexed with his lameness, Alexander said, "Be of good cheer, father, and go on your way rejoicing, that at each step you may recall your valor."

472a On His Shield

Plutarch, Moralia, Sayings of Spartan Women III:241F (16)

Another, as she handed her son his shield, exhorted him, saying, "Either this or upon this."[1]

1. Referred to Gorgo as the author by Aristotle in his *Aphorisms*, as quoted by Stobaeus, *Florilegium* 7.31, but it is often spoken of as a regular Spartan custom. Cf., for example, the scholium on Thucydides 2.39. Ancient writers were not agreed whether the second half meant to fall upon the shield (dead or wounded) or to be brought home dead upon it. In support of the second (traditional) interpretation cf. 472c and Valerius Maximus 2.7, externa 2.

472b Keep Shield Safe

Plutarch, Moralia, Sayings of Spartan Women III:241F (17)

Another, as her son was going forth to war, said, as she gave the shield into his hands, "This shield your father kept always safe for you; do you, therefore, keep it safe, or cease to live."

472c On His Shield

Plutarch, Moralia, Sayings of Spartans III:235A–B (35)

Tynnichus, when his son Thrasybulus was slain, bore it sturdily; and this epigram was written on him:

> Lifeless to Pitane came, on his shield upborne, Thrasybulus;
> Seven the wounds he received, pierced by the Argive spears;
> All in the front did he show them; and him with his blood-
> stained body
> Tynnichus placed on the pyre, saying these words in his eld:
> "Let the poor cowards be mourned, but with never a tear shall
> I bury
> You, my son, who are mine, yea, and are Sparta's as well."

473   *Only One Man*
Plutarch, Moralia, Bravery of Women III:258E–F

It came to pass that Chiomara,[1] the wife of Ortiagon, was made a prisoner of war along with the rest of the women at the time when the Romans under Gnaeus[2] overcame in battle the Galatians in Asia. The officer[3] who obtained possession of her used his good fortune as soldiers do, and dishonored her. He was, naturally, an ignorant man with no self-control when it came to either pleasure or money. He fell a victim, however, to his love of money, and when a very large sum in gold had been mutually agreed upon as the price for the woman, he brought her to exchange for the ransom to a place where a river, flowing between, formed a boundary. When the Galatians had crossed and given him the money and received Chiomara, she, by a nod, indicated to one man that he should smite the Roman as he was affectionately taking leave of her. And when the man obediently struck off the Roman's head, she picked it up and, wrapping it in the folds of her garment, departed. When she came to her husband and threw the head down before him, he said in amazement, "A noble thing, dear wife, is fidelity." "Yes," said she, "but it is a nobler thing that only one man be alive who has been intimate with me."

> 1. This is printed as one of the fragments of Polybius, 21.38 (22.21), from whom it is possible that Plutarch copied the story. Cf. also Livy, 38.24; Valerius Maximus 6.1, externa 2; Florus, *Epitome of Roman History* 1.27.6 (2.11.6).
> 2. Gnaeus Manlius Vulso; the battle took place in 189 B.C.E.
> 3. A centurion, according to the Roman account.

474   *The Gold of Pythes*
Plutarch, Moralia, Bravery of Women III:262D–263A

It is said the wife of Pythes,[1] contemporary with Xerxes, was wise and good. Pythes himself, as it appears, came by chance upon some gold mines, and, delighting in the wealth from them not with moderation, but insatiably and beyond measure, he himself spent all his time over them, and put the citizens down there also, and compelled all alike to dig or carry or wash out the gold, performing no other work and carrying on no other activity. Many perished and all were completely exhausted, when the women, coming to the door of the wife of Pythes, made supplication. She bade them depart and not lose heart; then she summoned the goldsmiths whom she trusted most, secluded them, and ordered them to make golden loaves of bread, cakes of all sorts, fruit, and whatever else in the way of dainties and food she knew Pythes liked best. When these had all been made, Pythes arrived home from abroad; for he had been traveling. And when he called for dinner, his wife caused a golden table to be set before him which contained nothing edible, but everything of gold. At first Pythes was delighted with the mimic food, but when he had gazed his fill, he called for something to eat; and she served to him a golden replica of whatever he chanced to express a desire for. By this time he was in a high dudgeon and shouted out that he was hungry, whereupon she said, "But it is you who have created for us a plentiful supply of these things, and of nothing else; for all skill in the trades has disappeared from among us; no one tills the soil, but we have forsaken the sowing and planting of crops in the soil and the sustaining food that comes from it, and we dig and delve for useless things, wasting our own strength and that of our people."

> 1. Cf. Polyaenus, *Strategemata* 8.42; Herodotus, 7.27–29 and 38–39, where the name is given as Pythius.

475 *Perfume and Butter*
Plutarch, Moralia, Reply to Colotes XIV:1109B–C

There is a story that a Spartan lady came to visit Beronice, wife of Deiotarus.[1] No sooner did they come near each other than each turned away, the one (we are told) sickened by the perfume, the other by the butter. If then one sense-perception is no more true than another, we must suppose that the water is no more cold than hot, and that perfume or butter is no more sweet-smelling than ill-smelling; for he who asserts that the object itself is what appears one thing to one person and another to another has unwittingly said that it is both things at once.

> 1. Four Galatian kings or princes of the name are known. They belong to the first century B.C.E.

476 *The Mother of Biton and Cleobis*
Plutarch, Moralia, Fragment: A Woman, Too, Should Be Educated XV:133

Someone has composed an epigram on them as follows:

Here lie Biton and Cleobis, who placed a yoke on their own shoulders and drew their mother to the shrine of Hera. The people envied her for having such fine children for her sons, and she in her joy prayed to the goddess that her sons might be allotted the best of fortunes, since they had done this honor to their mother. And thereupon they laid them down to sleep and departed life in their youth, showing this to be the best and most blessed thing there is.

477 *The Wife of Pelopidas*
Plutarch, Pelopidas 20.1–2

It was at this time that Pelopidas, on leaving his house, when his wife followed him on his way in tears and begging him not to lose his life, said: "This advice, my wife, should be given to private men; but men in authority should be told not to lose the lives of others."

478 *The Daughter of Jason*
Plutarch, Pelopidas 28.3–4

But Thebe, who was a daughter of Jason, and Alexander's wife, learned from the keepers of Pelopidas how courageous and noble the man was, and conceived a desire to see him and talk with him. But when she came to him, woman that she was, she could not at once recognize the greatness of his nature in such dire misfortune, but judging from his hair and garb and maintenance that he was suffering indignities which ill befitted a man of his reputation, she burst into tears. Pelopidas, not knowing at first what manner of woman she was, was amazed; but when he understood, he addressed her as daughter of Jason; for his father was a familiar friend of his. And when she said, "I pity thy wife," he replied, "And I thee, in that thou wearest no chains, and yet endurest Alexander."

479a *Elpinice Too Old*
Plutarch, Pericles 10.5

Pericles was at that time one of the committee of prosecution appointed by the people, and on Elpinice's coming to him and supplicating him, said to her with a smile: "Elpinice, thou art an old woman, thou art an old woman, to attempt such tasks."

479b *Pericles and Elpinice*
Plutarch, Pericles 28.3–4

When Pericles, after his subjection of Samos, had returned to Athens, he gave honorable burial to those who had fallen in the war, and for the oration which he made, according to the custom, over their tombs, he won the greatest admiration. But as he came down from the bema, while the rest of the women clasped his hand and fastened wreaths and fillets on his head, as though he were some victorious athlete, Elpinice drew nigh and said: "This is admirable in thee, Pericles, and deserving of wreaths, in that thou hast lost us many brave citizens, not in a war with Phoenicians or Medes, like my brother Cimon, but in the subversion of an allied and kindred city." On Elpinice's saying this, Pericles with a quiet smile, it is said, quoted to her the verse of Archilochus:—

"Thou hadst not else, in spite of years, perfumed thyself."[1]

1. That is, "Thou art too old to meddle in affairs."

480 *Phocion An Ornament*
Plutarch, Phocion 19.3

And this very wife [of Phocion], when an Ionian woman who was her guest displayed the ornaments of gold and and precious stones worked into collars and necklaces, said: "My ornament is Phocion, who is now for the twentieth year a general of Athens."

481 *Flora the Courtesan*
Plutarch, Pompey 2.2

We are told that Flora the courtesan, when she was now quite old, always took delight in telling about her former intimacy with Pompey, saying that she never left his embraces without bearing the marks of his teeth.

482 *The Laws of the City and the Laws of Nature*
Plutarch, Solon 20.4

Dionysius, indeed, when his mother asked him to give her in marriage to one of his citizens, said that, although he had broken the laws of the city by being its tyrant, he could not outrage the laws of nature by giving in marriage where age forbade.

483a *A Third Off*
Suetonius, Lives of the Caesars, Julius 1.50.2

But beyond all others Caesar loved Servilia, the mother of Marcus Brutus, for whom in his first consulship he bought a pearl costing six million sesterces. During the civil war, too, besides other presents, he knocked down some fine estates to her in a public auction at a nominal price, and when some expressed their surprise at the low figure, Cicero wittily remarked: "It's a better bargain than you think, for there is a third off." And in fact it was thought that Servilia was prostituting her own daughter Tertia to Caesar.[1]

1. The word play on *tertia* (*pars*) and Tertia, daughter of Servilia, as well as on the two senses of *deducta*, is quite untranslatable. The first meaning is given in the translation, and the second is implied in the following sentence.

483b *A Third Off*
Macrobius, Saturnalia 2.2.5

When Caesar . . . was selling by auction the property of certain citizens, Servilia (the mother of Marcus Brutus) bought a valuable estate quite cheaply and so became the victim of a jest of Cicero's who said: "Of course you will the better understand Servilia's bargain if you realize that a third was knocked off the purchase of the estate (*tertia deducta*)."[1] For Servilia had a daughter, Junia Tertia (the wife of Gaius Cassius), whose favors—as well as her mother's —the dictator was then enjoying. In fact rumors and jokes about the profligacy of the elderly adulterer were rife at that time in Rome and gave people some amusement in their troubles.

> 1. The play upon the two meanings of *deducere*—"to deduct" and "to conduct a bride to her husband"—can hardly be kept in English.

484 *Nero Poisons Britannicus*
Suetonius, Lives of the Caesars, Nero 6.33.2

He [Nero] attempted the life of Britannicus by poison, not less from jealousy of his voice (for it was more agreeable than his own) than from fear that he might sometime win a higher place than himself in the people's regard because of the memory of his father. He procured the potion from an archpoisoner, one Locusta, and when the effect was slower than he anticipated, merely physicing Britannicus, he called the woman to him and flogged her with his own hand, charging that she had administered a medicine instead of a poison; and when she said in excuse that she had given a smaller dose to shield him from the odium of the crime, he replied: "It's likely that I am afraid of the Julian law."[1]

> 1. Against assassination, including poisoning, passed by Sulla and renewed by Julius Caesar.

485 *Galba Revolts, Nero Faints*
Suetonius, Lives of the Caesars, Nero 6.42.1

Thereafter, having learned that Galba also and the Spanish provinces had revolted, he [Nero] fainted and lay for a long time insensible, without a word and all but dead. When he came to himself, he rent his robe and beat his brow, declaring that it was all over with him; and when his old nurse tried to comfort him by reminding him that similar evils had befallen other princes before him, he declared that unlike all others he was suffering the unheard of and unparalleled fate of losing the supreme power while he still lived.

486 *The Unclean Garment*
Tosefta, Kelim Baba Batra 1:2–3

One time a certain woman who had woven a garment in cleanness came before R. Ishmael for [him] to examine her [concerning whether or not the garment indeed was to be deemed clean]. She said to him: "Rabbi, I know that the garment was not rendered unclean; however, it was not in my heart to guard it [from uncleanness]." As a result of the examination of her which R. Ishmael conducted, she said to him: "Rabbi, I know that a menstruating woman entered and pulled the cord [so that she may have conveyed uncleanness to the garment by her shaking the web] with me." Said R. Ishmael: "How great are the words of the sages, for they used to say, 'If one did not intend to guard it [from uncleanness], it is unclean.'"

A feminine person is present or referred to in the stories listed below, but some other feature has determined their location in another section.

Cicero: 502
Diogenes Laertius: 708, 1400
Epistle: 712
Gellius: 74, 365
Gospel: 12j, 77a, 78a, 91a, 233a, 233b, 236, 735, 1204
Hadith: 265
Lucian: 1403
Macrobius: 483b, 786
Phaedrus: 24, 372
Philostratus: 123, 375, 877
Plutarch: 6b, 31a, 40b, 41, 132, 136, 137, 149, 153, 162, 170, 176, 379, 380, 382, 383, 384, 385, 387, 388, 390, 391, 393, 394, 397, 398, 404a, 406, 610a, 877, 901, 903, 913, 952a, 952b, 959, 962, 981, 988, 992, 1059a, 1098, 1362, 1480, 1481
Sifra: 1366
Sifre: 1367
Suetonius: 354, 409, 411, 412, 414, 415a, 418, 419, 420, 952c, 1150, 1169
Testament: 422

Adult: General

In addition to exchanges with specific persons, famous people frequently address people in general, or an anonymous person, or an animal. Anecdotes of this type display a greater interest in topics like courage, cowardice, foolishness, self-conceit, memory, justice, mercy, wealth, integrity, loneliness, and friendship. It is thus the topic, and not the discussion partner, that lies closest to the surface in these accounts.

487 *The Lion and the Bowman*
Babrius, Aesopic Fables 1

A man came on a mountain to hunt, skilled in shooting with the bow. All the animals turned to flight and were full of fear as they fled. Only the lion had the courage to challenge the man to fight with him. "Wait," said the man to him, "don't be so fast, nor count on victory; first get acquainted with my messenger; after that you'll know what's best for you to do." Then standing a short distance away he let fly an arrow, and the arrow buried itself in the lion's soft belly. Fear overcame the lion and he dashed away in flight to the lonely glens. Not far away stood a fox, who told him to pick up his courage and make a stand. But the lion replied: "You're not going to fool me, nor catch me in a trap; when he sends me such a stinging messenger as this, I know without waiting any longer how formidable he is in his own person."

488 *The Farmer Who Lost His Mattock*
Babrius, Aesopic Fables 2

A farmer while digging trenches in his vineyard lost his mattock and thereafter began a search to find out whether some one of the rustics present with him had stolen it. Each one denied having taken it. Not knowing what to do next, he brought all his servants into the city for the purpose of putting them under oath before the gods; for people suppose that those among the gods who are simpletons live in the country, and that those who dwell within the city walls are unerring and observe everything that goes on. When they had entered the gates of the city and were bathing their feet at a fountain, after laying aside their wallets, a public crier began to call out that a thousand drachmas would be paid for information revealing the whereabouts of property that had been stolen from the god's temple. When the farmer heard this, he said: "How useless for me to have come! How could this god know about other thieves, when he doesn't know who those were who stole his own property? Instead, he is offering money in the hope of finding some man who knows about them."

489a *The Shepherd and the She-Goat*
Babrius, Aesopic Fables 3

Once a goatherd had need to call in the she-goats, in order to drive them into the fold, and as he called some of them came, but others lingered. Down in the ravine one of the disobedient goats was still cropping the fragrant leaves of goatswort and mastich when the goatherd hit her horn with a stone thrown from a distance and broke it off. Then he entreated her: "Don't, I beg you, goat and fellow-slave, in the name of Pan who watches o'er these glens, don't, friend goat, betray me to the master. I didn't mean to throw that stone so straight." "And how," said she, "am I to hide a deed that is self-evident? My horn shouts out the truth, even though I hold my tongue."

489b *The Shepherd and the She-Goat*
Phaedrus, Aesopic Fables, Appendix 24

A shepherd, after breaking the horn of a she-goat with his staff, began to beg her not to betray him to his master. "Even though I have been injured outrageously," she said, "still I shall keep quiet; but the obvious fact will cry out and proclaim your guilt."

490 *The Arab and His Camel*
Babrius, Aesopic Fables 8

An Arab put a heavy load on his camel and asked him whether he preferred to take the high road or the low road. And the camel, not without inspiration, replied: "So the straight road is barred, is it?"

491 *The Farmer and the Stork*
Babrius, Aesopic Fables 13

In the furrows of his field a farmer fixed a thin-spun net and caught the cranes, those enemies of land new-sown. A limping stork besought him thus (for with the cranes a stork too had been taken): "I'm not a crane, I don't destroy the seed, I'm a stork, my color plainly marks me out, and storks are the most loyal and dutiful of all winged creatures; I nurse my father and care for him when he is ill." The man replied: "Sir Stork, what way of life you're pleased to live I do not know, but this I do know: I caught you with those who lay waste my work; die, therefore, you shall in their company, for in their company I caught you."

492a *The Fox and the Woodcutter*
Babrius, Aesopic Fables 50

A fox was fleeing, and behind him as he fled a hunter ran in close pursuit. The fox was tired out and, seeing a woodcutter, called to him saying: "By the gods who save, hide me in these poplars which you just now cut, and don't reveal me to the hunter." The woodsman gave his oath not to betray him, and the fox went into hiding. The hunter came up and asked the man whether a fox had hidden there, or was still in flight. "I did not see him," said the wood cutter, but with his finger he pointed out the place where the rogue lay hidden. The hunter did not linger, but, believing what he heard, went on. The wily fox, thus freed from imminent danger, peeped out from underneath the dense foliage of the poplar, fawning and grinning evilly. "You owe me thanks," the old man said, "I saved your life." "Oh yes, of course," the fox replied, "was I not witness to it all? Goodbye, therefore, you'll not escape the god of oaths; you saved me with your words, indeed, but with your finger you destroyed me."

492b The Hare and the Herdsman
Phaedrus, Aesopic Fables, Appendix 28

A hare fleeing with speedy foot from a hunter was seen by a herdsman as he crept into a thicket. "By the gods above, I beg of you, herdsman," he said, "by all your hopes, don't point me out; I have never done any harm to this field." The countryman answered: "Don't be afraid; hide and you have no need to worry." And now the hunter in pursuit comes up: "I say, herdsman, has a hare come this way?" "He came, but he went off in this direction, to the left"; and so saying the herdsman indicated by a wink (and a nod) the direction to his right. The hunter hurrying on did not understand and passed out of sight. Then said the herdsman: "Aren't you grateful to me for concealing you?" "I certainly do not deny," said the hare, "that to your tongue I feel very grateful and say thanks; but as for your eyes, which played me false, I'd like to see you deprived of them."

493 A Double Standard of Justice
Babrius, Aesopic Fables 117

Once when a ship had gone down with all its crew and passengers on board, a man who saw it declared that the gods' decrees were unjust; because, for the sake of one impious man who had boarded the ship, many others who were innocent went to their death along with him. While he was saying this a swarm of ants came upon him, as often happens, eager to feed upon the chaff of his wheat; and being bitten by one of them he trampled down the majority. Then Hermes appeared and said, striking him with his wand: "How now, won't you endure to have the gods judge you the way you judge the ants?"

494a The Serpent Fatal to the Merciful Man
Babrius, Aesopic Fables 143

A farmer picked up a viper that was almost dead from the cold, and warmed it. But the viper, after stretching himself out, clung to the man's hand and bit him incurably, thus killing (the very one who wanted to save him). Dying, the man uttered these words, worthy to be remembered: "I suffer what I deserve, for showing pity to the wicked."

494b The Serpent Fatal to the Merciful Man
Phaedrus, Aesopic Fables 4.20

He who brings aid to the wicked afterwards suffers for it. A man picked up a venomous serpent benumbed by the cold and warmed it in his bosom, showing pity to his own cost; for when the serpent revived he immediately killed the man. When another serpent asked him why he did this, he replied: "To teach men not to be good to those who are no good."

495a Themistocles on Memory
Cicero, Academica 2.1.2

And this form of memory is recorded as having been present in a remarkable degree in Themistocles, whom we rank as easily the greatest man of Greece, and of whom the story is told that when somebody[1] offered to impart to him the *memoria technica* that was then first coming into vogue, he replied that he would sooner learn to forget—no doubt this was because whatever he heard or saw remained fixed in his memory.

1. The lyric poet Simonides of Ceos (556–467 B.C.E.), the inventor of the system.

495b *Themistocles on Memory*
Cicero, De Finibus 2.32.104

And again, what is the sense of the maxim that the Wise Man will not let past blessings fade from memory, and that it is a duty to forget past misfortunes? To begin with, have we the power to choose what we shall remember? Themistocles at all events, when Simonides or someone offered to teach him the art of memory, replied that he would prefer the art of forgetting; "for I remember," said he, "even things I do not wish to remember, but I cannot forget things I wish to forget."

496 *Tarquin in Exile*
Cicero, De Amicitia 15.53

For can anyone love either the man whom he fears, or the man by whom he believes himself to be feared? Yet tyrants are courted under a pretence of affection, but only for a season. For when by chance they have fallen from power, as they generally do, then is it known how poor they were in friends. And this is illustrated by the remark said to have been made by Tarquin as he was going into exile: "I have learned what friends of mine are true and what are false, now that I am no longer able to reward or punish either."

497 *On Wealth*
Cicero, De Officiis 1.8.25

Again, men seek riches partly to supply the needs of life, partly to secure the enjoyment of pleasure. With those who cherish higher ambitions, the desire for wealth is entertained with a view to power and influence and the means of bestowing favors; Marcus Crassus, for example, not long since declared that no amount of wealth was enough for the man who aspired to be the foremost citizen of the state, unless with the income from it he could maintain an army. Fine establishments and the comforts of life in elegance and abundance also afford pleasure, and the desire to secure it gives rise to the insatiable thirst for wealth. Still, I do not mean to find fault with the accumulation of property, provided it hurts nobody, but unjust acquisition of it is always to be avoided.

498 *Effrontery and Courage*
Cicero, De Officiis 1.19.63

This, then, is a fine saying of Plato's: "Not only must all knowledge that is divorced from justice be called cunning rather than wisdom," he says, "but even the courage that is prompt to face danger, if it is inspired not by public spirit, but by its own selfish purposes, should have the name of effrontery rather than of courage." And so we demand that men who are courageous and high-souled shall at the same time be good and straightforward, lovers of truth, and foes to deception; for these qualities are the center and soul of justice.

499 *No Retreat*
Cicero, De Officiis 1.24.84

Many, on the other hand, have been found who were ready to pour out not only their money but their lives for their country and yet would not consent to make even the slightest sacrifice of personal glory—even though the interests of their country demanded it. For example, when Callicratidas, as Spartan admiral in the Peloponnesian War, had won many signal successes, he spoiled everything at the end by refusing to listen to the proposal of those who thought he ought to withdraw his fleet from the Arginusae and not to risk an engagement with the Athenians. His answer to them was that "the Spartans could build another fleet, if they lost that one, but could not retreat without dishonor to himself." And yet what he did dealt only a slight blow to Sparta; there was another which proved disastrous, when Cleombrotus in fear of criticism recklessly went into battle against Epaminondas. In consequence of that, the Spartan power fell.

500 *The Old Republic and the New Despotism*
Cicero, De Officiis 2.8.26–27

Let me add, however, that as long as the empire of the Roman People maintained itself by acts of service, not of oppression, wars were waged in the interest of allies or to safeguard our supremacy; the end of our wars was marked by acts of clemency or by only a necessary degree of severity; the senate was a haven of refuge for kings, tribes, and nations; and the highest ambition of our magistrates and generals was to defend our provinces and allies with justice and honor. And so our government could be called more accurately a protectorate of the world than a dominion. This policy and practice we had begun gradually to modify even before Sulla's time; but since his victory we have departed from it altogether. For the time had gone by when any oppression of the allies could appear wrong, seeing that atrocities so outrageous were committed against Roman citizens. In Sulla's case, therefore, an unrighteous victory disgraced a righteous cause. For when he had planted his spear[1] and was selling under the hammer in the forum the property of men who were patriots and men of wealth, and, at least, Roman citizens, he had the effrontery to announce that "he was selling his spoils." After him came one who, in an unholy cause, made an even more shameful use of victory; for he did not stop at confiscating the property of individual citizens, but actually embraced whole provinces and countries in one common ban of ruin.

> 1. The Romans were accustomed to set up a spear as a sign of an auction-sale—a symbol derived from the sale of booty taken in war.

501 *The Way to Glory Is Justice*
Cicero, De Officiis 2.12.43

But as there is a method not only of acquiring money but also of investing it so as to yield an income to meet our continuously recurring expenses—both for the necessities and for the more refined comforts of life—so there must be a method of gaining glory and turning it to account. And yet, as Socrates used to express it so admirably, "the nearest way to glory—a short cut, as it were—is to strive to be what you wish to be thought to be." For if anyone thinks that he can win lasting glory by pretence, by empty show, by hypocritical talk and looks, he is very much mistaken. True glory strikes deep roots and spreads its branches wide; but all pretences soon fall to the ground like fragile flowers, and nothing counterfeit can be lasting. There are very many witnesses to both facts; but for brevity's sake, I shall confine myself to one family: Tiberius Gracchus, Publius' son, will be held in honor as long as the memory of Rome shall endure; but his sons were not approved by patriots while they lived, and since they are dead they are numbered among those whose murder was justifiable.

502   *Wealth No Inducement Nor Bar to Personal Service*
Cicero, De Officiis 2.20.71

We must, of course, put forth every effort to oblige all sorts and conditions of men, if we can. But if it comes to a conflict of duty on this point, we must, I should say, follow the advice of Themistocles; when someone asked his advice whether he should give his daughter in marriage to a man who was poor but honest or to one who was rich but less esteemed, he said: "For my part, I prefer a man without money to money without a man."[1] But the moral sense of today is demoralized and depraved by our worship of wealth. Of what concern to any one of us is the size of another man's fortune? It is, perhaps, an advantage to its possessor; but not always even that. But suppose it is: he may, to be sure, have more money to spend; but how is he any the better man for that? Still, if he is a good man, as well as a rich one, let not his riches be a hindrance to his being aided, if only they are not the motive to it; but in conferring favors our decision should depend entirely upon a man's character, not on his wealth. The supreme rule, then, in the matter of kindnesses to be rendered by personal service is never to take up a case in opposition to the right nor in defense of the wrong. For the foundation of enduring reputation and fame is justice, and without justice there can be nothing worthy of praise.

> 1. Cf. 639.

503   *Official Integrity*
Cicero, De Officiis 2.21.75

But the chief thing in all public administration and public service is to avoid even the slightest suspicion of self-seeking. "I would," says Gaius Pontius, the Samnite, "that fortune had withheld my appearance until a time when Romans began to accept bribes, and that I had been born in those days! I should then have suffered them to hold their supremacy no longer." Aye, but he would have had many generations to wait; for this plague has only recently infected our nation. And so I rejoice that Pontius lived then instead of now, seeing that he was so mighty a man! It is not yet a hundred and ten years since the enactment of Lucius Piso's bill to punish extortion; there had been no such law before. But afterward came so many laws, each more stringent than the other, so many men were accused and so many convicted, so horrible a war was stirred up on account of the fear of what our courts would do to still others, so frightful was the pillaging and plundering of the allies when the laws and courts were suppressed, that now we find ourselves strong not in our own strength but in the weakness of others.

504   *Cato on Estate Profits*
Cicero, De Officiis 2.25.89

Outward advantages also may be weighed against one another: glory, for example, may be preferred to riches, an income derived from city property to one derived from the farm. To this class of comparisons belongs that famous saying of old Cato's: when he was asked what was the most profitable feature of an estate, he replied: "Raising cattle successfully." What next to that? "Raising cattle with fair success." And next? "Raising cattle with slight success." And fourth? "Raising crops." And when his questioner said, "How about money-lending?" Cato replied: "How about murder?" From this as well as from many other incidents we ought to realize that experiences have often to be weighed against one another and that it is proper for us to add this fourth division in the discussion of moral duty.

505 *Idleness and Loneliness*
Cicero, De Officiis 3.1.1

Cato, who was of about the same years, Marcus, my son, as that Publius Scipio who first bore the surname of Africanus, has given us the statement that Scipio used to say that he was never less idle than when he had nothing to do and never less lonely than when he was alone. An admirable sentiment, in truth, and becoming to a great and wise man. It shows that even in his leisure hours his thoughts were occupied with public business and that he used to commune with himself when alone; and so not only was he never unoccupied, but he sometimes had no need for company. The two conditions, then, that prompt others to idleness—leisure and solitude—only spurred him on. I wish I could say the same of myself and say it truly. But if by imitation I cannot attain to such excellence of character, in aspiration, at all events, I approach it as nearly as I can; for as I am kept by force of armed treason away from practical politics and from practice at the bar, I am now leading a life of leisure. For that reason I have left the city and, wandering in the country from place to place, I am often alone.

506 *On Finishing a Work of Art*
Cicero, De Officiis 3.2.10

For if a writer has finished two divisions of a threefold subject, the third must necessarily remain for him to do. Besides, he promises at the close of the third book that he will discuss this division also in its proper turn. We have also in Posidonius a competent witness to the fact. He writes in one of his letters that Publius Rutilius Rufus, who also was a pupil of Panaetius', used to say that "as no painter had been found to complete that part of the Venus of Cos which Appelles had left unfinished (for the beauty of her face made hopeless any attempt adequately to represent the rest of the figure), so no one, because of the surpassing excellence of what Panaetius did complete, would venture to supply what he had left undone."

507 *A Farmer Responds to Question on Planting*
Cicero, De Senectute 7.25

And if you ask a farmer, however old, for whom he is planting, he will unhesitatingly reply, "For the immortal gods, who have willed not only that I should receive these blessings from my ancestors, but also that I should hand them on to posterity."

508 *Themistocles' Favorite Voice*
Cicero, Pro Archia 20

For indeed there is no man to whom the Muses are so distasteful that he will not be glad to entrust to poetry the eternal emblazonment of his achievements. It is related that the great Athenian hero, Themistocles, when asked what recital or what voice he loved best to hear, replied, "That which bears most eloquent testimony to my prowess."

509 *Peripatetics on Desire*
Cicero, Tusculan Disputations 4.19.43

And indeed they [the Peripatetics] do not only praise lust of this sort (for anger is as I defined it lately the lust of vengeance), but they say that this selfsame kind of emotion, call it lust or desire, has been bestowed by nature for purposes of the highest utility; for no one is able to do anything really well except he has a lust for it. Themistocles walked by night in a public place because he was, he said, unable to sleep, and in answer to questions replied that he was kept awake by the trophies of Miltiades. Who has not heard of the sleeplessness of Demosthenes? who said that he was grieved if ever he had been beaten by the diligence of workmen rising before the break of day.

510a *How Much There Is I Do Not Need*
Cicero, Tusculan Disputations 5.32.91

Almost all philosophers of every school, except such as corrupt nature has turned away from right reason, have been able to show this same spirit. When a great quantity of gold and silver was being carried in a procession, Socrates said, "How much there is I do not need."

510b *How Much There Is I Do Not Need*
Diogenes Laertius, Lives of the Eminent Philosophers 2.25

Often when he [Socrates] looked at the multitude of wares exposed for sale, he would say to himself, "How many things I can do without!"

511 *Darius Drinks Muddy Water*
Cicero, Tusculan Disputations 5.34.97

And similiar reasoning is also applied to food, and the costly splendor of banquets is belittled, because they say nature is contented with little elaboration. For who does not see that need is the seasoning for all such things? When Darius in his flight drank muddy water polluted by corpses he said he had never had a more delightful drink; obviously he had never before been thirsty when he drank.

512a *Socrates on Walking*
Cicero, Tusculan Disputations 5.34.97

Socrates, it is said, would walk hard till evening, and when he was asked in consequence why he did so, he replied that by walking he was getting hunger as a relish to make a better dinner.

512b *Socrates on Walking*
Athenaeus, Deipnosophists 4.157E

And Socrates was many a time found walking up and down in front of his house in the late afternoon, and to those who asked, "What are you doing at this hour?" he would reply, "Gathering a relish for my dinner."

513a On One's Country
Cicero, Tusculan Disputations 5.37.108

Finally, in facing all mischances the easiest is the method of those who refer the aims they follow in life to the standard of pleasure, and this means that they can live happily wherever this is provided. And so Teucer's saying can be fitted to every condition: "One's country is wherever one does well."[1] Socrates, for instance, on being asked to what country he claimed to belong, said, "To the world"; for he regarded himself as a native and citizen of the world.

> 1. From the *Teucer* of Pacuvius, cf. Aristophanes, *Plutus* 1151.

513b On One's Country
Plutarch, Moralia, On Exile VII:600F (5)

For man, as Plato says, is "no earthly" or immovable "plant," but a "celestial" one,—the head, like a root, keeping the body erect—inverted to point to heaven. Thus Heracles spoke well when he said

an Argive I

Or Theban, for I boast no single city;
There is no fort in Greece but is my country;

whereas the saying of Socrates is still better, that he was no Athenian or Greek, but a "Cosmian" (as one might say "Rhodian" or "Corinthian"), because he did not shut himself up within Sunium and Taenarus and the Ceraunian mountains.

514 Asclepiades on Blindness
Cicero, Tusculan Disputations 5.39.113

It is related that Asclepiades,[1] no obscure follower of the Eretrian school, on being asked by someone what blindness had brought him, answered that he had one more boy in his retinue;[2] for just as the most utter poverty would be endurable if we could bring ourselves to do as certain Greeks do daily,[3] so blindness could readily be borne, should we be supplied with aids to our infirmities.

> 1. Pupil of Menedemus whose sect of philosophy took its name from Eretria in Euboea.
> 2. Rich men when they went out in public were attended by a large retinue of friends; poor philosophers went by themselves.
> 3. I.e., be parasites or beggars.

515 Thales on Hiding from the Gods
Diogenes Laertius, Lives of the Eminent Philosophers 1.36

Someone asked him [Thales] whether a man could hide an evil deed from the gods: "No," he replied, "nor yet an evil thought."

516 Thales Answers Questions
Diogenes Laertius, Lives of the Eminent Philosophers 1.36

Being asked what is difficult, he [Thales] replied, "To know oneself." "What is easy?" "To give advice to another." "What is most pleasant?" "Success." "What is the divine?" "That which has neither beginning nor end."

517 *Diminishing Crime*

Diogenes Laertius, Lives of the Eminent Philosophers 1.59

Asked how crime could most effectually be diminished, he [Solon] replied, "If it caused as much resentment in those who are not its victims as in those who are," adding, "Wealth breeds satiety, satiety outrage."

518 *Questions that Do Not Concern the Impious*

Diogenes Laertius, Lives of the Eminent Philosophers 1.86

When an impious man asked him [Bias] to define piety, he was silent; and when the other inquired the reason, "I am silent," he replied, "because you are asking questions about what does not concern you."

519 *The Safest Vessels*

Diogenes Laertius, Lives of the Eminent Philosophers 1.104

To the question what vessels were the safest his [Anacharsis'] reply was, "Those which have been hauled ashore."

520 *Anaxagoras Concerned with Native Land*

Diogenes Laertius, Lives of the Eminent Philosophers 2.7

When someone inquired, "Have you no concern for your native land?" he [Anaxagoras] replied, "I am greatly concerned with my native land," and pointed to the sky.

521 *Antisthenes on the Advantage of Philosophy*

Diogenes Laertius, Lives of the Eminent Philosophers 6.6

When he [Antisthenes] was asked what advantage had accrued to him from philosophy, his answer was, "The ability to converse with myself."

522 *Diogenes on Good Greek Men*

Diogenes Laertius, Lives of the Eminent Philosophers 6.27

Being asked where in Greece he [Diogenes] saw good men, he replied, "Good men nowhere, but good boys at Lacedaemon."

523 *Diogenes Gathers Crowd by Whistling*

Diogenes Laertius, Lives of the Eminent Philosophers 6.27

When one day he [Diogenes] was gravely discoursing and nobody attended to him, he began whistling, and as people clustered about him, he reproached them with coming in all seriousness to hear nonsense, but slowly and contemptuously when the theme was serious.

524 *Diogenes Calls For Men*

Diogenes Laertius, Lives of the Eminent Philosophers 6.32

One day he [Diogenes] shouted out for men, and when people gathered, hit out at them with his stick, saying, "It was men I called for, not scoundrels."

525 No Meaner Receptacle
Diogenes Laertius, Lives of the Eminent Philosophers 6.32

Someone took him [Diogenes] into a magnificent house and warned him not to expectorate, whereupon having cleared his throat he discharged the phlegm into the man's face, being unable, he said, to find a meaner receptacle.

526 Diogenes Sees No Horns
Diogenes Laertius, Lives of the Eminent Philosophers 6.38–39

To one who by argument had proved conclusively that he had horns, he [Diogenes] said, touching his forehead, "Well, I for my part don't see any."

527 The Proper Time for Lunch
Diogenes Laertius, Lives of the Eminent Philosophers 6.40

To one who asked what was the proper time for lunch, he [Diogenes] said, "If a rich man, when you will; if a poor man, when you can."

528 Look Out
Diogenes Laertius, Lives of the Eminent Philosophers 6.41

To one who had brandished a beam at him [Diogenes] and then cried, "Look out,"[1] he replied, "What, are you intending to strike me again?"

    1. Cf. 545.

529 Errors of Conduct and Mistakes in Grammar
Diogenes Laertius, Lives of the Eminent Philosophers 6.42

Seeing someone perform religious purification, he [Diogenes] said, "Unhappy man, don't you know that you can no more get rid of errors of conduct by sprinklings than you can of mistakes in grammar?"

530 Full Felicity
Diogenes Laertius, Lives of the Eminent Philosophers 6.44

Hence to a man whose shoes were being put on by his servant, he [Diogenes] said, "You have not attained to full felicity, unless he wipes your nose as well; and that will come, when you have lost the use of your hands."

531 Diogenes Plays the Dog
Diogenes Laertius, Lives of the Eminent Philosophers 6.46

At a feast certain people kept throwing all the bones to him [Diogenes] as they would have done to a dog. Thereupon he played a dog's trick and drenched them.

532 A Sneeze from the Left
Diogenes Laertius, Lives of the Eminent Philosophers 6.48

A very superstitious person addressed him thus, "With one blow I will break your head." "And I," said Diogenes, "by a sneeze from the left will make you tremble."

533 Diogenes Became Philosopher through Exile
Diogenes Laertius, Lives of the Eminent Philosophers 6.49

When someone reproached him [Diogenes] with his exile, his reply was, "Nay, it was through that, you miserable fellow, that I came to be a philosopher."

534 *The Right Time to Marry*
Diogenes Laertius, Lives of the Eminent Philosophers 6.54

Being asked what was the right time to marry, Diogenes replied, "For a young man not yet: for an old man never at all."

535 *Diogenes on the Best Wine*
Diogenes Laertius, Lives of the Eminent Philosophers 6.54

To the question what wine he [Diogenes] found pleasant to drink, he replied, "That for which other people pay."

536 *What Kind of Hound Is Diogenes?*
Diogenes Laertius, Lives of the Eminent Philosophers 6.55

Being asked what kind of hound he was, he [Diogenes] replied, "When hungry, a Maltese; when full, a Molossian—two breeds which most people praise, though for fear of fatigue they do not venture out hunting with them. So neither can you live with me, because you are afraid of the discomforts."

537 *Do the Wise Eat Cakes?*
Diogenes Laertius, Lives of the Eminent Philosophers 6.56

Being asked if the wise eat cakes, "Yes," he [Diogenes] said, "Cakes of all kinds, just like other men."

538 *People Laugh at Diogenes*
Diogenes Laertius, Lives of the Eminent Philosophers 6.58

When someone said, "Most people laugh at you," his [Diogenes'] reply was, "And so very likely do the asses at them; but as they don't care for the asses, so neither do I care for them."

539 *Whither and Whence?*
Diogenes Laertius, Lives of the Eminent Philosophers 6.59

He [Diogenes] was returning from Lacedaemon to Athens; and on someone asking, "Whither and whence?" he replied, "From the men's apartments to the women's."

540 *Diogenes on Votive Offerings*
Diogenes Laertius, Lives of the Eminent Philosophers 6.59

When someone expressed astonishment at the votive offerings in Samothrace, Diogenes said, "There would have been far more, if those who were not saved had set up offerings."

541 *Great Crowd, Few Men*
Diogenes Laertius, Lives of the Eminent Philosophers 6.60

He [Diogenes] was returning from Olympia, and when somebody inquired whether there was a great crowd, "Yes," he said, "a great crowd, but few who could be called men."

542 *Diogenes on Dirty Places*
Diogenes Laertius, Lives of the Eminent Philosophers 6.63

When someone reproached him for going into dirty places, Diogenes replied, "The sun too visits cesspools without being defiled."

543 Dirty Loaves in the Temple
Diogenes Laertius, Lives of the Eminent Philosophers 6.64

When he [Diogenes] was dining in a temple, and in the course of the meal loaves not free from dirt were put on the table, he took them up and threw them away, declaring that nothing unclean ought to enter a temple.

544 The Fool and the Psaltery
Diogenes Laertius, Lives of the Eminent Philosophers 6.65

Observing a fool tuning a psaltery, "Are you not ashamed," said he [Diogenes], "to give this wood concordant sounds, while you fail to harmonize your soul with life?"

545 Warnings
Diogenes Laertius, Lives of the Eminent Philosophers 6.66

When someone first shook a beam at him and then shouted "Look out," Diogenes struck the man with his staff and added "Look out."[1]

1. Cf. 528.

546 A Mina from a Spendthrift
Diogenes Laertius, Lives of the Eminent Philosophers 6.67

He [Diogenes] asked a spendthrift for a mina. The man inquired why it was that he asked others for an obol but him for a mina. "Because," said Diogenes, "I expect to receive from others again, but whether I shall ever get anything from you again lies on the knees of the gods."

547 Diogenes on Banishing Hunger
Diogenes Laertius, Lives of the Eminent Philosophers 6.69

While he [Diogenes] was masturbating in public, he said, "Would that it were as easy to banish hunger by rubbing the belly."

548 Zeno Relaxes at a Drinking Party
Diogenes Laertius, Lives of the Eminent Philosophers 7.26

When he [Zeno] was asked why he, though so austere, relaxed at a drinking-party, he said, "Lupins too are bitter, but when they are soaked become sweet."

549 When Will the Kingdom Come?
Epistle, 2 Clement 12.2 (Funk-Bihlmeyer: 76)

For when the Lord himself was asked by someone when his kingdom would come, he said, "When the two will be one, and the outside as the inside, and the male with the female neither male nor female."

550 Country before Friends
Gellius, Attic Nights 1.3.18

But that is the very point on which we most need instruction, but which the teachers make least clear, namely, how far and to what degree indulgence must be allowed to friendship. The sage, Chilo, whom I mentioned above, turned from the path to save a friend. But I can see how far he went; for he gave unsound advice to save his friend. Yet even as to that he was in doubt up to his last hour whether he deserved criticism and censure. "Against one's fatherland," says Cicero, "one must not take up arms for a friend."[1]

> 1. Cicero, *De Amicitia* 36.

551 *Love and Hate*
Gellius, Attic Nights 1.3.30

Now this Chilo, with whom I began this little discussion, is the author not only of some other wise and salutory precepts, but also of the following, which has been found particularly helpful, since it confines within due limits those two most ungovernable passions, love and hatred. "So love," said he, "as if you were possibly destined to hate; and in the same way, hate as if you might perhaps afterwards love."[1]

> 1. Cicero, *De Amicitia* 59, attributes this saying to Bias, another of the seven sages, as do also Aristotle, Diogenes Laertius and Valerius Maximus.

552 *Friendship and Enmity*
Gellius, Attic Nights 1.3.31

Of this same Chilo the philosopher Plutarch, in the first book of his treatise *On the Soul*, wrote as follows:[1] "Chilo of old, having heard a man say that he had no enemy, asked him if he had no friend, believing that enmities necessarily followed and were involved in friendships."

> 1. Plutarch, *Moralia, On the Soul* XV: Fragment 174.

553 *Gods Supply Virtue*
Gellius, Attic Nights 1.6.7

This other passage also from the same address of Metellus in my opinion deserves constant reading, not less by Heaven! than the writings of the greatest philosophers. His words are these: "The immortal gods have mighty power, but they are not expected to be more indulgent to us than our parents. But parents, if their children persist in wrongdoing, disinherit them. What different application of justice then are we to look for from the immortal gods, unless we put an end to our evil ways? Those alone may fairly claim the favor of the gods who are not their own worst enemies. The immortal gods ought to support, not supply, virtue."

554 *Bias' Syllogism on Marriage*
Gellius, Attic Nights 5.11.1-2

Some think that the famous answer of the wise and noble Bias, like of Protagoras of which I have just spoken, was *antistrephon*.[1] For Bias, being asked by a certain man whether he should marry or lead a single life, said: "You are sure to marry a woman either beautiful or ugly; and if beautiful, you will share her with others, but if ugly, she will be a punishment.[2] But neither of these things is desirable; therefore do not marry."

> 1. The "convertible" argument [which is equally strong for both sides of a question] is described in *Attic Nights* 5.10.
> 2. In the Greek there is a word-play on *koine* and *poine*, which it does not seem possible to reproduce in English. Perhaps, a flirt or a hurt, or, a harlot or a hard lot.

555 *Philosophers Wait for Pupils*
Gellius, Attic Nights 7.10.5

"But nowadays," said Taurus, "we may see the philosophers themselves running to the doors of rich young men, to give them instruction, and there they sit and wait until nearly noonday, for their pupils to sleep off all last night's wine."

556 *One Who Has Much Needs Much*
Gellius, Attic Nights 9.8.3

I recall that Favorinus once, amid loud and general applause, rounded off this thought, putting it into the fewest possible words: "It is not possible for one who wants fifteen thousand cloaks not to want more things; for if I want more than I possess, by taking away from what I have I shall be contented with what remains."

557 *The Sayings of Publius Nigidius*
Gellius, Attic Nights 11.11.1–4

These are the words of Publius Nigidius, a man of great eminence in the pursuit of liberal arts, whom Marcus Cicero highly respected because of his talent and learning: "There is a difference between telling a falsehood and lying. One who lies is not himself deceived, but tries to deceive another; he who tells a falsehood is himself deceived." He also adds this: "One who lies deceives, so far as he is able; but one who tells a falsehood does not himself deceive, any more than he can help." He also had this on the same subject: "A good man," says he, "ought to take pains not to lie, a wise man, not to tell what is false; the former affects the man himself, the latter does not." With variety, by Heaven! and neatness has Nigidius distinguished so many opinions relating to the same thing, as if he were constantly saying something new.

558 *Peregrinus on Secrecy and Sin*
Gellius, Attic Nights 12.11.4–5

If, however, there were any who were neither so endowed by nature nor so well disciplined that they could easily keep themselves from sinning by their own willpower, he [Peregrinus] thought that such men would all be more inclined to sin whenever they thought that their guilt could be concealed and when they had hope of impunity because of such concealment. "But," said he, "if men know that nothing at all can be hidden for very long, they will sin more reluctantly and more secretly."

559 *On Consulting the Ear*
Gellius, Attic Nights 13.21.1–8

Valerius Probus was once asked, as I learned from one of his friends, whether one ought to say *has urbis* or *has urbes* and *hanc turrem* or *hanc turrim*. "If," he replied, "you are either composing verse or writing prose and have to use those words, pay no attention to the musty, fusty rules of the grammarians, but consult your own ear as to what is to be said in any given place. What it favors will surely be the best." Then the one who had asked the question said: "What do you mean by 'consult my ear'?" and he told me that Probus answered: "Just as Vergil did his, when in different passages he has used *urbis* and *urbes*, following the taste and judgement of his ear. For in the first *Georgic*, which," said he, "I have read in a copy corrected by the poet's own hand, he wrote *urbis* with an *i*. These are the words of the verses:[1]

O'er cities (*urbis*) if you choose to watch, and rule
Our lands, O Caesar great.

But turn and change it so as to read *urbes*, and somehow you will make it duller and heavier. On the other hand, in the third *Aeneid* he wrote *urbes* with an *e*:[2]

An hundred mighty cities (*urbes*) they inhabit.

Change this too so as to read *urbis* and the word will be too slender and colorless, so great indeed is the different effect of combination in the harmony of neighboring sounds. Moreover, Vergil also said *turrim*, not *turrem*, and *securim*, not *securem*:

A turret (*turrim*) on sheer edge standing,[3]

and

Has shaken from his neck the ill-aimed axe (*securim*).

These words have, I think, a more agreeable lightness than if you should use the form in *e* in both places." But the one who asked the question, a boorish fellow surely and with untrained ear, said: "I don't just understand why you say that one form is better and more correct in one place and the other in the other." Then Probus, now somewhat impatient, retorted: "Don't trouble then to inquire whether you ought to say *urbis* or *urbes*. For since you are the kind of man that I see you are and err without detriment to yourself, you will lose nothing whichever you say."

1. Virgil, *Georgic* 1.25.
2. Virgil, *Aeneid* 3.106.
3. Ibid., 2.460.
4. Ibid., 2.224.

560   *Epictetus Chides Wicked Philosopher*
Gellius, Attic Nights 17.19.3

But that is still more severe which Arrian in his work *On the Dissertations of Epictetus*,[1] has written that this philosopher [Epictetus] used to say. "For," says Arrian, "when he perceived that a man without shame, persistent in wickedness, of abandoned character, reckless, boastful, and cultivating everything else except his soul—when he saw such a man taking up also the study and pursuit of philosophy, attacking natural history, practicing logic and balancing and investigating many problems of that kind, he used to invoke the help of gods and men, and usually amid his exclamations chided the man in these terms: "O man, where are you storing these things? Consider whether the vessel be clean. For if you take them into your self-conceit, they are lost; if they are spoiled, they become urine or vinegar or something worse, if possible."

1. 2.19; cf. Aulus Gellius, *Attic Nights* 1.2.8.

561   *Favorinus on Praise and Censure*
Gellius, Attic Nights 19.3.1

Favorinus the philsosopher used to say that it was more shameful to be praised faintly and coldly than to be censured violently and severely: "For," said he, "the man who reviles and censures you is regarded as unjust and hostile towards you in proportion to the bitterness of his invective, and therefore he is usually not believed. But one who praises grudgingly and faintly seems to lack a theme; he is regarded as the friend of a man whom he would like to praise but as unable to find anything in him which he can justly commend."

562a   *Drink from Jesus*
Gospel, John 7:37–39 (NIV)

On the last and greatest day of the Feast, Jesus stood and said in a loud voice, "If anyone is thirsty, let him come to me and drink. Whoever believes in me, as the Scripture has said, streams of living water will flow from within him." By this he meant the Spirit, whom those who believed in him were later to receive. Up to that time the Spirit had not been given, since Jesus had not yet been glorified.

562b   *Drink from Jesus' Mouth*
Gospel, Thomas 108

Jesus said, "Whoever drinks from my mouth will become like me; I myself shall become that person, and the hidden things will be revealed to that one."

563a   *Preaching to Other Cities Also*
Gospel, Luke 4:42–44 (NIV)

At day break Jesus went out to a solitary place. The people were looking for him and when they came to where he was, they tried to keep him from leaving them. But he said, "I must preach the good news of the kingdom of God to the other towns also, because that is why I was sent." And he kept on preaching in the synagogues of Judea.

563b   *Preaching to Other Cities Also*
Gospel, Mark 1:35–39 (NIV)

Very early in the morning, while it was still dark, Jesus got up, left the house and went off to a solitary place, where he prayed. Simon and his companions went to look for him, and when they found him, they exclaimed: "Everyone is looking for you!" Jesus replied, "Let us go somewhere else—to the nearby villages—so I can preach there also. That is why I have come." So he traveled throughout Galilee, preaching in their synagogues and driving out demons.

564   *Man Works on Sabbath*
Gospel, Luke 6:4 (Codex D, Aland: 66)

On the same day he [Jesus] saw a man working on the Sabbath and said to him, "Man, if you know what you are doing, you are blessed. But if you do not know, you are accursed and a transgressor of the law."

565a   *John the Baptist Beheaded*
Gospel, Luke 9:7–9 (NIV)

Now Herod the tetrarch heard about all that was going on. And he was perplexed, because some were saying that John had been raised from the dead, others that Elijah had appeared, and still others that one of the prophets of long ago had come back to life. But Herod said, "I beheaded John. Who, then is this I hear such things about?" And he tried to see him.

565b *John the Baptist Beheaded*
Gospel, Mark 6:14–16 (NIV)

King Herod heard about this, for Jesus' name had become well known. Some were saying, "John the Baptist has been raised from the dead, and that is why miraculous powers are at work in him." Others said, "He is Elijah." And still others claimed, "He is a prophet, like one of the prophets of long ago." But when Herod heard this, he said, "John, the man I beheaded, has been raised from the dead!"

565c *John the Baptist Beheaded*
Gospel, Matthew 14:1–2 (NIV)

At that time Herod the tetrarch heard the reports about Jesus, and he said to his attendants, "This is John the Baptist; he has risen from the dead! That is why miraculous powers are at work in him."

566 *Narrow Door*
Gospel, Luke 13:22–30 (NIV)

Then Jesus went through the towns and villages, teaching as he made his way to Jerusalem. Someone asked him, "Lord, are only a few people going to be saved?" He said to them, "Make every effort to enter through the narrow door, because many, I tell you, will try to enter and will not be able to. Once the owner of the house gets up and closes the door, you will stand outside knocking and pleading, 'Sir, open the door for us.' But he will answer, 'I don't know you or where you come from.' Then you will say, 'We ate and drank with you, and you taught in our streets.' "But he will reply, 'I don't know you or where you come from. Away from me, all you evildoers!' There will be weeping there, and gnashing of teeth, when you see Abraham, Isaac and Jacob and all the prophets in the kingdom of God, but you yourselves thrown out. People will come from east and west and north and south, and will take their places at the feast in the kingdom of God. Indeed there are those who are last who will be first, and first who will be last."[1]

1. Cf. Gospel, Thomas 4.

567a *Giving a Banquet*
Gospel, Luke 14:15–24 (NIV)

When one of those at the table with him heard this, he said to Jesus, "Blessed is the man who will eat at the feast in the kingdom of God." Jesus replied: "A certain man was preparing a great banquet and invited many guests. At the time of the banquet he sent his servant to tell those who had been invited, 'Come, for everything is now ready.' "But they all alike began to make excuses. The first said, 'I have just bought a field, and I must go and see it. Please excuse me.' "Another said, 'I have just bought five yoke of oxen, and I'm on my way to try them out. Please excuse me.' "Still another said, 'I just got married, so I can't come.' "The servant came back and reported this to his master. Then the owner of the house became angry and ordered his servant, 'Go out quickly into the streets and alleys of the town and bring in the poor, the crippled, the blind and the lame.' "'Sir,' the servant said, 'what you ordered has been done, but there is still room.' "Then the master told his servant, 'Go out to the roads and country lanes and make them come in, so that my house will be full. I tell you, not one of those men who were invited will get a taste of my banquet.'"

567b Giving a Banquet
Gospel, Luke 14:12–14 (NIV)

Then Jesus said to his host, "When you give a luncheon or dinner, do not invite your friends, your brothers or relatives, or your rich neighbors; if you do, they may invite you back and so you will be repaid. But when you give a banquet, invite the poor, the crippled, the lame, the blind, and you will be blessed. Although they cannot repay you, you will be repaid at the resurrection of the righteous."

567c Giving a Banquet
Gospel, Thomas 64

Jesus said, "A person was receiving guests. When he had prepared the dinner, he sent his servant to invite the guests. The servant went to the first and said to that one, 'My lord invites you.' The guest said, 'Some merchants owe me money, and they are coming to me tonight. I must go and give instructions to them. Please excuse me from dinner.' The servant went to another and said to that one, 'My lord invites you.' The guest said to the servant, 'I have bought a house, and I have been called away for a day. I shall have no time.' The servant went to another and said to that one, 'My lord invites you.' The guest said to the servant, 'My friend is to be married, and I am to arrange the dinner. I shall not be able to come. Please excuse me from dinner.' The servant went to another and said to that one, 'My lord invites you.' The guest said to the servant, 'I have bought an estate, and I am going to collect the rent. I shall not be able to come. Please excuse me.' The servant returned and said to the lord, 'Those whom you invited to dinner have asked to be excused.' The lord said to his servant, 'Go out on the streets, and bring back whomever you find to have dinner.' Buyers and merchants [will] not enter the places of my Father."

568a Parable of the Ten Pounds
Gospel, Luke 19:11–27 (NIV)

While they were listening to this, he went on to tell them a parable, because he was near Jerusalem and the people thought that the kingdom of God was going to appear at once. He said: "A man of noble birth went to a distant country to have himself appointed king and then to return. So he called ten of his servants and gave them ten minas. Put this money to work,' he said, 'until I come back.' "But his subjects hated him and sent a delegation after him to say, 'We don't want this man to be our king.' "He was made king, however, and returned home. Then he sent for the servants to whom he had given the money, in order to find out what they had gained with it. "The first one came and said, 'Sir, your mina has earned ten more.' "'Well done, my good servant!' his master replied. 'Because you have been trustworthy in a very small matter, take charge of ten cities.' "The second came and said, 'Sir, your mina has earned five more.' "His master answered, 'You take charge of five cities.' "Then another servant came and said, 'Sir, here is your mina; I have kept it laid away in a piece of cloth. I was afraid of you, because you are a hard man. You take out what you did not put in and reap what you did not sow.' "His master replied, 'I will judge you by your own words, you wicked servant! You knew, did you, that I am a hard man, taking out what I did not put in, and reaping what I did not sow? Why then didn't you put my money on deposit, so that when I came back, I could have collected it with interest?" Then he said to those standing by, 'Take his mina away from him and give it to the one who has ten minas.' "'Sir,' they said, 'he already has ten!' "He replied, 'I tell you that to everyone who has, more will be given, but as for the one who has nothing, even what he has will be taken away. But those enemies of mine who did not want me to be king over them—bring them here and kill them in front of me.'"

568b *Parable of the Talents*
Gospel, Matthew 25:14–30 (NIV)

"Again, it will be like a man going on a journey, who called his servants and entrusted his property to them. To one he gave five talents of money, to another two talents, and to another one talent, each according to his ability. Then he went on his journey. The man who had received the five talents went at once and put his money to work and gained five more. So also, the one with the two talents gained two more. But the man who had received the one talent went off, dug a hole in the ground and hid his master's money. After a long time the master of those servants returned and settled accounts with them. The man who had received the five talents brought the other five. 'Master,' he said, 'you entrusted me with five talents. See, I have gained five more.' "His master replied, 'Well done, good and faithful servant! You have been faithful with a few things; I will put you in charge of many things. come and share your master's happiness!' "The man with the two talents also came, 'master,' he said, 'you entrusted me with two talents; see, I have gained two more.' "His master replied, 'Well done, good and faithful servant! You have been faithful with a few things; I will put you in charge of many things. Come and share your master's happiness!' "Then the man who had received the one talent came. 'Master,' he said, 'I knew that you are a hard man, harvesting where you have not sown and gathering where you have not scattered seed. so I was afraid and went out and hid your talent in the ground. See, here is what belongs to you.' "His master replied, 'You wicked, lazy servant! So you knew that I harvest where I have not sown and gather where I have not scattered seed? Well then, you should have put my money on deposit with the bankers, so that when I returned I would have received it back with interest. "'Take the talent from him and give it to the one who has the ten talents. For everyone who has will be given more, and he will have an abundance. Whoever does not have, even what he has will be taken from him. And throw that worthless servant outside, into the darkness, where there will be weeping and gnashing of teeth.'

568c *Parable of the Talents*
Gospel, Nazoreans 18

Since the gospel that has come down to us in Hebrew characters levels the threat not against the one who hid [the talent], but against the one who lived a life of debauchery (for there were three servants: one who squandered his master's money with prostitutes and dancehall girls,[1] a second who multiplied the investment, and a third who hid the talent; one received approval, one was merely rebuked, and the other was locked up in prison), I wonder whether the threat in Matthew that follows upon the completion of the word directed against the one who did nothing, is not actually leveled against him, but against the first servant who ate and drank regularly in the company of drunks (by epanalepsis [a rhetorical figure involving resumption]).

1. Cf. 838.

568d Receiving More
Gospel, Thomas 41

Jesus said, "Whoever has something in hand will be given more, and whoever has nothing will be deprived of even the little that person has."

568e Receiving More
Gospel, Matthew 13:10–12 (NIV)

The disciples came to him and asked, "Why do you speak to the people in parables?" He replied, "The knowledge of the secrets of the kingdom of heaven has been given to you, but not to them. Whoever has will be given more, and he will have an abundance. Whoever does not have, even what he has will be taken from him.

568f Receiving More
Gospel, Mark 4:24–25 (NIV)

"Consider carefully what you hear," he continued. "With the measure you use, it will be measured to you—and even more. Whoever has will be given more; whoever does not have, even what he has will be taken from him."

569a Rest for the Weary
Gospel, Matthew 11:25–30 (NIV)

At that time Jesus said, "I praise you, Father, Lord of heaven and earth, because you have hidden these things from the wise and learned, and revealed them to little children. Yes, Father, for this was your good pleasure. "All things have been committed to me by my Father. No one knows the Son except the Father, and no one knows the Father except the Son and those to whom the Son chooses to reveal him. "Come to me, all you who are weary and burdened, and I will give you rest. Take my yoke upon you and learn from me, for I am gentle and humble in heart, and you will find rest for your souls. For my yoke is easy and my burden is light."

569b Rest for the Weary
Gospel, Thomas 90

Jesus said, "Come to me, for my yoke is easy and my lordship is gentle, and you will find rest your yourselves."

570 Be Worshippers of God and Brothers
Hadith, Bukhārī, adab, 57

Bishr b. Muḥammad reported to us saying, 'Abd Allāh informed us on the authority of Ma'mar, who had it from Ḥammām b. Munabbih, who in turn heard Abū Hurayra report that the Prophet said: Beware of suspicion for suspicion is the worst of false tales. Do not be busybodies nor spy on others. Avoid jealousy. Do not break off relations with each other and do not hate one another. Be worshippers of God and brothers!"

571 No Spitting in Mosque
Hadith, Bukhārī, adab, 75

Mūsā b. Ismā'īl and Juwayrīya related to us from Nafi', who had it from 'Abd Allāh b. 'Umar, who said: while the Prophet was praying he saw sputum on the wall of the mosque, on the side of the direction for prayer (qibla). He rubbed it off with his hand angrily and said, "Whenever anyone is at prayer he should not spit in front of him because God is present in front of him."

572   On Heat and Fire
Hadith, Mālik, wuqūt al-ṣalāt, 7

Yaḥyā related to me from Mālik, who had it from Zayd b. Aslam and ‘Aṭā b. Yasār that: The Messenger of God said, "The scorching heat is part of the blast of hell fire. So when the heat is intense, put off the prayer time until it gets cooler." He continued, "The fire complained to its Lord saying, 'O Lord part of me has eaten another part.' So he granted it two emanations, one for the winter and one for the summer."

573   Dirt for Flatterers
Hadith, Tirmidhī, zuhd, 43

Bundār, ‘Abd al-Raḥmān b. Mahdī and Sufyān informed us from Ḥabīb b. abī Thābit from Mujāhid from Abū Ma‘mar who said: A man got up and started praising a certain prince. Al-Miqdād b. al-Aswad threw dirt in his face and said, "The Messenger of God directed us to throw dirt in the face of flatterers."

574   Freedom from Hope and Fear
Lucian, Demonax 20

When a man asked him what he thought was the definition of happiness, Demonax replied, "Only the free man is happy." And when the other said that free men were numerous, he responded, "But I have in mind the man who neither hopes nor fears anything." He said, "But how can one achieve this? For the most part we are all slaves of hope and fear." "Why, if you observe human affairs you will find that they do not afford justification either for hope or for fear, since, whatever you may say, pains and pleasures are alike destined to end."

575   Demonax and the Mourner
Lucian, Demonax 25

He went to a man who was mourning the death of a son and had shut himself up in the dark, and told him that he was a magician and could raise the boy's ghost for him if only he would name three men who had never mourned for anyone. When the man hesitated for a long time and was perplexed—I suppose he could not name a single one—Demonax said, "You ridiculous fellow, do you think then that you alone suffer beyond endurance, when you see that nobody is unacquainted with mourning?"

576   On the Immortality of the Soul
Lucian, Demonax 32

When a man asked if he thought that the soul was immortal, he [Demonax] said, "Yes, but no more so than everything else."

577   Weigh the Ashes
Lucian, Demonax 39

Moreover, when questions were unanswerable he always had an apt retort ready. When a man asked him banteringly, "If I should burn a thousand pounds of wood,

Demonax, how many pounds of smoke would it make?" he replied, "Weigh the ashes; all the rest will be smoke."

578 Demonax Reproached with Cowardice
Lucian, Demonax 42

When he [Demonax] was taking a bath and hesitated to enter the steaming water, a man reproached him with cowardice. "Tell me," said he, "was my country at stake in the matter?"

579 Word from Hades
Lucian, Demonax 43

When someone asked him, "What do you think it is like in Hades?" he [Demonax] replied, "Wait a bit, and I'll send you word from there!"

580 Honey for Fools?
Lucian, Demonax 52

When someone asked him, "Do *you* eat honey-cakes?" he [Demonax] replied, "What! do you think the bees lay up their honey just for fools?"

581 Recognizing the Kingdom
Martyrdom, Peter 9 <Acts of Peter 38> (Lipsius-Bonnet 1:94)

Concerning these things the Lord said in a mystery, "Unless you make the things on the right as those on the left and the things on the left as those on the right and the things above as those below and the things behind as those before, you will not recognize the kingdom."

582 One Floating Skull
Mishnah, Abot 2:6

Also [Hillel] saw one skull floating on the face of the water. He said to it: "Because you drowned [others] they drowned you, and in the end they that drowned you shall be drowned."

583 Tarfon Places Himself in Danger
Mishnah, Berakhot 1:3

R. Tarfon said: "I was going on the road and I reclined to recite the [evening] *Shema* according to the words of the House of Shammai, and [in doing so] I placed myself in danger from robbers." They said to him: "You deserved to lose your life, for you transgressed the words of the House of Hillel."

584 Aesop Concerning the Success of the Wicked
Phaedrus, Aesopic Fables 2.3

When a certain man had been torn by the bite of a vicious dog he dipped a piece of bread in his own blood and tossed it to the evildoer, because he had heard that this was a remedy for such a wound. Then said Aesop: "Don't let any more dogs see you doing this, lest they devour us alive when they learn that guilt is rewarded in this way." The success of the wicked lures many others into evil ways.

585 *The Butcher and the Ape*
Phaedrus, Aesopic Fables 3.4

Someone saw an ape hanging in a butcher's shop among the other commodities and viands, and asked what the flavor was like; whereupon the butcher replied in jest: "It tastes as bad as it looks." This, I suppose, has been told more for the sake of a laugh than with regard to the truth; for I have often met with handsome persons who were scoundrels, and have known many with ugly features to be the best of men.

586 *Aesop and the Saucy Fellow*
Phaedrus, Aesopic Fables 3.5

Success invites many to their ruin. A saucy fellow threw a stone at Aesop and hit him. "Good for you!" said Aesop; then he gave him a penny and added: "So help me, I haven't any more, but I'll show you where you can get some. Look, here comes a rich and influential man; throw a stone at him the way you did at me, and you will get an adequate reward." The fellow was persuaded and did as he was advised. But his hope deceived him and frustrated his impudent audacity, for he was arrested and paid the penalty on the cross.

587 *Socrates to His Friends*
Phaedrus, Aesopic Fables 3.9

The name of friend is common enough, but loyalty is rare. When Socrates had laid the foundations of a small house for himself—incidentally, I do not refuse to die that man's death if only I may achieve his fame, and like him, I will submit to malice if my dust may be vindicated—one or other of the people, in the course of conversation usual on such occasions, remarked: "What, so small a house for so great a man?" "I only wish," he replied, "that I could fill it with real friends."

588 *The Horse and the Wild Boar*
Phaedrus, Aesopic Fables 4.4

A wild boar in wallowing muddied the shallow water where a horse was accustomed to quench his thirst. The result was a quarrel between them. He of the sounding hoof, enraged at the beast, sought the help of a man, and, after taking him up on his back, returned, elated, against his enemy. When the knight with his weapons had killed this enemy he is said to have spoken as follows to the horse: "I am very glad to have brought you help in response to your entreaties; for I have captured a prize, and have come to know how useful you are." And so he compelled the horse in spite of himself to submit to the reins. Then, in deep dejection the horse said to himself: "I was a fool; while looking for revenge in a small matter, I have found slavery for myself." This fable will serve to warn hot-tempered men that it is better to suffer an injury with impunity than to put one's self in the power of another.

589 *The Bald Man and the Fly*
Phaedrus, Aesopic Fables 5.3

A fly bit the bare head of a bald man, and in trying to crush it he gave himself a hard slap. Thereupon the fly mocked him saying: "You wanted to avenge with death the sting of a little insect; what will you do to yourself, now that you have added insult to injury?" The man replied: "I can easily get back into my own good graces, since I know that it was not my intention to injure myself, but as for you, miserable creature of a despised species, who delight in drinking human blood, I should be glad to be rid of you at the cost of even greater discomfort." As you will see by this example, it is fitting that one should be pardoned who does wrong by accident; but as for him who injures anyone intentionally, no punishment, I reckon, is too great for him.

590   *Aesop and the Writer*
Phaedrus, Aesopic Fables Appendix 9

A certain man had recited to Aesop some poor compositions, in the course of which he had inappropriately sounded his own praise at great length. Wishing, therefore, to know what the old man thought of it, he said: "I hope I have not appeared to you to be too proud of myself? The confidence that I feel in my own genius is no illusion." Aesop, who was completely worn out by listening to the miserable volume, replied: "For my part, I emphatically endorse your bestowing praise on yourself; for it will never come to you from any other source."

591   *The Traveler and the Raven*
Phaedrus, Aesopic Fables, Appendix 23

A man journeying through the country on a byway heard someone call "Hail!" He paused for a moment, but when he saw that no one was there, quickened his pace. Again the same sound greeted him from some hidden place. Feeling reassured by the friendly voice, he halted, in order that whoever it was might receive the like civility from himself. When he had remained a long while looking about in perplexity, and had lost enough time to have walked several miles, a raven appeared and, flying overhead, once more interjected his "Hail!" Perceiving then that he had been fooled, the traveler said: "Damn you, miserable bird, for detaining me like that when I was in a hurry."

592   *How a Man of Worth Responds to Threats*
Philo, Every Good Man Is Free 145–146

So then, too, the man of worth may say to his prospective purchaser, "Then you will have lessons in self-control." If one threatens him with banishment, he can say, "Every land is my native country"; if with loss of money, "A moderate livelihood suffices me"; if the threat takes the form of blows or death, he can say, "These bugbears do not scare me; I am not inferior to boxers or pancratiasts, who though they see but dim shadows of true excellence, since they only cultivate robustness of body, yet endure both bravely. For the mind within me which rules the body is by courage so well-braced and nerved, that it can stand superior to any kind of pain."

593   *Diogenes Marvels at Freedman's Folly*
Philo, Every Good Man Is Free 157

Thus Diogenes the Cynic, seeing one of the so-called freedmen pluming himself, while many heartily congratulated him, marveled at the absence of reason and discernment. "A man might as well," he said, "proclaim that one of his servants became from this day a grammarian, a geometrician, or musician, when he had no idea whatever of the art."

594a   *The Axe of Dionysius*
　　　　Philo, On Providence, Fragment 2 from Eusebius,
　　　　Preparation for the Gospel 7:14, 29–30

Another proof is the way in which he [Dionysius] is said to have treated a person who asserted the felicity of the tyrant's life. Having invited him to a dinner which had been provided on a very magnificent and costly scale he ordered a sharp-edged axe to be suspended over him by a very slender thread. When after taking his place on the couch the guest suddenly saw this, he had neither the courage in the tyrant's presence to rise and remove himself nor the power in his terror to enjoy the dishes provided, and so regardless of the abundance and wealth of the pleasures before him, he lay with neck and eye strained upwards, expecting his own destruction. Dionysius perceived this and said: "Do you now understand what this glorious and much coveted life of ours really is?"

594b   *The Sword of Damocles*
　　　　Cicero, Tusculan Disputations 5.21.61–62

For when one of his [Dionysius'] flatterers, named Damocles, dilated in conversation upon his troops, his resources, the splendors of his despotism, the magnitude of his treasures, the stateliness of his palaces, and said that no one had ever been happier: "Would you then, Damocles," said he, "as this life of mine seems to you so delightful, like to have a taste of it yourself and make trial of my good fortune?" On his admitting his desire to do so Dionysius had him seated on a couch of gold covered with beautiful woven tapestries embroidered with magnificent designs, and had several sideboards set out with richly chased gold and silver plate. Next a table was brought and chosen boys of rare beauty were ordered to take their places and wait upon him with eyes fixed attentively upon his motions. There were perfumes, garlands; incense was burnt; the tables were loaded with the choicest banquet: Damocles thought himself a lucky man. In the midst of all this display Dionysius had a gleaming sword, attached to a horse-hair, let down from the ceiling in such a way that it hung over the neck of this happy man. And so he had no eye either for those beautiful attendants, or the richly-wrought plate, nor did he reach out his hand to the table; presently the garlands slipped from their place of their own accord; at length he besought the tyrant to let him go, as he was sure he had no wish to be happy. Dionysius seems (does he not?) to have avowed plainly that there was no happiness for the man who was perpetually menaced by some alarm. Moreover it was not even open to him to retrace his steps to the path of justice, to restore to his fellow citizens their freedom and their rights; for with the inconsiderateness of youth he had entangled himself in such errors and been guilty of such acts as made it impossible for him to be safe if he once began to be sane.

595   *Damis Replies to Critic*
　　　　Philostratus, Life of Apollonius 1.19

It was a lazy fellow and malignant who tried to pick holes in him [Damis], and remarked that he had recorded well enough a lot of things, for example, the opinions and ideas of his hero [Apollonius], but that in collecting such trifles as these he reminded him of dogs who pick up and eat the fragments which fall from a feast. Damis replied thus: "If banquets there be of gods, and gods take food, surely they must have attendants whose business it is that not even the parcels of ambrosia that fall to the ground should be lost."

596 *The Gardens of Tantalus*
Philostratus, Lives of the Sophists 1.20 (513)

And when someone asked him [Isaeus, the Assyrian sophist] what sort of bird and what sort of fish were the best eating, "I have ceased," replied Isaeus, "to take these matters seriously, for I now know that I used to feed on the gardens of Tantalus."[1] Thus he indicated to his questioner that all pleasures are a shadow and a dream.

> 1. A proverb of fleeting joys; cf. Philostratus, *Life of Apollonius* 4.25.

597 *Antiochus Fears Own Temper*
Philostratus, Lives of the Sophists 2.4 (568)

Antiochus the sophist was born at Aegae in Cilicia of so distinguished a family that even now his descendants are made consuls. When he was accused of coward-ice in not appearing to speak before the assembly and taking no part in public business, he said, "It is not you but myself that I fear." No doubt that was because he knew that he had a bitter and violent temper, and that he could not control it.

598 *Sexual Pleasures*
Plato, Republic 1.329C

Once someone, on coming up to Sophocles the poet, said: "Sophocles, how do you feel about sexual pleasures? Are you still able to have sex with women?" And he replied, "Hush, fellow! I am delighted to have escaped them, as though I have run away from some raging and savage master."

599 *Sleep and Sex Remind Alexander of Mortality*
Plutarch, Alexander 22.6 (3)

And he [Alexander] used to say that sleep and sexual intercourse, more than anything else, made him conscious that he was mortal, implying that both weari-ness and pleasure arise from one and the same natural weakness.

600 *Lyra Rises by Decree*
Plutarch, Caesar 59.6 (3)

At any rate, Cicero the orator, we are told, when someone remarked that Lyra would rise on the morrow, said: "Yes, by decree," implying that men were com-pelled to accept even this dispensation.

601 *Anonymous Censoring of Opimius*
Plutarch, Caius Gracchus 17.6

However, what vexed the people more than this or anything else was the erection of a temple of Concord by Opimius;[1] for it was felt that he was priding himself and exulting and in a manner celebrating a triumph in view of all this slaughter of citizens. Therefore at night, beneath the inscription on the temple, somebody carved this verse: "A work of mad discord produces a temple of Con-cord."

> 1. Opimius restored the temple of Concord which had been built by Camillus (see Plutarch, *Camillus* 42.4).

602 *Victory in Sacrifice*
Plutarch, Caius Marius 26.2

It is said, too, that Marius offered sacrifice, and that when the victims had been shown to him, he cried with a loud voice: "Mine is the victory."

603 *On Loud Orators*
Plutarch, Cicero 5.6 (4)

Now, Cicero's delivery contributed not a little to his persuasive power. Moreover, of those orators who were given to loud shouting he used to say jestingly that they were led by their weakness to resort to clamor as cripples were to mount upon a horse.

604 *Bribe Wasted*
Plutarch, Cicero 17.4 (3)

At another time, too, he [Lentulus] was under prosecution and had bribed some of the jurors, and when he was acquitted by only two votes, he said that what he had given to the second juror was wasted money, since it would have sufficed if he had been acquitted by one vote only.

605 *Demetrius Smitten by Painting*
Plutarch, Demetrius 22.3

And Apelles says he [Demetrius] was so smitten with amazement on beholding the work[1] that his voice actually failed him, and that when at last he had recovered it, he cried, "Great is the toil and astonishing the work," remarking, however, that it had not the graces which made the fame of his own paintings touch the heavens.

> 1. A painting done by Protogenes the Caunian which illustrated the story of Ialysus. It had taken Protogenes seven years to complete the painting.

606 *Voice of One Hurt*
Plutarch, Demosthenes 11.2–3

A story is told of a man coming to him [Demosthenes] and begging his services as advocate, and telling at great length how he had been assaulted and beaten by someone. "But certainly," said Demosthenes, "you got none of the hurts you describe." Then the man raised his voice and shouted: "I, Demosthenes, no hurts?" "Now, indeed," said Demosthenes, "I hear the voice of one who is wronged and hurt."

607 *Dionysius On Guard*
Plutarch, Dion 9.6

He [Dionysius] used to say, too, that he was on his guard against friends who were men of sense, because he knew that they would rather be tyrants than subjects of a tyrant.

608a *Lycurgus' Short, Sententious Sayings*
Plutarch, Lycurgus 19.3–4

And indeed Lycurgus himself seems to have been short and sententious in his speech, if we may judge from his recorded sayings; that, for instance, on forms of government, to one who demanded the establishment of democracy in the city: "Go thou," said he, "and first establish democracy in thy household." That, again, to one who inquired why he ordained such small and inexpensive sacrifices: "That we may never omit," said he, "to honor the gods." Again, in the matter of athletic contests, he allowed the citizens to engage only in those where there was no stretching forth of hands.[1] There are also handed down similar answers which he made by letter to his fellow-citizens. When they asked how they could ward off an invasion of enemies, he answered: "By remaining poor, and by not desiring to be greater the one than the other." And when they asked about fortifying their city, he answered: "A city will be well fortified which is surrounded by brave men and not by bricks." Now regarding these and similar letters, belief and scepticism are alike difficult.

> 1. After the manner of men begging their conquerors to spare their lives.

608b *Fortified by Men*
Philostratus, Lives of the Sophists 1.20 (513)

Moreover, a concise form of expression and the summing up of every argument into a brief statement was peculiarly an invention of Isaeus, as was clearly shown in many instances, but especially in the following. He had to represent the Lacedaemonians debating whether they should fortify themselves by building a wall, and he condensed his argument into these few words from Homer, "'And shield pressed on shield, helm on helm, man on man.'[1] Thus stand fast, Lacedaemonians, these are our fortifications!"

> 1. Homer, *Iliad* 16.215. On the later fortification of Sparta cf. Pausanias 1.13. This was a famous theme and was inspired by the saying *Non est Sparta lapidibus circumdata* (Seneca, *Suasoriae* 2.3).

609 *Spartan Apophthegms*
Plutarch, Lycurgus 20.1–3

Of their [the Spartans'] aversion to long speeches, the following apophthegms are proof. King Leonidas, when a certain one discoursed with him out of all season on matters of great concern, said: "My friend, the matter urges, but not the time." Charilaüs, the nephew of Lycurgus, when asked why his uncle had made so few laws, answered: "Men of few words need few laws." Archidamidas, when certain ones found fault with Hecataeus the Sophist for saying nothing after being admitted to their public mess, answered: "He who knows how, knows also when to speak." Instances of the pungent sayings not devoid of grace, of which I spoke,[1] are the following. Demaratus, when a troublesome fellow was pestering him with ill-timed questions, and especially with the oft repeated query who was the best of the Spartans, answered at last: "He who is least like thee." And Agis, when certain ones were praising the Eleians for their just and honorable conduct of the Olympic games, said: "And what great matter is it for the Eleians to practice righteousness one day in five years?" And Theopompus, when a stranger kept saying, as he showed him kindness, that in his own city he was called a lover of Sparta, remarked: "My good Sir, it were better for thee to be called a lover of thine own city."

> 1. Plutarch, *Lycurgus* 9.1.

610a *Spartans Belong Wholly to Their Country*
Plutarch, Lycurgus 25.3–5

In a word, he [Lycurgus] trained his fellow-citizens to have neither the wish nor the ability to live for themselves; but like bees they were to make themselves always integral parts of the whole community, clustering together about their leader, almost beside themselves with enthusiasm and noble ambition, and to belong wholly to their country. This idea can be traced also in some of their utterances. For instance, Paedaretus, when he failed to be chosen among the three hundred best men, went away with a very glad countenance, as if rejoicing that the city had three hundred better men than himself. And again, Polycratidas, one of an embassy to the generals of the Persian king, on being asked by them whether the embassy was there in a private or a public capacity, replied: "If we succeed, in a public capacity; if we fail, in a private." Again, Argileonis, the mother of Brasidas, when some Amphipolitans who had come to Sparta paid her a visit, asked them if Brasidas had died nobly and in a manner worthy of Sparta. Then they greatly extolled the man and said that Sparta had not such another, to which she answered: "Say not so, Strangers; Brasidas was noble and brave, but Sparta has many better men than he."

610b *Paedaretus Not Among Three Hundred*
Plutarch, Moralia, Sayings of Kings and Commanders III:191F

When Paedaretus[1] was not chosen to be one of the three hundred, an honor which ranked highest in the State, he departed, cheerful and smiling, with the remark that he was glad if the State possessed three hundred citizens better than himself.

1. Spartan general at the time of the Peloponnesian war.

610c *Three Hundred Better Than Himself*
Plutarch, Moralia, Sayings of Spartans III:231B (3)

When he was not chosen as one of the three hundred, which was rated as the highest honor in the State, he went away cheerful and smiling; but when the Ephors called him back, and asked why he was laughing, he said, "Because I congratulate the State for having three hundred citizens better than myself."

611 *Against Extravagance*
Plutarch, Marcus Cato 8.1–2

Again, inveighing against the prevalent extravagance, he [Cato] said: "It is a hard matter to save a city in which a fish sells for more than an ox."

612 *Men Who Do Not Know the Road*
Plutarch, Marcus Cato 8.5–6

Of those who were eager to hold high office frequently, he [Cato] said that like men who did not know the road, they sought to be ever attended on their way by lictors, lest they go astray.

613 *Why Cato Was Hated*
Plutarch, Marcus Cato 8.8–9

His enemies hated him, he [Cato] used to say, because he rose every day before it was light and, neglecting his own private matters, devoted his time to the public interests.

614 *Prefers to Do Right*
Plutarch, Marcus Cato 8.9

He [Cato] also used to say that he preferred to do right and get no thanks, rather than to do ill and get no punishment; and that he had pardon for everybody's mistakes except his own.

615 *Wise Men Profit from Fools*
Plutarch, Marcus Cato 9.4

Wise men, he [Cato] said, profited more from fools than fools from wise men; for the wise shun the mistakes of fools, but fools do not imitate the successes of the wise.

616 *Blushes Better than Pallor*
Plutarch, Marcus Cato 9.4

He [Cato] said he liked to see blushes on a young man's face rather than pallor, and that he had no use for a soldier who plied his hands on the march, and his feet in battle, and whose snore was louder than his war-cry.

617 *On the Lover*
Plutarch, Marcus Cato 9.5

As for the lover, he [Cato] said his soul dwelt in the body of another.

618 *On Repentance*
Plutarch, Marcus Cato 9.6

And as for repentance, he [Cato] said he had indulged in it himself but thrice in his whole life: once when he entrusted a secret to his wife; once when he paid ship's fare to a place instead of walking thither; and once when he remained intestate a whole day.

619 *Abuse Unusual and Unpleasant*
Plutarch, Marcus Cato 9.7

And when he [Cato] was reviled by a man who led a life of shameless debauchery, he said: "I fight an unequal battle with you: you listen to abuse calmly, and utter it glibly; while for me it is unpleasant to utter it, and unusual to hear it."

620 *On Statues*
Plutarch, Marcus Cato 19.4

And yet, before this time he [Cato] used to laugh at those who delighted in such honors, saying that, although they knew it not, their pride was based simply on the work of statuaries and painters, whereas his own images, of the most exquisite workmanship, were borne about in the hearts of fellow-citizens. And to those who expressed their amazement that many men of no fame had statues, while he had none, he used to say: "I would much rather have men ask why I have no statue, than why I have one."

621 *Teaching Noble Tales*
Plutarch, Moralia, The Education of Children I:3E–F

For youth is impressionable and plastic, and while such minds are still tender lessons are infused deeply into them; but anything which has become hard is with

difficulty softened. For just as seals leave their impression in soft wax, so are lessons impressed upon the minds of chidren while they are young. And, as it seems to me, Plato, that remarkable man, quite properly advises nurses,[1] even in telling stories to children, not to choose at random, lest perchance their minds be filled at the outset with foolishness and corruption. Phocylides,[2] too, the poet, appears to give admirable advice in saying:
Should teach while still a child
The tale of noble deeds.

> 1. Plato, *Republic* 377 E.
> 2. Bergk, *Poetae Lyrici Graeci* 2.448 (frag. 13).

622a *The Friends of Kings*
Plutarch, Moralia, Sayings of Kings and Commanders III:174B

Orontes, the son-in-law of King Artaxerxes[1], became involved in disgrace because of an accusation, and, when the decision was given against him, he said that, as mathematicians' fingers are able to represent tens of thousands at one time, and at another time only units, so it was the same with the friends of kings: at one time they are omnipotent and at another time almost impotent.

> 1. King of Persia, 465–425 B.C.E.

622b *The Friends of Kings*
Diogenes Laertius, Lives of the Eminent Philosophers 1.59

He [Solon] used to say that those who had influence with tyrants were like the pebbles employed in calculations; for, as each of the pebbles represented now a large and now a small number, so the tyrants would treat each one of those about them at one time as great and famous, at another as of no account.

623 *Honorable and Righteous*
Plutarch, Moralia, Sayings of Kings and Commanders III:182C (8)

When somebody remarked that all things are honorable and righteous for kings, he [Antigonus] said, "Yes indeed, for kings of the barbarians; but for me only the honorable things are honorable and the righteous righteous."

624a *Iphicrates Commands All*
Plutarch, Moralia, Sayings of Kings and Commanders III:187A (6)

A certain speaker interrogated him [Iphicrates[1]] in the Assembly: "Who are you that you are so proud? Are you cavalryman or man-at-arms or archer or targeteer?" "None of these," he replied, "but the one who understands how to direct all of them."

> 1. Famous Athenian general, early part of fourth century B.C.E. A collection of his deeds and sayings may be found in Polyaenus, *Strategemata*, 3.9.

624b *Iphicrates Commands All*
Plutarch, Moralia, Chance II:99E (5)

Somebody asked Iphicrates the general, as though undertaking to expose him, who he was, since he was "neither a man-at-arms, nor archer, nor targeteer"; and he answered, "I am the man who commands and makes use of all these."

624c *Iphicrates Commands All*
Plutarch, Moralia, Can Virtue Be Taught? VI:440B (3)

Yet when Callias, son of Charias, asked the general Iphicrates, "Who are you? Bowman, targeteer, horseman, or hoplite?" Iphicrates replied, "None of these, but the one who commands them all."

625a *Lysander Uses Deception*
Plutarch, Moralia, Sayings of Kings and Commanders III:190E (2)

To those who found fault with him [Lysander[1]] for accomplishing most things through deception (a procedure which they asserted was unworthy of Heracles) he used to say in reply that where the lion's skin does not reach it must be pieced out with the skin of the fox.[2]

1. Spartan general at the time of the Peloponnesian war.
2. Cf. Leutsch and Schneidewin, *Paroemigraphi Graeci* 1.30.

625b *Lysander Uses Deception*
Plutarch, Moralia, Sayings of Spartans III:229B (3)

In answer to those who blamed him [Lysander] because of his carrying out most of his designs through deception, which they said was unworthy of Heracles, and gaining his successes by wile in no straightforward way, he said laughing that where he could not get on with the lion's skin it must be pieced out with the skin of the fox.

625c *Lysander Uses Deception*
Plutarch, Lysander 7.4

Those who demanded that the descendants of Heracles should not wage war by deceit he [Lysander] held up to ridicule, saying that "where the lion's skin will not reach, it must be patched out with the fox's."

626a *Bravery and Justice*
Plutarch, Moralia, Sayings of Kings and Commanders III:190F (3)

When he [Agesilaus] was questioned about bravery and uprightness and asked which was the better, he said, "We have no need of bravery if we are all upright."

626b *Bravery and Justice*
Plutarch, Moralia, Sayings of Spartans III:213C (62)

Being asked once which was better of the virtues, bravery or justice, he [Agesilaus] said that there is no use for bravery unless justice is also in evidence, and if all men should become just they would have no need of bravery.

626c *Bravery and Justice*
Plutarch, Agesilaus 23.5

And yet in his discourse he [Agesilaus] was always declaring that justice was the first of the virtues; for valor was of no use unless justice attended it, and if all men should be just, there would be no need of valor. And to those who said, "This is the pleasure of the Great King,"[1] he would say, "How is he greater than I unless he is also more just?"

1. Artaxerxes II, King of Persia ca. 436–358 B.C.E.

626d *Greater If More Just*
>Plutarch, Moralia, Sayings of Kings and Commanders III:190F (2)

Regarding their custom of calling the king of the Persians the Great King, he [Agesilaus[1]] said, "In what respect is he greater than I, unless he is more upright and self-restrained?"[2]

>1. King of Sparta, 398–360 B.C.E.
>2. Cf. Xenophon, *Agesilaus* 8.4.

626e *Greater If More Just*
>Plutarch, Moralia, Progress in Virtue I:78D

So too Agesilaus remarked in regard to the Great King, "In what is he greater than I, unless he be more just?"

626f *Greater If More Just*
>Plutarch, Moralia, On Inoffensive Self-Praise VII:545A

Useful too against public and private enemies are such remarks as these:

"Unhappy they whose sons oppose my power,"[1] and Agesilaus' saying about the King of the Persians (who was called "Great"): "Wherein greater than I, if not more just?"

>1. Homer, *Iliad* 6.127, quoted also by Aristides, *Orationes* 49.108.

626g *Happy If Just*
>Plato, Gorgias 470E

Polus: Then no doubt you'll say even of the Great King that you don't know whether he is happy, Socrates.

Socrates: It will be no more than the truth; I don't know what degree of enlightenment and virtue he has attained.

Polus: What? Does happiness depend entirely on that?

Socrates: Yes, Polus, in my opinion it does; I maintain that men and women are happy if they are honorable and upright, but miserable if they are vicious and wicked.

627a *Big Shoes on Small Foot*
>Plutarch, Moralia, Sayings of Spartans III:208C (3)

When someone praised an orator for his ability in making much of small matters, Agesilaus said that a shoemaker is not a good craftsman who puts big shoes on a small foot.[1]

>1. Cf. Cicero, *De oratore* 1.54 (231).

627b *Big Introduction for Small Subject*
>Plutarch, Moralia, Sayings of Spartans III:224C

Labotas, when someone spoke at very great length, said, "Why, pray, such a big introduction to a small subject? For proportionate to the topic should be the words you use."

628   Living according to Reason
Plutarch, Moralia, Sayings of Spartans III:216F (3)

When someone said that he [Alcamenes[1]] lived a straitened life while possessed of plenty of property, he said, "Yes, for it is a noble thing for one who possesses much to live according to reason and not according to his desires."

1. King of Sparta, 779–742 B.C.E.

629   Laws Have Authority
Plutarch, Moralia, Sayings of Spartans III:230F (1)

Pausanias,[1] the son of Pleistoanax, in answer to the question why it was not permitted to change any of the ancient laws in their country, said, "Because the laws ought to have authority over the men, and not the men over the laws."

1. King of Sparta, 408–394 B.C.E.

630a   Obedience Better
Plutarch, Moralia, Sayings of Spartans III:236E (71)

Another [Spartan], in the thick of the fight, was about to bring down his sword on an enemy when the recall sounded, and he checked the blow. When someone inquired why, when he had his enemy in his power, he did not kill him, he said, "Because it is better to obey one's commander than to slay an enemy."[1]

1. Cf. Plutarch, *Comparison of Pelopidas and Marcellus* 3 (317 D).

630b   Obedience Better
Plutarch, Moralia, Roman Questions IV:273F (39)

Is it because sheer necessity alone constitutes a warrant to kill a human being, and he who does so illegally and without the word of command is a murderer? For this reason Cyrus also praised Chrysantas who, when he was about to kill an enemy, and had his weapon raised to strike, heard the recall sounded and let the man go without striking him, believing that he was now prevented from so doing.

630c   Obedience Better
Epictetus, Discourses 2.6.15

But Chrysantas, when he was on the point of striking the foe, refrained because he heard the bugle sounding the recall; it seemed so much more profitable to him to do the bidding of his general than to follow his own inclination.

630d   Obedience Better
Xenophon, Cyropaedia 4.1.3

[Cyrus]: But as to Captain Chrysantas, who fought next to me, I have no need to make enquiry from others, for I myself know how gallant his conduct was; in everything else he did just as I think all of you also did; but when I gave the word to retreat and called to him by name, even though he had his sword raised to smite down an enemy he obeyed me at once and refrained from what he was on the point of doing and proceeded to carry out my order; not only did he himself retreat but he also with instant promptness passed the word on to the others; and so he succeeded in getting his division out of range before the enemy discovered that we were retreating or drew their bows or let fly their javelins. And thus by his obedience he is unharmed himself and he has kept his men unharmed.

631 Parmeno's Pig

Plutarch, Moralia, Table-Talk 5 VIII:674B–C

"What emotion or what external happening made people admire Parmeno's pig so much that it has become proverbial? You know the story: one time when Parmeno was already famous for his mimicry, some competitors put on a rival show, but the populace, being prejudiced in favor of Parmeno, said, 'Good enough!—but nothing, compared with Parmeno's sow.'[1] Then one of the performers stepped forward with a sucking pig concealed under his arm; but the people, even when they heard the genuine squeal, murmured, 'Well, what's this compared to Parmeno's pig?' Thereupon the fellow let the pig go in the crowd to prove that their judgement was based on prejudice instead of truth. This plainly demonstrates that the very same sensation will not produce a corresponding effect a second time in people's minds unless they believe that intelligence or conscious striving is involved in the performance."

> 1. F.C. Babbit's Index to Plutarch, Moralia, vol. 1 (Loeb Classical Library) identifies Parmeno as a famous comic actor of the latter part of the 4th century B.C.E., but the Paroemiographi Graecii, 1.412, surprisingly makes him a painter and the pig a painted one so realistic that everyone thought that his squeal could be heard.

632a Radiance of Ambition

Plutarch, Moralia, A Pleasant Life Impossible XIV:1099B–D

"Again, any remarkable quality in the bodily pleasures is plainly enough enjoyed by men of action too. They too 'eat food' and 'drink the sparkling wine'[1] and banquet with their friends, and do so with keener zest, I think, after their struggles and exploits, for instance, Alexander and Agesilaus, yes, and Phocion too and Epameinondas, than when, like these, they had done no more than rub down by a fire and get exercise in the gentle jouncing of their litters[2]; but men of action regard these pleasures as inconsiderable, preoccupied as they are by other greater ones. Thus what need to mention Epameinondas' refusal to dine when he saw that the dinner was an extravagance for his friend, saying 'I thought this was a sacrifice and dinner, not a scandal and outrage?' What need to mention this, when Alexander rejected Ada's cooks, saying that he had better seasoners himself, for his breakfast night marches, and for his dinner light breakfasting? And when Philoxenus wrote to suggest the purchase of handsome boys, Alexander[3] came within an ace of relieving him from his command. Yet who had greater liberty to do what he pleased? But as Hippocrates[4] says that of two pains the lesser is dimmed by the greater, those of statesmanlike action and ambition are so radiant and splendid that in the blaze of mental joy the bodily pleasures are obliterated and extinguished."

> 1. Homer, Iliad 5.341.
> 2. Epicurus' poor health caused him to use a litter (Diogenes Laertius 10.7).
> 3. Cf. 131.
> 4. Aphorisms 2.46. Thus the greater fire destroys the less (Theophrastus, On the Senses 18, On Fire 10) and the greater light the less (cf. On the Sublime 17.2).

632b Alexander's Mastery over Food

Plutarch, Alexander 22.7–10 (4–5)

He [Alexander] had also the most complete mastery over his appetite, and showed this both in many other ways, and especially by what he said to Ada, whom he honored with the title of Mother and made queen of Caria.[1] When, namely, in the kindness of her heart, she used to send him day by day many viands and sweetmeats, and finally offered him bakers and cooks reputed to be very skillful, he said he wanted none of them, for he had better cooks which had been given him by his tutor, Leonidas; for his breakfast, namely, a night march, and for his supper, a light breakfast. "And this same Leonidas," he said, "used to come and open my chests of bedding and clothing, to see that my mother did not hide there for me some luxury or superfluity."

> 1. Cf. Arrian, *Anabasis* 1.23.8.

632c   *Night Marches for Breakfast*
Plutarch, Moralia, Advice about Keeping Well II:127B (9)

And it is reported that Alexander said when he discharged the chefs of Ada that he had better ones always to take with him—his night marches for breakfast, and for dinner his frugal breakfast.

632d   *Night Marches for Breakfast*
Plutarch, Moralia, Sayings of Kings and Commanders III:180A (9)

Ada, queen of the Carians, made it a point of honor to be always sending to him fancy dishes and sweetmeats prepared in unusual ways by the hands of artists and chefs, but he said he had better fancy cooks—his night marches for his breakfast, and for his dinner his frugal breakfast.

632e   *Purchase of Handsome Boys*
Plutarch, Alexander 22.1–2 (1)

Moreover, when Philoxenus, the commander of his forces on the sea-board, wrote that there was with him a certain Theodorus, of Tarentum, who had two boys of surpassing beauty to sell, and inquired whether Alexander would buy them, Alexander was incensed, and cried out many times to his friends, asking them what shameful thing Philoxenus had ever seen in him that he should spend his time in making such disgraceful proposals. And on Philoxenus himself he heaped much reproach in a letter, bidding him send Theodorus to perdition, merchandise and all.

632f   *Purchase of Handsome Boys*
Plutarch, Moralia, Fortune of Alexander IV:333A (12)

But let us compare the actions of men who are admitted to be philosophers. Socrates forbore when Alcibiades spent the night with him. But when Philoxenus, the governor of the coast-lands of Asia Minor, wrote to Alexander that there was in Ionia a youth, the like of whom for bloom and beauty did not exist, and inquired in his letter whether he should send the boy on to him, Alexander wrote bitterly in reply, "Vilest of men, what deed of this sort have you ever been privy to in my past that now you would flatter me with the offer of such pleasures?"

633   *On Detail*
Plutarch, Moralia, Fragments: A Three-Foot Mortar XV:62

Plutarch strongly rebuts those critics who make fun of Hesiod for his petty detail; he says that Plato discoursed on the proper size of domestic utensils,[1] and Lycurgus on the making of doors, to ensure that they should be unornamented and made by saw and axe alone.[2] We should therefore welcome Hesiod's instructions about the measurements of mortar, pestle, axle, and wedge. Moreover, the ancients attached much importance to these things: among other inventors, they honored Pamphos because he was the original inventor of the lamp and introduced lamplight into temples and into private use, and they gave the deme of Pithos[3] its name because its members conceived the idea of molding jars (*pithoi*). So it is not costly elaboration that we should admire, but the procuring of useful objects, cheap and simple though they may be.

1. *Laws*, 746 E.
2. Cf. Plutarch, *Lycurgus* 13.
3. An attic deme in the upper Cephisus-valley.

634   *Numa Trusts in Gods*
Plutarch, Numa 15.6

And Numa himself, as they say, had such implicit confidence in the gods, that once, when a message was brought to him that enemies were coming up against the city, he smiled and said: "But I am sacrificing."

635   *Slanderer Tolerated*
Plutarch, Pyrrhus 8.5

Again, in Ambracia there was a fellow who denounced and reviled him, and people thought that Pyrrhus ought to banish him. "Let him remain here," said Pyrrhus, "and speak ill of us among a few, rather than carry his slanders around to all mankind."

636   *Draco on the Death Penalty*
Plutarch, Solon 17.2

And Draco himself, they say, being asked why he made death the penalty for most offenses, replied that in his opinion the lesser ones deserved it, and for the greater ones no heavier penalty could be found.

637   *The Best City*
Plutarch, Solon 18.5

And we are told a saying of his [Solon's] which is consonant with this law. Being asked, namely, what city was best to live in, "That city," he replied, "in which those who are not wronged, no less than those who are wronged, exert themselves to punish the wrongdoers."

638   *Solon on Tyranny*
Plutarch, Solon 30.4–5

Then it was, too, that he [Solon] uttered the famous saying, that earlier it had been easier for them to hinder the tyranny, while it was in preparation; but now it was a greater and more glorious task to uproot and destroy it when it had been already planted and was grown.

639   *Themistocles' Business Dealings*
Plutarch, Themistocles 18.5

Again, with the desire to be somewhat peculiar in all that he did, when he [Themistocles] offered a certain estate for sale, he bade proclamation to be made that it had an excellent neighbor into the bargain. Of two suitors for his daughter's hand, he chose the likely man in preference to the rich man, saying that he wanted a man without money rather than money without a man.[1]

    1. Cf. 502.

640   *Dionysius Ashamed of Corinth*
Plutarch, Timoleon 15.1–3

However, certain sayings of his are preserved from which it would appear that he [Dionysius] accommodated himself to his present circumstances not ignobly. Once, namely, when he landed at Leucadia, a city which had been colonized by Corinthians, just like Syracuse, he said he had the same feelings as young men who have been guilty of misdemeanors; for just as these pass their time merrily with their brothers, but shun their fathers from a feeling of shame, so he was ashamed to live in their common mother-city, and would gladly dwell there with them.

641   *Augustus on Haste*
Suetonius, Lives of the Caesars, Augustus 2.25.4

He [Augustus] thought nothing less becoming in a well-known trained leader than haste and rashness, and, accordingly, favorite sayings of his were: "More haste, less speed"; "Better a safe commander than a bold"; and "That is done quickly enough which is done well enough."

642   *The Golden Hook*
Suetonius, Lives of the Caesars, Augustus 2.25.4

He [Augustus] used to say that a war or a battle should not be begun under any circumstances, unless the hope of gain was clearly greater than the fear of loss; for he likened such as grasped at slight gains with no slight risk to those who fished with a golden hook, the loss of which, if it were carried off, could not be made good by any catch.

643   *Augustus Builds in Marble*
Suetonius, Lives of the Caesars, Augustus 2.28.3

Since the city was not adorned as the dignity of the empire demanded, and was exposed to flood and fire, he [Augustus] so beautified it that he could justly boast that he had found it built of brick and left it in marble.

644   *Bravery of Augustus*
Suetonius, Lives of the Caesars, Augustus 2.43.5

It chanced that at the time of the games which he had vowed to give in the circus, he [Augustus] was taken ill and headed the sacred procession lying in a litter; again, at the opening of the games with which he dedicated the theater of Marcellus, it happened that the joints of his curule chair gave way and he fell on his back. At the games for his grandsons, when the people were in a panic for fear the theater should fall, and he could not calm them or encourage them in any way, he left his own place and took his seat in the part which appeared most dangerous.

645   *No Honors for Augustus*
Suetonius, Lives of the Caesars, Augustus 2.52.1

Although well aware that it was usual to vote temples even to proconsuls, he [Augustus] would not accept one even in a province save jointly in his own name and that of Rome. In the city itself he refused this honor most emphatically, even melting down the silver statues which had been set up in his honor in former times and with the money coined from them dedicating golden tripods to Apollo of the Palatine. When the people did their best to force the dictatorship upon him, he knelt down, threw off his toga from his shoulders and with bare breast begged them not to insist.

646a   *Penny to Elephant*
Suetonius, Lives of the Caesars, Augustus 2.53.2

He [Augustus] did not if he could help it leave or enter any city or town except in the evening or at night, to avoid disturbing anyone by the obligations of ceremony. In his consulship he commonly went through the streets on foot, and when he was not consul, generally in a closed litter. His morning receptions were open to all, including even the commons, and he met the requests of those who approached him with great affability, jocosely reproving one man because he presented a petition to him with as much hesitation "as he would a penny to an elephant."

646b   *Penny to Elephant*
Macrobius, Saturnalia 2.4.3

To a man who was nervously presenting a petition to him, now holding out his hand and now withdrawing it, he [Augustus] said: "Do you think you are handing a penny to an elephant?"[1]

1. Quintilian 6.3.59.

647   *Vacillating Claudius*
Suetonius, Lives of the Caesars, Claudius 5.16.1

When he [Claudius] had removed the mark of censure affixed to one man's name, yielding to the entreaties of the latter's friends, he said: "But let the erasure be seen."

648   *Lightning Strikes*
Suetonius, Lives of the Caesars, Domitian 8.15.2

For eight successive months so many strokes of lightning occurred and were reported, that at last he [Vespasian] cried: "Well, let him now strike whom he will."

649   *Nero Signs Death Warrant*
Suetonius, Lives of the Caesars, Nero 6.10.2

When he was asked according to custom to sign the warrant for the execution of a man who had been condemned to death, he [Nero] said: "How I wish I had never learned to write!"

650 *Nero Sings*

Suetonius, Lives of the Caesars, Nero 6.20.2

Even when he [Nero] took a short time to rest his voice, he could not keep out of sight but went to the theater after bathing and dined in the orchestra with the people all about him promising them in Greek, that when he had wetted his whistle a bit, he would ring out something good and loud.

651 *Earth Consumed by Fire*

Suetonius, Lives of the Caesars, Nero 6.38.1

When someone in general conversation said:
"When I am dead, be earth consumed by fire,"[1]
he [Nero] rejoined "Nay, rather while I live."

1. A line put by Dio, 58.23, into the mouth of Tiberius. It is believed to be from the *Bellerophon*, a lost play of Euripides.

652 *Tiberius Hesitates*

Suetonius, Lives of the Caesars, Tiberius 3.24.1–25.1

Though Tiberius did not hesitate at once to assume and to exercise the imperial authority, surrounding himself with a guard of soldiers, that is, with the actual power and the outward sign of sovereignty, yet he refused the title for a long time, with barefaced hypocrisy now upbraiding his friends who urged him to accept it, saying that they did not realise what a monster the empire was, and now by evasive answers and calculating hesitancy keeping the senators in suspense when they implored him to yield, and fell at his feet. Finally, some lost patience, and one man cried out in the confusion: "Let him take it or leave it." Another openly voiced the taunt that others were slow in doing what they promised, but that he was slow to promise what he was already doing. At last, as though on compulsion, and complaining that a wretched and burdensome slavery was being forced upon him, he accepted the empire, but in such fashion as to suggest the hope that he would one day lay it down. His own words are: "Until I come to the time when it may seem right to you to grant an old man some repose." The cause of hesitation was fear of the dangers which threatened him on every hand, and often led him to say that he was "holding a wolf by the ears."[1]

1. A Greek proverb; cf. Terence, *Phormio* 506.

653 *Vespasian Quotes Homer*

Suetonius, Lives of the Caesars, Vespasian 8.23.1

He [Vespasian] also quoted Greek verses with great timeliness, saying of a man of tall stature and monstrous parts:
"Striding along and waving a lance that casts a long shadow."[1]

1. Homer, *Iliad* 7.213.

654 *Satan Attacks Job*

Testament, Job 20:1–10b (1)

Then after all my belongings were destroyed, Satan learned that nothing could move me to contempt. And he went away and requested my body from the Lord so he might inflict me with a plague. And then the Lord delivered me into his hands to treat my body as he wished, but over my soul he did not give him authority. And he approached me while I was sitting on my throne and was grieving over the annihilation of my children. And he was like a blast of wind and overturned my throne. And I spent three hours underneath my throne unable to get out. And he struck me with a cruel plague from head to toe. And with great frustration and distress I went out of the city, and as I sat on the dung heap my body became infested with worms. And fluids from my body saturated the ground with moisture. There were many worms in my body, and if a worm wriggled off, I would pick it up and return it to the same place saying: "Stay in the same place you were put until you are given orders by your commander."

655   *On the Passover Sacrifice*
Tosefta, Pisha 4:13

One time the 14th [of Nisan] fell on the Sabbath. They asked Hillel the Elder: "Does the Passover offering override the Sabbath?" He said to them: "And do we have only one Passover offering in the year which overrides the Sabbath? We have more than 300 Passover offerings in the year, and they [all] override the Sabbath." The whole courtyard collected against him. He said to them: "The continual offering is a community sacrifice and the Passover offering is a community sacrifice. Just as the continual offering, which is a community sacrifice, overrides the Sabbath, so the Passover offering, which is a community sacrifice, overrides the Sabbath. Another matter: It is said concerning the continual offering *its season* (Num. 28:2), and *its season* (Num. 9:2) is said concerning the Passover offering. Just as the continual offering, concerning which *its season* is said, overrides the Sabbath, so the Passover offering, concerning which *its season* is said, overrides the Sabbath. And furthermore, [it is an] *a fortiori* [argument]. Since the continual offering, which does not produce liability to [the punishment of] cutting off, overrides the Sabbath, the Passover offering, which does produce the liability to [the punishment of] cutting off, how much the more should it override the Sabbath. And further, I have received from my masters [the tradition] that the Passover offering overrides the Sabbath, and not [merely] the first Passover offering [overrides the Sabbath], but [also] the Passover offering of the individual [overrides the Sabbath]." They said to him: "What will be the rule for the people who do not bring knives and Passover offerings to the Sanctuary [before the Sabbath, so as to prevent themselves from needing to do forbidden labor on the Sabbath itself]?" He said to them: "Leave them alone. The holy spirit is upon them. If they are not prophets, they are the disciples of prophets."

656   *Asking Gods for Good Gifts*
Xenophon, Memorabilia 1.3.2

And again, when he [Socrates] prayed he asked simply for good gifts,[1] "for the gods know best what things are good."

1. Xenophon, *Cyropaedia*, 1.6.5.

657   *Knowing What to Do But Doing the Opposite*
Xenophon, Memorabilia 3.9.4

When asked further whether he [Socrates] thought that those who know what they ought to do and yet do the opposite are at once wise and vicious, he answered: "No; not so much that, as both unwise and vicious. For I think that all men have a choice between various courses, and choose and follow the one which they think conduces most to their advantage. Therefore I hold that those who follow the wrong course are neither wise nor prudent."

658 *Counsel a Despot*
Xenophon, Memorabilia 3.9.12

If anyone objected that a despot may refuse to obey a good counselor, "How can he refuse," he [Socrates] would ask, "when a penalty waits on disregard of good counsel? All disregard of good counsel is bound surely to result in error, and his error will not go unpunished."

659 *Despot Can Kill a Loyal Subject?*
Xenophon, Memorabilia 3.9.13

If anyone said that a despot can kill a loyal subject, "Do you think," he [Socrates] retorted, "that he who kills the best of his allies suffers no loss, or that his loss is trifling? Do you think that this conduct brings him safety, or rather swift destruction?"

660 *Best Pursuit*
Xenophon, Memorabilia 3.9.14

When someone asked him [Socrates] what seemed to him the best pursuit for a man, he answered: "Doing well."

661 *Is Good Luck a Pursuit?*
Xenophon, Memorabilia 3.9.14–15

Questioned further, whether he thought good luck a pursuit, he [Socrates] said: "On the contrary, I think luck and doing are opposite poles. To hit on something right by luck without search I call good luck, to do something well after study and practice I call doing well; and those who pursue this seem to me to do well. And the best men and dearest to the gods," he added, "are those who do their work well; if it is farming, as good farmers; if medicine, as good doctors; if politics, as good politicians. He who does nothing well is neither useful in any way nor dear to the gods."

662 *Greeting Not Returned*
Xenophon, Memorabilia 3.13.1

On a man who was angry because his greeting was not returned: "Ridiculous!" he [Socrates] exclaimed; "you would not have been angry if you had met a man in worse health; and yet you are annoyed because you have come across someone with ruder manners!"

663 *Mixing Ingredients When Eating*
Xenophon, Memorabilia 3.14.5–6

On another occasion he [Socrates] noticed one of the company at dinner tasting several dishes with each bite of bread. "Can you imagine," he asked, "a meal more extravagant and more ruinous to the victuals than his who eats many things together, and crams all sorts of sauces into his mouth at once? At any rate by mixing more ingredients than the cooks, he adds to the cost, and since he mixes ingredients that they regard as unsuitable in a mixture, if they are right, then he is wrong and is ruining their art. Yet it is surely ridiculous for a master to obtain highly skilled cooks, and then, though he claims no knowledge of the art, to alter their confections? There's another drawback, too, attaching to the habit of eating many things together. For if many dishes are not provided, one seems to go short because one misses the usual variety: whereas he who is accustomed to take one kind of meat along with one bit of bread can make the best of one dish when more are not forthcoming."

664   *Good Feeding Equals Eating*
Xenophon, Memorabilia 3.14.7

He [Socrates] used to say too that the term "Good feeding" in Attic was a synonym for "eating."

665   *Even the Wealthy Need Education*
Xenophon, Memorabilia 4.1.5

Those who prided themselves on riches and thought they had no need of education, supposing that their wealth would suffice them for gaining the objects of their wishes and winning honor among men, he [Socrates] admonished thus. "Only a fool," he said, "can think it possible to distinguish between things useful and things harmful without learning: only a fool can think that without distinguishing these he will get all he wants by means of his wealth and be able to do what is expedient: only a simpleton can think that without the power to do what is expedient he is doing well and has made good or sufficient provision for his life: only a simpleton can think that by his wealth alone without knowledge he will be reputed good at something, or will enjoy a good reputation without being reputed good at anything in particular.

Adult: Leaders

Representative leaders of society appear in many of these anecdotes. The eminent, such as emperors, kings, general, philosophers, priests, and teachers, display their wit and wisdom, virtue and vanity, in verbal exchanges. Such persons confront one another when they are at the peak of their powers; in so doing they exhibit the culture, craft, and clout of those who maintain a specific social identity with pride and persistence.

666a *John and the Priest*
Acts, John 56–57 (Lipsius-Bonnet 2.1:178–179)

Now one day as John was sitting (there), a partridge flew by and came and played in the dust before him. And John was amazed as he witnessed it. But a certain priest, who was one of his auditors, came and approached John and saw the partridge playing in the dust before him. And he was offended; he said to him, "At his age, can such a man take pleasure in a partridge playing in the dust?" But John knew in his spirit what he was thinking, and said to him: "It would be better for you, my son, to watch a partridge playing in the dust than to foul yourself with shameful and impious practices. He who waits for the repentance and conversion of all men has brought you here for this purpose. For I have no need of a partridge playing in the dust; the partridge is your own soul."

When the elder heard this and realized that he was not unknown but that the apostle of Christ had revealed to him all that was in his heart, he fell prostrate on the ground and cried out: "Now I know that God inhabits you, blessed John! How happy is the man who has not tempted God through you; for the man who tempts you tempts the untemptable." And he entreated him to pray for him; and John instructed him and gave him injunctions, and sent him away to his house, and glorified God who is over all.

666b *John and the Hunter*
John Cassan, Conferences 24.21
(Petschenig: 697–698; trans. from James: 241)

It is told that the most blessed Evangelist John, when he was quietly stroking a partridge with his hands, suddenly saw one in the habit of a hunter coming to him. He wondered that a man of such repute and fame should demean himself to such small and humble amusements, and said, "Art thou that John whose eminent and widespread fame hath enticed me also with great desire to know thee? Why then art thou taken up with mean amusements?" The blessed John said to him, "What is that which thou carriest in thy hand?" "A bow," said he. "And why," said he, "dost thou not bear it about always stretched?" He answered him, "I must not, lest by

196

constant bending the strength of its vigor be wrung and grow soft and perish, and when there is need that the arrows be shot with much strength at some beast, the strength being lost by excess of continual tension, a forceful blow cannot be dealt." "Just so," said the blessed John, "let not this little and brief relaxation of my mind offend thee, young man, for unless it doth sometimes ease and relax by some remission the force of its tension, it will grow slack through unbroken vigor and will not be able to obey the power of the spirit."

667   *The Grieving Man*
Acts, Peter, from Codex Cambrai 254 (de Bruyne, 1908:153)

In speaking to a man who bitterly complained at the death of his daughter, Peter said, "She has escaped so many assaults of the devil, so many struggles with the body, so many disasters of the world she has escaped! And you shed tears, as if you did not know what you yourself have achieved."

668   *Daniel Slays Dragon*
Apocryphal Daniel, Bel and the Dragon 23–32

There was also a great dragon, which the Babylonians revered. The king said to Daniel, "You cannot say that this is not a living god, so worship him." Daniel answered, "I will worship the Lord my God, for he is a living God. But with your permission, O King, I will kill the dragon without sword or stick." "You have my permission," said the king. Then Daniel took pitch, fat, and hair, and he brewed them together and made patties and fed them to the snake. The snake swallowed them and burst open. Then he said, "Look at what you were worshipping!"

669   *Heracles and the Ox-Driver*
Babrius, Aesopic Fables 20

An ox-driver was bringing his wagon home from the village when it fell into a deep ravine. Instead of doing something about it, as the situation required, he stood by idly and prayed for help to Heracles, of all the gods the one whom he really worshipped and held in honor. Suddenly the god appeared in person beside him and said: "Take hold of the wheels. Lay the whip on your oxen. Pray to the gods only when you are doing something to help yourself. Otherwise your prayers will be useless."

670   *Yes and No*
Babrius, Aesopic Fables 54

A eunuch went to a sacrificing seer to consult him about the prospect of having children. The sacrificer, spreading out the sacred liver of the victim, said: "When I look at this it tells me that you'll be a father; but when I look into your face you seem to be not even a man."

671   *Custom Stales*
Babrius, Aesopic Fables 61

A hunter was returning from the mountain successful in the chase, and a fisherman was going along with his basket full of fish. The two, as luck would have it, met each other. The hunter's fancy was for fish, lately swimming in the sea; the fisher thought that he preferred the wild game of the hills. So what they had they exchanged, one with the other, and thereafter always traded catches; it added to the pleasure of their meals. Finally, someone said to them: "Nay, but you'll spoil the benefit of these good things by too much use, then each of you will want again the thing he used to have."

672   *Interested Only in the Tracks*
Babrius, Aesopic Fables 92

A timid hunter was tracking a lion in the deep-shaded woods on the mountain. Meeting a woodcutter near a tall pine tree, he said to him: "Tell me, I beseech you, in the name of the Nymphs, have you seen the tracks of a lion whose lair is hereabouts?" "You come at a most fortunate time," the woodcutter replied, "I will show you the lion himself right now." The hunter turned pale and said, with chattering teeth: "No, no, don't favor me with more than what I ask; tell me about the tracks, but don't show me the lion."

673   *Enemy Infiltration*
Babrius, Aesopic Fables 113

A man gathering his sheep into the fold at evening was about to enclose a tawny wolf along with the flock. His dog, seeing this, said to him, "How can you be in earnest about saving the sheep when you bring this fellow in among us?"

674   *On Civic Courage*
Cicero, De Officiis 1.22.78

What achievement in war, then, was ever so great? What triumph can be compared with that? For I may boast to you, my son Marcus; for to you belong the inheritance of that glory of mine and the duty of imitating my deeds. And it was to me, too, that Gnaeus Pompey, a hero crowned with the honors of war, paid this tribute in the hearing of many, when he said that his third triumph would have been gained in vain, if he were not to have through my services to the state a place in which to celebrate it. There are, therefore, instances of civic courage that are not inferior to the courage of the soldier. Nay, the former calls for even greater energy and greater devotion than the latter.

675a   *Hands and Eyes*
Cicero, De Officiis 1.40.144

Such orderliness of conduct is, therefore, to be observed, that everything in the conduct of our life shall balance and harmonize, as in a finished speech. For it is unbecoming and highly censurable, when upon a serious theme, to introduce such jests as are proper at dinner, or any sort of loose talk. When Pericles was associated with the poet Sophocles as his colleague in command and they had met to confer about official business that concerned them both, a handsome boy chanced to pass and Sophocles said: "Look, Pericles; what a pretty boy!" How pertinent was Pericles' reply: "Hush, Sophocles, a general should keep not only his hands but his eyes under control." And yet, if Sophocles had made this same remark at a trial of athletes, he would have incurred no just reprimand. So great is the significance of both place and circumstance. For example, if anyone, while on a journey or on a walk, should rehearse to himself a case which he is preparing to conduct in court, or if he should under similar circumstances apply his closest thought to some other subject, he would not be open to censure; but if he should do that same thing at a dinner, he would be thought ill-bred, because he ignored the proprieties of the occasion.

675b *Hands and Eyes*
Plutarch, Pericles 8.5

Once also when Sophocles, who was general with him on a certain naval expedition, praised a lovely boy, he [Pericles] said: "It is not his hands only, Sophocles, that a general must keep clean, but his eyes as well."

676a *Seriphian and Athenian*
Cicero, De Senectute 3.8

For example, there is a story that when, in the course of a quarrel, a certain Seriphian[1] had said to Themistocles, "Your brilliant reputation is due to your country's glory, not your own," Themistocles replied, "True, by Hercules, I should never have been famous if I had been a Seriphian, nor you if you had been an Athenian."

> 1. Seriphos, an island of the Cyclades group, a symbol of smallness and insignificance.

676b *Seriphian and Athenian*
Plutarch, Themistocles 18.3

And when he [Themistocles] was told by the Seriphian that it was not due to himself that he had got reputation, but to his city, "True," said he, "but neither should I, had I been a Seriphian, have achieved reputation, nor wouldst thou, hadst thou been an Athenian."

677a *Lost and Recaptured City*
Cicero, De Senectute 4.11

It was in my own hearing that Salinator,[1] who had fled to the citadel after losing the town, remarked to him [Q. Fabius] in a boasting tone: "Through my instrumentality, Q. Fabius, you have recaptured Tarentum." "Undoubtedly," said Fabius, laughing, "for if you had not lost it I should never have recaptured it."

> 1. Cicero blunders here, for it was M. Livius Macatus, a relation of Salinator, who held the citadel, Livy 27.34.7.

677b *Lost and Recaptured City*
Plutarch, Fabius Maximus 23.3

Now there was a certain Marcus Livius, who commanded the garrison of Tarentum when Hannibal got the city to revolt. He occupied the citadel, however, and was not dislodged from this position, but held it until the Romans again got the upper hand of the Tarentines. This man was vexed by the honors paid to Fabius, and once, carried away by his jealousy and ambition, said to the senate that it was not Fabius, but himself, who should be credited with the capture of Tarentum. At this Fabius laughed, and said: "You are right; had you not lost the city, I had not taken it."

678a *Cyrus Good Life*
Cicero, De Senectute 17.59

To show you that Xenophon regarded nothing more befitting royalty than zeal in husbandry, let me recall the incident in the same book, related by Socrates in a conversation with Critobulus. Cyrus the Younger, a Persian prince, eminent for his intelligence and the glory of his rule, was visited at Sardis by Lysander the Spartan, a man of the highest virtue, who brought presents from the allies. Among other courtesies to Lysander while his guest, Cyrus showed him a certain carefully planted park. After admiring the stateliness of the trees, regularly placed in quincunx rows,[1] the clean and well-cultivated soil, and the sweet odors emanating from the flowers, Lysander then remarked: "I marvel not only at the industry, but also at the skill of the man who planned and arranged this work." "But it was I," Cyrus answered, "who planned it all; mine are the rows and mine the arrangement, and many of those trees I set out with my own hands." After gazing at the prince's purple robe, the beauty of his person, his Persian costume adorned with much gold and many precious stones, Lysander said: "With good reason, Cyrus, men call you happy, since in you good fortune has been joined with virtue."

    1. Virgil, *Georgics* 2.277.

678b *Cyrus' Good Life*
Xenophon, Oeconomicus 4.20

Further the story goes that when Lysander came to him bringing the gifts from the allies, this Cyrus showed him various marks of friendliness, as Lysander himself related once to a stranger at Megara, adding besides that Cyrus personally showed him round his paradise at Sardis.

679 *Sulla Pays Bad Poet*
Cicero, Pro Archia 25

Accordingly, if Archias were not legally a Roman citizen already, it would have been beyond his power, presumably, to win the gift of citizenship from some military commander. Sulla, no doubt, who gave it so freely to Spaniards and Gauls, would have refused it to the request of my client. It will be remembered that once at a public meeting some poetaster from the crowd handed up to that great man a paper containing an epigram upon him, improvised in somewhat unmetrical elegiacs. Sulla immediately ordered a reward to be paid him out of the proceeds of the sale which he was then holding, but added the stipulation that he should never write again. He accounted the diligent efforts of a poet worthy of some reward, bad though that poet was; and think you he would not have eagerly sought out my client, whose literary powers were so magnificent, and whose pen was so ready?

680 *Dionysius Learns Pain Is Real*
Cicero, Tusculan Disputations 2.25.60

But what, you will say, have we in time of peace, at home, in our easy chairs? You call me back to the philosophers who do not often step into the battle-line, and one of whom, Dionysius of Heraclea,[1] a person certainly of little resolution, after learning from Zeno to be brave was taught by pain to forget his lesson. For upon an attack of kidney trouble, even amid his shrieks, he kept on crying out that the opinions he had himself previously held about pain were false. And on being asked by Cleanthes,[2] his fellow-pupil, what was the reason that had seduced him from his former opinion, he replied: "Because if, after I had given such devoted attention to philosophy, I yet proved unable to bear pain, that would be sufficient proof that pain was evil. Now I have spent many years in studying philosophy and am unable to bear pain; pain is therefore an evil." Then Cleanthes stamped with his foot upon the ground and, according to the story, recited a line from the *Epigoni*:[3]

> Do you hear this, Amphiaraus, in your home beneath the
> earth?

meaning Zeno and grieving that Dionysius was false to his teaching.

1. A native of Magna Graecia, who for his desertion of Zeno was named *meta-themenos*, turncoat.
2. Cleanthes was Zeno's successor as head of the Stoic school.
3. A tragedy of Aeschylus translated by Accius: Amphiaraus the Argive seer went with Adrastus on the expedition against Thebes and was swallowed up by the earth. Cleanthes applies the line to his master Zeno who was numbered amongst the dead.

681 *Posidonius Refuses to Admit Evil of Pain*
Cicero, Tusculan Disputations 2.25.61

It was not so with our Posidonius,[1] whom I have often seen with my own eyes, and I shall repeat the story Pompey liked to tell, that after reaching Rhodes on giving up Syria[2] he felt a wish to hear Posidonius; but on learning that he was seriously ill with an attack of gout in the joints he wished at all events to go to see so famous a philosopher: when he had seen him and offered his respects, he paid him distinguished compliments and said that he regretted that he was not able to hear him, but Posidonius said, "You can hear me, nor will I suffer bodily pain to be a reason for allowing a man of your eminence to visit me for nothing." And accordingly Pompey related that from his sick bed the philosopher had earnestly and fully discussed this very proposition, "that there is nothing good except what is honorable," and as often as a paroxysm[3] of pain attacked him, continually repeated: "It is no use, pain! for all the distress you cause I shall never admit that you are an evil."

1. A native of Syria, a Stoic philosopher and teacher and friend of Cicero.
2. Pompey returned to Italy from his command in the East in 62 B.C.E.
3. *Faces*, torches, used metaphorically here for accesses of pain.

682 *Piso Takes Share*
Cicero, Tusculan Disputations 3.20.48

The famous Piso, named Frugi, had spoken consistently against the Corn-law.[1] When the law was passed, in spite of his consular rank, he was there to receive the corn. Gracchus noticed Piso standing in the throng; he asked him in the hearing of the Roman people what consistency there was in coming for the corn under the terms of the law which he had opposed. "I shouldn't like it, Gracchus, to come into your head to divide up my property among all the citizens; but should you do so I should come for my share." Did not the words of this serious and sagacious statesman show with sufficient clearness that the public inheritance was squandered by the Sempronian law?

1. The *Lex Frumentaria* of 123 B.C.E., by which cheap corn was distributed to citizens, was proposed by C. Sempronius Gracchus and hence called *lex Sempronia*.

683 *Archytas and Bailiff*
Cicero, Tusculan Disputations 4.36.78

Either the victims of angry men's attempted onslaught must be withdrawn from their reach until of themselves they gain self-control (but what is to control oneself except to bring together the scattered parts of the soul again into their place?) or, if they have any power of taking revenge, they must be begged and entreated to put it off to another time, until their anger cools down; but cooling down surely implies a fire in the soul kindled against the consent of reason: and hence the approval given to the utterance of Archytas[1] who on becoming angry with his bailiff said, "What a visitation you would have got if I had not been angry!"

1. A Pythagorean philosopher of Plato's time.

684 *Fortune Dependent on Cordage Undesirable*
Cicero, Tusculan Disputations 5.14.40

For how will he be able to feel assured of either strength of body or security of fortune? And yet no one can be happy except when good is secure and certain and lasting. What is so then in the goods of such thinkers? I am led to think that to them applies the saying of the Laconian who, when a certain trader boasted of the number of ships he had despatched to every distant coast, remarked: "The fortune that depends on cordage is not quite one to be desired." Or is there any question that nothing that can escape our grasp ought to be reckoned as one in kind with that which makes the fullness of happy life?

685 *Seasonings of the Lacedaemonians*
Cicero, Tusculan Disputations 5.34.98

Again! do we not know of the fare put before the Lacedaemonians at their public meals? When the tyrant Dionysius[1] dined with them he said that the black broth[2] which was the staple of the meal was not to his taste; whereupon the cook who had made it said: "No wonder; for you did not have the seasoning." "What is that, pray?" said the tyrant. "Toil in hunting, sweat, a run down to the Eurotas, hunger, thirst; for such things are the seasonings of the feasts of Lacedaemonians."

1. Dionysius the Elder.
2. Cf. Athenaeus 9.379.

686 *Delightful Dinners*
Cicero, Tusculan Disputations 5.35.100

Timotheus,[1] who bore a great name at Athens and was a leading man in the State, after dining, we are told, with Plato and being much delighted with the entertainment, said, when he saw him next day: "Your dinners are indeed delightful, not only at the time, but on the following day as well." Why so? because we cannot make proper use of our minds when our stomachs are filled with meat and drink.

1. Son of Conon and Athenian general between 378–356 B.C.E.

687 *Zacchaeus Repents*
Clement of Alexandria, Stromateis 4.6.35 <possibly quoted from the Traditions of Matthias> (Staehlin-Fruechtel 2.3:263–264)

When Zacchaeus, a chief tax-collector—but some say Matthias—heard that the Lord had seen fit to be with him, he said, "Look, Lord, I will give half of my belongings as alms, and if I have extorted anything from anyone, I will repay it four times." Then the Lord said, "The Son of Man has come today and has found that which was lost."

688 *Solon on Natural Beauty*
Diogenes Laertius, Lives of the Eminent Philosophers 1.51

There is a story that Croesus in magnificent array sat himself down on his throne and asked Solon if he had ever seen anything more beautiful. "Yes," was the reply, "cocks and pheasants and peacocks; for they shine in nature's colors, which are ten thousand times more beautiful."

689 *The Best Rule*
Diogenes Laertius, Lives of the Eminent Philosophers 1.77

And, when Croesus inquired what is the best rule, he [Pittacus] answered, "The rule of the shifting wood," by which he meant the law.

690a *Cutting Down the Prominent*
Diogenes Laertius, Lives of the Eminent Philosophers 1.100
Thrasybulus to Periander

"I made no answer to your herald; but I took him into a cornfield, and with a staff smote and cut off the over-grown ears of corn, while he accompanied me. And if you ask him what he heard and what he saw, he will give his message. And this is what you must do if you want to strengthen your absolute rule: put to death those among the citizens who are pre-eminent, whether they are hostile to you or not. For to an absolute ruler even a friend is an object of suspicion."

690b *Cutting Down the Prominent*
Frontinus, Stratagems 1.1.4

Tarquin the Proud,[1] having decided that the leading citizens of Gabii should be put to death, and not wishing to confide this purpose to anyone, gave no response to the messenger sent to him by his son, but merely cut off the tallest poppy heads with his cane, as he happened to walk about in the garden. The messenger, returning without an answer, reported to the young Tarquin what he had seen his father doing. The son thereupon understood that the same thing was to be done to the prominent citizens of Gabii.

> 1. The surname Superbus, here given to Tarquinius Priscus the father, is usually applied only to his son, the last Roman king.

691 *The Benefits of the Mysteries in Hades*
Diogenes Laertius, Lives of the Eminent Philosophers 6.4

When he [Antisthenes] was being initiated into the Orphic mysteries, the priest said that those admitted into these rites would be partakers of many good things in Hades. "Why then," said he, "don't you die?"

692 *Plato's Pride*
Diogenes Laertius, Lives of the Eminent Philosophers 6.8

And one day he [Antisthenes] visited Plato, who was ill, and seeing the basin into which Plato had vomited, remarked, "The bile I see, but not the pride."

693 *Release from Pains*
Diogenes Laertius, Lives of the Eminent Philosophers 6.18

Once too Diogenes, when he came to him [Antisthenes], brought a dagger. And when Antisthenes cried out, "Who will release me from these pains?" replied,

"This," showing him the dagger. "I said," quoth the other, "from the pains, not from life."

694 Diogenes' Pride Exposed
Diogenes Laertius, Lives of the Eminent Philosophers 6.26

And one day when Plato had invited to his house friends coming from Dionysius, Diogenes trampled upon his carpets and said, "I trample upon Plato's vainglory." Plato's reply was, "How much pride you expose to view, Diogenes, by seeming not to be proud."

695a Diogenes Defeats Men
Diogenes Laertius, Lives of the Eminent Philosophers 6.33

When someone boasted that at the Pythian games he had vanquished men, Diogenes replied, "Nay, I defeat men, you defeat slaves."

695b Diogenes Defeats Men
Diogenes Laertius, Lives of the Eminent Philosophers 6.43

At Olympia, when the herald proclaimed Dioxippus to be victor over the men, Diogenes protested, "Nay, he is victorious over slaves, I over men."

696 Plato's Man
Diogenes Laertius, Lives of the Eminent Philosophers 6.40

Plato had defined Man as an animal, biped and featherless, and was applauded. Diogenes plucked a fowl and brought it into the lecture-room with the words, "Here is Plato's man."

697 Diogenes Believes in the Gods
Diogenes Laertius, Lives of the Eminent Philosophers 6.42

When Lysias the druggist asked him [Diogenes] if he believed in the gods, he said, "How can I help believing in them when I see a god-forsaken wretch like you?"

698 Diogenes before Philip
Diogenes Laertius, Lives of the Eminent Philosophers 6.43

Dionysius the Stoic says that after Chaeronea he [Diogenes] was seized and dragged off to Philip, and being asked who he was, replied, "A spy upon your insatiable greed." For this he was admired and set free.

699 Alexander to Antipater
Diogenes Laertius, Lives of the Eminent Philosophers 6.44

Alexander having on one occasion sent a letter to Antipater at Athens by a certain Athlios, Diogenes, who was present, said;

Graceless son [athlios] of graceless sire [athliou] to graceless wight [athlion] by graceless squire [athliou].

700 *Hail Chanticleer*
Diogenes Laertius, Lives of the Eminent Philosophers 6.48
The musician who was always deserted by his audience he [Diogenes] greeted with a "Hail chanticleer," and when asked why he so addressed him, replied, "Because your song makes every one get up."

701 *The Best Bronze*
Diogenes Laertius, Lives of the Eminent Philosophers 6.50
On being asked by a tyrant what bronze is best for a statue, he [Diogenes] replied, "That of which Harmodius and Aristogiton were molded."

702 *Plato's Ideas*
Diogenes Laertius, Lives of the Eminent Philosophers 6.53
As Plato was conversing about Ideas and using the nouns "tablehood" and "cuphood," he [Diogenes] said, "Table and cup I see; but your tablehood and cuphood, Plato, I can nowise see." "That's readily accounted for," said Plato, "for you have the eyes to see the visible table and cup; but not the understanding by which ideal tablehood and cuphood are discerned."

703 *Plato on Diogenes*
Diogenes Laertius, Lives of the Eminent Philosophers 6.54
On being asked by somebody, "What sort of man do you consider Diogenes to be?" Plato said, "A Socrates gone mad."[1]

    1. Cf. Aelian, *Varia Historia* 14.33.

704 *The Statue of Aphrodite*
Diogenes Laertius, Lives of the Eminent Philosophers 6.60
When Phryne set up a golden statue of Aphrodite in Delphi, Diogenes is said to have written upon it: "From the licentiousness of Greece."

705 *Diogenes the Hound*
Diogenes Laertius, Lives of the Eminent Philosophers 6.60
Alexander once came and stood opposite him [Diogenes] and said, "I am Alexander the great king." "And I," said he, "am Diogenes the Cynic."[1] Being asked what he had done to be called a hound, he said, "I fawn on those who give me anything, I yelp at those who refuse, and I set my teeth in rascals."

    1. Literally "Diogenes the Hound."

706 *Sweet Scent or Ill Odor?*
Diogenes Laertius, Lives of the Eminent Philosophers 6.66
To one with perfumed hair he [Diogenes] said, "Beware lest the sweet scent on your head cause an ill odor in your life."

707 *Plato's Begging*
Diogenes Laertius, Lives of the Eminent Philosophers 6.67
Being reproached with begging when Plato did not beg, "Oh yes," says he [Diogenes], "he does, but when he does so—
    He holds his head down close, that none may hear."[1]

    1. Homer, *Odyssey* 1.157, 4.70.

708 *Didymon Plays the Oculist*
Diogenes Laertius, Lives of the Eminent Philosophers 6.68

When Didymon, who was a rake, was once treating a girl's eye, "Beware," says Diogenes, "lest the oculist instead of curing the eye should ruin the pupil."

709 *Alexander and Crates*
Diogenes Laertius, Lives of the Eminent Philosophers 6.93

When Alexander inquired whether he [Crates] would like his native city to be rebuilt, his answer was, "Why should it be? Perhaps another Alexander will destroy it again."

710 *Zeno Tells Envoys about Abuse*
Diogenes Laertius, Lives of the Eminent Philosophers 7.24

Now those who inquired of him [Zeno] were ambassadors from King Ptolemy, and they wanted to know what message they should take back from him to the king. On being asked how he felt about abuse, he replied, "As an envoy feels who is dismissed without an answer."

711 *Chrysippus on Following the Multitude*
Diogenes Laertius, Lives of the Eminent Philosophers 7.182

Once when somebody reproached him [Chrysippus] for not going with the multitude to hear Ariston, he replied, "If I had followed the multitude, I should not have studied philosophy."

712 *The Peasant's Daughter*
Epistle, Pseudo Titus (de Bruyne, 1925:50)

Consider and take note of the event about which the following account informs us: A peasant had a girl who was a virgin. She was also his only daughter, and he consequently entreated Peter to offer a prayer for her. After he had prayed, the apostle told the father that the Lord would give her what was good for her soul. The girl immediately dropped dead. What a worthy reward—ever pleasing to God—to escape one's shameless flesh and crush the pride of life. But this distrustful old man, failing to recognize the worth of the heavenly grace, i.e. the divine blessing, besought Peter again that his only daughter be raised from the dead. And some days later, after she had been raised, a man who passed himself off as a believer came into the house of the old man to stay with him, and seduced the girl, and the two of them never appeared again.

713 *Philometor Overawed by Maximus*
Eunapius, Lives of the Philosophers 470

Near the door he [Maximus] was met by Philometor who was entering in high spirits with many of his friends, and with a loud voice Maximus called out to him from some distance: "Friend Philometor, I adjure you in Heaven's name, cease to burn wood to no purpose." Perhaps he said this with some inner knowledge of the malpractices in which the other was engaged. Thereupon Philometor was over-awed by Maximus, believed him to be divine, and ceased his plotting, even ridiculing the course of action that he had entered on before.

714 *Libanius Prefers Title of Sophist*
Eunapius, Lives of the Philosophers 496

When the later emperors offered him [Libanius] the very highest of all honors—
for they bade him use the honorary title of pretorian prefect—he refused, saying
that the title of sophist was more distinguished.

715a *Pericles Disputes Wrestling Fall*
Eunapius, Lives of the Philosophers 498

The ancient writers relate that when Archidamus was asked whether he was
stronger than Pericles, he replied: "Nay, even when I throw Pericles a fall, he still
carries off the victory by declaring that he has not been thrown at all."

715b *Pericles Disputes Wrestling Fall*
Plutarch, Pericles 8.4

When Archidamus, the king of the Lacedaemonians, asked him [Thucydides]
whether he or Pericles was the better wrestler, he replied: "Whenever I throw him
in wrestling, he disputes the fall, and carries his point, and persuades the very men
who saw him fall."

716 *Fabius Retains Honor*
Frontinus, Stratagems 1.8.2

When Hannibal had proved no match for Fabius either in character or in
generalship, in order to smirch him [Fabius] with dishonor, he spared his lands,
when he ravaged all others. To meet this assault, Fabius transferred the title to his
property to the State, thus, by his loftiness of character, preventing his honor from
falling under the suspicion of his fellow-citizens.[1]

    1. 217 B.C.E. Cf. Livy 22.23.1–8; Plutarch, *Fabius Maximus* 7. Polyaenus 1.36.2
attributes a similar act to Pericles.

717a *Fabricius Would Rather Rule*
Frontinus, Stratagems 4.3.2

When Cineas, ambassador of the Epirotes, offered Fabricius a large amount of
gold, the latter rejected it, declaring that he preferred to rule those who had gold
rather than to have it himself.[1]

    1. 280 B.C.E. Usually this story is related of Manius Curius. Cf. Valerius Maximus
4.3.5; Pliny, *Natural History* 19.26 (27).

717b *Fabricius Would Rather Rule*
Gellius, Attic Nights 1.14.1–2

Julius Hyginus, in the sixth book of his work *On the Lives and Deeds of Famous
Men*, says that a deputation from the Samnites came to Gaius Fabricius, the
Roman general, and after mentioning his many important acts of kindness and
generosity to the Samnites since peace was restored, offered him a present of a
large sum of money, begging that he would accept and use it. And they said that
they did this because they saw that his house and mode of life were far from
magnificent, and that he was not so well provided for as his high rank demanded.
Thereupon Fabricius passed his open hands from his ears to his eyes, then down to
his nose, his mouth, his throat, and finally to the lower part of his belly; then he

replied to the envoys: "So long as I can restrain and control all those members which I have touched, I shall never lack anything; therefore I cannot accept money, for which I have no use, for those who, I am sure, do have use for it."

717c Manius Curius Would Rather Rule
Cicero, De Senectute 16.55–56

Well, then, it was in this sort of life that Manius Curius passed his remaining years after he had triumphed over the Samnites, the Sabines, and Pyrrhus; and, as I gaze upon his country house (for it is not far from mine), I cannot sufficiently admire the frugality of the man or the spirit of the age in which he lived. When the Samnites had brought him a great mass of gold as he sat before the fire, he declined their gift with scorn; "for," said he, "it seems to me that the glory is not in having the gold, but in ruling those who have it." Think you that such a mighty soul could not make old age happy?

717d No Need for Money
Plutarch, Moralia, Sayings of Romans III:194F (2)

When the Samnites came to him [Manius Curius] after their defeat and offered him money, he happened to be cooking turnips in pots. He made answer to the Samnites that he had no need of money when he could make his dinner from this sort of food; and for him it was better than having money to hold sway over those who had it.

717e No Need for Money
Plutarch, Marcus Cato 2.1–2

Near his [Marcus Cato's] fields was the cottage which had once belonged to Manius Curius, a hero of three triumphs. To this he would often go, and the sight of the small farm and the mean dwelling led him to think of their former owner, who, though he had become the greatest of the Romans, had subdued the most warlike nations, and driven Pyrrhus out of Italy, nevertheless tilled this little patch of ground with his own hands and occupied this cottage, after three triumphs. Here it was that the ambassadors of the Samnites once found him seated at his hearth cooking turnips, and offered him much gold; but he dismissed them, saying that a man whom such a meal satisfied had no need of gold, and for his part he thought that a more honorable thing than the possession of gold was the conquest of its possessors.

717f No Need for Money
Athenaeus, Deipnosophists 10.419A

Manius Curius, the Roman general, lived the whole time on turnips; and when the Sabines sent him a large sum of gold, he said he had no need of gold so long as he dined on turnips. This is recorded by Megacles in his book On Famous Men.[1]

> 1. F. Jacoby, Die Fragmente der griechischen Historiker 4.443.

717g No Need for Money
Cicero, De Re Publica 3.28.40

Fabricius, I suppose, felt the lack of the wealth of Pyrrhus, and Curius of the riches of the Samnites![1] . . . Our glorious Cato, when he went out to his farm in the Sabine country, as we have heard him say, often visited the hearth of this man, sitting in whose home he had declined the gifts of the Samnites, once his enemies, but then under his protection.

1. The allusion is to the incorruptibility of Roman magistrates of the past.

718a   *Cannot Prevent Us from Dying*
Frontinus, Stratagems 4.5.12

A certain Spartan noble, when Philip declared he would cut them off from many things, unless the state surrendered to him, asked: "He won't cut us off from dying in defense of our country, will he?"[1]

1. Cf. Valerius Maximus 6.4, externa 4.

718b   *Cannot Prevent Us from Dying*
Plutarch, Moralia, Sayings of Spartans III:219B

When someone said to Astycratidas, after the defeat of Agis their king in the battle against Antipater in the vicinity of Megalopolis, "What will you do, men of Sparta? Will you be subject to the Macedonians?" he said, "What! Is there any way in which Antipater can forbid us to die fighting for Sparta?"

718c   *Cannot Prevent Us from Dying*
Cicero, Tusculan Disputations 5.14.42

Did the Lacedaemonians in answer to Philip's threat, when he wrote that he would prevent all their efforts, ask him whether he also intended to "prevent" them from dying: and shall not the true man of whom we are in quest be more readily found with such a spirit than a whole community? Again, when to this fortitude of which we are speaking there is linked temperance to have control of all the emotions, what element of happy life can fail the man whom fortitude can deliver from distress and fear, while temperance can both call him away from lust and forbid him to give way to transports of immoderate eagerness? That this is virtue's work I should show, had not the previous day's discussions made it fully plain.

719   *Hortensius Stranger to Muses*
Gellius, Attic Nights 1.5.3

But when Sulla was on trial, and Lucius Torquatas, a man of somewhat boorish and uncouth nature, with great violence and bitterness did not stop with calling Hortensius an actor in the presence of the assembled jurors, but said that he was a posturer and a Dionysia—which was the name of a notorious dancing-girl—then Hortensius replied in a soft and gentle tone: "I would rather be a Dionysia, Torquatus, yes, a Dionysia, than like you, a stranger to the Muses, to Venus and to Dionysus."

720   *The Cheapness of Silence or Speech*
Gellius, Attic Nights 1.15.10

Again, Cato . . . upbraiding the same Marcus Caelius, tribune of the commons, for the cheapness at which not only his speech but also his silence could be bought, says: "For a crust of bread he can be hired either to keep silence or to speak."

721   An Overzealous Advocate
Gellius, Attic Nights 1.22.6

I remember happening to be present in the court of a praetor who was a man of learning, and that on that occasion an advocate of some repute pleaded in such fashion that he wandered from the subject and did not touch upon the point at issue. Thereupon the praetor said to the man whose case was before him: "You have no counsel." And when the pleader protested, saying "I am present for the honorable gentlemen," the praetor wittily retorted: "You surely present too much, but you do not represent your client."[1]

> 1. It is difficult to reproduce the word-play on *superesse*, "be present for" and "be superfluous." There is a pun also on *adesse*, "be present" and "help, assist."

722   The Difference between the Styles of Plato and Lysias
Gellius, Attic Nights 2.5.1

Favorinus used to say of Plato and Lysias: "If you take a single word from a discourse of Plato or change it, and do it with the utmost skill, you will nevertheless mar the elegance of his style; if you do the same to Lysias, you will obscure his meaning."

723a   Diogenes, Governor of Free Men
Gellius, Attic Nights 2.18.9

Diogenes the Cynic also served as a slave, but he was a freeborn man, who was sold into slavery. When Xeniades of Corinth wished to buy him and asked whether he knew any trade, Diogenes replied: "I know how to govern free men."[1] Then Xeniades, in admiration of his answer, bought him, set him free, and entrusting to him his own children, said: "Take my children to govern."

> 1. The word for free men and children is the same (*liberi*), but it seems impossible to reproduce the word play in English.

723b   Diogenes, Governor of Free Men
Macrobius, Saturnalia 1.11.42–43

Diogenes the Cynic was also a slave, although he was in fact a free man who had been sold into slavery. When Xeniades of Corinth, wishing to buy him, asked him whether he knew anything in the way of trade, he replied: "I know how to govern free men (*liberi*)." Whereupon Xeniades, struck by this reply, bought him and set him free, and entrusted his children to him, with the words: "Take my children (*liberi*) and govern them."

724a   Front or Rear
Gellius, Attic Nights 3.5.1–2

Plutarch tells us that Arcesilaüs the philosopher used strong language about a certain rich man, who was too pleasure-loving, but nevertheless had a reputation for uprightness and freedom from sensuality. For when he observed the man's affected speech, his artfully arranged hair, and his wanton glances, teeming with seduction and voluptuousness, he said: "It makes no difference with what parts of your body you debauch yourself, front or rear."

724b *Front or Rear*
Plutarch, Moralia, Table-Talk 7 IX:705E

Arcesilaüs said it makes no difference if a man is licentious in front or in the rear.

724c *Front or Rear*
Plutarch, Moralia, Advice about Keeping Well II:126A (7)

If the saying of Arcesilaüs addressed to the adulterous and licentious appears too bitter, to the effect that 'it makes no difference whether a man practises lewdness in the front parlor or in the back hall,' yet it is not without its application to our subject. For in very truth, what difference does it make whether a man employ aphrodisiacs to stir and excite licentiousness for the purposes of pleasure, or whether he stimulate his taste by odours and sauces to require, like the itch, continual scratchings and ticklings?

725 *Fabricius Backs Rufinus*
Gellius, Attic Nights 4.8.1–6

Fabricius Luscinus was a man of great renown and great achievements. Publius Cornelius Rufinus was, to be sure, a man energetic in action, a good warrior, and a master of military tactics, but thievish and keen for money. This man Fabricius neither respected nor treated as a friend, but hated him because of his character. Yet when consuls were to be chosen at a highly critical period for the State, and Rufinus was a candidate while his competitors were without military experience and untrustworthy, Fabricius used every effort to have the office given to Rufinus. When many men expressed surprise at his attitude, in wishing an avaricious man, towards whom he felt bitter personal enmity, to be elected consul, he said: "I would rather be robbed by a fellow-citizen than sold by the enemy."

726 *The Jester and the Censor*
Gellius, Attic Nights 4.20.4–6

The man who was to take the oath was a jester, a sarcastic dog, and too much given to buffoonery. Thinking that he had a chance to crack a joke, when the censor asked him, as was customary, "Have you, to the best of your knowledge and belief a wife?" he replied: "I indeed have a wife, but not by Heaven! such a one as I could desire."[1] Then the censor reduced him to a commoner for his untimely quip, and added that the reason for his action was a scurrilous joke made in his presence.

> 1. The joke, which seems untranslatable, is of course on the double meaning of *ex sententia*, "according to your opinion" and "according to your wish."

727 *The Knight and the Censors*
Gellius, Attic Nights 4.20.11

Sabinus Masurius too in the seventh book of his *Memoirs* relates a third instance of severity. He says: "When the censors Publius Scipio Nasica and Marcus Popilius were holding a review of the knights, they saw a horse that was very thin and ill-kept, while its rider was plump and in the best of condition. 'Why is it', said they, 'that you are better cared for than your mount?' 'Because,' he replied, 'I take care of myself, but Statius, a worthless slave, takes care of the horse.' This answer did not seem sufficiently respectful, and the man was reduced to a commoner, according to custom."

728a   *The Wit of Hannibal*
Gellius, Attic Nights 5.5.1-7

In collections of old tales it is recorded that Hannibal the Carthaginian made a highly witty jest when at the court of King Antiochus. The jest was this: Antiochus was displaying to him on the plain the gigantic forces which he had mustered to make war on the Roman people, and was maneuvering his army glittering with gold and silver ornaments. He also brought up chariots with scythes, elephants with turrets, and horsemen with brilliant bridles, saddlecloths, neck-chains and trappings. And then the king, filled with vainglory at the sight of an army so great and so well-equipped, turned to Hannibal and said: "Do you think that all this can be equalled and that it is enough for the Romans?" Then the Carthaginian, deriding the worthlessness and cowardice of the king's troops in their costly armor, replied: "I think all this will be enough, yes, quite enough, for the Romans, even though they are most avaricious." Absolutely nothing could equal this remark for wit and sarcasm; the king had inquired about the size of his army and asked for a comparative estimate; Hannibal in his reply referred to it as booty.

728b   *The Wit of Hannibal*
Macrobius, Saturnalia 2.2.2-3

Hannibal of Carthage made this most witty jest, when he was living in exile at the court of King Antiochus. Here it is. Antiochus was holding a review, on some open ground, to display the huge forces which he had mustered for war against the Roman people, and the troops were marching past, gleaming with accoutrements of silver and gold. Chariots too, fitted with scythes were brought on to the field, elephants with towers on their backs, and cavalry with glittering reins, housings, neck chains, and trappings. Glorying in the sight of his large and well-equipped army, the king then turned to Hannibal and said: "Do you think that all these will do for the Romans?" The Carthaginian, in mockery of the king's troops, who for all their costly equipment were cowardly and unwarlike, replied: "Yes, I think they will certainly do for the Romans—although the Romans can do with quite a lot." There could not have been a neater or more pungent remark. The king's question had referred, of course, to the size of the army, and he had asked if it could be regarded as a match for the Romans, but Hannibal's reply referred to the booty it would provide.

729   *Scipio Orders a Court Appearance*
Gellius, Attic Nights 6.1.7-11

These popular beliefs about Scipio seemed to be confirmed and attested by many remarkable actions and sayings of his. Of these the following is a single example: He was engaged in the siege of a town[1] in Spain, which was strongly fortified and defended, protected by its position, and also well provisioned; and there was no prospect of taking it. One day he sat holding court in his camp, at a point from which there was a distant view of the town. Then one of the soldiers who were on trial before him asked in the usual way on what day and in what place he bade them give bail for their appearance. Then Scipio, stretching forth his hand towards the very citadel of the town which he was besieging, said: "Appear the day after tomorrow in yonder place." And so it happened; on the third day, the day on which he had ordered them to appear, the town was captured, and on that same day he held court in the citadel of the place.

1. According to Valerius Maximus 3.7.1, the town was Badia.

730a   *Albinus Writes in Greek*
Gellius, Attic Nights 11.8.1–5

Marcus Cato is said to have rebuked Aulus Albinus with great justice and neatness. Albinus, who had been counsel with Lucius Lucullus, composed a *Roman History* in the Greek language. In the introduction to his work he wrote to this effect: that no one ought to blame him if had written anything then in those books that was incorrect or inelegant; "for," he continues, "I am a Roman, born in Latium, and the Greek language is quite foreign to me"; and accordingly he asked indulgence and freedom from adverse criticism in case he had made many errors. When Marcus Cato had read this, "Surely, Aulus," said he, "you are a great trifler in preferring to apologize for a fault rather than avoid it. For we usually ask pardon either when we have erred through inadvertence or done wrong under compulsion. But tell me, I pray you," said he, "who compelled you to do that for which you ask pardon before doing it." This is told in the thirteenth book of Cornelius Nepos' work *On Famous Men*.

730b   *Albinus Writes in Greek*
Macrobius, Saturnalia Book 1 Praefatio 13–15

But here I am indeed imprudent, and I have incurred that neat rebuke which Marcus Cato[1] gave to the Aulus Albinus who was consul with Lucullus. This Albinus composed a *History of Rome* in Greek and wrote in the preface to the effect that no one ought to criticize him for any lack of arrangement, or faults of style, "for," said he, "I am a Roman, born in Latium, and the Greek language is altogether foreign to me"; and on that ground he claimed the privilege of being excused from censure for any mistakes he might have made. After reading this, Marcus Cato said: "Upon my word, Aulus, you carry your trifling too far in choosing to apologize for a fault instead of refraining from committing it. As a rule, one asks for pardon after making a mistake through inadvertence or after doing wrong under compulsion; but who, pray, compelled you to do that for which you would ask pardon in advance?"

1. See Cicero, *Brutus* 81.

731a   *Paid for Holding Tongue*
Gellius, Attic Nights 11.9.1–2

Critolaus has written[1] that envoys came from Miletus to Athens on public business, perhaps for the purpose of asking aid. Then they engaged such advocates as they chose to speak for them, and the advocates, according to their instructions, addressed the people in behalf of the Milesians. Demosthenes vigorously opposed the demands of the Milesians, maintaining that the Milesians did not deserve aid, nor was it to the interest of the State to grant it. The matter was postponed to the next day. The envoys came to Demosthenes and begged him earnestly not to speak against them; he asked for money, and received the amount which he demanded. On the following day, when the case was taken up again, Demosthenes, with his neck and shoulders wrapped in thick wool, came forward before the people and said that he was suffering from quinsy and hence could not speak against the Milesians. Then one of the populace cried out that it was not quinsy, but "silver-insy" from which Demosthenes was suffering. Demosthenes himself, too, as Critolaus also relates, did not afterwards conceal that matter, but actually made a boast of it. For when he had asked Aristodemus, the player, what sum he had received for acting and Aristodemus[2] had replied "a talent," Demothenes rejoined: "Why, I got more than that for holding my tongue."

1. C. Mueller, *Fragmenta Historicorum Graecorum* 4.373.
2. Famous actors made large sums of money; according to Pliny, *Natural History* 7.129, the celebrated Roman actor Roscius made 500,000 sesterces yearly.

731b *Paid for Holding Tongue*
Gellius, Attic Nights 11.10.1–6

The story which in the preceding chapter we said was told by Critolaus about Demosthenes, Gaius Gracchus, in the speech *Against the Aufeian Law*, applied to Demades in the following words: "For you, fellow citizens, if you wish to be wise and honest, and if you inquire into the matter, will find that none of us comes forward here without pay. All of us who address you are after something, and no one appears before you for any purpose except to carry something away. I myself, who am now recommending you to increase your taxes, in order that you may the more easily serve your own advantage and administer the government, do not come here for nothing; but I ask of you, not money, but honor and your good opinion. Those who come forward to persuade you not to acccept this law, do not seek honor from you, but money from Nicomedes; those also who advise you to accept it are not seeking a good opinion from you but from Mithridates a reward and an increase of their possessions; those, however, of the same rank and order who are silent are your very bitterest enemies, since they take money from all and are false to all. You, thinking that they are innocent of such conduct, give them your esteem; but the embassies from the kings, thinking it is for their sake that they are silent, give them great gifts and rewards. So in the land of Greece, when a Greek tragic actor boasted that he had received a whole talent for one play, Demades, the most eloquent man of his country, is said to have replied to him: 'Does it seem wonderful to you that you have gained a talent by speaking? I was paid ten talents by the king for holding my tongue.' Just so, these men now receive a very high price for holding their tongues."

731c *Paid for Holding Tongue*
Pseudo-Plutarch, Moralia, Lives of the Ten Orators X:848B

Once when Polus the actor told him [Demosthenes] that he received a talent as pay for acting two days, he replied, "And I five talents for being silent one day."

731d *Silver Quinsy*
Plutarch, Demosthenes 25.3–6 (2–5)

A few days afterwards, however, while they were making an inventory of the treasure, Harpalus[1] saw that Demosthenes was eyeing with pleasure a cup of barbarian make, with a keen appreciation of its fashion and of the ornamental work upon it. He therefore bade him poise it in his hand and see how heavy the gold was. And when Demosthenes was amazed at its weight and asked how much it would amount to, Harpalus smiled and said, "For you it will amount to twenty talents;" and as soon as night was come he sent him the cup with the twenty talents. Now, Harpalus was skillful in detecting the character of a man who had a passion for gold, by means of the look that spread over his face and the glances of his eyes. For Demosthenes could not resist, but was overcome by the bribe, and now that he had, as it were, admitted a garrison into his house, promptly went over to the side of Harpalus. Next day, after swathing his neck carefully in woolen bandages, he went forth into the assembly; and when he was urged to rise and speak, he made signs that his voice was ruined. The wits, however, by way of raillery, declared that the orator had been seized overnight, not with an ordinary quinsy, but with a silver quinsy. And afterwards, when the people learned that he had been bribed, and would not permit him, when he wished it, to have a hearing and make his defense, but were angry and raised a tumult against him, someone rose and said jokingly: "Men of Athens, will you not listen to the man who holds the cup?"[2]

1. Alexander's treasurer. He came to Athens in 324 B.C.E.
2. At feasts, the cup passed from guest to guest, and the one who held it had the right of uninterrupted speech or song.

732   *Menander and Philemon*
Gellius, Attic Nights 17.4.1–2

In contests in comedy Menander was often defeated by Philemon, a writer by no means his equal, owing to intrigue, favor, and partisanship. When Menander once happened to meet his rival, he said: "Pray pardon me, Philemon, but really, don't you blush when you defeat me?"

733   *Diogenes and the Logician*
Gellius, Attic Nights 18.13.7–8

I must tell you how wittily Diogenes paid back a sophism of that kind which I have mentioned above, proposed with insulting intent by a logician of the Platonic school. For when the logician had asked: "You are not what I am, are you?" and Diogenes had admitted it, he added: "But I am a man." And when Diogenes had assented to that also and the logician had concluded: "Then you are not a man," Diogenes retorted: "That is a lie, but if you want it to be true, begin your proposition with me."

734   *A Stoic Philosopher on Fear*
Gellius, Attic Nights 19.1.10

"What does this mean, Sir philosopher, that when we were in the danger you were afraid and turned pale, while I neither feared nor changed color?" And the philosopher hesitating for a moment about the propriety of answering him said: "If in such a terrible storm I did show a little fear, you are not worthy to be told the reason for it. But, if you please, the famous Aristippus, the pupil of Socrates, shall answer for me,[1] who on being asked on a similar occasion by a man much like you why he feared, though a philosopher, while his questioner on the contrary had no fear, replied that they had not the same motives, for his questioner need not be very anxious about the life of a worthless coxcomb, but he himself feared for the life of an Aristippus."

1. F. W. A. Mullach, *Fragmenta Philosophorum Graecorum* 2.407.16.

735   *A Wedding at Cana*
Gospel, John 2:1–11 (NIV)

On the third day a wedding took place at Cana in Galilee. Jesus' mother was there, and Jesus and his disciples had also been invited to the wedding. When the wine was gone, Jesus' mother said to him, "They have no more wine." "Dear woman, why do you involve me?" Jesus replied. "My time has not yet come." His mother said to the servants, "Do whatever he tells you." Nearby stood six stone water jars, the kind used by the Jews for ceremonial washing, each holding from twenty to thirty gallons. Jesus said to the servants, "Fill the jars with water"; so they filled them to the brim. Then he told them, "Now draw some out and take it to the master of the banquet." They did so, and the master of the banquet tasted the water that had been turned into wine. He did not realize where it had come from, though the servants who had drawn the water knew. Then he called the bridegroom aside and said, "Everyone brings out the choice wine first and then the cheaper wine after the guests have had too much too drink; but you have saved the best till now." This, the first of his miraculous signs, Jesus performed in Cana of Galilee. He thus revealed his glory, and his disciples put their faith in him.

736   *Kingdom and Being Born Anew*
Gospel, John 3:1–10 (NIV)

Now there was a man of the Pharisees named Nicodemus, a member of the Jewish ruling council. He came to Jesus at night and said, "Rabbi, we know you are a teacher who has come from God. For no one could perform the miraculous signs you are doing if God were not with him." In reply Jesus declared, "I tell you the truth, no one can see the kingdom of God unless he is born again. How can a man be born when he is old?" Nicodemus asked. "Surely he cannot enter a second time into his mother's womb to be born!" Jesus answered, "I tell you the truth, no one can enter the kingdom of God unless he is born of water and the Spirit. Flesh gives birth to flesh, but the Spirit gives birth to spirit. You should not be surprised at my saying, 'You must be born again.' The wind blows wherever it pleases. You hear its sound, but you cannot tell where it comes from or where it is going. So it is with everyone born of the Spirit." "How can this be?" Nicodemus asked. "You are Israel's teacher," said Jesus, "and do you not understand these things?

737a   *Jesus' Word Heals Officer's Son*
Gospel, John 4:46–54 (NIV)

Once more he visited Cana in Galilee, where he had turned the water into wine. And there was a certain royal official whose son lay sick at Capernaum. When this man heard that Jesus had arrived in Galilee from Judea, he went to him and begged him to come and heal his son, who was close to death. "Unless you people see miraculous signs and wonders," Jesus told him, "you will never believe." The royal official said, "Sir, come down before my child dies." Jesus replied, "You may go. Your son will live." The man took Jesus at his word and departed. While he was still on the way, his servants met him with the news that his boy was living. When he inquired as to the time when his son got better, they said to him, "The fever left him yesterday at the seventh hour." Then the father realized that this was the exact time at which Jesus had said to him, "Your son will live." So he and all his household believed. This was the second miraculous sign that Jesus performed, having come from Judea to Galilee.

737b   *Jesus' Word Heals Centurion's Servant*
Gospel, Luke 7:2–10 (NIV)

There [in Capernaum] a centurion's servant, whom his master valued highly, was sick and about to die. The centurion heard of Jesus and sent some elders of the Jews to him, asking him to come and heal his servant. When they came to Jesus, they pleaded earnestly with him, "This man deserves to have you do this, because he loves our nation and has built our synagogue." So Jesus went with them. He was not far from the house when the centurion sent friends to say to him: "Lord, don't trouble yourself, for I do not deserve to have you come under my roof. That is why I did not even consider myself worthy to come to you. But say the word, and my servant will be healed. For I myself am a man under authority, with soldiers under me. I tell this one, 'Go,' and he goes; and that one, 'Come,' and he comes. I say to my servant, 'Do this,' and he does it." When Jesus heard this he was amazed at him, and turning to the crowd following him, he said, "I tell you, I have not found such great faith even in Israel." Then the men who had been sent returned to the house and found the servant well.

737c *Jesus' Word Heals Centurion's Servant*
Gospel, Matthew 8:5–13 (NIV)

When Jesus had entered Capernaum, a centurion came to him, asking for help. "Lord," he said, "my servant lies at home paralyzed and in terrible suffering." Jesus said to him, "I will go and heal him." The centurion replied, "Lord, I do not deserve to have you come under my roof. But just say the word, and my servant will be healed. For I myself am a man under authority, with soldiers under me. I tell this one, 'Go," and he goes; and that one, 'Come,' and he comes. I say to my servant, 'Do this,' and he does it." When Jesus heard this, he was astonished and said to those following him, "I tell you the truth, I have not found anyone in Israel with such great faith. I say to you that many will come from the east and the west, and will take their places at the feast with Abraham, Isaac and Jacob in the kingdom of heaven. But the subjects of the kingdom will be thrown outside, into the darkness, where there will be weeping and gnashing of teeth." Then Jesus said to the centurion, "Go! It will be done just as you believed it would." And his servant was healed at that very hour.

738 *Jesus' Word Heals Man by Pool*
Gospel, John 5:1–9 (NIV)

Some time later, Jesus went up to Jerusalem for a feast of the Jews. Now there is in Jerusalem near the Sheep Gate a pool, which in Aramaic is called Bethesda and which is surrounded by five covered colonnades. Here a great number of disabled people used to lie—the blind, the lame, the paralyzed. One who was there had been an invalid for thirty-eight years. When Jesus saw him lying there and learned that he had been in this condition for a long time, he asked him, "Do you want to get well?" "Sir," the invalid replied, "I have no one to help me into the pool when the water is stirred. While I am trying to get in, someone else goes down ahead of me." Then Jesus said to him, "Get up! Pick up your mat and walk." At once the man was cured; he picked up his mat and walked.[1]

1. Cf. 1212; Mark 2:1–12; Matthew 9:1–8.

739 *John's Statements True*
Gospel, John 10:40–42 (NIV)

Then Jesus went back across the Jordan to the place where John had been baptizing in the early days. Here he stayed and many people came to him. They said, "Though John never performed a miraculous sign, all that John said about this man was true," And in that place many believed in Jesus.

740 *The High Priest Questions Jesus*

Gospel, John 18:19–23 (NIV)

Meanwhile, the high priest questioned Jesus about his disciples and his teaching. "I have spoken openly to the world," Jesus replied. "I always taught in synagogues or at the temple, where all the Jews come together. I said nothing in secret. Why question me? Ask those who heard me. Surely they know what I said." When Jesus said this, one of the officials nearby struck him in the face. "Is this the way you answer the high priest?" he demanded. "If I said something wrong," Jesus replied, "testify as to what is wrong. But if I spoke the truth, why did you strike me?"

741 *Pilate's Question*

Gospel, John 18:33–38a (NIV)

Pilate then went back inside the palace, summoned Jesus and asked him, "Are you the king of the Jews?" "Is that your own idea," Jesus asked, "or did others talk to you about me?" "Am I a Jew?" Pilate replied. "It was your people and your chief priests who handed you over to me. What is it you have?" Jesus said, "My kingdom is not of this world. If it were, my servants would fight to prevent my arrest by the Jews. But now my kingdom is from another place." "You are a king, then!" said Pilate. Jesus answered, "You are right in saying I am a king. In fact, for this reason I was born, and for this I came into the world, to testify to the truth. Everyone on the side of truth listens to me." What is truth?" Pilate asked. With this he went out again to the Jews and said, "I find no basis for a charge against him."

742a *The Good Samaritan*

Gospel, Luke 10:25–37 (NIV)

On one occasion an expert in the law stood up to test Jesus. "Teacher," he asked, "what must I do to inherit eternal life?" "What is written in the Law?" he replied, "How do you read it?" He answered: "'Love the Lord your God with all your heart and with all your soul and with all your strength and with all your mind'; and, 'Love your neighbor as yourself.'"[1] "You have answered correctly," Jesus replied, "Do this and you will live." But he wanted to justify himself, so he asked Jesus, "And who is my neighbor?" In reply Jesus said: "A man was going down from Jerusalem to Jericho, when he fell into the hands of robbers. They stripped him of his clothes, beat him and went away, leaving him half dead. A priest happened to be going down the same road, and when he saw the man, he passed by on the other side. So too, a Levite, when he came to the place and saw him, passed by on the other side. But a Samaritan, as he traveled, came where the man was; and when he saw him, he took pity on him. He went to him and bandaged his wounds, pouring on oil and wine. Then he put the man on his own donkey, took him to an inn and took care of him. The next day he took out two silver coins and gave them to the innkeeper. 'Look after him,' he said, 'and when I return, I will reimburse you for any extra expense you may have.' "Which of these three do you think was a neighbor to the man who fell into the hands of robbers?" The expert in the law replied, "The one who had mercy on him." Jesus told, "Go and do likewise."

1. Cf. Gospel, Thomas 25.

742b   *Rich Man*

Gospel, Luke 18:18-30 (NIV)

A certain ruler asked him, "Good teacher, what must I do to inherit eternal life?" "Why do you call me good?" Jesus answered, "No one is good—except God alone. You know the commandments: 'Do not commit adultery, do not murder, do not steal, do not give false testimony, honor your father and mother.' " "All these I have kept since I was a boy," he said. When Jesus heard this, he said to him, "You still lack one thing. Sell everything you have and give to the poor, and you will have treasure in heaven. Then come, follow me." When he heard this, he became very sad, because he was a man of great wealth. Jesus looked at him and said, "How hard it is for the rich to enter the kingdom of God! Indeed, it is easier for a camel to go through the eye of a needle than for a rich man to enter the kingdom of God." Those who heard this asked, "Who then can be saved?" Jesus replied, "What is impossible with men is possible with God." Peter said to him, "We have left all we had to follow you!" "I tell you the truth," Jesus said to them, "no one who has left home or wife or brothers or parents or children for the sake of the kingdom of God will fail to receive many times as much in this age and, in the age to come, eternal life."

742c   *Rich Man*

Gospel, Mark 10:17-22 (NIV)

As Jesus started on his way, a man ran up to him and fell on his knees before him. "Good teacher," he asked, "what must I do to inherit eternal life?" "Why do you call me good?" Jesus answered. "No one is good—except God alone. You know the commandments: 'Do not murder, do not commit adultery, do not steal, do not give false testimony, do not defraud, honor your father and mother.'" [1] "Teacher," he declared, "all these I have kept since I was a boy." Jesus looked at him and loved him. "One thing you lack," he said. "Go, sell everything you have and give to the poor, and you will have treasure in heaven. Then come, follow me." At this the man's face fell. He went away sad, because he had great wealth.

1. Exodus 20:12-16; Deuteronomy 5:16-20.

742d   *Rich Man*

Gospel, Nazoreans 16, from Origen, *On Matthew* 15.14
(Klostermann: 389-390)

It says: The other rich man said to him, "Master, what good thing must I do that I may live?" Jesus said to him, "Man, do what is in the law and the prophets." He answered, "I have done that." He said to him, "Go and sell all you possess and distribute it among the poor, and come, follow me." But the rich man then began to scratch his head, for it did not please him. And the Lord said to him, "How can you say, I have done what is in the law and the prophets? For it is written in the law: Love your neighbor as yourself; and behold, many of your brothers, sons of Abraham, are clothed in filth and die of hunger, while your house is full of many good things, and nothing at all comes out of it for them." And he turned and said to Simon, his disciple, who was sitting by him, "Simon, son of Jonah, it is easier for a camel to go through the eye of a needle than for a rich man to enter into the kingdom of heaven."

742e   The Great Commandment
Gospel, Mark 12:28–34 (NIV)

One of the teachers of the law came and heard them debating. Noticing that Jesus had given them a good answer, he asked him, "Of all the commandments, which is the most important?" "The most important one," answered Jesus, "is this: 'Hear, O Israel, the Lord our God, the Lord is one. Love the Lord your God with all your heart and with all your soul and with all your mind and with all your strength.'[1] The second is this: 'Love your neighbor as yourself.'[2] There is no commandment greater than these." "Well said, teacher," the man replied. "You are right in saying that God is one and there is no other but him. To love him with all your heart, with all your understanding and with all your strength, and to love your neighbor as yourself is more important than all burnt offerings and sacrifices."[3] When Jesus saw that he had answered wisely, he said to him, "You are not far from the kingdom of God." And from then on no one dared ask him any more questions.

1. Deuteronomy 6:4.
2. Leviticus 19:18.
3. 1 Samuel 15:22; Hosea 6:6; Micah 6:6–8.

742f   The Great Commandment
Gospel, Matthew 22:34–40 (NIV)

Hearing that Jesus had silenced the Sadducees, the Pharisees got together. One of them, an expert in the law, tested him with this question: "Teacher, which is the greatest commandment in the Law?" Jesus replied: "'Love the Lord your God with all your heart and with all your soul and with all your mind.'[1] This is the first and greatest commandment. And the second is like it: 'Love your neighbor as yourself.'[2] All the Law and the Prophets hang on these two commandments."

1. Deuteronomy 6:4.
2. Leviticus 19:18.

743   Cleansing Ten Lepers
Gospel, Luke 17:11–19 (NIV)

Now on his way to Jerusalem, Jesus traveled along the border between Samaria and Galilee. As he was going into a village, ten men who had leprosy met him. They stood at a distance and called out in a loud voice, "Jesus, Master, have pity on us!" When he saw them, he said, "Go, show yourselves to the priests." And as they went, they were cleansed. One of them, when he saw he was healed, came back, praising God in a loud voice. He threw himself at Jesus' feet and thanked him—and he was a Samaritan. Jesus asked, "Were not all ten cleansed? Where are the other nine? Was no one found to return and give praise to God except this foreigner?" Then he said to him, "Rise and go; your faith has made you well."

744   Jesus and Zacchaeus
Gospel, Luke 19:1–10 (NIV)

Jesus entered Jericho and was passing through. A man was there by the name of Zacchaeus: he was a chief tax collector and was wealthy. He wanted to see who Jesus was, but being a short man he could not, because of the crowd. So he ran ahead and climbed a sycamore-fig tree to see him, since Jesus was coming that way. When Jesus reached the spot, he looked up and said to him, "Zacchaeus, come down immediately. I must stay at your house today." So he came down at once and welcomed him gladly. All the people saw this and began to mutter, "He has gone to be the guest of a 'sinner.'" But Zacchaeus stood up and said to the Lord, "Look, Lord! Here and now I give half of my possessions to the poor, and if I have cheated anybody out of anything, I will pay back four times the amount." Jesus said to him, "Today salvation has come to this house, because this man, too, is a son of Abraham. For the Son of Man came to seek and to save what was lost."

745   *The Two Thieves*
Gospel, Luke 23:39–43 (NIV)

One of the criminals who hung there hurled insults at him: "Aren't you the Christ? Save yourself and us!" But the other criminal rebuked him. "Don't you fear God," he said, "since you are under the same sentence? We are punished justly, for we are getting what our deeds deserve. But this man has done nothing wrong." Then he said, "Jesus, remember me when you come into your kingdom." Jesus answered him, "I tell you the truth, today you will be with me in paradise."

746a   *John the Baptist*
Gospel, Matthew 11:7–15 (NIV)

As John's disciples were leaving, Jesus began to speak to the crowd about John: "What did you go out into the desert to see? A reed swayed by the wind? If not, what did you go out to see? A man dressed in fine clothes? No, those who wear fine clothes are in kings' palaces.[1] Then what did you go out to see? A prophet? Yes, I tell you, and more than a prophet. This is the one about whom it is written: "'I will send my messenger ahead of you, who will prepare your way before you.'[2] I tell you the truth: Among those born of women there has not risen anyone greater than John the Baptist; yet he who is least in the kingdom of heaven is greater than he.[3] From the days of John the Baptist until now, the kingdom of heaven has been forcefully advancing, and forceful men lay hold of it. For all the Prophets and the Law prophesied until John. And if you are willing to accept it, he is the Elijah who was to come. He who has ears, let him hear."

1. Cf. Gospel, Thomas 78.
2. Malachi 3:1.
3. Cf. Gospel, Thomas 46.

746b   *John the Baptist*
Gospel, Luke 7:24–28 (NIV)

After John's messengers left, Jesus began to speak to the crowd about John: "What did you go out into the desert to see? A reed swayed by the wind? If not, what did you go out to see? A man dressed in fine clothes? No, those who wear expensive clothes and indulge in luxury are in palaces. But what did you go out to see? A prophet? Yes, I tell you, and more than a prophet. This is the one about whom it is written: "'I will send my messenger ahead of you, who will prepare your way before you.' I tell you, among those born of women there is no one greater than John; yet the one who is least in the kingdom of God is greater than he."

746c *John the Baptist*
Gospel, Luke 16:16 (NIV)

"The Law and the Prophets were proclaimed until John. Since that time, the good news of the kingdom of God is being preached, and everyone is forcing his way into it."

747a *Jesus and John the Baptist*
Gospel, Matthew 11:16–19 (NIV)

"To what can I compare this generation? They are like children sitting in the marketplaces and calling out to others: '"We played the flute for you, and you did not dance; we sang a dirge, and you did not mourn.' For John came neither eating nor drinking, and they say, 'He has a demon.' The Son of Man came eating and drinking, and they say, 'Here is a glutton and a drunkard, a friend of tax collectors and "sinners."' But wisdom is proved right by her actions."

747b *Jesus and John the Baptist*
Gospel, Luke 7:31–35 (NIV)

"To what, then, can I compare the people of this generation? What are they like? They are like children sitting in the marketplace and calling out to each other: '"We played the flute for you, and you did not dance; we sang a dirge, and you did not cry.' For John the Baptist came neither eating bread nor drinking wine, and you say, 'He has a demon.' The Son of Man came eating and drinking, and you say, 'Here is a glutton and a drunkard, a friend of tax collectors and "sinners."' But wisdom is proved right by all her children."

748 *Son of Man as Dyer*
Gospel, Philip 54 (CG II, 63:25–30)

The Lord went into the dye-works of Levi. He took seventy-two colors and threw them into the cauldron. He took them all out white and said, "Even so came the Son of Man [as] a dyer."

749 *Modesty Part of Faith*
Hadith, Bukhārī, adab, 77

Aḥmad b. Yūsuf, 'Abd al-'Azīz b. abī Salama and Ibn Shihāb related, on the authority of Sālim, who had it from 'Abd Allāh b. 'Umar who said, The Prophet passed by a man who was reproving his brother for being so modest, saying, "You are so modest that it will be harmful to you." The Messenger of God said, "Leave him alone, for modesty is a part of faith."

750 *The One You Love*
Hadith, Bukhārī, aḥkām, 10

'Uthmān b. abī Shayba and Jarīr related to us from Manṣūr and Sālim b. abī al-Ja'd, who had it from Anas b. Mālik who said: As the Prophet and I were going out of the mosque we met a man at the gate. He said, "O Messenger of God, when will be the Hour?" The Prophet said, "How have you prepared for it?" The man appeared to be distressed. Then he said, "O Messenger of God, I have not prepared much for it in the way of fasting, prayer and almsgiving, but I love God and His Messenger." The Prophet said, "You will be with the one you love."

751 *Faith First*

Hadith, Ibn Ḥanbal, 6604

Ḥasan informed us from Ibn Lihay'a who had it from Ḥuyyā b. 'Abd Allāh from Abū 'Abd al-Raḥmān al-Ḥubulī from 'Abd Allāh b. 'Amr who said: A man came to the Messenger of God and said, "O Messenger of God, I recite the Qur'ān but I find my head does not understand it." The Messenger of God replied, "Your heart lacks faith, for truly, faith is given to a believer first, then the Qur'ān."

752 *An Ill Muslim Gentleman*

Hadith, Muslim, dhikr, 7

Abū al-Khaṭṭāb, Ziyād b. Yaḥyā al-Ḥassānī and Muḥammad b. abī 'Adiyā related to us on the authority of Ḥumayd who had it from Thābit, who reported from Anas that: The Messenger of God visited a Muslim gentleman whose health had so declined that he was weak like a chicken. The Messenger of God said to him, "Did you pray and ask God about your condition?" He said, "Yes, I have said, 'O God, any punishment that you are going to impose upon me in the hereafter, give it to me now instead.'" The Messenger of God said, "God be glorified! You cannot bear that (or, you are in no position to do that).[1] Why did you not say, 'O God, give us blessing in this world and blessing in the hereafter, and preserve us from the fire of hell?'" The Prophet made this supplication for him and he became well.

1. Variant reading.

753 *On Fraud*

Hadith, Tirmidhī, Buyū', 72

'Alī b. Ḥujr and Ismā'īl b. Ja'far reported from Al-'Alā' b. 'Abd al-Raḥmān and his father who heard from Abu Hurayra. The Messenger of God passed by a pile of grain. He put his hand into the midst of it, and his fingers encountered moisture. He exclaimed, "O merchant, what is this?" The owner of the produce said, "It has been damaged by the rain, O Messenger of God." Then he replied: "If that is the case, why not put the damaged grain on top of the pile so that people can see it." Then he concluded, "Whoever practices fraud is not one of us."

754 *Mosollamus Disproves Bird's Divination*

Josephus, Against Apion 1.201–204 (22)

"When I [Hecataeus] was on the march towards the Red Sea, among the escort of Jewish cavalry which accompanied us was one named Mosollamus,[1] a very intelligent man, robust, and, by common consent, the very best of bowmen, whether Greek or barbarian. This man, observing that a number of men were going to and fro on the route and that the whole force was being held up by a seer who was taking the auspices, inquired why they were halting. The seer pointed out to him the bird he was observing, and told him that if it stayed in that spot it was expedient for them all to halt; if it stirred and flew forward, to advance; if backward, then to retire. The Jew, without saying a word, drew his bow, shot and struck the bird, and killed it. The seer and some others were indignant, and heaped curses upon him. 'Why so mad, you poor wretches?' he retorted; and then, taking the bird in his hands, continued, 'Pray, how could any sound information about our march be given by this creature, which could not provide for its own safety? Had it been gifted with divination, it would not have come to this spot, for fear of being killed by an arrow of Mosollamus the Jew.'"

1. Hellenized form of Meshullam (Ezra 8:16).

755 Daniel and the King
Lives of the Prophets: Daniel 14–20

Daniel caused the seven years (the meaning of his "seven times") to become seven months. The mystery of the seven times was fulfilled upon the king, for in seven months he was restored, and in the (remaining) six years and five months he was doing penance to the Lord and confessing his wickedness. When his sin had been forgiven, the kingdom was given back to him. He ate neither bread nor flesh in the time of his repentance, for Daniel had bidden him eat pulse and greens while appeasing the Lord. The king named the prophet Baltasar because he wished to make him a joint heir with his children; but the holy man said: "Far be it from me to forsake the heritage of my fathers and join in the inheritances of the uncircumcised." He also did for the other Persian kings many wonderful things which were not written down. He died there, and was buried with great honor, by himself, in the royal sepulcher.

756 Ear Not Cheated
Lucian, Demonax 12

When Favorinus[1] was told by someone that Demonax was making fun of his lectures and particularly of the laxity of their rhythm, saying that it was vulgar and effeminate and not by any means appropriate to philosophy, he went to Demonax and asked him, "Who are you to libel my compositions?" "A man," he said, "with an ear that is not easy to cheat."

1. An eunuch from Arles, of considerable repute as a sophist.

757 The Qualifications of Demonax
Lucian, Demonax 12

The sophist [Favorinus] kept at him and asked, "What qualifications had you, Demonax, to leave school and commence philosophy?" "Those you lack," he replied.

758 Favorinus Asks Demonax about Philosophy
Lucian, Demonax 13

Another time the same man [Favorinus] went to him and asked what philosophical school he favored most. Demonax replied, "Why, who told you that I was a philosopher?"

759 Philosopher Not Told by Beard
Lucian, Demonax 13

As Demonax left, he broke into a very hearty laugh; and when Favorinus asked him what he was laughing at, he replied, "It seemed to me ridiculous that you should think a philosopher can be told by his beard when you yourself have none."

760 Pythagoras Is Calling
Lucian, Demonax 14

When the Sidonian sophist[1] was once showing his powers at Athens, and was voicing his own praise to the effect that he was acquainted with all philosophy—

but I may as well cite his very words: "If Aristotle calls me to the Lyceum, I shall go with him; if Plato calls me to the Academy, I shall come; if Zeno calls, I shall spend my time in the Stoa; if Pythagoras calls, I shall hold my tongue."[2] Well, Demonax arose in the midst of the audience and said: "Ho" (addressing him by name), "Pythagoras is calling you!"

1. Otherwise unknown.
2. Alluding to the Pythagorean vow of silence.

761 *Demonax and Pytho*
Lucian, Demonax 15

When a handsome young fellow named Pytho, who belonged to one of the aristocratic families in Macedonia, was quizzing him, putting a trick-question to him and asking him to give the logical answer, Demonax said, "I know this much, my boy, that is a baffling question, and so are you!" Enraged at the pun, the other said threateningly, "I'll show you in short order that you've a man to deal with!" Whereupon Demonax laughingly inquired, "Oh, you will send for your man, then?"

762 *Doctor before Proconsul*
Lucian, Demonax 16

When an athlete, whom he [Demonax] had ridiculed for letting himself be seen in gay clothes although he was an Olympic champion, struck him on the head with a stone and drew blood, each of the bystanders was as angry as if he himself had been struck, and they shouted, "Go to the proconsul!" But Demonax said, "No, not to the proconsul, but for the doctor!"

763 *Boy Like Mother*
Lucian, Demonax 18

A Roman senator in Athens introduced his son to him, a handsome boy, but girlish and weak, saying, "My son here pays his respects to you." "A dear boy," said Demonax, "worthy of you and like his mother!"

764 *The Rebuke of Peregrinus*
Lucian, Demonax 21

When Peregrinus Proteus rebuked him for laughing a great deal and making sport of mankind, saying, "Demonax, you're not at all doggish!" he answered, "Peregrinus, you are not at all human!"

765 *Reflecting on Antipodes*
Lucian, Demonax 22

When a scientist was talking of the Topsy-turvy people (Antipodes), he [Demonax] made him get up, took him to a well, showed him their own reflection in the water and asked: "Is that the sort of topsy-turvy people you mean?"

766 *The Spell of Demonax*
Lucian, Demonax 23

When a fellow claimed to be a magician and to have spells so powerful that by their agency he could prevail on everybody to give him whatever he wanted, Demonax said, "Don't be amazed, for I am in the same business myself. Follow me to the bread-seller's if you like, and you shall see me persuade her to give me bread with a single spell and a tiny charm"—implying that a coin is as good as a spell.

767   Dead Slave Finds Fault
Lucian, Demonax 24

When the famous Herodes [Atticus] was mourning the premature death of Polydeuces [a favorite slave] and wanted a chariot regularly made ready and horses put to it just as if the boy were going for a drive, and dinner regularly served for him, Demonax went to him and said, "I am bringing you a message from Polydeuces." Herodes was pleased and thought that Demonax, like everyone else, was falling in with his mourning; so he said, "Well, what does Polydeuces want, Demonax?" "He finds fault with you," he replied, "for not going to join him at once!"

768   Atticism Criticized
Lucian, Demonax 26

He [Demonax] also liked to poke fun at those who use obsolete and unusual words in conversation. For instance, to a man who had been asked a certain question by him and had answered in an excessively Attic manner, he said, "I asked you now, but you answer me as if I had asked in Agamemnon's day."

769   The Two Philosophers
Lucian, Demonax 28

On seeing two philosophers very ignorantly debating a given subject, one asking silly questions and the other giving answers that were not at all to the point, he [Demonax] said, "Doesn't it seem to you, friends, that one of these fellows is milking a he-goat and the other is holding a sieve for him!"

770   Agathocles Illogical
Lucian, Demonax 29

When Agathocles the Peripatetic was boasting that he was first among the logicians—that there was no other, he [Demonax] said: "Come now, Agathocles; if there is no other, you are not first: if you are first, then there are others."

771   The New Quest of the Golden Fleece
Lucian, Demonax 31

When he saw Apollonius the philosopher leaving the city with a multitude of disciples (he was called away to be tutor to the emperor), Demonax remarked, "There goes Apollonius and his Argonauts!"[1]

> 1. Alluding to Apollonius of Rhodes and his poem on the Argonauts, and implying that this was another quest of the Golden Fleece.

772   Orator Recites to Fool
Lucian, Demonax 36

An orator whose delivery was wretched was advised by him to practice and exercise. When he replied, "I am always reciting to myself," Demonax said, "Then no wonder you recite that way, with a fool for a hearer!"

773 *On the Worth of Prophecy*
Lucian, Demonax 37

On seeing a prophet make public predictions for money, he [Demonax] said, "I don't see on what ground you claim the fee. If you think you can change destiny in any way, you ask too little, however much you ask; but if everything is to turn out as ordained by god, what good is your prediction?"

774 *A Wooden Adversary*
Lucian, Demonax 38

When a Roman officer, well-developed physically, gave him an exhibition of sword-practice on a post, and asked, "What do you think of my swordsmanship, Demonax?" he replied, "Fine, if you have a wooden adversary!"

775 *Roman Citizenship*
Lucian, Demonax 40

A man named Polybius, quite uneducated and ungrammatical, said: "The emperor has honored me with the Roman citizenship." "Oh, why didn't he make you a Greek instead of a Roman?" said he [Demonax].

776 *The Clothes of Sheep*
Lucian, Demonax 41

On seeing an aristocrat who placed great importance on the breadth of his purple band, Demonax taking hold of the garment and calling his attention to it, said in his ear, "A sheep wore this before you, and he was but a sheep for all that!"

777 *Admetus' Epitaph*
Lucian, Demonax 44

A vile poet named Admetus told him that he had written an epitaph in a single line and had given instructions in his will to have it carved on his tombstone. I may as well quote it exactly:

"Earth, in thy bosom receive Admetus' husk; he's a god now!" Demonax said with a laugh: "The epitaph is so fine that I wish it were already carved!"

778 *Spartan Equality*
Lucian, Demonax 46

He [Demonax] saw a Spartan beating a slave and said, "Stop treating him as your equal!"[1]

1. Whipping was a feature of Spartan training.

779 *The Disciple of Hyperides*
Lucian, Demonax 48

Above all, he [Demonax] made war on those who cultivate philosophy in the spirit of vainglory and not in the spirit of truth. For example, on seeing a Cynic with cloak and wallet, but with a bar [*hyperon*] instead of a staff, who was making an uproar and saying that he was the follower of Antisthenes, Crates, and Diogenes, Demonax said, "Don't lie! You are really a disciple of Hyperides!"

780   *The Punishment for Bold Speech*
Lucian, Demonax 50

His remark to the proconsul was at once clever and cutting. The man was one of the sort that use pitch to remove hair from their legs and their whole bodies. When a Cynic mounted a stone and charged him with this, accusing him of effeminacy, he was angry, had the fellow hauled down and was on the point of confining him in the stocks or even sentencing him to exile. But Demonax, who was passing by, begged him to pardon the man for making bold to speak his mind in the traditional Cynic way. The proconsul said, "Well, I will let him off for you this time, but if he ever dares to do such a thing again, what shall be done to him?" "Have him depilated!" replied Demonax.

781   *On Exercising Authority*
Lucian, Demonax 51

One to whom the emperor had entrusted the command of legions and of the most important province asked Demonax what was the best way to exercise authority. "Don't lose your temper," he said, "Do little talking and much listening."

782   *Demonax and Rufinus*
Lucian, Demonax 54

Noting that Rufinus the Cypriote (I mean the lame man of the school of Aristotle) was spending much time in the walks of the Lyceum, he [Demonax] remarked: "Pretty cheeky, I call it—a lame Peripatetic (Stroller)!"

783   *The Daughters of Epictetus*
Lucian, Demonax 55

When Epictetus rebuked him [Demonax] and advised him to get married and have children, saying that a philosopher ought to leave nature a substitute when he is gone, his answer was very much to the point, "Then give me one of your daughters, Epictetus!"[1]

1. Epictetus never married.

784   *Herminus and the Ten Sentences*
Lucian, Demonax 56

His reply to Herminus the Aristotelian deserves mention. Aware that, although he was an out-and-out scoundrel and had done a thousand misdeeds, he sang the praises of Aristotle and had his Ten Sentences (the Categories) on his tongue's end, Demonax said: "Herminus, you really need ten sentences!"

785   *Demonax and the Philosophers*
Lucian, Demonax 61–62

He [Demonax] had a good word even for Thersites, calling him a mob-orator of the Cynic type.

When he was once asked which of the philosophers he liked, he said: "They are all admirable, but for my part I revere Socrates, I marvel at Diogenes, and I love Aristippus."

786 *No Sow in House*
Macrobius, Saturnalia 1.6.30

As for Tremellius, he got the surname "Scropha" from the following incident. He was at his country estate with his children and household when his slaves stole and killed a sow (*scropha*) which was wandering away from a neighbor's land. The neighbor summoned guards and surrounded the other's whole estate, to prevent any possible removal of the animal, and then called on the master to return it to him. But Tremellius had heard from his bailiff what had happened and so put the dead body of the sow under some rugs on which his wife was lying and invited the neighbor to make a search. When they came to the bedroom, Tremellius swore that there was no sow in his house, "Except," said he, pointing to the bed, "the one lying in those rugs."

787 *For the Road*
Macrobius, Saturnalia 2.2.4

In the days of old . . . there used to be a sacrifice known as "For the road," and it was the custom at it for everything left over from the sacrificial feast to be burned. Hence the point of a jest of Cato's. For, when a certain Albidius, after devouring all his property, finally lost by fire the house which was all that remained to him of his possessions, Cato observed that it was a "Sacrifice for the road" since the man had burned what he could not have devoured.

788 *Cobbler Grinds Gall*
Macrobius, Saturnalia 2.2.6

Plancus happened to be in counsel for a friend, and wishing to discredit a hostile witness, whom he knew to be a cobbler, asked him how he made his living. The man neatly replied: "Grinding gall (*gallam subigo*)," for cobblers make use of gallnuts for their work, and by the double entendre[1] cleverly turned the question so as to charge Plancus with adultery, for stories were going round of his association with one Maevia Galla, a married woman.

> 1. The pun depends on an indecent use of the verb *subigere*. For the use of galls in dressing leather, see Pliny, *Natural History* 16.9.26.

789 *The Luck of Mucius*
Macrobius, Saturnalia 2.2.8

Mucius . . . was the most ill-natured of men; and so, finding him looking even gloomier than usual, Publius remarked: "Either Mucius has been unlucky or someone else has been lucky."

790 *Modeling Done in Dark*
Macrobius, Saturnalia 2.2.10

Servilius Genimus happened to be dining at the house of Lucius Mallius, who was held to be the best portrait painter in Rome, and noticing how misshapen his host's sons were, observed: "Your modeling, Mallius, does not come up to your painting." "Naturally," replied Mallius, "for the modeling is done in the dark but the painting by daylight."

791a *Consul of the Day*
Macrobius, Saturnalia 2.2.13

Marcus Otacilius Pitholaus . . . on the occasion of the consulship of Caninius Revilus which lasted only one day remarked: "We used to have Priests of the Day but now we have consuls of a day (*diales*)."[1]

> 1. The point of the jest is the punning reference to the Priest of Jupiter (or *Diespiter*, i.e., "Father of the Day"; see Aulus Gellius 5.12), who was known as the *Flamen Dialis*, and to the connection of the word *Dialis* with *dies*, "day."

791b *Consul of the Day*
Macrobius, Saturnalia 2.3.5

The consulship of Vatinius which lasted for only a few days gave Cicero an opportunity for some humorous sayings which had wide currency. "Vatinius' term of office," he said, "has presented a remarkable portent, for in his consulship there has been neither winter, spring, summer, nor autumn." And again, when Vatinius complained that Cicero had found it too much trouble to come to see him in his sickness, he replied: "It was my intention to come while you were consul, but night overtook me." Cicero, however, was thought to be getting his own back here and to have had in mind the retort made by Vatinius to his boast that he had returned from exile borne in triumph on the shoulders of the people: "How, then, did you get those varicose veins in your legs?"[1]

> 1. Cf. Quintilian 11.3.143 and Sidonius, *Epistles* 5.5.

791c *Consul of the Day*
Macrobius, Saturnalia 2.3.6

Caninius Revilus . . . was consul for only a single day and mounted the rostrum to assume office and at the same time to relinquish it. Cicero therefore, who welcomed every chance to make a humorous remark, referred to him slightingly as "a notional consul" and said later of him: "He has at any rate done this: he has obliged us to ask in whose consulship he was consul," adding, "We have a wide awake consul in Caninius, for while in office he never slept a wink."

791d *Consul of the Day*
Macrobius, Saturnalia 7.3.10

But there are other gibes which are not so unkind (suggesting, as it were, the bite of the beast that has lost its teeth), for example, Cicero's reference to a consul whose term of office lasted for only a single day: "We are accustomed," he said, "to having Priests of the Day, but now we have Consuls of a day (*diales*)." And it was of the same man that he said: "Our Consul is wide awake indeed, for while in office he has not slept a wink"; and again, on being reproached by this same man for not calling on him during his consulate, Cicero replied: "I was on my way, but night overtook me."

792 *Nothing Ready Yet*
Macrobius, Saturnalia 2.3.7

Pompey found Cicero's witticisms tiresome, and the following sayings of Cicero were current: "I know whom to avoid, but I do not know whom to follow." Again, when he had come to join Pompey, to those who were saying that he was late in coming he retorted: "Late? Not at all, for I see nothing ready here yet."

793   *Pompey Gives Citizenship to Deserter*
Macrobius, Saturnalia 2.3.8

And when Pompey had given Roman citizenship to a deserter [from Caesar], Cicero's comment was: "That was handsome of the man; he promises the Gauls a citizenship to which they have no right, and yet he can't restore our own city to us."

794   *Pompey Wishes Cicero Were Enemy*
Macrobius, Saturnalia 2.3.8

And so it was thought that Pompey was justified in saying of Cicero: "I wish to goodness he would go over to the enemy. He would then learn to fear us."

795   *The Whereabouts of Dolabella*
Macrobius, Saturnalia 2.3.8

Afterward, when Pompey asked him [Cicero] where his son-in-law, Dolabella, was, he replied: "With your [former] father-in-law."[1]

> 1. Pompey had married Caesar's daughter Julia, and her untimely death in 54 B.C.E. went far to break the bond between the two men.

796a   *Ill-Girt Boy*
Macrobius, Saturnalia 2.3.9

Cicero showed his teeth at Caesar too. In the first place, when (after Caesar's victory) he was asked how he had come to choose the wrong side, he replied: "The way he wore his toga took me in"; the point of the jest being that Caesar used to wear his toga in such a way that an edge hung loose in an effeminate manner as he walked, so that Sulla would seem to have foreseen the future when he said to Pompey: "I bid you beware of that ill-girt lad."

796b   *Ill-Girt Boy*
Suetonius, Lives of the Caesars, Julius 1.45.3

They say, too, that he [Julius] was remarkable in his dress; that he wore a senator's tunic with fringed sleeves reaching to the wrist, and always had a girdle over it, though rather a loose one; and this, they say, was the occasion of Sulla's *mot*, when he often warned the nobles to keep an eye on the ill-girt boy.

797a   *Laberius and Cicero*
Macrobius, Saturnalia 2.3.10

Then, when Laberius toward the end of the Games received from Caesar the honor of the gold ring of knighthood and went straightaway to the fourteen rows[1] to watch the scene from there—only to find that the knights had felt themselves affronted by the degradations of one of their order and his offhand restoration—as he was passing Cicero, in his search for a seat, the latter said to him: "I would have been glad to have you beside me were I not already pressed for room"; meaning by these words to snub the man and at the same time to make fun of the new Senate, whose numbers had been unduly increased by Caesar. Here, however, Cicero got as good as he gave, for Laberius replied: "I am surprised that you of all people should be pressed for room, seeing that you make a habit of sitting on two seats at once," thus reproaching Cicero with the fickleness of which that excellent and loyal citizen was unfairly accused.

1. Cf. Suetonius, *Lives of the Caesars*, Julius 1.39. By the *Lex Roscia theatralis* of 67 B.C.E. the first fourteen rows of seats in the theater, immediately behind the orchestra (where the senators sat), were reserved for the *equites*.

797b *Laberius and Cicero*
Macrobius, Saturnalia 7.3.8

It was Cicero, too, who, when remarking on his inability to give Laberius a seat beside him, said: "I should be glad to have you with me were I not already pressed for room"; whereupon that famous actor bitingly replied: "And yet it was always your way to sit on two seats"—thus taunting the great man with the fickleness of his political allegiance.

798 *The Servile State of Rome*
Macrobius, Saturnalia 2.3.12

And indeed his biting wit went even further; for, greeted by a certain Andron from Laodicea, he [Cicero] asked what had brought him to Rome and, hearing that the man had come as an envoy to Caesar to beg freedom for his city, he made open reference to the servile state of Rome by saying, in Greek, "If you are successful, put in a word for us too."

799 *Cicero and Cassius*
Macrobius, Saturnalia 2.3.13

The vigor of his [Cicero's] sarcasm could go beyond mere jesting and express his deep feelings, as for example, in his letter to Caius Cassius,[1] one of the men who murdered the dictator, in which he said: "I could wish you had asked me to your dinner on the Ides of March. Nothing, I assure you, would have been left over. But as things are, your leaving makes me feel anxious."[2]

1. Cicero, *Epistulae ad Familiares* 12.4.
2. The meaning is that, if Cicero had been in on the plot to murder Caesar, Antony too would have been killed.

800 *Cicero and Lepidus*
Macrobius, Saturnalia 2.3.16

And again, after a speech by Marcus Lepidus in the Senate, he [Cicero] observed: "For my part, I should not have rated *la pareille consonance* (*homoioptoton*)[1] so highly."

1. The text is corrupt and the point obsure, but it would seem that Cicero is punning on the proper name Lepidus and the adjective *lepidus*, "neat and agreeable."

801 *Never Look Round while Running*
Macrobius, Saturnalia 2.4.7

A man who had been struck by a stone when on active service and had a noticeable and unsightly scar on his forehead, was bragging loudly of his exploits and received this gentle rebuke from Augustus: "Never look round when you are running away."

802 *No Correction*
Macrobius, Saturnalia 2.4.8

To an ugly hunchback named Galba, who was pleading in court before him and kept on saying: "If you have any fault to find, correct me," he [Augustus] said: "I can offer you advice, but I certainly can't correct you."

803 *The Prosecution of Cassius*
Macrobius, Saturnalia 2.4.9

Since many of those who were prosecuted by Severus Cassius got off, but the architect of the Forum of Augustus kept putting off the completion of the work, the emperor jestingly remarked: "I could wish that Cassius would prosecute my Forum too—and get it off my hands."

804 *Cultivating Father's Memory*
Macrobius, Saturnalia 2.4.10

A certain Vettius had ploughed up a memorial to his father, whereupon Augustus remarked: "This is indeed cultivating your father's memory."

805 *Better to Be Herod's Pig*
Macrobius, Saturnalia 2.4.11

When he heard that Herod King of the Jews had ordered boys in Syria under the age of two years to be put to death and that the king's son was among those killed, he [Augustus] said: "I'd rather be Herod's pig than Herod's son."[1]

    1. Cf. 1191.

806 *Purple Too Dark*
Macrobius, Saturnalia 2.4.14

He [Augustus] once had reason to complain that some cloth of Tyrian purple which he had ordered was too dark. "Hold it up higher," said the tailor, "and look at it from below." This provoked the witty retort: "Have I to walk on my roof garden before people at Rome can say that I am well dressed?"

807 *The Forgetful Servant*
Macrobius, Saturnalia 2.4.15

He [Augustus] once had occasion too to complain of the forgetfulness of the servant whose duty it was to tell him the names of the persons he met; and so, when the servant asked him whether he had any orders for the Forum, he replied: "Yes, take these letters of introduction; for you know no one there."

808 *Pillow Conducive to Sleep*
Macrobius, Saturnalia 2.4.17

Hearing of enormous debts, amounting to more than twenty million sesterces, which a certain Roman knight had successfully concealed while he lived, he [Augustus] gave orders that the man's pillow should be bought for him at the sale by auction of the estate, explaining to those who expressed surprise at his order: "The pillow must certainly be conducive to sleep, if that man in spite of all his debts should have slept on it."

809 *Augustus Commends Cato*
Macrobius, Saturnalia 2.4.18

He [Augustus] happened to visit a house in which Cato had lived, and, when Strabo to flatter Augustus spoke slightingly of Cato's obstinacy, he replied: "To seek to keep the established constitution unchanged argues a good citizen and a good man." And he meant what he said, for in thus praising Cato he also in his own interest discouraged any attempt to change the form of government.

810 *Man Resembles Augustus*
Macrobius, Saturnalia 2.4.20

An unkind quip made by a man from one of the provinces is well known. In appearance he closely resembled the emperor, and on his coming to Rome the likeness attracted general attention. Augustus sent for the man and on seeing him said: "Tell me, young man, was your mother ever in Rome?" "No," replied the other, and not content to leave it at that, added: "But my father was—often."

811 *Pollio and Augustus*
Macrobius, Saturnalia 2.4.21

During the triumvirate Augustus wrote some lampoons on Pollio, but Pollio only observed: "For my part I am saying nothing in reply; for it is asking for trouble to write against a man who can write you off."

812 *Curtius Dines with Augustus*
Macrobius, Saturnalia 2.4.22

A certain Curtius, a Roman knight given to good living, was dining with Augustus and, when a skinny thrush was placed before him, asked whether he might let it go (*mittere*). "Of course you may," said his host. Whereupon Curtius at once "let it go"—through a window.

813 *Nothing for Senator*
Macrobius, Saturnalia 2.4.23

After Augustus, unasked, had paid the debts of a certain senator who was a friend of his (they came to four million sesterces) the only thanks he got was a letter saying: "But you have given me nothing for myself."

814 *Whatever Sum You Think Fit*
Macrobius, Saturnalia 2.4.24

Whenever he [Augustus] undertook some public works his freedman Licinius used to advance large sums of money, and on one occasion this Licinius, following his usual practice, gave the emperor a promissory draft for a hundred thousand sesterces. Now in this draft a part of the line drawn over the written sign which represented the amount of the advance extended beyond the writing, thus leaving an empty space below the line, and Augustus took the opportunity to add to the former entry a second C, with his own hand, carefully filling up the empty space and copying his freedman's handwriting. In this way he doubled the sum contributed. Licinius pretended not to have noticed the additon made to the draft, but afterward, when some other work had been begun, he gently reproached the emperor for what he had done, by presenting him with a draft similarly written and saying as he did so: "Toward the cost of a new work, Sire, I advance—whatever sum you think fit."

815   *Augustus and the Knight*
Macrobius, Saturnalia 2.4.25

As censor, too, Augustus showed a remarkable tolerance which won him high praise. A Roman knight was being reprimanded by him on the ground that he had squandered his property but was able to show publicly that he had in fact increased it. The next charge brought up against him was failure to comply with the marriage laws.[1] To this he replied that he had a wife and three children and then added: "I suggest, Sire, that in future, when you have occasion to inquire into the affairs of respectable persons, the inquiry be entrusted to respectable persons."

     1. Laws to check the prevalence of celibacy.

816   *Soldier Goes Unpunished*
Macrobius, Saturnalia 2.4.26

There is, moreover, the story of the soldier from whom he [Augustus] tolerated language which was not only blunt but recklessly rude. While he was staying at a certain country house he spent restless nights, his sleep being broken by the frequent hooting of an owl. He therefore gave orders for the bird to be caught, and a soldier who happened to be an expert fowler brought it to him. The man expected to receive a handsome reward, but the emperor only complimented him and ordered him to be given a thousand sesterces. Whereupon the fellow had the audacity to say: "I'd sooner let it live," and let the bird go. It is surely remarkable that Augustus took no offense at this insolence but allowed the soldier to go away unpunished.

817   *Augustus Appears for Soldier*
Macrobius, Saturnalia 2.4.27

An old soldier who found himself in danger of losing an action at law in which he was the defendant accosted the Emperor in a public place with a request that he would appear for him in court. Augustus at once chose one of his suite to act as counsel and introduced the litigant to him. But the soldier, stripping his sleeve and showing his scars, shouted at the top of his voice: "When you were in danger at Actium, I didn't look for a substitute but I fought for you in person." The emperor blushed, and, fearing to be thought both haughty and ungrateful, appeared in court on the man's behalf.

818   *Busy at the Mill*
Macrobius, Saturnalia 2.4.28

He [Augustus] presented the musicians of the slave dealer Toronius Flaccus with a quantity of corn as a reward for the pleasure which they had given him at dinner, although he had shown his appreciation of other such entertainments by generous gifts of money. And when, some time later, he asked Toronius to allow them to play again at dinner, the latter excused himself by saying: "They are busy at the mill."

819a *Bird Trainer*
Macrobius, Saturnalia 2.4.29

Among those who welcomed him [Augustus] on his return in state from his victory at Actium was a man with a raven which he had taught to say: "Greetings to Caesar, our victorious commander." Augustus was charmed by this compliment and gave the man twenty thousand sesterces for the bird. But the bird's trainer had a partner, and, when none of this large sum of money had come his way, he told the Emperor that the man had another raven and suggested that he should be made to produce it as well. The bird was produced and repeated the words which it had been taught to say; they were: "Greetings to Antony, our victorious commander." Augustus, however, instead of being at all angry, simply told the first man to share the money with his mate.

819b *Bird Trainer*
Macrobius, Saturnalia 2.4.30

He [Augustus] was greeted in a similar way[1] by a parrot, and he ordered that bird to be bought, and a magpie too, which he fancied for the same trick. These examples encouraged a poor cobbler to try to train a raven to repeat a like form of greeting, but the bird remained dumb, and the man, ruined by the cost incurred, used often to say to it: "Nothing to show for the trouble and expense." One day, however, the raven began to repeat its lesson, and Augustus as he was passing heard the greeting. "I get enough of such greetings at home," he replied. But the bird also recalled the words of his master's customary lament and added: "Nothing to show for the trouble and expense." This made the Emperor laugh, and he ordered the bird to be bought, giving more for it than he had given for any of the others.[2]

1. I.e., "Greetings to Caesar, our victorious commander."
2. For the reference to talking birds and to ways of training them to talk, see Pliny, *Natural History* 10.58–59.117–120.

820 *If I Had More, I Should Give More*
Macrobius, Saturnalia 2.4.31

As he [Augustus] went down from his residence on the Palatine, a seedy-looking Greek used to offer him a complimentary epigram. This the man did on many occasions without success, and Augustus, seeing him about to do it again, wrote a short epigram in Greek with his own hand and sent it to the fellow as he drew near. The Greek read it and praised it, expressing admiration in both words and by his looks. Then, coming up to the imperial chair, he put his hand in a shabby purse and drew out a few pence, to give them to the emperor, saying as he did so: "I swear by thy Good Fortune, Augustus, if I had more, I should give you more." There was laughter all around, and Augustus, summoning his steward, ordered him to pay out a hundred thousand sesterces to the Greek.

821 *Fruit for Vatinius*
Macrobius, Saturnalia 2.6.1

Let me turn back now from stories of women to stories of men and from risque jests to seemly humor. The lawyer Cascellius had a reputation for a remarkably outspoken wit, and here is one of his best known quips. Vatinius had been stoned by the populace at a gladiatorial show which he was giving, and so he prevailed on the aediles to make a proclamation forbidding the throwing of anything but fruit into the arena. Now it so happened that Cascellius at that time was asked by a client to advise whether a fircone was a fruit or not, and his reply was: "If you propose to throw one at Vatinius, it is."

822   Splitting the Ship
Macrobius, Saturnalia 2.6.2

Then there is the story that, when a merchant asked him [Cascellius] how to split a ship with a partner, he replied: "If you split the ship, it will be neither yours nor your partner's."

823   Ability Ill Housed
Macrobius, Saturnalia 2.6.3

A jest that went the rounds was one directed by Marcus Lollius at the distinguished speaker Galba, who . . . was hampered by a bodily deformity: "Galba's intellectual ability is ill housed."

824   Currying Hunchbacks
Macrobius, Saturnalia 2.6.4

The same Galba was the victim of a crueler sneer from Orbilius the schoolmaster, when the latter had come into court to give evidence against a defendant. Galba, seeking to disconcert the witness, pretended to be unaware of his profession and asked him: "What's your job?" The reply was: "Currying hunchbacks in the sun."[1]

1. Cf. Suetonius, *De Grammaticis* 9.

825   Return Passage to Dyrrachium
Macrobius, Saturnalia 2.6.6

When Publius Clodius told Decimus Laberius that he was angry with him for refusing to produce a mime for him at his request, Laberius said: "What of it? All that you can do is to give me a return passage to Dyrrachium"—a mocking allusion to Cicero's exile.

826   Tall, Not Great
Macrobius, Saturnalia 2.7.12–13

Having once begun to talk about the stage, I must not omit to mention Pylades, a famous actor in the time of Augustus, and his pupil Hylas, who proceeded under his instruction to become his equal and his rival. On the question of the respective merits of these two actors popular opinion was divided. Hylas one day was performing a dramatic dance the closing theme of which was *The Great Agamemnon*, and by his gestures he represented the subject as a man of mighty stature. This was more than Pylades could stand, and from his seat in the pit he shouted: "You are making him merely tall, not great."

827   Using the Eyes
Macrobius, Saturnalia 2.7.15

On another occasion, when Hylas was dancing *Oedipus*, Pylades criticized him for moving with more assurance than a blind man could have shown, by calling out: "You are using your eyes."

828 *Ungrateful Augustus*
Macrobius, Saturnalia 2.7.19

Moreover, when the popular disturbances caused by the rivalry between him [Pylades] and Hylas brought on him the displeasure of Augustus, he retorted: "And you, Sire, are ungrateful, for you would do well to let the populace busy themselves with our affairs."

829 *Holes in Ears*
Macrobius, Saturnalia 7.3.7

Thus Octavius, who regarded himself as of noble birth, once said to Cicero, when the latter was reading aloud: "I can't hear what you are saying," to which the other replied: "And yet you certainly used to have good holes in your ears"—the point of the gibe being that Octavius was said to be of Libyan extraction, and it is a custom of the Libyans to pierce their ears.

830 *White and Black*
Macrobius, Saturnalia 7.3.13

I should agree that philosophers too have sometimes, under provocation, had recourse to a gibe of the more bitter kind. For a royal freedman, lately raised to unexpected wealth, once invited a number of philosophers to dinner and, to make fun of the oversubtlety of their inquiries, said that he would be glad to know why the dish of which they were eating was of a uniform color, although its ingredients were both black beans and white beans; whereat the philosopher Aridices angrily retorted: "Perhaps you, for your part, would tell us why the marks made by white whiplashes and black whiplashes look alike."

831 *Diogenes on Antisthenes*
Macrobius, Saturnalia 7.3.21

Gibes which take the form of straightforward chaff, such as the following, please those at whom they are aimed; if, for example, you rally a brave man for being careless of his own safety and seeking to die for others, or charge a generous man with wasting his substance by thinking more of others than of himself. And it was in this seemingly disparaging way that Diogenes used to praise his master, Antisthenes the Cynic. "It was my master," he would say, "who turned me from a rich man into a beggar and made me live in a tub instead of in a roomy house." For this was a better way of putting it than had he said: "I owe him thanks for making me a lover of learning and a man of the highest virtue."

832 *Aristides "the Just"*
Nepos 3, Aristides 1.2-4

For although Aristides so excelled in honesty that he is the only one within the memory of man—at least, so far as we have heard—who was given the title of "the Just," yet his influence was undermined by Themistocles and he was exiled for ten years by that well-known process known as the shard-vote.[1] Aristides himself, when he realized that the excited populace could not be quieted, and, as he was withdrawing, saw a man in the act of voting that he should be banished, is said to have asked him why he did so, and what Aristides had done to be thought deserving of such a punishment. To which the man replied that he did not know

Aristides, but that he was displeased because he had worked so hard to be distinguished from other men by the surname of "the Just."[2]

1. An institution established by Cleisthenes after the expulsion of the Pisistratidae. The Prytanies and the popular assembly must first determine whether such a step was necessary. If they decided in the affirmative, each citizen wrote on a potsherd the name of the man whom he wished to banish. The one who had the greatest number of votes recorded against him, provided the total number of voters was 6000, was obliged to leave the city within ten days for an exile of ten, later of five, years, but without loss of rank or property. If the number of votes did not amount to 6000, no action was taken.
2. According to one version of the story, the man could not write and Aristides wrote his own name for him on the shard.

833 *Peace Is Won by War*
Nepos 15, Epaminondas 5.3-4

This man [Meneclides], observing that warfare brought glory to Epaminondas, used to urge the Thebans to seek peace rather than war, in order that they might not need the aid of that great man as their commander. To him Epaminondas said: "You are deceiving your fellow-citizens by using the wrong word, when you dissuade them from war; for under the name of peace it is slavery that you are recommending. As a matter of fact, peace is won by war; hence those who wish to enjoy it for a long time ought to be trained for war. Therefore if you wish to be the leading city of Greece you must frequent the camp and not the gymnasium."

834 *Agamemnon No Rival*
Nepos 15, Epaminondas 5.5-6

When this same Meneclides taunted him [Epaminondas] with not having children or marrying, and especially with arrogance in thinking that he had equalled Agamemnon's renown in war, Epaminondas answered: "Cease, Meneclides, to taunt me about marriage; there is no one whose example in that regard I should be less willing to follow"; and, in fact, Meneclides was suspected of adultery. "Further, in supposing that I regard Agamemnon as a rival, you are mistaken; for he, with all Greece at his back, needed fully ten years to take one city, while I, on the contrary, with this city of ours alone, and in a single day, routed the Lacedaemonians and freed all Greece."[1]

1. At Leuctra, 371 B.C.E.

835 *Asylum with the Athenians*
Nepos 15, Epaminondas 6.1-3

Again, when he [Epaminondas] had entered the assembly of the Arcadians, urging them to conclude an alliance with the Thebans and Argives, Callistratus, the envoy of the Athenians and the most eloquent orator of that time, advised them rather to ally themselves with the people of Attica, and in his speech made many attacks upon the Thebans and Argives. For example, he declared that the Arcadians ought to bear in mind the character of some of the citizens that those two cities had produced, since from them they could form an estimate of the rest. Thus from Argos came Orestes and Alcmaeon, the matricides; from Thebes, Oedipus, who, after killing his father, begot children from his mother. In replying to him Epaminondas, after having first discussed the other questions, finally came to these two taunts. He was amazed, he said, at the folly of the Attic orator, who did not understand that those men were all blameless at the time of their birth in their native land, but after they had committed their crimes and had been exiled from their country, they had found asylum with the Athenians.

836 *Epaminondas' Immortal Daughter*
Nepos 15, Epaminondas 10.1–2

Epaminondas never took a wife. Because of this he was criticized by Pelopidas, who had a son of evil reputation; for his friend said that the great Theban did a wrong to his country in not leaving children. Epaminondas replied, "Take heed that you do not do her a greater wrong in leaving such a son as yours. And besides, I cannot lack offspring; for I leave as my daughter the battle of Leuctra, which is certain, not merely to survive me, but even to be immortal."[1]

> 1. Cf. Theon, *Progymnasmata* 213.15–214.3 (Walz).

837 *All Foes Yield to Eumenes*
Nepos 18, Eumenes 11.3–5

But Eumenes, after having been in prison for some time, said to Onomarchus, who held the chief command of the guards, that he was surprised that he had been thus confined for three full days; that it was not in accordance with Antiochus' usual wisdom thus to mistreat a defeated enemy; why did he not bid him be executed or set free? Since it seemed to Onomachus that this remark was over-arrogant, he retorted: "Well, if that was your feeling, why did you not die in battle rather than fall into the hands of your enemy?" To which Eumenes answered: "Would that what you say had happened; but the reason that it did not is because I have never encountered a foeman stronger than myself; for I have never joined battle with anyone that he did not yield to me."

838 *Jesus in the Temple*
Papyrus Oxyrhynchus 840 (Grenfell and Hunt 5:6–7)

And he [Jesus] took them and brought them into the place of purification itself and walked about in the temple. And a certain Pharisee, a chief priest named Levi, approached and spoke with them and said to the Savior, "Who permitted you to walk in this place of purification and to view these holy vessels, without having washed and without your disciples having washed even their feet? On the contrary, while still defiled, you have walked in this temple which is a clean place, in which no one who has not washed himself and changed his clothes walks or dares view these holy vessels." Immediately the Savior stood still, along with the disciples, and answered him, "Are you who are here in the temple therefore clean?" He said, "I am clean, for I have washed in David's pool and have gone down by one stair and come up by the other and have put on clean, white clothes, and then I came and looked at these holy vessels." The Savior answered and said to him, "Woe to you blind who do not see. You have washed yourself in these poured-out waters in which dogs and swine have wallowed night and day, and you have washed and wiped the outer skin which harlots and flute-girls[1] also anoint, wash, wipe, and beautify for the lust of men, whereas within they are full of scorpions and wickedness of every kind. But I and my disciples, who you say have not washed, have been washed in waters of eternal life which come down from . . . But woe to those who . . ."

> 1. Cf. 568c.

839 *The Bullock, the Lion, and the Robber*
Phaedrus, Aesopic Fables 2.1

A lion was standing over a bullock which he had brought down. A robber came up and demanded a share in the spoil. "I would give it to you," said the lion, "were you not in the habit of taking things for yourself without leave," and thus he rebuffed the rogue. By chance an innocent wayfarer came upon the same place and, on seeing the wild beast, began to retrace his steps. "You have nothing to fear," the lion said to him benignly, "and you may boldly take the portion to which your modesty entitles you." Then, having divided the carcass, he made off from the woods, in order to provide free access for the man. This is a shining example altogether, and worthy of praise; but the truth is that greed is rich and modesty poor.

840 *The Two Mules and the Robbers*
Phaedrus, Aesopic Fables 2.7

Two mules were going along heavily laden with packs; one was carrying baskets containing money, the other sacks bulging with full loads of barley. The one who carries riches on his back arches his neck high in the air and jingles his clear-toned bell by the tossing of his head; his companion, on the other hand, brings up the rear with a calm and quiet pace. Suddenly robbers rushed upon them from ambush. Amid the slaughter they wound the rich mule with a sword and pillage the money, but they neglect the paltry barley. Accordingly when the plundered mule bewailed his misfortune the other said: "For my part, I'm glad that I was despised; for I have lost nothing and have suffered no wound." Here is evidence that the little man is safe; great riches are exposed to risks.

841 *The Two Bald Men*
Phaedrus, Aesopic Fables 5.6

A bald man happened to find a comb in the street. Another equally destitute of hair came up and said: "Hey there, share in the profit!" The other man showed him the booty and added: "We have been favored by the will of the gods, but by an unkind fate we have found, as the saying goes, coals in place of a treasure." This complaint befits one who has been fooled by hope.

842 *Aesop and the Victorious Athlete*
Phaedrus, Aesopic Fables, Appendix 13

Once when the wise Phrygian saw that the victor in an athletic contest was too much inclined to boast about it, he asked him whether his opponent had been a man of greater strength than himself. "Don't say that," replied the athlete, "my strength proved to be much greater." "Well then, you simpleton," said Aesop, "what honor have you earned, if being the stronger, you prevailed over a weaker man? You might be tolerated, if you were telling us that you overcame by skill a man who was superior to you in bodily strength."

843 *Socrates and a Worthless Servant*
Phaedrus, Aesopic Fables, Appendix 27

A worthless slave was speaking ill of Socrates to his face. This fellow, as it happened, had seduced his master's wife, and Socrates was aware that this fact was known to the bystanders. Said he: "You are pleased with yourself because you please one whom you ought not to please, but you are not doing it with impunity because you displease the one whom you are bound to please."

844 *Calanus Refuses to Submit to Alexander*
Philo, Every Good Man Is Free 93–95

Calanus was an Indian by birth of the school of the gymnosophists. Regarded as possessed of endurance more than any of his contemporaries, by combining virtuous actions with laudable words he gained the admiration, not only of his fellow countrymen, but of men of other races, and, what is most singular of all, of enemy sovereigns. Thus Alexander of Macedon, wishing to exhibit to the Grecian world a specimen of the barbarians' wisdom, like a copy reproducing the original picture, began by urging Calanus to travel with him from India with the prospect of winning high fame in the whole of Asia and the whole of Europe; and when he failed to persuade him declared that he would compel him to follow him. Calanus' reply was as noble as it was apposite. "What shall I be worth to you, Alexander, for exhibiting to the Greeks if I am compelled to do what I do not wish to do?"

845 *Diogenes Cheerful in Captivity*
Philo, Every Good Man Is Free 122

And when he [Diogenes] was about to be brought to market with the other captives, he first sat down and took his dinner in the highest spirits, and gave some of it to those near him. To one of them who could not resign himself,[1] and indeed, was exceedingly dejected, he said, "Stop this repining and make the best of things, for

> E'en fair-haired Niobe took thought for food
> Though she had lost twelve children in the halls—
> Six daughters and six sons in prime of youth."[2]

1. Or perhaps "could not bring himself to accept the food," which fits better with the Homeric quotation.
2. Homer, *Iliad* 24.602ff.

846 *Diogenes Good at Ruling Men*
Philo, Every Good Man Is Free 123

Then when one of the prospective purchasers asked him what he was skilled at, he [Diogenes] said with all boldness, "at ruling men," a reply which, showing freedom, nobility, and natural kingliness, was clearly dictated by the soul within him.

847 *Diogenes Shames Buyer*
Philo, Every Good Man Is Free 124

It is said, for instance, that looking at one of the purchasers, an addict to effeminacy, whose face showed that he had nothing of the male about him, he [Diogenes] went up to him and said, "You should buy me, for you seem to me to need a husband," whereat the person concerned conscience-stricken into shame subsided, and the others were amazed at the courage and the aptness of the sally.

848 *Chaereas Ignores King's Anger*
Philo, Every Good Man Is Free 125

When he [Chaereas] was living in Alexandria by Egypt, he once incurred the anger of Ptolemy, who threatened him in no mild terms. Chaereas, considering that his own natural freedom was not a whit inferior to the other's kingship, replied:

> "Be King of Egypt; I care not for you—
> a fig for all your anger."[1]

1. Homer, *Iliad* 1.180f.

849 *Flute-Player Rebuts Rival*
Philo, Every Good Man Is Free 144

When a rival professional said to him in anger, "I'll buy you," he [Antigenidas the flute-player] answered him with great irony, "Then I'll teach you to play."

850 *Ladies of Quality*
Philostratus, Life of Apollonius 1.20

And as they fared on into Mesopotamia, the tax-gatherer who presided over the Bridge (*Zeugma*) led them into the registry and asked them what they were taking out of the country with them. And Apollonius replied: "I am taking with me temperance, justice, virtue, continence, valor, discipline." And in this way he strung together a number of feminine nouns or names. The other, already scenting his own perquisites, said: "You must then write down in the register these female slaves." Apollonius answered: "Impossible, for they are not female slaves that I am taking out with me, but ladies of quality."

851 *Advice to Babylonian King*
Philostratus, Life of Apollonius 1.37

And the king asking him what was the most stable and secure way of governing, Apollonius answered: "To respect many, and confide in few."

852 *Apollonius and the King of Babylon*
Philostratus, Life of Apollonius 1.38

One day the king was showing to him [Apollonius] the grotto under the Euphrates, and asked him what he thought of so wonderful a thing. Apollonius in answer belittled the wonder of the work and said: "It would be a real miracle, O king, if you went dry-shod through a river as deep as this and as unfordable." And when he was shown the walls of Ecbatana, and was told that they were the dwelling-place of gods, he remarked: "They are not the dwelling-place of gods at all, and I am not sure that they are of real men either; for, O king, the inhabitants of the city of Lacedaemon do not dwell within walls, and have never fortified their city." Moreover, on one occasion the king had decided a suit for some villages and was boasting to Apollonius of how he had listened to the one suit for two whole days. "Well," said the other, "you took a mighty long time, anyhow, to find out what was just." And when the revenues from the subject country came in on one occasion in great quantities at once, the king opened his treasury and showed his wealth to the sage, to induce him to fall in love with wealth; but he admired nothing that he saw and said: "This, for you, O king, represents wealth, but to me it is mere chaff." "How, then," said the other, "and in what manner can I best make use of it?" "By spending it," he said, "for you are king."

853 Apollonius Critiques Dion
Philostratus, Life of Apollonius 5.40

Dion's philosophy struck Apollonius as being too rhetorical and overmuch adapted to please and flatter, and that is why he addressed to him by way of correction the words: "You should use a pipe and a lyre, if you want to tickle men's senses, and not speech."

854 Crates and Alexander
Philostratus, Life of Apollonius 7.2

The other Crates, when Alexander had declared that he would rebuild Thebes for his sake, replied that he would never stand in need of a country or of a city which anyone could raze to the ground by mere force of arms.

855 The Son of Athene
Philostratus, Life of Apollonius 7.24

Another man came and said that he was being prosecuted because at a public sacrifice in Tarentum, where he held office, he had omitted to mention in the public prayers that Domitian was the son of Athene. Said Apollonius: "You imagined that Athene could not possibly have a son, because she is a virgin for ever and ever; but you forgot, me thinks, that this goddess once on a time bore a dragon to the Athenians."

856 Apollonius and the Informant
Philostratus, Life of Apollonius 7.27

On the next day he [Apollonius] was haranguing them in a discourse of the same tenor, when a man was sent into the prison privately by Domitian to listen to what he said. In his deportment this person had a downcast air, and, as he himself admitted, looked as if he ran a great risk. He had great volubility of speech, as is usually the case with sycophants who have been chosen to draw up eight or ten informations. Apollonius saw through the trick and talked about themes which could in no way serve his purpose; for he told his audience about rivers and mountains, and he described wild animals and trees to them, so that they were amused, while the informer gained nothing to his purpose. And when he tried to draw him away from these subjects and get him to abuse the tyrant, "My good friend," said Apollonius, "you say what you like, for I am the last man in the world to inform against you; but if I find anything to blame in the Emperor, I'll say it to his face."

857 Insolent Chaerephon
Philostratus, Lives of the Sophists 1.intro (483)

There was at Athens a certain Chaerephon, not the one who used to be nick-named "Boxwood" in Comedy,[1] because he suffered from anemia due to hard study, but the one I now speak of had insolent manners and made scurrilous jokes; he rallied Gorgias for his ambitious efforts, and said, "Gorgias, why is it that beans blow out my stomach, but do not blow up the fire?"[2] But he was not at all disconcerted by the question and replied, "This I leave for you to investigate; but here is a fact which I have long known, that the earth grows canes[3] for such as you."

1. Cf. Eupolis, *Kolakes*, fr. 165 Kock; scholiast on *Wasps* 1408 and on *Clouds* 496; Athenaeus 4.164F–165A.
2. There is a play on the verb, which means both "inflate" and "blow the bellows."
3. The jest lies in the ambiguity of the meaning and also the application here of this word, which is originally "hollow reed," such as that used by Prometheus to steal fire from heaven, but was also the regular word for a rod for chastisement.

858 *Lovers Need Not Instruments of War*
Philostratus, Lives of the Sophists 1.2 (485)

Leon of Byzantium was in his youth a pupil of Plato, but when he reached man's estate he was called a sophist because he employed so many different styles of oratory, and also because his repartees were so convincing. For example, when Philip brought an army against Byzantium, Leon went out to meet him and said, "Tell me, Philip, what moved you to begin war on us?" And when he replied, "Your birthplace, the fairest of cities, lured me on to love her, and that is why I have come to my charmer's door," Leon retorted, "They come not with swords to the beloved's door who are worthy of requited love. For lovers need not the instruments of war but of music."[1] And Byzantium was freed, after Demosthenes had delivered many speeches to the Athenians on her behalf, while Leon had said but these few words to Philip himself.

1. Cf. Philostratus, *Life of Apollonius* 7.42.

859 *Antiphon on Tyrants*
Philostratus, Lives of the Sophists 1.15 (500)

He [Antiphon of Rhamnus] was put to death in Sicily by Dionysius the tyrant,[1] and I ascribe to Antiphon himself rather than to Dionysius the responsibility for his death. For he used to run down the tragedies of Dionysius, though Dionysius prided himself more on these than on his power as a tyrant; and once when the tyrant was interested in finding out where the best kind of bronze was produced, and asked the bystanders what continent or island produced the best bronze, Antiphon, who happened to be there, said "The best I know of is at Athens, of which the statues of Harmodius and Aristogeiton[2] have been made."

1. Philostratus confuses the orator Antiphon with a poet of the same name, who is said by Plutarch, *Moralia*, How to Tell a Flatterer from a Friend I:68A–B, to have been put to death for his rash epigram. The Athenian orator was executed in 411 and the tyranny of Dionysius did not begin until about 404.
2. Who overthrew the tyrants at Athens.

860 *Barking and Biting*
Philostratus, Lives of the Sophists 1.19 (511)

And once when a tax-collector behaved insolently to him in the law court, and said, "Stop barking at me," Nicetes replied with ready wit, "I will, by Zeus, if you too will stop biting[1] me."

1. I.e. like a noxious insect; this seems to have been a favorite retort.

861 *Isaeus Ends Eye Trouble*
Philostratus, Lives of the Sophists 1.20 (513)

But when he [Isaeus, the Assyrian sophist] attained to manhood he so transformed himself as to be thought to have become another person, for he discarded both from his countenance and from his mind the frivolity that had seemed to come to the surface in him; no longer did he, even in the theater, hearken to the sounds of the lyre and the flute; he put off his transparent garments and his many-colored cloaks, reduced his table, and left off his amours as though he had lost the eyes he had before. For instance, when Ardys the rhetorician asked him whether he considered some woman or other handsome, Isaeus replied with much discretion, "I have ceased to suffer from eye trouble."

862 *The Shield of Ajax*
Philostratus, Lives of the Sophists 1.21 (519–520)

He [Scopelian] excelled also in the use of "covert allusion" and ambiguous language, but he was even more admirable in his treatment of the more vigorous and grandiloquent themes, and especially those relating to the Medes, in which occur passages about Darius and Xerxes; for in my opinion he surpassed all the other sophists, both in phrasing these allusions and in handing down that sort of eloquence for his successors to use; and in delivering them he used to represent dramatically the arrogance and levity that are characteristic of the barbarians. It is said that at these times he would sway to and fro more than usual, as though in a Bacchic frenzy, and when one of Polemo's pupils said of him that he beat a loud drum, Scopelian took to himself the sneering jest and retorted, "Yes, I do beat a drum, but it is the shield of Ajax."

863 *The Strength of Polemo*
Philostratus, Lives of the Sophists 1.22 (525)

Dionysius heard Polemo defend the suit, and as he left the court he remarked, "This athlete possesses strength, but it does not come from the wrestling-ground." When Polemo heard this he came to Dionysius' door and announced that he would declaim before him. And when he had come and Polemo had sustained his part with conspicuous success, he went up to Dionysius, and leaning shoulder to shoulder with him, like those who begin a wrestling match standing, he wittily turned the laugh against him by quoting
"Once O once they were strong, the men of Miletus."[1]

1. For this iambic response of Apollo which became a proverb for the degenerate cf. Aristophanes, *Plutus* 1003. It occurs also as a fragment of Anacreon.

864 *Polemo Expells Antoninus*
Philostratus, Lives of the Sophists 1.25 (534–535)

Moreover, the Emperor reconciled his own son Antoninus with Polemo, at the time when he handed over his scepter and became a god instead of a mortal. I must relate how this happened. Antoninus was proconsul of the whole of Asia without exception, and once he took up his lodging in Polemo's house because it was the best in Smyrna and belonged to the most notable citizen. However, Polemo arrived home at night from a journey and raised an outcry at the door that he was outrageously treated in being shut out of his own house, and next he compelled Antoninus to move to another house. The Emperor was informed of this, but he held no inquiry into the affair, lest he should reopen the wound. But in considering what would happen after his death, and that even mild natures are often provoked by persons who are too aggressive and irritating, he became anxious about Polemo. Accordingly in his last testament on the affairs of the Empire, he wrote, "And Polemo, the sophist, advised me to make this arrangement." By this means he opened the way for him to win favor as a benefactor, and forgiveness enough and to spare. And in fact Antoninus used to jest with Polemo about what had happened in Smyrna, thus showing that he had by no means forgotten it, though by the honors with which he exalted him on every occasion he seemed to pledge himself not to bear it in mind. This is the sort of jest he would make. When Polemo came to Rome, Antoninus embraced him, and then said, "Give Polemo a lodging and do not let anyone turn him out of it." And once when a tragic actor who had performed at the Olympic games in Asia, over which Polemo presided, declared that he would prosecute him, because Polemo had expelled him at the beginning of the play, the Emperor asked the actor what time it was when he was expelled from the theater, and when he replied that it happened to be at noon, the Emperor made this witty comment, "But it was midnight when he expelled *me* from his house, and I did not prosecute him."

865 *Ruler Forced to Come to Polemo*
Philostratus, Lives of the Sophists 1.25 (535)

And once when the ruler of the Bosporus, a man who had been trained in all the culture of Greece, came to Smyrna in order to learn about Ionia, Polemo not only did not take his place among those who went to salute him, but even when the other begged him to visit him he postponed it again and again, until he compelled the king[1] to come to his door with a fee of ten talents.

> 1. At this date there were kings of the Bosporus under the protectorate of Rome.

866 *Asclepius Appears to Polemo*
Philostratus, Lives of the Sophists 1.25 (535)

Again, when he [Polemo] came to Pergamon suffering from a disease of the joints, he slept in the temple, and when Asclepius appeared to him and told him to abstain from drinking anything cold, "My good sir," said Polemo, "but what if you were doctoring a cow?"

867 *Polemo Follows Timocrates*
Philostratus, Lives of the Sophists 1.25 (536)

This proud and haughty temper he [Polemo] contracted from Timocrates[1] the philosopher, with whom he associated for four years when he came to Ionia. It would do no harm to describe Timocrates also. This man came from the Pontus and his birthplace was Heraclea whose citizens admire Greek culture. At first he devoted himself to the study of writings on medicine and was well versed in the theories of Hippocrates and Democritus. But when he had once heard Euphrates of Tyre, he set full sail for his kind of philosophy. He was irascible beyond measure, so much so that while he was arguing his beard and the hair on his head stood up like a lion's when it springs to the attack. His language was fluent, vigorous and ready, and it was on this account that Polemo, who loved this headlong style of oratory, valued him so highly. At any rate, when a quarrel arose between Timocrates and Scopelian, because the latter had become addicted to the use of pitch-plasters and professional "Hair-removers,"[2] the youths who were then residing in Smyrna took different sides, but Polemo, who was the pupil of both men, became one of the faction of Timocrates and called him "the father of my eloquence." And when he was defending himself before Timocrates for his speeches against Favorinus, he cowered before him in awe and submission, like boys who fear blows from their teachers when they have been disobedient.

1. Lucian, *Demonax* 3, praises Timocrates.
2. This was a mark of effeminacy and foppishness.

868   Herodes Praises Eloquence of Polemo
Philostratus, Lives of the Sophists 1.25 (539)

When the Emperor Marcus asked him [Herodes], "What is your opinion of Polemo?" Herodes gazed fixedly before him and said,

"The sound of swift-footed horses strikes upon mine ears;"[1]
thus indicating how resonant and far-echoing was his eloquence.

1. Homer, *Iliad* 10.535.

869   Polemo Teacher of Herodes
Philostratus, Lives of the Sophists 1.25 (539)

And when Varus the consul asked him what teachers he had had, he [Herodes] replied, "This man and that, while I was being taught, but Polemo, when I was teaching others."

870   Herodes Recommends Polemo
Philostratus, Lives of the Sophists 1.25 (539)

Herodes gave Polemo leave not to appear after him to give an exhibition of his oratory, and not to have to maintain a theme after him, and allowed him to depart from Smyrna by night, lest he should be compelled to do this, since Polemo thought it outrageous to be compelled to do anything. And from that time forward he never failed to commend Polemo, and to think him beyond praise. For instance, in Athens, when Herodes had brilliantly maintained the argument about the war trophies, and was being complimented on the fluency and vigor of his speech, he said, "Read Polemo's declamation, and then you will know a great man."

871   Memory Work as Punishment
Philostratus, Lives of the Sophists 1.25 (541)

On another occasion, when the proconsul was putting to the torture a bandit who had been convicted on several charges, and declared that he could not think of any penalty for him that would match his crimes, Polemo who was present said, "Order him to learn by heart some antiquated stuff." For though this sophist had learned by heart a great number of passages, he nevertheless considered that this is the most wearisome of all exercises.

872   The Agony of Declamation
Philostratus, Lives of the Sophists 1.25 (541)

Again, on seeing a gladiator dripping with sweat out of sheer terror of the life-and-death struggle before him, he [Polemo] remarked, "You are in as great an agony as though you were going to declaim."

873 *The Sophist's Diet*
Philostratus, Lives of the Sophists 1.25 (541)

Again, when he [Polemo] met a sophist who was buying sausages, sprats, and other cheap dainties of that sort, he said, "My good sir, it is impossible for one who lives on this diet to act convincingly the arrogance of Darius and Xerxes."

874 *Polemo Makes Fun of Favorinus*
Philostratus, Lives of the Sophists 1.25 (541)

When Timocrates the philosopher remarked to him that Favorinus had become a chatterbox, Polemo said wittily, "And so is every old woman," thus making fun of him for being like a eunuch.

875 *A Solecism of the Hand*
Philostratus, Lives of the Sophists 1.25 (541)

Again, when a tragic actor at the Olympic games in Smyrna pointed to the ground as he uttered the words, "O Zeus!" then raised his hands to heaven at the words, "and Earth!" Polemo, who was presiding at the Olympic games, expelled him from the contest, saying, "The fellow has committed a solecism with his hand."

876 *Atticus Finds Fortune*
Philostratus, Lives of the Sophists 2.1 (547–548)

His [Hipparchus'] son Atticus, however, the father of Herodes, was not over-looked by Fortune after he had lost his wealth and become poor, but she revealed to him a prodigious treasure in one of the houses which he had acquired near the theater. And since, on account of its vastness, it made him cautious rather than overjoyed, he wrote the following letter to the Emperor: "O Emperor, I have found a treasure in my own house. What commands do you give about it?" To which the Emperor (Nerva at that time was on the throne) replied, "Use what you have found." But Atticus did not abandon his caution and wrote that the extent of the treasure was beyond his station. "Then misuse your windfall," replied the Emperor, "for yours it is."[1] Hence Atticus became powerful, but Herodes still more so, for besides his father's fortune his mother's also, which was not much less, helped to make him affluent.

    1. Suidas tells the story of Herodes himself.

877 *Controlling Grief a Gift*
Philostratus, Lives of the Sophists 2.1 (558)

But when his other daughter, whom he called Elpinice, died also, he [Herodes] lay on the floor, beating the earth and crying aloud, "O my daughter, what offerings shall I consecrate to thee? What shall I bury with thee?" Then Sextus the philosopher who chanced to be present said, "No small gift will you give your daughter if you control your grief for her."

878 *Loving the Trojans*
Philostratus, Lives of the Sophists 2.1 (559)

His [Herodes'] quarrel with the Quintilii[1] began, as most people assert, over the Pythian festival, when they held different views about the musical competition;

but some say that it began with the jests that Herodes made to Marcus at their expense. For when he saw that, though they were Trojans, the Emperor thought them worthy of the highest honors, he said, "I blame Homer's Zeus also, for loving the Trojans."

1. These brothers are mentioned by Cassius Dio 71.33.

879 Herodes Rebukes Cassius for Treason
Philostratus, Lives of the Sophists 2.1 (563)

Moreover, the story is told that when Cassius[1] the governor of the Eastern provinces was plotting treason against Marcus, Herodes rebuked him in a letter that ran thus: "Herodes to Cassius. You have gone mad." We must regard this letter as not merely a rebuke but also as a strong demonstration by one who, to defend the Emperor, took up the weapons of the intelligence.

1. For the conspiracy and death of Cassius in Syria see Cassius Dio 71.22.

880 False Accusations Reach Only Ears
Philostratus, Lives of the Sophists 2.1 (563)

But how stoutly Herodes bore himself in the face of abuse will appear also from what he once said to the Cynic Proteus[1] at Athens. For this Proteus was one of those who have the courage of their philosophy, so much so that he threw himself into a bonfire at Olympia; and he used to dog the steps of Herodes and insult him in a semi-barbarous dialect. So once Herodes turned round and said, "You speak ill of me, so be it, but why in such bad Greek?" And when Proteus became still more persistent with his accusations, he said, "We two have grown old, you in speaking ill of me and I in hearing you." By which he implied that, though he heard him, he laughed him to scorn, because he was convinced that false accusations reach the ears but wound no deeper.[2]

1. Lucian in his *Peregrinus* gives a full account of the self-immolation, of which he was an eyewitness, of Peregrinus Proteus the Cynic philosopher. This took place in C.E. 165.
2. An echo of Aeschines, *On the False Embassy* 149.

881 Caesar Pays Attention to Alexander
Philostratus, Lives of the Sophists 2.5 (570–571)

After he [Alexander] had reached manhood he went on an embassy to Antoninus on behalf of Seleucia, and malicious gossip became current about him, that to make himself look younger he used artificial means. Now the Emperor seemed to be paying too little attention to him, whereupon Alexander raised his voice and said: "Pay attention to me, Caesar." The Emperor, who was much irritated with him for using so unceremonious a form of address, retorted: "I am paying attention, and I know you well. You are the fellow who is always arranging his hair, cleaning his teeth, and polishing his nails, and always smells of myrrh."

882 Alexander at Athens
Philostratus, Lives of the Sophists 2.5 (574)

Herodes thus characterized him [Alexander] because he had observed that the sophist knew how to combine a sober and tempered eloquence with a bold use of sophistic modes of thought; and when he himself declaimed before Alexander he raised his eloquence to a higher pitch, because he knew that Alexander took the keenest pleasure in intensity and force; and he introduced into his speech rhythms more varied than those of the flute and the lyre, because he considered that Alexander was especially skillful in elaborate variations. The theme elected by his audience was, "The wounded in Sicily implore the Athenians who are retreating thence to put them to death with their own hands."[1] In the course of this argument, with tears in his eyes, he uttered that famous and often quoted supplication: "Ah, Nicias! Ah, my father! As you hope to see Athens once more!" Whereupon they say that Alexander exclaimed, "O Herodes, we sophists are all of us merely small slices of yourself!"[2] And that Herodes was delighted beyond measure by this eulogy, and yielding to his innate generosity presented him with ten pack-animals, ten horses, ten cup-bearers, ten shorthand writers, twenty talents of gold, a great quantity of silver, and two lisping children from the deme Collytus, since he was told that Alexander liked to hear childish voices. This, then, is what happened to Alexander at Athens.

> 1. This theme is based on the narrative of Thucydides 7.75.
> 2. An echo of the famous saying of Aeschylus that his plays were "slices" from Homer's splendid feasts.

883   *Antiochus Parodies Alexander's Style*
Philostratus, Lives of the Sophists 2.5 (574)

Antiochus made fun of this style, and despised Alexander for indulging too much in the luxury of fine-sounding words; and so when he came before the public at Antioch he began his speech with the words: "Ionias, Lydias, Marsyases, foolishness, propose me themes."[1]

> 1. The point lies in the magniloquent use of the plural and the hackneyed allusions.

884   *Hermogenes Loses Eloquence with Age*
Philostratus, Lives of the Sophists 2.7 (577–578)

Hermogenes, who was born at Tarsus, by the time he was fifteen had attained such a reputation as a sophist that even the Emperor Marcus became eager to hear him. At any rate Marcus made the journey to hear him declaim, and was delighted with his formal discourse, but marveled at him when he declaimed extempore, and gave him splendid presents. But when Hermogenes arrived at manhood his powers suddenly deserted him, though this was not due to any apparent disease, and this provided the envious with an occasion for their wit. For they declared that his words were in very truth "winged," as Homer says, and that Hermogenes had molted them, like wing-feathers. And once Antiochus the sophist, jesting at his expense, said, "Lo, here is that fellow Hermogenes, who among boys was an old man, but among the old is a boy."[1]

> 1. A parody of Pindar, *Nemean Odes* 3.72.

885   *Rufinus, Son of Apollonius*
Philostratus, Lives of the Sophists 2.19 (599)

Apollonius of Naucratis taught rhetoric as the rival of Heracleides, when the latter held the chair at Athens. He devoted himself to political oratory of a type restrained and moderate, but little suited to controversy; for it lacks rhetorical amplitude and force. He was a libertine in love, and from one of his lawless intrigues he had a son named Rufinus who succeeded him as a sophist, but produced nothing that was his own or from the heart, but always clung to his father's phrases and epigrams. When he was criticized for this by a learned man, he said, "The laws allow me to use my patrimony." "The laws allow it, certainly," said the other, "but only to those that are born within the law."

886 *Alexander and Apollonius*
Philostratus, Lives of the Sophists 2.20 (601)

While he [Apollonius of Athens] was on an embassy to the Emperor Severus at Rome, he entered the lists against the sophist Heracleides to compete in declamation, and Heracleides came out of the encounter with the loss of his privileges of exemption,[1] while Apollonius carried off gifts. Heracleides spread a false report about Apollonius that he was to set out forthwith to Libya, when the Emperor was staying there and was gathering about him the talented from all parts, and he said to Apollonius: "It is a good time for you to read the speech *Against Leptines*."[2] "Nay, for you rather," retorted Apollonius, "for indeed it also was written on behalf of exemptions."

1. From certain taxes and expensive public services, i.e. "liturgies."
2. The law of Leptines abolished all exemptions from public charges. In 355 B.C.E. Demosthenes by his speech *Against Leptines* secured the repeal of the law. Hercleides may be punning on the word Leptis where the Emperor was born.

887 *Philostratus on the Indictment of a Tyrant*
Philostratus, Lives of the Sophists 2.31 (625)

Philostratus of Lemnos once met him [Aelian] when he was holding a book in his hands and reading it aloud in an indignant and emphatic voice, and he asked him what he was studying. He replied, "I have composed an indictment of Gynnis,[1] for by that name I call the tyrant who has just been put to death, because by every sort of wanton wickedness he disgraced the Roman Empire." On which Philostratus retorted, "I should admire you for it, if you had indicted him while he was alive." For he said that while it takes a real man to try to curb a living tyrant, anyone can trample on him when he is down.

1. The "womanish man," applied to Heliogabalus, who was put to death in 222. This diatribe is lost.

888 *Aemilius Rebukes Perseus' Cowardice*
Plutarch, Aemilius Paulus 26.7-12

Accordingly, having most confidence in Nasica, he [Perseus] called for him; but since Nasica was not there, after bewailing his misfortune and carefully weighing the necessity under which he lay, he gave himself into the power of Gnaeus, thus making it most abundantly clear that his avarice was a less ignoble evil than the love of life that was in him, and that led him to deprive himself of the only things which Fortune cannot take away from the fallen, namely pity. For when at his request he was brought to Aemilius, Aemilius saw in him a great man whose fall was due to the resentment of the gods and his own evil fortune, and rose up and came to meet him, accompanied by his friends, and with tears in his eyes; but Perseus, a most shameful sight, after throwing himself prone before him and then clasping his knees, broke out into ignoble cries and supplications. These Aemilius could not abide and would not hear; but looking upon him with a distressed and sorrowful countenance, said: "Why, wretched man, dost thou free Fortune from thy strongest indictment against her, by conduct which will make men think that thy misfortunes are not undeserved, and that thy former prosperity, rather than thy present lot, was beyond thy deserts? And why dost thou deprecate my victory, and make my success a meager one, by showing thyself no noble or even fitting antagonist for Romans? Valor in the unfortunate obtains great reverence even among their enemies, but cowardice, in Roman eyes, even though it meet with success, is in every way a most dishonorable thing."

889   *Death Preferable to Disgrace*
Plutarch, Aemilius Paulus 34.3–4

And yet Perseus had sent to Aemilius begging not to be led in the procession and asking to be left out of the triumph. But Aemilius, in mockery, as it would seem, of the king's cowardice and love of life, had said: "But this at least was in his power before, and is so now, if he should wish it," signifying death in preference to disgrace.

890   *Pharnabazus and Agesilaus*
Plutarch, Agesilaus 12.1–5

After this, Pharnabazus desired to have a conference with him [Agesilaus], and Apollophanes of Cyzicus, who was a guest-friend of both, brought the two together. Agesilaus, with his friends, came first to the appointed place, and throwing himself down in a shady place where the grass was deep, there awaited Pharnabazus. And when Pharnazbus came, although soft cushions and broidered rugs had been spread for him, he was ashamed to see Agesilaus reclining as he was, and threw himself down likewise, without further ceremony, on the grassy gound, although he was clad in raiment of wonderful delicacy and dyes. After mutual salutations, Pharnabazus had plenty of just complaints to make, since, although he had rendered the Lacedaemonians many great services in their war against the Athenians, his territory was now being ravaged by them. But Agesilaus, seeing the Spartans with him bowed to the earth with shame and at a loss for words (for they saw that Pharnabazus was a wronged man), said: "We, O Pharnabazus, during our former friendship with the King, treated what belongs to him in a friendly way, and now that we have become his enemies, we treat it in a hostile way. Accordingly, seeing that thou also desirest to be one of the King's chattels, we naturally injure him through thee. But from the day when thou shalt deem thyself worthy to be called a friend and ally of the Greeks instead of a slave of the King, consider this army, these arms and ships, and all of us, to be guardians of thy possessions and of thy liberty, without which nothing in the world is honorable or even worthy to be desired." Upon this, Pharnabazus declared to him his purposes. "As for me, indeed," he said, "if the King shall send out another general in my stead, I will be on your side; but if he entrusts me with the command, I will spare no efforts to punish and injure you in his behalf." On hearing this, Agesilaus was delighted, and said, as he seized his hand and rose up with him, "O Pharnabazus, I would that such a man as thou might be our friend rather than our enemy."[1]

> 1. Cf. Xenophon, *Hellenica* 4.1.28–38, where Agesilaus adds a promise to respect, in future, the property of Pharnabazus, even in case of war.

891   *Acquit Him*
Plutarch, Agesilaus 13.4

At any rate, there is in circulation a letter of his [Agesilaus'] to Hidrieus the Carian, which runs as follows: "As for Nicias, if he is innocent, acquit him; if he is guilty, acquit him for my sake; but in any case acquit him."

892 Callipides the Buffoon
Plutarch, Agesilaus 21.4

Once upon a time Callipides the tragic actor, who had a name and fame among the Greeks and was eagerly courted by all, first met him [Agesilaus] and addressed him, then pompously thrust himself into his company of attendants, showing plainly that he expected the king to make him some friendly overtures, and finally said: "Dost thou not recognize me, O King?" The king fixed his eyes upon him and said: "Yea, art thou not Callipides the buffoon?" For this is how the Lacedaemonians describe actors.

893a Health and Sanity
Plutarch, Agesilaus 21.5

Again, Menecrates the physician, who, for his success in certain desperate cases, had received the surname of Zeus, and had the bad taste to employ the appellation, actually dared to write the king a letter beginning thus: "Menecrates Zeus to King Agesilaus, greeting." To this Agesilaus replied: "King Agesilaus to Menecrates, health and sanity."

893b Health and Sanity
Plutarch, Moralia, Sayings of Kings and Commanders III:191A (5)

Menecrates the physician, who was addressed by the title of 'Zeus,' wrote in a letter to him: "Menecrates Zeus to King Agesilaus, health and happiness." Agesilaus wrote in reply: "King Agesilaus to Menecrates, health and sanity!"

893c Health and Sanity
Plutarch, Moralia, Sayings of Spartans III:213A (59)

Menecrates the physician, who, because of his success in curing certain persons who had been given up to die, had come to be called Zeus, used to drag in this title on all occasions, and even went so far in his effrontery as to write to Agesilaus in this fashion: "Menecrates Zeus to King Agesilaus, health and happiness." Agesilaus did not read any further, but wrote in reply,
"King Agesilaus to Menecrates, health and sanity!"[1]

> 1. Ascribed to Philip of Macedon by Aelian, *Varia Historia* 12.51; cf. 893d.

893d Health and Sanity
Athenaeus, Deipnosophists 7.289D

In a letter to King Philip he [Menecrates] wrote as follows: "Zeus-Menecrates to Philip, greeting: You are king of Macedonia, but I am king of Medicine. You can destroy healthy people whensoever you wish, but I can save the ailing, and the robust who follow my prescriptions I can keep alive without sickness until old age comes. Therefore, while you are attended by a bodyguard of Macedonians, I am attended by all posterity. For I, Zeus, give them life." In answer to him Philip wrote, treating him as a crazy man: "Philip to Menecrates, come to your senses!"[1]

> 1. Philip, in an excellent pun, substituted for *chairein* (rejoice!), the common greeting to open a letter, the closing statement *hygiainein* (be of sound health!).

894   *Public Friendship Enough*
Plutarch, Agesilaus 23.6

And when, after the peace was concluded, the Great King [Artaxerxes II] sent him [Agesilaus] a letter proposing guest-friendship, he would not accept it, saying that the public friendship was enough, and that while that lasted there would be no need of a private one.

895   *Antalcidas and the Athenian*
Plutarch, Agesilaus 31.5

It is also said that Antalcidas, when an Athenian was disputing with him over the valor of the two peoples and said, "Yet we have often driven you away from the Cephisus," replied, "But we have never driven you away from the Eurotas."

896   *No Argives Buried in Laconia*
Plutarch, Agesilaus 31.6

And a similar retort was made by a Spartan of lesser note to the Argive who said, "Many of you lie buried in the lands of the Argos"; the Spartan answered: "But not a man of you in the lands of Laconia."

897   *Inexperience Feared*
Plutarch, Agesilaus 38.1–2

Then Nectanabis sought to encourage Agesilaus by saying that although the enemy were numerous, they were a mixed rabble of artisans whose inexperience in war made them contemptible. "Indeed," said Agesilaus, "it is not their numbers that I fear, but the inexperience and ignorance of which you speak, which it is hard to overcome by stratagems. For stratagems array unexpected difficulties against men who try to defend themselves against them, if they suspect and await them; but he who does not await nor even suspect any stratagem gives no hold to the opponent who is trying to outwit him, just as, in a wrestling bout, he who does not stir gives no advantage to his antagonist."

898   *Agis Defers to Aratus*
Plutarch, Agis 15.1

Aratus, when Agis joined him near Corinth, was still deliberating whether or not to meet the enemy in open battle. Here Agis displayed great ardor, and courage which was sane and calculating. For he declared that in his opinion it was best to fight a decisive battle and not to abandon the gate of the Peloponnesus and suffer the enemy to pass inside: "However," he said, "I will do as seems best to Aratus, for Arataus is an older man, and is general of the Achaeans; I did not come hither to be their leader or to give them orders, but to give them aid and share their expedition."

899   *Pericles Studies Accounts*
Plutarch, Alcibiades 7.2

He [Alcibiades] once wished to see Pericles, and went to his house. But he was told that Pericles could not see him; he was studying how to render his accounts to the Athenians. "Were it not better for him," said Alcibiades, as he went away, "to study how not to render his accounts to the Athenians?"

900 *Timon and Alcibiades*
Plutarch, Alcibiades 16.6

Timon the misanthrope once saw Alcibiades, after a successful day, being publicly escorted home from the assembly. He did not pass him by nor avoid him, as his custom was with others, but met him and greeted him, saying: "It's well you're growing so, my child; you'll grow big enough to ruin all this rabble."

901 *Alexander's Response to Pausanias after Philip's Death*
Plutarch, Alexander 10.6–8 (4)

And so when Pausanias, who had been outrageously dealt with at the instance of Attalus and Cleopatra and could get no justice at Philip's hands, slew Philip, most of the blame devolved upon Olympias, on the ground that she had added her exhortations to the young man's anger and incited him to the deed; but a certain amount of accusation attached itself to Alexander also. For it is said that when Pausanias, after the outrage that he had suffered, met Alexander, and bewailed his fate, Alexander recited to him the iambic verse of the "Medeia":[1]

"The giver of the bride, the bridegroom, and the bride." However, he did seek out the participants in the plot and punished them, and was angry with Olympias for her savage treatment of Cleopatra during his absence.[2]

> 1. The *Medeia* of Euripides, 5.289 (Kirchhoff). The text makes the verse suggest the murder of Attalus, Philip, and Cleopatra.
> 2. "After his death Olympias killed Philip's infant son, together with his mother Cleopatra, niece of Attalus, by dragging them over a bronze vessel filled with fire" (Pausanias 8.7.5).

902a *Alexander Visits Diogenes*
Plutarch, Alexander 14.1–5 (1–3)

And now a general assembly of the Greeks was held at the Isthmus, where a vote was passed to make an expedition against Persia with Alexander, and he was proclaimed their leader. Thereupon many statesmen and philosophers came to him with their congratulations, and he expected that Diogenes of Sinope also, who was tarrying in Corinth, would do likewise. But since that philosopher took not the slightest notice of Alexander, and continued to enjoy his leisure in the suburb Craneion, Alexander went in person to see him; and he found him lying in the sun. Diogenes raised himself up a little when he saw so many persons coming towards him, and fixed his eyes upon Alexander. And when that monarch addressed him with greetings, and asked if he wanted anything, "Yes," said Diogenes, "stand a little out of my sun." It is said that Alexander was so struck by this, and admired so much the haughtiness and grandeur of the man who had nothing but scorn for him, that he said to his followers, who were laughing and jesting about the philosopher as they went away, "But verily, if I were not Alexander, I would be Diogenes."

902b *Alexander Visits Diogenes*
Diogenes Laertius, Lives of the Eminent Philosophers 6.38

When he [Diogenes] was sunning himself in the Craneum, Alexander came and stood over him and said, "Ask of me anything you desire." To which he replied, "Stand out of my light."

902c *Alexander Visits Diogenes*
Cicero, Tusculan Disputations 5.32.92

But Diogenes,[1] certainly, was more outspoken, in his quality of Cynic, when Alexander asked him to name anything he wanted: "Just now," said he, "stand a bit away from the sun." Alexander had apparently interfered with his basking in the heat. And in fact Diogenes, to show how far superior he was to the King of Persia in the conditions of his life, used to argue that while he had no needs, nothing would ever be enough for the king; he did not miss the pleasures with which the king could never be sated, the king could never enjoy the pleasures of the philosopher.

1. Cf. Cicero, *Tusculan Disputations* 1.104.

902d *If Not Alexander, Then Diogenes*
Diogenes Laertius, Lives of the Eminent Philosophers 6.32

Alexander is reported to have said, "Had I not been Alexander, I should have liked to be Diogenes."

903 *Alexander Forces Delphic Oracle*
Plutarch, Alexander 14.6–7 (4)

And now, wishing to consult the god concerning the expedition against Asia, he [Alexander] went to Delphi; and since he chanced to come on one of the inauspicious days, when it is not lawful to deliver oracles, in the first place he sent a summons to the prophetess. And when she refused to perform her office and cited the law in her excuse, he went up himself and tried to drag her to the temple, whereupon, as if overcome by his ardor, she said: "Thou art invincible, my son!" On hearing this, Alexander said he desired no further prophecy, but had from her the oracle which he wanted.

904 *Seers Foretell Alexander's Success*
Plutarch, Alexander 14.8–9 (5)

Moreover, when he [Alexander] set out upon his expedition,[1] it appears that there were many signs from heaven, and, among them, the image of Orpheus at Leibethra (it was made of cypress-wood) sweated profusely at about that time. Most people feared the sign, but Aristander bade Alexander be of good cheer, assured that he was to perform deeds worthy of song and story, which would cost poets and musicians much toil and sweat to celebrate.[2]

1. In the early Spring of 334 B.C.E.
2. Cf. Arrian, *Anabasis* 1.11.2.

905 *Alexander Pays Tribute to Athena and Achilles*
Plutarch, Alexander 15.7–8 (4)

Then, going up to Ilium, he [Alexander] sacrificed to Athena and poured libations to the heroes. Furthermore, the gravestone of Achilles he anointed with oil, ran a race by it with his companions, naked, as is the custom, and then crowned it with garlands, pronouncing the hero happy in having, while he lived, a faithful friend, and after death, a great herald of his fame.

906   *Alexander Prefers Achilles' Lyre to Paris' Lyre*
Plutarch, Alexander 15.9 (5)

As he [Alexander] was going about and viewing the sights of the city, someone asked him if he wished to see the lyre of Paris. "For that lyre," said Alexander, "I care very little; but I would gladly see that of Achilles, to which he used to sing the glorious deeds of brave men."[1]

> 1. See Homer, *Iliad* 9.185–191.

907   *Amyntas Interprets Alexander's Tactics for Darius*
Plutarch, Alexander 20.1–3 (1–2)

Now, there was in the army of Darius a certain Macedonian who had fled from his country, Amyntas by name, and he was well acquainted with the nature of Alexander. This man, when he saw that Darius was eager to attack Alexander within the narrow passes of the mountains, begged him to remain where he was, that he might fight a decisive battle with his vast forces against inferior numbers in plains that were broad and spacious. And when Darius replied that he was afraid the enemy would run away before he could get at them, and Alexander thus escape him, "Indeed," said Amyntas, "on this point, O king, thou mayest be without fear; for he will march against thee, nay, at this very moment, probably, he is on the march."

908a   *Alexander's Rebuke of Leonidas' Stinginess with Incense*
Plutarch, Alexander 25.5–8 (4–5)

Moreover, as he [Alexander] was dispatching great quantities of the spoils home to Olympias and Cleopatra and his friends, he sent also to Leonidas his tutor five hundred talents' weight of frankincense and a hundred of myrrh, in remembrance of the hope with which that teacher had inspired his boyhood. It would seem, namely, that Leonidas, as Alexander was one day sacrificing and taking incense with both hands to throw upon the altar-fire, said to him:—"Alexander, when thou hast conquered the spice-bearing regions thou canst be thus lavish with thine incense; now, however, use sparingly what thou hast." Accordingly, Alexander now wrote him: "I have sent thee myrrh and frankincense in abundance, that thou mayest stop dealing parsimoniously with the gods."

908b   *Alexander's Rebuke of Leonidas' Stinginess with Incense*
Plutarch, Moralia, Sayings of Kings and Commanders III:179E–F (4)

On a time when he [Alexander[1]] was offering incense to the gods with lavish hand, and often taking up handfuls of the frankincense, Leonidas, who had been his attendant in boyhood, happening to be present, said, "My boy, you may offer incense thus lavishly when you have made yourself master of the land that bears it." And so, when Alexander had become master of it, he sent a letter to Leonidas: "I have sent to you a half-ton of frankincense and cassia, so that you may never again count any petty cost in dealing with the gods, since you know that we are now masters of the land that bears these fragrant things."[2]

> 1. Alexander the Great, born 356, king of Macedon 336–323 B.C.E.
> 2. Cf. Pliny, *Natural History* 12.32 (62).

909 *Alexander's Dream about Pharos Island*
Plutarch, Alexander 26.4–7 (2–4)

Then, in the night, as he [Alexander] lay asleep, he saw a wonderful vision. A man with very hoary locks and of a venerable aspect appeared to stand by his side and recite these verses:

"Now, there is an island in the much-dashing sea,
In front of Egypt; Pharos is what men call it."[1] Accordingly, he rose up at once and went to Pharos, which at that time was still an island, a little above the Canobic mouth of the Nile, but now it has been joined to the mainland by a causeway. And when he saw a site of surpassing natural advantages (for it is a strip of land like enough to a broad isthmus, extending between a great lagoon and a stretch of sea which terminates in a large harbor), he said he saw now that Homer was not only admirable in other ways, but also a very wise architect, and ordered the plan of the city to be drawn in conformity with this site.

1. Homer, *Odyssey* 4.354f.

910a *Mispronouncing "My Son" as "Son of Zeus"*
Plutarch, Alexander 27.9 (5)

And some say that the prophet [of Ammon], wishing to show his friendliness by addressing him [Alexander] with "O paidion," or *O my son*, in his foreign pronunciation ended the words with "s" instead of "n," and said, "O paidios," and that Alexander was pleased at the slip in pronunciation, and a story became current that the god had addressed him with "O pai Dios," or *O son of Zeus*.

910b *Zeus Makes Noblest His Own*
Plutarch, Alexander 27.10–11 (6)

We are told, also, that he [Alexander] listened to the teachings of Psammon the philosopher in Egypt, and accepted most readily this utterance of his, namely, that all mankind are under the kingship of God, since in every case that which gets the mastery and rules is divine. Still more philosophical, however, was his own opinion and utterance on this head, namely that although God was indeed a common father of all mankind, still, He made peculiarly His own the noblest and best of them.

910c *Zeus Makes Noblest His Own*
Plutarch, Moralia, Sayings of Kings and Commanders III:180D (15)

In the shrine of Ammon he [Alexander] was hailed by the prophetic priest as the son of Zeus. "That is nothing surprising," said he; "for Zeus is by nature the father of all, and he makes the noblest his own."

911a *Anaxarchus Queries about Divine Power to Thunder*
Plutarch, Alexander 28.4–5 (2–3)

Once, too, there came a great peal of thunder, and all were terrified at it; whereupon Anaxarchus the sophist who was present said to Alexander: "Couldst thou, the son of Zeus, thunder like that?" At this, Alexander laughed and said: "Nay, I do not wish to cause fear in my friends, as thou wouldst have me do, thou who despisest my suppers because, as thou sayest, thou seest the tables furnished with fish, and not with satraps' heads." For, in fact, we are told that Anaxarchus, on seeing a present of small fish which the king had sent to Hephaestion, had uttered the speech above mentioned, as though he were disparaging and ridiculing those who undergo great toils and dangers in the pursuit of eminence and power, since in the way of enjoyments and pleasures they have little or nothing more than other men.

911b Anaxarchus Queries about Divine Power To Thunder
Athenaeus, Deipnosophists 6.250F-251A

On one occasion when he [Anaxarchus] was traveling with the king [Alexander] there came a violent clap of thunder so extraordinary that everybody cowered in fear, and he said, "Can it be that you, Alexander, the son of Zeus, did that?" Alexander laughed and said, "No, for I don't want to be so terrifying as you would have me, when you urge me to have the heads of satraps and kings brought to me when I am dining."

912a Alexander Counters Parmenio
Plutarch, Alexander 29.7-9 (4)

When Darius sent to him a letter and friends,[1] begging him to accept ten thousand talents as ransom for the captives, to hold all the territory this side of the Euphrates, to take one his daughters in marriage, and on these terms to be his ally and friend, Alexander imparted the matter to his companions. "If I were Alexander," said Parmenio, "I would accept these terms." "And so indeed would I," said Alexander, "were I Parmenio." But to Darius he wrote: "Come to me, and thou shalt receive every courtesy; but otherwise I shall march at once against thee."[2]

1. This was during the siege of Tyre, according to Arrian (*Anabasis* 2.25.1).
2. This was but the conclusion of an arrogant letter. Cf. Arrian, *Anabasis* 2.25.3.

912b Alexander Counters Parmenio
Plutarch, Moralia, Sayings of Kings and Commanders III:180B (11)

When Darius offered him two million pounds, and also offered to share Asia equally with him, Parmenio said, "I would take it if I were Alexander." "And so indeed would I," said Alexander, "if I were Parmenio." But he made answer to Darius that the earth could not tolerate two suns, nor Asia two kings.[1]

Cf. Diodorus 17.54; Longinus, *De sublimitate* 9.4; Valerius Maximus 6.4, externa 3.

913 Alexander's Honorable Funeral for Darius' Wife
Plutarch, Alexander 30.2-6 (1-3)

One of the eunuchs of the bed-chamber who had been captured with the women, Teireos by name, ran away from the camp, made his way on horseback to Darius, and told him of the death of his wife. Then the king, beating upon his head and bursting into lamentation, said: "Alas for the evil genius of the Persians, if the sister and wife of their king must not only become a captive in her life, but also in her death be deprived of royal burial." "Nay, O King," answered the chamberlain, "as regards her burial, and her receiving every fitting honor, thou hast no charge to make against the evil genius of the Persians. For neither did my mistress Stateira, while she lived, or thy mother or thy children, lack any of their former great blessings except the light of thy countenance, which Lord Oromazdes will cause to shine again with luster; nor after her death was she deprived of any funeral adornment, nay, she was honored with the tears of enemies. For Alexander is as gentle after victory as he is terrible in battle."

914   *Alexander Confronts Fallen Statue of Xerxes*
Plutarch, Alexander 37.5 (3)

On beholding a great statue of Xerxes which had been carelessly overthrown by a throng that forced its way into the palace, Alexander stopped before it, and accosting it as if it had been alive, said: "Shall I pass on and leave thee lying there, because of thine expedition against the Hellenes, or, because of thy magnanimity and virtue in other ways, shall I set thee up again?" But finally, after communing with himself a long time in silence, he passed on.

915   *Ariston Expects Golden Beaker for Head of Slain Enemy*
Plutarch, Alexander 39.2 (1–2)

Ariston, the captain of the Paeonians, having slain an enemy, brought his head and showed it to Alexander, saying: "In my country, O King, such a gift as this is rewarded with a golden beaker." "Yes," said Alexander with a laugh, "an empty one; but I will pledge thy health with one which is full of pure wine."

916   *Alexander Rewards Commoner Carrying Heavy Load of Gold*
Plutarch, Alexander 39.3 (2)

Again, a common Macedonian was driving a mule laden with some of the royal gold, and when the beast gave out, took the load on his own shoulders and tried to carry it. The king [Alexander], then, seeing the man in great distress and learning the facts of the case, said, as the man was about to lay his burden down, "Don't give out, but finish your journey by taking this load to your own tent."

917   *Mazaeus Refuses Alexander's Second Province*
Plutarch, Alexander 39.9 (6)

Again, though the son of Mazaeus, the most influential man at the court of Darius, already had a province, Alexander gave him a second and a larger one. He, however, declined it, saying: "O King, formerly there was one Darius, but now thou hast made many Alexanders."

918   *Alexander's Victory over a Lion*
Plutarch, Alexander 40.4–5 (3–4)

Accordingly, he [Alexander] exerted himself yet more strenuously in military and hunting expeditions, suffering distress and risking his life, so that a Spartan ambassador who came up with him as he was bringing down a great lion, said: "Nobly, indeed, Alexander, hast thou struggled with the lion to see which should be king." This hunting-scene Craterus dedicated at Delphi, with bronze figures of the lion, the dogs, the king engaged with the lion, and himself coming to his assistance; some of the figures were molded by Lysippus, and some by Leochares.

919   *Lysimachus Questions Tale of Amazons*
Plutarch, Alexander 46.4 (2)

And the story is told that many years afterwards Onesicritus was reading aloud to Lysimachus, who was now king, the fourth book of his history, in which was the tale of the Amazon, at which Lysimachus smiled gently and said: "And where was I at the time?"

920   *Alexander Agrees with Punishment of Philotas*
Plutarch, Alexander 49.10–12 (6)

After the king [Alexander] had once given ear to such speeches and suspicions, the enemies of Philotas brought up countless accusations against him. Consequently he was arrested and put to the question, the companions of the king standing by at the torture, while Alexander himself listened behind a stretch of tapestry. Here, as we are told, on hearing Philotas beset Hephaestion with abject and pitiful cries and supplications, he said: "So faint-hearted as thou art, Philotas, and so unmanly, couldst thou have set hand to so great an undertaking?"

921   *Discussion of Weather by Callisthenes and Anaxarchus*
Plutarch, Alexander 52.8–9 (5)

It is said that once at supper the conversation turned upon seasons and weather, and that Callisthenes, who held with those who maintain that it is more cold and wintry there than in Greece, was stoutly opposed by Anaxarchus, whereupon he said: "You surely must admit that it is colder here than there; for there you used to go about in winter in a cloak merely, but here you recline at table with three rugs thrown over you."

922   *Alexander Criticizes Callisthenes' Life Style*
Plutarch, Alexander 53.1–2

Moreover, the other sophists and flatterers in the train of Alexander were annoyed to see Callisthenes eagerly courted by the young men on account of his eloquence, and no less pleasing to the older men on account of his mode of life, which was well-ordered, dignified, and independent, and confirmed the reason given for his sojourn abroad, namely, that he had gone to Alexander from an ardent desire to restore his fellow-citizens to their homes and re-people his native city.[1] And besides being envied on account of his reputation, he also at times by his own conduct furnished material for his detractors, rejecting invitations for the most part, and when he did go into company, by his gravity and silence making it appear that he disapproved or disliked what was going on, so that even Alexander said in allusion to him:—

"I hate a wise man even to himself unwise."[2]

1. Olynthus, which had been destroyed by Philip in 347 B.C.E.
2. An iambic trimeter from an unknown play of Euripides (A. Nauck, *Tragicorum Graecorum Fragmenta*, p. 652)

923a   *Honor in Time of Sedition*
Plutarch, Alexander 53.3–6 (3–5)

It is said, moreover, that once when a large company had been invited to the king's supper, Callisthenes was bidden, when the cup came to him, to speak in praise of the Macedonians, and was so successful on the theme that the guests rose up to applaud him and threw their garlands at him; whereupon Alexander said that, in the language of Euripides, when a man has for his words

"A noble subject, it is easy to speak well;"[1]

"But show us the power of your eloquence," said he, "by a denunciation of the Macedonians, that they may become even better by learning their faults." And so

Callisthenes began his palinode, and spoke long and boldly in denunciaton of the Macedonians, and after showing that faction among the Greeks was the cause of the increase of Philip's power, added:

"But in a time of sedition, the base man too is in honor."[2] This gave the Macedonians a stern and bitter hatred of him, and Alexander declared that Callisthenes had given a proof, not of his eloquence, but of his ill-will towards the Macedonians.

1. *Bacchae*, 260 (Kirchhoff).
2. A proverb in hexameter verse, attributed to Callimachus, the Alexandrian poet and scholar (310–235 B.C.E.).

923b *Honor in Time of Sedition*
Plutarch, Moralia VI:479A (2)

Just as in the same body the combination of moist and dry, cold and hot, sharing one nature and diet, by their consent and agreement engender the best and most pleasant temperament and bodily harmony—without which, they say, there is not any joy or profit either "in wealth" or

> In that kingly rule which makes men
> Like to gods—

but if overreaching and factious strife be engendered in them, they corrupt and destroy the animal most shamefully; so through the concord of brothers both family and household are sound and flourish, and friends and intimates, like an harmonious choir, neither do nor say, nor think, anything discordant;

Even the base wins honor in a feud: a slandering servant, or a flatterer who slips in from outside, or a malignant citizen.

923c *Honor in Time of Sedition*
Plutarch, Nicias 11.3

Above all else, his [Nicias'] way of life, which was not genial nor popular but unsocial and aristocratic, seemed alien and foreign: and since he often opposed the people's desires and tried to force them against their wishes into the way of their advantage, he was burdensome to them. To tell the simple truth, it was a struggle between the young men who wanted war and the elderly men who wanted peace; one party proposed to ostracise Nicias, the other Alcibiades.

"But in a time of sedition, the base man too is in honor," and so in this case also the people divided into two factions, and thereby made room for the most aggressive and mischievous men.

924 *Aristotle Criticizes Callisthenes' Common Sense*
Plutarch, Alexander 54.1-3 (1-2)

This, then, according to Hermippus, is the story which Stroebus, the slave who read aloud for Callisthenes, told to Aristotle, and he says that when Callisthenes was aware of the alienation of the king, twice or thrice, as he was going away from him, he recited the verse:

"Dead is also Patroclus, a man far braver than thou art."[1] What Aristotle said, then, would seem to have been no idle verdict, namely, that Callisthenes showed great ability as a speaker, but lacked common sense.

1. Achilles to Hector in Homer, *Iliad* 21.107.

925 *Callisthenes Suggests Hermolaüs Kill Alexander*
Plutarch, Alexander 55.3-4 (2-3)

For this reason also, when the conspiracy of Hermolaüs and his associates against Alexander was discovered, it was thought that the accusations of his detractors had an air of probability. They said, namely, that when Hermolaüs put the question to him how he might become a most illustrious man, Callisthenes said: "By killing the most illustrious"; and that in inciting Hermolaüs to the deed he bade him have no fear of the golden couch, but remember that he was approaching a man who was subject to sickness and wounds.

926 *Captured Acuphis Rebuts Alexander*
Plutarch, Alexander 58.7-9 (4-5)

And when, after he [Alexander] had put a stop to the fighting, ambassadors came from the beleaguered cities to beg for terms, they were amazed, to begin with, to see him in full armor and without an attendant; and besides, when a cushion was brought him for his use, he ordered the eldest of the ambassadors, Acuphis by name, to take it for his seat. Acuphis, accordingly, astonished at his magnanimity and courtesy, asked what he wished them to do in order to be his friends. "Thy countrymen," said Alexander, "must make thee their ruler, and send me a hundred of their best men." At this Acuphis laughed, and said: "Nay, O King, I shall rule better if I send to thee the worst men rather than the best."[1]

1. Cf. Arrian, *Anabasis* 5.2.1-3.

927 *Taxiles Confronts Alexander*
Plutarch, Alexander 59.1-5 (1-3)

Taxiles, we are told, had a realm in India as large as Egypt, with good pasturage, too, and in the highest degree productive of beautiful fruits. He was also a wise man in his way, and after he had greeted Alexander, said: "Why must we war and fight with one another, Alexander, if thou art not come to rob us of water or of necessary sustenance, the only things for which men of sense are obliged to fight obstinately? As for other wealth and possessions, so-called, if I am thy superior therein, I am ready to confer favors; but if thine inferior, I will not object to thanking you for favors conferred." At this Alexander was delighted, and clasping the king's hand, said: "Canst thou think, pray, that after such words of kindness our interview is to end without a battle? Nay, thou shalt not get the better of me; for I will contend against thee and fight to the last with my favors, that thou mayest not surpass me in generosity." So, after receiving many gifts and giving many more, at last he lavished upon him a thousand talents in coined money.

928a *Like a King*
Plutarch, Alexander 60.14 (8)

Porus was taken prisoner, and when Alexander asked him how he would be treated, said: "Like a king"; and to another question from Alexander whether he had anything else to say, replied: "All things are included in my 'like a king.'"

928b *Like a King*
Plutarch, Moralia, Sayings of Kings and Commanders III:181E (31)

Porus, after the battle, was asked by Alexander, "How shall I treat you?" "Like a king," said he. Asked again if there were nothing else, he said, "Everything is included in those words." Marveling at his sagacity and manliness, Alexander added to his kingdom more land than he had possessed before.[1]

1. Cf. Arrian, *Anabasis* 5.19.2.

928c *Like a King*
Plutarch, Moralia, Fortune of Alexander IV:332E (11)

It occurs to me to introduce here an incident touching Porus. For when Porus was brought as a captive before Alexander, the conqueror asked how he should treat him. "Like a king, Alexander," said Porus. When Alexander asked again if there were nothing else, "No," said he, "for everything is included in that word."

928d *Like a King*
Plutarch, Moralia, Control of Anger VI:458B

And so Porus, when he was taken captive, requested Alexander to treat him "like a king." When Alexander asked, "Is there nothing more?" "In the words 'like a king,'" replied Porus, "there is everything."

929a *Alexander Questions the Gymnosophists*
Plutarch, Alexander 64.1–12 (1–5)

He [Alexander] captured ten of the Gymnosophists who had done most to get Sabbas to revolt, and had made the most trouble for the Macedonians. These philosophers were reputed to be clever and concise in answering questions, and Alexander therefore put difficult questions to them, declaring that he would put to death him who first made an incorrect answer, and then the rest, in an order determined in like manner; and he commanded one of them, the oldest, to be judge in the contest. The first one, accordingly, being asked which, in his opinion, were more numerous, the living or the dead, said that the living were, since the dead no longer existed. The second, being asked whether the earth or the sea produced larger animals, said the earth did, since the sea was but a part of the earth. The third, being asked what animal was most cunning, said: "That which up to this time man has not discovered." The fourth, when asked why he had induced Sabbas to revolt, replied: "Because I wished him either to live nobly or to die nobly." The fifth, being asked which, in his opinion, was older, day or night, replied: "Day, by one day"; and he added, upon the king expressing amazement, that hard questions must have hard answers. Passing on, then, to the sixth, Alexander asked how a man could be most loved; "If," said the philosopher, "he is most powerful, and yet does not inspire fear." Of the three remaining, he who was asked how one might become a god instead of man, replied: "By doing something which a man cannot do"; the one who was asked which was the stronger, life or death, answered: "Life, since it supports so many ills." And the last, asked how long it were well for a man to live, answered: "Until he does not regard death as better than life." So, then, turning to the judge, Alexander bade him give his opinion. The judge declared that they had answered one worse than another. "Well, then," said Alexander, "thou shalt die first for giving such a verdict." "That cannot be, O King," said the judge, "unless thou falsely saidst that thou wouldst put to death first him who answered worst."

929b *Night and Day*
Diogenes Laertius, Lives of the Eminent Philosophers 1.36
To the question which is older, day or night, he [Thales] replied: "Night is the older by one day."

930 *Calanus and Dandamis*
Plutarch, Alexander 65.1–4 (1–3)
These philosophers [the ten gymnosophists], then, he [Alexander] dismissed with gifts; but to those who were in the highest repute and lived quietly by themselves he sent Onesieritus, asking them to pay him a visit. Now, Onesieritus was a philosopher of the school of Diogenes the Cynic. And he tells us that Calanus very harshly and insolently bade him strip off his tunic and listen naked to what he had to say, otherwise he would not converse with him, not even if he came from Zeus; but he says that Dandamis was gentler, and that after hearing fully about Socrates, Pythagoras, and Diogenes, he remarked that the men appeared to him to have been of good natural parts but to have passed their lives in too much awe of the laws. Others, however, say that the only words uttered by Dandamis were these: "Why did Alexander make such a long journey hither?"

931 *Calanus Illustrates Government with Hide*
Plutarch, Alexander 65.5–8 (3–4)
Calanus, nevertheless, was persuaded by Taxiles to pay a visit to Alexander. His real name was Sphines, but because he greeted those whom he met with "Cale," the Indian word of salutation, the Greeks called him Calanus. It was Calanus, as we are told, who laid before Alexander the famous illustration of government. It was this. He threw down upon the ground a dry and shriveled hide, and set his foot upon the outer edge of it; the hide was pressed down in one place, but rose up on others. He went all round the hide and showed that this was the result wherever he pressed the edge down, and then at last he stood in the middle of it, and lo! it was all held down firm and still. The similitude was designed to show that Alexander ought to put most constraint upon the middle of his empire and not wander far away from it.

932 *Alexander Imprisons Abuletes*
Plutarch, Alexander 68.6–7 (3–4)
For these reasons he [Alexander] sent Nearchus back to the sea, determined to fill all the regions along the sea with wars, while he himself, marching down from Upper Asia, chastised those of his commanders who had done wrong. One of the sons of Abuletes, Oxyartes, he slew with his own hand, running him through with a spear; and when Abuletes failed to furnish him with the necessary provisions, but brought him instead three thousand talents in coin, Alexander ordered the money to be thrown to his horses. And when they would not touch it, "Of what use to us, then," he cried, "is the provision you have made?" and threw Abuletes into prison.

933 *Men Bring Charges against Antipater*
Plutarch, Alexander 74.4–5 (2–3)
And at another time, when Cassander would have said something in opposition to those who were bringing charges against Antipater, Alexander interrupted him, saying: "What meanest thou? Would men come so long a journey if they had not been wronged and were making false charges?" And when Cassander declared that

this very fact of their coming a long distance away from the proofs showed that they were making false charges, Alexander burst out laughing and said: "These are the famous sophisms of Aristotle's disciples for either side of the question; but ye shall rue the day if it appear that ye have done these men even a slight wrong."

934 *Antony Rewards Liberally*
Plutarch, Antony 4.4

To one of his friends he [Antony] ordered that two hundred and fifty thousand drachmas should be given (a sum which the Romans call "decies"). His steward was amazed, and in order to show Antony the magnitude of the sum, deposited the money in full view. Antony, passing by, asked what that was; and when his steward told him it was the gift which he had ordered, he divined the man's malice and said: "I thought that decies was more; this is a trifle; therefore add as much more to it."

935 *Controversy over Taxes*
Plutarch, Antony 24.4–5

But finally, when he [Antony] was imposing a second contribution on the cities, Hybreas, speaking in behalf of Asia, plucked up courage to say this: "If thou canst take a contribution twice in one year, thou hast power also to make summer for us twice, and harvest-time twice." These words were rhetorical, it is true, and agreeable to Antony's taste; but the speaker added in plain and bold words that Asia had given him two hundred thousand talents; "If," said he, "thou hast not received this money, demand it from those who took it; but if thou didst receive it, and hast it not, we are undone."

936 *Prosper, Victor*
Plutarch, Antony 65.3

Caesar [Julius], we are told, who had left his tent while it was yet dark and was going round to visit his ships, was met by a man driving an ass. Caesar asked the man his name, and he, recognizing Caesar, replied: "My name is Prosper, and my ass's name is Victor." Therefore, when Caesar afterwards decorated the place with the beaks of ships, he set up bronze figures of an ass and a man.

937 *Timon Loves Alcibiades*
Plutarch, Antony 70.1

Now, Timon was an Athenian, and lived about the time of the Peloponnesian War, as may be gathered from the plays of Aristophanes and Plato. For he is represented in their comedies as peevish and misanthropical; but though he avoided and repelled all intercourse with men, he was glad to see Alcibiades, who was then young and headstrong, and showered kisses upon him. And when Apemantus was amazed at this and asked the reason for it, Timon said he loved the youth because he knew that he would be a cause of many ills to Athens.

938 *Caesar Pardons Philostratus*
Plutarch, Antony 80.1–3

And now Caesar [Julius] himself drove into the city, and he was conversing with Areius the philosopher, to whom he had given his right hand, in order that Areius might at once be conspicuous among the citizens, and be admired because of the marked honor shown him by Caesar. After he had entered the gymnasium and ascended a tribunal there made for him, the people were beside themselves with fear and prostrated themselves before him, but he bade them rise up and said that he acquitted the people of all blame, first because of Alexander, their founder; second, because he admired the great size and beauty of the city; and third, to gratify his companion, Areius. This honor Caesar bestowed upon Areius, and pardoned many other persons also at his request. Among these was Philostratus, a man more competent to speak extempore than any sophist that ever lived, but he improperly represented himself as belonging to the school of the Academy. Therefore Caesar, abominating his ways, would not listen to his entreaties. So Philostratus, having a long white beard and wearing a dark robe, would follow behind Areius, ever declaiming this verse:

"A wise man will a wise man save, if wise he be."[1]

When Caesar learned of this, he pardoned him, wishing rather to free Areius from odium than Philostratus from fear.

1. An iambic trimeter from an unknown poet (A. Nauck, *Tragicorum Graecorum Fragmenta*, p. 921).

939 *Erginus Betrays Corinth*
Plutarch, Aratus 18.2–4

There were in Corinth four brothers, Syrians by race, one of whom, Diocles by name, was serving as a mercenary soldier in the citadel. The other three, after stealing some gold plate of the king's, came to Aegias, a banker in Sicyon with whom Aratus did business. A portion of the gold they disposed of to him at once, but the remainder was being quietly exchanged by one of them, Erginus, in frequent visits. Erginus thus became well acquainted with Aegias, and having been led by him into conversation about the garrison in the citadel, said that as he was going up to see his brother he had noticed in the face of the cliff a slanting fissure leading to where the wall of the citadel was at its lowest. Thereupon Aegias fell to jesting with him, and said: "Do you, then, best of men, thus for the sake of a little gold plate rifle the king's treasure, when it is in your power to sell a single hour's work for large sums of money? Don't you know that burglars as well as traitors, if they are caught, have only one death to die?" Erginus burst out laughing, and as a first step agreed to make trial of Diocles (saying that he had no confidence at all in his other brothers), and a few days afterwards came back and bargained to conduct Aratus to the wall at a spot where it was not more than fifteen feet in height and to aid in the rest of the enterprise together with Diocles.

940 *Persaeus Learns Lesson from Aratus*
Plutarch, Aratus 23.5

And at a later time, as we are told, when he [Persaeus] was leading a life of leisure, and someone remarked that in his opinion the wise man only could be a good general, "Indeed," he replied, "there was a time when I too particularly liked this doctrine of Zeno's; but now, since the lesson I got from the young man of Sicyon [Aratus], I am of another mind."

941 *Aristides as Arbitrator*
Plutarch, Aristides 4.2

And again, when he [Aristides] was serving as private arbitrator between two men, on one of them saying that his opponent had done Aristides much injury,

"Tell me rather," he said, "whether he has done thee any wrong; it is for thee, not for myself, that I am seeking justice."

942   *Great Instead of Small*
Plutarch, Artaxerxes 4.4

Indeed, when a certain Omisus brought him a single pomegranate of surpassing size, he [Artaxerxes] said: "By Mithra, this man would speedily make a city great instead of small were he entrusted with it."

943   *Power To Say And Do*
Plutarch, Artaxerxes 5.1

To Eucleidas the Lacedaemonian, who would often say bold and impudent things to him, he [Artaxerxes] sent this word by his officer of the guard: "It is in thy power to say what thou pleasest, but it is in mine both to say and to do."

944   *Artaxerxes Amused by Witless Teribazus*
Plutarch, Artaxerxes 5.2

Again, when he [Artaxerxes] was hunting once and Teribazus pointed out that the king's coat was rent, he asked him what was to be done. And when Teribazus replied, "Put on another for thyself, but give this one to me," the king did so saying, "I give this thee, Teribazus, but I forbid thee to wear it." Teribazus gave no heed to the command (being not a bad man, but rather light-headed and witless), and at once put on the king's coat, and decked himself with necklaces and women's ornaments of royal splendor. Everybody was indignant at this (for it was a forbidden thing); but the king merely laughed and said: "I permit thee to wear the trinkets as a woman, and the robe as a madman."

945a   *Cow's Milk for Ailment*
Plutarch, Artaxerxes 22.5–6

With Timagoras the Athenian, however, who sent to him by his secretary, Beluris, a secret message in writing, the king [Artaxerxes] was so pleased that he gave him ten thousand darics, and eighty milk cows to follow in his train because he was sick and required cow's milk; and besides, he sent him a couch, with bedding for it, and servants to make the bed (on the ground that the Greeks had not learned the art of making beds), and bearers to carry him down to the seacoast, enfeebled as he was. Moreover, during his presence at court, he used to send him a most splendid supper, so that Ostanes, the brother of the king, said: "Timagoras, remember this table; it is no slight return which thou must make for such an array." Now this was a reproach for his treachery rather than a reminder of the king's favor. At any rate, for his venality, Timagoras was condemned to death by the Athenians.

945b   *Cow's Milk for Ailment*
Plutarch, Pelopidas 30.6

Timagoras, at any rate, was condemned and executed by the Athenians, and if this was because of the multitude of gifts which he took, it was right and just; for he took not only gold and silver, but also an expensive couch and slaves to spread it, since, as he said, the Greeks did not know how; and besides, eighty cows with their cow-herds, since, as he said, he wanted cow's milk for some ailment; and, finally, he was carried down to the sea in a litter, and had a present of four talents from the King with which to pay his carriers.

946a Brutus Will Wait
Plutarch, Brutus 8.3

And again, when certain ones were accusing Brutus to him, and urging him to be on his guard against him, he [Caesar] laid his hand upon his breast and said: "What? Think ye not that Brutus can wait for this poor flesh"?

946b Brutus Will Wait
Plutarch, Caesar 62.6 (3)

Once, too, when certain persons were actually accusing Brutus to him, the conspiracy being already on foot, Caesar would not heed them, but laying his hand upon his body said to the accusers: "Brutus will wait for this shriveled skin," implying that Brutus was worthy to rule because of his virtue, but that for the sake of ruling he would not become a thankless villain.

947 Brutus on Justice and Power
Plutarch, Brutus 35.1–6

But on the following day Lucius Pella, a Roman who had been praetor and had enjoyed the confidence of Brutus, being denounced by the Sardians as an embezzler of the public moneys, was condemned by Brutus and disgraced; and the matter vexed Cassius beyond measure. For a few days before, when two friends of his had been convicted of the same misdeeds, he had privately admonished them but publicly acquitted them, and continued to employ them. He therefore found fault with Brutus on the ground that he was too observant of law and justice at a time which demanded a policy of kindness. But Brutus bade him remember the Ides of March, on which they had slain Caesar, not because he was himself plundering everybody, but because he enabled others to do this; since, if there is any good excuse for neglecting justice, it had been better for us to endure the friends of Caesar than to suffer our own to do wrong. "For in the one case," said he, "we should have had the reputation of cowardice merely; but now, in addition to our toils and perils, we are deemed unjust."

948 The Punishment of Jesters
Plutarch, Brutus 45.6–9

Among the prisoners there was a certain Volumnius, an actor, and Saculio, a buffoon, to whom Brutus paid no attention; but the friends of Brutus brought them forward and denounced them for not refraining even now from insolent and mocking speeches to them. Brutus had nothing to say, being concerned about other matters, but Messala Corvinus gave his opinion that they should be publicly flogged and then sent back naked to the enemy's generals in order to let these know what sort of boon companions they required on their campaigns. At this some of the bystanders burst out laughing, but Publius Casca, the one who first smote Caesar, said: "It is not meet for us to celebrate the funeral rites of Cassius with jests and mirth; and thou, Brutus, wilt show what esteem thou hast for the memory of that general according as thou punishest or shieldest those who will abuse and revile him." To this Brutus, in high dudgeon said: "Why, then, do ye inquire of me, Casca, instead of doing what seems best to you?"

949 *Messala Ever Right*
Plutarch, Brutus 53.3

And it is said that Messala himself was once praised by Octavius because, though at Philippi he had been most hostile to him and Antony for the sake of Brutus, at Actium he had been a most zealous adherent of his; whereupon Messala said: "Indeed, O Caesar, I have ever been on the better and juster side."

950 *Cicero Sees through Caesar*
Plutarch, Caesar 4.8–9 (4)

At all events, the man who is thought to have been the first to see beneath the surface of Caesar's public policy and to fear it, as one might fear the smiling surface of the sea, and who comprehended the powerful character hidden beneath his kindly and cheerful exterior, namely Cicero, said that in most of Caesar's political plans and projects he saw a tyrannical purpose; "On the other hand," said he, "when I look at his hair, which is arranged with so much nicety, and see him scratching his head with one finger, I cannot think that this man would ever conceive of so great a crime as the overthrow of the Roman constitution."

951 *Caesar Revives Party of Marius*
Plutarch, Caesar 6.1–7 (1–4)

There were two parties in the city, that of Sulla, which had been all powerful since his day, and that of Marius, which at that time was in an altogether lowly state, being cowed and scattered. This party Caesar wished to revive and attach to himself, and therefore, when the ambitious efforts of his aedileship were at their height, he had images of Marius secretly made, together with trophy-bearing Victories, and these he ordered to be carried by night and set up on the Capitol. At day-break those who beheld all these objects glittering with gold and fashioned with the most exquisite art (and they bore inscriptions setting forth the Cimbrian successes of Marius) were amazed at the daring of the man who had set them up (for it was evident who had done it) and the report of it quickly spreading brought everybody together for the sight. But some cried out that Caesar was scheming to usurp sole power in the state when he thus revived honors which had been buried by laws and decrees, and that this proceeding was a test of the people, whose feelings towards him he had previously softened, to see whether they had been made docile by his ambitious displays and would permit him to amuse himself with such innovations. The partisans of Marius, however, encouraged one another and showed themselves on a sudden in amazing numbers, and filled the Capitol with their applause. Many, too, were moved to tears of joy when they beheld the features of Marius, and Caesar was highly extolled by them, and regarded as above all others worthy of his kinship with Marius. But when the senate met to discuss these matters, Catulus Lutatius, a man of the highest repute at that time in Rome, rose up and denounced Caesar, uttering the memorable words: "No longer, indeed, by sapping and mining, Caesar, but with engines of war art thou capturing the government." Caesar, however, defended himself against this charge and convinced the senate, whereupon his admirers were still more elated and exhorted him not to lower his pretensions for any man, since the people would be glad to have him triumph over all opposition and be the first man in the state.

952a *Wife without Suspicion*
Plutarch, Caesar 10.8–9 (6)

Caesar divorced Pompeia at once, but when he was summoned to testify at the trial, he said he knew nothing about the matters with which Clodius was charged. His statement appeared strange, and the prosecutor therefore asked, "Why, then, didst thou divorce thy wife?" "Because," said Caesar, "I thought my wife ought not even to be under suspicion."

952b *Wife without Suspicion*
Plutarch, Cicero 29.6–9 (5–7)

However, since the people at this time set themselves against those who combined and testified against him [Clodius], the jurors were frightened and surrounded themselves with a guard, and most of them cast their voting-tablets with the writing on them confused.[1] But nevertheless those who were for acquittal appeared to be in the majority; and some bribery also was said to have been used. This led Catulus to say, when he met the jurors, "It was indeed as a measure of safety that you asked for your guard; you were afraid that someone would take your money away from you."[2] And Cicero, when Clodius told him that as a witness he had found no credit with the jurors, said: "Nay, twenty-five of the jurors gave me credit, for so many voted against you; and thirty of them gave you no credit, for they did not vote to acquit you until they had got your money."[3] Caesar, however, when summoned as a witness, gave no testimony against Clodius, and denied that he had condemned his wife for adultery, but said that he had put her away because Caesar's wife must be free not only from shameful conduct, but even from shameful report.

> 1. Each juror was provided with three tablets, on one of which was marked A (*absolvo*); on a second C (*condemno*); and on a third N.L. (*non liquet*). The jurors voted by placing one of these tablets in the urn. Plutarch must have misunderstood his source.
> 2. Cf. Cicero, *Epistulae ad Atticum* 1.16.5.
> 3. Cf. Cicero, ibid. 16.10.

952c *Wife without Suspicion*
Suetonius, Lives of the Caesars, Julius 1.74.2

When summoned as a witness against Publius Clodius, the paramour of his wife Pompeia, charged on the same count with sacrilege, Caesar declared that he had no evidence, although both his mother Aurelia and his sister Julia had given the same jurors a faithful account of the whole affair; and on being asked why it was then that he had put away his wife, he replied: "Because I maintain that the members of my family should be free from suspicion, as well as from accusation."

953a *Stamp on the Ground*
Plutarch, Caesar 33.5 (4)

Favorinus bade him [Caesar] stamp on the ground; for once, in a boastful speech to the senate, he told them to take no trouble or anxious thought about preparations for the war, since when it came he had but to stamp upon the earth to fill Italy with armies.

953b *Stamp on the Ground*
Plutarch, Pompey 57.5

When someone said that if Caesar should march upon the city, they did not see any forces with which to defend it from him, with a smiling countenance and calm mien he [Pompey] bade them be in no concern; "For," said he, "in whatever part of Italy I stamp upon the ground, there will spring up armies of foot and horse."

954 *Caesar Breaks into Treasury*
Plutarch, Caesar 35.6–9 (3–4)

When the tribune Metellus tried to prevent Caesar's taking money from the reserve funds of the state, and cited certain laws, Caesar said that arms and laws had not the same season. "But if thou art displeased at what is going on, for the present get out of the way, since war has no use for free speech; when, however, I have come to terms and laid down my arms, then thou shalt come before the people with thy harangues. And in saying this I waive my own just rights; for thou art mine, thou and all of the faction hostile to me whom I have caught." After this speech to Metellus, Caesar walked towards the door of the treasury and when the keys were not to be found, he sent for smiths and ordered them to break in the door.

955 *Caesar Threatens Metellus*
Plutarch, Caesar 35.10 (4)

Metellus once more opposed him, and was commended by some for so doing; but Caesar, raising his voice, threatened to kill him if he did not cease his troublesome interference. "And thou surely knowest, young man," said he, "that it is more unpleasant for me to say this than to do it."

956a *Discontent with Pompey*
Plutarch, Caesar 41:2–4 (2)

All the rest, however, reviled Pompey for trying to avoid a battle, and sought to goad him on by calling him Agamemnon and King of Kings, implying that he did not wish to lay aside his sole authority, but plumed himself on having so many commanders dependent upon him and coming constantly to his tent. And Favonius, affecting Cato's boldness of speech, complained like a mad man because that year also they would be unable to enjoy the figs of Tusculum because of Pompey's love of command. Afranius, too, who had lately come from Spain, where he had shown bad generalship, when accused of betraying his army for a bribe, asked why they did not fight with the merchant who had bought the provinces from him.

956b *No Figs of Tusculum*
Plutarch, Pompey 67.3

And Favonius was no less displeasing to him [Pompey] than those who used a bolder speech, when he bawled out his untimely jest: "O men, this year, also, shall we eat no figs of Tusculum?"

957 *Caesar and the Seer*
Plutarch, Caesar 43:3–4 (2)

As he [Caesar] was holding a lustration and review of his forces and had sacrificed the first victim, the seer at once told him that within three days there would be a decisive battle with the enemy. And when Caesar asked him whether he also saw in the victims any favorable signs of the issue, "Thou thyself," said the seer, "canst better answer this question for thyself. For the gods indicate a great change and revolution of the present status to the opposite. Therefore, if thou thinkest thyself well off as matters stand, expect the worse fortune; if badly off, the better."

958   *A Portent of Victory*
Plutarch, Caesar 47:3–6 (2)

Moreover, at Patavium, Caius Cornelius, a man in repute as a seer, a fellow citizen and acquaintance of Livy the historian, chanced that day to be sitting in the place of augury. And to begin with, according to Livy, he discerned the time of the battle, and said to those present that even then the event was in progress and the men were going into action. And when he looked again and observed the signs, he sprang up in a rapture crying: "Thou art victorious, O Caesar!" The bystanders being amazed, he took the chaplet from his head and declared with an oath that he would not put it on again until the event had borne witness to his art.

959   *No Need of Egyptian Advisers*
Plutarch, Caesar 48.9 (5)

When, however, Potheinus bade him go away now and attend to his great affairs, assuring him that later he would get his money with thanks, Caesar replied that he had no need whatever of Egyptians as advisers, and secretly sent for Cleopatra from the country.

960   *Courted as Superior*
Plutarch, Caesar 60:6–8 (4–5)

But afterwards he [Caesar] made his disease an excuse for his behavior, saying that the senses of those who are thus afflicted do not usually remain steady when they address a multitude standing, but are speedily shaken and whirled about, bringing on giddiness and insensibility. However, what he said was not true; on the contrary, he was very desirous of rising to receive the senate; but one of his friends, as they say, or rather one of his flatterers, Cornelius Balbus, restrained him saying: "Remember that thou art Caesar, and permit thyself to be courted as a superior."

961a   *Ides Not Gone*
Plutarch, Caesar 63.5–6 (3)

A certain seer warned Caesar to be on his guard against a great peril on the day of the month of March which the Romans call the Ides; and when the day had come and Caesar was on his way to the senate-house, he greeted the seer with a jest and said: "Well, the Ides of March are come," and the seer said to him softly, "Aye, they are come, but they are not gone."

961b   *Ides Not Gone*
Suetonius, Lives of the Caesars, Julius 1.81.4

Both for these reasons and because of poor health he [Julius] hesitated for a long time whether to stay at home and put off what he had planned to do in the senate; but at last, urged by Decimus Brutus not to disappoint the full meeting which had for some time been waiting for him, he went forth almost at the end of the fifth hour; and when a note revealing the plot was handed him by someone on the way, he put it with others which he held in his left hand, intending to read them presently. Then, after several victims had been slain, and he could not get favorable omens, he entered the House in defiance of portents, laughing at Spurinna and calling him a false prophet, because the Ides of March were come without bringing him harm; though Spurinna replied that they had of a truth come, but they had not gone.

962 Caius Rebukes Effeminate Man
Plutarch, Caius Gracchus 4.4

There are on record also many things which Caius said about her in the coarse style of forensic speech, when he was attacking one of his enemies: "What, said he, "dost thou abuse Cornelia, who gave birth to Tiberius?" And since the one who had uttered the abuse was charged with effeminate practices, "With what effrontery," said Caius, "canst thou compare thyself with Cornelia? Hast thou borne children as she did? And verily all Rome knows that she refrained from commerce with men longer than thou hast, though thou art a man."

963 A Test of Power
Plutarch, Caius Marius 33.2

We are told that Publius Silo, who had the greatest authority and power among the enemy, once said to him, "If thou art a general, Marius, come down and fight it out with us"; to which Marius answered, "Nay, but do thou, if thou art a great general, force me to fight it out with you against my will."

964 Marius a Fugitive
Plutarch, Caius Marius 40.3–4

The Roman governor of Africa at this time was Sextilius, a man who had received neither good nor ill at the hands of Marius, but whom, as it was expected, pity alone would move to give him aid. Hardly, however, had Marius landed with a few companions, when an official met him, stood directly in front of him, and said: "Sextilius the governor forbids thee, Marius, to set foot in Africa; and if thou disobeyest, he declares that he will uphold the decrees of the Senate and treat thee as an enemy of Rome." When he heard this, Marius was rendered speechless by grief and indignation, and for a long time kept quiet, looking sternly at the official. Then, when asked by him what he had to say, and what answer he would make to the governor, he answered with a deep groan: "Tell him, then, that thou hast seen Caius Marius a fugitive, seated amid the ruins of Carthage." And it was not inaptly that he compared the fate of that city with his own reversal of fortune.

965 Woe to the Vanquished
Plutarch, Camillus 28.3–5

All this, however, brought no relief to the besieged, for famine increased upon them, and their ignorance of what Camillus was doing made them dejected. No messenger could come from him because the city was now closely watched by the Barbarians. Wherefore, both parties being in such a plight, a compromise was proposed, at first by the outposts as they encountered one another. Then, since those in authority thought it best, Sulpicius, the military tribune of the Romans, held a conference with Brennus, and it was agreed that on the delivery of a thousand pounds of gold by the Romans, the Gauls should straightway depart out of the city and the country. Oaths were sworn to these terms, and the gold was brought to be weighed. But the Gauls tampered with the scales, secretly at first, then they openly pulled the balance back out of its poise. The Romans were incensed at this, but Brennus, with a mocking laugh, stripped off his sword, and added it, belt and all, to the weights. When Sulpicius asked, "What means this?" "What else," said Brennus, "but woe to the vanquished?" and the phrase passed at once into a proverb.

966   Cato's Days and Nights
Plutarch, Cato the Younger 6.1–2

At suppers, he [Cato] would throw dice for the choice of portions; and if he lost, and his friends bade him choose first, he would say it was not right, since Venus was unwilling. At first, he would drink once after supper and then leave the table; but as time went on he would allow himself to drink very generously, so that he often tarried at his wine till early morning. His friends used to say that the cause of this was his civic and public activities; he was occupied with these all day, and so prevented from literary pursuits, wherefore he would hold intercourse with the philosophers at night and over the cups. For this reason, too, when a certain Memmius remarked in company that Cato spent his entire nights in drinking, Cicero answered him by saying: "Thou shouldst add that he spends his entire days in throwing dice."

967   The Proverbial Cato
Plutarch, Cato the Younger 19.3–5

At one time he [Cato] opposed Clodius the demagogue, who was raising agitation and confusion as a prelude to great changes, and was calumniating to the people priests and priestesses, among whom Fabia, a sister of Cicero's wife Terentia, was in danger of conviction. But Cato put Clodius to such shame that he was forced to steal away from the city; and when Cicero thanked him, Cato told him he ought to be thankful to the city, since it was for her sake that all his public work was done. In consequence of this, he was held in high repute, so that an orator, at a trial where the testimony of a single witness was introduced, told the jurors that it was not right to give heed to a single witness, not even if he were Cato; and many already, when speaking of matters that were strange and incredible, would say, as though using a proverb, "This is not to be believed even though Cato says it."

968a   Talk Like Cato
Plutarch, Cato the Younger 19.5

Again, when a corrupt and extravagant man was expatiating in the senate on frugality and self-restraint, Amnaeus sprang to his feet and said: "Who can endure it, my man, when you sup like Lucullus, build like Crassus, and yet harangue us like Cato?"

968b   Talk Like Cato
Plutarch, Lucullus 40.3

Once when a youthful senator had delivered a tedious and lengthy discourse, all out of season, on frugality and temperance, Cato rose and said; "Stop there! you get wealth like Crassus, you live like Lucullus, but you talk like Cato."

969 *No Fault in Sulpicius*
Plutarch, Cato the Younger 49.1–2

But Caesar, though he devoted himself to his armies in Gaul and was busy with arms, nevertheless employed gifts, money and above all friends, to increase his power in the city. Presently, therefore, the admonitions of Acto roused Pompey from the great incredulity which he had indulged in up to this time, so that he had forebodings of his peril. However, he was still given to hesitation and spiritless delays in checking or attacking he threatening evil, and therefore Cato determined to stand for the consulship, that he might at once deprive Caesar of his armed forces or convict him of his hostile designs. But his competitors were both acceptable men, and Sulpicius had actually derived much benefit from Cato's repute and power in the city, and was therefore thought to be acting in an improper and thankless manner. But Cato had no fault to find with him. "Pray, what wonder is it," said he, "if a man will not surrender to another what he regards as the greatest of all good things?"

970 *The Pride of Statyllius*
Plutarch, Cato the Younger 65.4–5

But there was one Statyllius, a man who was young in years, but minded to be strong in purpose and to imitate Cato's calmness. This man Cato insisted should take ship; for he was a notorious hater of Caesar. But when Statyllius would not consent, Cato turned his eyes upon Appolonides the Stoic and Demetrius the Peripatetic, saying: "It is your task to reduce this man's swollen pride and restore him to conformity with his best interests."

971 *Apollonius and Cicero*
Plutarch, Cicero 4.6–7 (4–5)

Apollonius, we are told, not understanding the Roman languge, requested Cicero to declaim in Greek, with which request Cicero readily complied, thinking that in this way faults could better be corrected. After he had declaimed, his other hearers were astounded and vied with one another in their praises, but Apollonius was not greatly moved while listening to him, and when he had ceased sat for a long time lost in thought; then, since Cicero was distressed at this, he said: "Thee, indeed, O Cicero, I admire and commend; but Greece I pity for her sad fortune, since I see that even the only glories which were left to us, culture and eloquence, are through thee to belong also to the Romans."

972 *Cicero and Verres*
Plutarch, Cicero 7.6–8 (5–6)

For instance, "verres" is the Roman word for a castrated porker; when, accordingly, a freedman named Caecilius, who was suspected of Jewish practices, wanted to thrust aside the Sicilian accusers and denounce Verres himself, Cicero said, "What has a Jew to do with a Verres?" Moreover, Verres had a young son, who had the name of lending himself to base practices. Accordingly, when Cicero was reviled by Verres for effeminacy, "you ought," said he, "to revile your sons at home."

973 *Cicero and Vatinius*
Plutarch, Cicero 9.3

Again, there was Vatinius, a man who had a harsh manner and one which showed contempt for the magistrates before whom he pleaded; his neck also was covered with swellings. As this man once stood at Cicero's tribunal and made some request of him, Cicero did not grant it at once, but took a long time for deliberation, whereupon Vatinius said that he himself would not have stuck at the matter had he been praetor. At this Cicero turned upon him and said: "But I have not the neck that you have."

974 *Cicero as Head*
Plutarch, Cicero 14.3–7 (2–5)

For Catiline was again a candidate for the consulship, and had determined to kill Cicero in the very tumult of the elections. Moreover, even the heavenly powers seemed, by earthquakes and thunderbolts and apparitions, to foreshow what was coming to pass. And there were also human testimonies which were true, indeed, but not sufficient for the conviction of a man of reputation and great power like Catiline. For this reason Cicero postponed the day of the elections, and summoning Catiline to the senate, examined him concerning what was reported. But Catiline, thinking that there were many in the senate who were desirous of a revolution, and at the same time making a display of himself to the conspirators, gave Cicero the answer of a madman: "What dreadful thing, pray," said he, "am I doing, if, when there are two bodies, one lean and wasted, but with a head, and the other headless, but strong and large, I myself become a head for this?"

975 *Cicero Confronts Catiline*
Plutarch, Cicero 16.3–5 (3–4)

Then Cicero went forth and summoned the senate to the temple of Jupiter Stesius (or Stator, as the Romans say), which was situated at the beginning of the Via Sacra, as you go up to the Palatine hill. Thither Catiline also came with the rest in order to make his defense; no senator, however, would sit with him, but all moved away from the bench where he was. And when he began to speak he was interrupted by outcries, and at last Cicero rose and ordered him to depart from the city, saying that, since one of them did his work with words and the other with arms, the city-wall must needs lie between them.[1]

1. Cf. Cicero, *In Catilinam* 1.5.10.

976 *Demosthenes Best at Length*
Plutarch, Cicero 24.6 (3)

And when he [Cicero] was asked which of the speeches of Demosthenes he thought the best, he replied, "the longest."

977 *Cicero and Munatius*
Plutarch, Cicero 25.1

For instance, he [Cicero] once served as advocate for Munatius, who was no sooner acquitted than he prosecuted a friend of Cicero's, Sabinus, whereupon, it is said, Cicero was so transported with anger as to say: "Was it, pray, on your own merits, Munatius, that you were acquitted, and not because I spread much darkness about the court when before there was light?"

978 *Exercising Eloquence*
Plutarch, Cicero 25.2

And again, he [Cicero] gained great applause by an encomium on Marcus Crassus from the rostra, and a few days afterwards as publicly reviled him, whereupon Crassus said: "What, did you not stand there yourself a day or two ago and praise me?" "Yea," said Cicero, "exercising my eloquence by way of practice on a bad subject."

979 *No Old Crassus*
Plutarch, Cicero 25.3–4 (3)

Again, Crassus once said that no Crassus had lived in Rome to be older than sixty years, and then tried to deny it, exclaiming, "What could have led me to say this?" "You knew," said Cicero, "that the Romans would be delighted to hear it, and by that means you tried to court their favor."

980 *Covetous Crassus*
Plutarch, Cicero 25.4 (3–4)

And when Crassus expressed his satisfaction with the Stoics because they represented the good man as rich, "Consider," said Cicero, "whether your satisfaction is not rather due to their declaration that all things belong to the wise." Now, Crassus was accused of covetousness.

981 *Worthy of Crassus*
Plutarch, Cicero 25.5 (4)

Again, one of the sons of Crassus who was thought to resemble a certain Axius, and on this account had brought his mother's name into scandalous connection with that of Axius, once made a successful speech in the senate, and when Cicero was asked what he thought of him, he answered with the Greek words "Axios Krassou" [Worthy of Crassus].

982 *Perish the Wretch Who Lied*
Plutarch, Cicero 26.3–4 (2–3)

Now, Vatinius himself had swellings on his neck, and once when he was pleading a case Cicero called him a tumid orator. Again, after hearing that Vatinius was dead, and after a little learning for a surety that he was alive, "Wretchedly perish, then," said Cicero, "the wretch who lied."

983 *No Long Postponement*
Plutarch, Cicero 26.4–5 (3–4)

And again, Caesar once got a decree passed that the land in Campania should be divided among his soldiers, and many of the senators were dissatisfied, and Lucius Gellius, who was about the oldest of them, declared that it should never be done while he was alive; whereupon Cicero said: "Let us wait, since Gellius does not ask for a long postponement."

984 *Octavius Cannot Hear*
Plutarch, Cicero 26.5–6 (4)

There was a certain Octavius, too, who was reputed to be of African descent; to this man, who at a certain trial said that he could not hear Cicero, the orator replied, "And yet your ear is not without a perforation."[1]

1. Usually the mark of a slave.

985 *Credibility Greater Than Eloquence*
Plutarch, Cicero 26.6–7 (4–5)

And when Metellus Nepos declared that Cicero had brought more men to death as a hostile witness than he had saved from it as an advocate, "Yes," said Cicero, "I admit that my credibility is greater than my eloquence."

986 *Tomorrow You Are Nobody*
Plutarch, Cicero 26.8–9 (5–6)

There was Publius Sextius, too, who retained Cicero as an advocate in a case, along with others, and then wanted to do all the speaking himself, and would allow no one else a word; when it was clear that he was going to be acquitted by the jurors and the vote was already being given, "Use your opportunity today, Sextius," said Cicero, "for tomorrow you are going to be a nobody."

987 *Publius Consta Knows Nothing*
Plutarch, Cicero 26.9 (6)

Publius Consta, too, who wanted to be a lawyer, but was ignorant and stupid, was once summoned by Cicero as witness in a case; and when he kept saying that he knew nothing, "Perhaps," said Cicero, " you think you are being questioned on points of law."

988 *Difficult Question*
Plutarch, Cicero 26.9–10 (6–7)

Again, in a dispute with Cicero, Metellus Nepos asked repeatedly, "Who is your father?" "In your case," said Cicero, "your mother has made the answer to this question rather difficult." Now, the mother of Nepos was thought to be unchaste, and he himself a fickle sort of man.

989 *Nepos Acts More Wisely Than Usual*
Plutarch, Cicero 26.10–12 (7–8)

He [Nepos] once suddenly deserted his office of tribune and sailed off to join Pompey in Syria, and then came back from there with even less reason. Moreover, after burying his teacher Philagrus with more than usual ceremony, he set upon his tomb a raven in stone; whereupon Cicero remarked: "In this you have acted more wisely than is your wont, for he taught you to fly rather than to speak."

990 *Marcus Appius and Cicero*
Plutarch, Cicero 26.12 (8)

And again, when Marcus Appius prefaced his speech in a case by saying that his friend had begged him to exhibit diligence, eloquence, and fidelity, "And then," said Cicero, "are you so hard-hearted as to exhibit none of those great qualities which your friend demanded?"

991 *Cicero and Marcus Aquinius*
Plutarch, Cicero 27.1–3 (1–2)

Now this use of very biting jests against enemies or legal opponents seems to be part of the orator's business; but his indiscriminate attacks for the sake of raising a laugh made many people hate Cicero. And I will give a few instances of this also. Marcus Aquinius, who had two sons-in-law in exile, he called Adrastus.[1]

> 1. Adrastus, mythical king of Argos, gave his two daughters in marriage to Tydeus and Polyneices, both of whom were fugitives from their native cities.

992 *Voconius' Daughters*
Plutarch, Cicero 27.4 (2)

And when he [Cicero] met Voconius escorting three very ugly daughters, he cried out:—

"It was against the will of Phoebus that he begat children."[1]

> 1. An iambic trimeter from some lost tragedy, perhaps the Oedipus of Euripides.

993 *Cried Aloud for Freedom*
Plutarch, Cicero 27.5–6 (3)

Again, when Marcus Gellius, who was thought to be of servile birth, had read letters to the senate in a loud and clear voice, "Do not marvel," said Cicero, "he too is one of those who have cried aloud for their freedom."

994 *Better Placarding*
Plutarch, Cicero 27.6 (3)

And when Faustus, the son of the Sulla who was dictator at Rome and placarded many people for death, got into debt, squandered much of his substance, and placarded his household goods for sale, Cicero said he liked this placarding better than his father's.

995 *No Panthers in Cilicia*
Plutarch, Cicero 36.6 (5)

When Caelius the orator asked Cicero to send him panthers from Cilicia for a certain spectacle at Rome, Cicero, pluming himself upon his exploits, wrote to him that there were no panthers in Cilicia; for they had fled to Caria in indignation because they alone were warred upon, while everything else enjoyed peace.[1]

> 1. Cf. Cicero, *Epistulae ad Familiares* 2.2.2.

996 *Soldier or Guardian*
Plutarch, Cicero 38.3–4

When Domitius, then, was advancing to a post of command a man who was no soldier, with the remark that he was gentle in his disposition and prudent, "Why, then," said Cicero, "do you not keep him as a guardian of your children?"

997 *Greek as Prefect*
Plutarch, Cicero 38.4–5 (4)

And when certain ones were praising Theophanes the Lesbian, who was prefect of engineers in the camp, because he had given excellent consolation to the Rhodians on the loss of their fleet, "What a blessing it is," said Cicero, "to have a Greek as prefect!"

998   *Gloomy Friends*
Plutarch, Cicero 38.5–6 (4–5)
Again, when Caesar was successful for the most part and in a way was laying siege to them,[1] Lentulus said he had heard that Caesar's friends were gloomy, to which Cicero replied: "You mean that they are ill-disposed to Caesar."

    1. At Dyrrhachium. See Plutarch, *Caesar* 39; Caesar, *Civil War* 3.41–55.

999   *Pompey Besieged*
Plutarch, Cicero 38.6–7 (5)
And when a certain Marcius, who had recently come from Italy, spoke of a report which prevailed in Rome that Pompey was besieged, "And then," said Cicero, "did you sail off that you might see with your own eyes and believe?"

1000   *War with Jackdaws*
Plutarch, Cicero 38.7–8 (5–6)
Again, after the defeat, when Nonnius said they ought to have good hopes, since seven eagles were left in the camp of Pompey, "Your advice would be good," said Cicero, "if we were at war with jackdaws."

1001   *Generalship Costs Camp*
Plutarch, Cicero 38.8 (6)
And when Labienus, insisting on certain oracles, said that Pompey must prevail, "Yes," said Cicero, "this is the generalship that has now cost us our camp."

1002   *Let Proscriptions End*
Plutarch, Cicero 49.1–2 (1)
When Cicero's extremities[1] were brought to Rome, it chanced that Antony was conducting an election, but when he heard of their arrival and saw them, he cried out, "Now let our proscriptions have an end."

    1. His head and hands.

1003   *Miltiades Requests Honors*
Plutarch, Cimon 8.1
[When Miltiades] asked for a crown of olive merely, Sophanes the Deceleian rose up in the midst of the assembly and protested. His speech was ungracious, but it pleased the people of that day. "When," said he, "thou hast fought out alone a victory over the Barbarians, then demand to be honored alone."

1004   *Rhoesaces and Cimon*
Plutarch, Cimon 10.8–9
It is told, indeed, that one Rhoesaces, a Barbarian who had deserted from the King, came to Athens with large moneys, and being set upon fiercely by the public informers, fled for refuge to Cimon, and deposited at his door two platters, one filled with silver, the other with golden Darics. Cimon, when he saw them, smiled, and asked the man whether he preferred to have Cimon as his hireling or his friend, and on his replying, "As my friend," "Well, then," said Cimon, "take this money with thee and go thy way, for I shall have the use of it when I want it if I am thy friend."

1005 *Lachartus and Cimon*
Plutarch, Cimon 17.1

After he [Cimon] had given aid to the Lacedaemonians, he was going back home with his forces through the Isthmus of Corinth, when Lachartus upbraided him for having introduced his army before he had conferred with the citizens. "People who knock at doors," said he, "do not go in before the owner bids them"; to which Cimon replied, "And yet you Corinthians, O Lachartus, did not so much as knock at the gates of Cleonae and Megara, but hewed them down and forced your way in under arms, demanding that everything be opened up to the stronger."

1006 *Tyrtaeus Evaluated*
Plutarch, Cleomenes 2.3

For Leonidas of old, as we are told, when asked what manner of poet he thought Tyrtaeus to be, replied: "A good one to inflame the souls of young men."

1007 *Aratus and Cleomenes Jest*
Plutarch, Cleomenes 4.2–3

But Cleomenes wrote him [Aratus] an ironical letter, inquiring, as from a friend, whither he had marched out in the night. Aratus wrote back that hearing of Cleomenes' intention to fortify Belbina he had gone down there to prevent it. Whereupon Cleomenes sent back word again that he believed this story to be true: "but those torches and ladders," said he, "if it is all one to thee, tell me for what purpose thou hadst them with thee." Aratus burst out laughing at the jest, and inquired what manner of youth this was. Whereupon Damocrates, the Lacedaemonian exile, replied: "If thou hast designs upon the Lacedaemonians, see that thou hastenest, before this young cock grows his spurs."

1008 *Cleomenes Proposes Alliance*
Plutarch, Cleomenes 24.1–4

At last the disaster became clear to the citizens, and some of them at once fled the city, taking with them what property they could lay hands on, while others banded together under arms, resisting and assaulting the enemy. These they were not strong enough to eject from the city, but they afforded a safe escape to the citizens who wished to flee, so that not more than a thousand persons were taken in the place; all the rest, together with their wives and children, succeeded in escaping to Messene. Moreover, the greater part of those who tried to save the city by fighting got off alive; but a few of them, all told, were captured, among whom were Lysandridas and Thearidas, men of the greatest reputation and influence in Megalopolis. Therefore the soldier had no sooner seized them than they brought them to Cleomenes. Then Lysandridas, when he saw Cleomenes from afar, cried out with a loud voice and said: "It is in thy power now, O king of the Lacedaemonians, to display an action fairer and more worthy of a king than any that has preceded it, and thereby win men's high esteem." But Cleomenes, conjecturing what the speaker wished, said: "What meanest thou, Lysandridas? Thou surely canst not bid me give your city back again to you." To which Lysandridas replied: "Indeed, that is just what I mean, and I advise thee in thine own interests not to destroy so great a city, but to fill it with friends and allies who are trusty and true by giving back to the Megalopolitans their native city and becoming the preserver of so large a people." Accordingly, after a short silence, Cleomones said: "It is difficult to believe that all this will happen, but with us let what makes for good repute always carry the day, rather than what brings gain." And with these words he sent the two men off to Messene attended by a herald from himself, offering to give back their city to the Megalopolitans on condition that they renounce the Achaean cause and be his friends and allies.

1009 Cleomenes No Longer Wants Horses
Plutarch, Cleomenes 35.1–2

While matters stood thus with him, Nicagoras the Messenian came to Alexandria, a man who hated Cleomenes, but pretended to be a friend. He had at one time sold Cleomenes a fine estate, and owing to the constant demands of war upon the king, as it would seem, had not received the money for it. And so now, when Cleomenes, who chanced to be taking a walk along the quay, saw Nicagoras landing from his vessel, he greeted him heartily and asked what errand brought him to Egypt. Nicagoras returned his greeting in a friendly manner, and said that he was bringing horses for the king, some fine ones for use in war. At this, Cleomenes gave a laugh and said: "I could wish that thou hadst rather brought sambuca-girls and catamites; for these now most interest the king."

1010 Crassus Asks for Escort
Plutarch, Crassus 6.2–3

But when Sulla crossed into Italy, he wished all the young men with him to take active part in the campaign, and assigned different ones to different undertakings. Crassus, being sent out to raise a force among the Marsi, asked for an escort, since his road would take him past the enemy. But Sulla was wroth, and said to him vehemently: "I give thee as an escort thy father, thy brother, thy friends and thy kinsmen, who were illegally and unjustly put to death, and whose murderer I am pursuing." Thus rebuked and incited, Crassus set out at once, and forcing his way vigorously through the enemy, raised a considerable force, and showed himself an eager partisan of Sulla in his struggles.

1011 How Great Is He?
Plutarch, Crassus 7.1

And once when someone said: "Pompey the Great is coming," Crassus fell to laughing and asked: "How great is he?"

1012 How Great a Pleasure
Plutarch, Crassus 7.5

It is true that once when Caesar had been captured by pirates in Asia and was held a close prisoner by them,[1] he exclaimed: "O Crassus, how great a pleasure wilt thou taste when thou hearest of my capture!"

1. See Plutarch, Caesar 2.

1013 Demetrius Leaves City in Freedom
Plutarch, Demetrius 9.5–6

Megara, however, was captured, and the soldiers would have plundered it had not the Athenians made strong intercession for its citizens; Demetrius also expelled its garrison and gave the city its freedom. While he was still engaged in this, he bethought himself of Stilpo the philosopher, who was famous for his election of a life of tranquility. Accordingly, Demetrius summoned him and asked him whether anyone had robbed him of anything. "No one," said Stilpo, "for I saw nobody carrying away knowledge." But nearly all the servants in the city were stolen away, and when Demetrius once more tried to deal kindly with the philosopher, and finally, on going away, said: "Your city, Stilpo, I leave in freedom," "Thou sayest truly," replied Stilpo, "for thou hast not left a single one of our slaves."

1014 *Demetrius Spares Artwork*
Plutarch, Demetrius 22.2

It happened, namely, that Protogenes the Caunian had been making a painting for them which illustrated the story of Ialysus, and this picture, nearly finished, had been captured by Demetrius in one of the suburbs of the city. The Rhodians sent a herald and begged Demetrius to spare and not destroy the work, whereupon he replied that he would rather burn the likenesses of his father than so great a labor of art.

1015 *Madness Sane*
Plutarch, Demetrius 24.3-5

Not so Cleaenetus the son of Cleomedon, who, in order to obtain a letter from Demetrius to the people and therewith to secure the remission of a fine of fifty talents which had been imposed upon his father, not only disgraced himself, but also got the city into trouble. For the people released Cleomedon from his sentence, but they passed an edict that no citizen should bring a letter from Demetrius before the assembly. However, when Demetrius heard of it and was beyond measure incensed thereat, they took fright again, and not only rescinded the decree, but actually put to death some of those who had introduced and spoken in favor of it, and drove others into exile; furthermore, they voted besides that it was the pleasure of the Athenian people that whatsoever King Demetrius should ordain in future, this should be held righteous towards the gods and just towards men. And when one of the better class of citizens declared that Stratocles was mad to introduce such a motion, Demochares of Leuconoe said: "He would indeed be mad not to be mad."

1016 *Demetrius Slays Alexander*
Plutarch, Demetrius 36.5-6

And so, when Demetrius rose up from table before supper was over, Alexander [who had delayed his plans to kill Demetrius], filled with fear, rose up also and followed close upon his heels towards the door. Demetrius, then, on reaching the door where his own bodyguards stood, said merely, "Smite any one who follows me," and quietly went out himself; but Alexander was cut down by the guards together with those of his friends who came to his aid. One of these, we are told, as he was smitten, said that Demetrius had got one day's start of them.

1017 *Erasistratus Pleads for Antiochus*
Plutarch, Demetrius 38.5-7

He [Erasistratus] took the risk one day [of convincing Seleucus to give his wife Stratonice to his son Antiochus], and told him [Seleucus] that love was the young man's [Antiochus'] trouble, a love that could neither be satisfied nor cured. The king was amazed, and asked why his son's love could not be satisfied nor cured. "Because, indeed," said Erasistratus, "he is in love with my wife." "Then canst thou not, O Erasistratus," said Seleucus, "since thou art my son's friend, give him thy wife in addition to thy friendship, especially when thou seest that he is the only anchor of our storm-tossed house?" "Thou art his father," said Erasistratus, "and yet thou wouldst not have done so if Antiochus had set his affections on Stratonice." "My friend," said Seleucus, "would that someone in heaven or on earth might speedily convert and turn his passion in this direction; since I would gladly let my kingdom also go, if I might keep Antiochus."

1018 *Spartans Send One*
Plutarch, Demetrius 42.1–2

For instance, he [Demetrius] kept an embassy from the Athenians, for whose favor he was more solicitous than for that of any other Greeks, two years in waiting; and when a single envoy came to him from Sparta, he thought himself despised, and was incensed. However, when he cried, "What meanest thou? Have the Spartans sent but one envoy?" he got the neat and laconic reply, "Yea, O king, to one man."

1019a *Ares is Lord*
Plutarch, Demetrius 42.5–6

And surely nothing so befits a king as the work of justice. For "Ares is tyrant," in the words of Timotheus,[1] but "Law is king of all things," according to Pindar;[2] and Homer speaks of kings as receiving from Zeus for protection and safe-keeping, not city-takers nor bronze-beaked ships, but "ordinances of justice";[3] and he calls a disciple and "confidant" of Zeus, not the most warlike or unjust or murderous of kings, but the most just.[4] Demetrius, on the contrary, was delighted to receive a surname most unlike those given to the king of the gods; for Zeus is surnamed City-guardian, or City-protector; but Demetrius, City-besieger. Thus a power devoid of wisdom advances evil to the place of good, and makes injustice co-dweller with fame.

1. T. Bergk, *Poetae Lyrici Graeci* 3.622.
2. Bergk, 1.439.
3. Homer, *Iliad* 1.238f.
4. Homer, *Odyssey* 19.179.

1019b *Ares is Lord*
Plutarch, Agesilaus 14.2

And it was most pleasing to the Greeks who dwelt in Asia to see the Persian viceroys and generals, who had long been insufferably cruel, and had reveled in wealth and luxury, now fearful and obsequious before a man who went about in a paltry cloak, and at one brief and laconic speech from him [Agesilaus] conforming themselves to his ways and changing their dress and mien, insomuch that many were moved to cite the words of Timotheus:

"Ares is Lord; of gold Greece hath no fear."[1]

1. Cf. T. Bergk, *Poetae Lyrici Graeci* 3.622.

1020   *Arguments Smell of Lampwicks*
Plutarch, Demosthenes 8.3–5 (3–4)

Demosthenes was rarely heard to speak on the spur of the moment, but though the people often called upon him by name as he sat in the assembly, he would not come forward unless he had given thought to the question and was prepared to speak upon it. For this, many of the popular leaders used to rail at him, and Pytheas, in particular, once told him scoffingly that his arguments smelt of lampwicks. To him, then, Demosthenes made a sharp answer. "Indeed," said he, "thy lamp and mine, O Pytheas, are not privy to the same pursuits."

1021   *Demosthenes' Frenzied Speech*
Plutarch, Demosthenes 9.4–5

And [Demetrius] the Phalerian says that once, as if under inspiration, he [Demosthenes] swore the famous metrical oath to the people:—
   "By earth, by springs, by rivers, and by streams."[1]
Of the comic poets, one calls him a "rhopoperperethras," or trumpery-braggart,[2] and another, ridiculing his use of the antithesis, says this:—
   (First slave) "My master, as he took, retook."
   (Second slave(?)) "Demosthenes would have been delighted to
      take over this phrase."[3]

   1. T. Kock, *Comicorum Atticorum Fragmenta* 2.128.
   2. Ibid., 3.461.
   3. Ibid., 2.80.

1022   *Aesion Praises Demosthenes*
Plutarch, Demosthenes 11.3–4

And Hermippus tells us that Aesion,[1] when asked his opinion of the ancient orators as compared with those of his own time, said that one would have listened with admiration when the older orators discoursed to the people decorously and in the grand manner, but that the speeches of Demosthenes, when read aloud, were far superior in point of arrangement and power.

   1. A contemporary of Demosthenes.

1023   *Demosthenes Likened to Sow*
Plutarch, Demosthenes 11.5–6 (5)

For instance, when Demades said: "Demosthenes teach me! As well might the sow teach Athena." "It was this Athena," said Demosthenes, "that was lately found playing the harlot in Collytus."

1024   *Thieves of Brass*
Plutarch, Demosthenes 11.6 (5–6)

And to the thief nicknamed Brazen, who attempted to make fun of him [Demosthenes] for his late hours and his writing at night, "I know," he said, "that I annoy you with my lighted lamp. But you, men of Athens, must not wonder at the thefts that are committed, when we have thieves of brass, but house walls of clay."

1025   *Character of Demosthenes*
Plutarch, Demosthenes 13.3–4 (2–3)

For he [Demosthenes] was not like Demades, who apologized for his change of policy by saying that he often spoke at variance with himself, but never at variance with the interests of the city; nor like Melanopus, who, though opposed politically to Callistratus, was often bought over by him, and then would say to people: "The man is my enemy, it is true, but the interests of the city shall prevail"; nor like Nicodemus the Messenian, who first attached himself to Cassander, and then again advocated the interests of Demetrius, but said that he was not contradicting himself, for it was always advantageous to listen to one's masters.

1026   Not Praise Fit for King
Plutarch, Demosthenes 16.3–4 (2)

As regards all other marks of honor and kindly attention, however, Philip did not treat Demosthenes as well as the others, but courted rather the party of Aeschines and Philocrates. And so when these lauded Philip as most powerful in speaking, most fair to look upon, and indeed, as a most capable fellow-drinker, Demosthenes had to say in bitter raillery that the first encomium was appropriate for a sophist, the second for a woman, and the third for a sponge, but none of them for a king.

1027   Asses' Milk
Plutarch, Demosthenes 27.5 (3–4)

Pytheas, we are told, said that just as we think that a house into which asses' milk is brought must certainly have some evil in it, so also a city must of necessity be diseased into which an Athenian embassy comes; whereupon Demosthenes turned the illustration against him by saying that asses' milk was given to restore health, and the Athenians came to bring salvation to the sick.

1028   Funny Consul
Plutarch, Demosthenes and Cicero 1.5

And we are told that when Cato prosecuted Murena, Cicero, who was then consul, defended him, and because of Cato's beliefs made much fun of the Stoic sect, in view of the absurdities of their so-called paradoxes;[1] and when loud laughter spread from the audience to the jurors, Cato, with a quiet smile, said to those who sat by: "What a funny man we have, my friends, for consul!"

     1. Cf. Cicero, *Pro Murena* 29–31.

1029   Power, Wisdom, and Justice
Plutarch, Demosthenes and Cicero 3.4

And when in Rome itself he [Cicero] was appointed consul in name, but really received the power of a dictator and sole ruler against Catiline and his conspirators, he bore witness to the truth of Plato's prophecy[1] that states would then have respite from evil, when in one and the same person, by some happy fortune, great power and wisdom should be conjoined with justice.

     1. Plato, *Republic* 473.

1030   No Virtuous Man
Plutarch, Dion 5.1–4

At this meeting the general subject was human virtue, and most of the discussion turned upon manliness. And when Plato set forth that tyrants least of all men had this quality, and then, treating of justice, maintained that the life of the just was blessed, while that of the unjust was wretched, the tyrant [Dionysius], as if convicted by arguments, would listen to them, and was vexed with the audience because they admired the speaker and were charmed by his utterances. At last he got exceedingly angry and asked the philsopher why he had come to Sicily. And when Plato said that he was come to seek a virtuous man, the tyrant answered and said: "Well, by the gods, it appears that you have not yet found such an one."

1031 *Dionysius and Gelon*
Plutarch, Dion 5.9

The tyrant [Dionysius] was ridiculing the government of Gelon, and when he said that Gelon himself, true to his name, became the laughing stock ("gelos") of Sicily, the rest of his hearers pretended to admire the joke, but Dion was disgusted and said: "Indeed, thou art now tyrant because men trusted thee for Gelon's sake; but no man hereafter will be trusted for thy sake."

1032 *Dionysius Safely Munificent*
Plutarch, Dion 19.3

The tyrant offered him, too, presents of money, much money and many times, but Plato would not accept them. Whereupon Aristippus of Cyrene, who was present on one of these occasions, said that Dionysius was safely munificent; for he offered little to men like him, who wanted more, but much to Plato, who would take nothing.

1033 *Dionysius Not Topic*
Plutarch, Dion 20.2–4

Dionysius sought to disprove his enmity to Plato by giving banquets in his honor and making kind provisions for his journey, and went so far as to say something like this to him: "I suppose, Plato, thou wilt bring many dire accusations against me to the ears of your fellow philosophers." To this Plato answered with a smile: "Heaven forbid that there should be such a dearth of topics for discussion in the Academy that anyone mention thee."

1034 *Master of Own Sword Has No Superior*
Plutarch, Eumenes 10.2

Moreover, when Antigonus demanded to be addressed by him as a superior, Eumenes replied: "I regard no man as my superior so long as I am master of my sword."

1035 *Fabius Leaves Gods*
Plutarch, Fabius Maximus 22.5

While everything else was carried off as plunder, it is said that the accountant asked Fabius what his orders were concerning the gods, for so he called their pictures and statues; and that Fabius answered: "Let us leave their angered gods for the Tarentines."

1036 Lucullus and Pompey
Plutarch, Lucullus 39.4

He [Lucullus] also had country establishments near Tusculum, with observatories, and extensive open banqueting halls and cloisters. Pompey once visited these, and chided Lucullus because he had arranged his country seat in the best possible way for summer, but had made it uninhabitable in winter. Whereupon Lucullus burst out laughing and said: "Do you suppose, then, that I have less sense than cranes and storks, and do not change residences according to the seasons?"

1037 Praetor Receives Two Hundred Cloaks
Plutarch, Lucullus 39.5

A praetor was once making ambitious plans for a public spectacle, and asked of him some purple cloaks for the adornment of a chorus. Lucullus replied that he would investigate, and if he had any, would give them to him. The next day he asked the praetor how many he wanted, and on his replying that a hundred would suffice, bade him take twice that number. The poet Flaccus[1] alluded to this when he said that he did not regard a house as wealthy in which the treasures that were overlooked and unobserved were not more than those which met the eye.

    1. *Epistles* 1.6.45f.

1038a No Thrush
Plutarch, Lucullus 40.2–3

A saying of Pompey's, when he was ill, was certainly very popular. His physicians had prescribed a thrush for him to eat, and his servants said that a thrush could not be found anywhere in the summer season except where Lucullus kept them fattening. Pompey, however, would not suffer them to get one from there, but bade them prepare something else that was easily to be had, remarking as he did so to his physician, "What! must a Pompey have died if a Lucullus were not luxurious?"

1038b No Thrush
Plutarch, Pompey 2.6

Once when he [Pompey] was sick and loathed his food, a physician prescribed thrush for him. But when, on inquiry, his servants could not find one for sale (for it was past the season for them), and someone said they could be found at Lucullus's where they were kept year round, "What then," said he, "if Lucullus were not luxurious must Pompey have died?" and paying no regard to the physician he took something that could easily be procured.

1039 Lucullus Dines with Lucullus
Plutarch, Lucullus 41.2

And once, when he [Lucullus] was dining alone, and a modest repast of one course had been prepared for him, he was angry, and summoned the servant who had the matter in charge. The servant said that he did not suppose, since there were no guests, that he wanted anything very costly. "What sayest thou?" said the master, "dost thou not know that today Lucullus dines with Lucullus?"

1040 *King Dislikes Spartan Broth*
Plutarch, Lycurgus 12.7

And it is said that one of the kings of Pontus actually bought a Spartan cook for the sake of having this broth, and then, when he tasted it, disliked it; whereupon the cook said: "O King, those who relish this broth must first have bathed in the river Eurotas."

1041 *Lycurgus on Luxury*
Plutarch, Lycurgus 13.3–4

As in later times Epaminondas is reported to have said at his own table, that such a meal did not comport with treachery, so Lycurgus was the first to see clearly that such a house does not comport with luxury and extravagance.

1042a *No Adulterers in Sparta*
Plutarch, Lycurgus 15.10

And a saying is reported of one Geradas,[1] a Spartan of very ancient type, who, on being asked by a stranger what the punishment for adulterers was among them, answered: "Stranger, there is no adulterer among us." "Suppose then," replied the stranger, "there should be one." "A bull," said Geradas, "would be his forfeit, a bull so large that it could stretch over Mount Taygetus and drink from the river Eurotas." Then the stranger was astonished and said: "But how could there be a bull so large?" To which Geradas replied, with a smile: "But how could there be an adulterer in Sparta?"

  1. The name is Geradatas in 1042b.

1042b *No Adulterers in Sparta*
Plutarch, Moralia, Sayings of Spartans III:228C (20)

So strict in those times was the virtue of the women, and so far removed from the laxity of morals which later affected them, that in the earlier days the idea of adultery among them was an incredible thing. There is still recalled a saying of a certain Geradatas, a Spartan of the very early times, who, on being asked by a foreigner what was done to adulterers in their country, since he saw that there had been no legislation by Lycurgus on that subject, said, "Sir, there is never an adulterer in our country." But when the other retorted with, "Yes, but if there should be?" Geradatas said, "His penalty is to provide an enormous bull which by stretching his neck over Mount Taygetus can drink from the river Eurotas." And when the other in amazement said, "But how could there ever be a bull of that size?" Geradatas laughed and said, "But how could there ever be an adulterer in Sparta, in which wealth and luxury and adventitious aids to beauty are held in disesteem, and respect and good order and obedience to authority are given the highest place?"

1043 *Spartan Swords Reach Enemies*
Plutarch, Lycurgus 19.2

King Agis, accordingly, when a certain Athenian decried the Spartan swords for being so short, and said that jugglers on the stage easily swallowed them, replied: "And yet we certainly reach our enemies with these daggers."

1044 Lacedaemonians Learned No Evil
Plutarch, Lycurgus 20.4

And Pleistoanax, the son of Pausanias, when an Athenian orator declared that the Lacedaemonians had no learning, said: "True, we are indeed the only Hellenes who have learned no evil from you."

1045 A Spartan Wrestler of Integrity
Plutarch, Lycurgus 22.4

And they tell of a certain Spartan who refused to be bought off from a contest at Olympia by large sums of money, and after a long struggle outwrestled his antagonist. When some one said to him then: "What advantage, O Spartan, hast thou got from thy victory?" he answered, with a smile: "I shall stand in front of my king when I fight our enemies."

1046 Lysander and Cyrus
Plutarch, Lysander 4.3

At a banquet which Cyrus gave him [Lysander] as he was to depart, the prince begged him not to reject the tokens of his friendliness, but to ask plainly for whatever he desired, since nothing whatsoever would be refused him. "Since, then," said Lysander in reply, "thou art so very kind, I beg and entreat thee, Cyrus, to add an obol to the pay of my sailors, that they may get four obols instead of three."

1047 Aristonous the Harper
Plutarch, Lysander 18.5

However, when Aristonous the harper, who had been six times victor at the Pythian games, told Lysander in a patronizing way that if he should be victorious again, he would have himself proclaimed under Lysander's name, "That is," Lysander replied, "as my slave?"

1048 To Survive a Curse
Plutarch, Marcus Cato 8.6–7

Of one of his enemies who had the name of leading a disgraceful and disreputable life, he [Cato] said: "This man's mother holds the wish that he may survive her to be no pious prayer, but a malignant curse."

1049 Ancestral Lands Sold
Plutarch, Marcus Cato 8.7

Pointing to the man who had sold his ancestral fields lying near the sea, he [Cato] pretended to admire him, as stronger than the sea. "This man," said he, "has drunk down with ease what the sea found it hard to wash away."

1050 King by Nature Carnivorous
Plutarch, Marcus Cato 8.7–8

When King Eumenes paid a visit to Rome, the Senate received him with extravagant honors, and the chief men of the city strove who should be most about him. But Cato clearly looked upon him with suspicion and alarm. "Surely," someone said to him, "he is an excellent man, and a friend of Rome." "Granted," said Cato, "but the animal known as king is by nature carnivorous."

1051 *Worthy Kings*
Plutarch, Marcus Cato 8.8

He [Cato] said further that not one of the kings whom men so lauded was worthy of comparison with Epaminondas, or Pericles, or Themistocles, or Manius Curius, or with Hamilcar, surnamed Barcas.

1052 *Roman Embassy Deficient*
Plutarch, Marcus Cato 9.1–2

The Romans once chose three ambassadors to Bithynia, of whom one was gouty, another had had his head trepanned, and the third was deemed a fool. Cato made merry over this, and said that the Romans were sending out an embassy which had neither feet, nor head, nor heart.

1053 *Polybius Returns*
Plutarch, Marcus Cato 9.3

The Senate voted that the men be allowed to return, and a few days afterwards Polybius tried to get admission to that body again, with a proposal that the exiles be restored to their former honors in Achaia, and asked Cato's opinion on the matter. Cato smiled and said that Polybius, as if he were another Odysseus, wanted to go back into the cave of the Cyclops for a cap and belt which he had left there.

1054 *Palate Too Sensitive*
Plutarch, Marcus Cato 9.5

A certain epicure wished to enjoy his society, but he [Cato] excused himself, saying that he could not live with a man whose palate was more sensitive than his heart.

1055 *Against Fat Knights*
Plutarch, Marcus Cato 9.5

Railing at the fat knight, he [Cato] said, "Where can such a body be of service to the state, when everything between its gullet and its groins is devoted to belly?"

1056 *Poison or Bills Worse?*
Plutarch, Marcus Cato 9.7

To a tribune of the people who had been accused of using poison, and who was trying to force the passage of a useless bill, he [Cato] said: "Young man, I know not which is worse, to drink your mixtures, or to enact your bills."

1057a *Frank Speech*
Plutarch, Moralia, How to Tell a Flatterer I:71E–F

For as Lysander, we are told, said to the man from Megara, who in the council of the allies was making bold to speak for Greece, that "his words needed a country to back them"; so it may well be that every man's frank speaking needs to be backed by character, but this is especially true in the case of those who admonish others and try to bring them to their sober senses. Plato at any rate used to say that he admonished Speusippus by his life, as to be sure, the mere sight of Xenocrates in the lecture-room, and a glance from him, converted Polemon and made him a changed man. But the speech of a man light-minded and mean in character, when it undertakes to deal in frankness, results only in evoking the retort:

Wouldst thou heal others, full of sores thyself![1]

1. From Euripides; cf. A. Nauck, *Tragicorum Graecorum Fragmenta*, Euripides No. 1086.

1057b *Words Lack City*

Plutarch, Lysander 22.1

And when a Megarian, in some conference with him, grew bold in speech, he [Lysander] said: "Thy words, Stranger, lack a city."

1057c *Words Need Backing*

Plutarch, Moralia, Sayings of Kings and Commanders III:190F (5)

When a man from Megara used frank speech towards him [Lysander] in the general council, he said, "Your words need a country to back them."

1057d *Words Need Backing*

Plutarch, Moralia, Sayings of Spartans III:229C (8)

When a Megarian in the common council used plain words to him [Lysander], he said, "My friend, your words need a city to back them."

1057e *Words Need Backing*

Plutarch, Moralia, Sayings of Spartans III:212E (56)

When a man from Megara boasted greatly about his city, Agesilaus said, "Young man, your words need a great power to back them."

1057f *Admonish Others with Own Life*

Plutarch, Moralia, On Brotherly Love VI:491F–492A (21)

It was in this way that Plato reclaimed his nephew Speusippus from great self-indulgence and debauchery, not by either saying or doing to him anything that would cause him pain, but when the young man was avoiding his parents, who were always showing him to be in the wrong and upbraiding him, Plato showed himself friendly and free from anger to Speusippus and so brought about in him great respect and admiration for Plato himself and for philosophy. Yet many of Plato's friends used to rebuke him for not admonishing the youth, but Plato would say that he was indeed admonishing him: by his own, the philosopher's, manner of life, showing him a way to distinguish the difference between what is shameful and what is honorable.

1057g *Full of Sores Thyself*

Plutarch, Moralia, How to Profit by One's Enemies II:88C–D (4)

If you wish to distress the man who hates you, do not revile him as lewd, effeminate, licentious, vulgar, or illiberal, but be a man yourself, show self-control, be truthful, and treat with kindness and justice those who have to deal with you. And if you are led into reviling, remove yourself as far as possible from the things for which you revile him. Enter within the portals of your soul, look about to see if there be any rottenness there, lest some vice lurking somewhere within whisper to you the words of the tragedian:

Wouldst thou heal others, full of sores thyself?

1057h *Full of Sores Thyself*
> Plutarch, Moralia, Reply to Colotes XIV:1110E (8)

Accordingly the slime and confusion in which Colotes says those people become mired who say of things "no more this than that" are slime and confusion that he dumps on himself and his master. Is it here alone that our friend turns out to be a "Healer of others, full of sores himself?" Not at all; in his second charge he fails even more signally to notice that along with Democritus he expels Epicurus from the company of the living.

1058 *On Democracy*
> Plutarch, Moralia, Dinner of the Seven Wise Men II:154D–F

Mnesiphilus the Athenian,[1] a warm friend and admirer of Solon's, said, "I think it is no more than fair, Periander, that the conversation, like the wine, should not be apportioned on the basis of wealth or rank, but equally to all, as in a democracy, and that it should be general. Now in what has just been said dealing with dominion and kingdom, we who live under a popular government have no part. Therefore I think that at this time each of you ought to contribute an opinion on the subject of republican government, beginning again with Solon." It was accordingly agreed to do this, and Solon began by saying, "But you, Mnesiphilus, as well as all the rest of the Athenians, have heard the opinion which I hold regarding government. However, if you wish to hear it again now, I think that a State succeeds best, and most effectively perpetuates democracy, in which persons uninjured by a crime, no less than the injured person, prosecute the criminal and get him punished." Second was Bias, who said that the most excellent democracy was that in which the people stood in as much fear of the law as of the despot. Following him Thales said that it was the one having citizens neither too rich nor too poor. After him Anacharsis said that it was the one in which, all else being held in equal esteem, what is better is determined by virtue and what is worse by vice. Fifth, Cleobulus said that a people was most righteous whose public men dreaded censure more than they dreaded the law. Sixth, Pittacus said that it was where bad men are not allowed to hold office, and good men are not allowed to refuse it. Chilon, turning to the other side, declared that the best government is that which gives greatest heed to laws and least heed to those who talk about them. Finally, Periander once more concluded the discussion with the decisive remark, that they all seemed to him to approve a democracy which was most like an aristocracy.

> 1. Mnesiphilus, according to Plutarch, *Themistocles* 2 (112 D), handed down the political wisdom of Solon to Themistocles. At any rate Herodotus, 8.57, represents Mnesiphilus as advising Themistocles against withdrawing the Greek fleet from Salamis. Cf. also Plutarch, *Moralia*, On the Malice of Herodotus XI:869 D–E (36).

1059a *The Story of Enalus*
> Plutarch, Moralia, Dinner of the Seven Wise Men II:163A–D (20)

Pittacus thereupon said that it was a famous story,[1] and one mentioned by many, to this effect. An oracle had been given to those who were setting out to found a colony in Lesbos that when their voyage should bring them to a reef which is called "Midland," then they should cast into the sea at that place a bull as an offering to Poseidon, and to Amphitrite and the Nymphs of the sea a living virgin. The commanders were seven in number, all kings, and the eighth was Echelaus, designated by the oracle at Delphi to head the colony, although he was young and still unmarried. The seven, or as many as had unmarried daughters, cast lots, and the lot fell upon the daughter of Smintheus. Her they adorned with fine raiment and golden ornaments as they arrived opposite the spot, and purposed, as soon as they had offered prayer, to cast her into the sea. It happened that one of the company on board, a young man of no origin as it seems, was in love with her. His name, according to a tradition still preserved, was Enalus. He, conceiving a despairing desire to help the maiden in her present misfortune at the critical moment hurriedly clasped her in his arms, and threw himself with her into the sea. Straightway a rumor spread, having no sure foundation, but nevertheless carrying conviction to many in the community, regarding their safety and rescue. Later, as they say, Enalus appeared in Lesbos, and told how they had been borne by dolphins through the sea, and put ashore unharmed on the mainland. Other things he related more miraculous even than this, which astonished and fascinated the crowd, and he gave good grounds for believing them all by a deed which he did; for when a towering wave precipitated itself on the shores of the island, and the people were in a state of terror, he, all by himself, went to meet the sea, and cuttlefish followed him to the shrine of Poseidon, the biggest of which brought a stone with him, and this stone Enalus took and dedicated there, and this we call Enalus. "And in general," he continued, "if a man realizes a difference between the impossible and the unfamiliar, and between false reasoning and false opinion, such a man, Chilon, who would neither believe nor disbelieve at haphazard, would be most observant of the precept, 'Avoid extremes,'as you have enjoined."

1. The story is briefly mentioned by Plutarch, *Moralia*, The Cleverness of Animals XII:984E (36).

1059b *The Story of Enalus*
Athenaeus, Deipnosophists 11.466C–E

Anticleides of Athens, in the sixth book of his *Returns*, relates the story of Gras, who led the colony to Lesbos with other chieftains, and says that an oracle told them to let down into the sea as they sailed across a maiden as offering to Poseidon; he writes also the following: "Some of the people in Methymna tell the story of the maiden who was dropped into the sea, and they declare that one of the leaders, whose name was Enalus, had fallen in love with her and dived off the ship to save the girl. At that moment they were both hidden by a wave and disappeared from sight, but some time after, when Methymna was already settled, Enalus appeared and related the manner of life he had led,[1] and he said that the girl was staying with the Nereids, while he himself had fed the horses of Poseidon; and finally, when a great wave came sweeping on he plunged along with it and emerged with a cup made of gold so marvelous that the gold they[2] had, when compared with it, was no better than copper."

1. Something has been lost after "the manner of."
2. That is, the people to whom he related the adventure.

1060a *Dionysius Helped by Plato*
Plutarch, Moralia, Sayings of Kings and Commanders III:176D (3)

He [Dionysius the Younger[1]] was compelled to abdicate, and when a man said to him, "What help have Plato and philosophy given to you?" his answer was: "The power to submit to so great a change of fortune without repining."

1. Ruler of Syracuse, 367–343 B.C.E.

1060b *Dionysius Helped by Plato*
Plutarch, Timoleon 15.4

And again, in Corinth, when a stranger somewhat rudely derided him [Dionysius] about his associations with philosophers, in which he used to take delight when he was a tyrant, and finally asked him what good Plato's wisdom did him now, "Dost thou think," said he, "that I have had no help from Plato, when I bear my change of fortune as I do?"

1061 *Physician Has Key*
Plutarch, Moralia, Sayings of Kings and Commanders III:177F (9)

When the keybone of his [Philip's] shoulder had been broken in battle,[1] and the attending physician insistently demanded a fee every day, he said, "Take as much as you wish; for you have the key in your charge!"[2]

> 1. Cf. Demosthenes, *Oration* 18 (*De Corona*), 67 (p. 247), and Aulus Gellius 2.27.
> 2. The pun depends on the fact that *kleis* means both "key" and "collarbone."

1062 *Decision Appealed*
Plutarch, Moralia, Sayings of Kings and Commanders III:178F–179A (24)

While he [Philip] was hearing the case of Machaetas, he was near falling asleep, and did not give full attention to the rights of the case, but decided against Machaetas. And when Machaetas exclaimed that he appealed from the decision, Philip, thoroughly enraged, said, "To whom?" And Machaetas replied, "To you yourself, Your Majesty, if you will listen awake and attentive." At the time Philip merely ended the sitting, but when he had gained more control of himself and realized that Machaetas was treated unfairly, he did not reverse his decision, but satisfied the judgement with his own money.[1]

> 1. Of an old woman in Stobaeus, *Florilegium* 13.29 (quoted from Serenus) and Valerius Maximus 6.2, externa 1; in the latter place is the more familiar appeal from "Philip drunk to Philip sober."

1063a *Greatest Gifts to Anaxarchus*
Plutarch, Moralia, Sayings of Kings and Commanders III:179F–180A (7)

He [Alexander] bade his manager give to Anaxarchus, the philosopher, as much as he asked for; and when the manager said that he asked for twenty thousand pounds, Alexander said, "He does well, for he knows that he has a friend who is both able and willing to make such presents."

1063b *Greatest Gifts to Anaxarchus*
Plutarch, Moralia, Fortune of Alexander IV:331E (10)

It is recorded by several authors that he [Alexander] considered the musician Anaxarchus the most valuable of all his friends, that he gave ten thousand gold pieces to Pyrrhon of Elis the first time he met him, that he sent to Xenocrates, the friend of Plato, fifty talents as a gift, and that he made Onesicritus, the pupil of Diogenes the Cynic, chief pilot of his fleet.

1063c *Greatest Gifts to Anaxarchus*
Plutarch, Alexander 8.5

However, that eager yearning for philosophy which was imbedded in his [Alexander's] nature and which ever grew with his growth, did not subside from his soul, as is testified by the honor in which he held Anaxarchus, by his gift of fifty talents to Xenocrates, and by the attentions which he so lavishly bestowed upon Dandamis and Calanus.

1064 Ruler Trusts in Good Man

Plutarch, Moralia, Sayings of Kings and Commanders III:181C–D (26)

When another man who held a seemingly impregnable rock surrendered himself together with his stronghold to Alexander, Alexander bade him to continue to rule, and gave him additional country to govern, saying that "this person seems to me to show sense in trusting himself to a good man rather than to a strong place."

1065a Offspring of the Sun

Plutarch, Moralia, Sayings of Kings and Commanders III:182C (7)

When Hermodotus in his poems wrote of him [Antigonus] as "The Offspring of the Sun," he said, "The slave who attends to my chamber-pot is not conscious of that!"

1065b Offspring of the Sun

Plutarch, Moralia, Isis and Osiris V:360D (24)

Hence the elder Antigonus, when a certain Hermodotus in a poem proclaimed him to be "the Offspring of the Sun and a god," said, "the slave who attends to my chamberpot is not conscious of any such thing!"

1066 Gift Fit to Give

Plutarch, Moralia, Sayings of Kings and Commanders III:182E (15)

When Thrasyllus the Cynic asked him for a shilling, he [Antigonus] said "That is not a fit gift for a king to give." And when Thrasyllus said, "then give me two hundred pounds," he retorted, "But that is not a fit gift for a Cynic to receive."[1]

1. The story is told more fully by Seneca, De Beneficiis 2.17.1.

1067 True Words without Crown and Purple

Plutarch, Moralia, Sayings of Kings and Commanders III:184D–E (1)

Antiochus,[1] who made his next[2] campaign against the Parthians, in a hunt and chase wandered away from his friends and servants, and unrecognized entered the hut of some poor people. At dinner he brought in the subject of the king, and heard that, in general, he was a decent man, but that he entrusted most matters to friends who were scurvy fellows, and overlooked and often desregarded matters that were imperative through being too fond of hunting. At the time he said nothing; but at daybreak some of his bodyguards arrived at the hut, and his identity was disclosed when the purple and the crown were brought to him. "Howbeit," said he, "since the day when I donned you, yesterday was the first time that I heard true words about myself."

1. Antiochus VII, king of Syria, 137–128 B.C.E.
2. The first campaign was against Jerusalem in 133 B.C.E.

1068 *Achilles or Homer?*
Plutarch, Moralia, Sayings of Kings and Commanders III:185A (2)

Being asked whether he [Themistocles[1]] would rather have been Achilles or Homer, he said, "How about you yourself? Would you rather be the victor at the Olympic games or the announcer of the victor?"[2]

> 1. Leader of the Athenians against the Persians in 480 B.C.E.
> 2. The remark is attributed to Alexander by Dio Chrysostom, *Oration* 2 (22 M., 79 R).

1069a *No Crown for Those Who Lag*
Plutarch, Moralia, Sayings of Kings and Commanders III:185A–B (4)

When Adeimantus lacked the courage to risk a naval battle, and said to Themistocles, who was exhorting and urging on the Greeks, "Themistocles, in the games they always scourge the runners who start before the signal is given," Themistocles replied, "Yes, Adeimantus, but they do not crown those who are left behind in the race."[1]

> 1. Adeimantus is the speaker here, as in Herodotus 8.59; but see 1096b, where the remark is attributed not to the Corinthian Adeimantus, but to Eurybiades the Spartan, who was in command of the fleet.

1069b *No Crown for Those Who Lag*
Plutarch, Themistocles 11.1–3

When Eurybiades, who had command of the fleet on account of the superior claims of Sparta, but who was faint-hearted in time of danger, wished to hoist sail and make for the Isthmus, where the infantry also of the Peloponnesians had been assembled, it was Themistocles who spoke against it, and it was then, they say, that these memorable sayings of his were uttered. When Eurybiades said to him, "Themistocles, at the games those who start too soon get a caning," "Yes," said Themistocles, "but those who lag behind get no crown." And when Eurybiades lifted up his staff as though to smite him, Themistocles, said: "Smite, but hear me." Then Eurybiades was struck with admiration at his calmness, and bade him speak, and Themistocles tried to bring him back to his own position.

1070a *Phocion Refuses Riches*
Plutarch, Moralia, Sayings of Kings and Commanders III:188C (9)

When Alexander the king sent him [Phocion[1]] twenty thousand pounds as a present, he asked those who brought the money why it was that, when there were so many Athenians, Alexander offered this to him only. They replied that their king considered him only to be upright and honorable. "Then," said he, "let him suffer me both to seem and to be such."[2]

> 1. Upright Athenian general and statesman, fourth century B.C.E.
> 2. Cf. Aelian, *Varia Historia* 9.9.

1070b *Phocion Refuses Riches*
Plutarch, Phocion 18.1–3

The story about the money, indeed, is generally admitted, namely, that Alexander sent him a present of a hundred talents. When this was brought to Athens, Phocion asked the bearers why in the world, when there were so many Athenians, Alexander offered such a sum to him alone. They replied: "Because Alexander judges that thou alone art a man of honor and worth." "In that case," said Phocion, "let him suffer me to be and be thought such always." But when the messengers accompanied him to his home and saw there a great simplicity—his wife kneading bread, while Phocion with his own hands drew water from the well and washed his feet—they were indignant, and pressed the money upon him still more urgently, declaring it an intolerable thing that he though a friend of the king should live in such poverty. Phocion accordingly, seeing a poor old man walking the street in a dirty cloak, asked them if they considered him inferior to this man. "Heaven forbid!" they cried. "And yet this man," said Phocion, "has less to live upon than I, and finds it sufficient. And, in a word," said he, "if I make no use of this great sum of money, it will do men no good to have it; or, if I use it, I shall bring myself, and the king as well, under the calumnies of the citizens." So the treasure went back again from Athens, after it had showed the Greeks that the man who did not want so great a sum was richer than the man who offered it.

1071a *Justice as Boundary*
Plutarch, Moralia, Sayings of Romans III:204A (8)

When Phraates, king of the Parthians, sent to him [Pompey], claiming the right to set his boundary at the river Euphrates, he said that the Romans set justice as their boundary towards the Parthians.

1071b *Justice as Boundary*
Plutarch, Pompey 33.6

Not long after this, Phraates the Parthian sent a demand for the young man, on the plea that he was his son-in-law, and a proposition that the Euphrates be adopted as a boundary between his empire and that of the Romans. Pompey replied that as for Tigranes, he belonged to his father more than his father-in-law; and as for a boundary, the just one would be adopted.

1072 *Cured Soldier Less Daring*
Plutarch, Pelopidas 1.1–2

There was a soldier of Antigonus who was venturesome, but had miserable health and an impaired body. When the king asked him the reason for his pallor, the man admitted that it was a secret disease, whereupon the king took compassion on him and ordered his physicians, if there were any help for him, to employ their utmost skill and care. Thus the man was cured; but then the good fellow ceased to court danger and was no longer a furious fighter, so that even Antigonus rebuked him and expressed his wonder at the change. The man, however, made no secret of the reason, but said: "O King, it is thou who hast made me less daring, by freeing me from those ills which made me set little value on life."

1073 *Serious Business for the Morrow*
Plutarch, Pelopidas 10.3–4

For there came a messenger from Athens, from Archias the hierophant to his namesake Archias, who was his guest-friend, bearing a letter which contained no empty nor false suspicion, but stated clearly all the details of the scheme that was on foot, as was subsequently learned. At the time, however, Archias was drunk, and the bearer of the letter was brought to him and put it into his hands saying: "The sender of this bade thee read it at once; for it is on serious business." Then Archias answered with a smile: "Serious business for the morrow"; and when he had received the letter he put it under his pillow, and resumed his casual conversation with Phillidas. Wherefore these words of his are a current proverb to this day among the Greeks.

1074 *Pelopidas and the Tyrant*
Plutarch, Pelopidas 28.1-3

As for Pelopidas, after the tyrant [Alexander of Pherae] had brought him back to Pherae, at first he suffered all who desired it to converse with him, thinking that his calamity had made him a pitiful and contemptible object; but when Pelopidas exhorted the lamenting Phereans to be of good cheer, since now certainly the tyrant would meet with punishment, and when he sent a message to the tyrant himself, saying that it was absurd to torture and slay the wretched and innocent citizens day by day, while he spared him, a man most certain, as he knew, to take vengeance on him if he made his escape; then the tyrant, amazed at his high spirit and his fearlessness, said: "And why is Pelopidas in haste to die?" To which Pelopidas replied: "That thou mayest the sooner perish, by becoming more hateful to the gods than now."

1075a *Not Destined to Ascend*
Plutarch, Pelopidas 34.4

Therefore the Spartan's advice was better, who, when he greeted Diagoras, the Olympian victor, who had lived to see his sons crowned at Olympia, yes, and the sons of his sons and daughters, said: "Die now, Diagoras; thou canst not ascend to Olympus."

1075b *Not Destined to Ascend*
Cicero, Tusculan Disputations 1.46.111

Indeed he will even be ready to die in the midst of prosperity; for no accumulation of successes can afford so much delight as their diminution will cause annoyance. This seems to be the meaning of the well-known utterance of the Lacedaemonian who, when Diagoras of Rhodes, a famous Olympian victor, had seen his two sons victorious on one day at Olympia, approached the old man and, congratulating him, said, "Die, Diagoras, for you are not destined to ascend to heaven." Such achievements the Greeks think glorious—too much so perhaps— or rather thought so in that day, and he, who spoke in this way to Diagoras, considered it very glorious for three Olympian victors to come from one home, and judged it inexpedient for the father to linger longer in life exposed to the buffets of fortune.

1076 *The Good Piper*
Plutarch, Pericles 1.5

Therefore it was a fine saying of Antisthenes, when he heard that Ismenias was an excellent piper: "But he's a worthless man," said he, "otherwise he wouldn't be so good a piper."

1077 Agatharchus and Zeuxis
Plutarch, Pericles 13.2

And yet they say that once on a time when Agatharchus the painter was boasting loudly of the speed and ease with which he made his figures, Zeuxis heard him, and said, "Mine take, and last, a long time."

1078 Wait for Time
Plutarch, Pericles 18.2

So when he [Pericles] saw that Tolmides, son of Tolmaeus, all on account of his previous good-fortune and of the exceeding great honor bestowed upon him for his wars, was getting ready, quite inopportunely, to make an incursion into Boeotia, and that he had persuaded the bravest and most ambitious men of military age to volunteer for the campaign—as many as a thousand of them, aside from the rest of his forces—he tried to restrain and dissuade him in the popular assembly, uttering then that well remembered saying, to wit, that if he would not listen to Pericles, he would yet do full well to wait for that wisest of all counselors, Time.

1079 Performance, Not Practice, Admired
Plutarch, Philopoemen 13.3

[Philopoemen] was averse to inactivity, and wished to keep his skill as a commander in war, like any other possession, all the while in use and exercise. And he made this evident by what he once said about King Ptolemy. When certain persons were extolling that monarch because he carefully drilled his army day by day, and carefully and laboriously exercised himself in arms, "And yet who," said Philopoemen, "can admire a king of his years for always practicing but never performing anything?"

1080 Aristaenus Eager to See Greek Fate
Plutarch, Philopoemen 17.3

Aristaenus the Megalopolitan was a man of the greatest influence among the Achaeans, but he always paid court to the Romans and thought that the Achaeans ought not to oppose or displease them in any way. As this man was once speaking in the assembly, we are told that Philopoemen listened to him a while in silent indignation, but at last, overcome by anger, said to him: "My man, why art thou eager to behold the fated end of Greece?"

1081 Philopoemen Scorns General
Plutarch, Philopoemen 18.2

For it is recorded that at some conference, when others present were lavishing praise upon one who was reputed to be a redoubtable general, Philopoemen contemptously said: "Yet why should any account be made of this man, who has been taken alive by his enemies?"

1082 Laughter Costs Tears
Plutarch, Phocion 5.1

Therefore, when Chares once made the Athenians laugh by speaking of Phocion's frowning brows, "No harm," said Phocion, "has come to you from this brow of mine; but these men's laughter has cost the city many a tear."

1083 *Phocion Bests Demosthenes*
Plutarch, Phocion 9.5

And when Demosthenes, one of the orators in opposition to him, said to him, "The Athenians will kill thee, Phocion, should they go crazy," he replied: "But they will kill thee, should they come to their senses."

1084 *Phocion's Counsel Ignored*
Plutarch, Phocion 9.6

At another time Lycurgus heaped much abuse upon him in the assembly, and above all because, when Alexander demanded ten citizens of Athens, Phocion counselled their surrender; Phocion, however, merely said: "I have given this people much good and profitable counsel, but they will not listen to me."

1085 *Archibiades Not Really Spartan*
Plutarch, Phocion 10.1

There was a certain Archibiades, nicknamed Laconistes, because, in imitation of the Spartans, he let his beard grow to an extravagant size, always wore a short cloak, and had a scowl on his face. Phocion was once stormily interrupted in the council, and called upon this man for testimony and support in what he said. But when the man rose up and gave such counsel as was pleasing to the Athenians, Phocion seized him by the beard and said: "O Archibiades, why, then didst thou not shave thyself?"

1086 *Aristogeiton Lame*
Plutarch, Phocion 10.2

Again, when Aristogeiton the public informer, who was always warlike in the assemblies and tried to urge the people on to action, came to the place of muster leaning on a staff and with both legs bandaged, Phocion spied him from the tribunal when he was far off, and cried out: "Put down Aristogeiton, too, as lame and worthless."

1087 *Victory, Not Location, Important*
Plutarch, Phocion 16.1–3

Presently, the relations between Athens and Philip were altogether hostile, and, in Phocion's absence, other generals were chosen to conduct the war. But when Phocion returned with his fleet from the islands, to begin with, he tried to persuade the people, since Philip was peaceably inclined and greatly feared the peril of war, to accept the terms of settlement which he offered. And when one of those who haunted the law-courts in the capacity of public informer opposed him, and said, "Canst thou dare, O Phocion, to divert the Athenians from war when they are already under arms?" "I can," said he, "and that, too, though I know that while there is a war thou wilt be under my orders, but when peace has been made I shall be under thine." When, however, he could not prevail, but Demosthenes carried the day and was urging the Athenians to join battle with Philip as far from Attica as possible, "My good Sir," said Phocion, "let us not ask where we can fight, but how we shall be victorious. For in that case the war will be at a long remove; but wherever men are defeated every terror is close at hand."

1088 An Actor's Vanity
Plutarch, Phocion 19.2-3

And once when the Athenians were witnessing an exhibition of new tragedies, the actor who was required to take the part of a queen asked the choregus to furnish him with a great number of attendant women in expensive array; and when he could not get them, he was indignant, and kept the audience waiting by his refusal to come out. But the choregus, Melanthius, pushed him before the spectators, crying: "Dost thou not see that Phocion's wife always goes out with one maidservant? Thy vanity will be the undoing of our womenfolk." His words were plainly heard by the audience, and were received with tumultuous applause.

1089 On Spartan Polity
Plutarch, Phocion 20.3

And once Demades said to him: "Phocion, why shouldn't we try to persuade the Athenians to adopt the Spartan polity? For if thou sayest the word, I am ready to introduce and support the requisite law." But Phocion replied: "Indeed, it would very well become thee, with so strong a scent of ointment upon thee, and wearing such a mantle as thine, to recommend to the Athenians the public mess-halls of the Spartans and to extol Lycurgus."

1090 Pytheas Silenced
Plutarch, Phocion 21.1

To Pytheas, who at that time was just beginning to address the Athenians, but was already loquacious and bold, Phocion said: "Hold thy peace, thou who art but a newly bought slave of the people!"

1091 Phocion's Good
Plutarch, Phocion 23.1

Leosthenes, who plunged the city into the Lamian war much to Phocion's displeasure, once asked him derisively what good he had done the city during the many years in which he had been general. "No slight good," said Phocion, "in that its citzens are buried in their own sepulchers."

1092 Leosthenes Fruitless
Plutarch, Phocion 23.2

Again, when Leosthenes was talking very boldly and boastfully in the assembly, Phocion said: "Thy speeches, young man, are like cypress trees, which are large and towering but bear no fruit."

1093 Prerequisites For War
Plutarch, Phocion 23.2

And when Hypereides confronted him with the question, "When then, O Phocion, wilt thou counsel the Athenians to go to war?" "Whenever," said Phocion, "I see the young men willing to hold their places in the ranks, the rich to make contributions and the orators to keep their thievish hands away from the public moneys."

1094 *Leosthenes' Success*
Plutarch, Phocion 23.3

When many were admiring the force got together by Leosthenes, and were asking Phocion what he thought of the city's preparations, "They are good," said he, "for the short course;[1] but it is the long course which I fear in war, since the city has no other moneys, or ships, or men-at-arms." And events justified his fears. For at first Leosthenes achieved brilliant successes, conquering the Boeotians in battle, and driving Antipater into Lamia. Then, too, they say that the city came to cherish high hopes, and was continuously holding festivals and making sacrifices of glad tidings. Phocion, however, when men thought to convict him of error and asked him if he would not have been glad to have performed these exploits, replied: "By all means; but I am glad to have given the advice I did." And again, when the glad tidings came in quick succession by letter and messenger from the camp, "When, pray," said he, "will our victories cease?"

> 1. The short course in the foot-races was straight away, the length of the stadium; the long course was ten times back and forth.

1095 *Phocion Acquires Friend*
Plutarch, Phocion 24.1–2

But Leosthenes was killed, and then those who feared that Phocion, if he were sent out as general, would put a stop to the war, arranged with a certain obscure person to rise in the assembly and say that he was a friend and intimate associate of Phocion, and therefore advised the people to spare him and keep him in reserve, since they had none other like him, and to send out Antiphilus to the army. This course was approved by the Athenians, whereupon Phocion came forward and said that he had never been intimately associated with the person, nor in any way familiar or acquainted with him; "But now," said he, "from this very day I make thee a friend and close companion, for thou hast counselled what was for my advantage."

1096 *Phocion Bargains with Antipater*
Plutarch, Phocion 27.4–5

Phocion, however, besought Antipater to spare them [the Athenians] the [Macedonian] garrison, to which Antipater, as we are told, replied: "O, Phocion, we wish to gratify thee in all things, except those which will ruin thee and us." But some tell a different story, and say that Antipater asked whether, in case he indulged the Athenians in the matter of the garrison, Phocion would go surety that his city would abide by the peace and stir up no trouble; and that when Phocion was silent and delayed his answer, Callimedon, surnamed Carabus, an arrogant man and a hater of democracy, sprang to his feet and cried: "But even if the fellow should prate such nonsense, Antipater, wilt thou trust him and give up what thou hast planned to do?"

1097 *Gift for Phocus Refused*
Plutarch, Phocion 30.1

When Menyllus offered Phocion a gift of money, he replied that neither was Menyllus better than Alexander, nor was there any stronger reason why the man who would not accept it then should take it now. Menyllus, however, begged him to take the money for his son Phocus at least, whereupon Phocion said: "For

Phocus, should he be converted to sobriety of life, his patrimony will be enough; but as he is now, nothing is sufficient."

1098 *Phocus Led by Passion*
Plutarch, Phocion 38.2

This son of Phocion [Phocus], we are told, turned out to be a man of no worth in general, and once, being enamoured of a girl who was kept in a brothel, chanced to hear Theodorus the Atheist discourse in the Lyceum as follows: "If there is no disgrace in ransoming a man beloved, the same is true of a woman loved; what is true of a comrade, is true also of a mistress." Accordingly, his passion leading him to think the argument sound, he ransomed his mistress.

1099 *Pompey as Proconsuls*
Plutarch, Pompey 17.4

On this occasion, too, they say that a certain senator asked with amazement if Philippus thought it necessary to send Pompey out as proconsul. "No indeed!" said Philippus, "but as pro-consuls," implying that both the consuls of that year were good for nothing.

1100a *Dead Man Does Not Bite*
Plutarch, Pompey 77.3–4

The opinions of the other counselors were so far divergent that some advised to drive Pompey away, and others to invite him in and receive him. But Theodotus, making a display of his powerful speech and rhetorical art, set forth that neither course was safe for them, but that if they received Pompey they would have Caesar for an enemy and Pompey for a master; while if they rejected him, Pompey would blame them for casting him off, and Caesar for making him continue his pursuit; the best course, therefore, was to send for the man and put him to death, for by so doing they would gratify Caesar and have nothing to fear from Pompey. To this he smilingly added, we are told, "A dead man does not bite."

1100b *Dead Man Does Not Bite*
Plutarch, Brutus 33.3–5

When Pompey the Great, after he had been stripped of his great power by Caesar, put in as a fugitive at Pelusium in Egypt, the guardians of the boy king were holding a council with their friends, at which opinions differed. Some thought they should receive Pompey, others thought they should repulse him from Egypt. But a certain Theodotus, of Chios, who was attached to the king as a paid teacher of rhetoric, and was at this time deemed worthy of a place in the council for lack of better men, declared that both were wrong, both those who would admit and those who would reject Pompey; for there was but one advantageous course in view of the circumstances, and that was to receive him and put him to death. And he added, as he closed his speech, "A dead man does not bite."

1101 *Pyrrhus Best General*
Plutarch, Pyrrhus 8.2

It is said also that Antigonus, when asked who was the best general, replied, "Pyrrhus, if he lives to be old."

1102 Alexander Leads Pyrrhus in Dream
Plutarch, Pyrrhus 11.2

That night Pyrrhus dreamed that he was called by Alexander the Great, and that when he answered the call he found the king lying on a couch, but met with kindly speech and friendly treatment from him, and received a promise of his ready aid and help. "And how, O King," Pyrrhus ventured to ask, "when thou art sick, canst thou give me aid and help?" "My name itself will give it," said the king, and mounting a Nisaean horse he led the way.

1103 Neither Gold Nor Beast Impress Fabricius
Plutarch, Pyrrhus 20.1-3

The embassy was headed by Caius Fabricius, who, as Cineas reported, was held in highest esteem at Rome as an honorable man and good soldier, but was inordinately poor. To this man, then, Pyrrhus privately showed kindness and tried to induce him to accept gold, not for any base purpose, indeed, but calling it a mark of friendship and hospitality. But Fabricius rejected the gold, and for that day Pyrrhus let him alone; on the following day, however, wishing to frighten a man who had not yet seen an elephant, he ordered the largest of these animals to be stationed behind a hanging in front of which they stood conversing together. This was done; and at a given signal the hanging was drawn aside and the animal suddenly raised his trunk, and held it over the head of Fabricius and emitted a harsh and frightful cry. But Fabricius calmly turned and said with a smile to Pyrrhus: "Your gold made no impression on me yesterday, neither does your beast today."

1104 Fabricius Lauds Epicurus
Plutarch, Pyrrhus 20.3-4

Again, at supper, where all sorts of topics were discussed, and particularly that of Greece and her philosophers, Cineas happened somehow to mention Epicurus, and set forth the doctrines of that school concerning the gods, civil government, and the highest good, explaining that they made pleasure the highest good, but would have nothing to do with civil government on the ground that it was injurious and the ruin of felicity, and that they removed the Deity as far as possible from feelings of kindness or anger or concern for us, into a life that knew no care and was filled with ease and comfort. But before Cineas was done, Fabricius cried out and said: "O Hercules, may Pyrrhus and the Samnites cherish these doctrines, as long as they are at war with us."

1105 High Character of Fabricius
Plutarch, Pyrrhus 20.4

Thus Pyrrhus was led to admire the high spirit and character of the man [Fabricius], and was all the more eager to have friendship with his city instead of waging war against it; he even privately invited him, in case he brought about the settlement, to follow his fortunes and share his life as the first and foremost of all his companions and generals. But Fabricius, as we are told, said quietly to him: "Nay, O King, this would not be to thy advantage; for the very men who now admire and honor thee, if they should become acquainted with me, would prefer to have me as their king rather than thee."

1106   *Spartans Confront Pyrrhus*
Plutarch, Pyrrhus 26.11

And when the Spartan ambassadors upbraided him for making war upon them without previous declaration, he [Pyrrhus] said: "Yet we know that you Spartans also do not tell others beforehand what you are going to do." Whereupon one of those who were present, Mandrocleidas by name, said to him in the broad Spartan dialect: "If thou art a god, we shall suffer no harm at thy hands; for we have done thee no wrong; but if a man, another will be found who is even stronger than thou."

1107   *The Wit of Anacharsis*
Plutarch, Solon 5.1-2

Anacharsis came to Athens, knocked at Solon's door, and said that he was a stranger who had come to make ties of friendship and hospitality with him. On Solon's replying that it was better to make one's friendships at home, "Well then," said Anacharsis, "do thou, who art at home, make me thy friend and guest." So Solon, admiring the man's ready wit, received him graciously and kept him with him some time.

1108   *False Story Produces Grief*
Plutarch, Solon 6.1-3

On his visit to Thales at Miletus, Solon is said to have expressed astonishment that his host was wholly indifferent to marriage and the getting of children. At the time Thales made no answer, but a few days afterwards he contrived to have a stranger say that he was just arrived after ten days' journey from Athens. When Solon asked what news there was at Athens, the man, who was under instructions what to say, answered: "None other than the funeral of a young man, who was followed to the grave by the whole city. For he was the son, as I was told, of an honored citizen who excelled all others in virtue; he was not at the funeral of his son; they told me that he had been traveling abroad for a long time." "O the miserable man!" said Solon; "pray, what was his name?" "I heard the name," the man said, "but I cannot recall it; only there was great talk of his wisdom and justice." Thus every answer heightened Solon's fears, and at last, in great distress of soul, he told his name to the stranger and asked him if it was Solon's son that was dead. The man said it was; whereupon Solon began to beat his head and to do and say everything else that betokens a transport of grief. But Thales took him by the hand and said, with a smile, "This it is, O Solon, which keeps me from marriage and the getting of children; it overwhelms even thee, who art the most stout-hearted of men. But be not dismayed at this story, for it is not true."

1109   *Solon and Aesop*
Plutarch, Solon 28.1

Now it so happened that Aesop, the writer of fables, was in Sardis, having been summoned thither by Croesus, and receiving much honor at his hands. He was distressed that Solon met with no kindly treatment, and said to him by way of advice: "O Solon, our converse with kings should be either as rare, or as pleasing as is possible." "No, indeed!" said Solon, "but either as rare or as beneficial as is possible."

1110 *Peisistratus Plays Role Badly*

Plutarch, Solon 30.1

Now when Peisistratus, after inflicting a wound upon himself,[1] came into the market place riding a chariot, and tried to exasperate the populace with the charge that his enemies had plotted against his life on account of his political opinions, and many of them greeted the charge with angry cries, Solon drew near and accosted him, saying: "O son of Hippocrates, thou art playing the Homeric Odysseus badly; for when he disfigured himself it was to deceive his enemies,[2] but thou dost it to mislead thy fellow-citizens."

1. Cf. Herodotus, 1.59; Aristotle, *Constitution of Athens* 14.1.
2. Homer, *Odyssey* 4.244–264.

1111 *Sulla Rich*

Plutarch, Sulla 1.2

For instance, we are told that when he [Sulla] was putting on boastful airs after his campaign in Libya, a certain nobleman said to him: "How canst thou be an honest man, when thy father left thee nothing, and yet thou art so rich?"

1112 *Sulla Bought Office*

Plutarch, Sulla 5.2

And so it happened that, during his praetorship, when he [Sulla] angrily told Caesar [Julius] that he would use his own authority against him, Caesar laughed and said: "You do well to consider the office your own, for you bought it."

1113 *Mithridates and Sulla Reconciled*

Plutarch, Sulla 24.1–3

They met, accordingly, at Dardanus, in the Troad, Mithridates having two hundred ships there, equipped with oars, twenty thousand men at arms from his infantry force, six thousand horse, and a throng of scythe-bearing chariots; Sulla on the other hand, having four cohorts and two hundred horse. When Mithridates came towards him and put out his hand, Sulla asked him if he would put a stop to the war on the terms which Archelaus had made, and as the king was silent, Sulla said: "But surely it is the part of suppliants to speak first, while victors need only to be silent." Then Mithridates began a defense of himself, and tried to shift the blame for the war partly upon the gods, and partly upon the Romans themselves. But Sulla cut him short, saying that he had long ago heard from others, but now knew of himself, that Mithridates was a very powerful orator, since he had not been at a loss for plausible arguments to defend such baseness and injustice as his. Then he reproached him bitterly and denounced him for what he had done, and asked him again if he would keep the agreements made through Archelaus. And when he said that he would, then Sulla greeted him with an embrace and a kiss, and later, bringing to him Ariobarzanes and Nicomedes the kings, he reconciled him with them. Mithridates, accordingly, after handing over to Sulla seventy ships and five hundred archers, sailed away to Pontus.

1114 *The Clever Magistrate*

Plutarch, Themistocles 5.4–5

So he [Themistocles] once said to Simonides of Ceos, who had made an improper request from him when he was magistrate: "You would not be a good poet if you should sing contrary to the measure; nor I a clever magistrate if I should show favor contrary to the law."

1115   Pouch for Heart
Plutarch, Themistocles 11.5

And again, when the Eretrian tried to argue somewhat against him [Themistocles], "Indeed!" said he, "what argument can ye make about war, who, like the cuttle fish, have a long pouch in the place where your heart ought to be?"

1116   Themistocles and Aristides
Plutarch, Themistocles 16.1–3

After the sea-fight, Xerxes, still furious at his failure, undertook to carry moles out into the sea on which he could lead his infantry across to Salamis against the Hellenes, damming up the intervening strait. But Themistocles, merely by way of sounding Aristides, proposed, as though he were in earnest, to sail with the fleet to Hellespont and break the span of boats there, "in order," said he, "that we may capture Asia in Europe." Aristides, however, was displeased with the scheme and said: "Now indeed the Barbarian with whom we have fought consults his ease and pleasure, but should we shut up in Hellas and bring under fearful compulsion a man who is lord of such vast forces, he will no longer sit under a golden parasol to view the spectacle of the battle at his ease, but he will dare all things, and, superintending everything in person, because of his peril, will rectify his previous remissness and take better counsel for the highest issues thus at stake. We must not, then," said he, "tear down the bridge that is already there, Themistocles, nay rather, we must build another alongside it, if that be possible, and cast the fellow out of Europe in a hurry." "Well, then," said Themistocles, "if that is what is thought for the best, it is high time for us all to be studying and inventing a way to get him out of Hellas by the speediest route."

1117   Both Come to Senses
Plutarch, Themistocles 18.2

Again, to one who had once been a beauty, Antiphates, and who had at that time treated him [Themistocles] disdainfully, but afterwards courted him because of the reputation he had got, "Young man," said he, "'tis late, 'tis true, but both of us have come to our senses."

1118   The Festival and the Day After
Plutarch, Themistocles 18.4

Again, when one of his fellow-generals, who thought he had done some vast service to the city, grew bold with Themistocles, and began to compare his own services with his, "With the Festival-day," said he, "the Day After once began a contention, saying: 'Thou art full of occupations and wearisome, but when I come, all enjoy at their leisure what has been richly provided beforehand'; to which the Festival-day replied: 'True, but had I not come first, thou hadst not come at all.' So now," said he, "had I not come at that day of Salamis, where would thou and thy colleagues be now?"

1119 *"I Have Themistocles the Athenian"*
Plutarch, Themistocles 28.4

But in converse with his friends it is said that he [the Persian King] congratulated himself over what he called the greatest good fortune, and prayed Arimanius ever to give his enemies such minds as to drive their best men away from them; and then sacrificed to the gods, and straightway betook himself to his cups; and in the night, in the midst of his slumbers, for very joy called thrice: "I have Themistocles the Athenian."

1120 *No Brains to Cover*
Plutarch, Themistocles 29.5

And when Demaratus the Spartan, being bidden to ask a gift, asked that he might ride in state through Sardis, wearing his tiara upright after the manner of the Persian kings, Mithropaustes the King's cousin said, touching the tiara of Demaratus: "This tiara of thine hath no brains to cover; indeed thou wilt not be Zeus merely because thou graspest the thunderbolt."

1121 *Timoleon as Tyrannicide or Fratricide?*
Plutarch, Timoleon 7.1–2

But the grief of Timoleon over what had been done, whether it was due to pity for his dead brother or to reverence for his mother, so shattered and confounded his mental powers that almost twenty years passed without his setting his hand to a single conspicuous or public enterprise. Accordingly, when he had been nominated general, and the people had readily approved of it and given him their votes, Telecleides who was at that time the foremost man in the city for reputation and influence, rose up and exhorted Timoleon to be a noble and brave man in his enterprises. "For if," said he, "thou contendest successfully, we shall think of thee as a tyrannicide; but if poorly, as a fratricide."

1122 *The Greatest Ill of Tyranny*
Plutarch, Timoleon 15.5

Further, when Aristoxenus the musician and certain others inquired what his complaint against Plato was and what its origin, he [Dionysius] told them that of the many ills with which tyranny abounded there was none so great as this, that not one of those reputed to be friends speaks frankly with the tyrant; for indeed it was by such friends that he himself had been deprived of Plato's good will.

1123 *Dionysius Returns Mocking Jest*
Plutarch, Timoleon 15.6

Again, when one of those who wish to be witty, in mockery of Dionysius shook out his robe on coming into his presence,[1] as if into the presence of a tyrant, Dionysius turned the jest upon him by bidding him do so when he went from his presence, that he might not take anything in the house away with him.

1. To show that no weapon was concealed there.

1124 *Elder Dionysius Found Time to Write*
Plutarch, Timoleon 15.7

And when Philip of Macedon, at a banquet, began to talk in banter about the lyric poems and tragedies which Dionysius the Elder had left behind him, and pretended to wonder when that monarch found time for these compositions, Dionysius not inaptly replied by saying: "When thou and I and all those whom men call happy are busy at the bowl."

1125 *Diogenes Indignant*
Plutarch, Timoleon 15.8–9

Now, Plato did not live to see Dionysius when he was in Corinth, but he was already dead. Diogenes of Sinope, however, on meeting him for the first time said: "How little thou deservest, Dionysius, thus to live!" Upon this Dionysius stopped and said: "It is good of thee, O Diogenes, to sympathize with me in my misfortunes." "How is that?" said Diogenes, "Dost thou suppose that I am sympathizing with thee? Nay I am indignant that such a slave as thou, and one so worthy to have grown old and died in the tyrant's estate, just as thy father did, should be living here with us in mirth and luxury."

1126 *Philip Alone*
Plutarch, Titus Flaminius 17.2

Again, when he [Titus Flaminius] held his first conference with Philip concerning a truce and peace, and Philip remarked that Titus had come with many attendants while he himself had come alone, Titus answered, "Yes, thou hast made thyself alone by slaying thy friends and kindred."

1127 *Titus Rebukes Deinocrates the Messenian*
Plutarch, Titus Flaminius 17.3

Again, when Deinocrates the Messenian, who had taken too much wine at a drinking-party in Rome, and after putting on a woman's robe executed a dance, on the following day asked Titus to assist him in his plan to separate Messene from the Achaean league, Titus said he would consider the matter: "But I am amazed," said he, "that when thou hast matters of so great moment in hand thou canst dance and sing at a drinking-party."

1128 *Hannibal First of Generals*
Plutarch, Titus Flamininus 21.3–4

Moreover, we are told that the two men met again at Ephesus, and in the first place, that when, as they were walking about together, Hannibal took the side which more properly belonged to Scipio as the Superior, Scipio suffered it and walked about without paying any heed to it; and again, that when they fell to discussing generals and Hannibal declared Alexander to have been the mightiest of generals, and next to him Pyrrhus, and third himself, Scipio asked with a great smile, "And what wouldst thou have said if I had not conquered thee? To which Hannibal replied: "In that case, Scipio, I should not have counted myself third, but first of generals."[1]

1. Cf. Livy 35.14.

1129 *Commander Bitten*
Sifre, Deuteronomy 322

One time [when] a royal regiment was in Judea, a commander of horsemen ran after an Israelite on a horse in order to kill him, but he did not reach him. Before he reached him a snake bit [the commander] on the heel. [The Israelite] said to him: "Because we are strong, you are delivered into our hands. *Were it not that their rock had sold them.*" (Deut. 32:34).

1130   Augustus Abuses Captives
Suetonius, Lives of the Caesars, Augustus 2.13.1-2

He [Augustus] did not use his victory with moderation, but after sending Brutus' head to Rome, to be cast at the feet of Caesar's statue, he vented his spleen upon the most distinguished of his captives, not even sparing them insulting language. For instance, to one man who begged humbly for burial, he is said to have replied: "The birds will soon settle that question."

1131   Captives Abuse Augustus
Suetonius, Lives of the Caesars, Augustus 2.13.2

When two others, father and son, begged for their lives, he [Augustus] is said to have bidden them cast lots or play *mora*,[1] to decide which should be spared, and then to have looked on while both died, since the father was executed because he offered to die for his son, and the latter thereupon took his own life. Because of this the rest, including Marcus Favonius, the well-known imitator of Cato, saluted Antony respectfully as *Imperator*[2], when they were led out in chains, but lashed Augustus to his face with the foulest abuse.

> 1. A game still common in Italy, in which the contestants thrust out their fingers (*micare digitis*), the one naming correctly the number thrust out by his opponent being the winner.
> 2. The term applied to a victorious general by his soldiers.

1132   Augustus Sleeps until Signal
Suetonius, Lives of the Caesars, Augustus 2.16.1-2

The Sicilian war was among the first that he [Augustus] began, but it was long drawn out by many interruptions, now for the purpose of rebuilding his fleets, which he twice lost by shipwreck due to storms, and that, too, in the summer; and again by making peace at the demand of the people, when supplies were cut off and there was a severe famine. Finally, after new ships had been built and twenty thousand slaves set free and trained as oarsmen, he made the Julian harbor at Baiae by letting the sea into the Lucrine lake and lake Avernus. After drilling his forces there all winter, he defeated Pompey between Mylae and Naulochus, though just before the battle he was suddenly held fast by so deep a sleep that his friends had to awaken him to give the signal. And it was this, I think, that gave Antony opportunity for the taunt: "He could not even look with steady eyes at the fleet when it was ready for battle, but lay in a stupor on his back, looking up at the sky, and did not rise or appear before the soldiers until the enemy's ships had been put to flight by Marcus Agrippa."

1133   Augustus Sees King, Not Corpses
Suetonius, Lives of the Caesars, Augustus 2.18.1

About this time he [Augustus] had the sarcophagus and body of Alexander the Great brought forth from its shrine,[1] and after gazing on it, showed his respect by placing upon it a golden crown and strewing it with flowers; and being then asked whether he wished to see the tomb of the Ptolemies as well, he replied, "My wish was to see a king, not corpses."

> 1. The sacred precinct at Alexandria (Strabo, 17.1.8) containing the tombs of Alexander and of the kings.

1134 Stopping Evil
Suetonius, Lives of the Caesars, Augustus 2.51.2–3

Again, when he was hearing a case against Aemilius Aelianus of Corduba and it was made the chief offense, amongst other charges, that he was in the habit of expressing a bad opinion of Caesar, Augustus turned to the accuser with assumed anger and said: "I wish you could prove the truth of that. I'll let Aelianus know that I have a tongue as well as he, for I'll say even more about him"; and he made no further inquiry either at the time or afterwards. When Tiberius complained to him of the same thing in a letter, but in more forcible language, he replied as follows: "My dear Tiberius, do not be carried away by the ardor of youth in this matter, or take it too much to heart that anyone speak evil of me; we must be content if we can stop anyone from doing evil to us."

1135 Caligula Executes Sick Praetor
Suetonius, Lives of the Caesars, Caligula 4.29.2

An ex-praetor who had retired to Anticyra for his health sent frequent requests for an extention of his leave, but Caligula had him put to death, adding that a man who had not been helped by so long a course of hellebore needed to be bled.

1136 Caligula Tortures Hesitant Actor
Suetonius, Lives of the Caesars, Caligula 4.33.1

As a sample of his humor, he [Caligula] took his place beside a statue of Jupiter, and asked the tragic actor Apelles which of the two seemed to him the greater, and when he hesitated, Caligula had him flayed with whips, extolling his voice from time to time, when the wretch begged for mercy, as passing sweet even in his groans.

1137 Caligula Scorns Seneca
Suetonius, Lives of the Caesars, Caligula 4.53.2

When about to begin a harangue, he [Caligula] threatened to draw the sword of his nightly labors, and he had such scorn of a polished and elegant style that he used to say that Seneca, who was very popular just then, composed "mere school exercises," and that he was "sand without lime."

1138 Death Acceptable Excuse
Suetonius, Lives of the Caesars, Claudius 5.15.3

One man in making excuses for a witness that the emperor had summoned from one of the provinces, said that he could not appear, but for a long time would give no reason; at last, after a long series of questions, he said: "He's dead; I think the excuse is a lawful one."

1139 *Knight Admonished*
Suetonius, Lives of the Caesars, Claudius 5.16.1

Another [knight] who was notorious for corruption and adultery he [Claudius] merely admonished to be more restrained in his indulgence, or at any rate more circumspect, adding, "For why should I know what mistress you keep?"

1140 *Claudius Jests about Gladiator*
Suetonius, Lives of the Caesars, Claudius 5.21.5

When they called for Palumbus[1] he [Claudius] promised that they should have him, "if he could be caught."

> 1. "The Dove," nickname of a gladiator.

1141 *Claudius Devoted to Freedmen*
Suetonius, Lives of the Caesars, Claudius 5.28

But most of all [of his freedmen] he [Claudius] was devoted to his secretary Narcissus and his treasurer Pallas, and he gladly allowed them to be honored in addition by a decree of the senate, not only with immense gifts, but even with the insignia of quaestors and praetors. Besides this he permitted them to amass such wealth by plunder, that when he once complained of the low state of his funds, the witty answer was made that he would have enough and to spare, if he were taken into partnership by his two freedmen.

1142 *Thief Invited Back*
Suetonius, Lives of the Caesars, Claudius 5.32

When a guest was suspected of having stolen a golden bowl the day before, he [Claudius] invited him again the next day, but set before him an earthenware cup.

1143 *Claudius Remembers Cold Water*
Suetonius, Lives of the Caesars, Claudius 5.40.2

He [Claudius] gave us one of his reasons for supporting a candidate for the quaestorship, that the man's father had once given him cold water when he was ill and needed it.

1144 *No Flies with Domitian*
Suetonius, Lives of the Caesars, Domitian 8.3.1

At the beginning of his reign he [Domitian] used to spend hours in seclusion every day, doing nothing but catch flies and stab them with a keenly-sharpened stylus. Consequently when someone once asked whether anyone was in there with Caesar, Vibius Crispus made the witty reply: "Not even a fly."

1145 *Lamia Slain for Jests*
Suetonius, Lives of the Caesars, Domitian 8.10.2

He [Domitian] slew Aelius Lamia for joking remarks, which were reflections on him, it is true, but made long before and harmless. For when Domitian had taken away Lamia's wife, the latter replied to someone who praised his voice: "I practice continence"; and when Titus urged him to marry again, he replied: "Are you too looking for a wife?"

1146 Mockery of Galba

Suetonius, Lives of the Caesars, Galba 7.12.3

The following tales too were told in mockery of him, whether truly or falsely: that when an unusually elegant dinner was set before him, he [Galba] groaned aloud; that when his duly appointed steward presented his expense account, he handed him a dish of beans in return for his industry and carefulness; and that when the flute player Canus greatly pleased him, he presented him with five denarii, which he took from his own purse with his own hand.

1147 Soldier Slays Otho

Suetonius, Lives of the Caesars, Galba 7.19.2

When one of the soldiers had boasted that he had slain Otho, he [Galba] asked him, "On whose authority?"

1148 Jesting about Caesar

Suetonius, Lives of the Caesars, Julius 1.20.2

From that time on Caesar managed all the affairs of state alone and after his own pleasure; so that sundry witty fellows, pretending by way of jest to sign and seal testamentary documents, wrote "Done in the consulship of Julius and Caesar," instead of "Bibulus and Caesar," writing down the same man twice, by name and by surname. Presently too the following verses were on everyone's lips:
"In Caesar's year, not Bibulus', an act took place of late;
For naught do I remember done in Bibulus' consulate."

1149 Caesar and Nicomedes

Suetonius, Lives of the Caesars, Julius 1.49.1–4

There was no stain on his [Julius'] reputation for chastity except his intimacy with King Nicomedes, but that was a deep and lasting reproach, which laid him open to insults from every quarter. I say nothing of the notorious lines of Licinius Calvus:
"Whate'er Bithynia had, and Caesar's paramour."
I pass over, too, the invectives of Dolabella and the elder Curio, in which Dolabella calls him "the queen's rival, the inner partner of the royal couch," and Curio, "the brothel of Nicomedes and the stew of Bithynia." I take no account of the edicts of Bibulus, in which he posted his colleague as "the queen of Bithynia," saying that "of yore he was enamoured of a king, but now of a king's estate." At this same time, so Marcus Brutus declares, one Octavius, a man whose disordered mind made him somewhat free with his tongue, after saluting Pompey as "king" in a crowded assembly, greeted Caesar as "queen." But Gaius Memmius makes the direct charge that he acted as cup-bearer to Nicomedes with the rest of his wantons at a large dinner-party, and that among the guests were some merchants from Rome, whose names Memmius gives. Cicero, indeed, is not content with having written in sundry letters that Caesar was led by the king's attendants to the royal apartments, that he lay on a golden couch arrayed in purple, and that the virginity of this son of Venus was lost in Bithynia; but when Caesar was once addressing the senate in defense of Nysa, daughter of Nicomedes, and was enumerating his obligations to the king, Cicero cried: "No more of that, pray, for it is well known what he gave you, and what you gave him in turn." Finally, in his Gallic triumph

his soldiers, among the bantering songs which are usually sung by those who follow the chariot, shouted these lines, which became a by-word:

> "All the Gauls did Caesar vanquish, Nicodemus vanquished
>   him;
> Lo! now Caesar rides in triumph, victor over all the Gauls,
> Nicomedes does not triumph, who subdued the conquerer."

1150   *Caesar's Reputation for Vice*
Suetonius, Lives of the Caesars, Julius 1.52.3

But to remove all doubt that he [Julius] had an evil reputation both for shameless vice and for adultery, I have only to add that the elder Curio in one of his speeches calls him "every woman's man and every man's woman."

1151   *Self-Restraint of Caesar*
Suetonius, Lives of the Caesars, Julius 1.75.1

He [Julius] certainly showed admirable self-restraint and mercy, both in his conduct of the civil war and in the hour of victory. While Pompey announced that he would treat as enemies those who did not take up arms for the government, Caesar gave out that those who were neutral and of neither party should be numbered with his friends.

1152   *Arrogance of Caesar*
Suetonius, Lives of the Caesars, Julius 1.77.1

No less arrogant were his [Julius'] public utterances, which Titus Ampius records: that the state was nothing, a mere name without body or form; that Sulla did not know his ABC's when he laid down his dictatorship; that men ought now to be more circumspect in addressing him, and to regard his word as law. So far did he go in his presumption, that when a soothsayer once reported direful innards without a heart, he said: "They will be more favorable when I wish it; it should not be regarded as a portent, if a beast has no heart."[1]

> 1. Playing on the double meaning of *cor*, also regarded as the seat of intelligence.

1153   *Pontius Aquila Insults Caesar*
Suetonius, Lives of the Caesars, Julius 1.78.2

And this action of his seemed the more intolerable, because when he [Julius] himself in one of his triumphal processions rode past the benches of the tribunes, he was so incensed because a member of the college, Pontius Aquila by name, did not rise, that he cried: "Come then, Aquila, take back the republic from me, you tribune"; and for several days he would not make a promise to any one without adding, "That is, if Pontius Aquila will allow me."

1154a   *Not King, But Caesar*
Suetonius, Lives of the Caesars, Julius 1.79.2

But from that time on he [Julius] could not rid himself of the odium of having aspired to the title of monarch, although he replied to the commons, when they hailed him as king, "I am Caesar and no king,"[1] and at the Lupercalia, when the consul Antony several times attempted to place a crown upon his head as he spoke from the rostra, he put it aside and at last sent it to the Capitol, to be offered to Jupiter Optimus Maximus.

1. With a pun on *Rex* as a Roman name; cf. Horace, *Satires* 1.7.

1154b *Not King, But Caesar*
Plutarch, Caesar 60:1–4 (1–2)

But the most open and deadly hatred towards him [Caesar] was produced by his passion for the royal power. For the multitude this was a first cause of hatred, and for those who had long smothered their hate, a most specious pretext for it. And yet those who were advocating this honor for Caesar actually spread abroad among the people a report that from the Sibylline books it appeared that Parthia could be taken if the Romans went up against it with a king, but otherwise could not be assailed; and as Caesar was coming down from Alba into the city they ventured to hail him as king. But at this the people were confounded, and Caesar, disturbed in mind, said that his name was not King, but Caesar, and seeing that his words produced an universal silence, he passed on with no very cheerful or contented looks.

1155 *Nero and Helius*
Suetonius, Lives of the Caesars, Nero 6.23.1

To avoid being distracted or hindered in any way while busy with these contests, he [Nero] replied to his freedman Helius, who reminded him that the affairs of the city required his presence, in these words: "However much it may be your advice and your wish that I should return speedily, yet you ought rather to counsel me and to hope that I may return worthy of Nero."

1156 *Nero Insults Dead Claudius*
Suetonius, Lives of the Caesars, Nero 6.33.1

After Claudius' death he [Nero] vented on him every kind of insult, in act and word, charging him now with folly and now with cruelty; for it was a favorite joke of his to say that Claudius had ceased "to play the fool"[1] among mortals.

1. The pun on *morari*, "to linger, remain," and *morari*, "to play the fool," seems untranslatable.

1157 *Claudius Praises Otho*
Suetonius, Lives of the Caesars, Otho 7.1.3

Claudius also enrolled him [Otho] among the patricians, and after praising him in the highest terms, added these words: "a man of greater loyalty than I can even pray for in my own children."

1158 *Otho Dreams*
Suetonius, Lives of the Caesars, Otho 7.7.2

It is said that he [Otho] had a fearful dream that night, uttered loud groans, and was found by those who ran to his aid lying on the ground beside his couch; that he tried by every kind of expiatory rite to propitiate the shade of Galba, by whom he dreamt that he was ousted and thrown out; and that next day, as he was taking the auspices, a great storm arose and he had a bad fall, whereat he muttered from time to time:

"With long pipes what concern have I?"[1]

1. Proverb for undertaking something beyond one's powers. Cf. Cicero, *Ad Atticum* 2.16.

1159 *Tiberius Loathes Flattery*
Suetonius, Lives of the Caesars, Tiberius 3.27.1

He [Tiberius] so loathed flattery that he would not allow any senator to approach his litter, either to pay his respects or on business, and when an ex-consul in apologizing to him attempted to embrace his knees, he drew back in such haste that he fell over backward.

1160 *Jester Condemned*
Suetonius, Lives of the Caesars, Tiberius 3.57.2

When a funeral was passing by and a jester called aloud to the corpse to let Augustus know that the legacies which he had left to the people were not yet being paid, Tiberius had the man hauled before him, ordered that he be given his due and put to death, and bade him go tell the truth to his father.

1161 *Pompeius Threatened*
Suetonius, Lives of the Caesars, Tiberius 3.57.2

Shortly afterwards, when a Roman knight called Pompeius stoutly opposed some action in the senate, Tiberius threatened him with imprisonment, declaring that from a Pompeius he would make of him a Pompeian, punning cruelly on the man's name and the fate of the old party.

1162 *Carnulus Commits Suicide to Escape Execution*
Suetonius, Lives of the Caesars, Tiberius 3.61.5

Those who wished to die were forced to live; for he [Tiberius] thought death so light a punishment that when he heard that one of the accused, Carnulus by name, had anticipated his execution, he cried: "Carnulus has given me the slip."

1163 *Tiberius Refuses a Prisoner a Speedy Execution*
Suetonius, Lives of the Caesars, Tiberius 3.61.5

When he [Tiberius] was inspecting the prisons and a man begged for a speedy death, he replied: "I have not yet become your friend."

1164 *Go to Morbovia*
Suetonius, Lives of the Caesars, Vespasian 8.14

When he [Vespasian] was in terror at being forbidden Nero's court, and asked what on earth he was to do or where he was to go, one of the ushers put him out and told him to "go to Morbovia;"[1] But when the man later begged for forgiveness, Vespasian confined his resentment to words, and those of about the same number and purport.

1. A made-up name from *morbus* "illness", the expression is equivalent to "go to the devil."

1165 Fox Changes Fur
Suetonius, Lives of the Caesars, Vespasian 8.16.3

Some say that he [Vespasian] was naturally covetous and was taunted with it by an old herdsman of his, who on being forced to pay for the freedom for which he earnestly begged Vespasian when he became emperor, cried: "The fox changes his fur, but not his nature."

1166 Vespasian Feeds Commons
Suetonius, Lives of the Caesars, Vespasian 8.18

To a mechanical engineer, who promised to transport some heavy columns to the Capitol at small expense, he [Vespasian] gave no mean reward for his invention, but refused to make use of it, saying: "You must let me feed my poor commons."

1167 Vespasian's Strained Expression
Suetonius, Lives of the Caesars, Vespasian 8.20

He [Vespasian] was well built, with strong, sturdy limbs, and the expression of one who was straining. Apropos of which a witty fellow, when Vespasian asked him to make a joke on him also, replied rather cleverly: "I will, when you have finished relieving yourself."

1168 A Lesson in Pronunciation
Suetonius, Lives of the Caesars, Vespasian 8.22

When an ex-consul called Mestrius Florus called his attention to the fact that the proper pronunciation was plaustra[1] rather than plostra, he [Vespasian] greeted him next day as "Flaurus."

> 1. Plaustra was the urban form of the word for "wagons."

1169 A Passion for Vespasian
Suetonius, Lives of the Caesars, Vespasian 8.22

When he was importuned by a woman, who said that she was dying with love for him, he [Vespasian] took her to his bed and gave her four hundred thousand sesterces for her favors. Being asked by his steward how he would have the sum entered in his accounts, he replied: "To a passion for Vespasian."

1170 Cerylus Changes Names to Laches
Suetonius, Lives of the Caesars, Vespasian 8.23.1

And [Vespasian said] of the freedman Cerylus, who was very rich, and to cheat the privy purse of its dues at his death had begun to give himself out as freeborn, changing his name to Laches:

"O Laches, Laches,
When you are dead, you'll change your name at once
To Cerylus again."[1]

> 1. Menander, Fr. 223.2, Koch.

1171 Vespasian Appoints "Brother"
Suetonius, Lives of the Caesars, Vespasian 8.23.2

Having put off one of his favorite attendants, who asked for a stewardship for a pretended brother, he [Vespasian] summoned the candidate himself, and after compelling him to pay him as much money as he had agreed to give his advocate, appointed him to the position without delay. On his attendant's taking up the matter again, he said: "Find yourself another brother; the man that you thought was yours is mine."

1172 *Muleteer's Pay*
Suetonius, Lives of the Caesars, Vespasian 8.23.2

On a journey, suspecting that his muleteer had gone down to shoe the mules merely to make delay and give time for a man with a lawsuit to approach the emperor, he [Vespasian] asked how much he was paid for shoeing the mules and insisted on a share of the money.

1173 *Vespasian Interprets Omens*
Suetonius, Lives of the Caesars, Vespasian 8.23.3

For when among other portents the Mausoleum[1] opened on a sudden and a comet appeared in the heavens, he [Vespasian] declared that the former applied to Junia Calvina of the family of Augustus, and the latter to the king of the Parthians, who wore his hair long.

1. Of Augustus; see Suetonius, *Lives of the Caesars*, Augustus 2.100.4.

1174 *Helper Receives Wages*
Testament, Job 12:1–6 (4)

Occasionally a man would come to me cheerful at heart saying, "I am not well off enough to aid the destitute. Nevertheless I wish at least to serve the poor at your table." And when he was given permission, he would serve and eat. And when it was evening, when he was leaving for home, he would receive payment. And if he did not want to take it, he was compelled by me saying, "I know you are a laboring man welcoming and anticipating your wage, and you must accept it!" And I did not allow the wage earner's pay to remain with me in my house.

1175 *Lord Gives and Takes*
Testament, Job 19:1–4

Now when another messenger came and made clear to me the annihilation of my children, I was deeply disturbed and I ripped my clothes saying to the one who reported to me, "How then were you saved?" And then after I understood what had happened I cried out saying,

"The Lord gave, the Lord took away.
As it seemed good to the Lord, so also it happened.
May the name of the Lord be blessed."

1176 *Healing from the Lord*
Testament, Job 38:9 (6)–13b (13)

Then Sophar also replied and said,

"We are not searching for something beyond us, but we want to know if you possess a sound mind. And behold we truly know that your intelligence has not changed. What then do you want us to do for you? For behold, since we are traveling we have present with us our own physicians from our three kingdoms, and if you wish you may be treated by them likewise."

But I answered and said:

"My healing and treatment are from the Lord, who even created the physicians."

1177   Reuben and the Philosopher
Tosefta, Shebuot 3:6

One time R. Reuben spent the Sabbath in Tiberias, and one philosopher found him. He said to him: "Which is the one who is hated in the world?" [Reuben] said to him: "The one who denies his Creator." [The philosopher] said to him: "How [does he deny Him]?" [Reuben] said to him: "*Honor your father and your mother. Do not murder. Do not commit adultery. Do not steal. Do not bear false witness against your neighbor. Do not covet.* Behold, a man does not deny a thing until he denies [its] essential part. And a man commits a sin only after he has denied [the existence] of the one who commanded concerning it."

1178   Pharnabazus to Revolt or Serve
Xenophon, Agesilaus 3.5

And Pharnabazus too came and parleyed with Agesilaus, and made agreement with him that if he were not himself appointed the Persian general, he would revolt from the Great King. "But," he said, "if I become general, I shall make war on you, Agesilaus, with all my might."

1179   Agesilaus on a Ruler's Honor
Xenophon, Agesilaus 4.6

On receiving from Tithraustes an offer of gifts unnumbered if only he would leave his country, Agesilaus answered: "Among us, Tithraustes, a ruler's honor requires him to enrich his army rather than himself, and to take spoils rather than gifts from the enemy."

1180   Agesilaus Demands Proof of Friendship
Xenophon, Agesilaus 8.3

Thus, when the Persian envoy who came with Calleas, the Lacedaemonian, handed him a letter from the Great King containing offers of friendship and hospitality, he [Agesilaus] declined to accept it. "Tell his Majesty," he said to the bearer, "that there is no need for him to send me private letters, but, if he gives proof of friendship for Lacedaemon, and goodwill towards Greece, I on my part will be his friend with all my heart. But if he is found plotting against them, let him not hope to have a friend in me, however many letters I may receive."

1181   Making a Person a Politician
Xenophon, Memorabilia 1.6.15

On yet another occasion Antiphon [the Sophist] asked him [Socrates]: "How can you suppose that you make politicians of others, when you yourself avoid politics even if you understand them?" "How now, Antiphon?" he retorted, "should I play a more important part in politics, by engaging in them alone or by taking pains to turn out as many competent politicians as possible?"

1182 *No Pleasure in Eating*
Xenophon, Memorabilia 3.13.2

On another who declared that he found no pleasure in eating: "Acumenus," he [Socrates] said, "has a good prescription for that ailment." And when asked "What?" he answered, "Stop eating; and you will then find life pleasanter, cheaper, and healthier."

1183 *Dialogue on Washing and Eating*
Xenophon, Memorabilia 3.13.3

On yet another who complained that the drinking water at home was warm: "Consequently," he [Socrates] said, "when you want warm water to wash in, you will have it at hand." "But it's too cold for washing," objected the other. "Then do your servants complain when they use it both for drinking and washing?" "Oh no: indeed I have often felt surprised that they are content with it for both these purposes." "Which is the warmer to drink, the water in your house or Epidaurus water?"[1] "Epidaurus water." "And which is the colder to wash in, yours or Oropus water?"[2] "Oropus water." "Then reflect that you are apparently harder to please than servants and invalids."

1. The hot spring in the precincts of Asclepius' temple at Epidaurus.
2. The spring by the temple of Amphiaraus at Oropus in Boeotia.

1184 *Gaining Assent through Argument*
Xenophon, Memorabilia 4.6.15

Accordingly, whenever he [Socrates] argued, he gained a greater measure of assent from his hearers than any man I have known. He said that Homer gave Odysseus the credit of being "a safe speaker"[1] because he had a way of leading the discussion from one acknowledged truth to another.

1. Homer, *Odyssey* 8.171.

A leader or representative of a social group or type is present or referred to in the stories listed below, but some other feature has determined their location in another section.

Adult: Groups

Anecdotes of this type feature groups such as Atheneans, Spartans, Samaritans, Pharisees, Sadducees, Stoics, Ambassadors, Scribes, Judges, Farmers, and Senators. Groups in these narratives speak and act in unison. The interaction of individuals with representatives of the public sphere involves praise, censor, command, request, or appeal.

1185   *On Courage*
Cicero, De Officiis 1.19.62

But if the exaltation of spirit seen in times of danger and toil is devoid of justice and fights for selfish ends instead of for the common good, it is a vice; for not only has it no element of virtue, but its nature is barbarous and revolting to all our finer feelings. The Stoics, therefore, correctly define courage as "that virtue which champions the cause of right." Accordingly, no one has attained to true glory who has gained a reputation for courage by treachery and cunning; for nothing that lacks justice can be morally right.

1186   *A Spartan Responds to Athenians Ignoring an Old Man at a Play*
Cicero, De Senectute 18.63–64

For example, there is a story that when an old man entered the theater at Athens during the dramatic performances, not one of his countrymen in that vast crowd offered him a place; but when he came to the special seats occupied by the Lacedaemonians and assigned to them because they were ambassadors, all of them arose, it is said, and invited him to sit down. After this action had been greeted by the whole audience with repeated applause, one of the Spartans remarked: "These Athenians know what politeness is, but they won't practice it."

1187   *Xenocrates and the Ambassadors*
Cicero, Tusculan Disputations 5.32.91

When ambassadors brought fifty talents to Xenocrates[1] from Alexander, a large sum for those days, particularly at Athens, he carried off the ambassadors to sup with him in the Academy and put before them just enough to be sufficient, without any display. On their asking him the next day to whom he required them to count out the money: "What?" he said, "Did not yesterday's pot-luck show you that I have no need of money?" And when he saw their faces fall he accepted thirty minas to avoid appearing scornful of the king's generosity.

1. Cf. Cicero, *Tusculan Disputations* 1.20.

1188   *Solon Inflames Athenians*
Diogenes Laertius, Lives of the Eminent Philosophers 1.46–47

His [Solon's] greatest service was this: Megara and Athens laid rival claims to his birthplace Salamis, and after many defeats the Athenians passed a decree punishing with death any man who should propose a renewal of the Salaminian war. Solon, feigning madness, rushed into the Agora with a garland on his head; there he had his poem on Salamis read to the Athenians by the herald and roused them to fury. They renewed the war with the Megarians and, thanks to Solon, were victorious. These were the lines which did more than anything else to inflame the Athenians:

> Would I were citizen of some mean isle
> Far in the Sporades! For men shall smile
> And mock me for Athenian: "Who is this?"
> "An Attic slave who gave up Salamis";

and

> Then let us fight for Salamis and fair fame,
> Win the beloved isle, and purge our shame!

1189 *Diogenes Calls Demosthenes Demagogue*
Diogenes Laertius, Lives of the Eminent Philosophers 6.34

When some strangers expressed a wish to see Demosthenes, he [Diogenes] stretched out his middle finger and said, "There goes the demagogue of Athens."

1190 *Diogenes Urged to Be Initiated*
Diogenes Laertius, Lives of the Eminent Philosophers 6.39

The Athenians urged him [Diogenes] to become initiated, and told him that in the other world those who have been initiated enjoy a special privilege. "It would be ludicrous," quoth he, "if Agesilaus and Epaminondas are to dwell in the mire, while certain folk of no account will live in the Isles of the Blest because they have been initiated."

1191 *Better to Be a Megarian's Ram*
Diogenes Laertius, Lives of the Eminent Philosophers 6.41

At Megara he [Diogenes] saw the sheep protected by leather jackets, while the children went bare. "It's better," he said, "to be a Megarian's ram than his son."[1]

> 1. Where the wool was of fine quality, as near Tarentum (Horace, *Carmina* 2.6.10 *"pellitis ovibus"*), the fleeces were protected by coverings of skin, partly against damage from brambles and partly to preserve the color (Varro, *Rerum Rusticarum* 2.2). Cf. 805.

1192 *Sacrificing for a Son*
Diogenes Laertius, Lives of the Eminent Philosophers 6.63

Certain parents were sacrificing to the gods, that a son might be born to them. "But," said he [Diogenes], "do you not sacrifice to ensure what manner of man he shall turn out to be?"

1193 *Omens Too Trivial*
Eunapius, Lives of the Philosophers 466

In my researches concerning this man [Eustathius], I have come upon evidence of the following, namely that the whole of Greece prayed to see him and implored the gods that he might visit them. Moreover, the omens and those who were skilled to interpret them agreed that this would come to pass. But when they proved to be mistaken, for he did not visit Greece, the Greeks sent an embassy to him and chose for this embassy their most famous wise men. The purpose of their mission was to discuss with the renowned Eustathius this question: "Why did not the facts accord with these omens?" He listened to them, and then investigated and sifted the evidence of men who were famed in this science and had a wide renown, and cross-examined them, asking what was the size, color, and shape of the omens. Then, as his manner was, he smiled at them, on hearing the true facts (for as falsehood has no place in the choir of the gods,[1] so too it has none in their utterance), and said: "Nay, these omens did not foretell this visit from me." Then he said something that in my judgement was too high for a mere mortal, for this was his reply: "The omens revealed were too trivial and too tardy for such dignity as mine."

1. An echo of Plato, *Phaedrus* 247A; a rhetorical commonplace.

1194 *Two Dogs and a Wolf*
Frontinus, Stratagems 1.10.4

Scorylo, a chieftain of the Dacians, though he knew that the Romans were torn with the dissensions of the civil wars, yet did not think he ought to venture on any enterprise against them, inasmuch as a foreign war might be the means of uniting the citizens in harmony. Accordingly he pitted two dogs in combat before the populace, and when they became engaged in a desperate encounter, exhibited a wolf to them. The dogs straightway abandoned their fury against each other and attacked the wolf. By this illustration, Scorylo kept the barbarians from a movement which could only have benefited the Romans.

1195 *Soldiers Fight for All*
Frontinus, Stratagems 1.11.5

When Agesilaus, general of the Spartans, had his camp near the allied city of Orchomenos and learned that very many of his soldiers were depositing their valuables within their fortifications, he commanded the townspeople to receive nothing belonging to his troops, in order that his soldiers might fight with more spirit, when they realized that they must fight for all their possessions.[1]

1. Cf. Polyaenus 2.1.18.

1196 *Fabius Maximus Causes Famine*
Frontinus, Stratagems 3.4.1

Fabius Maximus, having laid waste the lands of the Campanians, in order that they might have nothing left to warrant the confidence that a siege could be sustained, withdrew at the time of the sowing, that the inhabitants might plant what seed they had remaining. Then, returning, he destroyed the new crop and thus made himself master of the Campanians, whom he had reduced to famine.[1]

1. 215 or 211 B.C.E. Cf.Livy 23.48.1–2 and 25.13.

1197a *Small Portion of Land*
Frontinus, Stratagems 4.3.12

When in honor of his defeat of the Sabines, the Senate offered Manius Curius a larger amount of ground than the discharged troops were receiving, he was content with the allotment of ordinary soldiers, declaring that that man was a bad citizen who was not satisfied with what the rest received.[1]

1. Cf. Valerius Maximus 4.3.5; Pliny, *Natural History* 18.4.

1197b *Small Portion of Land*

Plutarch, Moralia, Sayings of Romans III:194E (1)

When some complained against Manius Curius because he apportioned to each man but a small part of the land taken from the enemy, and made the most of it public land, he prayed that there might never be a Roman who would regard as small the land that gave him enough to live on.

1197c *Pittacus Content with One Hundred Acres*

Nepos 8, Thrasybulus 4.2

For Pittacus, who was numbered among the Seven Sages, well said, when the people of Mytilene wished to make him a present of many thousand acres of land: "Do not, I beg of you, give me a gift that may excite the jealousy of many and the cupidity of still more. But out of what you offer I desire no more than one hundred acres,[1] which will be a token of my moderation and your good-will."

> 1. According to Plutarch, Pittacus measured the amount which he would accept by the distance that he could hurl a spear.

1198 *Gaius Fabricius and the Samnites*

Gellius, Attic Nights 1.14.1–2

Julius Hyginus, in the sixth book of his work *On the Lives and Deeds of Famous Men*, says that a deputation from the Samnites came to Gaius Fabricius, the Roman general, and after mentioning his many important acts of kindness and generosity to the Samnites since peace was restored, offered him a present of a large sum of money, begging that he would accept and use it. And they said that they did this because they saw that his house and mode of life were far from magnificent, and that he was not so well provided for as his high rank demanded. Thereupon Fabricius passed his open hands from his ears to his eyes, then down to his nose, his mouth, his throat, and finally to the lower part of his belly; then he replied to the envoys: "So long as I can restrain and control all those members which I have touched, I shall never lack anything; therefore I cannot accept money, for which I have no use, from those who, I am sure, do have use for it."

1199 *Scipio Refuses to Give Account*

Gellius, Attic Nights 4.18.7–12

There is also another celebrated act of his [Scipio Africanus]. Certain Petilii, tribunes of the commons, influenced they say by Marcus Cato, Scipio's personal enemy, and instigated to appear against him, insisted most vigorously in the senate on his rendering an account of the money of Antiochus and of the booty taken in that war; for he had been deputy to his brother Lucius Scipio Asiaticus, the commander in that campaign. Thereupon Scipio arose, and taking a roll from the fold of his toga, said that it contained an account of all the money and all the booty; that he brought it to be publicly read and deposited in the treasury. "But that," said he, "I shall not do now, nor will I so degrade myself." And at once, before them all, he tore the roll across with his own hands and rent it into bits, indignant that an account of money taken in war should be required of him, to whose account the salvation of the Roman State and its power ought to be credited.

1200 Gnaeus Flavius Sits
Gellius, Attic Nights 7.9.5–6

"This same Gnaeus Flavius, son of Annius, is said to have come to call upon a sick colleague. When he arrived and entered the room, several young nobles were seated there. They treated Flavius with contempt and none of them was willing to rise in his presence. Gnaeus Flavius, son of Annius, the aedile, laughed at this rudeness; then he ordered his curule chair to be brought and placed it on the threshold, in order that none of them might be able to go out, and that all of them against their will might see him sitting on his chair of state."[1]

1. Aulus Gellius quotes this passage from Piso's *Annals*.

1201 Julianus Hears Rash Young Orator
Gellius, Attic Nights 9.15.1–11

With the rhetorician Antonius Julianus I had withdrawn to Naples during the season of the summer holidays, wishing to escape the heat of Rome. And there was there at the time a young man of the richer class studying with tutors in both languages, and trying to gain a command of Latin eloquence in order to plead at the bar in Rome; and he begged Julianus to hear one of his declamations. Julianus went to hear him and I went along with him. The young fellow entered the room, made some preliminary remarks in a more arrogant and presumptious style than became his years, and then asked that subjects for debate be given him. There was present there with us a pupil of Julianus, a man of ready speech and good ability, who was already offended that in the hearing of a man like Julianus the fellow should show such rashness and should dare to test himself in extempore speaking. Therefore, to try him, he proposed a topic for debate that was not logically constructed, of the kind which the Greeks call "unsolvable." The subject was this kind: "Seven judges are to hear the case of a defendant, and judgement is to be passed in accordance with the decision of a majority of their number. When the seven judges had heard the case, two decided that the defendant ought to be punished with exile; two, that he ought to be fined; the remaining three, that he should be put to death. The execution of the accused is demanded according to the decision of the three judges, but he appeals." As the young man had heard this, without any reflection and without waiting for other subjects to be proposed, he began at once with incredible speed to reel off all sorts of principles and apply them to that same question, pouring out floods of confused and meaningless words and a torrent of verbiage. All the other members of his company, who were in the habit of listening to him, showed their delight by loud applause, but Julianus blushed and sweat from shame and embarrassment. But when after many thousand lines of drivel the fellow at last came to an end and we went out, his friends and comrades followed Julianus and asked him for his opinion. Whereupon Julianus very wittily replied, "Don't ask me what I think; without controversy[1] this young man is eloquent."

1. *Sine controversia* is of course used in a double sense: "without question," and "without an opponent" (i.e., when there is no one to argue against him).

1202a On Toil and Shameful Pleasure
Gellius, Attic Nights, 16.1.3–4

Later I read that same sentiment in the speech of Marcus Cato which he delivered at Numantia to the Knights. Although it is expressed somewhat loosely and diffusely compared with the Greek which I have given, yet, since it is prior in time and more ancient, it ought to seem worthy of greater respect. The words in the speech are as follows: "Bear in mind, that if through toil you accomplish a good deed, that toil will quickly pass from you, the good deed will not leave you so long as you live; but if through pleasure you do anything dishonorable, the pleasure will quickly pass away, that dishonorable act will remain with you forever."

1202b *On Toil and Shameful Pleasure*
Gellius, Attic Nights 16.1.2

When I was still young and a schoolboy, I heard that this Greek sentiment which I have subjoined was uttered by the philosopher Musonius, and since it a true and brilliant saying, expressed briefly and roundly, I very willingly committed it to memory: "If you accomplish anything noble with toil, the toil passes, but the noble deed endures. If you do anything shameful with pleasure, the pleasure passes, but the shame endures."

1203a *Jesus Clears Temple*
Gospel, John 2:13–22 (NIV)

When it was almost time for the Jewish Passover, Jesus went up to Jerusalem. In the temple courts he found men selling cattle, sheep and doves, and others sitting at tables exchanging money. So he made a whip out of cords, and drove all from the temple area, both sheep and cattle; he scattered the coins of the money changers and overturned their tables. To those who sold doves he said, "Get these out of here! How dare you turn my Father's house into a market!" His disciples remembered that it is written: "Zeal for your house will consume me."[1] Then the Jews demanded of him, "What miraculous sign can you show us to prove your authority to do all this?" Jesus answered them, "Destroy this temple, and I will raise it again in three days." The Jews replied, "It has taken forty-six years to build this temple, and you are going to raise it in three days?"[2] But the temple he had spoken of was his body. After he was raised from the dead, his disciples recalled what he had said. Then they believed the Scripture and the words that Jesus had spoken.

1. Psalm 69:9.
2. Cf. Gospel, Thomas 71.

1203b *Jesus Clears Temple*
Gospel, Luke 19:45–46 (NIV)

Then he entered the temple area and began driving out those who were selling. "It is written," he said to them, "'My house will be a house of prayer'; but you have made it 'a den of robbers.'"

1. Isaiah 56:7; Jeremiah 7:11.

1203c *Jesus Clears Temple*
Gospel, Mark 11:15–18 (NIV)

On reaching Jerusalem, Jesus entered the temple area and began driving out those who were buying and selling there. He overturned the tables of the money changers and the benches of those selling doves, and would not allow anyone to carry merchandise through the temple courts. And as he taught them, he said, "Is it not written: "'My house will be called a house of prayer for all nations'? But you have made it 'a den of robbers.'" The chief priests and the teachers of the law heard this and began looking for a way to kill him, for they feared him, because the whole crowd was amazed at his teaching.

1203d *Jesus Clears Temple*
Gospel, Matthew 21:12–13 (NIV)

Jesus entered the temple area and drove out all who were buying and selling there. He overturned the tables of the money changers and the benches of those selling doves. "It is written," he said to them, "'My house will be called a house of prayer,' but you are making it a 'den of robbers.'"

1. Isaiah 56:7; Jeremiah 7:11.

1204 *Samaritans Believe*
Gospel, John 4:39–42 (NIV)

Many of the Samaritans from that town believed in him because of the woman's testimony, "He told me everything I ever did." So when the Samaritans came to him, they urged him to stay with them, and he stayed two days. And because of his words many more became believers. They said to the woman, "We no longer believe just because of what you said; now we have heard for ourselves, and we know that this man really is the Savior of the world."

1205a *Prophet Without Honor*
Gospel, John 4:43–45 (NIV)

After the two days he left for Galilee. (Now Jesus himself had pointed out that a prophet has no honor in his own country.[1]) When he arrived in Galilee, the Galileans welcomed him. They had seen all that he had done in Jerusalem at the Passover Feast, for they also had been there.

1. Cf. Gospel, Thomas 31.

1205b *Prophet Without Honor*
Gospel, Mark 6:1–6 (NIV)

Jesus left there and went to his hometown, accompanied by his disciples. When the Sabbath came, he began to teach in the synagogue, and many who heard him were amazed. "Where did this man get these things?" they asked. "What's this wisdom that has been given him, that he even does miracles! Isn't this the carpenter? Isn't this Mary's son and the brother of James, Joseph, Judas and Simon? Aren't his sisters here with us?" And they took offense at him. Jesus said to them, "Only in his hometown, among his relatives and in his own house is a prophet without honor." He could not do any miracles there except lay his hands on a few sick people and heal them. And he was amazed at their lack of faith.

1205c *Prophet Without Honor*
Gospel, Matthew 13:53–58 (NIV)

When Jesus had finished these parables, he moved on from there. Coming to his hometown, he began teaching the people in their synagogue, and they were amazed. "Where did this man get this wisdom and these miraculous powers?" they asked. "Isn't this the carpenter's son? Isn't his mother's name Mary, and aren't his brothers James, Joseph, Simon and Judas? Aren't all his sisters with us? Where then did this man get all these things?" And they took offense at him. But Jesus said to them, "Only in his hometown and in his own house is a prophet without honor." And he did not do many miracles there because of their lack of faith.

1206 *Judge with Right Judgment*
Gospel, John 7:14–24 (NIV)

Not until halfway through the Feast did Jesus go up to the temple courts and begin to teach. The Jews were amazed and asked, "How did this man get such learning without having studied?" Jesus answered, "My teaching is not my own. It comes from him who sent me. If anyone chooses to do God's will, he will find out whether my teaching comes from God or whether I speak on my own. He who speaks on his own does so to gain honor for himself, but he who works for the honor of the one who sent him is a man of truth; there is nothing false about him. Has not Moses given you the law? Yet not one of you keeps the law. Why are you trying to kill me?" "You are demon-possessed," the crowd answered. "Who is trying to kill you?" Jesus said to them, "I did one miracle, and you are all astonished. Yet, because Moses gave you circumcision (though actually it did not come from Moses, but from the patriarchs), you circumcise a child on the Sabbath. Now if a child can be circumcised on the Sabbath so that the law of Moses may not be broken, why are you angry with me for healing the whole man on the Sabbath? Stop judging by mere appearances and make a right judgment."

1207 *One with the Father*
Gospel, John 10:22–30 (NIV)

Then came the Feast of Dedication at Jerusalem. It was winter, and Jesus was in the temple area walking in Solomon's Colonnade. The Jews gathered around him, saying, "How long will you keep us in suspense? If you are the Christ, tell us plainly." Jesus answered, "I did tell you, but you do not believe because you are not my sheep. My sheep listen to my voice; I know them, and they follow me. I give them eternal life, and they shall never perish; no one can snatch them out of my hand. My Father, who has given them to me, is greater than all; no one can snatch them out of my Father's hand. I and the Father are one."

1208 *The Grain of Wheat*
Gospel, John 12:20–26 (NIV)

Now there were some Greeks among those who went up to worship at the Feast. They came to Philip, who was from Bethsaida in Galilee, with a request. "Sir" they said, "we would like to see Jesus." Philip went to tell Andrew; Andrew and Philip in turn told Jesus. Jesus replied, "The hour has come for the Son of Man to be glorified. I tell you the truth, unless a kernel of wheat falls to the ground and dies, it remains only a single seed. But if it dies, it produces many seeds. The man who loves his life will lose it, while the man who hates his life in this world will keep it for eternal life. Whoever serves me must follow me; and where I am, my servant also will be. My Father will honor the one who serves me.

1209 *The Seamless Tunic*
Gospel, John 19:23–25a (NIV)

When the soldiers crucified Jesus, they took his clothes, dividing them into four shares, one for each of them, with undergarment remaining. This garment was seamless, woven in one piece from top to bottom. "Let's not tear it," they said to one another. "Let's decide by lot who will get it." This happened that the scripture might be fulfilled which said, "They divided my garments among them and cast lots for my clothing."[1] So this is what the soldiers did. Near the cross of Jesus stood his mother, his mother's sister, Mary the wife of Clopas, and Mary Magdalene.

1. Psalm 22:18.

1210 *Pierced But No Bone Broken*
Gospel, John 19:31–37 (NIV)

Now it was the day of Preparation, and the next day was to be a special Sabbath. Because the Jews did not want the bodies left on the crosses during the Sabbath, they asked Pilate to have the legs broken and the bodies taken down. The soldiers therefore came and broke the legs of the first man who had been crucified with Jesus, and then those of the other. But when they came to Jesus and found that he was already dead, they did not break his legs. Instead, one of the soldiers pierced Jesus' side with a spear, bringing a sudden flow of blood and water. The man who saw it has given testimony, and his testimony is true. He knows that he tells the truth, and he testifies so that you also may believe. These things happened so that the scripture would be fulfilled: "Not one of his bones will be broken,"[1] and, as another scripture says, "They will look on the one they have pierced."[2]

1. Exodus 12:46.
2. Zechariah 12:10.

1211 *John Replies to Questioners*
Gospel, Luke 3:10–14 (NIV)

What should we do then?" the crowd asked. John answered, "The man with two tunics should share with him who has none, and the one who has food should do the same." Tax collectors also came to be baptized. "Teacher," they asked, "what should we do?" "Don't collect any more than you are required to," he told them. Then some soldiers asked him, "And what should we do?" He replied, "Don't extort money and don't accuse people falsely—be content with your pay."

1212 *Jesus Heals Paralytic*
Gospel, Luke 5:17–26 (NIV)

One day as he was teaching, Pharisees and teachers of the law, who had come from every village of Galilee and from Judea and Jerusalem, were sitting there. And the power of the Lord was present for him to heal the sick. Some men came carrying a paralytic on a mat and tried to take him into the house to lay him before Jesus. When they could not find a way to do this because of the crowd, they went up on the roof and lowered him on his mat through the tiles into the middle of the crowd, right in front of Jesus. When Jesus saw their faith, he said, "Friend, your sins are forgiven." The Pharisees and the teachers of the law began thinking to themselves, "Who is this fellow who speaks blasphemy? Who can forgive sins but God alone?" Jesus knew what they were thinking and asked, "Why are you think-ing these things in your hearts? Which is easier to say, 'Your sins are forgiven,' or to say, 'Get up and walk'? But that you may know that the Son of Man has authority on earth to forgive sins . . . ." He said to the paralyzed man, "I tell you, get up, take your mat and go home." Immediately he stood up in front of them, took what he had been lying on and went home praising God. Every one was amazed and gave praise to God. They were filled with awe and said, "We have seen remarkable things today."[1]

    1. Cf. 738; Mark 2:1–12; Matthew 9:1–8.

1213a *Physicians and the Sick*
Gospel, Luke 5:29–32 (NIV)

Then Levi held a great banquet for Jesus at his house, and a large crowd of tax collectors and others were eating with them. But the Pharisees and the teachers of the law who belonged to their sect complained to his disciples, "Why do you eat and drink with tax collectors and 'sinners'?" Jesus answered them, "It is not the healthy who need a doctor, but the sick. I have not come to call the righteous, but sinners to repentance."

1213b *Physicians and the Sick*
Gospel, Mark 2:15–17 (NIV)

While Jesus was having dinner at Levi's house, many tax collectors and "sinners" were eating with him and his disciples, for there were many who followed him. When the teachers of the law who were Pharisees saw him eating with the "sinners" and tax collectors, they asked his disciples: "Why does he eat with tax collectors and 'sinners'?" On hearing this, Jesus said to them, "It is not the healthy who need a doctor, but the sick. I have not come to call the righteous, but sinners."

1213c *Physicians and the Sick*
Gospel, Matthew 9:10–13 (NIV)

While Jesus was having dinner at Matthew's house, many tax collectors and "sinners" came and ate with him and his disciples. When the Pharisees saw this, they asked his disciples, "Why does your teacher eat with tax collectors and 'sinners'?" On hearing this, Jesus said, "It is not the healthy who need a doctor, but the sick. But go and learn what this means: 'I desire mercy, not sacrifice.'[1] For I have not come to call the righteous, but sinners."

    1. Hosea 6:6.

1213d *Physicians and the Sick*
Plutarch, Moralia, Sayings of Spartans III:230F (2)

When, in Tegea, after he [Pausanius] had been exiled,[1] he commended the Spartans, someone said, "Why did you not stay in Sparta instead of going into exile?" And he said, "Because physicians, too, are wont to spend their time, not among the healthy, but where the sick are."

    1. In 394 B.C.E.

1213e *Physicians and the Sick*
Diogenes Laertius, Lives of the Eminent Philosophers 6.6

One day when he [Antisthenes] was censured for keeping company with evil men, the reply he made was, "Physicians attend to their patients without getting the fever themselves."

1213f *Physicians and the Sick*
Diogenes Laertius, Lives of the Eminent Philosophers 2.70

In answer to one who remarked that he always saw philosophers at rich men's doors, he [Aristippus] said, "So, too, physicians are in attendance on those who are sick, but no one for that reason would prefer being sick to being a physician."

1214a *Man with the Withered Hand*
Gospel, Luke 6:6–11 (NIV)

On another Sabbath he went into the synagogue and was teaching, and a man was there whose right hand was shriveled. The Pharisees and the teachers of the law were looking for a reason to accuse Jesus, so they watched him closely to see if he would heal on the Sabbath. But Jesus knew what they were thinking and said to the man with the shriveled hand, "Get up and stand in front of everyone." So he got up and stood there. Then Jesus said to them, "I ask you which is lawful on the Sabbath: to do good or to do evil, to save life or to destroy it?" He looked around at them all, and then said to the man, "Stretch out your hand." He did so, and his hand was completely restored. But they were furious and began to discuss with one another what they might do to Jesus.

1214b *Healing of the Man with Dropsy*
Gospel, Luke 14:1–6 (NIV)

One Sabbath, when Jesus went to eat in the house of a prominent Pharisee, he was being carefully watched. There in front of him was a man suffering from dropsy. Jesus asked the Pharisees and experts in the law, "Is it lawful to heal on the Sabbath or not?" But they remained silent. So taking hold of the man, he healed him and sent him away. Then he asked them. "If one of you has a son or an ox that falls into a well on the Sabbath day, will you not immediately pull him out?" And they had nothing to say.

1214c *Man with a Withered Hand*
Gospel, Matthew 12:9–12 (NIV)

Going on from that place, he went into their synagogue, and a man with a shriveled hand was there. Looking for a reason to accuse Jesus, they asked him, "Is it lawful to heal on the Sabbath?" He said to them, "If any of you has a sheep and it falls into a pit on the Sabbath will you not take hold of it and lift it out? How much more valuable is a man than a sheep! Therefore it is lawful to do good on the Sabbath."

1214d *Man with the Withered Hand*
Gospel, Nazoreans 10

In the Gospel which the Nazarenes and the Ebionites use . . . the man who had the withered hand is described as a mason who pleaded for help as follows: I was a mason and earned my livelihood with my hands; I beg you, Jesus, restore my health that I may not have to beg for my bread in shame.

1215a *Jesus and John the Baptist*
Gospel, Luke 7:18–23 (NIV)

John's disciples told him about all these things. Calling two of them, he sent them to the Lord to ask, "Are you the one who was to come, or should we expect someone else?" When the men came to Jesus, they said, "John the Baptist sent us to you to ask, 'Are you the one who was to come, or should we expect someone else?'" At that very time Jesus cured many who had diseases, sicknesses and evil spirits, and gave sight to many who were blind. So he replied to the messengers, "Go back and report to John what you have seen and heard: The blind receive sight, the lame walk, those who have leprosy are cured, the deaf hear, the dead are raised, and the good news is preached to the poor. Blessed is the man who does not fall away on account of me."

    1. Cf. Isaiah 29:18–19; 35:5–6; 61:1.

1215b *Jesus and John the Baptist*
Gospel, Matthew 11:2–6 (NIV)

When John heard in prison what Christ was doing, he sent his disciples to ask him, "Are you the one who was to come, or should we expect someone else?" Jesus replied, "Go back and report to John what you hear and see: The blind receive sight, the lame walk, those who have leprosy are cured, the deaf hear, the dead are raised, and the good news is preached to the poor.[1] Blessed is the man who does not fall away on account of me."

1216 *Repent or Perish*
Gospel, Luke 13:1–9 (NIV)

Now there were some present at that time who told Jesus about the Galileans whose blood Pilate had mixed with their sacrifices. Jesus answered, "Do you think that these Galileans were worse sinners than all the other Galileans because they suffered this way? I tell you, no! But unless you repent, you too will all perish. Or those eighteen who died when the tower in Siloam fell on them—do you think they were more guilty than all the others living in Jerusalem? I tell you, no! But unless you repent, you too will all perish." Then he told this parable: "A man had a fig tree, planted in his vineyard, and he went to look for fruit on it, but did not find any. So he said to the man who took care of the vineyard, 'For three years now I've been coming to look for fruit on this fig tree and haven't found any. Cut it down! Why should it use up the soil?' "'Sir,' the man replied, 'leave it alone for one more year, and I'll dig around it and fertilize it. If it bears fruit next year, fine! If not, then cut it down.'"[1]

    1. Cf. Luke 6:43–45.

1217a *The Lament over Jerusalem*
Gospel, Luke 13:31–35 (NIV)

At that time some Pharisees came to Jesus and said to him, "Leave this place and go somewhere else. Herod wants to kill you." He replied, "Go tell that fox, 'I will drive out demons and heal people today and tomorrow, and on the third day I will reach my goal.' In any case, I must keep going today and tomorrow and the next day—for surely no prophet can die outside Jerusalem! "O Jerusalem, Jerusalem, you who kill the prophets and stone those sent to you, how often I have longed to gather your childrien together, as a hen gathers her chicks under her wings, but you were not willing! Look, your house is left to you desolate. I tell you, you will not see me again until you say, 'Blessed is he who comes in the name of the Lord.' "

1217b *The Lament over Jerusalem*
Gospel, Matthew 23:37–39 (NIV)

"O Jerusalem, Jerusalem, you who kill the prophets and stone those sent to you, how often I have longed to gather your children together, as a hen gathers her chicks under her wings, but you were not willing. Look, your house is left to you desolate. For I tell you, you will not see me again until you say, 'Blessed is he who comes in the name of the Lord.'"

1218a *Jesus Speaks in Parables*
Gospel, Luke 15:1–32 (NIV)

Now the tax collectors and "sinners" were all gathering around to hear him. But the Pharisees and the teachers of the law muttered, "This man welcomes sinners and eats with them." Then Jesus told them this parable: "Suppose one of you has a hundred sheep and loses one of them. Does he not leave the ninety-nine in the open country and go after the lost sheep until he finds it? And when he finds it, he joyfully puts it on his shoulders and goes home. Then he calls his friends and neighbors together and says, 'Rejoice with me; I have found my lost sheep.' I tell you that in the same way there will be more rejoicing in heaven over one sinner who repents than over ninety-nine righteous persons who do not need to repent.[1] "Or suppose a woman has ten silver coins and loses one. Does she not light a lamp, sweep the house and search carefully until she finds it? And when she finds it, she calls her friends and neighbors together and says, 'Rejoice with me; I have found my lost coin.' In the same way, I tell you, there is rejoicing in the presence of the angels of God over one sinner who repents." Jesus continued: "There was a man who had two sons. The younger one said to his father, 'Father, give me my share of the estate.' So he divided his property between them. "Not long after that, the younger son got together all he had, set off for a distant country and there squandered his wealth in wild living. After he had spent everything, there was a severe famine in that whole country, and he began to be in need. So he went and hired himself out to a citizen of that country, who sent him to his fields to feed pigs. He longed to fill his stomach with the pods that the pigs were eating, but no one gave him anything. "When he came to his senses, he said, 'How many of my father's hired men have food to spare, and here I am starving to death! I will set out and go back to my father and say to him: Father, I have sinned against heaven and against you. I am no longer worthy to be called your son; make me like one of your hired men.' So he got up and went to his father. "But while he was still a long way off, his father saw him and was filled with compassion for him; he ran to his son, threw his arms around him and kissed him. "The son said to him, 'Father, I have sinned against heaven and against you. I am no longer worthy to be called your son.' "But the father said to his servants, 'Quick! Bring the best robe and put it on him. Put a ring on his finger and sandals on his feet. Bring the fattened calf and kill it. Let's have a feast and celebrate. For this son of mine was dead and is alive again; he was lost and is found.' So they began to celebrate. Meanwhile, the older son was in the field. When he came near the house, he heard music and dancing. So he called one of the servants and asked him what was going on. Your brother has come,' he replied, 'and your father has killed the fattened calf because he has him back safe and sound.' "The older brother became angry and refused to go in. So his father went out and pleaded with him. But he answered his father, 'Look! All these years I've been slaving for you and never disobeyed your orders. Yet you never gave me even a young goat so I could celebrate with my friends. But when this son of yours who has squandered your property with prostitutes comes home, you kill the fattened calf for him!' "'My son,' the father said, 'you are always with me, and everything I have is yours. But we had to celebrate and be glad, because this brother of yours was dead and is alive again; he was lost and is found.'"

1. Cf. Gospel, Thomas 107.

1218b *Parable of the Lost Sheep*
Gospel, Matthew 18:12–14 (NIV)

"What do you think? If a man owns a hundred sheep, and one of them wanders away, will he not leave the ninety-nine on the hills and go to look for the one that wandered off? And if he finds it, I tell you the truth, he is happier about that one sheep than about the ninety-nine that did not wander off. In the same way your Father in heaven is not willing that any of these little ones should be lost."

1219a *Authority of Jesus Questioned*
Gospel, Luke 20:1–8 (NIV)

One day as he was teaching the people in the temple courts and preaching the gospel, the chief priests and the teachers of the law, together with the elders, came up to him. "Tell us by what authority you are doing these things," they said. "Who gave you this authority?" He replied, "I will also ask you a question. Tell me, John's baptism—was it from heaven or from men?" They discussed it among themselves and said, "If we say, 'From heaven,' he will ask, 'Why didn't you believe him?' But if we say, 'From men,' all the people will stone us, because they are persuaded that John was a prophet." So they answered, "We don't know where it was from." Jesus said, "Neither will I tell you by what authority I am doing these things."

1219b *Authority of Jesus Questioned*
Gospel, Mark 11:27–33 (NIV)

They arrived again in Jerusalem, and while Jesus was walking in the temple courts, the chief priests, the teachers of the law and the elders came to him. "By what authority are you doing these things?" they asked. "And who gave you authority to do this?" Jesus replied, "I will ask you one question. Answer me, and I will tell you by what authority I am doing these things. John's baptism—was it from heaven, or from men? Tell me!" They discussed it among themselves and said, "If we say, 'From heaven,' he will ask, 'Then why didn't you believe him?'" But if we say, 'From men' . . . ." (They feared the people, for everyone held that John really was a prophet.) So they answered Jesus, "We don't know." Jesus said, "Neither will I tell you by what authority I am doing these things."

1219c *Authority of Jesus Questioned*
Gospel, Matthew 21:23–27 (NIV)

Jesus entered the temple courts, and while he was teaching, the chief priests and the elders of the people came to him. "By what authority are you doing these things?" they asked. "And who gave you this authority?" Jesus replied, "I will also ask you one question. If you answer me, I will tell you by what authority I am doing these things. John's baptism—where did it come from?" Was it from heaven, or from men?" They discussed it among themselves and said, "If we say, 'From heaven,' he will ask, 'Then why didn't you believe him?' But if we say, 'From men'—we are afraid of the people, for they all hold that John was a prophet." So they answered Jesus, "We don't know." Then he said, "Neither will I tell you by what authority I am doing these things.

1220a *Resurrection and Marriage*
Gospel, Luke 20:27–40 (NIV)

Some of the Sadducees, who say there is no resurrection, came to Jesus with a question. "Teacher," they said, "Moses wrote for us that if a man's brother dies and leaves a wife but no children, the man must marry the widow and have children for his brother. Now there were seven brothers. The first one married a woman and died childless. The second and then the third married her, and in the same way the seven died, leaving no children. Finally, the woman died too. Now then, at the resurrection whose wife will she be, since the seven were married to her?" Jesus replied, "The people of this age marry and are given in marriage. But those who are considered worthy of taking part in that age and in the resurrection from the dead will neither marry nor be given in marriage, and they can no longer die; for they are like the angels. They are God's children, since they are children of the resurrection. But in the account of the bush, even Moses showed that the dead rise, for he calls the Lord 'the God of Abraham, and the God of Isaac, and the God of Jacob.'[1] He is not the God of the dead, but of the living, for to him all are alive." Some of the teachers of the law responded, "Well said, teacher!" And no one dared to ask him any more questions.

1. Exodus 3:2–16.

1220b *Resurrection and Marrriage*
Gospel, Mark 12:18–27 (NIV)

Then the Sadducees, who say there is no resurrection, came to him with a question. "Teacher," they said, "Moses wrote for us that if a man's brother dies and leaves a wife but no children, the man must marry the widow and have children for his brother. Now there were seven brothers. The first one married and died without leaving any children. The second one married the widow, but he also died, leaving no child. It was the same with the third. In fact, none of the seven left any children. Last of all, the woman died too. At the resurrection whose wife will she be, since the seven were married to her?" Jesus replied, "Are you not in error because you do not know the Scriptures or the power of God? When the dead rise, they will neither marry nor be given in marriage; they will be like the angels in heaven. Now about the dead rising—have you not read in the book of Moses, in the account of the bush, how God said to him, 'I am the God of Abraham, the God of Isaac, and the God of Jacob? He is not the God of the dead, but of the living. You are badly mistaken!"

1220c *Resurrection and Marriage*
Gospel, Matthew 22:23–33 (NIV)

That same day the Sadducees, who say there is no resurrection, came to him with a question. "Teacher," they said, "Moses told us that if a man dies without having children, his brother must marry the widow and have children for him. Now there were seven brothers among us. The first one married and died, and since he had no children, he left his wife to his brother. The same thing happened to the second and third brother, right on down to the seventh. Finally, the woman died. Now then, at the resurrection, whose wife will she be of the seven, since all of them were married to her?" Jesus replied, "You are in error because you do not know the Scriptures or the power of God. At the resurrection people will neither marry nor be given in marriage; they will be like the angels in heaven. But about the resurrection of the dead—have you not read what God said to you, 'I am the God of Abraham, the God of Isaac, and the God of Jacob'? He is not the God of the dead but of the living." When the crowds heard this they were astonished at his teaching.

1221a *Question about David's Son*
Gospel, Luke 20:41–44 (NIV)
Then Jesus said to them, "How is it that they say the Christ is the Son of David? David himself declares in the Book of Psalms:
"'The Lord said to my Lord:
"Sit at my right hand
until I make your enemies
a footstool for your feet."'[1]
David calls him 'Lord.' How then can he be his son?"

1. Psalm 110:1.

1221b *Question about David's Son*
Gospel, Mark 12:35–37 (NIV)
While Jesus was teaching in the temple courts, he asked, "How is it that the teachers of the law say that the Christ is the son of David? David himself, speaking by the Holy Spirit, declared:
"'The Lord said to my Lord:
"Sit at my right hand
until I put your enemies
under your feet."'
David himself calls him 'Lord.' How then can he be his son?" The large crowd listened to him with delight.

1221c *Question about David's Son*
Gospel, Matthew 22:41–45 (NIV)
While the Pharisees were gathered together, Jesus asked them, "What do you think about the Christ? Whose son is he?" "The son of David," they replied. He said to them, "How is it then that David, speaking by the Spirit, calls him 'Lord'? For he says,
'The Lord said to my lord:
"Sit at my right hand
until I put your enemies
under your feet."'
If then David calls him 'Lord,' how can he be his son?" No one could say a word in reply, and from that day on no one dared to ask him any more questions.

1222a *Man with an Unclean Spirit*
Gospel, Mark 1:21–28 (NIV)
They went to Capernaum, and when the Sabbath came, Jesus went into the synagogue and began to teach. The people were amazed at his teaching, because he taught them as one who had authority, not as the teachers of the law. Just then a man in their synagogue who was possessed by an evil spirit cried out, "What do you

want with us, Jesus of Nazareth? Have you come to destroy us? I know who you are—the Holy One of God?" "Be quiet!" said Jesus sternly. "Come out of him!" The evil spirit shook the man violently and came out of him with a shriek. The people were all so amazed that they asked each other, "What is this? A new teaching—and with authority! He even gives orders to evil spirits and they obey him." News about him spread quickly over the whole region of Galilee.

1222b *Man with Unclean Spirit*
Gospel, Luke 4:31–37 (NIV)

Then he went down to Capernaum, a town in Galilee, and on the Sabbath began to teach the people. They were amazed at his teaching, because his message had authority. In the synagogue there was a man possessed by a demon, an evil spirit. He cried out at the top of his voice, "Ha! What do you want with us, Jesus of Nazareth? Have you come to destroy us? I know who you are—the Holy One of God!" "Be quiet!" Jesus said sternly. "Come out of him!" Then the demon threw the man down before them all and came out without injuring him. All the people were amazed and said to each other, "What is this teaching? With authority and power he gives orders to evil spirits and they come out!" And the news about him spread throughout the surrounding area.

1223a *Plucking Grain on the Sabbath*
Gospel, Mark 2:23–28 (NIV)

One Sabbath Jesus was going through the grainfields, and as his disciples walked along, they began to pick some heads of grain. The Pharisees said to him, "Look, why are they doing what is unlawful on the Sabbath?" He answered, "Have you never read what David did when he and his companions were hungry and in need? In the days of Abiathar the high priest, he entered the house of God and ate the consecrated bread, which is lawful only for priests to eat.[1] And he also gave some to his companions." Then he said to them, "The Sabbath was made for man, not man for the Sabbath. So the Son of Man is Lord even of the Sabbath."[2]

1. 1 Samuel 21:1–6.
2. Cf. Gospel, Thomas 27.

1223b *Plucking Grain on the Sabbath*
Gospel, Luke 6:1–5 (NIV)

One Sabbath Jesus was going through the grainfields, and his disciples began to pick some heads of grain, rub them in their hands and eat the kernels. Some of the Pharisees asked, "Why are you doing what is unlawful on the Sabbath?" Jesus answered them, "Have you never read what David did when he and his companions were hungry? He entered the house of God, and taking the consecrated bread, he ate what is lawful only for priests to eat. And he also gave some to his companions." Then Jesus said to them, "The Son of Man is Lord of the Sabbath."

1223c *Plucking Grain on the Sabbath*
Gospel, Matthew 12:1–8 (NIV)

At that time Jesus went through the grainfields on the Sabbath. His disciples were hungry and began to pick some heads of grain and eat them. When the Pharisees saw this, they said to him, "Look! Your disciples are doing what is unlawful on the Sabbath." He answered, "Haven't you read what David did when he and his companions were hungry? He entered the house of God, and he and his companions ate the consecrated bread—which was not lawful for them to do, but only for the priests.[1] Or haven't you read in the Law that on the Sabbath the priests in the temple desecrate the day and yet are innocent?[2] I tell you that one greater than the temple is here. If you had know what these words mean, 'I desire mercy, not sacrifice,'[3] you would not have condemned the innocent. For the Son of Man is Lord of the Sabbath."

1. 1 Samuel 21:1-6.
2. Numbers 28:9-10.
3. Hosea 6:6.

1224   *Multitude at the Seaside*
Gospel, Mark 3:7-12 (NIV)

Jesus withdrew with his disciples to the lake, and a large crowd from Galilee followed. When they heard all he was doing, many people came to him from Judea, Jerusalem, Idumea, and the regions across the Jordan and around Tyre and Sidon. Because of the crowd he told his disciples to have a small boat ready for him, to keep the people from crowding him. For he had healed many, so that those with diseases were pushing forward to touch him. Whenever the evil spirits saw him, they fell down before him and cried out, "You are the Son of God." But he gave them strict orders not to tell who he was.

1225a   *Teaching about Divorce*
Gospel, Mark 10:2-9 (NIV)

Some Pharisees came and tested him by asking, "Is it lawful for a man to divorce his wife?" "What did Moses command you?" he replied. They said, "Moses permitted a man to write a certificate of divorce and send her away."[1] It was because your hearts were hard that Moses wrote you this law," Jesus replied. "But at the beginning of creation God 'made them male and female.'[2] 'For this reason a man will leave his father and mother and be united to his wife, and the two will become one flesh.[3] So they are no longer two, but one. Therefore what God has joined together, let man not separate."

1. Deuteronomy 24:1-4.
2. Genesis 1:27.
3. Genesis 2:24.

1225b   *Teaching about Divorce*
Gospel, Matthew 19:1-6 (NIV)

When Jesus had finished saying these things, he left Galilee and went into the region of Judea to the other side of the Jordan. Large crowds followed him, and he healed them there. Some Pharisees came to him to test him. They asked, "Is it lawful for man to divorce his wife for any and every reason?" "Haven't you read," he replied, "that at the beginning the Creator 'made them male and female,' and said, 'For this reason a man will leave his father and mother and be united to his wife, and the two will become one flesh'? So they are no longer two, but one. Therefore what God has joined together, let man not separate."

1226   *John Condemns the Pharisees and Sadducees*
Gospel, Matthew 3:7-10 (NIV)

But when he [John] saw many of the Pharisees and Sadducees coming to where he was baptizing, he said to them: "You brood of vipers! Who warned you to flee from the coming wrath? Produce fruit in keeping with repentance. And do not think you can say to yourselves, 'We have Abraham as our father.' I tell you that out of these stones God can raise up children for Abraham. The ax is already at the root of the trees, and every tree that does not produce good fruit will be cut down and thrown into the fire."[1]

1. Cf. Luke 3:7–9.

1227 Woe on Unrepentant Cities
Gospel, Matthew 11:20–24 (NIV)

Then Jesus began to denounce the cities in which most of his miracles had been performed, because they did not repent. "Woe to you, Korazin! Woe to you, Bethsaida! If the miracles that were performed in you had been performed in Tyre and Sidon, they would have repented long ago in sackcloth and ashes.[1] But I tell you, it will be more bearable for Tyre and Sidon on the day of judgment than for you. And you, Capernaum, will you be lifted up to the skies? No, you will go down to the depths. If the miracles that were performed in you had been performed in Sodom, it would have remained to this day. But I tell you that it will be more bearable for Sodom on the day of judgment than for you."[2]

1. Cf. Gospel, Nazoreans 27.
2. Cf. Luke 10:12–15.

1228a Tradition of the Elders
Gospel, Matthew 15:1–11 (NIV)

Then some Pharisees and teachers of the law came to Jesus from Jerusalem and asked, "Why do your disciples break the tradition of the elders? They don't wash their hands before they eat!" Jesus replied, "And why do you break the command of God for the sake of your tradition? For God said, 'Honor your father and mother' and 'Anyone who curses his father or mother must be put to death.'[1] But you say that if a man says to his father or mother, 'Whatever help you might otherwise have received from me is a gift devoted to God,' he is not to 'honor his father' with it. Thus you nullify the word of God for the sake of your tradition. You hypocrites! Isaiah was right when he prophesied about you: "'These people honor me with their lips, but their hearts are far from me. They worship me in vain; their teachings are but rules taught by men.'"[2] Jesus called the crowd to him and said, "Listen and understand. What goes into a man's mouth does not make him 'unclean,' but what comes out of his mouth, that is what makes him 'unclean.'"

1. Exodus 20:12; Deuteronomy 5:16; Exodus 21:17; Leviticus 20:9.
2. Isaiah 29:13.

1228b Tradition of the Elders
Gospel, Mark 7:1–8 (NIV)

The Pharisees and some of the teachers of the law who had come from Jerusalem gathered around Jesus and saw some of his disciples eating food with hands that were "unclean," that is, unwashed. (The Pharisees and all the Jews do not eat unless they give their hands a ceremonial washing, holding to the tradition of the elders. When they come from the marketplace they do not eat unless they wash. And they observe many other traditions, such as the washing of cups, pitchers and kettles.) So the Pharisees and teachers of the law asked Jesus, "Why don't your disciples live according to the tradition of the elders instead of eating their food with 'unclean' hands?" He replied, "Isaiah was right when he prophesied about you hypocrites; as it is written: "'These people honor me with their lips, but their hearts are far from me. They worship me in vain; their teachings are but rules taught by men.' You have let go of the commands of God and are holding on to the traditions of men."

1229 *The Children's Confession*
Gospel, Matthew 21:14–16 (NIV)

The blind and the lame came to him at the temple, and he healed them. But when the chief priests and the teachers of the law saw the wonderful things he did and the children shouting in the temple area, "Hosanna to the Son of David," they were indignant. "Do you hear what these children are saying?" they asked him. "Yes," replied Jesus, "have you never read, "'From the lips of children and infants you have ordained praise'?"[1]

1. Psalm 8:2.

1230 *Two Young Men Fight*
Hadith, Muslim, al-birr wa-l-ṣila wa-l-ādāb, 16

Aḥmad b. 'Abd Allāh b. Yūnus, Zuhayr and Abū al-Zubayr related from Jābir, who said: Two young men were fighting, one from the Emigrants and one from the Helpers. The Emigrant called to his fellow Emigrants, and the Helper called to his fellow Helpers. Then the Messenger of God went out to them and said, "What is this, proceedings of the Time of Ignorance?" They said, "No, O Messenger of God, it is just that two young men were fighting and one of them hit the other on his back." Then he said, "Well, that is not so bad, but a man should help his brother, whether he is doing wrong or has been wronged. If his brother is doing wrong then he should hinder him from doing so. That is his help. If the brother has been wronged then he should help to obtain justice for him."

1231 *Death Only Way to Pacify People*
Josephus, Jewish War 1.91–92 (4, 4)

His victories, however, by which he [Alexander Jannaeus] wasted his realm brought him little satisfaction; desisting, therefore, from hostilities, he endeavored to conciliate his subjects by persuasion. But his change of policy and inconsistency of character only aggravated their hatred; and when he inquired what he could do to pacify them, they replied "Die; even death would hardly reconcile us to one guilty of your enormities."

1232 *Young Men Exult in Death*
Josephus, Jewish War 1. 651–653 (33.3)

While they [the doctors of the law] were discoursing in this strain, a rumor spread that the king [Herod] was dying; the news caused the young men to throw themselves more boldly into the enterprise. At mid-day, accordingly, when numbers of people were perambulating the temple, they let themselves down from the roof by stout cords and began chopping off the golden eagle with hatchets. The king's captain,[1] to whom the matter was immediately reported, hastened to the scene with a considerable force, arrested about forty of the young men and conducted them to the king. Herod first asked them whether they had dared to cut down the golden eagle; they admitted it. "Who ordered you to do so?" he continued. "The law of our fathers." "And why so exultant, when you will shortly be put to death?" "Because, after our death, we shall enjoy greater felicity."

1. Perhaps "the captain of the Temple" is intended (cf. Acts 4:1; 5:24).

1233 *Fortune an Imaginary Blessing*
Lucian, Demonax 8

Some of them, who were seemingly favored by fortune, he [Demonax] reminded that they were elated over imaginary blessings of brief span.

1234 *Misfortune Ends in Time*
Lucian, Demonax 8

Others, who were bewailing poverty, fretting at exile or finding fault with old age or sickness, he [Demonax] laughingly consoled, saying that they failed to see that after a little while they would have surcease of worries and would find oblivion of their fortunes, good and bad, and lasting liberty.

1235 *Demonax, Athena, and the Mysteries*
Lucian, Demonax 11

Hence all Athens, high and low, admired him [Demonax] enormously and always viewed him as a superior being. Yet in office he ran counter to public opinion and won from the masses quite as much hatred as his prototype[1] by his freedom of speech and action. He too had his Anytus and his Meletus who combined against him and brought the same charges that their predecessors brought against Socrates, asserting that he had never been known to sacrifice and was the only man in the community uninitiated in the Eleusinian mysteries. In reply to this, with right good courage he wreathed his head, put on a clean cloak, went to the assembly and made his defense, which was in part good-tempered, in part more caustic than accorded with his scheme of life. Regarding his never having offered sacrifice to Athena, he said: "Do not be surprised, men of Athens, that I have not hitherto sacrificed to her: I did not suppose that she had any need of my offerings." Regarding the other charge, the matter of the mysteries, he said that he had never joined them in the rite because if the mysteries were bad, he would not hold his tongue before the uninitiate but would turn them away from the cult, while if they were good, he would reveal them to everybody out of his love for humanity. So the Athenians, who already had stones in both hands to throw at him, became good-natured and friendly toward him at once, and from that time on they honored, respected and finally admired him. Yet in the very beginning of his speech he had used a pretty caustic introduction, "Men of Athens, you see me ready with my garland: come, sacrifice me like your former victim, for on that occasion your offering found no favor with the gods!"

1. Socrates.

1236 *The Mysteries and Foreigners*
Lucian, Demonax 34

Once, on hearing the proclamation which precedes the mysteries, he [Demonax] made bold to ask the Athenians publicly why they exclude foreigners, particularly as the founder of the rite, Eumolpus, was a foreigner and a Thracian to boot!

1237 *Athletes Called Lions*
Lucian, Demonax 49

When he [Demonax] saw many of the athletes fighting foul and breaking the rules of the games by biting instead of boxing, he said: "No wonder the athletes of the present day are called 'lions' by their hangers-on!"

1238 *Pretty Late for Honoring Cynegirus*
Lucian, Demonax 53

On seeing near the Painted Porch a statue with its hand cut off, he [Demonax] remarked that it was pretty late in the day for the Athenians to be honoring Cynegirus[1] with a bronze statue.

> 1. Brother of Aeschylus, who lost his hand at Marathon, and the Painted Porch was so called from a fresco by Polygnotus representing the battle.

1239 *The Gladiatorial Show*
Lucian, Demonax 57

When the Athenians, out of rivalry with the Corinthians, were thinking of holding a gladiatorial show, he [Demonax] came before them and said: "Don't pass this resolution, men of Athens, without first pulling down the altar of Mercy."

1240 *The Bronze Statue*
Lucian, Demonax 58

When he [Demonax] went to Olympia and the Eleans voted him a bronze statue, he said, "Don't do this, men of Elis, for fear you may appear to reflect on your ancestors because they did not set up statues either to Socrates or to Diogenes."

1241 *Dancing as Madman*
Macrobius, Saturnalia 2.7.16

Once, when Pylades had come on to dance *Hercules the Madman*, some of the spectators thought that he was not keeping to action suited to the stage. Whereupon he took off his mask and turned on his critics with the words: "Fools, my dancing is intended to represent a madman."[1]

> 1. Cf. Lucian, *Of Pantomime* 83.

1242 *Phocion's Moderation*
Nepos 19, Phocion 1.2–4

In fact, he [Phocion] was always in moderate circumstances, although he might have acquired great wealth because of the frequent offices and commissions which the people conferred upon him. When he had refused the gift of a large sum of money from King Philip, the king's envoys urged him to take it, at the same time reminding him that even if he himself could readily do without such things, yet he ought to consider his children, who would find it difficult with narrow means to live up to the great glory inherited from their father. But he replied to them: "If they are like me, they will live on this same little farm which has brought me to my present rank; but if they are going to be different, I do not wish their luxury to be nourished and grow at my expense."[1]

> 1. That is, at the expense of his good name.

1243 *Jesus Confronts Lawyers and Rulers*
Papyrus Egerton 2, 1 verso 1–19 (Mayeda: 27–28)

[And Jesus said] to the lawyers, "[Punish] everyone who transgresses [against the law] and not me, [for he (the transgressor) does not know] how he does what he does." [And he turned to the] rulers of the people and spoke this saying, "[Search] the scriptures in which you think you have life. These are [the ones which] testify concerning me. Do not think that I have come to accuse [you] to my Father. Moses is [he who] accuses you, on whom you have set your hope." And when they said, "We know indeed that God spoke to Moses, but we do not know [where you are from]," Jesus answered and said, "Now your unbelief is accursed. . . ."

1244 *From Cobbler to Physician*
Phaedrus, Aesopic Fables 1.14

A bungling cobbler, desperately in want, had resorted to practicing medicine in a strange locality, and peddling what he falsely called an "antidote," built up a reputation for himself by verbal tricks of advertising. So it happened that when <the king's minister> lay gravely ill and all but gone, <our physician was called in. Whereupon> the king of the city, to test his skill, called for a cup; then pouring water into it, but pretending to mix poison with the "antidote," he ordered the man to drink it off himself, for a reward that he displayed. In mortal fear the cobbler then confessed that his high standing as a physician was not due to any knowledge of the art but to the gullibility of the crowd. The king then summoned an assembly and said to the people: "How crazy you are, you may judge for yourselves. You have no hesitation about putting your lives at the mercy of a man to whose care no one in want of shoes ever trusted his feet." This, I dare say, strikes home at those whose gullibility provides an income for impostors.

1245 *The Panther and the Shepherds*
Phaedrus, Aesopic Fables 3.2

Those who are scorned usually pay in the same coin. Once a panther inadvertently fell into a pit. The country people saw her there. Some of them brought clubs, others piled stones on her; still others felt sorry for her, as being likely to die, though no one harmed her, and these tossed bread to her that she might keep herself alive. Night came on and the men went home unconcerned, thinking that they would find her dead on the following day. But the panther, having recruited her failing strength, with a quick leap freed herself from the pit and hastened to her lair at a swift pace. After a few days she sallied forth again, slaughtered the sheep and killed the shepherds themselves, and laid everything to waste in the exercise of her violent and savage fury. Hereupon even those who had spared the beast began to be afraid for themselves; they made no complaint about lost property but only begged for their lives. But she said to them: "I remember who attacked me with stones, and who gave me bread. As for you, cease to be afraid; I return as an enemy only to those who injured me."

1246 *The Ass and the Priests of Cybele*
Phaedrus, Aesopic Fables 4.1

Whoever is born to ill luck not only runs out the course of life in sorrow but is also dogged after death by the hard misery of his fate. The Galli, priests of Cybele, on their begging circuits used to take an ass around with them as porter for their luggage. When this ass was dead from overwork and beating they stripped off his hide and made themselves tambourines of it. Afterwards, when they were asked by someone what they had done with their pet, this is how they put it: "He thought that after death he would rest in peace, but, behold, new blows are heaped upon him, dead though he is."

1247 *On Fortune*
Phaedrus, Aesopic Fables 4.18

When a certain man was complaining about his ill fortune, Aesop invented the following story to comfort him. A ship had been badly tossed about by fierce storms so that its passengers were in tears and fear of death, when suddenly the weather changed and took on a serene aspect; the ship began to ride safely, borne along by favorable winds, which raised the spirits of the sailors to an excessive pitch of joy. Hereupon the pilot, made wise by danger in the past, remarked: "One must be cautious in rejoicing and slow to complain, for the whole of life is a blend of grief and joy."

1248 *The Buffoon and the Country Fellow*
Phaedrus, Aesopic Fables 5.5

Through perverse partiality men often go wrong and, while standing up for an opinion founded on their own error, are compelled by plain facts to regret their mistake. A rich man, about to put on some splendid shows, invited everybody by promise of reward to exhibit whatever new attraction each one could. Professional actors entered this contest, competing for fame. Among them was a buffoon, well known for his urban wit, who announced that he had a kind of exhibition that had never yet been presented on any stage. The rumor spreading stirred up much excitement in the city. Seats that had formerly been left empty now proved insufficient to accommodate the crowd. When he actually took his place on the stage, alone, without any equipment and without any helpers, anticipation automatically hushed the crowd. Suddenly he lowered his head into his bosom and with his own voice imitated that of a pig so well that spectators insisted that there was a real pig beneath his cloak and demanded that the cloak be shaken out. When this was done and nothing was found they loaded the man with many praises and honored him with the greatest applause. A country fellow saw this happening and said: "By George, he won't win against me," and at once offered to do the same thing better the next day. An even greater crowd assembled. By this time their minds were obsessed with partisanship. You could see that they came to jeer, not to judge the quality of the performance. Both actors came forth on the stage. First the buffoon ran through his scale of squeals, started the audience applauding, and stirred them to cheers. Then the country fellow, pretending that he had a pig hidden under his clothes—as of course he had, although no one noticed it, since no pig was found the day before—gave a good tug at the ear of the real pig that he had hidden there, and, because it hurt, the voice of nature was perforce evoked. The crowd roared that the buffoon had given a much better imitation, and they would have had the rustic hustled off the stage. But he confronted them with the real pig from the folds of his cloak and by clear evidence exposed their shameful mistake. "Look," said he, "this pig makes it plain what kind of judges you are!"

1249 *Diogenes Elicits Food from Captors*
Philo, Every Good Man Is Free 121

Thus it was with the cynic philosopher Diogenes. So great and lofty was his spirit, that when captured by robbers, who grudgingly provided him with the barest minimum of food, he still remained unmoved by his present position and had no fear of the cruelty of those who held him in their power. "It is surely very preposterous," he said, "that while sucking pigs and sheep when they are going to be sold are fed up with greater care to make them fat and well favored, man the best of animals should be reduced to a skeleton by want of food and constant privations and so fetch a lower price," and then received adequate allowances of food.

1250 *Chief Men Laud Abraham in His Grief*
Philo, On Abraham 260–261

Now, when the chief men of the country came to sympathize [at the death of Abraham's wife] and saw nothing of the sort of mourning which was customary with themselves, no wailing, no chanting of dirges, no beating of breasts either of men or of women, but a quiet sober air of sorrow pervading the whole house, they were profoundly amazed, though indeed the rest of his life had struck them with admiration. Then, as the greatness and glory of his virtue in all its pre-eminence were more than they could keep to themselves, they approached him and exclaimed: "Thou art a king from God among us."

1251 *Apollonius at the Temple in Antioch*
Philostratus, Life of Apollonius 1.16

He [Apollonius] also visited the great Antioch, and passed into the Temple of Apollo of Daphne, to which the Assyrians attach the legend of Arcadia. For they say that Daphne, the daughter of Ladon, there underwent her metamorphosis, and they have a river flowing there, the Ladon, and a laurel tree is worshipped by them which they say is the one substituted for the maiden; and cypress trees of enormous height surround the Temple, and the ground sends up springs both ample and placid, in which they say Apollos purifies himself by ablution. And there it is that the earth sends up a shoot of cypress, they say in honor of Cyparissus, an Assyrian youth; and the beauty of the shrub lends credence to the story of his metamorphosis . . . . Apollonius, when he beheld a Temple so graceful and yet the home of no serious studies, but only of men half-barbarous and uncultivated, remarked: "O Apollo, change these dumb dogs into trees, so that at least as cypresses they may become vocal." And when he had inspected the springs, and noted how calm and quiet they were, and how not one of them made the least babble, he remarked: "The prevailing dumbness of this place does not permit even the springs to speak." And when he saw the Ladon he said: "it is not your daughter alone that underwent a change, but you too, so far as one can see, have become a barbarian after being a Hellene and an Arcadian."

1252 *Sparta Rejuvenated*
Philostratus, Life of Apollonius 4.27

The career of our sage in Olympia was as follows: when Apollonius was on his way up to Olympia, some envoys of the Lacedaemonians met him and asked him to visit their city; there seemed, however, to be no appearance of Sparta about them, for they conducted themselves in a very effeminate manner and reeked of luxury. And seeing them to have smooth legs, and sleek hair, and that they did not even wear beards, nay were even dressed in soft raiment, he sent such a letter to the Ephors that the latter issued a public proclamation and forbade the use of pitch plasters in the baths,[1] and drove out of the city the women who professed to rejuvenate dandies,[2] and they restored the ancient regime in every respect. The consequence was that the wrestling grounds were filled once more with the youth, and the jousts and the common meals were restored, and Lacedaemon became once more like herself. And when he learned that they had set their house in order, he sent them an epistle from Olympia, briefer than any cipher dispatch of ancient Sparta; and it ran as follows:

"Apollonius to the Ephors sends salutation.

"It is the duty of men not to fall into sin, but of noble men, to recognise that they are doing so."

1. Adhesive plasters were used to remove superfluous hair from the body.
2. Literally "hair-pluckers".

1253 *Apollonius Advises Spartans*
Philostratus, Life of Apollonius 4.33

Here is another incident that happened in Lacedaemon. A letter came from the Emperor heaping reproaches upon the public assembly of the Lacedaemonians, and declaring that in their license they abused liberty, and this letter had been addressed to them at the instance of the governor of Greece, who had maligned them. The Lacedaemonians then were at a loss what to do, and Sparta was divided against herself over the issue, whether in their reply to the letter they should try to appease the Emperor's wrath or take a lofty tone towards him. Under the circumstances they sought the counsel of Apollonius and asked him how to pitch the tone of their letter. And he, when he saw them to be divided on the point, came forward in their public assembly and delivered himself of the following short and concise speech: "Palamedes discovered writing not only in order that people might write, but also in order that they might know what they must not write."

1254 *Citizens Quarrel in Antioch*
Philostratus, Life of Apollonius 6.38

The ruler of Syria had plunged Antioch into a feud, by disseminating among the citizens suspicions such that when they met in assembly they all quarrelled with one another. But a violent earthquake happening to occur, they were all cowering, and as is usual in the case of heavenly portents, praying for one another. Apollonius accordingly stepped forward and remarked: "It is God who is clearly anxious to reconcile you to one another, and you will not revive these feuds since you cherish the same fears."

1255 *Ephesian Celebration Interrupted*
Philostratus, Life of Apollonius 7.7

On another occasion when after the murder of Sabinus, one of his [Domitian's] own relations, Domitian was about to marry Julia, who was herself the wife of the murdered man, and Domitian's own niece, being one of the daughters of Titus, Ephesus was about to celebrate the marriage with sacrifice, only Apollonius interrupted the rites, by exclaiming: "O thou night of the Danaids of yore, how unique thou wast!"

1256 Apollonius Protects Sheep

Philostratus, Life of Apollonius 8.22

But certain persons accused him [Apollonius] of avoiding attendance on governors at their visits, and of influencing his hearers rather to live in retirement instead; and one of them uttered the jest that he drove away his sheep as soon as he found any forensic orator approaching. "Yes, by Zeus," said Apollonius, "lest these wolves should fall upon my flock."

1257 Leon Wins over Athenians

Philostratus, Lives of the Sophists 1.2 (485)

When this Leon [of Byzantium] came on an embassy to Athens, the city had long been disturbed by factions and was being governed in defiance of established customs. When he came before the assembly he excited universal laughter, since he was fat and had a prominent paunch, but he was not at all embarrassed by the laughter. "Why," said he, "do ye laugh, Athenians? Is it because I am so stout and so big? I have a wife at home who is much stouter than I, and when we agree the bed is large enough for us both, but when we quarrel not even the house is large enough." Thereupon the citizens of Athens came to a friendly agreement, thus reconciled by Leon, who had so cleverly improvised to meet the occasion.[1]

> 1. Diogenes Laertius 4.37 tells the same story about Arcesilaus the head of the Academy. Athenaus says that Leon told this anecdote not about himself but about Python.

1258 Favorinus Insulted

Philostratus, Lives of the Sophists 1.8 (490)

He [Favorinus] was appointed high priest,[1] whereupon he appealed to the established usage of his birthplace, pleading that, according to the laws on such matters, he was exempt from public services because he was a philosopher. But when he saw that the Emperor intended to vote against him on the ground that he was not a philosopher, he forestalled him in the following way. "O Emperor," he cried, "I have had a dream of which you ought to be informed. My teacher Dio appeared to me, and with respect to this suit admonished and reminded me that we come into the world not for ourselves alone, but also for the country of our birth.[2] Therefore, O Emperor, I obey my teacher, and I undertake this public service." Now the Emperor had acted thus merely for his own diversion, for by turning his mind to philosopher and sophists he used to lighten the responsibilites of Empire. The Athenians, however, took the affair seriously, and, especially the Athenian magistrates themselves, hastened in a body to throw down the bronze statue of Favorinus as though he were the Emperor's bitterest enemy. Yet on hearing of it Favorinus showed no resentment or anger at the insult, but observed, "Socrates himself would have been the gainer, if the Athenians had merely deprived him of a bronze statue, instead of making him drink hemlock."

> 1. The high priest was president of the public games in the cities of his district and provided them at his own expense as a "liturgy."
> 2. An echo of Demosthenes, On the Crown 205, and perhaps also of Plato, Crito 50.

1259 Aeschines Praises Rival Demosthenes

Philostratus, Lives of the Sophists 1.18 (510)

Accordingly we must limit the eloquence of Aeschines to three orations, which are: Against Timarchus, In Defense of the Embassy, and the speech Against Ctesi-

phon. There is also extant a fourth work of his, the *Letters*, which, though they are few, are full of learning and character. What that character was he clearly showed at Rhodes. For once after he had read in public his speech *Against Ctesiphon*, they were expressing their surprise that he had been defeated after so able a speech, and were criticizing the Athenians as out of their senses, but Aeschines said, "You would not marvel thus if you had heard Demosthenes in reply to these arguments." Thus he not only praised his enemy but also acquitted the jury from blame.

1260   *Nicetes Fears Public*
Philostratus, Lives of the Sophists 1.19 (511)
Though he [Nicetes of Smyrna] was deemed worthy of the highest honor in Smyrna, which left nothing unsaid in its loud praise of him as a marvelous man and a great orator, he seldom came forward to speak in the public assembly; and when the crowd accused him of being afraid, "I am more afraid," said he, "of the public when they praise than when they abuse me."

1261   *Smyrna a Grove*
Philostratus, Lives of the Sophists 1.21 (516)
He [Scopelian] frequented the rhetoricians' schools of oratory as a pupil of Nicetes of Smyrna, who had conspicuous success as a declaimer, though in the law courts he was an even more vigorous orator. When the city of Clazomenae begged Scopelian to declaim in his native place, because they thought it would greatly benefit Clazomenae if so talented a man should open a school there, he declined politely, saying that the nightingale does not sing in a cage; and he regarded Smyrna as, so to speak, a grove in which he could practice his melodious voice, and thought it best worth his while to let it echo there. For while all Ionia is, as it were, an established seat of the Muses, Smyrna holds the most important positon, like the bridge in musical instruments.

1262   *Words, Not Bread*
Philostratus, Lives of the Sophists 1.23 (526)
Lollianus of Ephesus was the first to be appointed to the chair of rhetoric[1] at Athens, and he also governed the Athenian people, since he held the office of strategus in that city. The functions of this office were formerly to levy troops and lead them to war, but now it has charge of the food-supplies and the provision-market. Once when a riot arose in the bread-sellers' quarter, and the Athenians were on the point of stoning Lollianus, Pancrates the Cynic, who later professed philosophy at the Isthmus, came forward before the Athenians, and by simply remarking, "Lollianus does not sell bread but words," he so diverted the Athenians that they let fall the stones that were in their hands.

   1. I.e., the municipal, as distinct from the Imperial chair.

1263   *The Wondrous Rainbow*
Philostratus, Lives of the Sophists 1.24 (528)
His style in his discourses may be gathered from the following. He [Marcus] was trying to show how rich and how many-sided is the art of the sophists, and taking the rainbow as the image of an oration, he began his discourse thus: "He who sees the rainbow only as a single color does not see a sight to marvel at, but he who sees

how many colors it has, marvels more."[1] Those who ascribe this discourse to Alcinous the Stoic fail to observe the style of his speech, they fail to observe the truth, and are most dishonest men, in that they try to rob the sophist even of what he wrote about his own art.

> 1. Iris was the daughter of Thaumas whose name means "Wonder." The play on "to wonder" seems to echo Plato, *Theaetetus* 155C–D: "philosophy begins in wonder." Plato goes on to apply the image of the rainbow (Iris) to philosophy.

1264 *No Return without Shield*
Philostratus, Lives of the Sophists 1.24 (528)

The most characteristic example of the style of Marcus is his speech of the Spartan advising the Lacedaemonians not to receive the men who had returned from Sphacteria without their weapons. He began this argument as follows: "As a citizen of Lacedaemon who till old age has kept his shield, I would gladly have slain these men who have lost theirs."

1265 *Athenians Accomplished Judges of Oratory*
Philostratus, Lives of the Sophists 1.25 (535)

Let this suffice to show how mild an Emperor could be, and how arrogant a mere man. For in truth Polemo was so arrogant that he conversed with cities as his inferiors, Emperors as not his superiors, and the gods as his equals. For instance, when he gave a display to the Athenians of extempore speeches on first coming to Athens, he did not condescend to utter an encomium on the city, though there were so many things that one might say in honor of the Athenians; nor did he make a long oration about his own renown, although this style of speech is likely to win favor for sophists in their public declamations. But since he well knew that the natural disposition of the Athenians needs to be held in check rather than encouraged to greater pride, this was his introductory speech: "Men say, Athenians, that as an audience you are accomplished judges of oratory. I shall soon find out."

1266 *Herodes Wishes to Equal Polemo*
Philostratus, Lives of the Sophists 1.25 (539)

And at the Olympic games when all Greece acclaimed him [Herodes], crying, "You are the equal of Demosthenes!" he replied, "I wish I were the equal of the Phrygian," applying this name to Polemo because in those days Laodicea counted as part of Phrygia.

1267 *Polemo on Poetry and Prose*
Philostratus, Lives of the Sophists 1.25 (539)

He [Polemo] used to say that the works of prose writers needed to be brought out[1] by armfuls, but the works of poets by the wagon-load.

> 1. The meaning of the verb is obscure, but as "bury" and "publish" are improbable, Polemo seems to mean that the student, for his training as a sophist, must take out from his store of books more poets than prose writers.

1268 *Polemo's Joints Like Stone-Quarries*
Philostratus, Lives of the Sophists 1.25 (543)

When the doctors were regularly attending him [Polemo] for hardening of the joints, he exhorted them to "dig and carve in the stone-quarries of Polemo."

1269 *Herodes Criticized for Statues of Sons*
Philostratus, Lives of the Sophists 2.1 (559)

And when the Quintilii during their proconsulship of Greece censured him [Herodes] for putting up the statues of these youths [his foster sons] on the ground that they were an extravagance, he retorted, "What business is it of yours if I amuse myself with my poor marbles?"

1270 *Herodes Praised in Greece*
Philostratus, Lives of the Sophists 2.1 (564–565)

And when all Greece was loud in applause of Herodes and called him one of the Ten,[1] he was not abashed by such a compliment, though it seems magnificent enough, but replied to his admirers with great urbanity, "Well, at any rate I am better than Andocides."

1. The Ten Attic Orators of the canon.

1271 *Money Makes No Man*
Philostratus, Lives of the Sophists 2.10 (591)

To Chrestus of Byzantium, the sophist, Greece does less than justice, since it neglects a man who received from Herodes the best education of any Hellene, and himself educated many remarkable men. Among these were Hippodromus the sophist, Philiscus, Isagoras the tragic poet, famous rhetoricians, namely Nicomedes of Pergamon, Acylas from Eastern Galatia, and Aristaenetus of Byzantium; and among well-known philosophers, Callaeschrus the Athenian, Sospis the curator of the altar, and several others worthy of mention. He taught in the days of the sophist Adrian and had then a hundred pupils who paid fees, the best of them those whom I have mentioned. After Adrian had been installed in the chair at Rome, the Athenians voted to send an embassy on behalf of Chrestus to ask for him from the Emperor the chair at Athens. But he came before them in the assembly and broke up the embassy, saying many memorable things in his discourse, and he ended with these words: "The ten thousand drachmae[1] do not make a man."

1. This was the salary of the chair.

1272 *Victory to Clemens*
Philostratus, Lives of the Sophists 2.27 (616)

Clemens of Byzantium was a tragic actor whose like has never yet been seen for artistic skill. But since he was winning his victories at a time when Byzantium was being besieged,[1] he used to be sent away without the reward of victory, lest it should appear that a city that had taken up arms against the Romans was being proclaimed victor in the person of one of her citizens. Accordingly, after he had performed brilliantly in the Amphictyonic games, the Amphictyons were on the point of voting that he should not receive the prize, because for the reason that I have mentioned they were afraid. Whereupon Hippodromus sprang up with great energy and cried, "Let these others go on and prosper by breaking their oath and giving unjust decisions, but by my vote I award the victory to Clemens."

1. The siege of Byzantium lasted C.E. 193–196 when it was taken by Severus. See Dio Cassius 75.10 for the story of its courageous defense by the Byzantines.

1273 Hippodromus Compared to Polemo
Philostratus, Lives of the Sophists 2.27 (616)

At any rate, on one occasion when the Greeks were acclaiming him [Hippodromus] with flatteries, and even compared him with Polemo, "Why," said he, "do you liken me to immortals?"[1] This answer, while it did not rob Polemo of his reputation for being divinely inspired, was also a refusal to concede to himself any likeness to so great a genius.

1. Homer, *Odyssey* 16.187.

1274 The Benevolence of Hippodromus
Philostratus, Lives of the Sophists 2.27 (617)

For when Philostratus of Lemnos,[1] his [Hippodromus'] own pupil, aged twenty-two, was about to try his chances in an extempore oration, Hippodromus gave him many useful hints for the art of panegyric, namely what one ought and ought not to say. And when all Greece called on Hippodromus to come forward himself without delay, he replied, "I will not strip for a fight with my own entrails." Having said this, he put off the declamation till the day of the sacrifice.[2] I have said enough to show that he was a man truly well-educated, with a benevolent and humane disposition.

1. The biographer's son-in-law, the author of the *Imagines*.
2. The last day of the festival.

1275 Lenient Quirinus
Philostratus, Lives of the Sophists 2.29 (621)

When the informers in Asia found fault with him [Quirinus] for being more lenient in his prosecutions than accorded with the evidence furnished by them, he said, "Nay, it were far better that you should adopt my clemency than I your ruthlessness."

1276 No Reward for Causing Desolation
Philostratus, Lives of the Sophists 2.29 (621)

And when they [the informers in Asia] cited a small town for the payment of many myriads of drachmae, Quirinus did indeed win the case, though much against his will, but when the informers came to him and said, "This case when it comes to the Emperor's ears will greatly enhance your reputation," he retorted, "It suits you but not me to win rewards for making a town desolate."

1277 Not Kings, But Kinglets
Plutarch, Agesilaus 2.3

Archidamus was fined by the ephors for marrying a little woman, "For she will bear us," they said, "not kings, but kinglets."

1278a Dead Could Have Conquered Barbarians
Plutarch, Agesilaus 16.4

When he [Agesilaus] learned that a great battle had been fought near Corinth, and that men of the highest repute had suddenly been taken off, and that although few Spartans altogether had been killed, the loss of their enemies was very heavy, he was not seen to be rejoiced or elated, but fetched a deep groan and said: "Alas for Hellas, which has by her own hands destroyed so many brave men! Had they lived, they could have conquered in battle all the Barbarians in the world."

1278b *Dead Could Have Conquered Barbarians*
Xenophon, Agesilaus, 7.5

Now when a report reached Agesilaus that eight Lacedaemonians and near ten thousand of the enemy had fallen at the battle of Corinth, instead of showing pleasure, he actually exclaimed: "Alas for thee, Hellas! those who now lie dead were enough to defeat all the barbarians in battle had they lived!"

1279 *Agesilaus Angered by Corinthians*
Plutarch, Agesilaus 22.1–3

While he [Agesilaus] was lingering in the territory of Corinth, he seized the Heraeum, and as he was watching his soldiers carry off the prisoners and booty, messengers came from Thebes to treat for peace. But he had always hated that city, and thinking this an advantageous time also for insulting it, pretended neither to see nor hear its ambassadors when they presented themselves. But his pride soon had a fall; for the Thebans had not yet departed when messengers came to him with tidings that the Spartan division had been cut to pices by Iphicrates. This was the greatest disaster that had happened to the Spartans in a long time; for they lost many brave men, and those men were overwhelmed by targeteers and mercenaries, though they were men-at-arms and Lacedaemonians. At once, then, Agesilaus sprang up to go to their assistance, but when he learned that it was all over with them, he came back again to the Heraeum, and ordering the Boeotians then to come before him, gave them an audience. But they returned his insolence by making no mention of peace, but simply asking safe conduct into Corinth. Agesilaus was wroth at this, and said: "If you wish to see your friends when they are elated at their successes, you can do so tomorrow in all safety."

1280 *Agesilaus Rebukes Allies*
Plutarch, Agesilaus 26.3–5

Moreover, the allies of the Lacedaemonians were offended at Agesilaus, because, as they said, it was not upon any public ground of complaint, but by reason of some passionate resentment of his own, that he sought to destroy the Thebans. Accordingly, they said they had no wish to be dragged hither and thither to destruction every year, they themselves so many, and the Lacedaemonians, with whom they followed, so few. It was at this time, we are told, that Agesilaus, wishing to refute their argument from numbers, devised the following scheme. He ordered all the allies to sit down by themselves indiscriminately, and the Lacedaemonians apart by themselves. Then his herald called upon the plotters to stand up first, and after them the smiths, next, the carpenters in their turn, and the builders, and so on through all the handicrafts. In response, almost all of the allies rose up, but not a man of the Lacedaemonians; for they were forbidden to learn or practice a manual art.[1] Then Agesilaus said with a laugh: "You see, O men, how many more soldiers than you we are sending out."

1. Cf. Plutarch, *Lycurgus* 24.2.

1281a *Mountain Travails, Bears Mouse*
Plutarch, Agesilaus 36.4–5

As soon as he [Agesilaus] landed in Egypt,[1] the chief captains and governors of the king came down to meet him and pay him honor. There was great eagerness and expectation on the part of the other Egyptians also, owing to the name and fame of Agesilaus, and all ran together to behold him. But when they saw no brilliant array whatever, but an old man lying in some grass by the sea, his body small and contemptible, covered with a cloak that was coarse and mean, they were moved to laughter and jesting, saying that here was an illustration of the fable, "a mountain is in travail, and then a mouse is born."

    1. 361 B.C.E.

1281b *Mountain Travails, Bears Mouse*
Athenaeus, Deipnosophists 14.616D

And Tachos, the king of Egypt, because of a joke made at the expense of Agesilaus, the king of Sparta (for he was short of stature), when Agesilaus arrived to be his ally, was reduced to private station because Agesilaus renounced the alliance. The joke was this: "The mountain was in travail-pains and Zeus was affrighted; but it brought forth—a mouse."[1] When Agesilaus heard that, he said in anger, "I shall one day look to you like a lion."

    1. Horace, *Ars Poetica* 139; Phaedrus, *Aesopic Fables* 4.24.

1282 *Sparta Swallows in One Gulp*
Plutarch, Alcibiades 15.2–4

After this battle of Mantinea, the oligarchs of Argos, "The Thousand," set out at once to depose the popular party and make the city subject to themselves; and the Lacedaemonians came and deposed the democracy. But the populace took up arms again and got the upper hand.[1] Then Alcibiades came and made the people's victory secure. He also persuaded them to run long walls down to the sea, and so to attach their city completely to the naval dominion of Athens. He actually brought carpenters and masons from Athens, and displayed all manner of zeal, thus winning favor and power for himself no less than for his city. In like manner he persuaded the people of Patrae to attach their city to the sea by long walls.[2] Thereupon someone said to the Patrensians: "Athens will swallow you up!" "Perhaps so," said Alcibiades, "but you will go slowly, and feet first, whereas Sparta will swallow you head first, and at one gulp."

    1. 417 B.C.E.
    2. 419 B.C.E.

1283 *No Trust for Own Life*
Plutarch, Alcibiades 22.1–2

Alcibiades had no sooner sailed away than he robbed the Athenians of Messana.[1] There was a party there who were on the point of surrendering the city to the Athenians, but Alcibiades knew them, and gave the clearest information of their design to the friends of Syracuse in the city, and so brought the thing to naught. Arrived at Thurii, he left his trireme and hid himself so as to escape all quest. When someone recognised him and asked, "Can you not trust your country,

Alcibiades?" "In all else," he said, "but in the matter of life I wouldn't trust even my own mother not to mistake a black for a white ballot when she cast her vote."

    1. In September, 415 B.C.E.

1284 *Alcibiades Elected General*
Plutarch, Alcibiades 33.2–3

At this time,[1] therefore, the people had only to meet in assembly, and Alcibiades addressed them. He lamented and bewailed his own lot, but had only little and moderate blame to lay upon the people. The entire mischief he ascribed to a certain evil fortune and envious genius of his own. Then he descanted at great length upon the vain hopes which their enemies were cherishing, and wrought his hearers up to courage. At last they crowned him with crowns of gold, and elected him general with sole powers by land and sea. They voted also that his property be restored to him, and that the Eumolpidae and Heralds revoke the curses wherewith they had cursed him at the command of the people. The others revoked their curses, but Theodorus the High Priest said: "Nay, I invoked no evil upon him if he does no wrong to the city."

    1. In the early summer of 408 B.C.E.

1285 *Satyr Dream Means Victory over Tyre*
Plutarch, Alexander 24.8–9 (4–5)

In another dream, too, Alexander thought he saw a satyr who mocked him at a distance, and eluded his grasp when he tried to catch him, but finally, after much coaxing and chasing, surrendered. The seers, dividing the word "satyros" into two parts, said to him, plausibly enough, "Tyre is to be thine." And a spring is pointed out, near which Alexander dreamed he saw the satyr.

1286 *Alexander Implies Divinity in Letter to Athenians*
Plutarch, Alexander 28.1–2 (1)

In general, he [Alexander] bore himself haughtily towards the Barbarians, and like one fully persuaded of his divine birth and parentage, but with the Greeks it was within limits and somewhat rarely that he assumed his own divinity. However, in writing to the Athenians concerning Samos, he said: "I cannot have given you that free and illustrious city; for ye received it from him who was then your master and was called my father," meaning Philip.

1287 *Theater Contest between Athenodorus and Thessalus*
Plutarch, Alexander 29.1–4 (1–2)

When he [Alexander] had returned from Egypt into Phoenicia,[1] he honored the gods with sacrifices and solemn processions, and held contests of dithyrambic choruses and tragedies which were made brilliant, not only by their furnishings, but also by the competitors who exhibited them. For the kings of Cyprus were the choregi, or exhibitors, just like, at Athens, those chosen by lot from the tribes, and they competed against each other with amazing ambition. Most eager of all was the contention between Nicocreon of Salamis and Pasicrates of Soli. For the lot assigned to these exhibitors the most celebrated actors, to Pasicrates Athenodorus, and to Nicocreon Thessalus, in whose success Alexander himself was interested. He did not reveal this interest, however, until, by the votes of the judges, Athenodorus had been proclaimed victor. But then, as it would appear, on leaving the theater, he said that he approved the decision of the judges, but would gladly have given up a part of his kingdom rather than to have seen Thessalus vanquished.

1. Early in 331 B.C.E.

1288 *Lysimachus and Hagnon Criticize Callisthenes*
Plutarch, Alexander 55.1–2 (1)

The king having been thus alienated, in the first place, Hephaestion found credence for his story that Callisthenes had promised him to make obeisance to the king and then had been false to his agreement. Again, men like Lysimachus and Hagnon persisted in saying that the sophist went about with lofty thoughts as if bent on abolishing a tyranny, and that the young men flocked to him and followed him about as if he were the only freeman among so many tens of thousands.

1289 *Seers Interpret Oily Spring as Good Omen*
Plutarch, Alexander 57.5–9 (3–5)

However, a better portent occurred and put an end to his [Alexander's] dejection. The Macedonian, namely, who was set over those in charge of the royal equipage, Proxenus by name, as he was digging a place for the king's tent along the river Oxus, uncovered a spring of liquid which was oily and fatty; but when the top of it was drawn off, there flowed at once a pure and clear oil, which appeared to differ from olive oil neither in odor nor in flavor, and in smoothness and luster was altogether the same, and that too though the country produced no olive trees. It is said, indeed, that the Oxus itself also has a very soft water, which gives sleekness to the skin of those who bathe in it. However, that Alexander was marvelously pleased is clear from what he writes to Antipater, where he speaks of this as one of the greatest omens vouchsafed to him from Heaven. The seers, however, held that the omen foreshadowed an expedition which would be glorious, but difficult and toilsome; for oil, they said, was given to men by Heaven as an aid to toil.

1290 *Alexander Tries to Cross River Hydaspes in a Storm*
Plutarch, Alexander 60.1–6 (1–3)

Of his campaign against Porus[1] he himself has given an account in his letters. He [Alexander] says, namely, that the river Hydaspes flowed between the two camps, and that Porus stationed his elephants on the opposite bank and kept continual watch of the crossing. He himself, accordingly, day by day caused a great din and tumult to be made in his camp, and thereby accustomed the Barbarians not to be alarmed. Then, on a dark and stormy night, he took a part of his infantry and the best of his horsemen, and after proceeding along the river to a distance from where the enemy lay, crossed over to a small island. Here rain fell in torrents, and many tornadoes and thunderbolts dashed down upon his men; but nevertheless, although he saw that many of them were being burned to death by the thunderbolts, he set out from the islet and made for the opposite banks. But the Hydaspes, made violent by the storm and dashing high against its bank, made a great breach in it, and a large part of the stream was setting in that direction; and the shore between the two currents gave his men no sure footing, since it was broken and slippery. And here it was that he is said to have cried: "O Athenians, can ye possibly believe what peril I am undergoing to win glory in your eyes?"

1. See Arrian, *Anabasis* 5.9–19. It was in the spring of 326 B.C.E.

1291 *Small Rotten Senate-House*
Plutarch, Antony 23.3

But when the Megarians wished to show him [Antony] something fine to rival Athens, and thought that he ought to see their senate-house, he went up and took a view of it; and when they asked him what he thought of it, "It is small," he said, "but rotten."

1292 *Hang Yourselves before Tree Cut Down*
Plutarch, Antony 70.2-3

We are told also that once when the Athenians were holding an assembly, he [Timon] ascended the bema, and the strangeness of the thing caused deep silence and great expectancy; then he said: "I have a small building lot, men of Athens, and a figtree is growing in it, from which many of my fellow citizens have already hanged themselves. Accordingly, as I intend to build a house there, I wanted to give public notice to that effect, in order that all of you who desire to do so may hang yourselves before the fig tree is cut down."

1293 *Aratus Deceives Spies*
Plutarch, Aratus 6.4-5

In the meantime some spies of Nicocles appeared in Argos and were reported to be secretly going about and watching the movements of Aratus. As soon as it was day, therefore, Aratus left his house and showed himself openly in the market-place, conversing with his friends; then he annointed himself in the gymnasium, took with him from the palestra some of the young men who were wont to drink and make holiday with him, and went back home; and after a little one of his servants was seen carrying garlands through the market place, another buying lights, and another talking with the women that regularly furnished music of harp and flute at banquets. When the spies saw all this, they were completely deceived, and with loud laughter said to one another: "Nothing, you see, is more timorous than a tyrant, since even Nicocles, though master of so great a city and so large a force, is in fear of a stripling who squanders on pleasures and mid-day banquets his means of subsistence in exile."

1294 *Aristides Elected Overseer*
Plutarch, Aristides 4.2-5

When he [Aristides] was elected overseer of the public revenues, he proved clearly that large sums had been embezzled, not only by his fellow-officials, but also by those of former years, and particularly by Themistocles:
"The man was clever, but of his hand had no control."
For this cause, Themistocles banded many together against Aristides, prosecuted him for theft at the auditing of his accounts, and actually got a verdict against him, according to Idomeneus. But the first and best men of the city were incensed at this, and he was not only exempted from his fine, but even appointed to administer the same charge again. Then he pretended to repent him of his former course, and made himself more pliable, thus giving pleasure to those who were stealing the common funds by not examining them or holding them to strict account, so that they gorged themselves with the public moneys, and then lauded Aristides to the skies, and pleaded with the people in his behalf, eagerly desirous that he be once more elected to his office. But just as they were about to vote, Aristides rebuked the

Athenians. "Verily," said he, "when I served you in office with fidelity and honor, I was reviled and persecuted; but now that I am flinging away much of the common funds to thieves, I am thought to be an admirable citizen. For my part, I am more ashamed of my present honor than I was of my former condemnation, and I am sore distressed for you, because it is more honorable in your eyes to please base men than to guard the public moneys."

1295 *Spartanizing Medes*
Plutarch, Artaxerxes 22.2

For Agesilaus, as it would appear, when someone said to him: "Alas for Greece, now that the Spartans are medizing," replied, "Are not the Medes rather spartanizing?"

1296 *Threats from Brutus*
Plutarch, Brutus 2.6–8

For instance, when he [Brutus] had already embarked upon the war, he wrote to the Pergamenians: "I hear that ye have given money to Dolabella; if ye gave it willingly confess that ye have wronged me; if unwillingly, prove it by giving willingly to me." Again, to the Samians: "Your counsels are paltry, your subsidies slow; what, think ye, will be the end of this?" And in another letter: "The Xanthians ignored my benefactions, and have made their country a grave for their madness; but the Patareans entrusted themselves to me, and now enjoy their freedom in all its fullness. It is in your power also to choose the decision of the Patareans or the fate of the Xanthians."

1297 *Senate Aids Caesar*
Plutarch, Caesar 14.3–5 (2–3)

In the senate the opposition of men of the better sort gave him [Caesar] the pretext which he had long desired, and crying with loud adjurations that he was driven forth into the popular assembly against his wishes, and was compelled to court its favor by the insolence and obstinacy of the senate, he hastened before it, and stationing Crassus on one side of him and Pompey on the other, he asked them if they approved his laws. They declared that they did approve them, whereupon he urged them to give him their aid against those who threatened to oppose him with swords. They promised him such aid, and Pompey actually added that he would come up against swords with sword and buckler too.

1298 *Dissension in the Senate*
Plutarch, Caesar 30.4–6 (2)

But in the Senate, Scipio, the father-in-law of Pompey, introduced a motion that if by a fixed day Caesar did not lay down his arms he should be declared a public enemy. And when the consuls put the question whether Pompey should dismiss his soldiers, and again whether Caesar should, very few senators voted for the first, and all but a few for the second; but when Antony again demanded that both should give up their commands, all with one accord assented. Scipio, however, made violent opposition, and Lentulus the consul cried out that against a robber there was need of arms, not votes; whereupon the senate broke up, and the senators put on the garb of mourning in view of the dissension.

1299 *Agrippa Tells Fable*
Plutarch, Caius Marcius Coriolanus 6.2–4

The chief spokesman was Menenius Agrippa, and after much entreaty of the people and much plain speaking in behalf of the senate, he concluded his discourse with a celebrated fable. He said, namely, that all the other members of man's body once revolted against the belly, and accused it of being the only member to sit idly down in its place and make no contribution to the common welfare, while the rest underwent great hardships and performed great public services only to minister to its appetites; but that the belly laughed at their simplicity in not knowing that it received into itself all the body's nourishment only to send it back again and duly distribute it among the other members. "Such, then," said Agrippa, "is the relation of the senate, my fellow-citizens, to you; the matters for deliberation which there receive the necessary attention and disposition bring to you all and severally what is useful and helpful."[1]

1. Cf. Livy 2.32.9–11; Dionysius of Halicarnassus, *Roman Antiquities* 6.86.

1300 *Slight Fall Atones*
Plutarch, Camillus 5.5–7

At any rate the city was taken by storm, and the Romans were pillaging and plundering its boundless wealth, when Camillus, seeing from the citadel what was going on, at first burst into tears as he stood, and then, on being congratulated by the bystanders, lifted up his hands to the gods and prayed, saying: "O greatest Jupiter, and ye gods who see and judge men's good and evil deeds, ye surely know that it is not unjustly, but of necessity and in self-defense that we Romans have visited its iniquity upon this city of hostile and lawless men. But if, as counterpoise to this our present success, some retribution is due to come upon us, spare, I beseech you, the city and the army of the Romans, and let it fall upon my own head, though with as little harm as may be." With these words, as the Romans' custom is after prayer and adoration, he wheeled himself about to the right, but stumbled and fell as he turned. The bystanders were confounded, but he picked himself up again from his fall and said: "My prayer is granted! a slight fall is my atonement for the greatest good fortune."

1301 *Camillus Appointed Dictator*
Plutarch, Camillus 39.1–2

After this, Licinius Stolo stirred up the great dissension in the city which brought the people into collision with the Senate. The people insisted that, when two consuls were appointed, one of them must certainly be a plebian, and not both patricians. Tribunes of the people were chosen, but the multitude prevented the consular elections from being duly held. Owing to this lack of magistrates, matters were getting more and more confused, and so Camillus was for the fourth time appointed dictator by the Senate, though much against the wishes of the people. He was not eager for the office himself, nor did he wish to oppose men whose many and great struggles gave them the right to say boldly to him: "Your achievements have been in the field with us, rather than in politics with the patricians; it is through hate and envy that they have now made you dictator; they hope that you will crush the people if you prevail, or be crushed yourself if you fail."

1302 *Blunt Force By Kindness*
Plutarch, Cato The Younger 12.3–5

He [Cato] therefore arranged his journey as follows. At daybreak, he would send forward his baker and his cook to the place where he intended to lodge. These would enter the city with great decorum and little stir, and if Cato had no family friend or acquaintance there, they would prepare a reception for him at an inn, without troubling anybody; or, in case there was no inn, they would apply to the magistrates for hospitality, and gladly accept what was given. But frequently they were distrusted and neglected, because they raised no tumult and made no threats in their dealings with the magistrates. In such a case, Cato would find their work not done when he arrived, and he himself would be more despised than his servants when men saw him, and would awaken suspicion, as he sat upon the baggage without saying a word, that he was a man of low condition and very timid. However, he would then call the magistrates to him and say: "Ye miserable wretches, lay aside this inhospitality. Not all men who come to you will be Catos. Blunt by your kind attentions the power of those who only want an excuse for taking by force what they do not get with men's consent."

1303 *Cato Unheeded*
Plutarch, Cato the Younger 52.1–2

But when Ariminum was occupied and Caesar was reported to be marching against the city with an army, then all eyes were turned upon Cato, both those of the common people and those of Pompey as well; they realized that he alone had from the outset foreseen, and first openly foretold, the designs of Caesar. Cato therefore said: "Nay, men, if any of you had heeded what I was ever foretelling and advising, ye would now neither be fearing a single man nor putting your hopes in a single man."

1304 *Cato Deserted by Three Hundred*
Plutarch, Cato the Younger 61.1–2

Accordingly, Cato decided to detain the bearers of the letters until he felt sure of the attitude of the three hundred. For the Romans of senatorial rank were eager in his cause, and after promptly manumitting their slaves, were arming them; but as for the three hundred, since they were men engaged in navigation and money-lending and had the greater part of their property in slaves, the words of Cato did not long abide in their minds, but lapsed away. For just as porous bodies readily receive heat and as readily yield it up again and grow cold when the fire is removed, in like manner these men when they saw Cato, were filled with warmth and kindled into flame, but when they came to think matters over by themselves, their fear of Caesar drove away their regard for Cato and for honor. "Who, pray, are we," they said, "and who is he whose commands we are refusing to obey? Is he not Caesar, upon whom the whole power of Rome devolved? And not one of us is a Scipio, or a Pompey, or a Cato. But at a time when all men are led by fear to think more humbly than they ought to think, at such time shall we fight in defense of the liberty of Rome, and wage war in Utica against a man before whom Cato, with Pompey the Great, fled and gave up Italy? And shall we give our slaves freedom in opposition to Caesar, we who ourselves have only as much freedom as he may wish to give us? Nay, before it is too late, poor wretches, let us know ourselves, crave the conqueror's grace, and send men to entreat him."

1305   *They Have Lived*
Plutarch, Cicero 22.3–4 (2)

When Cicero had passed through the forum and reached the prison, he delivered Lentulus to the public executioner with the order to put him to death. Then Cethegus in his turn, and so each one of the others, he brought down to the prison and had him executed. And seeing that many members of the conspiracy were still assembled in the forum in ignorance of what had been done and waiting for night to come, with the idea that the men were still living and might be rescued, he cried out to them with a loud voice and said: "They have lived."

1306   *Cicero Praised*
Plutarch, Cicero 22.5–7 (3–5)

It was now evening, and Cicero went up through the forum to his house, the citizens no longer escorting him on his way with silent decorum, but receiving him with cries and clapping of hands as he passed along, calling him the savior and founder of his country. And many lights illuminated the streets, since people placed lamps and torches at their doors. The women, too, displayed lights upon the housetops in honor of the man, and that they might see him going up to his home in great state under escort of the noblest citizens. Most of these had brought to an end great wars and entered the city in triumph, and had added to the Roman dominion no small extent of land and sea; but they now walked along confessing to one another that to many of the commanders and generals of the time the Roman people were indebted for wealth and spoils and power, but for preservation and safety to Cicero alone, who had freed them from so peculiar and so great a peril.

1307   *Cicero Returns from Exile*
Plutarch, Cicero 33.7–8 (5)

Thus Cicero came home in the sixteenth month after his exile; and so great was the joy of the cities and the eagerness of men to meet him that what was said by Cicero afterwards fell short of the truth. He said, namely, that Italy had taken him on her shoulders and carried him into Rome.[1]

> 1. Cf. Cicero, *Post Reditum in Senatu* 15.39.

1308   *Moist Dough*
Plutarch, Cleomenes 27.1

And Demades, when the Athenians once ordered that their triremes should be launched and manned, but had no money, said: "Dough must be moistened before it is kneaded."

1309a   *War Has No Fixed Rations*
Plutarch, Cleomenes 27.1

It is also said that Archidamus of old,[1] towards the beginning of the Peloponnesian war, when the allies ordered their contributions for the war to be fixed, said: "War has no fixed rations."

> 1. Archidamus II, king of Sparta, 469–427 B.C.E.

1309b *War Has No Fixed Rations*
Plutarch, Moralia, Sayings of Spartans III:219A (7)

In the Peloponnesian war, when his allies sought to know how much money would be sufficient, and said it was only fair that he [Archidamus, son of Agesilaus] set a limit to their contributions, he said, "War does not feed on fixed rations."

1309c *War Has No Fixed Rations*
Plutarch, Moralia, Sayings of Kings and Commanders III:190A

When the allies said in the Peloponnesian war it was only right that Archidamus set a limit to their contributions, he said, "War does not feed on fixed rations."

1309d *War Has No Fixed Rations*
Plutarch, Crassus 2.7–8

He [Crassus] held that anything else was to be done for him by his slaves, but his slaves were to be governed by their master. For household management, as we see, is a branch of finance in so far as it deals with lifeless things; but a branch of politics when it deals with men.[1] He was not right, however, in thinking, and in saying too, that no one was rich who could not support an army out of his substance; for "war has no fixed rations," as King Archidamus said, and therefore the wealth requisite for war cannot be determined.

    1. Cf. Aristotle, *Politics* 1.1253b, 32.

1309e *War Has No Fixed Rations*
Plutarch, Demosthenes 17.4 (3)

It was at this time, as Theophrastus says, when the allies were demanding that their contributions be fixed within limits, that Crobylus[1] the popular leader said: "War has no fixed rations."

    1. The familiar name for Hegesippus, the Athenian orator.

1310 *Cleomenes a Lion*
Plutarch, Cleomenes 33.5–6

But afterwards, when Ptolemy's weakness intensified his cowardice, and, as is wont to happen where there is no sound judgement, his best course seemed to him to lie in fearing everybody and distrusting all men, it led the courtiers to be afraid of Cleomenes, on the ground that he had a strong following among the mercenaries; and many of them were heard to say: "There goes the lion up and down among these sheep."

1311 *Stratocles Gives False Report*
Plutarch, Demetrius 11.3

Again, when the Athenians suffered their naval defeat near Amorgus, before the tidings of the disaster could reach the city he [Stratocles] put a garland on his head and drove through the Cerameicus, and after announcing that the Athenians were victorious, moved a sacrifice of glad tidings and made a generous distribution of meat to the people by tribes. Then, a little later, when the wrecks were brought home from the battle and the people in their wrath called him out, he faced the tumult recklessly and said: "What harm have I done you, pray, if for two days you have been happy?"

1312 *Counsels against Wishes*
Plutarch, Demosthenes 14.4 (3)

And even Theopompus tells us that, when the Athenians nominated him [Demosthenes] to conduct a certain impeachment, and, on his refusal, raised a tumult against him, he rose and said: "Men of Athens, I will serve you as a counselor, even though you do not wish it; but not as a false accuser, even though you wish it."

1313 *On Surrender*
Plutarch, Demosthenes 23.5–6 (4)

It was on this occasion that Demosthenes told the Athenians the story of how the sheep surrendered their dogs to the wolves, comparing himself and his fellow orators to dogs fighting in defense of the people, and calling Alexander "the Macedonian arch-wolf." Moreover, he said further: "Just as grain merchants sell their whole stock by means of a few kernels of wheat which they carry about with them in a bowl as a sample, so in surrendering us you unwittingly surrender also yourselves, all of you."

1314 *Generous Enemies*
Plutarch, Demosthenes 26.3–4 (2–3)

At any rate, we are told that when he [Demosthenes] was in flight at a short distance from the city, he learned that some of the citizens who were his enemies were in pursuit of him, and therefore wished to hide himself; and when they called upon him loudly by name, and came up near to him, and begged him to accept from them provision for his journey, declaring that they were bringing money from home for this very purpose, and were pursuing him only in order to get it to him; and when at the same time they exhorted him to be of good courage and not to be pained at what had happened, Demosthenes broke out all the more into cries of grief, saying, "Surely I must be distressed to leave a city where my enemies are as generous as I can hardly find friends to be in another."

1315 *Lucullus' Account*
Plutarch, Lucullus 41.1–2

It is said, for instance, that he [Lucullus] entertained for many successive days some Greeks who had come up to Rome, and that they, with genuinely Greek scruples, were at last ashamed to accept his invitation, on the ground that he was incurring so much expense every day on their account; whereupon Lucullus said to them with a smile, "Some of this expense, my Grecian friends, is indeed on your account; most of it, however, is on account of Lucullus."

1316 *Soüs Outwits Cleitorians*
Plutarch, Lycurgus 2.1–2

It is also related of this Soüs that when he was besieged by the Cleitorians in a rough and waterless place, he agreed to surrender to them the land which he had conquered if he himself and all his men with him should drink from the adjacent spring. After the oaths to this agreement were taken, he assembled his men and offered his kingdom to the one who should not drink; no one of them, however, could forbear, but all of them drank, whereupon Soüs himself went down last of all to the water, sprinkled his face merely, while the enemy were still at hand to see, and then marched away and retained his territory, on the plea that all had not drunk.

1317 *Grain Like Divided Estate*
Plutarch, Lycurgus 8.4

And it is said that on returning from a journey some time afterwards, as he [Lycurgus] traversed the land just after the harvest, and saw the heaps of grain standing parallel and equal to one another, he smiled, and said to them that were by: "All Laconia looks like a family estate newly divided among many brothers."

1318 *Archidamus Posits Enough Spartans*
Plutarch, Lycurgus 20.4

And Archidamus, when someone asked him how many Spartans there were, replied: "Enough, good Sir, to keep evil men away."

1319a *Serious Pupils of Lycurgus*
Plutarch, Lycurgus 20.5–6

And even from their [Lycurgus' pupils] jests it is possible to judge of their character. For it was their wont never to talk at random, and to let slip no speech which did not have some thought or other worth serious attention. For instance, when one of them was invited to hear a man imitate the nightingale, he said: "I have heard the bird herself." And another, on reading the epitaph:—

> "Tyranny's fires they were trying to quench when panoplied
> Ares Slew them; Selinus looked down from her gates on their
>   death,"

said: "The men deserved to die; they should have let the fires burn out entirely." And a youth, when someone promised to give him game-cocks that would die fighting, said, "Don't do that, but give me some of the kind that kill fighting." Another, seeing men seated on stools in a privy, said: "May I never sit where I cannot give place to an elder." The character of their apophthegms, then, was such as to justify the remark that love of wisdom rather than love of bodily exercise was the special characteristic of a Spartan.

1319b *The Bird Herself*
Plutarch, Agesilaus 21.5

And again, when he [Agesilaus] was invited to hear the man who imitated the nightingale, he declined, saying: "I have heard the bird herself."

1320 *Spartan Freedom and Slavery*
Plutarch, Lycurgus 28.5

And therefore in later times, they say, when the Thebans made their expedition into Laconia,[1] they ordered the Helots whom they captured to sing the songs of Terpander, Aleman, and Spendon the Spartan; but they declined to do so, on the plea that their masters did not allow it, thus proving the correctness of the saying: "In Sparta the freeman is more a freeman than anywhere else in the world, and the slave more a slave."

1. Under Epaminondas, 369 B.C.E.

1321   *Sparta Safe Because of Obedience*
Plutarch, Lycurgus 30.3

Wherefore, I for one am amazed at those who declare that the Lacedaemonians knew how to obey, but did not understand how to command, and quote with approval the story of King Theopompus, who, when someone said that Sparta was safe and secure because her kings knew how to command, replied: "Nay, rather because her citizens know how to obey."

1322   *Theban Victory Like Pupils Thrashing Tutor*
Plutarch, Lycurgus 30.6

To this position of Sparta Stratonicus would seem to have mockingly alluded when, in jest, he proposed a law that the Athenians should conduct mysteries and processions, and that the Eleians should preside at games, since herein lay their special excellence, but that the Lacedaemonians should be cudgelled if the others did amiss.[1] This was a joke; but Antisthenes the Socratic, when he saw the Thebans in high feather after the battle of Leuctra,[2] said in all seriousness that they were just like little boys strutting about because they had thrashed their tutor.

> 1. Cf. chapter 18.4.
> 2. In 371 B.C.E., when the Thebans under Epaminondas broke the supremacy of Sparta.

1323   *Spears Upright or Leveled?*
Plutarch, Lysander 22.2

And when the Boeotians tried to play a double game with him, he [Lysander] asked them whether he should march through their territory with spears upright, or leveled.

1324   *Cato's Mean Nature*
Plutarch, Marcus Cato 5.1–2

These things were ascribed by some to the man's [Cato's] parsimony; but others condoned them in the belief that he lived in this contracted way only to correct and moderate the extravagance of others. However, for my part, I regard his treatment of his slaves like beasts of burden, using them to the uttermost, and then when they were old, driving them off and selling them, as the mark of a very mean nature, which recognizes no tie between man and man but that of necessity. And yet we know that kindness has a wider scope than justice. Law and justice we naturally apply to men alone; but when it comes to beneficence and charity, these often flow in streams from the gentle heart, like water from a copious spring, even down to dumb beasts. A kindly man will take good care of his horses even when they are worn out with age, and of his dogs, too, not only in their puppyhood, but when their old age needs nursing.

1325   *Pay Half as Much*
Plutarch, Moralia, Sayings of Kings and Commanders III:172F (2)

After fixing the amount of the taxes which his subjects were to pay, he [Darius[1]] sent for the leading men of the provinces, and asked them if the taxes were not perhaps heavy; and when the men said that the taxes were moderate, he ordered that each should pay only half as much.[2]

1. Darius I, king of Persia 521–485 B.C.E.
2. The same story with variations may be found in Polyaenus, *Strategemata*, 7.11.3. Nothing to this effect is to be found in Herodotus' account of Darius' taxation, 3.86–95.

1326   *Dionysius Chosen General*
Plutarch, Moralia, Sayings of Kings and Commanders III:175D

Dionysius the Elder[1], when the speakers who were to address the people were drawing by lot the letters of the alphabet to determine their order of speaking, drew the letter M; and in answer to the man who said, "Muddle-head you are, Dionysius," he replied, "No! Monarch I am to be," and after he had addressed the people he was at once chosen general by the Syracusans.[2]

1. Ruler of Syracuse, 405–367 B.C.E.
2. Cf. Diodorus 13.91–92.

1327a   *Laws Sleep for a Day*
Plutarch, Moralia, Sayings of Kings and Commanders III:191C (10)

After the battle of Leuctra, since the law decrees that all who run away in battle shall lose their citizenship, and the Ephors saw that the State was destitute of men, they, wishing to abrogate this penalty, invested Agesilaus with authority to revise the laws. He came forward into their midst, and ordered that beginning with the morrow all laws should be in full force.[1]

1. Cf. Polyaenus, *Strategemata* 2.1.13.

1327b   *Laws Sleep for a Day*
Plutarch, Moralia, Sayings of Spartans III:214B–C (73)

In the battle of Leuctra many Spartans ran away to escape the enemy, and these were liable to disgrace as provided by the law. The Ephors, seeing the State bereft of men when it was in great need of soldiers, wished to do away with the disgrace, and also to observe the laws. Accordingly they chose Agesilaus as lawgiver; and he, coming into the public meeting, said, "I would not become a lawgiver to enact another set of laws, for in the present laws I would make no addition, subtraction, or revision. It is good that our present laws be in full force, beginning with the morrow."

1327c   *Laws Sleep for a Day*
Plutarch, Agesilaus 30.4

So they chose Agesilaus as a lawgiver for the occasion. And he, without adding to or subtracting from or changing the laws in any way, came into the assembly of the Lacedaemonians and said that the laws must be allowed to sleep for that day, but from that day on must be in sovereign force. By this means he at once saved the laws for the city and the men from infamy.

1327d   *Laws Sleep for a Day*
Plutarch, Agesilaus and Pompey 2.2

On the other hand, when we consider the remedy which Agesilaus applied to the perplexity of the state in dealing with those who had played the coward, after the disaster at Leuctra, when he urged that the laws should slumber for that day, there was never another political device like it, nor can we find anything in Pompey's career to compare with it; on the contrary, he did not even think it incumbent upon him to abide by the laws which he himself had made, if he might only display the greatness of his power to his friends. But Agesilaus, when he confronted the necessity of abrogating the laws in order to save his fellow-citizens, devised a way by which the citizens should not be harmed by the laws, nor the laws be abrogated to avoid such harm.

1328a *Stopped Brevity of Speech*
Plutarch, Moralia, Sayings of Kings and Commanders III:193D (16)

When the Spartans accused the Thebans of a long list of serious offenses, he [Epaminondas] retorted, "These Thebans, however, have put a stop to your brevity of speech!"

1328b *Stopped Brevity of Speech*
Plutarch, Moralia, On Inoffensive Self-Praise VII:545A (15)

Useful too against public and private enemies are such remarks as these: . . . Epameinondas' reply to the Lacedaemonians when they denounced the Thebans: "We have at any rate put a stop to your Laconic speech."

1329a *Fancy Gifts Refused*
Plutarch, Moralia, Sayings of Spartans III:210C (24)

The Thasians, as he [Agesilaus] was marching through their country with his army, sent to him flour, geese, sweetmeats, honey-cakes, and other costly foods and drinks of all kinds. The flour alone he accepted, but the rest of the things he bade those who had brought them to carry back because these were of no use to the Spartans. But when the Thasians importuned him and begged him by all means to take all, he gave orders to distribute them among the Helots. And when the Thasians inquired the reason, he said, "It is not in keeping that those who practice manly virtues should indulge in such gourmandizing, for things that allure the servile crowd are alien to free men."[1]

> 1. Cf. 1329b–c, where the scene is laid in Egypt. In Aelian, *Varia Historia* 3.20 and 1329d, the story is told of Lysander.

1329b *Fancy Gifts Refused*
Plutarch, Agesilaus 36.6

When all manner of hospitable gifts were brought to him [Agesilaus], he accepted the flour, the calves, and the geese, but rejected the sweetmeats, the pastries, and the perfumes, and when he was urged and besought to take them, ordered them to be carried and given to his Helots.

1329c *Fancy Gifts Refused*
Nepos 17, Agesilaus 8.3–4

When the report of the Spartan's arrival had reached the king's officers, they hastened to bring to his camp gifts of every kind. When they inquired for Agesilaus, they could hardly believe that he was one of those who were then at meat. When they offered him in the name of the king what they had brought, he refused everything except some veal and similar kinds of food which his circumstances made necessary; perfumes, garlands and desserts he distributed among his servants, the rest he ordered to be taken back. Such conduct led the barbarians to hold him in still greater contempt, since they supposed that he had made his choice through lack of acquaintance with fine things.

1329d *Fancy Gifts Refused*
Athenaeus, Deipnosophists 14.656B–C

The Thasians, too, sent to Agesilaus when he went to their aid all kinds of small cattle and steers well fattened, and besides these cakes and every possible variety of sweetmeats. Agesilaus accepted the sheep and the large cattle, but as for the cakes and the sweetmeats, at first he did not know what they were, since they were kept covered. But when he saw them, he commanded that they be taken away, saying that it was not lawful for Spartans to use such viands. And when the Thasians [Egyptians?] insisted he replied, pointing out the Helots to them, "Take and give them to those fellows yonder," explaining that it was much better for them to be corrupted by eating the stuff than that he and the Spartans with him should be.

1330 *Better to Be of Worth*
Plutarch, Moralia, Sayings of Spartans III:230E (5)

When some people were amazed at the costliness of the raiment found among the spoils of the barbarians, he [Pausanias[1]] said that it would have been better for them to be themselves men of worth than to possess things of worth.[2]

1. Regent of Sparta from 479 B.C.E.; commander at Plataea.
2. Cf. Plato, *Laws* 870 B; Cicero, *Paradoxa Stoicorum* 6.1–3 (42–52).

1331a *Orders Harsher Than Death*
Plutarch, Moralia, Sayings of Spartans III:235B–C (54)

After the defeat of Agis, Antipater demanded fifty boys as hostages, but Eteocles, who was Ephor, said they would not give boys, lest the boys should turn out to be uneducated through missing the traditional discipline; and they would not be fitted for citizenship either. But the Spartans would give, if he so desired, either old men or women to double the number. And when Antipater made dire threats if he should not get the boys, the Spartans made answer with consent, "If the orders you lay upon us are harsher than death, we shall find it easier to die."

1331b *Require Nothing Dishonorable*
Plutarch, Moralia, How to Tell a Flatterer I:64D (23)

No, we would choose not even to have knowledge of our friends' dishonorable actions; how then can we possibly choose to cooperate in them and to share in the unseemly conduct? As the Lacedaemonians, defeated in battle by Antipater, in making terms of peace bade him prescribe any penalty he would, but nothing dishonorable, so a friend, if need befall for his services that involves expense, danger, or labor, is foremost in insisting, without excuse or hesitation, that he be called upon and that he do his share, but wherever disgrace goes with it, he is also foremost in begging to be left alone and spared from participation.

1332 *Spartans on Liberty*
Plutarch, Moralia, Sayings of Spartans III:236A (63)

Bulis and Sperchis of Sparta went as volunteers to Xerxes king of the Persians, to render satisfaction which Sparta owed according to an oracle, because the people had killed the heralds sent to them by the Persian. These men came before Xerxes and bade him make away with them in any manner he desired, as representing the Spartans. But when he, filled with admiration, let them go free, and was insistent that they remain with him, they said, "And how should we be able to live here, abandoning our country and laws and those men in whose behalf we made such a long journey to die?" And when Indarnes[1] the general besought them at greater length, and said that they would receive equal honor with the friends of the king who stood highest in advancement, they said, "You seem to us not to know what is the reward of liberty, which no man of sense would exchange for the kingdom of the Persians."[2]

> 1. Hydarnes in Herodotus 7.135.
> 2. Cf. Dio Chrysostom, *Oration* 76. ad fin.; Stobaeus, *Florilegium* 7.70, and 39.27 (quoting Serenus). The ultimate source is probably Herodotus 7.134–136.

1333 *Nicias Makes People Wait*
Plutarch, Nicias 7.5

It is said, for instance, that once when the assembly was in session, the people sat out on the Pynx a long while waiting for him [Nicias] to address them, and that late in the day he came in all garlanded for dinner and asked them to adjourn the assembly to the morrow. "I'm busy today," he said, "I'm going to entertain some guests, and have already sacrificed to the gods."

1334 *Giving Rather Than Receiving*
Plutarch, Nicias and Crassus 1.3

And for this practice Lycurgus the orator, in later times, boldly took to himself credit before the people, when accused of buying up one of these informers; "I am glad indeed," he said, "that after such a long political career among you, I have been detected in giving rather than receiving money."

1335 *Philip Surveys Dead*
Plutarch, Pelopidas 18.5

It is said, moreover, that the band was never beaten, until the battle of Chaeroneia;[1] and when, after the battle, Philip was surveying the dead, and stopped at the place where the three hundred were lying, all where they had faced the long spears of his phalanx, with their armor, and mingled with one another, he was amazed, and on learning that this was the band of lovers and beloved, burst into tears and said: "Perish miserably they who think that these men did or suffered aught disgraceful."

> 1. 338 B.C.E.

1336 *Pericles Wins Support*
Plutarch, Pericles 14.1–2

Thucydides and his party kept denouncing Pericles for playing fast and loose with the public moneys and annihilating the revenues. Pericles therefore asked the people in assembly whether they thought he had expended too much, and on their declaring that it was altogether too much, "Well then," said he, "let it not have been spent on your account, but mine, and I will make the inscriptions of dedication in my own name." When Pericles had said this, whether it was that they admired his magnanimity or vied with his ambition to get the glory of his works, they cried out with a loud voice and bade him take freely from the public funds for his outlays, and to spare naught whatsoever. And finally he ventured to undergo with Thucydides the contest of the ostracism, wherein he secured his rival's banishment,[1] and the dissolution of the faction which been arrayed against him.

1. 442 B.C.E.

1337 Bribe Enemies, Not Friends
Plutarch, Philopoemen 15.6

Then Philopoemen, who was pleased by what he heard, went in person to Sparta, and counseled the people there not to try to bribe good men who were their friends, and by whose virtues they could profit without payment of money, but rather to buy and corrupt the bad men who were ruining the city by their factious conduct in the assembly, to the end that such might have their mouths stopped in consequence of their venality, and so be less annoying to their fellow citizens; for it was better, he said, to take away freedom of speech from their enemies rather than from their friends.

1338 Philopoemen Distressed over Roman Victory
Plutarch, Philopoemen 17.1–2

He [Philopoemen] was distressed because he was not general of the Achaeans at that time, and kept saying that he begrudged the Romans their victory. "For if I had been general," he said, "I would have cut off all these fellows in their taverns."

1339 Phocion Alone Opposes
Plutarch, Phocion 8.3

Indeed, when an oracle from Delphi was read out in the assembly, declaring that when the rest of the Athenians were of like mind, one man had a mind at variance with the city, Phocion came forward and bade them seek no further, since he himself was the man in question; for there was no one but he who disliked everything they did.

1340 Debt Comes First
Plutarch, Phocion 9.1

The Athenians were once asking contributions for a public sacrifice, and the rest were contributing, but Phocion, after being many times asked to give, said: "Ask from these rich men; for I should be ashamed to make a contribution to you before I have paid my debt to this man here," pointing to Callicles the money-lender.

1341 The Coward and the Ravens
Plutarch, Phocion 9.2

And once when his audience would not cease shouting and crying him down, he [Phocion] told them this fable. "A coward was going forth to war, but when some ravens croaked, he laid down his arms and kept quiet; then he picked them up and was going forth again, and when the ravens croaked once more, he stopped, and said at last: "You may croak with all your might, but you shall not get a taste of me."

1342 *Phocion Accused of Cowardice*
Plutarch, Phocion 9.2

And at another time, when the Athenians urged him to lead forth against the enemy, and called him an unmanly coward, because he did not wish to do so, he [Phocion] said: "Ye cannot make me bold, nor can I make you cowards. However, we know one another."

1343 *Safety First*
Plutarch, Phocion 9.3

And again, in a time of peril, when the people were behaving very harshly towards him and demanding that he [Phocion] render up accounts of his general-ship, "My good friends," said he, "make sure of your safety first."

1344 *People Fortunate to Have Phocion*
Plutarch, Phocion 9.3

Again, when they had been humble and timorous during a war, but then, after peace had been made, were getting bold and denouncing Phocion on the ground that he had robbed them of the victory, "Ye are fortunate," said he, "in having a general who knows you; since otherwise ye had long ago perished."

1345 *Fight with Words*
Plutarch, Phocion 9.4

Once, too, when the people were unwilling to adjudicate with the Boeotians a question of territory, but wanted to go to war about it, he [Phocion] counseled them to fight with words, in which they were superior, and not with arms in which they were inferior.

1346 *Speech Not Forced*
Plutarch, Phocion 9.4

Again, when he was speaking and they would not heed or even consent to hear him, he [Phocion] said: "Ye can force me to act against my wishes, but ye shall not compel me to speak against my judgement."

1347 *Polyeuctus Poor Soldier*
Plutarch, Phocion 9.5

Again, when he saw Polyeuctus the Sphettian, on a hot day, counseling the Athenians to go to war with Philip, and then, from much panting and sweating since he was really very corpulent, frequently gulping down water, Phocion said: "It is meet that ye should be persuaded by this man to go to war; for what do ye think he would do under breastplate and shield, when the enemy were near, if, in making you a premeditated speech, he is in danger of choking to death?"

1348 *Hypereides Criticizes Athenians*
Plutarch, Phocion 10.3

And yet we are told that Hypereides once said to the people: "Do not ask, men of Athens, merely whether I am bitter, but whether I am paid for being bitter," as if the multitude were led by their avarice to fear and attack those only who are troublesome and vexatious, and not rather all who use their power to gratify their insolence or envy or wrath or contentiousness.

1349 *Generals Bring Fear*
Plutarch, Phocion 14.2–3

And now Philip, cherishing great anticipations, went to the Hellespont with all his forces, expecting to get the Chersonesus, and at the same time Perinthus and Byzantium, into his power. The Athenians were eager to give aid to their allies, but their orators strove successfully to have Chares sent out as commander, and he, after sailing thither, did nothing worthy of the forces under his order, nor would the cities even receive his armament into their harbors. On the contrary, he was held in suspicion by all of them, and wandered about exacting money from the allies and despised by the enemy, so that the people of Athens, instigated by their orators, were incensed at him, and repented of having sent aid to the Byzantians. Then Phocion rose in the assembly and declared that they must not be angry at their allies who showed distrust, but at their generals who were distrusted, "For these," said he, "make you to be feared even by those who can be saved only by your help."

1350 *Doing Well Saves Greeks*
Plutarch, Phocion 16.4–5

In general, Phocion thought that the policy and kindly overtures of Philip should be accepted by the Athenians; but when Demades brought in a motion that the city should participate with the Greeks in the common peace and in the Congress, Phocion would not favor it before they found out what demands Philip was going to make upon the Greeks. His opinion did not prevail, owing to the crisis, and yet as soon as he saw that the Athenians were repenting of their course, because they were required to furnish Philip with triremes and horsemen, "This is what I feared," said he, "when I opposed your action; but since you agreed upon it, you must not repine or be dejected, remembering that our ancestors also were sometimes in command, and sometimes under command, but by doing well in both positions saved both their city and the Greeks."

1351 *Phocion on Military Superiority*
Plutarch, Phocion 21.1

When Alexander wrote asking the Athenians to send him triremes, and the orators opposed the request, and the council bade Phocion speak upon the matter, "I tell you, then," he said, "either to be superior in arms or to be friends with those who are superior."

1352 *News of Alexander's Death*
Plutarch, Phocion 22.3–4

Asclepiades the son of Hipparchus was the first one to bring to the Athenians the tidings that Alexander was dead. Thereupon Demades urged them to pay no heed to the report, since, had it been true, the whole earth would long ago have been filled with the stench of the body. But Phocion, who saw that the people were bent on revolution, tried to dissuade them and restrain them. And when many of them sprang towards the bema, and shouted that the tidings brought by Ascelpiades were true and that Alexander was dead, "Well, then," said Phocion, "if he is dead today, he will be dead tomorrow, and the day after. Therefore we can deliberate in quiet and with greater safety."

1353 *War No Hardship for Elderly Phocion*
Plutarch, Phocion 24.3

Afterwards, however, seeing that they [the Athenians calling for war] would not desist, but continued to clamor, he [Phocion] ordered the herald to make proclamation that every man in Athens under sixty years of age should take provisions for five days and follow him at once from the assembly. Thereupon a great tumult arose, the elderly men leaping to their feet and shouting their dissent. "It is no hardship," said Phocion, "for I who am to be your general am in my eightieth year."

1354 *Laws Irrelevant before Swords*
Plutarch, Pompey 10.2

Perpenna at once abandoned Sicily to him [Pompey], and he recovered the cities there. They had been harshly used by Perpenna, but Pompey treated them all with kindness except the Mamertines in Messana. These declined his tribunal and jurisdiction on the plea that they were forbidden by an ancient law of the Romans, at which Pompey said: "Cease quoting laws to us that have swords girt about us!"

1355 *To Sail Is Necessary*
Plutarch, Pompey 50.1–2

Having thus been set over the administration and management of the grain trade, Pompey sent out his agents and friends in various directions, while he himself sailed to Sicily, Sardinia and Africa, and collected grain. When he was to set sail with it, there was a violent storm at sea, and the ship-captains hesitated to put out; but he led the way on with a loud voice: "To sail is necessary; to live is not." By this exercise of zeal and courage attended by good fortune, he filled the sea with ships and the markets with grain, so that the excess of what he provided sufficed also for foreign peoples, and there was an abundant overflow, as from a spring, for all.

1356 *Victory a Ruin*
Plutarch, Pyrrhus 21.9

We are told that Pyrrhus said to one who was congratulating him on his victory, "If we are victorious in one more battle with the Romans, we shall be utterly ruined."

1357 *No Victory without Honor*
Plutarch, Sertorius 23.3–5

So Mithridates sent envoys to Iberia carrying letters and oral propositions to Sertorius, the purport of which was that Mithridates for his part promised to furnish money and ships for the war, but demanded that Sertorius confirm him in the possession of the whole of Asia, which he yielded to the Romans by virtue of the treaties made with Sulla. Sertorius assembled a council which he called a senate, and here the rest urged him to accept the king's proposals and be well content with them; for they were asked to grant a name and an empty title to what was not in their possession, and would receive therefore that of which they stood most in need. Sertorius, however, would not consent to this. He said he had no objection to Mithridates taking Bithynia and Cappadocia, countries used to kings and of no concern whatever to the Romans; but a province which Mithridates had taken away and held when it belonged in the justest manner to the Romans, from which he had been driven by Fimbria in war, and which he had renounced by treaty with Sulla, this province Sertorius said he would not suffer to become the king's again; for the Roman state must be increased by his exercise of power, and he must not exercise power at the expense of the state. For to a man of noble spirit victory is to be desired if it comes with honor, but with shame not even life itself.

1358 *Fools Decide Cases*
Plutarch, Solon 5.3

It was Anacharsis, too, who said, after attending a session of the assembly, that he was amazed to find that among the Greeks, the wise men pleaded cases, but the fools decided them.

1359 *The Best Laws*
Plutarch, Solon 15.2

Therefore when he [Solon] was afterwards asked if he had enacted the best laws for the Athenians, he replied, "The best they would receive."

1360 *Themistocles and a Critic*
Plutarch, Themistocles 11:3–5

But on a certain one saying that a man without a city had no business to advise men who still had cities of their own to abandon and betray them, Themistocles addressed his speech with emphasis to him, saying: "It is true, thou wretch, that we have left behind us our houses and our city walls, not deeming it meet for the sake of such lifeless things to be in subjection; but we still have a city, the greatest in the Hellas, our two hundred triremes, which now are ready to aid you if you choose to be saved by them; but if you go off and betray us for the second time, straightway many a Hellene will learn that Athenians have won for themselves a city that is free and a territory that is far better than the one they cast aside." When Themistocles said this, Eurybiades began to reflect, and was seized with fear lest the Athenians go away and abandon him.

1361 *Themistocles a Plane-Tree*
Plutarch, Themistocles 18.3

And he [Themistocles] also used to say of the Athenians that they did not really honor and admire him for himself but treated him for all the world like a plane-tree, running under his branches for shelter when it stormed, but when they had fair weather all about them, plucking and docking him.

1362 *Song of the Bottiaean Maidens*
Plutarch, Theseus 16.2

And he [Aristotle] says that the Cretans once, in fulfillment of an ancient vow, sent an offering of their first born to Delphi, and that some descendants of those Athenians were among the victims, and went forth with them; and that when they were unable to support themselves there, they first crossed over into Italy and dwelt in that country round about Iapygia, and from there journeyed again into Thrace and were called Bottiaeans; and that this was the reason why the maidens of Bottiaea, in performing a certain sacrifice, sing as an accompaniment: "To Athens let us go!"

1363 *Nasica Leads Senators against Tiberius*
Plutarch, Tiberius Gracchus 19.1–4

Tiberius, accordingly, reported this [the plot to kill him] to those who stood about him, and they at once girded up their togas, and breaking in pieces the spearshafts with which the officers keep back the crowd, distributed the fragments among themselves, that they might defend themselves against their assailants. Those who were farther off, however, wondered at what was going on and asked what it meant. Whereupon Tiberius put his hand to his head, making this visible sign that his life was in danger, since the questioners could not hear his voice. But his opponents, on seeing this, ran to the senate and told that body that Tiberius was asking for a crown; and that his putting his hand to his head was a sign having that meaning. All the senators, of course, were greatly disturbed, and Nasica demanded that the consul should come to the rescue of the state and put down the tyrant. The consul replied with mildness that he would resort to no violence and would put no citizen to death without trial; if, however, the people, under persuasion or compulsion from Tiberius, should vote anything that was unlawful, he would not regard this vote as binding. Thereupon Nasica sprang to his feet and said: "Since then the chief magistrate betrays the state, do ye who wish to succor the laws follow me." With these words he covered his head with the skirt of his toga and set out for the Capitol. All the senators who followed him wrapped their togas about their left arms and pushed aside those who stood in their path, no man opposing them, in view of their dignity, but all taking to flight and trampling upon one another.

1364 *Titus Warns Achaeans*
Plutarch, Titus Flaminius 17.2

When he [Titus] was trying to dissuade the Achaeans from appropriating the island of Zacynthos, he said it would be dangerous for them, like a tortoise, to stick their head out of its Peloponnesian shell.

1365a *Antiochus' Army Nothing But Syrians*
Plutarch, Titus Flaminius 17.4

And once more, when an embassy from Antiochus was recounting to the Achaeans the vast multitude of the king's forces and enumerating them all by their various appellations, Titus said that once, when he was dining with a friend, he criticised the multitude of meals that were served, wondering where he had obtained so varied a supply; whereupon his host told him they were all swine's flesh, and differed only in the way they were cooked and dressed. "And so in your case," said he, "men of Achaia, do not be astonished when you hear of the Spearbearers and Lance-bearers and Foot-companions in the army of Antiochus; for they are all Syrians and differ only in the way they are armed."[1]

1. Cf. Livy 35.49.

1365b *Antiochus' Army Nothing But Syrians*
Plutarch, Moralia, Sayings of Romans III:197C–D (4)

When Antiochus the king, with a great force, arrived in Greece, and all were terror-stricken at the great numbers of the men and their armament, Flamininus told a story for the benefit of the Achaeans as follows: He said he was in Chalcis dining with a friend, and was amazed at the great number of the meats served. But his friend said that these were all pork, differing only in their seasoning and the way they were cooked. "So then," he said, "do not you, either, be amazed at the king's forces when you hear the names: 'pikemen,' 'panoplied,' 'foot-guards,' 'archers with two horses.' For all these are but Syrians differing from one another only in their paraphernalia."

1366 *Impudent Student Dies*
Sifra 45

It once happened that one of his students was rendering [legal] decisions in [R. Eliezer]'s presence. [R. Eliezer] said to his wife, Imma Shalom: "He will no longer live after the end of the Sabbath." And when he died after the Sabbath, sages entered and said to [Eliezer]: "Rabbi, you are a prophet!" He said to them: "I am neither a prophet nor the son of a prophet. However, thus I received from my teachers, that anyone who renders legal decisions in the presence of his teacher deserves death."

1367 *Sabta Serves Peor*
Sifre, Numbers 131

One time Sabta of Ulan hired his donkey to a gentile woman. When she reached the edge of the territory, she said to him: "Wait until I enter the temple of [the territory's] idol." When she came out, he said to her: "Wait for me until I enter and do as you have done." She said to him: "Is it possible that you, a Jew [will enter and serve the idol]?" He entered [and uncovered himself] and wiped himself on the nose of Peor. Then all the gentiles laughed and said: "No man has served [Peor] like this before!"

1368 *Augustus Revives Ancient Dress*
Suetonius, Lives of the Caesars, Augustus 2.40.5

He [Augustus] desired also to revive the ancient fashion of dress, and once when he saw in an assembly a throng of men in dark cloaks, he cried out indignantly, "Behold them Romans, lords of the world, the nation clad in the toga,"[1] and he directed the aediles never again to allow anyone to appear in the Forum or its neighborhood except in the toga and without a cloak.

1. Virgil, *Aeneid* 1.282.

1369 *The Largess of Augustus*
Suetonius, Lives of the Caesars, Augustus 2.42.2–3

Again, when the people demanded largess which he had in fact promised, he [Augustus] replied: "I am a man of my word"; but when they called for one which had not been promised, he rebuked them in a proclamation for their shameless impudence, and declared that he would not give it, even though he was intending to do so. With equal dignity and firmness, when he had announced a distribution of money and found that many had been manumitted and added to the list of citizens, he declared that those to whom no promise had been made should receive nothing, and gave the rest less than he had promised, to make the appointed sum suffice. Once indeed in a time of great scarcity when it was difficult to find a remedy, he expelled from the city the slaves that were for sale, as well as the schools of gladiators, all foreigners with the exception of physicians and teachers, and a part of the household slaves; and when grain at last became more plentiful, he writes: "I was strongly inclined to do away forever with distributions of grain, because through dependence on them agriculture was neglected; but I did not carry out my purpose, feeling sure that they would one day be renewed through desire for popular favor." But from that time on he regulated the practice with no less regard for the interests of the farmers and grain-dealers than for those of the populace.

1370   *Augustus Offered Title*
Suetonius, Lives of the Caesars, Augustus 2.58.1–2

The whole body of citizens with a sudden unanimous impulse proffered him [Augustus] the title of Father of his Country: first the commons, by a deputation sent to Antium, and then, because he declined it, again at Rome as he entered the theater, which they attended in throngs, all wearing laurel wreaths; the senate afterwards in the House, not by a decree or by acclamation, but through Valerius Messala. He, speaking for the whole body, said: "Good fortune and divine favor attend thee and thy house, Caesar Augustus; for thus we feel that we are praying for lasting prosperity for our country and happiness for our city. The senate in accord with the people of Rome hails thee Father of thy Country." Then Augustus with tears in his eyes replied as follows (and I have given his exact words, as I did those of Messala): "Having attained my highest hopes, Fathers of the Senate, what more have I to ask of the immortal gods than that I may retain this same unanimous approval of yours to the very end of my life."

1371   *Caligula as Monster*
Suetonius, Lives of the Caesars, Caligula 4.22.1

So much for Caligula as emperor; we must now tell of his career as a monster. After he had assumed various surnames (for he was called "Pious," "Child of the Camp," "Father of the Armies," and "Greatest and Best of Caesars"), chancing to overhear some kings, who had come to Rome to pay their respects to him, disputing at dinner about the nobility of their descent, he cried:

"Let there be one Lord, one King."[1]

1. Homer, *Iliad* 2.204.

1372   *Caligula Jests about Executions*
Suetonius, Lives of the Caesars, Caligula 4.29.2

On signing the list of prisoners who were to be put to death later, he [Caligula] said that he was clearing his accounts. Having condemned several Gauls and Greeks to death in a body, he boasted that he had subdued Gallograecia.

1373a   *Bloodthirsty Caligula*
Suetonius, Lives of the Caesars, Caligula 4.30.1–3

He [Caligula] seldom had anyone put to death except by numerous slight wounds, his constant order, which soon became well-known, being: "Strike so that he may feel that he is dying." When a different man than he had intended had been killed, through a mistake in the names, he said that the victim too had deserved the same fate. He often uttered the familiar line of the tragic poet:[1]

"Let them hate me, so they but fear me."

He cften inveighed against all the senators alike, as adherents of Sejanus and informers against his mother and brothers, producing the documents which he pretended to have burned, and upholding the cruelty of Tiberius as forced upon him, since he could not but believe so many accusers. He constantly tongue-lashed the equestrian order as devotees of the stage and the arena. Angered at the rabble for applauding a faction which he opposed, he cried: "I wish the Roman people had but a single neck," and when the brigand Tetrinius was demanded, he said that those who asked for him were Tetriniuses also. Once a band of five *retiarii* in tunics, matched against the same number of *secutores*, yielded without a struggle; but when their death was ordered, one of them caught up his trident and slew all the victors. Caligula bewailed this in a public proclamation as a most cruel murder, and expressed his horror of those who had had the heart to witness it.

1. Accius, *Tragedies* 203.

1373b *Complaints about Tiberius*
Suetonius, Lives of the Caesars, Tiberius 3.59.2

These [complaints] at first he [Tiberius] wished to be taken as the work of those who were impatient of his reforms, voicing not so much their real feelings as their anger and vexation; and he used to say from time to time: "Let them hate me, provided they respect my conduct."

1374 *Power Amusing*
Suetonius, Lives of the Caesars, Caligula 4.32.3

At one of his more sumptuous banquets he [Caligula] suddenly burst into a fit of laughter, and when the consuls, who were reclining next him, politely inquired at what he was laughing, he replied: "What do you suppose, except that at a single nod of mine both of you could have your throats cut on the spot?"

1375 *Be Frugal or Caesar*
Suetonius, Lives of the Caesars, Caligula 4.37.1

In reckless extravagance he [Caligula] outdid the prodigals of all times in ingenuity, inventing a new sort of baths and unnatural varieties of food and feasts: for he would bathe in hot or cold perfumed oils, drink pearls of great price dissolved in vinegar, and set before his guests loaves and meats of gold, declaring that a man ought either to be frugal or Caesar.

1376 *Caligula Gains by Play*
Suetonius, Lives of the Caesars, Caligula 4.41.2

He [Caligula] did not even disdain to make money from play, and to increase his gains by falsehood and even by perjury. Having on one occasion given up his place to the player next him and gone into the courtyard, he spied two wealthy Roman knights passing by; he ordered them to be seized at once and their property confiscated and came back exultant, boasting that he had never played in better luck.

1377a *Claudius as Censor*
Suetonius, Lives of the Caesars, Claudius 5.16.1

He [Claudius] also assumed the censorship, which had long been discontinued, ever since the term of Plancus and Paulus, but in this office too he was variable, and both his theory and his practice were inconsistent. In his review of the knights he let off a young man of evil character, whose father said that he was perfectly satisfied with him, without any public censure,[1] saying "He has a censor of his own."

1. On this see 1377b.

1377b *Augustus as Censor*
Suetonius, Augustus 2.39

Having obtained ten assistants from the senate, he [Augustus] compelled each knight to render an account of his life, punishing some of those whose conduct was scandalous and degrading others; but the greater part he reprimanded with varying degrees of severity. The mildest form of reprimand was to hand them a pair of tablets publicly, which they were to read in silence on the spot. He censured some because they had borrowed money at low interest and invested it at a higher rate.

1378 *Sham Sea-Fight*
Suetonius, Lives of the Caesars, Claudius 5.21.6

Even when he [Claudius] was on the point of letting out the water from Lake Fucinus he gave a sham sea-fight first. But when the combatants cried out: "Hail, emperor, they who are about to die salute thee," he replied, "Or not," and after that all of them refused to fight, maintaining that they had been pardoned.

1379 *Claudius Jests in House*
Suetonius, Lives of the Caesars, Claudius 5.40.1

When a debate was going on about the butchers and vintners, he [Claudius] cried out in the House: "Now, pray, who can live without a snack?"

1380 *Claudius No Telegenius*
Suetonius, Lives of the Caesars, Claudius 5.40.3

When the people of Ostia made a public petition to him, he [Claudius] flew into a rage on the very tribunal and bawled out that he had no reason for obliging them; that he was surely free if anyone was. In fact every day, and almost every hour and minute, he would make such remarks as these; "What! do you take me for a Telegenius?"[1] "Scold me, but hands off!"

1. Obviously some man proverbial for his folly; but nothing is known about him.

1381 *Claudius Repents Marriage and Adoption*
Suetonius, Lives of the Caesars, Claudius 5.43

Towards the end of his life he [Claudius] had shown some plain signs of repentance for his marriage with Agrippina and his adoption of Nero; for when his freedmen expressed their approval of a trial in which he had the day before condemned a woman for adultery, he declared that it had been his destiny also to have wives who were all unchaste, but not unpunished.

1382   Caesar Chooses Gaul

Suetonius, Lives of the Caesars, Julius 1.22.1–2

Backed therefore by his father-in-law and son-in-law, out of all the numerous provinces he [Julius] made the Gauls his choice, as the most likely to enrich him and furnish suitable material for triumphs. At first, it is true, by the bill of Vatinius he received only Cisalpine Gaul with the addition of Illyricum; but presently he was assigned Gallia Comata as well by the senate, since the members feared that even if they should refuse it, the people would give him this also. Transported with joy at this success, he could not keep from boasting a few days later before a crowded house, that having gained his heart's desire to the grief and lamentation of his opponents, he would therefore from that time mount on their heads;[1] and when someone insultingly remarked that that would be no easy matter for any woman, he replied in the same vein that Semiramis too had been queen in Syria and the Amazons in days of old had held sway over a great part of Asia.

1. Used in a double sense, the second unmentionable.

1383   Caesar Insults Senate

Suetonius, Lives of the Caesars, Julius 1.79.1

To an insult which so plainly showed his contempt for the Senate he [Julius] added an act of even greater insolence; for at the Latin Festival, as he was returning to the city, amid the extravagant and unprecedented demonstrations of the populace, someone in the press placed on his statue a laurel wreath with a white fillet tied to it;[1] and when Epidius Marullus and Caesetius Flavus, tribunes of the commons, gave orders that the ribbon be removed from the wreath and the man taken off to prison, Caesar sharply rebuked and deposed them, either offended that the hint at regal power had been received with so little favor, or, as he asserted, that he had been robbed of the glory of refusing it.

1. The white fillet was emblematic of royalty.

1384   Senate Returns Thanks

Suetonius, Lives of the Caesars, Nero 6.10.2

He [Nero] greeted men of all orders off-hand and from memory. When the senate returned thanks to him, he replied, "When I shall have deserved them."

1385   Greeks Alone Worthy of Nero's Songs

Suetonius, Lives of the Caesars, Nero 6.22.3

When some of them begged him to sing after dinner and greeted his performance with extravagant applause, he [Nero] declared that "the Greeks were the only ones who had an ear for music and that they alone were worthy of his efforts."

1386   Humble Art Affords Bread

Suetonius, Lives of the Caesars, Nero 6.40.1

Astrologers had predicted to Nero that he would one day be repudiated, which was the occasion of that well known saying of his: "A humble art affords us daily bread."

1387 *Nero Exhibits Water Organs*
Suetonius, Lives of the Caesars, Nero 6.41.2

Not even on his arrival did he [Nero] personally address the senate or people, but called some of the leading men to his house and after a hasty consultation spent the rest of the day in exhibiting some water-organs of a new and hitherto unknown form, explaining their several features and lecturing on the theory and complexity of each of them; and he even declared that he would presently produce them all in the theater "with the kind permission of Vindex."

1388 *Tiberius Crunches Slowly*
Suetonius, Lives of the Caesars, Tiberius 3.21.2

I know that it is commonly believed, that when Tiberius left the room after this confidential talk, Augustus was overheard by his chamberlains to say: "Alas for the Roman people, to be ground by jaws that crunch so slowly!"

1389 *Good Shepherd Shears Flock*
Suetonius, Lives of the Caesars, Tiberius 3.32.2

To the governors who recommended burdensome taxes for his provinces, he [Tiberius] wrote in answer that it was the part of a good shepherd to shear his flock, not skin it.

1390 *Statue of Vespasian*
Suetonius, Lives of the Caesars, Vespasian 8.23.3

On the report of a deputation that a colossal statue of great cost had been voted him at public expense, he [Vespasian] demanded to have it set up at once, and holding out his open hand, said that the base was ready.

1391 *Job and the Traders*
Testament, Job 11:1–11 (12)

Now there were also some strangers who saw my good will, and they also desired to help with the distribution. And there were some others at the time without resources and not able to spend a thing. And they came and implored, saying:

> "We beg you, since we also are able to accomplish this distri-
> bution but we own nothing, be compassionate with us and
> provide us with money so we may go away to distant cities and,
> engaging in business, we may be able to carry out this distri-
> bution for the destitute. And after this we will restore to you
> what is yours."

And when I heard these things I would be glad that they would take anything at all from me as an arrangement for the poor. And readily accepting the note, I would give them as they wished—not taking from them any security except a note. And so they would go with my resources.

Now sometimes they would be successful in business and give to the poor. Then again, at other times they would be robbed and would come and implore me saying, "We beg you, be patient with us so we may see how we may restore your things to you." And I, without delay, would bring their note and read it, crowning the bearing of the burden with cancellation saying, "As long as I trusted you for the sake of the destitute, I will take nothing from you." And I would take nothing from my debtor.

1392 Kings Visit Job
Testament, Job 28:1-7 (6)
Now when I had completed twenty years with the plague the kings heard about the things that had happened to me. And they arose and came to me, each from his own region, to encourage me by a visit. And when they came near to me from a distance, they did not recognize me. And they cried out and wept as each one tore his own robe. And throwing dirt on themselves they sat beside me seven days and seven nights. But not even one of them spoke to me—and not because of their patience with me but because they had known me as one with much wealth while they were never comparable. For even when I would bring to them precious stones, they would marvel, and clapping their hands they would say, "Whenever the possessions of us three kings are brought together at the same place, they shall never match the brilliant stones of your kingdom. For you are more noble than those from the east."

1393 Agesilaus Refuses to Destroy Fellow Greeks
Xenophon, Agesilaus, 7.6
And when the Corinthian exiles told him [Agesilaus] that the city was about to be surrendered to them and pointed to the engines with which they were confident of taking the walls, he would not make an assault, declaring that Greek cities ought not to be enslaved, but chastened. "And if," he added, "we are going to annihilate the erring members of our own race, let us beware lest we lack men to help in the conquest of the barbarians."

1394a King Like Herdsman
Xenophon, Memorabilia 1.2.32
When the Thirty were putting to death many citizens of the highest respectability and were encouraging many in crime, Socrates had remarked: "It seems strange enough to me that a herdsman who lets his cattle decrease and go to the bad should not admit that he is a poor cowherd; but stranger still that a statesman, when he causes the citizens to decrease and go to the bad, should feel no shame nor think himself a poor statesman."

1394b King Like Herdsman
Xenophon, Cyropaedia 8.2.14
People quote a remark of his [Cyrus'] to the effect that the duties of a good shepherd and of a good king were very much alike; a good shepherd ought, while deriving benefit from his flocks, to make them happy (so far as sheep can be said to have happiness), and in the same way a king ought to make his people and his cities happy, if he would derive benefits from them.

1395 A List of Exemplary Actions
Xenophon, Memorabilia 4.4.2-4
When chairman in the Assemblies he [Socrates] would not permit the people to record an illegal vote, but, upholding the laws, resisted a popular impulse that might even have overborne any but himself. And when the Thirty laid a command

on him that was illegal, he refused to obey. Thus he disregarded their repeated injunction not to talk with young men; and when they commanded him and certain other citizens to arrest a man on a capital charge, he alone refused, because the command laid on him was illegal.[1] Again, when he was tried on the charge brought by Meletus, whereas it is the custom of defendants to curry favor with the jury and to indulge in flattery and illegal appeals, and many by such means have been known to gain a verdict of acquittal, he rejected utterly the familiar chicanery of the courts; and though he might easily have gained a favorable verdict by even a moderate indulgence in such stratagems, he chose to die through his loyalty to the laws rather than to live through violating them.

    1. Alluding to the famous case of Leon.

A specified group is present or referred to in the stories listed below, but some other feature has determined their location in another section.

Cicero: 70b, 717c, 1423
Eunapius: 198a
Frontinus: 65, 203a, 203c, 690b, 716
Gellius: 731a
Gospel: 88b, 225, 229a, 366, 367, 432, 743
Hadith: 253
Josephus: 754
Lucian: 1432
Nepos: 833, 835
Philo: 373
Philostratus: 878, 883, 884
Plutarch: 5, 6a, 33, 52, 172a, 172c, 173, 202b, 404a, 454, 461, 465a, 677b, 929a, 951, 952b, 965, 975, 983, 993, 1003, 1014, 1015, 1016, 1074, 1082, 1087, 1095, 1106, 1110, 1122, 1418
Suetonius: 53a, 1135, 1149

Adult: Youth

Boys jump on Muḥammad's back while he is praying; candid action by a child evokes Diogenes' praise; young people squander their life and money on drunkenness, gluttony, and possessions; a young man seeks advice about marriage; and young princes, orators, and senators receive advice from their elders. In antiquity as in our time, these anecdotes display encounters of the energy, creativity, folly, and naïveté of youth with the commendation and censure of adults.

1396 *Generosity of Two Kinds*
Cicero, De Officiis 2.15.53

Liberality is thus forestalled by liberality: for the more people one has helped with gifts of money, the fewer one can help. But if people are generous and kind in the way of personal service—that is, with their ability and personal effort—various advantages arise: first, the more people they assist, the more helpers they will have in works of kindness; and second, by acquiring the habit of kindness they are better prepared and in better training, as it were, for bestowing favors upon many. In one of his letters Philip takes his son Alexander sharply to task for trying by gifts of money to secure the good-will of the Macedonians: "What in the mischief induced you to entertain such a hope," he says, "as that those men would be loyal subjects to you whom you had corrupted with money? Or are you trying to do what you can to lead the Macedonians to expect that you will be not their king but their steward and purveyor?" "Steward and purveyor" was well said, because it was degrading for a prince; better still, when he called the gift of money "corruption." For the recipient goes from bad to worse and is made all the more ready to be constantly looking for one bribe after another.

1397 *Keep to Your Own Sphere*
Diogenes Laertius, Lives of the Eminent Philosophers 1.79–80

The story goes that a young man took counsel with him [Pittacus] about marriage, and received this answer, as given by Callimachus in his Epigrams[1]:

> A stranger of Atarneus thus inquired of Pittacus, the son of
>   Hyrrhadius:
> Old sire, two offers of marriage are made to me; the one bride
>   is in wealth and birth my equal;
> The other is my superior. Which is the better? Come now and
>   advise me which of the two I shall wed.
> So spake he. But Pittacus, raising his staff, an old man's weap-
>   on, said, "See there, yonder boys will tell you the whole
>   tale."

The boys were whipping their tops to make them go fast and
    spinning them in a wide open space.
"Follow in their track," said he. So he approached near, and
    the boys were saying, "Keep to your own sphere."
When he heard this, the stranger desisted from aiming at the
    lordlier match, assenting to the warning of the boys.
And, even as he led home the humble bride, so do you, Dion,
    keep to your own sphere.

    1. *Anthologia Palatina* 7.89.

1398 *Child Beats Diogenes in Plainness*
Diogenes Laertius, Lives of the Eminent Philosophers 6.37

One day, observing a child drinking out of his hands, he [Diogenes] cast away
the cup from his wallet with the words, "A child has beaten me in plainness of
living."

1399 *Dogs Don't Eat Beetroot*
Diogenes Laertius, Lives of the Eminent Philosophers 6.45

When some boys clustered round him [Diogenes] and said, "Take care he
doesn't bite us," he answered, "Never fear, boys, a dog does not eat beetroot."

1400 *An Intention Worse Than Nature's*
Diogenes Laertius, Lives of the Eminent Philosophers 6.65

Seeing a young man behaving effeminately, "Are you not ashamed," he [Dio-
genes] said, "that your own intention about yourself should be worse than nature's:
for nature made you a man, but you are forcing yourself to play the woman."

1401 *Boys Jump on Muḥammad*
Hadith, Albānī, 312

Abū Yaʿlā reported from ʿAlī b. Ṣāliḥ from ʿĀṣim from Zirr from ʿAbd Allāh b.
Masʿūd who said, The Prophet was praying, and when he prostrated himself al-
Ḥasan and al-Ḥusayn jumped on his back. When someone tried to prevent them
from doing this he motioned for them to leave the children alone. After he had
finished praying he took the two boys on his lap and said, "If anyone loves me, let
him love these two as well."

1402 *Advice to Young Men*
Hadith, Bukhārī, akhbār al-āḥād, 1

Muḥammad b. al-Muthannā, ʿAbd al-Wahhāb and Ayyūb related to us from Abū
Qilāba who had it from Mālik who said: We came to the Prophet as young men
about the same age and we stayed with him for twenty nights. The Messenger of
God was kind. When he thought that we were missing our families and longing to
see them he asked us about those whom we had left behind. We told him about
them, and he said, "Go back to your families, stay with them, teach them and give
them counsel." Then he mentioned some things that I remember and some that I
do not. He said, "Pray as you have seen me pray and when the time of prayer
comes, one of you should give the call to prayer, and the oldest among you should
lead the prayer."

1403   The Lost Ring
Lucian, Demonax 17

Finding a gold ring one day while he was out walking, he [Demonax] posted a notice in the public square asking the one who owned it and had lost it to come and get it by describing the weight of the setting, the stone, and the engravings on it. A pretty girl came to him saying that she had lost it; but as there was nothing right in her description, Demonax said, "Be off, girl, and don't lose your own ring, for you have not lost this one!"

1404   Herennius Cashiered
Macrobius, Saturnalia 2.4.6

His [Augustus'] reply to Herennius, a young man of bad character whom he had ordered to be cashiered, was a well-known example of his humor; for when the man begged for pardon saying: "How am I to return home? What shall I say to my father?" Augustus answered: "Tell your father that you didn't find me to your liking."

1405   Apollonius and the Drunkard
Philostratus, Life of Apollonius 1.9

For an Assyrian stripling came to Asclepius, and though he was sick, yet he lived the life of luxury, and being continually drunk, I will not say he lived, rather he was ever dying. He suffered then from dropsy, and finding his pleasure in drunkenness took no care to dry up his malady. On this account then Asclepius took no care of him, and did not visit him even in a dream. The youth grumbled at this, and thereupon the god, standing over him, said, "if you were to consult Apollonius you would be easier." He therefore went to Apollonius, and said: "What is there in your wisdom that I can profit by? for Asclepius bids me consult you." And he replied: "I can advise you of what, under the circumstances, will be most valuable to you; for I suppose you want to get well." "Yes, by Zeus," answered the other, "I want the health which Asclepius promises, but never gives." "Hush," said the other, "for he gives to those who desire it, but you do things that irritate and aggravate your disease, for you give yourself up to luxury, and you accumulate heavy meals upon your water-logged and worn-out stomach, and as it were, choke water with a flood of mud." This was a clearer response, in my opinion, than Heraclitus, in his wisdom, gave. For he said when he was visited by this affection that what he needed was someone to substitute a drought for his rainy weather, a very unintelligible remark, it appears to me, and by no means clear; but the sage restored the youth to health by a clear interpretation of the wise saw.

1406   Apollonius a Law-Giver
Philostratus, Life of Apollonius 1.17

And when a certain quibbler asked him [Apollonius] why he asked himself no questions, he replied: "Because I asked questions when I was a stripling; and it is not my business to ask questions now, but to teach people what I have discovered." "How then," the other asked him afresh, "O Apollonius, should the sage converse?" "Like a law-giver," he replied, "for it is the duty of the law-giver to deliver to the many the instructions of whose truth he has persuaded himself."

1407 *Apollonius and the Rich Young Man*
Philostratus, Life of Apollonius 5.22

It happened also that a young man was building a house in Rhodes who was a nouveau riche without any education, and he collected in his house rare pictures and gems from different countries. Apollonius then asked him how much money he had spent upon teachers and on education. "Not a farthing," he replied. "And how much upon your house?" "Twelve talents," he replied, "and I mean to spend as much again upon it." "And what," said the other, "is the good of your house to you?" "Why, as a residence, it is splendidly suited to my bodily training, for there are colonnades in it and groves, and I shall seldom need to walk out into the market place, but people will come in and talk to me with all the more pleasure, just as if they were visiting a temple." "And," said Apollonius, "are men to be valued more for themselves or for their belongings?" "For their wealth," said the other, "for wealth has the most influence." "And," said Apollonius, "my good youth, which is the best able to keep his money, an educated person or an uneducated?" And as the other made no answer, he added: "My good boy, it seems to me that it is not you that own the house, but the house that owns you. As for myself I would far rather enter a temple, no matter how small, and behold in it a statue of ivory and gold, than behold one of pottery and bad workmanship in a vastly larger one."

1408 *Apollonius and the Glutton*
Philostratus, Life of Apollonius 5.23

And meeting a young man who was young and fat and who prided himself upon eating more than anybody else, and on drinking more wine than others, he [Apollonius] remarked: "Then you, it seems, are the glutton." "Yes, and I sacrifice to the gods out of gratitude for the same." "And what pleasure," said Apollonius, "do you get by gorging yourself in this way?" "Why, everyone admires me and stares at me; for you have probably heard of Hercules, how people took as much pains to celebrate what he ate as what labors he performed." "Yes, for he was Hercules," said Apollonius; "but as for yourself, you scum, what good points are there about you? There is nothing left for you but to burst, if you want to be stared at."

1409 *Isaeus Rebukes Pupils*
Philostratus, Lives of the Sophists 1.20 (513)

When Dionysius of Miletus, who had been his pupil, delivered his declamations in a sing-song, Isaeus rebuked him, saying, "Young man from Ionia, I did not train you to sing."[1] And when a youth from Ionia admired in his presence the grandiloquent saying of Nicetes in his *Xerxes*, "Let us fasten Aegina to the king's ship," Isaeus burst into a loud laugh and said, "Madman, how will you put to sea?"

1. The Ionian rhetoricians were especially fond of such vocal effects.

1410 *Fragments of a Colossus*
Philostratus, Lives of the Sophists 2.10 (586)

When he was still a mere youth Adrian invited Herodes to hear him make a speech extempore. Herodes listened to him, not as some people unjustly accuse him, in an envious or scoffing spirit, but with his usual calm and kindly bearing, and afterwards he encouraged the youth, and ended by saying, "These might well be great fragments of a colossus."

411 Many Victories Teach Mistakes of Vanquished
Plutarch, Aemilius Paulus 17.1–4

Aemilius, after effecting a junction with Nasica, came down in battle array against the enemy. But when he saw how they were drawn up, and in what numbers, he was amazed, and came to a halt, considering with himself. His young officers, however, who were eager for battle, rode up and begged him not to delay, especially Nasica, who was emboldened by his success at Mount Olympus. But Aemilius, with a smile, said to him: "Yes, if I had thy youth; but many victories teach me the mistakes of the vanquished, and forbid me to join battle, immediately after a march, with a phalanx which is already drawn up and completely formed."

1412 Serapion, Playing Ball, Receives Gifts
Plutarch, Alexander 39.5 (3)

Again, to Serapion, one of the youths who played at ball with him, he [Alexander] used to give nothing because he asked for nothing. Accordingly, whenever Serapion had the ball, he would throw it to others, until the king said: "Won't you give it to me?" "No," said Serapion, "because you don't ask for it," whereat the king burst out laughing and made him many presents.

1413 Abuse Rather Than Cake
Plutarch, Cicero 26.7 (5)

Again, when a certain young man who was accused of having given his father poison in a cake put on bold airs and threatened to cover Cicero with abuse, "That," said Cicero, "I would rather have from you than a cake."

1414 Sacrifices for Parents
Plutarch, Marcus Cato 15.3

We are also told that a certain young man, who had got a verdict of civil outlawry against an enemy of his dead father, was passing through the forum on the conclusion of the case, and met Cato, who greeted him and said: "These are the sacrifices we must bring to the spirits of our parents; not lambs and kids, but the condemnations and tears of their enemies."

1415 Limping with Lame Man
Plutarch, Moralia, The Education of Children I:4A (6)

Now there is another point which should not be omitted, that in choosing the younger slaves, who are to be the servants and companions of young masters, those should be sought out who are, first and foremost, sound in character, who are Greeks as well, and distinct of speech, so that the children may not be contaminated by barbarians and persons of low character, and so take on some of their commonness. The proverb-makers say, and quite to the point, "If you dwell with a lame man, you will learn to limp."

1416   *Paid for Own Excellence*
Plutarch, Moralia, Sayings of Kings and Commanders III:183D (4)

When a young man, son of a brave father, but not himself having any reputation for being a good solider, suggested the propriety of his receiving his father's emoluments, Antigonus [the Second[1]] said, "My boy, I give pay and presents for the excellence of a man, not for the excellence of his father."

> 1. Antigonus Gonatas, king of Macedonia, 283–239 B.C.E.

1417   *Ashamed to Pluck Well*
Plutarch, Pericles 1.5

And so Philip once said to his son, who, as the wine went round, plucked the strings charmingly and skilfully, "Art not ashamed to pluck the strings so well?"

1418   *Pyrrhus Lenient with Drunkards*
Plutarch, Pyrrhus 8.5

And again, some young fellows indulged in abuse of him over their cups, and were brought to task for it. Pyrrhus asked them if they had said such things, and when one of them replied, "We did, O King; and we should have said still more than this if we had more wine," Pyrrhus laughed and dismissed them.

1419   *A Prediction about Themistocles*
Plutarch, Themistocles 2.1–2

In times of relaxation and leisure, when absolved from his lessons, he [Themistocles] would not play nor indulge his ease, as the rest of the boys did, but would be found composing and rehearsing to himself mock speeches. These speeches would be in accusation or defense of some boy or other. Wherefore his teacher was wont to say to him: "My boy, thou wilt be nothing insignificant, but something great, of a surety, either for good or for evil."

1420   *Britannicus Receives Gown of Manhood*
Suetonius, Lives of the Caesars, Claudius 5.43

When he [Claudius] expressed his intention of giving Britannicus the gown of manhood, since his stature justified it though he was still young and immature, he added: "That the Roman people may at last have a genuine Caesar."[1]

> 1. That is, a legitimate heir to the throne.

1421   *Vespasian Revokes Appointment*
Suetonius, Lives of the Caesars, Vespasian 8.8.3

To let slip no opportunity of improving military discipline, when a young man reeking with perfumes came to thank him for a commission which had been given him, Vespasian drew back his head in disgust, adding the stern reprimand: "I would rather you had smelt of garlic"; and he revoked the appointment.

A young person is present or referred to in the stories listed below, but some other feature has determined their location in another section.

Frontinus: 72
Gellius: 31b, 365

Gospel: 224b, 224c, 224d, 224e, 224f, 224g
Hadith: 97, 1230
Lucian: 761, 763
Macrobius: 723b
Phaedrus: 372
Philo: 373
Philostratus: 25
Plutarch: 35, 36, 44, 47a, 126, 178, 308, 334b, 395, 396a, 397, 399b, 400, 403, 404a, 405, 471a, 621, 937, 1487
Xenophon: 193

See also the section entitled "Youth": 5–24.

Old Age

Seniors like Solon, Sophocles, Diogenes, Demonax, and the Emperor Marcus exhibit more spirit and courage than youth in our anecdotes. They are still learning at a ripe old age. They adopt frugality rather than lead a life of luxury. They oppose tyrants rather than bend to their dictatorial commands. And they work hard rather than leaning on their oars as they near their goal. Accordingly, these seniors are models of self-control and candid insight into life in antiquity.

Old Age

1422 *Gorgias of Leontini Replies about His Age*
Cicero, De Senectute 5.13

Gorgias of Leontini rounded out one hundred and seven years and never rested from his pursuits or his labors. When someone asked him why he chose to remain so long alive, he answered: "I have no reason to reproach old age." A noble answer and worthy of a scholar!

1423 *Sophocles Acquitted after Reading "Oedipus at Colonus" to Jury*
Cicero, De Senectute 7.22

Sophocles composed tragedies to extreme old age; and when, because of his absorption in literary work, he was thought to be neglecting his business affairs, his sons hauled him into court in order to secure a verdict removing him from the control of his property on the ground of imbecility, under a law similar to ours, whereby it is customary to restrain heads of families from wasting their estates. Thereupon, it is said, the old man read to the jury his play, "Oedipus at Colonus," which he had just written and was revising, and inquired: "Does that poem seem to you to be the work of an imbecile?" When he had finished he was acquitted by the verdict of the jury.

1424a *Solon Grows Old Learning*
Cicero, De Senectute 8.26

And what of those who even go on adding to their store of knowledge? Such was the case with Solon, whom we see boasting in his verses that he grows old learning something every day.

1424b *Solon Grows Old Learning*
Plutarch, Solon 2.2

For he was admittedly a lover of wisdom, since even when he was well on in years he would say that he "grew old ever learning many things."

1424c *Solon Grows Old Learning*
Plutarch, Solon 31.3

Now Solon, after beginning his great work on the story or fable of the lost Atlantis, which, as he had heard from the learned men of Saïs,[1] particularly concerned the Athenians, abandoned it, not for lack of leisure, as Plato says, but rather because of his old age, fearing the magnitude of the task. For that he had abundant leisure, such verses as these testify:—
> "But I grow old ever learning many things;"[2]
and again,
> "But now the works of the Cyprus-born goddess are dear to my
>   soul,

Of Dionysus, too, and the Muses, which impart delights to
    men."[3]

1. There is no trace of any such work of Solon's, and the attribution of it to him is
probably a play of Plato's fancy.
2. Fragment 26 (Bergk).
3. Plato mentions the relationship of Critias, his maternal uncle, with Solon (*Char-
mides* 155A).

1425   *Milo of Crotona Bemoans Loss of Physical Strength in Old Age*
Cicero, De Senectute 9.27

For what utterance can be more pitiable than that of Milo of Crotona? After he
was already an old man and was watching the athletes training in the race-course,
it is related that, as he looked upon his shrunken muscles, he wept and said: "Yes,
but they now are dead."

1426   *Sophocles on Love and Old Age*
Cicero, De Senectute 14.47

It was an excellent reply that Sophocles made to a certain man who asked him,
when he was already old, if he still indulged in the delights of love. "Heaven
forbid!" he said. "Indeed I have fled from them as from a harsh and cruel master."[1]

   1. Plato, *Republic* 329B.

1427   *Lysander Reports on Sparta's Response to Elderly*
Cicero, De Senectute 18.63

Moreover, Lysander, the Spartan, of whom I just now spoke, is reported to have
said more than once that in Sparta old age has its most fitting abode; because
nowhere else is so much deference paid to age and nowhere else is it more
honored.

1428   *Boldness in Old Age*
Cicero, De Senectute 20.72

But old age has no certain term, and there is good cause for an old man living so
long as he can fulfil and support his proper duties and hold death of no account. By
this means old age actually becomes more spirited and more courageous than
youth. This explains the answer which Solon gave to the tyrant Pisistratus who
asked, "Pray, what do you rely upon in opposing me so boldly?" and Solon replied,
"Old age."

1429   *Diogenes Approaches the Goal*
Diogenes Laertius, Lives of the Eminent Philosophers 6.34

To those who said to him [Diogenes], "You are an old man; take a rest," "What?"
he replied, "if I were running in the stadium, ought I to slacken my pace when
approaching the goal? ought I not rather to put on speed?"

1430   *Old Man Walks to the Ka'ba*
Hadith, Bukhārī, jazā' al-ṣayd, 27

Ibn Salām and Al-Fazārī related to us from Ḥumayd al-Ṭawīl, who said that
Thābit told him from Anas that: The Prophet saw an old man walking supported
by his two sons. He said, "What is wrong with him?" They said, "He has vowed to

go on foot to the Kaʿba. The Prophet said, "God is not in need of this man's punishing himself." And he told him to ride.

1431 *The Bite of Charon*
Lucian, Demonax 45

A man saw on the legs of Demonax a discoloration of the sort that is natural to old people, and asked, "What's that, Demonax?" With a smile he said, "Charon [the ferryman of the Styx] has bit me!"

1432 *Demonax Silences Assembly*
Lucian, Demonax 64

Once when there was a party quarrel in Athens, he [Demonax] went into the assembly and just by showing himself reduced them to silence: then, seeing that they had already repented, he went away without a word.

1433 *What the Ass Said to the Old Shepherd*
Phaedrus, Aesopic Fables 1.15

A change of sovereignty brings to the poor nothing more than a change in the name of their master. The truth of this is shown by the following little tale. A timorous old man was pasturing an ass in a meadow. Alarmed by the sudden war cry of enemy soldiers approaching, he urged the ass to flee for fear of capture. But the stubborn beast replied: "I ask you, are you assuming that the conqueror will load me with two packs at a time?" "No," said the old man. "Then," said the ass, "what difference does it make to me whose slave I am, so long as I carry only one pack at a time?"

1434 *Aesop and the Farmer*
Phaedrus, Aesopic Fables 3.3

One who has learned by experience is commonly believed to be a surer prophet than a soothsayer, but the reason for this is not told; it will gain currency now for the first time, thanks to my fable. The ewes of a certain farmer who kept many flocks gave birth to lambs with human heads. Being greatly alarmed at this prodigy and in deep dejection, he hastened to consult the soothsayers. One of them replied that this thing had reference to the owner's life, and that he must avert the danger by the sacrifice of a victim; and another declared the meaning to be that his wife was an adulteress and his children spurious, but this omen could be disspelled at the cost of a larger sacrificial victim. Why say more? They all had different opinions and they increased the man's anxiety by the addition of greater anxiety. Aesop happened to be standing by, an old man of keen discernment, whom nature could never deceive; said he: "If you wish to take proper measures to avert this portent, farmer, give wives to your shepherds."

1435 *Concerning Relaxation and Tension*
Phaedrus, Aesopic Fables 3.14

A certain Athenian, on seeing Aesop in a crowd of boys playing with nuts, stopped and laughed at him as though he were crazy. As soon as he perceived this, the old man, who was one to laugh at others rather than one to be laughed at himself, placed an unstrung bow in the middle of the street and said: "Here now, Mr. Philosopher, interpret my symbolic action." The people gathered around. The man racked his brains for a long time and could see no point in the problem put to him. At last he gave up. Thereupon the winner in the battle of wits said: "You will soon break your bow if you keep it always bent; but if you unbend it, it will be ready to use when you want it." So it is. You should let your mind play now and then, that it may be better fitted for thinking when it resumes its work.

1436 *Aesop's Reply to an Inquisitive Fellow*
Phaedrus, Aesopic Fables 3.19

Once when Aesop was the only servant his master had, he was ordered to prepare dinner earlier than usual. So he went around to several houses in search of fire, and at last found a place to light his lamp. Then, since he had made too long a circuit on the way out, he took a shorter way back, and so returned straight through the Forum. "Aesop, what are you doing with a lamp at midday?" "I'm looking for a man," said he, and hurried away home. If that bore managed to get this answer into his head he must have seen that in the judgment of old Aesop he did not pass as a man—a fellow who saw fit to banter another inopportunely when he was busy.

1437 *The Weasel and the Mice*
Phaedrus, Aesopic Fables 4.2

A weasel, enfeebled by old age and no longer able to overtake the agile mice, rolled in the flour and threw herself down carelessly in a dark place. A mouse, thinking this was something to eat, came bounding, was caught, and fell a prey to death. Another did likewise, and after him a third also perished. After a few others there came an old fellow shriveled by the ages, who had escaped snares and mousetraps many a time. Clearly perceiving from afar the strategem of his crafty enemy, he said: "I wish you luck, you who are lying there, just as truly and sincerely as I believe that you are only flour."

1438 *A Dog and the Hunter*
Phaedrus, Aesopic Fables 5.10

A dog who had been bold and swift against all wild beasts, and had always so satisfied his master, began to grow feeble under the burden of years. One day when thrown into combat with a bristly boar he seized it by the ear, but owing to his decayed teeth his jaws lost their grip on the prey. The hunter was grieved at this and scolded the dog. But old Spartan replied: "It was not my spirit that failed you but my strength; praise me for what I was, if you condemn me now for what I am."

1439 *The Emperor Goes to School*
Philostratus, Lives of the Sophists 2.1 (557)

Here is another admirable saying of this Lucius. The Emperor Marcus was greatly interested in Sextus the Boeotian philosopher, attending his classes and going to his very door. Lucius had just arrived in Rome, and asked the Emperor, whom he met going out, where he was going and for what purpose. Marcus answered, "It is a good thing even for one who is growing old to acquire knowledge. I am going to Sextus the philosopher to learn what I do not yet know." At this Lucius raised his hand to heaven, and exclaimed, "O Zeus! The Emperor of the Romans is already growing old, but he hangs a tablet round his neck and goes to school, while my Emperor Alexander died at thirty-two!" What I have quoted is enough to show the kind of philosophy cultivated by Lucius, for these speeches suffice to reveal the man as a sip reveals the bouquet of wine.

1440a Lysimachus and Phoenix
Plutarch, Alexander 24.10 (6)

While the siege of the city was in progress, he [Alexander] made an expedition against the Arabians who dwelt in the neighborhood of Mount Antilibanus. On this expedition he risked his life to save his tutor, Lysimachus, who insisted on following him, declaring himself to be neither older nor weaker than Phoenix.

1440b Lysimachus and Phoenix
Plutarch, Alexander 5.8

The man, however, who assumed the character and the title of tutor was Lysimachus, a native of Acarnania, who had no general refinement, but because he called himself Phoenix,[1] Alexander Achilles, and Philip Peleus, was highly regarded and held a second place.

> 1. The preceptor of Achilles.

1441a Some Never Saw Alexander on Darius' Throne
Plutarch, Alexander 37.7 (4)

And it is said that when he [Alexander] took his seat for the first time under the golden canopy on the royal throne, Demaratus the Corinthian, a well-meaning man and a friend of Alexander's, as he had been of Alexander's father, burst into tears, as old men will, and declared that those Hellenes were deprived of great pleasure who had died before seeing Alexander seated on the throne of Darius.

1441b Some Never Saw Alexander on Darius' Throne
Plutarch, Alexander 56.1 (1)

Meanwhile Demaratus the Corinthian, who was now well on in years, was eagerly desirous of going up to Alexander; and when he had seen him, he said that those Greeks were deprived of a great pleasure who had died before seeing Alexander seated on the throne of Darius.

1442 Old Age Makes Fearless
Plutarch, Caesar 14.14 (8)

Considius, a very aged senator, once told Caesar that his colleagues did not come together because they were afraid of the armed soldiers. "Why then," said Caesar, "dost thou too not stay at home out of the same fear?' To this Considius replied: "Because my old age makes me fearless; for the short span of life that is still left me does not require much anxious thought."

1443 Deiotarus Builds at Twelfth Hour
Plutarch, Crassus 17.1–2

And finding that King Deiotarus, who was now a very old man, was founding a new city, he [Crassus] rallied him saying: "O King, you are beginning to build at the twelfth hour." The Galatian laughed and said: "But you yourself, Imperator, as I see, are not marching very early in the day against the Parthians."

1444 Crassus Seeks Seleucia
Plutarch, Crassus 18.1–2

No sooner had he [Crassus] begun to assemble his forces from their winter quarters than envoys came to him from Arsaces[1] with a wonderfully brief message.

They said that if the army had been sent out by the Roman people, it meant war without truce and without treaty; but if it was against the wishes of his country, as they were informed, and for his own private gain that Crassus had come up in arms against the Parthians and occupied their territory, then Arsaces would act with moderation, would take pity on the old age of Crassus, and release to the Romans the men whom he had under watch and ward rather than watching over him. To this Crassus boastfully replied that he would give his answer in Seleucia, whereupon the eldest of the envoys, Vagises, burst out laughing and said, pointing to the palm of his upturned hand: "O Crassus, hair will grow there before thou shalt see Seleucia."[2]

1. In subsequent passages called Hyrades.
2. Cf. Dio Cassius 40.16.

1445   *The Simplicity of Leotychides*
Plutarch, Lycurgus 13.5

It was because he was used to this simplicity that Leotychides the Elder, as we are told, when he was dining in Corinth, and saw the roof of the house adorned with costly panellings, asked his host if trees grew square in that country.

1446   *Disgraces Added to Old Age*
Plutarch, Marcus Cato 9.6–7

To an old man who was steeped in iniquity he [Cato] said: "Man, old age has disgraces enough of its own; do not add to them the shame of vice."

1447   *Cato's Last Case*
Plutarch, Marcus Cato 15.4

It is said that he [Cato] was defendant in nearly fifty cases, and in the last one when he was eighty-six years of age. It was in the course of this that he uttered the memorable saying: "It is hard for one who has lived among men of one generation, to make his defense before those of another."

1448   *Antigonus Craves Goodwill*
Plutarch, Moralia, Sayings of Kings and Commanders III:182B (3)

When all were astonished because, after he [Antigonus] had grown old, he handled matters with mildness and gentleness, he said, "Time was when I craved power, but now I crave repute and goodwill among men."

1449a   *Eudamidas and Xenocrates*
Plutarch, Moralia, Sayings of Kings and Commanders III:192A (1)

Eudamidas,[1] seeing Xenocrates, already well on in years, discussing philosophy with his pupils in the Academy, and being informed that he was seeking after virtue, said, "And when will he make use of it?"

1. Brother of Agis III, whom he succeeded in 331–330 B.C.E.

1449b   *Eudamidas and Xenocrates*
Plutarch, Moralia, Sayings of Spartans III:220D (1)

Eudamidas, the son of Archidamus and the brother of Agis, seeing Xenocrates in the Academy, already well on in years, discussing philosophy with his acquaintances, inquired who the old man was. Somebody said that he was a wise man and one of the seekers after virtue. "And when will he use it," said Eudamidas, "if he is only now seeking for it?"

1450 Man Who Slew Ox for Benefactor
Plutarch, Moralia, Greek Questions IV:298E–F (34)

Who was the man who slew an ox for his benefactor?[1]

Anchored off the island of Ithaca was a pirate vessel in which there chanced to be an old man with earthenware jars containing pitch. By chance a ferryman of Ithaca, by name Pyrrhias, put off to the ship and rescued the old man without asking for any reward, but because he had been persuaded by the old man and pitied him. He did, however, accept some of the jars, for the old man bade him do so. But when the pirates had departed and there was nothing to fear, the old man led Pyrrhias to the jars and in them showed him much gold and silver mixed with the pitch. So Pyrrhias, suddenly becoming rich, treated the old man well in various ways, and also slew an ox for him. Wherefore men make use of this as a proverbial expression: "No one but Pyrrhias has slain an ox for his benefactor."

> 1. Possibly "sacrificed an ox to his benefactor"; but an animal sacrifice to a living man seems incredible.

1451 Oldest Man and Senior General
Plutarch, Nicias 15.2

It is said that once at the War Department, when his fellow commanders were deliberating on some matter of general moment, he [Nicias] bade Sophocles the poet state his opinion first, as being the senior general on the Board. Thereupon Sophocles said: "I am the oldest man, but you are the senior general."

1452 Pericles and Anaxagoras
Plutarch, Pericles 16.7

And, besides, they say that Anaxagoras himself, at a time when Pericles was absorbed in business, lay on his couch all neglected, in his old age, starving himself to death, his head already muffled for departure, and that when the matter came to the ears of Pericles, he was struck with dismay, and ran at once to the poor man, and besought him most fervently to live, bewailing not so much that great teacher's lot as his own, were he now to be bereft of such a counselor in the conduct of the state. Then Anaxagoras—so the story goes—unmuffled his head and said to him, "Pericles, even those who need a lamp pour oil herein."

1453 Solon Opposes Play
Plutarch, Solon 29.4–5

Thespis was now beginning to develop tragedy, and the attempt attracted most people because of its novelty, although it was not yet made a matter of competitive contest. Solon, therefore, who was naturally fond of hearing and learning anything new, and who in his old age more than ever before indulged himself in leisurely amusement, yes, and in wine and song, went to see Thespis act in his own play, as the custom of the ancient poets was. After the spectacle, he accosted Thespis, and asked him if he was not ashamed to tell such lies in the presence of so many people. Thespis answered that there was no harm in talking and acting that way in play, whereupon Solon smote the ground sharply with his staff and said: "Soon, however, if we give play of this sort so much praise and honor, we shall find it in our solemn contracts."

1454 *Caligula a Viper*
Suetonius, Lives of the Caesars, Caligula 4.11.1

Yet even at that time he [Caligula] could not control his natural cruelty and viciousness, but he was a most eager witness of the tortures and executions of those who suffered punishment, reveling at night in gluttony and adultery, disguised in a wig and a long robe, passionately devoted besides to the theatrical arts of dancing and singing, in which Tiberius very willingly indulged him, in the hope that through these his savage nature might be softened. This last was so clearly evident to the shrewd old man, that he used to say now and then that to allow Gaius to live would prove the ruin of himself and of all men, and that he was rearing a viper for the Roman people and a Phaethon for the world.

1455 *Galba's Strength Unimpaired*
Suetonius, Lives of the Caesars, Galba 7.20.2

When someone had congratulated him on still looking young and vigorous, he [Galba] replied: "As yet my strength is unimpaired."[1]

1. Homer, *Iliad* 5.254; *Odyssey* 21.426.

An old man or old age as an issue is present in the stories listed below, but some other feature has determined their location in another section.

Cicero: 1186, 1456
Gellius: 75, 1467
Hadith: 266
Phaedrus: 590
Plutarch: 330b, 387, 463a, 479a, 479b, 482, 1042a, 1353
Suetonius: 1165

Death

In these anecdotes, Socrates, Diogenes, Anaxagoras, and Demonax show no concern about the place or manner of their burial. Theramenes drinks the cup of poison as a toast to the head of the jury who convicted him. Jesus drinks vinegar and dies with words from scripture on his lips. And Agesilaus requests that his deeds rather than statues commemorate him after his death. Expressing a conviction that death is neither to be wished for nor to be feared, these ancients approach their death as vigorously as they had approached their youth.

Death

1456 *Cyrus on Old Age and Youth*
Cicero, De Senectute 9.30

For example, Cyrus,[1] in Xenophon, in that discourse which he delivered when he was very old and on his death-bed, says that he had never felt that his old age was any less vigorous than his youth had been.

> 1. Cyrus the Elder, Xenophon *Cyropaedia* 8.7.6. But other authorities (Herodotus 1.24, Lucian, *Charon* 30) say that Cyrus died in battle with the Scythians.

1457 *Death of Theramenes*
Cicero, Tusculan Disputations 1.40.96

But if our minds are kept in suspense and torture and anguish of expectation and longing, ye immortal gods! how delightful should the journey prove which at its close leaves us no further care, no anxiety for the future! How charmed I am with Theramenes! How lofty a spirit is his! For though we shed tears as we read, nevertheless a notable man dies a death that is not pitiable: he was flung into prison by order of the thirty tyrants, and when he had swallowed the poison like a thirsty man he tossed the remainder out of the cup[1] to make a splash, and with a laugh at the sound it made, "I drink," said he, "to the health of the fair Critias," the man who had treated him abominably; I may explain that at their banquets the Greeks make a practice of naming the guest to whom they are going to pass the cup. This noble spirit jested with his last breath, though he already had within him the death his vitals had absorbed, and in reality he prophesied for the man he had toasted in the poison the death which shortly overtook him.[2]

> 1. The game *kottabos* was much in use at ancient Athenian banquets. Its object was to throw a small quantity of wine at a mark and make a sound in doing so. The mark was either a saucer floating in a big bowl of water or else a saucer attached to the rod of a special apparatus. Theramenes combined this with a toast. He was an Athenian statesman of moderate views and hence nicknamed *kothopnos*, "trimmer," and was put to death by the thirty tyrants, of whom Critias was the leader, in 404 B.C.E.
> 2. In the battle between the thirty tyrants and the exiles under Thrasybulus at Piraeus in 403 B.C.E., a year afterwards.

1458 *Penalty Can Be Paid*
Cicero, Tusculan Disputations 1.42.100

Let us on our side hold fast the principle of accounting nothing evil which has been bestowed by nature upon all mankind, and of realizing that if death be an evil it is an everlasting evil. For death seems to be the end of a wretched life; if death is wretched, there can be no end to its wretchedness. But why do I quote examples of Socrates and Theramenes, men pre-eminently famous for virtue and wisdom? There was a Lacedaemonian (and not so much as his name has been reported) who had such utter scorn of death that when, after being sentenced by the ephors, he was led out to execution with a cheerful and joyous look, and an enemy said to him, "Do you scorn the laws of Lycurgus?" he replied: "I am deeply grateful to him for inflicting upon me a penalty which I could pay without borrowing from friend or usurer." A man of whom Sparta could be proud!

1459 *Death of Socrates*
Cicero, Tusculan Disputations 1.43.103

Socrates' view on the subject is given clearly in the book which relates his death, of which we have already said so much.[1] For after he had discussed immortality of souls and the hour of death was close at hand, when asked by Crito how he wished to be buried, "My friends," said he, "I have indeed spent a deal of labor to no purpose, for I have not convinced our friend Crito that I shall fly hence and leave nothing of me behind. But all the same, Crito, if you can catch me or light upon me, you shall bury me as you think fit. But, believe me, none of you will come up with me when I have gone hence." That was indeed nobly said, for he gave his friend a free hand and yet showed that no thought of this sort troubled him at all.

   1. Plato, *Phaedo* 115.

1460 *Diogenes on Burial*
Cicero, Tusculan Disputations 1.43.104

Diogenes was rougher; his feeling it is true was the same, but like a Cynic he spoke more harshly and required that he should be flung out unburied. Upon which his friends said: "To the birds and wild beasts?" "Certainly not," said he, "but you must put a stick near me to drive them away with." "How can you, for you will be without consciousness?" they replied. "What harm, then, can the mangling of wild beasts do to me if I am without consciousness?" It was a noble saying of Anaxagoras[1] on his deathbed at Lampsacus, in answer to his friends' inquiry whether he wished in the event of need to be taken away to Clazomonae, his native land: "There is no necessity," said he, "for from any place the road to the lower world is just as far." Accordingly one principle must be adhered to in dealing with the whole purpose of burial, that it has to do with the body, whether the soul has perished or is still vigorous: in the body, however, it is plain that, when the soul has either been annihilated or made its escape, there is no remnant of sensation.

   1. Anaxagoras, an Ionian philosopher, 500–428 B.C.E., who lived for thirty years at Athens and was the friend of Pericles.

1461 *Two Best Things*
Cicero, Tusculan Disputations 1.48.114

There is further a story told of Silenus,[1] who had been taken captive by Midas and to gain his release had granted him, according to the record, the following boon: he instructed the king that it was far the best thing for man not to be born at all, but the next best was to die as soon as possible.

   1. A demigod, nurse and attendant of Dionysus.

1462 *The Two Pythagoreans*
Cicero, Tusculan Disputations 5.22.63

While, however, he [Dionysius] had a lively fear of the disloyalty of friends, how deeply he felt the need of them he disclosed in the affair of the two Pythagoreans,[1] one of whom he had accepted as surety for sentence of death, while the other had presented himself at the hour appointed for execution to discharge the surety: "Would," said he, "that I could be enrolled as a third in your friendship!"

   1. Damon and Phintias. Phintias was condemned to death for plotting against Dionysius, and Damon became bail for his friend's appearance at the appointed time.

1463   Power of a Blister-Beetle

Cicero, Tusculan Disputations 5.40.117

Let everything be piled up on one single man so that he loses together sight and hearing, suffers too the most acute bodily pains; and these in the first place commonly finish a man of themselves alone: but if, maybe, they are indefinitely prolonged and torture him notwithstanding more violently than he sees reason for enduring, what reason have we, gracious heaven, for continuing to suffer? For there is a haven close at hand, since death is at the same time an eternal refuge where nothing is felt. Theodorus said to Lysimachus when he threatened him with death, "A great achievement indeed of yours if you have got the power of a blister-beetle."

1464   Perses and Paulus

Cicero, Tusculan Disputations 5.40.118

When Perses begged not to be led in triumph, Paulus replied, "That is a thing *you* can settle." Much was said about death the first day, when we inquired into the nature of death; a good deal on the next day when pain was being discussed, and he who remembers it surely runs no risk of thinking either that death is not to be wished for or at any rate that it is to be feared.

1465   Socrates Dies in Own Garment

Diogenes Laertius, Lives of the Eminent Philosophers 2.35

When he [Socrates] was about to drink the hemlock, Apollodorus offered him a beautiful garment to die in: "What," said he, "is my own good enough to live in but not to die in?"

1466   Diogenes Questions Evil of Death

Diogenes Laertius, Lives of the Eminent Philosophers 6.68

Being asked whether death was an evil thing, Diogenes replied, "How can it be evil, when in its presence we are not aware of it?"

1467   The Successor to Aristotle

Gellius, Attic Nights 13.5.1–12

The philosopher Aristotle, being already nearly sixty-two years of age, was sickly and weak of body and had slender hope of life. Then the whole band of his disciples came to him, begging and entreating that he should himself choose a successor to his position and his office, to whom, as to himself, they might apply after his last day, to complete and perfect their knowledge of the studies into which he had initiated them. There were at the time in his school many good men, but two were conspicuous, Theophrastus and Eudemus, who excelled the rest in talent and learning. The former was from the island of Lesbos, but Eudemus from Rhodes. Aristotle replied that he would do what they asked, so soon as the opportunity came. A little later, in the presence of the same men who had asked him to appoint a master, he said that the wine he was then drinking did not suit his health, but was unwholesome and harsh; that therefore they ought to look for a foreign wine, something either from Rhodes or from Lesbos. He asked them to procure both kinds for him, and said that he would use the one which he liked the better. They went, sought, found, brought. Then Aristotle asked for the Rhodian and tasting it said: "This is truly a sound and pleasant wine." Then he called for the Lesbian. Tasting that also, he remarked: "Both are very good indeed, but the Lesbian is the sweeter." When he said this, no one doubted that gracefully, and at the same time tactfully, he had by those words chosen his successor, not his wine. This was Theophrastus, from Lesbos, a man equally noted for the fineness of his eloquence and of his life. And when, not long after this, Aristotle died, they accordingly all became followers of Theophrastus.

1468   *Jesus' Dying Words*
Gospel, John 19:28–30 (NIV)

Later, knowing that all was now completed, and so that the Scripture would be fulfilled, Jesus said, "I am thirsty."[1] A jar of wine vinegar was there, so they soaked a sponge in it, put the sponge on a stalk of the hyssop plant, and lifted it to Jesus' lips. When he had received the drink, Jesus said, "It is finished."[2] With that, he bowed his head and gave up his spirit.

> 1. Psalm 22:15.
> 2. Job 19:26, 27 (LXX).

1469   *Death of Jesus*
Gospel, Mark 15:33–39 (NIV)

At the sixth hour darkness came over the whole land until the ninth hour. And at the ninth hour Jesus cried out in a loud voice, "Eloi, Eloi, lama sabachthani?"— which means, "My God, my God, why have you forsaken me?"[1] When some of those standing near heard this, they said, "Listen, he's calling Elijah." One man ran, filled a sponge with wine vinegar, put it on a stick, and offered it to Jesus to drink. "Now leave him alone. Let's see if Elijah comes to take him down," he said. With a loud cry, Jesus breathed his last. The curtain of the temple was torn in two from top to bottom. And when the centurion, who stood there in front of Jesus, heard his cry and saw how he died, he said, "Surely this man was the Son of God!"

> 1. Psalm 22:1.

1470   *Demonax Decides to Die*
Lucian, Demonax 65

When he [Demonax] realised that he was no longer able to wait upon himself, he quoted to those who were with him the verses of the heralds at the games:

> Here endeth a contest awarding the fairest
> Of prizes: time calls, and forbids us delay.

Then, refraining from all food, he took leave of life in the same cheerful humor that people he met always saw him in.

1471   *Burial Instructions*
Lucian, Demonax 66

A short time before his death he [Demonax] was asked, "What orders have you to give about your burial?" He replied, "Don't make trouble! The stench will get me buried!"

1472 Death a Service to Living
Lucian, Demonax 66

Someone said, "Isn't it disgraceful that the body of such a man should be exposed for birds and dogs to devour?" Demonax answered, "I see nothing improper in it if even in death I am going to be of service to living creatures."

1473 Epaminondas Dies Unconquered
Nepos 15, Epaminondas 9.3

But Epaminondas, realizing that he had received a mortal wound, and at the same time that if he drew out the head of the lance, which was separated from the shaft and fixed in his body, he would at once die, retained it until news came that the Boeotians were victorious. As soon as he heard that, he cried: "I have lived long enough, since I die unconquered." Then he drew out the iron and at once breathed his last.

1474 Euphiletus and Phocion
Nepos 19, Phocion 4.3

As he [Phocion] was being led to execution, he was met by Euphiletus, who had been his intimate friend. When the latter said with tears in his eyes: "Oh, how unmerited is the treatment you are suffering, Phocion!" the prisoner replied: "But it is not unexpected; for nearly all the distinguished men of Athens have met this end."

1475 The Sparrow Gives Advice to the Hare
Phaedrus, Aesopic Fables 1.9

Let me point out in a few lines how foolish it is to admonish others while forgetting all danger to oneself. When a hare in the clutches of an eagle was uttering bitter moans, a sparrow meanwhile scoffed at him: "Where," says he, "is that famous agility of yours? What made your legs so laggard?" While the sparrow was still speaking, a hawk caught him off guard. The sparrow screamed and screamed, but his plaint was futile. It was soon over. "Aha," said the hare, still alive, "here is some comfort for me as I die. A moment ago you were gaily making fun of my misfortune; but now you are bewailing your own fate in the same tone of complaint."

1476 The Old Lion, the Boar, the Bull, and the Ass
Phaedrus, Aesopic Fables 1.21

Anyone who has lost the prestige that he once had becomes in his disastrous state subject to insult even by cowards. When a lion, worn out by age and bereft of his strength, lay feebly drawing his last breath a wild boar came up with foaming mouth and murderous tusks and with a thrust avenged an old wrong. Soon after a bull with angry horns gored the body of his foe. An ass, on seeing the wild beast maltreated with impunity, gave him a smashing kick in the face. Then, as he died, the lion said: "I resented the insults of the brave; but as for you, you disgrace to Nature, when I put up with you, as now at life's end I must, I seem to die a second death."

1477 *Death of Polemo*
Philostratus, Lives of the Sophists 1.25 (543–544)

But yet another version is nearer the truth, namely that he [Polemo] lies at Laodicea near the Syrian gate, where, in fact, are the sepulchers of his ancestors; that he was buried while still alive, for so he had enjoined on his nearest and dearest; and that, as he lay in the tomb, he thus exhorted those who were shutting up the sepulcher, "Make haste, make haste! Never shall the sun behold me reduced to silence!" And when his friends wailed over him, he cried with a loud voice, "Give me a body and I will declaim!"

1478 *Agis Betters His Murderers*
Plutarch, Agis 20.1

Agis, then, on his way to the halter, saw one of the officers shedding tears of sympathy for him. "My man," said he, "cease weeping; for even though I am put to death in this lawless and unjust manner, I have the better of my murderers."

1479 *Dying Darius Lauds Alexander*
Plutarch, Alexander 43.1–4 (1–2)

So, then, all were alike ready and willing; but only sixty, they say, were with Alexander when he burst into the camp of the enemy. There, indeed, they rode over much gold and silver that was thrown away, passed by many wagons full of women and children which were coursing hither and thither without their drivers and pursued those who were foremost in flight, thinking that Darius was among them. But at last they found him lying in a wagon, his body all full of javelins, at the point of death. Nevertheless, he asked for something to drink, and when he had drunk some cold water which Polystratus gave him, he said to him: "My man, this is the extremity of all my ill-fortune, that I receive good at thy hands and am not able to return it; but Alexander will requite thee for thy good offices, and the gods will reward Alexander for his kindness to my mother, wife, and children; to him, through thee, I give this right hand."

1480 *Antony Found Inferior to Cleopatra*
Plutarch, Antony 76.1–3

At daybreak, Antony in person posted his infantry on the hills in front of the city, and watched his ships as they put out and attacked those of the enemy; and as he expected to see something great accomplished by them, he remained quiet. But the crews of his ships as soon as they were near, saluted Caesar's crew with their oars, and on their returning the salute changed sides and so all the ships, now united into one fleet, sailed up towards the city prows on. No sooner had Antony seen this than he was deserted by his cavalry, which went over to the enemy, and after being defeated with his infantry he retired into the city, crying out that he had been betrayed by Cleopatra to those with whom he waged war for her sake. But she, fearing his anger and his madness, fled for refuge into her tomb and let fall the drop doors, which were made strong with bolts and bars; then she sent messengers to tell Antony that she was dead. Antony believed the message, and saying to himself: "Why dost thou longer delay, Antony? Fortune has taken away thy sole remaining excuse for clinging to life," he went into his chamber. Here, as he unfastened his breastplate and laid it aside, he said: "Cleopatra, I am not grieved to be bereft of thee, for I shall straightaway join thee; but I am grieved that such an imperator as I am has been found to be inferior to a woman in courage."

1481 Suicide of Antony
Plutarch, Antony 76.4–5

Now Antony had a trusty slave named Eros. Him Antony had long before engaged, in case of need, to kill him, and now demanded the fulfillment of his promise. So Eros drew his sword and held it up as though he would smite his master, but then turned his face away and slew himself. And as he fell at his master's feet Antony said: "Well done, Eros, though thou wast not able to do it thyself, thou teachest me what I must do"; and running himself through the belly he dropped upon the couch. But the wound did not bring a speedy death. Therefore as the blood ceased flowing after he had lain down, he came to himself and besought the bystanders to give him the finishing stroke. But they fled from the chamber, and he lay writhing and crying out, until Diomedes the secretary came from Cleopatra with orders to bring him to her in the tomb.

1482 Taurion Poisons Aratus
Plutarch, Aratus 52.1–3

For that the feelings which he [Philip] had cherished from the beginning towards Aratus had an admixture of shame and fear, was made plain by what he did to him at the last. For he desired to kill Aratus, and thought he could not be a free man while Aratus lived, much less a tyrant or a king. In a violent way, however, he made no attempt upon him, but ordered Taurion, one of his officers and friends, to do this in a secret way, preferably by poison, when the king was absent. So Taurion made an intimate companion of Aratus, and gave him poison, not of a sharp and violent sort, but one of those which first induce gentle heats in the body, and a dull cough, and then little by little bring on consumption. The thing was not hidden from Aratus, but since it was no use for him to convict the criminal, he calmly and silently drank his cup of suffering to the dregs, as if his sickness had been of a common and familiar type. However, when one of his intimate companions who was with him in his chamber saw him spit blood, and expressed surprise, "Such, my dear Cephalo," said Aratus, "are the wages of royal friendship."

1483 The Suicide of Brutus
Plutarch, Brutus 52.1–3

As the night advanced, Brutus turned, just as he sat, towards his servant Cleitus, and talked with him. And when Cleitus wept and made no answer, Brutus next drew Dardanus his shield-bearer aside and had some private conservation with him. Finally, he spoke to Volumnius himself in Greek, reminding him of their student life, and begged him to grasp his sword with him and help him drive home the blow. And when Volumnius refused, and the rest likewise, and someone said they must not tarry but fly, Brutus rose and said: "By all means must we fly; not with our feet, however, but with our hands."

1484 Scipio and Granius Petro
Plutarch, Caesar 16.8–9 (4)

Again, in Africa, Scipio captured a ship of Caesar's in which Granius Petro, who had been appointed quaestor, was sailing. Of the rest of the passengers Scipio made booty, but told the quaestor that he offered him his life. Granius, however, remarking that it was the custom with Caesar's soldiers not to receive but to offer mercy, killed himself with a blow of his sword.

1485a *Death of Cato*
Plutarch, Caesar 54.1–2 (1)

Being eager to take Cato alive, Caesar hastened toward Utica, for Cato was guarding that city, and took no part in the battle. But he learned that Cato had made away with himself, and he was clearly annoyed, though for what reason is uncertain. At any rate, he said: "Cato, I begrudge thee thy death; for thou didst begrudge me the preservation of thy life."

1485b *Death of Cato*
Plutarch, Cato the Younger 72.1–2

When Caesar learned from people who came to him that Cato was remaining in Utica and not trying to escape, but that he was sending off the rest, while he himself, his companions, and his son, were fearlessly going up and down, he thought it difficult to discern the purpose of the man, but since he made the greatest account of him, he came on with his army in all haste. When, however, he heard of his death, he said thus much only, as we are told: "O Cato, I begrudge thee thy death; for thou didst begrudge me the sparing of thy life."

1486 *Cleomenes Defeated*
Plutarch, Cleomenes 37.4–6

Well, then, as Ptolemy the son of Chrysermus was coming out of the palace, three of them [Cleomenes' followers] straightway fell upon him and slew him; and as another Ptolemy, who had the city in his charge, was driving towards them in a chariot, they rushed to meet him, scattered his servants and mercenaries, dragged him from his chariot, and slew him. Then they proceeded to the citadel, purposing to break open the prison and avail themselves of the multitude of prisoners. But the guards were too quick for them and barred the way securely, so that Cleomenes, baffled in this attempt also, roamed up and down through the city, not a man joining him but everybody filled with fear and flying from him. So, then, he desisted from his attempt, and saying to his friends, "It is no wonder, after all, that women rule over men who run away from freedom," he called upon them all to die in a manner worthy of their king and their past achievements.

1487 *Evils of Public Career*
Plutarch, Demosthenes 26.6–7 (4–5)

We are told, namely, that as he [Demosthenes] was leaving the city he lifted up his hands towards the acropolis and said: "O potent Guardian of the City, Athena, how, pray, canst thou take delight in those three most intractable beasts, the owl, the serpent, and the people?" Moreover, when young men came to visit and converse with him, he would try to deter them from public life, saying that if two roads had been presented to him in the beginning, one leading to the bema and the assembly, and the other straight to destruction, and if he could have known beforehand the evils attendant on a public career, namely fears, hatreds, calumnies and contentions, he would have taken that road which led directly to death.

1488 *Eumenes Waits for Death*
Plutarch, Eumenes 18.4

We are told, also, that Eumenes asked his keeper, Onomarchus, why in the world Antigonus, now that he had got a hated enemy in his hands, neither killed him speedily nor generously set him free; and when Onomarchus insolently told him it was not now, but on the field of battle, that he should have faced death boldly, "Yea, by Zeus," said Eumenes, "then, too, I did so; ask the men who fought with me; I know that none I met was a better man." "Well, then," said Onomarchus, "since now thou hast found thy better, why canst thou not bide his time?"

1489 *Fortune Reserves Theramenes*
Plutarch, Moralia, A Letter to Apollonius II:105B

While Theramenes, who afterwards became one of the Thirty Tyrants at Athens, was dining with several others, the house in which they were collapsed, and he was the only one to escape death; but as he was being congratulated by everybody, he raised his voice and exclaimed in a loud tone, "O Fortune, for what occasion are you reserving me?"

1490a *Army Like Blinded Cyclops*
Plutarch, Moralia, Sayings of Kings and Commanders III:181F (34)

When he [Alexander] had come to his end, Demades the orator said that the army of the Macedonians, because of its lack of leadership, looked like the Cyclops after his eye had been put out.[1]

1. In 1490b the saying is attributed to Leosthenes. Cf. also Demetrius Phalereus, *De elocutione* 284.

1490b *Army Like Blinded Cyclops*
Plutarch, Moralia, Fortune of Alexander IV:336F (4)

Then, immediately after Alexander's decease, Leosthenes said that his forces, as they wandered here and there and fell foul of their own efforts, were like the Cyclops after his blinding, groping about everywhere with his hands, which were directed at no certain goal; even thus did that vast throng roam about with no safe footing, blundering through want of a leader.

1490c *Army Like Blinded Cyclops*
Plutarch, Galba 1.4

Demades, indeed, after Alexander had died, likened the Macedonian army to the blinded Cyclops, observing the many random and disorderly movements that it made.

1491a *No Resentment against Athenians*
Plutarch, Moralia, Sayings of Kings and Commanders III:189A–B (19)

When the cup of hemlock was already being handed to him [Phocion], he was asked if he had any message for his son. "I charge and exhort him," said he, "not to cherish any ill feeling against the Athenians."[1]

1. Cf. Aelian, *Varia Historia* 12.49.

1491b *No Resentment against Athenians*
Plutarch, Phocion 36.3

And when one of his friends asked him if he [Phocion] had any message for his son Phocus, "Certainly," said he; "my message is that he cherish no resentment against the Athenians."

1492a *No Plaster or Paint*
Plutarch, Moralia, Sayings of Kings and Commanders III:191D (12)

When he [Agesilaus] was dying he gave orders that his friends have no 'plaster or paint' used, for this was the way he spoke of statues and portraits. "For," said he, "if I have done any noble deed, that is my memorial; but if none, then not all the statues in the world avail."[1]

> 1. Cf. Dio Chrysostom, *Oration* 35 (466M., 127R); Cicero, *Epistulae ad Familiares* 5.12.7.

1492b *No Plaster or Paint*
Plutarch, Moralia, Sayings of Spartans III:215A (79)

On his way home from Egypt death came to him [Agesilaus], and in his last hours he gave directions to those with him that they should not cause to be made any sculptured or painted or imitative representation of his person. "For if I have done any goodly deed, that shall be my memorial; but if not, then not all the statues in the world, the works of menial and worthless men, will avail."

1492c *No Plaster or Paint*
Plutarch, Agesilaus 2.2

We have no likeness of him [Agesilaus] (for he himself would not consent to one, and even when he lay dying forbade the making of "either statue or picture" of his person), but he is said to have been a little man of unimposing presence.

1492d *No Plaster or Paint*
Xenophon, Agesilaus 11.7

He [Agesilaus] would not allow a statue of himself to be set up, though many wanted to give him one, but on memorials of his mind he labored unceasingly, thinking the one to be the sculptor's work, the other his own, the one appropriate to the rich, the other to the good.

1493 *Pericles Gives Funeral Oration*
Plutarch, Pericles 8.6

Again, Stesimbrotus says that, in his funeral oration over those who had fallen in the Samian War, he [Pericles] declared that they had become immortal, like the gods; "the gods themselves," he said, "we cannot see, but from the honors which they receive, and the blessings which they bestow, we conclude that they are immortal."

1494 *No Mourning Due to Pericles*
Plutarch, Pericles 38.3–4

Being now near his [Pericles'] end,[1] the best of the citizens and those of his friends who survived were sitting around him holding discourse of his excellence and power, how great they had been, and estimating all his achievements and the number of his trophies—there were nine of these which he had set up as the city's victorious general. This discourse they were holding with one another, supposing that he no longer understood them but had lost consciousness. He had been attending to it all, however, and speaking out among them said he was amazed at their praising and commemorating that in him which was due as much to fortune as to himself, and which had fallen to the lot of many generals besides, instead of mentioning his fairest and greatest title to their admiration; "for," said he, "no living Athenian ever put on mourning because of me."

1. He died in the autumn of 429 B.C.E.

1495   *Suicide of Philopoemen*
Plutarch, Philopoemen 20.1–3

But Deinocrates, who feared that delay was the one thing most likely to save Philopoemen, and wished to forestall the efforts of the Achaeans, when night came on and the multitude of Messene had dispersed, opened the prison and sent in a public official with poison, ordering him to give it to Philopoemen and to stand by his side until he had drunk it. Now, Philopoemen was lying down wrapped in his soldier's cloak, not sleeping, but overwhelmed with trouble and grief. When, however, he saw a light and a man standing by him holding the cup of poison, he pulled himself together as much as his weakness permitted and sat up. Then taking the cup he asked the man if he had heard anything about the horsemen, and particularly about Lycortas, and on being told by him that the greater part of them had escaped, he nodded his head, and with a kindly look at the man said to him: "That is good news, if we have not wholly lost." Without another word and even without a sigh he drained the cup and laid himself down again.

1496   *Death of Cinna*
Plutarch, Pompey 5.1–2

On his [Pompey's] disappearance, there went a rumor through the camp which said that Cinna had slain the young man [Pompey], and in consequence of this those who had long hated Cinna and felt oppressed by him made an onslaught upon him. Cinna, as he fled, having been seized by one of the centurions who pursued him with drawn sword, clasped him by the knees and held out his seal-ring, which was of great price. But the centurion, with great insolence, said: "Indeed, I am not come to seal a surety, but to punish a lawless and wicked tyrant," and slew him.

1497   *Scipio Does Not Mourn Tiberius*
Plutarch, Tiberius Gracchus 21.4

Even Scipio Africanus, than whom no one would seem to have been more justly or more deeply loved by the Romans, came within a little of forfeiting and losing the popular favor because, to begin with, at Numantia, when he learned of the death of Tiberius, he recited in a loud voice the verse of Homer:[1]

"So perish also all others who on such wickedness venture."

1. Homer, *Odyssey* 1.47.

1498 *Death of Augustus*
Suetonius, Lives of the Caesars, Augustus 2.99.1

On the last day of his life he [Augustus] asked every now and then whether there was any disturbance without on his account; then calling for a mirror, he had his hair combed and his falling jaws set straight. After that, calling in his friends and asking whether it seemed to them that he had played the comedy of life fitly, he added the tag:

"Since well I've played my part, all clap your hands
And from the stage dismiss me with applause."

1499 *Nero without Friend or Foe*
Suetonius, Lives of the Caesars, Nero 6.47.3

Having therefore put off further consideration to the following day, he [Nero] awoke about midnight and finding that the guard of soldiers had left, he sprang from his bed and sent for all his friends. Since no reply came back from anyone, he went himself to their rooms with a few followers. But finding that all the doors were closed and that no one replied to him, he returned to his own chamber, from which now the very caretakers had fled, taking with them even the bed-clothing and the box of poison. Then he at once called for the gladiator Spiculus or any other adept at whose hand he might find death, and when no one appeared, he cried, "Have I then neither friend nor foe?"

1500 *Nero Hides*
Suetonius, Lives of the Caesars, Nero 6.48.3

Here the aforesaid Phaon urged him [Nero] to hide for a time in a pit, from which sand had been dug, but he declared that he would not go under ground while still alive, and after waiting for a while until a secret entrance into the villa could be made, he scooped up in his hand some water to drink from a pool close by, saying: "This is Nero's distilled water."[1]

> 1. Referring to a drink of his own contrivance, distilled water cooled in snow; cf. Pliny, *Natural History* 31.40.

1501 *Nero's Grave*
Suetonius, Lives of the Caesars, Nero 6.49.1

At last, while his companions one and all urged him to save himself as soon as possible from the indignities that threatened him, he [Nero] bade them dig a grave in his presence, proportioned to the size of his own person, collect any bits of marble that could be found, and at the same time bring water and wood for presently disposing of his body. As each of these things was done, he wept and said again and again: "What an artist the world is losing!"

1502 *Death of Nero*
Suetonius, Lives of the Caesars, Nero 6.49.4

He [Nero] was all but dead when a centurion rushed in, and as he placed a cloak to the wound, pretending that he had come to aid him, Nero merely gasped: "Too late!" and "This is fidelity!"

1503 *One Night Added*
Suetonius, Lives of the Caesars, Otho 7.11.1

When he [Otho] had thus made his preparations and was now resolved upon death, learning from a disturbance which meantime arose that those who were beginning to depart and leave the camp were being seized and detained as deserters, he said, "Let us add this one more night to our life."

1504 *Favor at Funeral*
Suetonius, Lives of the Caesars, Vespasian 8.19.2

Even at his [Vespasian's] funeral, Favor, a leading actor of mimes, who wore his mask and, according to the usual custom, imitated the actions and words of the deceased during his lifetime, having asked the procurators in a loud voice how much his funeral procession would cost, and hearing the reply "Ten million sesterces," cried out: "Give me a hundred thousand and fling me even into the Tiber."

1505 *Vespasian Turns into God*
Suetonius, Lives of the Caesars, Vespasian 8.23.4

And as death drew near, he [Vespasian] said: "Woe's me. Methinks I'm turning into a god."

The stories listed below refer to death, but other features in the stories have determined their location in another section.

Cicero: 58, 424
Gospel: 437a, 745
Hadith: 256, 260
Josephus: 1232
Philo: 1250
Philostratus: 26, 859
Plutarch: 459, 1278a, 1305

Bibliography of Sources

Jesus Traditions

Canonical Gospels

Revised Standard Version of the Bible. New Testament section, 2d ed. Division of Christian Education of the National Council of the Churches of Christ in the U.S.A., 1971, 1973.
Holy Bible, New International Version. Grand Rapids: Zondervan, 1973.

Gospel of Thomas

The Facsimile Edition of the Nag Hammadi Codices: Codex II. Leiden: E. J. Brill, 1974.

Other Jesus Traditions

Aland, Kurt, ed. *Synopsis Quattuor Evangeliorum.* 2d ed. Stuttgart: Württemberg, 1964.
Aphrahat. J. Parisot, ed., in *Patrologia Syriaca.* Rene Graffin, ed. Paris: Firmin-Didot, 1894–1926.
Bell, H. Idris, and Skeat, T. C. *Fragments of an Unknown Gospel and Other Early Christian Papyri.* London: British Museum, 1935.
Bihlmeyer, Karl, and Funk, Franz Xavier. *Die Apostolischen Väter.* Tübingen, J. C. B. Mohr, 1924.
Cassian, John. *Collations.* M. Petschenig, ed. Vindobonae: Geroldi, 1886.
Clements Alexandrinus. Otto Staehlin, ed. *Die griechischen christlichen Schriftsteller der ersten drei Jahr hunderte.* 3 vols. Leipzig: J. C. Hinrichs, 1905–1909.
De Bryne, D. "Nouveaux Fragments des Acts de Pierre, de Paul, de Jean, d'Andre, et de l'Apocalypse d'Elie." *Revue Benedictine* 25 (1908): 149–160.
_____, "Epistule Titi, Disciplii Pauli, De Dispositione Sanctimonii." *Revue Benedictine* 37 (1925): 47–72.
Funk, Robert W. *New Gospel Parallels.* 2 vols. Philadelphia: Fortress Press, 1985 (Sonoma, Calif.: Polebridge Press, 1987).
Grenfell, Bernard P., and Hunt, Arthur S. *The Oxyrhynchus Papyri: Part V.* London: Egypt Exploration Fund, 1908.
Hippolytus. Hans Achelis and G. Bonwetsch, eds. *Die griechischen christlichen Schriftsteller der ersten drei Jahr hunderte.* 4 vols. Leipzig: J. C. Hinrichs, 1897–1955.
Irenaeus, *Adversus Haereses.* William W. Harvey, ed. Cambridge: Cambridge University Press, 1857.
James, Montague Rhodes. *Apocryphal New Testament.* Oxford: Clarendon Press, 1926.
Lipsius, Richard Adelbert, and Bonnet, Maximilianus, eds. *Acta Apostolorum Apocrypha.* Darmstadt: Wissenschaftliche Buchgesellschaft, 1959 reprint of 1891 ed.
Mayeda, Goro. *Das Leben-Jesu Fragment Papyrus Egerton 2 und seine Stellung in der urchristlichen Literaturgeschichte.* Bern: Paul Haupt, 1946.
Migne, Jacques Paul. *Patrologiae Latina.* Paris: Migne, 1844–55.

Origen, *Zur überlieferung der Matthäuserklärung.* Erich Klostermann and Ernst Benz, eds. Berlin: Akademie-Verlag, 1933–1935.

Sachau, Edward C. *Alberuni's India.* Delhi: S. Chand, 1964.

Intertestamental Literature

The Apocrypha. Division of Christian Education of the National Council of Churches of Christ in the U.S.A., 1957, 1977.

The Testament of Job. Edited by Robert A. Kraft. Missoula, Mont.: Society of Biblical Literature & Scholars Press, 1974.

Torrey, Charles Cutler. *The Lives of the Prophets.* JBL Monograph Series 1. Society of Biblical Literature, 1946.

Rabbinic Sources

Albeck, H., ed. *Shishah Sidré Mishnah.* 6 vols. Jerusalem/Tel-Aviv, 1952–58.

Finkelstein, Louis, ed. *Siphre ad Deuteronomium.* New York: The Jewish Theological Seminary, 1969.

Horovitz, H. S., ed. *Siphre d'be Rab.* Jerusalem: Wahrmann Books, 1966.

———, and Rabin, I. A., eds. *Mekhilta d'Rabbi Ishmael.* Jerusalem: Bamberger and Wahrmann, 1960.

Lauterbach, J. Z. *Mekhilta de Rabbi Ishmael.* Philadelphia: Jewish Publication Society of America, 1933.

Lieberman, Saul, ed. *The Tosefta.* New York: The Jewish Theological Seminary, 1955–.

Weiss, Isaac H., ed. *Torat Cohanim.* New York: Om Publishing Co., 1946.

Zuckermandel, M. S., ed. *Tosefta.* Jerusalem: Wahrmann Books, 1963.

Islamic Hadith

Abū Dawud al-Sijistānī. *Sunan Abī Dawud.* Edited by Muhammad Muḥyī al-Dīn 'Abd al-Ḥamid. 4 vols. Cairo: Maṭba'at Muṣṭafā Muḥammad, n.d.

Al-Albānī, Muhammad Nāṣir al-Dīn. *Al-Ahādīth al-Ṣaḥīḥa.* 2 vols. Damascus: Manshūrāt al-Maktab al-Islāmī, 1959.

Al-Bukhārī, Muḥammad b. Ismā'īl. *Ṣaḥīḥ al-Bukhāri-.* 3 vols. Cairo: Dār wa-Maṭabi' al-Sha'b, n.d.

Ibn Ḥanbal, Aḥmad. *Al-Musnad.* Edited by Aḥmad Shakir. 14 vols. Cairo: Dar al-Ma'ārif, 1949–1955.

Mālik b. Anas. *Al-Muwatta'.* Edited by Muhammad Fu'ad 'Abd al-Bāqī. 2 vols. Cairo: Al-Ḥalabī, 1951.

Muslim b. al-Hajjāj. *Ṣaḥīḥ Muslim.* Edited by Muhammad Fu'ad 'Abd al-Bāqī. 5 vols. Cairo: Al-Ḥalabī, 1955.

Al-Mubārakfūrī, Muḥammad 'Abd al-Raḥmān. *Tuḥfat al-Aḥwadhī bi Sharḥ Jāmi' al-Tirmidhi-.* Edited by 'Abd al-Wahhāb 'Abd al-Laṭīf and 'Abd al Raḥmān Muḥammad 'Uthmān. 10 vols. Al-Madīna al-Munawwara: Al-Maktaba al- Salafiyya, 1963–1967.

Al-Ṭayālisī, Sulāymān b. Dawud. *Al-Musnad.* Edited by Abū al-Ḥasan al-Amruhi, et al. Hyderabad: Majlis Dā'irat al-Ma'ārif al-Niẓāmiyya, 1903.

Greek and Roman Writers

Athenaeus. *The Deipnosophists.* Translated by Charles Burton Gulick. Loeb Classical Library, 7 vols. New York: G. P. Putnam's Sons; London: William Heinemann, 1927–41.

Babrius and Phaedrus. Translated by Ben Edwin Perry. Loeb Classical Library. Cambridge: Harvard University Press; London: William Heinemann, 1965.

Cicero. *De Finibus Bonorum et Malorum.* Translated by H. Rackham. Loeb Classical Library, 2 vols. Cambridge: Harvard University Press; London: William Heinemann, 1914.

———, *De Natura Deorum; Academica.* Translated by H. Rackham. Loeb Classical Library. Cambridge: Harvard University Press; London: William Heinemann, 1933.

———, *De Officiis.* Translated by Walter Miller. Loeb Classical Library. Cambridge: Harvard University Press; London: William Heinemann, 1913.

———, *De Senectute, De Amicitia, De Divinatione.* Translated by William Armistead Falconer. Loeb Classical Library. Cambridge: Harvard University Press; London: William Heinemann, 1923.

———, *The Speeches.* Translated by N. H. Watts. Loeb Classical Library. Cambridge: Harvard University Press; London: William Heinemann, 1923.

———, *Tusculan Disputations.* Translated by J. E. King. Loeb Classical Library. Cambridge: Harvard University Press; London: William Heinemann, 1927.

Diogenes Laertius. *Lives of Eminent Philosophers.* Translated by R. D. Hicks. Loeb Classical Library, 2 vols. Cambridge: Harvard University Press; London: William Heinemann, 1925.

Frontinus. *The Strategems and the Aqueducts of Rome.* Translated by Charles E. Bennett. Loeb Classical Library. Cambridge: Harvard University Press; London: William Heinemann, 1925.

Gellius, Aulus. *The Attic Nights.* Translated by John C. Rolfe. Loeb Classical Library, 3 vols. Cambridge: Harvard University Press; London: William Heinemann, 1927–1928.

Josephus. *The Life, Against Apion.* Translated by H. St. J. Thackeray. Loeb Classical Library. Cambridge: Harvard University Press; London: William Heinemann, 1926.

———, *The Jewish War.* Translated by H. St. J. Thackeray. Loeb Classical Library, 2 vols. Cambridge: Harvard University Press; London: William Heinemann, 1926–1929.

Lucian. Translated by A. M. Harmon, K. Kilburn and M. D. MacLeod. Loeb Classical Library, 7 vols. Cambridge: Harvard University Press; London: William Heinemann, 1913–1961.

Lucius Annaeus Florus; Cornelius Nepos. Translated by E. S. Forster and J. C. Rolfe. Loeb Classical Library. Cambridge: Harvard University Press; London: William Heinemann, 1929.

Macrobius. *The Saturnalia.* Translated by Percival Vaughan Davies. New York: Columbia University Press, 1969.

Philo. Translated by F. H. Colson, G. H. Whitaker and J. W. Earp. Loeb Classical Library, 10 vols. Cambridge: Harvard University Press; London: William Heinemann, 1929–1962.

Philostratus and Eunapius. Translated by Wilmer Cave Wright. Loeb Classical

Library, 2 vols. Cambridge: Harvard University Press; London: William Heinemann, 1921.

Philostratus. *The Life of Apollonius of Tyana.* Translated by F. C. Conybeare. Loeb Classical Library, 2 vols. Cambridge: Harvard University Press; London: William Heinemann, 1912.

Plato. *The Republic.* Translated by Paul Shorey. Loeb Classical Library, 2 vols. Cambridge: Harvard University Press; London: William Heinemann, 1930–35.

Plutarch. *Lives.* Translated by Bernadotte Perrin. Loeb Classical Library, 11 vols. Cambridge: Harvard University Press; London: William Heinemann, 1914–1926.

———, *Moralia.* Translated by F. C. Babbitt, W. C. Helmbold, Phillip H. DeLacy, Benedict Einarson, P. A. Clement, H. B. Hoffleit, E. L. Minar, Jr., F. H. Sandbach, H. N. Fowler, Lionel Pearson, and Harold Cherniss. Loeb Classical Library, 15 vols. Cambridge: Harvard University Press; London: William Heinemann, 1927–1969.

Suetonius. Translated by J. C. Rolphe. Loeb Classical Library, 2 vols. Cambridge: Harvard University Press; London: William Heinemann, 1914.

Xenophon. *Memorabilia and Oeconomicus.* Translated by E. C. Marchant. Loeb Classical Library. Cambridge: Harvard University Press; London: William Heinemann, 1923.

———, *Scripta Minora.* Translated by E. C. Marchant. Loeb Classical Library. Cambridge: Harvard University Press; London: William Heinemann, 1918.

Edited Collections

Bergk, T. *Poetae Lyrici Graeci.* Leipzig, 1882 (reprint 1914–15).

Bernardakis, Gregorius N. *Plutarchi Chaeronensis Moralia.* Leipzig: Teubner, 1888–96.

Dindorf, L. *Historici Graeci Minores.* Leipzig: Teubner, 1870–71.

Jacoby, F. *Fragmente der griechischen Historiker.* Berlin, 1923–.

Kirchhoff, A. *Euripidis Tragoediae.* Berlin, 1867.

Kock, T. *Comicorum Atticorum Fragmenta.* 3 vols. Leipzig, 1880–88.

Leutsch, E. L. von & F. G. Schneidewin. *Corpus Paroemiographorum Graecorum.* Göttingen, 1839–51.

Mueller, C. *Fragmenta Historicorum Graecorum.* 5 vols. Paris, 1841–70.

Mullach, F. W. A. *Fragmenta Philosophorum Graecorum.* 3 vols. Paris, 1860–81.

Nauck, A. *Tragicorum Graecorum Fragmenta.* Leipzig, 1889.

Waltz, Christian. *Rhetores Graeci.* 7 vols. Stuttgart and Tübingen: J. G. Cottae, 1832–36.

Index of Names and Places

Note: Numbers in parentheses refer to footnotes

Index of Passages

Note: Numbers in parentheses refer to footnotes

New Testament

Early Christian Literature

Islamic Hadith and Qu'ran

Greek and Latin Authors

Index of Subjects

Note: Numbers in parentheses refer to footnotes

Design & typesetting: Polebridge Press, Sonoma, California

Printing & binding: BookCrafters, Chelsea, Michigan

Display & text type: Plantin